T0318557

CONSUMER, PROSUMER, PROSUMAGER

CONSUMER, PROSUMER, PROSUMAGER

How Service Innovations Will Disrupt the Utility Business Model

FEREIDOON SIOSHANSI

ACADEMIC PRESS

An imprint of Elsevier

Academic Press is an imprint of Elsevier
125 London Wall, London EC2Y 5AS, United Kingdom
525 B Street, Suite 1650, San Diego, CA 92101, United States
50 Hampshire Street, 5th Floor, Cambridge, MA 02139, United States
The Boulevard, Langford Lane, Kidlington, Oxford OX5 1GB, United Kingdom

Notices
Knowledge and best practice in this field are constantly changing. As new research and experience
broaden our understanding, changes in research methods, professional practices, or medical
treatment may become necessary.

Practitioners and researchers must always rely on their own experience and knowledge in evaluating
and using any information, methods, compounds, or experiments described herein. In using such
information or methods they should be mindful of their own safety and the safety of others, including
parties for whom they have a professional responsibility.

To the fullest extent of the law, neither the Publisher nor the authors, contributors, or editors, assume
any liability for any injury and/or damage to persons or property as a matter of products liability,
negligence or otherwise, or from any use or operation of any methods, products, instructions, or
ideas contained in the material herein.

Library of Congress Cataloging-in-Publication Data
A catalog record for this book is available from the Library of Congress

British Library Cataloguing-in-Publication Data
A catalogue record for this book is available from the British Library

ISBN: 978-0-12-816835-6

For information on all Academic Press publications
visit our website at https://www.elsevier.com/books-and-journals

Working together
to grow libraries in
developing countries

www.elsevier.com • www.bookaid.org

Publisher: Candice Janco
Acquisition Editor: Graham Nisbet
Editorial Project Manager: Ali Afzal-Khan
Production Project Manager: Kiruthika Govindaraju
Cover Designer: Harris Greg

Typeset by SPi Global, India

CONTENTS

AUTHOR BIOGRAPHIES

Ibtihal Abdelmotteleb is a research assistant in the smart and sustainable grids research group at the Institute for Research in Technology (IIT) of Universidad Pontificia Comillas in Madrid, Spain. She is currently enrolled in Erasmus Mundus Joint Doctorate on Sustainable Energy Technologies and Strategies Degree at Comillas Pontifical University.

Previously, she was a teaching assistant in the Electrical and Control engineering department at Arab Academy for Science, Technology and Maritime Transport in Cairo, Egypt.

Ibtihal obtained her BSc and MSc in Electrical and Control Engineering from AASTMT in Cairo, Egypt.

Jose Pablo Chaves Avila is a researcher at the Institute for Research in Technology (IIT) of Universidad Pontificia Comillas in Madrid, Spain.

José Pablo has been visiting scholar at the European University Institute, the Lawrence Berkeley National Laboratory, and the Massachusetts Institute of Technology. During his postdoc he participated in the Utility of the Future project, a joint project between IIT and MIT. He has more than 10 papers in peer-reviewed journals and conference proceedings.

He holds a Doctorate in sustainable energy technologies and strategies from Delft University of Technology.

Jim Baak is Senior Manager for Regulatory Affairs, West for Stem − a leading behind-the-meter energy storage software and services provider. He is focused on legislation and regulatory policies to support the transition of the energy industry to cleaner, more reliable and distributed future, enabled by advanced energy storage.

He has 30 years of experience in the energy industry including Vote Solar, PG&E, Powel Group, Utility.com, Alameda Municipal Power, and ElectriCities of NC. He has experience managing programs and developing policies for electric vehicles, solar energy, and energy storage.

He graduated magna cum laude with a BS in economics from the University of South Carolina.

Stephanie Bashir is founder of Nexa Advisory, which focuses on helping businesses and organizations find new opportunities and navigate complex problems in the energy transition by providing value-added future-proofed, customer-centric advice and solutions.

Stephanie has more than 16 years working for energy market leaders, most recently as Senior Director of Public Policy at AGL. She has held leadership roles spanning the energy value chain in technical, commercial, strategic, policy and advisory, with expertise in energy policy and regulation, energy technologies, innovation, networks, and grid modernization.

She completed the Company Directors Course, Australian Institute of Company Directors and Advanced Diploma in Business, MBS, Melbourne University.

Dierk Bauknecht is a senior researcher with the Oeko-Institut's Energy and Climate Division. Dierk has led a broad range of national and European projects on the integration of renewables into the power system, the governance of electricity system transformation, infrastructure regulation and smart grids, flexibility options and market design, power system modeling, European renewables policy.

Before joining the Oeko-Institut, he was modeling manager with a UK-based power market consultancy.

Dierk graduated in political science at the Freie Universität Berlin and holds an MSc in Science and Technology Policy and a doctorate from the University of Sussex, UK.

Ron Ben-David has served as chairman of Essential Services Commission (ESC) in state of Victoria, Australia since 2008. The Commission regulates electricity, gas, water, ports, freight rail, taxi as well as administrating Australia's largest white certificate scheme, the Victorian Energy Efficiency Scheme.

Dr. Ben-David has held senior roles in numerous government departments since joining the Victorian government including the Secretariat for the national review of climate change policy and has published on a wide range of topics including whether the retail energy market has delivered beneficial outcomes for consumers.

He holds a BSc in Optometry, BCom (Hons.) and PhD in Economics.

Philipp Blechinger is an international expert in island energy supply and energy system modeling, currently heading RLI's Off-Grid Systems research unit. He has more than 9 years of experience in the field of renewable energy and rural electrification projects in Germany and on international level. Before joining the Reiner Lemoine Institut (RLI) in 2011, he worked with financial and technical consultancies in Germany assessing the economic viability of PV, Geothermal and energy efficiency projects.

Philipp holds a PhD in Engineering from Technical University Berlin where he also graduated as Master in Economics and Engineering.

Audun Botterud is a Principal Research Scientist in Laboratory for Information and Decision Systems (LIDS) at MIT and in the Energy Systems Division at Argonne National Laboratory.

He was previously with SINTEF Energy Research in Trondheim, Norway. His research interests include power systems, electricity markets, energy economics, renewable energy, energy storage, and stochastic optimization. He is cochair for the IEEE Task Force on Bulk Power System Operations with Variable Generation.

Audun received a MSc in Industrial Engineering (1997) and a PhD in Electrical Power Engineering (2004), both from the Norwegian University of Science and Technology.

Joss Bracker is researcher with the Oeko-Institut's Energy and Climate Division in Freiburg, Germany. He has been working in several research and consultancy projects on national and European level. His fields of expertise are market integration of renewable energy, trading and markets for renewable electricity, electric mobility and voluntary green electricity markets (e.g., Guarantees of Origin, eco-labeling, electricity disclosure).

He studied Philosophy & Economics (BA) at the University of Bayreuth and University of Cape Town (SA) and holds a Master degree in Environmental Governance (MSc) from the University of Freiburg.

Mostyn Brown is a Consultant at Pöyry Management Consulting where he specializes in the price, policy, and regulatory risk governing the UK's renewable electricity markets. He also leads Pöyry's modeling of the EU ETS carbon market and increasingly works on projects relating to the digitalization of the energy system.

Prior to joining Pöyry, Mostyn carried out field research in Africa for Azuri Technologies who provide pay-as-you-go solar PV for off-grid households.

He has a DPhil in Biophysics from the University of Oxford.

Christoph Burger is senior lecturer at ESMT Berlin. Before joining in 2003, he worked 5 years in industry at Otto Versand and as vice president at the Bertelsmann Buch AG, 5 years at consulting practice Arthur D. Little, and 5 years as independent consultant focusing on private equity financing of SMEs.

His research focus is in innovation, blockchain, and energy markets. He is coauthor of the dena/ESMT studies on "Vulnerabilities in Smart Meter Infrastructure" and "Blockchain in the Energy Transition," the "ESMT Innovation Index – Electricity Supply Industry," and the book "The Decentralized Energy Revolution – Business Strategies for a New Paradigm."

Christoph studied business administration at the University of Saarbrücken, Germany, the Hochschule St. Gallen, Switzerland, and economics at the University of Michigan, Ann Arbor, USA.

Scott Burger is a PhD Candidate and Energy Fellow with the MIT Institute for Data, Systems, and Society and the MIT Energy Initiative.

Scott has previously served as the Managing Director of the MIT Clean Energy Prize, the Director of Operations for PRIME Coalition, the Director of Engineering for Circular Energy, and as an Analyst with GTM Research.

Scott holds a BS with distinction in Chemical Engineering from Washington University in St. Louis, and an SM in Technology and Policy from MIT.

Catherina Cader is a researcher at Reiner Lemoine Institute's Off-Grid team. She is an expert in spatial energy access planning using geographic information software (GIS).

She has international experience in rural electrification planning with a focus in sub-Saharan Africa and Southeast Asia. Her key expertise is in spatial data analysis as well as in providing GIS trainings on spatial electrification planning to governmental representatives and private sector stakeholders.

Catherina holds degrees in Environmental Management (BSc) and Geography (MSc, PhD).

Toby Couture is Founder and Director of E3 Analytics, an independent consultancy. He has over a decade of experience in the renewable energy and off-grid sectors with a focus on policy, strategy, and economic and financial analysis.

Prior to founding E3 Analytics in 2009, Mr. Couture worked as Energy and Financial Markets Analyst at the U.S. National Renewable Energy Lab (NREL) in Colorado.

He is a recipient of the Fulbright Scholarship, has a Master's degree in Environmental Policy from the University of Moncton in Canada, as well as an MSc in Financial and Commercial Regulation from the London School of Economics.

Franziska Flachsbarth is a research associate at the Freiburg branch of the Oeko-Institut's Energy and Climate Division. Her thematic emphasis is the German power grid as well as investment decisions. Her key activities at the Institute include the modeling of the future power system and data processing.

She studied Industrial Engineering focusing on energy grids and energy market modeling at the Brandenburg Technical University of Cottbus.

Pierre Germain is partner and cofounder of E-CUBE Strategy Consultants in Paris.

Pierre has over 20 years of experience in strategy and management consulting, working with more than 15 major European energy companies (production, network infrastructures, trading, marketing, etc.). He teaches courses at Mines de Paris, Sciences Po Paris, and IFP Energies Nouvelles. Pierre is the author or coauthor of more than a dozen publications with E-CUBE.

Pierre graduated from the Ecole Polytechnique and the Ecole des Mines de Paris.

Jean-Michel Glachant is the Director of the Florence School of Regulation and Loyola de Palacio Chair at the European University Institute. He regularly advises the European Commission and various European energy regulators, has been coordinator or scientific advisor of several European research projects, and is a research partner in the CEEPR at MIT and the EPRG at Cambridge University.

His main research interests are the building of a common European energy regulation and policy, the working of the European energy internal market, the industrial organization, and market strategy of energy companies. He has been first editor-in-chief of the Economics of Energy & Environmental Policy and is Vice-President of the International Association for Energy Economics. He is the author of numerous books and publications.

He has Master's degree and PhD in economics from La Sorbonne.

Tomas Gomez is a professor at the Engineering School of Universidad Pontificia Comillas in Madrid, Spain, and the Director of the Institute for Research in Technology (IIT) at the same university.

Previously, Prof. Gomez has been Vice-Rector of Research, Development, and Innovation of Comillas and served as commissioner at the Spanish Energy Regulatory Commission (CNE). He has been principal investigator in more than 80 joint research projects in the field of Electric Energy Systems in collaboration with Spanish, Latin American, and European institutions and has coauthored more than 100 articles in different specialized journals and conferences.

Prof. Gomez holds a PhD in Industrial Engineering from Universidad Politécnica Madrid, and an MSc in Electrical Engineering from Comillas.

Richard Gross is a research assistant at the Workgroup for Economic and Infrastructure Policy at Berlin University of Technology.

He participated in a study on the reorganization of the German utilities, including on-site visits and background research.

He is currently enrolled as a graduate student in Industrial Engineering at Berlin University of Technology.

Emi Minghui Gui is a PhD researcher in the School of Electrical Engineering and Telecommunications at the University of New South Wales, Australia. Her research interests include integration of sustainable distributed and decentralized energy infrastructure and business models, such as community microgrids.

Prior to her study, she worked for a number of energy companies in both Australia and Europe, including Australian Energy Market Operator, EnerNOC, IHS Emerging Energy Research and Essent Energy Trading, specialized in energy and renewable energy policy, network asset management, energy trading, and electricity market design.

She holds an MBA from Melbourne Business School and a Master of Engineering from Nanyang Technological University in Singapore.

Lucas Noura Guimarães is an energy associate at Madrona Law firm and Member of the Advisory Board of the Brazilian Institute for Energy Law Studies. He is an expert in the field of Energy Law regulation and renewable energy integration.

Previous to his current job, Lucas was energy associate at Vieira Rezende Law firm and partner at Claudio Girardi Law firm, where he advocated in cases related to Brazilian Energy Law. He also worked as an advisor to the Attorney General in the Brazilian National Agency for Electric Energy.

Lucas obtained a Bachelor of Laws and a Master of Laws from the University Center of Brasília and a PhD in Law from the Free University of Berlin.

Rudi A. Hakvoort is an associate professor at the Faculty of Technology, Policy and Management, TU Delft. He is an expert in the area of energy network regulation as well as design and regulation of liberalized energy markets.

Previously, Dr. Hakvoort directed the Market and Infrastructure department of the Dutch Office for Energy Regulation. He has been chairman of the working group on Congestion Management of the Council of European Energy Regulators. Dr. Hakvoort also serves as a consultant for energy utilities worldwide and contributes to training courses in the area of energy policy and regulation in Europe and beyond.

Dr. Hakvoort holds a MSc in Applied Physics and a PhD in Materials Science.

Christoph Heinemann is a Senior Researcher at the Freiburg branch of the Oeko-Institut's Energy and Climate Division. His key activities include the topics of integration of renewable energy, flexibility options, regulation and modeling of the future power system. Before he joined the Institute, he worked in the field of smart grids and innovative power products for 2 years.

He studied geography, political economy, and business studies at the University of Freiburg.

Udi Helman is the founder of Helman Analytics, an independent consultancy primarily advising a range of clients including commercial, research, governmental organizations on emerging technologies and wholesale markets.

Before becoming a consultant, he worked for over 15 years at the Federal Energy Regulatory Commission (FERC), the California ISO, and in the utility-scale solar industry. His publications include many in peer-reviewed journals as well as research studies with different organizations.

Udi has a PhD in energy economics from The Johns Hopkins University.

Etienne Jan is a manager at E-CUBE Strategy Consultants in Paris, where he works on the economics of flexible energy systems and on renewable energy sources.

More specifically, he focuses on the modeling of energy markets and on the evolution of market design. He is the coauthor of several publications under the reference E-CUBE, for example, on the value of flexibility for DSOs, on renewables and DR aggregation business models. Etienne is an adjunct lecturer in industrial economics and energy at Ecole des Mines de Paris.

Etienne graduated from the Ecole des Mines de Paris and with an MS from Columbia University.

Dominique Jamme is special advisor at CRE, the French energy regulatory commission. He is in charge of innovation, industrial affairs and prospective, and he is the Secretary of the Prospective committee set up by CRE in 2017.

Dominique held several positions at CRE and he has 15 years' experience in market design and regulation of gas and electricity sectors. Prior to his current position, he was CRE's director for networks, working in particular on networks tariffs, market design, balancing, investment in interconnections, smart grids, and European affairs.

Dominique graduated from Ecole Polytechnique, Paris and ENSTA Paristech.

James Johnston is the CEO and cofounder of Piclo, an innovative technology start-up based in London, UK with a mission to solve the energy trilemma.

Prior to founding Piclo (formally known as Open Utility), James spent 3 years researching building-integrated direct current microgrids at University of Strathclyde. James is also the founder of Solar Sketch, a design company for the solar industry and worked as a building services engineer at international engineering consultancy Arup.

James holds a BEng and MSc from University of Strathclyde in Mechanical Engineering.

Binod Prasad Koirala is a postdoctoral researcher at the Faculty of Behavioral, Management, and Social Sciences, University of Twente. His current research areas are community energy systems, distributed energy resources, as well as system integration.

Previously, Dr. Koirala has been working at the Faculty of Technology, Policy and Management, TU Delft and autonomous systems and mini-grids group of Fraunhofer ISE in Freiburg, Germany. He was DAAD WISE fellow at Fraunhofer IWES in Kassel, Germany.

Dr. Koirala holds a Bachelor of Technology in Electrical Engineering, Master of Science in Renewable Energy Management, and PhD in Sustainable Energy Technologies and Strategies.

Jean-Laurent Lastelle is Commissioner at CRE, the French energy regulatory commission, in charge of the Prospective Committee set up by CRE in 2017 currently focused on personal data privacy issues and European affairs. From 2013 to 2017, he was appointed advisor then Deputy Chief of Staff for the Presidency of the French Parliament.

Mr. Lastelle's career started at the Health Ministry where he dealt with the revision of Bioethics Law, after which he joined the Group Caisse des Dépôts as Chief of Staff for the retail activities.

Graduated from Sciences Po Paris and the French National School of Administration (ENA) in 2007, Jean-Laurent has been serving as a civil servant.

Sara Linowski is a research assistant at the Workgroup for Economic and Infrastructure Policy at Berlin University of Technology.

Her interests are energy sector reform and organizational change.

She is a graduate student in Industrial Engineering at Berlin University of Technology.

Iain MacGill is an Associate Professor in the School of Electrical Engineering and Telecommunications at the University of New South Wales, and Joint Director for the University's Centre for Energy and Environmental Markets (CEEM). Iain's teaching and research interests include electricity industry restructuring and the Australian National Electricity Market, sustainable energy technologies, and energy and climate policy.

Iain leads CEEM's research in Sustainable Energy Transformation including energy technology assessment, renewable energy integration, and Distributed Energy Systems including smart grids, distributed generation, and demand-side participation.

Dr. MacGill has a Bachelor of Engineering and a Masters of Engineering Science from the University of Melbourne, and a PhD on electricity market modeling from UNSW.

Bruce Mountain is the Director of the Victoria Energy Policy Centre at Victoria University and the cofounder of retail market data business, [MI] Retail Energy.

He has 27 years' experience as an advisor and researcher on a wide range of issues in the economics of energy and regulation in Australia, Britain, South Africa, and other countries.

He has a PhD in Economics from Victoria University, a Bachelor's and a Master's degree in Electrical Engineering from the University of Cape Town and qualified as a Chartered Management Accountant in England.

Tim Nelson is the Chief Economist at AGL Energy Ltd. where he leads the company's public policy advocacy and AGL's sustainability strategy. He has been instrumental in the development of AGL's Affordability Initiative, Greenhouse Gas Policy and Strategy and the Powering Australian Renewables Fund. He is a member of the Grattan Institute Energy Reference Group and on the Board of Sustainable Business Australia.

Tim is an Associate Professor at Griffith University and the author of numerous publications in peer-reviewed journals.

He holds a PhD in energy economics for which he was awarded the Chancellors Doctoral Research Medal, a degree in economics, and is a Chartered Secretary.

Setu Pelz is a member of the Off-Grid Systems Team at the Reiner Lemoine Institut and is currently pursuing a PhD in energy economics at the Europa-University Flensburg. From 2015 to 2017, Setu worked with two energy access companies in Kenya and Bangladesh. Prior to this, from 2011 to 2014 he worked as an engineer in the wind energy sector.

Setu holds a double degree in Mechanical Engineering and Business Management from RMIT University, Melbourne, Australia.

Guillermo Ivan Pereira is a PhD candidate in Sustainable Energy Systems at the University of Coimbra and MIT Portugal Program. His research centers on policy, technology, and business model adaptation for smart and sustainable electricity distribution.

Previously he worked as an innovation developer for smart grid and smart home applications at ISA, Intelligent Sensing Anywhere, Portugal. Here he collaborated with industry, universities, and governmental institutions to design and develop initiatives to advance energy efficiency across the EU.

He holds an MSc in Energy for Sustainability, Energy Systems and Policy from the University of Coimbra.

Ignacio J. Pérez-Arriaga is Professor and Director of the BP Chair on Energy and Sustainability at Comillas University in Spain, visiting professor at MIT since 2008, founder and director of Comillas' Institute for Research in Technology, and Professor and Director of Training at the Florence School of Regulation.

Professor Pérez-Arriaga is life member of the Spanish Royal Academy of Engineering, Fellow and Life Member of IEEE, and was a Commissioner at the Spanish Electricity Regulatory Commission among others. He serves as an advisor to institutions and governments in more than 35 countries.

He has MS and PhD degrees in Electrical Engineering from Comillas University, Spain and MIT.

Ian Schneider is a graduate student at MIT, working toward a PhD in Engineering Systems in the Institute for Data, Systems, and Society (IDSS) at MIT.

At MIT, Ian's main research interests include optimization and game theory. He is especially interested in using these tools to improve market design and policy related to renewable energy and electric power systems. Ian has also worked for Borrego Solar and the U.S. Department of Energy's Advanced Research Projects Agency (ARPA-E).

Ian received a BE from Dartmouth College and dual master's degrees in Electrical Engineering & Computer Science and Technology and Policy from MIT.

Patricia Pereira da Silva is a Professor at the Faculty of Economics of the University of Coimbra, where she teaches corporate finance, financial analyses, capital budgeting, financial accountancy, and introduction to management. She is also a faculty member at the MIT Portugal Program, lecturing Energy Economics and Markets and a faculty member of Energy for Sustainability Initiative also at the University of Coimbra.

Her research areas include energy economics and markets, finance, carbon markets, energy policy, and sustainable energy systems. She has been a visiting professor in Brazilian, North American, and European universities.

She received a PhD in Finance from the University of Coimbra.

Dominik Seebach is senior researcher with the Oeko-Institut's Energy and Climate Division in Freiburg, Germany. He has proficient expertise in the field of RES-E markets and the role of consumers in the context of environmental additionality in green energy markets.

Previous to his current job, Dominik has been working at Institute for Energy and Environment (Heidelberg, Germany) and at the EC DG JRC (Ispra, Italy).

He holds an MS in Environmental Earth Sciences (University Bayreuth, Germany).

David Shipworth is Professor of Energy and the Built Environment at the UCL Energy Institute. He is also Chair of the International Energy Agency's Demand Side Management Technology Collaboration Program and is the UK Government's Industry and Academic representative to the same.

His research focuses on ways to provide demand flexibility within the energy system and roles of consumers, regulators, and buildings in delivering these. He has a particular interest in peer-to-peer energy trading, time-of-use tariffs, and home energy management systems. He speaks and consults widely in the UK and internationally on peer-to-peer energy trading – particularly on the design, conduct, and evaluation of field trials for testing the consumer acceptability and response to different flexibility product offerings.

David holds a BA (Arch.) and a BArch (Hons.) from Deakin University, and a PhD in Complex Systems from Melbourne University.

Fereidoon Sioshansi is founder and president of Menlo Energy Economics, a consulting firm advising clients on energy-related issues. For 28 years, he has been the editor and publisher of *EEnergy Informer*, a monthly newsletter with international circulation.

His prior work experience includes working at So. Calif. Edison Co., EPRI, NERA and Global Energy Decisions, acquired by ABB. Since 2006, he has edited 10 volumes on different subjects including evolution of global electricity markets, distributed generation, future of utilities, and most recently innovation and disruption at the grid's edge.

He has a BS and MS in civil and structural engineering and an MS and PhD in economics from Purdue University.

Deborah Soule is a researcher at the MIT Initiative on the Digital Economy. She applies an interdisciplinary approach to research focusing on organizations and technologies.

Her research centers on the design, practice, and management of collaborative innovation in organizations, with attention to the roles of technology, diverse knowledge, and dispersed settings. Prior to academia, Deborah worked in Europe and Africa on information systems projects in multidisciplinary and multilingual settings.

Deborah earned her doctorate at Harvard Business School, her MBA from the University of Cape Town's Graduate School of Business, and a Bachelor of Science from Rhodes University in South Africa.

Aleks Smits is a Manager Policy & Research at AGL Energy where he has a research focus on network, grid modernization, and energy transformation policy. He is currently leading AGL's policy engagement on a number of significant reforms relating to energy market development.

Prior to his current role, Aleks has held both operational management and advisory roles within AGL's retail business and also as a market development advisor at the Australian Energy Market Operator (AEMO).

Aleks has a BA and LLB from the University of Adelaide, as well as a GDLP from the Law Society of South Australia.

Rachel Stanley is the Innovation Manager at Piclo where her main focus is the development of their local flexibility marketplace platform.

Prior to this role, Rachel has a decade of experience analyzing, developing, and implementing new business propositions in a pan-European utility company (E.ON) and numerous energy start-ups in areas including domestic and grid-based storage, local residential energy markets, and demand response.

Rachel holds a BSc in Psychology from the University of Sheffield, UK and an MA in Innovation and Social Entrepreneurship from Hult International Business School, USA.

Henny van der Windt is an associate professor at the Faculty of Science and Engineering, University of Groningen. He is an expert in the relationship between sustainability and science, with a specific focus on energy technology, local energy initiatives, and the energy transition.

Previously, Dr. van der Windt worked as postdoctoral researcher at NWO program Ethics and Policy at Groningen and as a research assistant at the Faculty of Mathematics and Natural Sciences, University of Groningen.

Dr. van der Windt also specializes in the field of nature protection and ecology and holds a PhD in Ecology.

Ellen van Oost is an associate professor at the Faculty of Behavioral, Management, and Social Sciences, University of Twente. She is an expert in the history of ICT, the coconstruction of users and technology, gender, and technology.

Dr. van Oost is a member of the Centre for Telematics and Information Technology and Institute for Governance Studies, both at the University of Twente. She is also engaged with diverse professional organizations (4S, EASST, Dutch Association for Women's Studies) and the Netherlands Graduate Research School of Science, Technology and Modern Culture.

Dr. van Oost holds MSc in mathematical engineering and PhD in the field of gender and technology.

Moritz Vogel is a researcher at the Freiburg branch of the Oeko-Institut's Energy and Climate Division. His key activities are located in the areas electricity market design, decentralized energy systems, integration of renewable energies, as well as flexibility mechanisms.

He studied environmental sciences at the University of Lüneburg and finished his studies with the Bachelor of Science degree. Afterward Moritz Vogel began the Master studies "Sustainability Economics and Management" at the University of Oldenburg, which he finished with a master's thesis at the German Institute for Economic Research in Berlin.

Christian von Hirschhausen is Professor of Economics at the Workgroup for Economic and Infrastructure Policy at Berlin Institute of Technology and is also Research Director at DIW Berlin, the German Institute for Economic Research.

Prof. von Hirschhausen focuses on the regulation and financing of infrastructure sectors, mainly energy, and is a regular advisor to industry and policymakers, among them the World Bank, the European Commission, European Investment Bank, and the corporate sector; he is also coorganizer of a speaker series entitled "Utilities of the Future."

Christian holds a Master of Economics from the University of Colorado in Boulder and a PhD in Industrial Economics from the Ecole Nationale Supérieure des Mines de Paris.

Ben Wealer is a research associate at the Workgroup for Economic and Infrastructure Policy at Berlin University of Technology and guest researcher at DIW Berlin.

His research focus is the restructuring of utilities in the transformation process, with special emphasis on the nuclear sector.

Ben holds an MSc in Industrial Engineering in the discipline of energy and resource management from TU Berlin.

Jeremy Webb is a visiting researcher at the Queensland University of Technology where he is focused on urban transport systems and modal choice. His doctoral thesis examined the historical evolution and the locking in of the automotive mode in urban transport systems. Choice modeling was used to determine the incentives needed to reduce private car usage and commit to public transport. More recently Dr. Webb has collaborated in a number of academic studies and projects focusing on the phenomenon of "peak car" and the likely uptake of shared electric autonomous vehicles in urban environments.

As a former diplomat and head of the Australian Department of Foreign Affairs and Trade's Economic Analysis Unit, he has been responsible for a wide range of reporting on global trade and investment issues.

Jeremy holds an MA from University of Hawaii, a Bachelor of Economics with honors from ANU, and PhD in Economics from QUT.

Jens Weinmann is Program Director at ESMT Berlin. Prior to that, he worked in a government-sponsored research project on electric mobility and at the economic consultancy ESMT Competition Analysis.

Jens' research focuses on the analysis of decision-making in regulation, competition policy, and innovation, with a special interest in energy and transport. He coauthored the dena/ESMT studies on "Vulnerabilities in Smart Meter Infrastructure" and "Blockchain in the Energy Transition," the "ESMT Innovation Index − Electricity Supply Industry," and the book "The Decentralized Energy Revolution − Business Strategies for a New Paradigm."

He graduated in energy engineering at the TU Berlin and received his PhD in Decision Sciences from London Business School. He also held fellowships at the Kennedy School of Government, Harvard University, and the Florence School of Regulation, European University Institute.

Florian Weiss is a research associate at the Workgroup for Economic and Infrastructure Policy at Berlin University of Technology.

His research focus is innovation and techno-economic aspects of the electrification process of rural areas in sub-Saharan Africa, as well as developing the related corporate strategies.

Florian teaches economic policy and corporate strategy, and is also enrolled in Industrial Engineering at the Berlin University of Technology.

Jake Whitehead is a Research Associate at the University of Queensland and Director of Transmobility Consulting in Brisbane, Australia. He specializes in the modeling and analysis of transportation policies focusing on the electric and autonomous vehicle markets.

Through his consulting firm he has worked extensively with Australian Governments to develop electric vehicle policies. He has also published widely on energy efficient and autonomous vehicle policies, and consumer preferences toward these transport innovations.

Jake holds a PhD and Licentiate in Transportation Science from the Royal Institute of Technology (KTH) in Sweden and a PhD, Masters, and Bachelor's degrees in Transport Engineering from Queensland University of Technology in Australia.

Clevo Wilson is a Professor of Economics at the Queensland University of Technology. He specializes in environmental, ecological, agricultural, energy, tourism, and development economics with a special interest in using environmental valuation techniques, both revealed and stated for policy decision-making.

He has published widely in diverse topics including energy and water conservation, agriculture, aquaculture, eco-tourism, and environmental sustainability.

Clevo has a PhD in Environmental and Resource Economics from St Andrews, Scotland, MSc in Economics from Glasgow University, an MPhil in Environment and Development from Cambridge, and a BA in Economics from the University of Peradeniya, Sri Lanka.

Stephen Woodhouse is Pöyry's Chief Digital Officer, responsible for the consultancy's digital transformation business. He has considerable experience in the energy industry, specializing in the changing energy markets and until recently led Pöyry's global practice in energy market design.

Stephen contributes to the global and EU debates on appropriate market designs for decarbonization, flexibility, capacity, and network access as well as working on electricity market reforms in over 30 countries. Before his current job, he worked for the UK's electricity regulator Ofgem, and previously as a consultant on global aviation emissions and high-speed rail.

Stephen has an MA in Economics from the University of Cambridge and has published numerous papers on electricity market design.

Timon Zimmermann is a research and teaching assistant at the Workgroup for Infrastructure Policy at Berlin University of Technology.

His research focuses on corporate strategy and sustainable development in both developed and emerging countries.

He is enrolled as a graduate student in Industrial Engineering at the Berlin University of Technology.

FOREWORD

The electricity sector has entered a new wave of radical changes. As we have already seen another wave three decades ago, we can better recognize that we are facing a new one, as radical if not more so than the last. Why? Because three pillars of the industry are simultaneously moving before our eyes, namely: the generation set, the consumption pattern, and the trading arrangements.

As further described in this volume, we learn that many consumers have become producers, of a kW size, while 30 years ago the efficient size of generation was 100,000 times bigger − in the hundreds of MW. And we explore what could become the role of a grid, the operation of the system, or the products exchanged in the wholesale and the retail markets, when more prosumers become active in fine tuning their consumption and self-generation via their own storage.

In this Foreword, I would like to insist more on another key component of this new wave of changes, its "*Weltgeist.*" As I discovered three decades ago, some common factors can influence different industries in a similar way: they are the "new world" trends. What was unique to the creation of all the first electricity wholesale markets, as the UK Pool, the Nord Pool, PJM, or California Power Exchange, was the various algorithms conceived to produce prices and the different tools used to combine those markets' bids equilibrium with the electricity system operation. However, what was common "state of mind" at that time was the wave of mainframes, computer programs, and dedicated terminals revolutionizing many other wholesale markets − the ones exchanging commodities, shares, bonds, or currencies. In many industries a similar computing revolution was booming. Digitalization of wholesale trade even pushed many old typical US "Exchanges," being non-for-profit cooperatives of traders, to become themselves "market-based" and "for-profit" companies.[1]

Something of the same magnitude is starting today, in a new wave of digitalization − and with more profound implications. To better identify what is happening we need a framework, an analytical framework. As I see it, there are six digitalization building blocks driving today's process

---

[1] Craig Pirrong "Exchanges: the quintessential manufactured markets" in Eric Brousseau & Jean-Michel Glachant, *The Manufacturing of Markets*, Cambridge University Press, 2014, pp 421-440.

of change, which can be grouped under infrastructure, market, and digital transformation:

- First, the *infrastructure changes*, which come in two components,
  - A – The proper digital infrastructures; and
  - B – The smart infrastructures internal to brick and mortar networks.
- Second, the *market changes*, which also come in two components:
  - A – The platforms for direct digital production/consumption; and
  - B – The platforms for interactions within two-sided markets.
- Third, the *digital frontier*, which can also be divided into two components,
  - A – Toward dis-intermediated Peer-to-Peer within digital communities; and
  - B – Toward "virtual resorts"[2] for Artificial Intelligence.

Let us visit them all, as they should give us an analytical compass helping to map the today's various changes covered in this book.

FIRST, *INFRASTRUCTURE CHANGES*

1.A The first basic infrastructures of today's digitalization process are the proper "*digital infrastructures*," which are strongly departing from what it was 30 years ago. A first monumental departure is the massive equipment of billions of "B2C" consumers with personal computers or portable devices, supported by Wi-Fi or 3G/4G wireless channels. A second departure, as transformative, is the rise of an interactive version of Internet and of cloud computing, the two giant twins supporting today's digital interactions. In 2018 we already have three billion people equipped with smart phones, and Internet users are assumed to be four billion. This gigantic infrastructure is, in a sense, universal as Internet and Android-iOS duopoly are interconnecting the various particular universes of the different devices and alternative operating systems.

1.B The other new infrastructures involved in the digitalization process are the "*Smart infrastructures internal to brick & mortar networks.*" Air transportation shows how traditional network industries can become deeply "digitalized," from ticketing and booking, to piloting of the planes equipped with automatic pilots – a reference for Artificial Intelligence.

---

[2]In this context – as further described below – the term "virtual resort," rather than "a community," is used to emphasize the fact that in a resort, like Disneyland, there are many rules that limit what the visitors within the resort can do. These rules are defined not by the users but by the owner/developer/manager of the resort. By contrast, in a "community," rules are typically designed and agreed by the members of the community itself on an equal footing. It is a subtle, yet important distinction.

However, most of these smart networks are not universal for access and usage, and work like "franchised territories" with proprietary norms and exclusive rights for their particular owners. It is because two types of digitalization of the brick and mortar networks have to be distinguished. The first is a *"back-office digitalization"*: it frames the network assets and their operation to keep delivering the preexisting traditional services as typical air transportation does. The second is a *"transformative digitalization"*: it reframes assets and their operations to permit delivering new and highly customized services to the consumers as Amazon currently does with its own home delivery loop for online shopping.

- Implications for electricity

  Traditional "smart grids" and "smart metering" in the electricity sector look more like "back-office" digitalization of the classical system and markets. They are not creating a universal interconnected space of operation, and – more important – not offering radically new services or personalized service options to consumers. However, a new wave of "smart grids" is arriving. It targets a *"smart grid redefined"* to lead the *"transformation of the electric utility."* It is conceived to address radical novelties popping up such as the rise of distributed energy resources, storage, microgrids, electric vehicles, smart homes, smart buildings, and smart cities.[3] Most of the existing "smart meters" are still far from this new redefinition of "smartness" for electricity networks and only do the back office of the classical grid and market services. Therefore the new digital revolution needs to focus somewhere else, perhaps behind the aging smart meter and in the behind-the-meter space?

SECOND, *MARKET CHANGES*

Deeper digitalization of markets brings many novelties, with one being the sparkling core of today's digital world: the *"platform"* – which comes in two forms:

2.A *Platforms for direct digital production/consumption.* This first type provides the digitalization of services being directly consumed on the platform by its users. These services are typically: Internet search; information data, e-books, e-journals; messaging and e-mails, etc. These companies maybe for profit, or not (think Wikipedia), but they all are *"digital providers."* These providers cannot be bypassed to access the "ready to use" digital services that they produce.

[3]Mani Vadari "*Smart Grid Redefined. Transformation of the Electric Utility*", Artech House, 2018.

Within this category, two types of digital providers can be distinguished:

- Firstly, the *"fully centralized"* platforms (as Google Search or Google Maps), where the digital provider is the only producer of the service being consumed; and

- Secondly, the *"half-decentralized"* platforms (as Gmail, Twitter, Instagram, or Wikipedia), where the users interact *"Peer-to-Peer"* to coproduce individual units of the services being consumed within the digital frame provided by the platform.

2.B *Platforms for interaction within two-sided markets.* These platforms are *"specialized intermediaries for two-sided markets."* They offer a *"digital marketplace"* that facilitates the matching of producers and consumers of particular goods, as dedicated platforms in a specialized *"two-sided market."* In this case, the platform operators and the users are not producing or consuming anything on the platform, contrary to the platforms of "direct digital production/consumption" seen previously. These *"Two-sided platforms"* only act as intermediaries, merely bringing the two sides together. They act as an auxiliary service permitting to show/search a particular product, to present/identify the product characteristics, and to select/locate a partner (buyer/supplier) who can be trusted into the settlement and delivery process.

Two types of such platforms coexist:

- The first ones are *"low interaction platforms,"* behaving like a "search engine" (such as Google Search) coupled to a "home delivery loop" (very typical of Amazon), or to a "direct use online" (as with Apple Music or Apple Store); and

- The second are *"high interaction platforms,"* which remedy with appropriate and sophisticated information, credibility, and incentives,[4] to what G. Akerlof, the 2001 Nobel Laureate in economics, identified as the deadlock of too deep asymmetry of information between buyers and sellers, as in his famous *"Market for 'Lemons'."*[5] These high interaction platforms are the backbone of the growing *"sharing economy"* allowing enterprises such as Uber, BlaBlaCar, or AirBnB[6] to thrive. They do what was considered impossible for decades until the arrival of the Internet and ubiquitous wireless connectivity.

---

[4]Sangeet Paul Choudary, *Platform Scale*, Plateformscalebook, 2015.

[5]George Akerlof, "The Market for 'Lemons': Quality Uncertainty and the Market Mechanism", *Quarterly Journal of Economics*, vol; 84, n°3, 1970, p. 488-500.

[6]Jean Tirole, *Economics for the common good*, Princeton University Press, 2017; Arun Sundararajan, *The Sharing Economy*, MIT Press, 2016.

- Implications for electricity
  Online retail via apps, similar to digital banking, could look like the centralized digital platforms of "direct" type, while the survival of online electricity suppliers with "light assets" is another key complementary dimension. The next big novelty seems to be the aggregators, who act as digital intermediaries centralizing interactions between the wholesale market and the balancing demand, or between the grid operators and the consumers. Two-sided markets too could and do appear. Think of grid operators succeeding into following the New York authorities' road map for "open platforms," and running "open distribution grids" where buyers and sellers do their own affairs as they wish for a full range of new products. Going a step further, "high interaction platforms" could appear by creating trust for the transacting parties as a prerequisite to start trading. Examples include peer-to-peer trading of distributed renewable self-generation, P2P storage, P2P electric vehicle charging stations,[7] and many others covered in this volume.

THIRD, *THE DIGITAL FRONTIER*

This digital frontier is more notional, being the frontier of both the practice and knowledge. However, so many radical innovations have already been made reality in the 21st century that we should not restrain ourselves from looking in this direction.

3.A *Toward dis-intermediated Peer to Peer within digital communities.* Among the contributions of E. Ostrom, the 2009 Nobel laureate in economics, was to highlight the significant role of "*Communities*" – pointing out that they are as important as that of markets, companies, and the state, in real economic and social life.[8] In this context, it is not very challenging to welcome the fifth digital form of transactions, where individuals eliminate all intermediaries and third parties from their direct economic relations and rely on the "community" for trading, verification, settlements, and management of conflicts.

Recently, this type of direct "*peer-to-peer*" trading without a central clearinghouse or intermediary has turned into the latest promising frontier

[7]Florence School of Regulation "Young Research Award 2018" to Fany Vanrykel "*Fostering Share&Charge through proper regulation*", University of Liège, Tax Institute, 4000 Liège, Belgium.

[8]Elinor Ostrom, *The Future of the Commons: Beyond Market Failures and Government Regulations*, Institute of Economic Affairs, London, 2012.

of "*blockchain networks*,"[9] further described in one of the chapters of this volume. The beauty of the distributed ledger is its ability to trace direct "peer-to-peer" trades or any form of transactions among the participants, thanks to sophisticated digital services offered within a community or a network of individuals.

Once fully developed, radically pure blockchain networks promise the end of all private intermediaries and public third parties. Some economists, however, believe that the magnitude of "*transaction costs*" including managing errors, misinterpretation, and conflicts among large number of traders may limit the scope of services offered by these networks, potentially barring their application to all types of goods and services.[10] Which explains why less radical, more realistic blockchain "clubs" appear more attractive. In this case, the trading takes place within a community of trusted peers with an implicit or explicit set of rules and common governance.

Beyond blockchain networks and clubs, other types of "digital communities" can act as larger, and less strictly organized entities having multiple purposes, for example, as an "*Energy Community*" or as a "smart city."[11]

3.B *Toward "virtual resorts" for Artificial Intelligence.* This ultimate digitalization form is very intuitive, while not yet used as a concept in academia or in practice.

Consider, for example, a future when cars will be self-driven. In this case, their users will voluntarily enter into a "virtual resort," a world of self-defined operational rules for transportation. In contrast to the disintermediated peer-to-peer world, in this case, a company will own the exclusive rights to design and operate the artificial intelligence network permitting each device to self-drive. Such a car universe would be a "single purpose AI resort."

Different types of AI resorts could appear if the areas of operations, the domain of services and products managed by the AI, were extended to various interactive devices; as the proclaimed "*Internet of Things*," which could become a network of multipurpose AI resorts.

Another form of entry into this multiple purpose AI world could be by the likes of Alexa, Amazon's ubiquitous smart home box or similar per-

---

[9]Don & Alex Tapscott, *Blockchain Revolution*, Penguin, 2016.

[10]Benito Arrunada, *Blockchain's Struggle to Deliver Impersonal Exchange*, Pompeu Fabra University, Barcelona, 2018.

[11]Bas Boorsma, *A New Digital Deal. Beyond smart cities. How to best leverage Digitalization for the benefit of our Communities*, Rainmaking Publications, 2017.

sonal assistant devices offered by Apple, Google, and others. As with Alexa, vocal personal assistants are conceived to transform any human voice dialog or interaction with the device potentially into an AI automated, "smart & learning," decision-making process.

- Implications for electricity
  It is easy to understand why the P2P trade, seen as a natural target for "two-sided" platforms, can easily become a Holy Grail for blockchain. The trust needed to support P2P exchange can obviously be gained within dis-intermediated networks, be they "pure blockchain," or hybrid, trusted "blockchain communities" described in the preceding section.

In a similar fashion, here or there, over time people can come to perceive renewables resources, distribution grids, storage assets, electric vehicles – in fact, all behind-the-meter assets – as scarce local resources in need of a community approach and a community governance. The new legislative energy package of European Commission has already proposed, in November 2016, to baptize the *"energy communities"* as a new category of players into the European energy field. Many variants of such a theme can occur in real life, including micro-grid private pools, smart neighborhood clubs, up to smart districts and smart cities. An electric car fleet of 100,000 units, say in 2030, will have a cumulated size of batteries from 3 to 6 GWh. Behind-the-meter assets are already big and will grow even bigger over time. And, naturally, the time will arrive for them to be properly aggregated and managed.

The building of AI resorts is not a utopia anymore nor an academic curiosity. Future self-driving cars, used by individuals, can also be owned by a fleet company, who will manage the portfolio, easily with 3–6 GWh of battery storage capacity. And such a fleet of behind-the-meter assets, most likely integrated with distributed generation and flexible loads, will be professionally managed with sophisticated algorithms as a business. With 15 million cars annually sold in the EU, assuming they are all electric, the added aggregate energy storage capacity of the batteries could amount to 450–900 GWh every year – a sizeable number compared to the average EU daily consumption of 8.5 TWh. Similar numbers apply to the US, China, India, and other parts of the world.

Roughly the same could apply to smart buildings and smart cities. In the case of California, which recently passed a "zero-net-energy" building code affecting virtually all new residential buildings starting in 2020, and other buildings in 2030, one can imagine smart communities of buildings with integrated electricity, heating, cooling, self-generation, and distributed storage managed by the communities. In this new future, even the "*Internet of Things*," interlinking tens of billions of professional and home appliances, looks like a realistic frontier.

Having explored the fundamental changes confronting us, I conclude with Herbert Simon, the recipient of the 1975 Turing Award for computing and 1978 Nobel Prize for economics. Back in the 1960s, he rightly observed that all computers are artificial intelligence units, because they substitute device algorithms to human intelligence. Today, we see his pioneering AI vision reformulated as the coming days of business and humanity. Simon was not afraid by the many uncertainties of the AI world we are entering in, or by the strong limits human rationality always has. In fact, he constructed a vision of the future despite the many uncertainties while cognizant of "*bounded rationality.*"[12] It is fully rational not to be afraid of the radical uncertainties of the world and genuine limits of reason as we think about the future, as long as we chain these two unescapable realities to our farsightedness.

Jean-Michel Glachant
Director, Florence School of Regulation
European University Institute
Florence, Italy

---

[12]Herbert Simon, *The Sciences of the Artificial*, MIT Press, 1969.

PREFACE

Earlier this year, Mr Sioshansi invited me to contribute to this upcoming volume of essays. At the time, I was developing some ideas for a paper I was scheduled to deliver at an upcoming consumer law conference. The paper would involve an exploration of the shortcomings of competition in a specific subset of retail services markets which included the retail energy market.

Although I hadn't yet written a word, I did have a title – *Competition, Neo-paternalism and the Nonsumer uprising.* I happily shared my untethered title with Mr Sioshansi who expressed great enthusiasm, particularly for my new class of customers to be known as "nonsumers." We left it there without any further discussion or elaboration.

Some months later, we reconnected. By now, I had written and delivered my paper with its detailed hypothesis about how competition manifests in different types of markets.[1] In the meantime, Mr Sioshansi had embraced the idea of energy nonsumers in an article in his newsletter.[2] We shared our respective writings only to realize we had attached almost diametrically opposed meanings to the term "nonsumer."

In my paper, a nonsumer market was defined as one where purchases were involuntary, largely inelastic, and intangible. The retail electricity market fits this description. Customers do not get to choose whether they consume electricity or not. It is an essential service without which household well-being would be severely jeopardized, and economic and social participation would be significantly hampered. For most households, there was little flexibility in how much electricity they required. Having made their investment in housing stock and appliances, customers had little discretion over how much energy they used. And despite these characteristics, most customers have little, if any, comprehension of the electricity they consume despite it being the most homogeneous of services. After all, how many customers can picture the value of a kilowatt hour of electricity?

---

[1]Ben-David, Ron (2018) *Competition, Neo-paternalism and the Nonsumer uprising* (15 May) https://www.esc.vic.gov.au/sites/default/files/documents/competition-neo-paternalism-and-the-nonsumer-uprising-paper.pdf.
[2]Sioshansi, Fereidoon (2018) *Prosumers turning into prosumagers; eventually nonsumer.* EEnergy Informer: The International Energy Newsletter July 2018, Vol 28, no 7.

In these markets, customers have very limited choices compared to other markets. Most importantly, they cannot exercise the ultimate sanction. They cannot walk away from the market. No matter how dissatisfied they might be with the prices or services on offer, they must still make the same purchase. Customers therefore become disinterested and passive participants in these markets. I called these disinterested and passive customers, "nonsumers."

I argued that competition in nonsumer markets manifests itself in completely different terms from how it operates in "regular" consumer markets. Competition sees electricity retailers focus on nonsumers' willingness to shop around rather than their willingness to pay. Instead of focusing on developing new value propositions to offer to customers, retailers in nonsumer markets focus on strategies that allow them to distinguish between those customers who do shop around and those who do not. The latter group pay higher prices than the former group, and possibly much higher prices despite receiving the same level of service.

This makes the competitive electricity market a rather unhappy experience for many customers (nonsumers). Sure, they might be able to reduce their costs by shopping around, but failure to shop around will see their electricity bills increase for no corresponding increase in the quality of service. And for those customers who are not able, willing, or interested enough to shop around, the consequences can sum to a very significant impost.

In other words, nonsumer markets require customers to be ever vigilant or face excessive prices even though they have little choice but to consume the service. It was no wonder, I argued, that nonsumers were distrustful and angry about how the retail electricity market was treating them.

In complete contrast to my rather bleak reference to nonsumers, Mr Sioshansi saw nonsumers as an ideal toward which electricity markets should, and will, ultimately evolve. His was a much sunnier picture. In his newsletter, Mr Sioshansi wrote[3]:

> And if the scenario envisioned does indeed materialize, it may give rise to communities of virtual nonsumers – in the sense that the entire community can become essentially self-sufficient in terms of net kWhs purchased from the grid, or in some cases, become a net generator of energy...
> It may sound like a pipedream, but it is not as farfetched as it seems.

It is fascinating how one term can connote such divergent meanings.

---

[3]ibid. p.12.

For me, nonsumer markets described the present state in which individuals are at the mercy of a market in which they have little effective bargaining power. For Mr Sioshansi, nonsumer markets represent an end-state in which customers come together in the pursuit of energy independence. Whereas my paper expressed deep concern about nonsumer markets, Mr Sioshansi expressed great enthusiasm.

Despite these polar differences, this volume of essays contains contributions that give great hope to both me and Mr Sioshansi. The developments described in this volume offer my nonsumers pathways out of their unhappy relationship with electricity markets. For Mr Sioshansi, these developments offer pathways for realizing his aspirations for energy users.

The essays in Part 1 of this volume highlight the potential for innovation in information management to fundamentally alter the way market participants interact with the electricity market. We are on the cusp of a data revolution with consequences we can hardly fathom. This revolution has the potential to completely reconfigure how households and businesses engage with the electricity market. Relationships and transactions that could hardly be imagined just a few years ago are now becoming possible.

Part 2 contains contributions that ignite the imagination. The commercial, regulatory, political, and legal challenges that lie before us are as exciting as they are immense. As our contributors make clear, these challenges are bearing down on us in a way that will leave us with few options. Energy suppliers, regulators, and policy makers must rise to these challenges or risk being washed away by them.

The contributions in Part 3 take us deeper into the opportunities that lie ahead. The stuff of science fiction only a few years ago is now on the verge of realization. The old models of service provision are entering their twilight. Service providers around the world need to adapt or make way. Indeed, if they are not already adapting, then these essays suggest that the destiny that awaits incumbent operators may already be foretold.

As a regulator, the challenges we face are mounting. The neat license categories that have worked so well for decades are struggling to keep pace with new business models. The distinction between retailer, distributor, and generator is blurring. This means we need a new flexible framework that doesn't require force-fitting new businesses into these old licensing categories.

Perhaps, however, the greatest challenge lies in the unpredictability of the customer experience in 5, 10, or 20 years from now. How will customers be supplied? Who will supply them? Who will own the assets? What will be the services they receive? For now, we have more questions than answers. But there is one answer that will remain unchanged. We know that even in the future, someone, somewhere, in some way will still be a consumer of electricity or a user of electricity-related assets, or both. Business models will rise and fall, but the consumer will live on. That is why we are reconfiguring our regulatory constructs so that they are tethered to the only thing that is certain about the future – the consumer. As a regulator, we are shifting from a framework based on obligations, to one based on customer entitlements; from compliance to outcomes.

Make no mistake. These changes are not mere legalities or semantic niceties. They fundamentally alter the role of regulation and the regulator. In doing so, they will alter the relationship between the regulator and service providers, and service providers and their customers. The regulator will no longer define the outer boundary of service providers' obligations. There will be no regulatory "to do" list for service providers to hide behind. They will be judged by the outcomes their customers experience and not by their mechanical compliance with a checklist of rules.

As the contributors to this volume make abundantly clear, the future is replete with endless imagination and intrigue. Fortunes will be made and lost. Value will be created and destroyed. Reputations will be enhanced or smashed. But when all is said and done, the only question that matters will be whether consumers, individually and collectively, are better off than they are today. The future beckons us.

Ron Ben-David
Chairperson, Essential Services Commission
Melbourne, VIC, Australia

INTRODUCTION

On 21 Jan 2015, *The Wall Street Journal* ran a front page story with the intriguing title of "Future Power Company: Your Home." The author, a journalist, had attended the annual convention of the American Homebuilders Association in Las Vegas, which featured a site visit to a zero net energy (ZNE) home built in the city's outskirts. The $700,000 house was extremely well insulated with double pane windows, super-efficient appliances, state-of-the art LED lighting, and a sophisticated home energy management system. Consequently, it consumed little electricity year-round. The visitors were told that, with a few solar panels added on the roof, the building would generate as much power as it consumed over the course of a year – this being sunny Nevada – thus meeting the definition of ZNE.

What was more surprising to the WSJ reporter, however, was not that the building was ZNE, but that a number of large US homebuilders at the convention announced that they would begin to offer such homes among their future inventory of new homes for sale to upscale segment of the market. According to the article, the builders saw a growing market niche developing for such a product. They were *interested* in selling ZNE homes as a profitable commercial product, not in response to mandatory regulation, a building code,[1] to save the planet or for other altruistic reasons.

The extra upfront cost of a ZNE house, these builders said, would be more than offset through lower energy costs over a relatively few years. Since most buildings last decades, the realized savings would far outstrip the extra initial investment.

Moreover, the homebuyers would not have to deal with the hassle of finding a qualified contractor to add solar panels on the roof after it has been built, or add more insulation or install efficient HVAC systems to save on heating and air conditioning costs, or replace the lights with LEDs, or change the appliances to more efficient variety – things that many homebuyers currently do if they wish to reduce their energy bills, which can be as high as $500 a month or more for anyone with a big house and a big HVAC system in a hot climate as in Nevada.

The WSJ article was intriguing in other ways too. If ZNE buildings with rooftop solar panels were to be offered as standard product – the same way

[1] Refer to Chapter 12 by Sioshansi for definition of recently adopted zero net energy building code in California.

that granite kitchen countertops are considered standard in most upscale homes today – that might eventually lead to entire ZNE neighborhoods – albeit affluent ones at first – with significant implications for the local distribution company.[2]

Affluent neighborhoods already tend to have more solar rooftops and own more electric vehicles (EVs) as a casual visit to Palo Alto, or Berkeley, California would suggest. If the cost of distributed storage falls, as is widely expected, these homes can go a step further by becoming even *less* dependent on the distribution network for net kWhs purchased while continuing to rely on the network for reliability and balancing services.

The rise of integrated energy services – touted by the likes of Tesla Energy, Sonnen, Stem and others[3] – is no longer considered *avant garde* as entrepreneurs and innovators continue to push the envelope on what products and services can be commercially offered just as homebuilders are beginning to offer ZNE houses among their standard products.

Much, of course, has happened since the publication of the WSJ article in 2015, allowing an increasing number of customers to move away from the traditional *bundled services* offered by the local distribution company at regulated tariffs. While the great majority of customers in most jurisdictions still rely on such bundled services, consumers in some parts of the world are gradually moving away from total reliance on the local distribution network for all their kWhs.

The best known example, of course, is customers – with or without ZNE homes – who invest in distributed generation (DG), usually in the form of rooftop solar PV panels. Depending on their consumption and generation profile, these consumers could become *net* producers or exporters of power during sunny hours of the day (Fig. I.1). In most jurisdictions this excess generation may be fed into the distribution network. The details, of course, vary from place to place based on the prevailing regulations. The important thing to note, however, is that these *consumers* – who now generate more than their consumption during certain hours of the day, become *prosumers*.

Going a step further, some prosumers may invest in distributed storage, allowing them the option to store some of the excess generation for use at later times. Electric vehicles (EVs), of course, are a form of distributed storage, as are batteries or other devices that can store energy in various forms

---

[2]One such a community of 2,900 homes is currently under construction in Prescott Valley, AZ, further described in Chapter 3.

[3]Further details in Chapter 3.

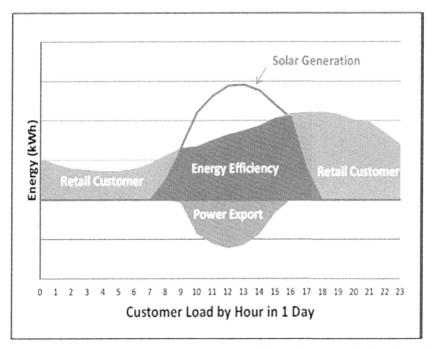

Fig. I.1 The first step: From consumer to prosumer. *(Source: Evaluating the benefits and costs of NEM laws in California, prepared for Vote Solar, Jan 2013.)*

or media, such as hot water stored in a tank. Tesla, Sonnen, Engie Storage, and a number of others are offering small-scale batteries suitable for households or small commercial customers precisely to do that. If the price of storage continues to fall, as is widely expected, some prosumers may decide to invest in distributed storage, making them *prosumagers*.

While today the number of prosumers and prosumagers is miniscule compared to the number of consumers, their numbers may grow over time as innovators take advantage of lower costs and improved technologies to carve out profitable niches. If successful, this will come at the expense of incumbent service providers.[4]

How might such scenarios evolve? The answer depends on the confluence of three important factors schematically depicted in Fig. I.2, which vary from one country or state to another.

The first and most important variable is retail electricity prices. The higher they are, the more incentive consumers have to become prosumers

---

[4]An earlier volume in these series covered the impact of distributed generation on the incumbents, followed by a volume examining the future of utilities and the latest looking at the potential impact of innovation and disruption at the grid's edge.

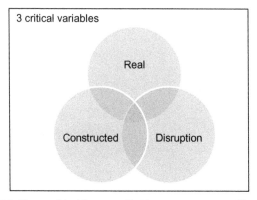

Fig. I.2 Three critical factors affecting consumer stratification.

by generating more of their own and/or using less through energy efficiency investments (Box I.1).

The second important factor is the role of prevailing policy and regulations affecting the relative economics of DERs vs. full reliance on bundled services from the distribution network. For example, the existence of generous feed-in-tariffs (FiTs) or net energy metering (NEM) determines how many consumers are likely to become prosumers (Box I.2). Conversely, in places where there are restrictions on how much of the excess solar PV

Box I.1 Distributed Energy Resources (DERs): A Primer
DERs refer to resources, devices, and/or assets generally on the customer side of the meter or behind the meter. Broadly speaking, DERs can be grouped into three categories:
- Distributed generation, mostly solar panels generating power, which can be locally used, fed into the distribution network, stored or potentially shared or traded with others;
- Energy efficiency investments such as improved insulation, more efficient appliances, lighting, HVAC systems, better monitoring and energy management and control systems – basically anything that reduces consumption; and
- Distributed energy storage systems (ESS), which can store some of the excess distributed generation for use at later times.

How big or important are the DERs? According to Navigant Research,[5] the global market for DERs can be expected to reach nearly 530 GW through 2026. In describing the main drivers for the growth, Roberto Rodriguez Labastida, senior research analyst with Navigant Research said:

[5]Navigant Research, Dec 2017.

Box I.1 Distributed Energy Resources (DERs): A Primer—*cont'd*

Technology advances, business model innovation, changing regulations, and sustainability and resilience concerns have brought DER into the core of the future deployment of energy infrastructure.

Adding,

...... the global proliferation of DER has begun to have a significant, and at times controversial, influence on the electricity industry.

Moreover,

... globally, distributed generation is expected to lead DER installations in 2017, and electric vehicle charging and flexibility technologies, such as demand response and energy storage, are expected to outpace competing solutions in the next decade.

The Navigant report notes that "... rapidly expanding investment in DER represents a major shift from the centralized, one-way electrical grid. This growth has generated both concern and optimism throughout the power industry as regulators and grid operators work to understand the evolving landscape that is redefining the relationship between utilities and customers."

Others broadly agree that as time goes on, more investments are likely on the customer side or behind-the-meter (BTM) as opposed to upstream of the meter, part of the decentralization of the electricity sector, which is likely to take place at different pace across the globe. Bloomberg New Energy Finance, for example, projects that by 2030 more than 40% of the installed generation capacity in Australia may be BTM – making that country among the leaders in decentralization.

As further explained in chapter by Helman, DER participation in the US wholesale markets may be in the range of 20–30% within the next 10–15 years.

Box I.2 Impact of Regulations on DERs

As further explained in several chapters of this volume, prevailing regulations play a critical role in how many customers invest in DERs. All else being equal, more customers can be expected to invest in DERs if regulation allows, encourages, and/or generously subsidizes them. For example, until recently the net energy metering (NEM) regulations in a number of states, such as California, were overly generous, which is among the reasons for California being home to roughly half of distributed solar PVs in the United States. High retail rates and plentiful sunshine also play a role. In states where NEM regulations do not exist or are not as generous, there is far less interest in solar PVs.

Continued

Box I.2 Impact of Regulations on DERs—*cont'd*

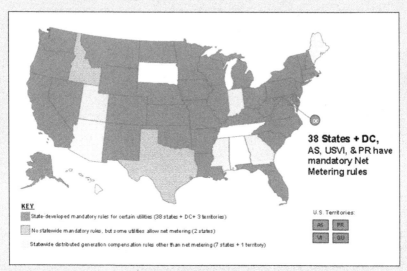

38 States + DC, AS, USVI, & PR have mandatory Net Metering rules

KEY

State-developed mandatory rules for certain utilities (38 states + DC+ 3 territories)

No statewide mandatory rules, but some utilities allow net metering (2 states)

Statewide distributed generation compensation rules other than net metering (7 states + 1 territory)

U.S. Territories:

AS PR
VI GU

Map of net energy metering regulation in the United States. *(Source: DSIRE USA http://programs.dsireusa.org/system/program/maps.)*

The prevalence of DERs, especially solar PVs, in other parts of the world is also largely explained by the relative generosity of the prevailing regulations. For example, Australia, for a while, had extremely generous feed-in-tariffs (FiTs), which explains why the country has the highest penetration of distributed solar PVs in the residential sector in the world.

The same explains why Germany, not a particularly sunny country, has over 40 GW of distributed solar capacity. The opposite is true in, say, Saudi Arabia, a sunny place with virtually no distributed solar generation to date. The explanation is extremely low, subsidized retail tariffs and lack of a NEM or FiT scheme.

The situation varies from place to place. In some countries feeding the excess solar generation to the grid is moderately to strongly discouraged, which results in relatively little interest in distributed solar.

Another critical issue is the regulatory determined value of the excess generation. If, for example, prosumers all allowed to receive a credit equal to the full retail price of electricity, tariffs are high and there is ample sunshine, then many will have the incentive to invest in solar PVs.

Change or modify regulations and what used to be a lucrative business may suddenly disappear, as has been experienced in many countries over the years. Potential changes in regulation are among the major risks in the DER business.

generation can be fed into the network and at what price, this often seriously limits their widespread adoption.

Third important factor is the continuous innovation and technological advancements that makes alternative service options feasible and commercially viable. Innovation, of course, inevitably leads to disruption.[6]

The significance of retail tariffs cannot be overstated. In places where electricity is inexpensive — for whatever reason — or heavily subsidized, customers have little or no incentive to invest in energy efficiency, self-generation, and/or storage. Take a country like Saudi Arabia, where electricity prices are currently heavily subsidized or free for some citizens. In such a case, why would any rational consumer wish to engage in DERs?

On the contrary, in Australia, Japan, and most of Europe, where retail prices are relatively high, consumers have strong incentives to invest in DERs. This explains the prevalence of distributed solar PVs in Australia or California (Fig. I.3).

The role of regulators is also critical — since the regulators not only set tariffs but also make the rules that either encourages or prohibits DERs — of which there are many examples. Aside from the retail tariff, the most important determinant of how many consumers may decide to become prosumers is the incentive to generate beyond self-consumption as described in Box I.3.

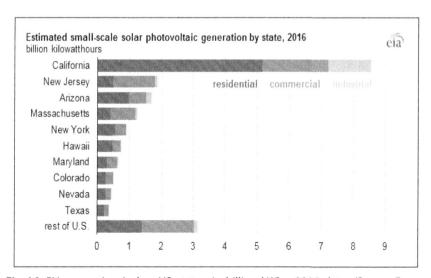

Fig. I.3 PV generation in key US states, in billion kWhs, 2016 data. *(Source: Energy Information Administration, Electric Power Monthly.)*

[6]Innovation and disruption at the Grid's edge, F. Sioshansi (Ed.), Academic Press, 2017.

Box I.3 How Much Is the Extra Generation Fed Into the Network Worth?

Historically, all kWhs moved in one direction, from the network to the customers. There was no self-generation, no storage, and certainly no kWhs feeding back into the network.

Initially, some regulators decided to encourage not only energy efficiency – as in California – but also to encourage distributed self-generation. In some cases, they introduced generous incentives for solar PV panels, which led to their rapid rise. Many of these regulators are now having second thoughts as the growth of distributed generation has cut into utility sales leading to concerns about "death spiral" for incumbent distribution utilities.[7]

In some places, say, California or states of Australia, the regulators are actively debating how best to react to the rapid uptake of distributed generation while in other places, the issue may not be on the radar screen yet.

The debate is largely focused on how much the excess or "net" distributed generation fed into the network is worth, namely:
- Should it get credit equal to full retail value;
- Should it get credit equal to the wholesale cost of generation; or
- Should the credit vary based its *cost-causality* and/or vary by time and location. For a sense of why it matters,
- The first option may lead to a 35 cents/kWh "credit" in a high retail price country;
- The second option may lead to a 10 cents/kWh credit or even less since more kWhs are being generated from essentially zero marginal cost renewable resources; and
- The third option may potentially lead to a negative "credit" during sunny hours of the day when the local distribution network may already be flooded with excess distribution generation and/or when wholesale prices may be negative due to utility-scale solar generation in excess of demand.[8]

The Energy Services Commission (ESC), the regulator in Victoria in Australia, recently proposed a *variable feed-in-tariff* to apply to any excess generation fed into the network.[9] These types of regulations will undoubtedly be needed in the coming years to prevent the so-called un-economic investment in solar panels – from societal perspective – where individuals may be better off but not necessarily the society as a whole.

Another thorny issue is the prevalent cross-subsidies when certain consumers become prosumers and prosumagers – in the process paying little for the upkeep of the distribution network, on which they still rely for backup, reliability, and balancing services.

Like everything else in regulation, things get rather complicated quickly, frequently politicized with polarized arguments from supporters and opponents of DERs, who often have radically opposing perspectives.

[7]Peter Kind, Disruptive Challenges: Financial Implications and Strategic Responses to a Changing Retail Electric Business, Edison Electric Institute, 2013.
[8]Negative electricity prices are becoming more frequent in more places.
[9]Victoria regulator introduces variable solar FiTs, EEnergy Informer, Apr. 2018, p. 1.

In the beginning, for example, feed-in-tariffs in Australia were extremely generous, which helped to kick-start the industry. But the uptake of rooftop solar in Australia may be attributed to high solar insolation, continuous decline in PV costs and high retail prices. While the premium feed-in tariffs were a factor in the beginning, they account for no more than 20% the total number of installed systems. Today Australia, a country with a population of 25 million, has over 2 million solar roofs, more distributed solar per capita than anywhere else.

Finally, without continuous advances in technology – say precipitous drop in cost of solar PV panels – there would not be the distributed solar revolution that has been experienced to date. Clearly, should the cost of distributed storage fall as rapidly as it did for solar panels, distributed storage is likely to become more viable over time as a resource.

What might be the likely evolution of consumers to prosumers to prosumagers – and more exotic versions? Driven by the three powerful variables outlined before, consumers are likely to self-select over time based on the relative costs, features, and merits of the options available to them.

For example, under prevailing net energy metering laws in California,[10] a consumer with monthly electricity bills of $500/month has strong incentives to install solar PV panels – either by buying them outright or leasing them – depending on the circumstances. The monthly bill savings are often more than sufficient to pay back for the investment in relatively short time.

The falling cost of solar PVs and stiff competition among solar installers suggests that they will continue to be attractive to many homeowners even with less generous subsidies. This phenomenon is exemplified by the experience of Energex, now Energy Queensland in Australia. As illustrated in Fig. I.4, the number of households with solar PVs continues to rise even after the super-premium FiT scheme was terminated. While the rate of growth is not as fast as it used to be, consumers in Queensland continue to invest in solar PVs.

In Spain and Portugal, on the other hand, the prevailing regulations until recently discouraged the sale of *excess* generation to the network, which means prosumers sized the units strictly for self-consumption, rather than for maximizing the credits received from selling the excess to the grid, as is currently the case in California. In other countries, notably Mexico, recent changes in regulations are expected to give rise to growth of solar PV panels. As explained by Guimaraes in Chapter 11, many Latin American countries currently have extremely low penetration levels for solar PVs despite

---

[10]Both tiered retail tariffs and NEM regulations have been modified recently in California, making them less lucrative than they used to be. Further regulatory decisions are expected in 2019 as further described in Chapter 12 by Sioshansi.

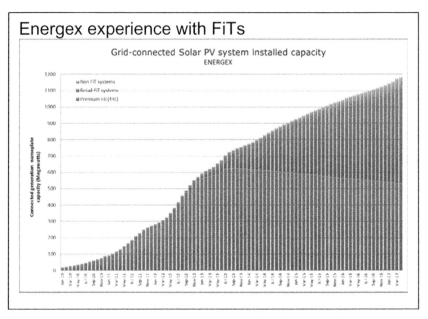

Fig. I.4 Experience in Australia illustrates that even after the termination of super generous FiTs, customers continue to install solar panels in Brisbane metropolitan area served by Energex, now called Energy Queensland. The portion on bottom of graph shows the rapid uptake of solar PVs after the launch of super premium, which has been phased out. *(Source: Energex.)*

ample sunshine and relatively high retail prices – a consequent of unfavorable regulations, which some countries are trying to rectify.

Needless to say, the issue of how much to pay for the "excess" generation fed into the network is controversial and is treated differently in different parts of the world by the regulators as outlined in Box I.3.

To recapture, given the growing number of options, over time, consumers will self-select and in the process may be, broadly speaking, *stratified* into four more-or-less distinct groups:

- Consumer refers to those who will continue to buy *all* kWhs from the distribution network and pay more or less the current regulated bundled rates. These consumers, while not entirely thrilled with their current supplier, may nevertheless not be sufficiently motivated and/or have attractive options to move away from the status quo[11];
- Prosumer refers to those who will invest in energy efficiency and/or self-generation, thereby reducing or virtually eliminating their *net* electricity purchase

---

[11]For many consumers with small monthly bills, the motivation to move away may not be worth the effort. Moreover, many who live in apartments in city centers do not have options to install solar panels and/or may not have a garage for a battery or an EV.

from the network. As will be noted elsewhere in this volume, most prosumers, however, will remain connected to the distribution network and dependent on the grid for balancing their variable generation and load;

- Prosumager refers to those who may go a step beyond prosumer by investing in distributed storage, making them even less dependent on the distribution network because they can store some of the excess generation for use at later times; and
- More exotic versions of prosumagers, including customers who may *trade* or *share* their energy generation and consumption imbalance with others. Such peer-to-peer (P2P) schemes may become feasible through intermediaries and/ or aggregators offering platforms where trading and sharing can take place. These *more exotic* options are currently in their infancy but are beginning to be introduced on pilot scale. It is a matter of time before they will eventually become widespread.[12]

Clearly, the interface and the relationship between consumers, prosumers, prosumagers and the more exotic varieties, and their service providers varies widely, and the retail rates and tariffs or whatever is paid for services rendered will have to evolve accordingly as schematically illustrated in Fig. I.5.

To what extent, how soon, and where such consumer stratification may take place is, of course, a matter of intense debate. Like many other developments, it is likely to start slowly, and initially only appeal to niche segments of customers. In its early stages, it is likely to be highly concentrated in certain areas or among certain class of customers depending on the three variables highlighted earlier. In Australia, for example, already 20% of residential customers have invested in solar roofs, while the penetration is currently much lower in California. While tariffs matter a great deal, prevailing regulation and

Consumers	Content with status quo: Bundled, regulated tariffs
	ALL kWhs provided by/thru existing network
	Maintain existing relationship/interface/tariffs
Prosumers	Take few/fewer *net* kWhs from network
	Require different pricing/service relationship
Prosumagers	Ditto, but even more so
	Radically different pricing/service/interface relationship
More exotic?	Service aggregated/enabled/assisted by intermediaries
	Semi-autonomous micro-grids of "nonsumers"
	P2P trading & transactive energy
	Integrated energy services

Fig. I.5 Interface and relationships of consumers, prosumers, and prosumagers with the distribution network service provider varies as outlined.

[12]Several chapters in this book describe early versions of such schemes.

policies matter even more, which means that the outcome will vary from one country to another and, in the case of the United States, from state to state.

The stratification of consumers and the resulting service options, among the main topics of this book, is important to all the existing stakeholders as well as a number of new players who are developing business models to serve the needs of the emerging market. As illustrated in Fig. I.6, with passage of time, growing numbers of consumers will have new service needs and requirements diverging from those of traditional full-service consumers on bundled regulated tariffs.

Eventually, a day may arrive where the bulk of the consumers will no longer be the traditional type – similar to what happened to telephone customers with so-called landlines – now a distinct minority or cable TV subscribers or DVD rental outlets.

As these examples illustrate, entire industries and business models have vanished in the recent past with advances in technology. For example, video rental companies gave way to cable TV, which is now increasingly being replaced with downstreaming services. Movie theaters, once among the big forms of entertainment, are increasingly finding it difficult to compete with the likes of Netflix and its counterparts who deliver original content on demand to so-called smart TV screens and/or mobile devices. A new generation of savvy millennials no longer watches TV, subscribes to print versions of newspapers, and rarely goes to a brick-and-mortar store for shopping.

Could the electricity sector eventually evolve to a state where the current pyramid shown in Fig. I.6 is flipped? And if that were to happen, what would be the implications? These, of course, are among the topics further explored in the following chapters.

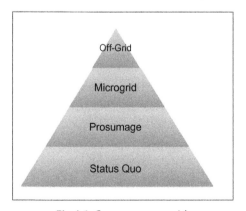

Fig. I.6 Consumer pyramid.

In this context, one of the most interesting questions is how would, or could, current consumers decide on where to end up in the pyramid of choice? Would they be able to make rational decisions on their own – given their limited time and lack of interest – or would they need the assistance of a third party, perhaps an intermediary or an aggregator? This is an important topic covered by a number of authors in the book.

Some who are studying such issues believe that as the number and complexity of the options proliferates, more consumes may decide to let a third party or a trusted professional to handle their portfolio of behind-the-meter assets in the same way that many small-scale investors allow a broker to handle their retirement savings or invest it in a managed index fund.

The answer to the how and who may assist consumers in deciding what is the best option for them is critical at least for two reasons:

- First, research in behavioral science suggests that the great majority of consumers are ill equipped and/or scarcely motivated to find what may be the best options available to them – say in places where competitive retail is available; and
- Second, the range of options available to the average consumer is likely to multiply over time as more behind-the-meter assets are offered and more service options and business models emerge.

If you think the average consumer is hopelessly unprepared to make good choices today (Box I.4), the future is likely to be far more daunting.

And for anyone who is concerned that many behind-the-meter investments made today are not optimally utilized, this is likely to get much worse. Consider, for example, a consumer with a $40,000 investment in solar panels, another $30,000 in distributed storage and an $80,000 Tesla EV – not uncommon in certain places. That is $150,000 of BTM investments that in all likelihood is not optimally used. Few people with such a portfolio know when or how best to charge or discharge the battery or the EV or how much of the excess solar generation to feed into the grid or at what time. Left to their own resources, many such BTM devices are likely to be poorly utilized and that would be a huge waste of resources.

Multiply such prosumagers by thousands and the numbers begin to add up. Policy makers and regulators should care and take necessary steps to encourage not only good BTM investments by individuals but also optimal levels of utilization and good outcomes for the society at large. As more countries reach high levels of BTM penetration already achieved in say Germany or Australia or California, the answer to these questions becomes more acute and pressing.

It must be noted that the preceding narrative mostly, but not exclusively, applies to developing countries – say the OECD economies – where the

Box I.4 If You Think It Is Complicated to Make the Right Choice, It'll Get Worse

Consumers face complicated decisions every day, say, in deciding where to buy a good set of tires or the lowest cost insurance for their car.

It turns out that deciding how to buy electricity and from whom – an option available to many in markets with competitive retail – is even more complicated. To start, the consumer has to know how much s/he is currently consuming, the load pattern and its variations over the year while comparing various tariffs and a myriad of options, discounts, and contract terms that are not typically easy to understand.

If the customer has already invested in solar panels, an EV and/or batteries – or is contemplating to do so – s/he must also consider a variety of feed-in prices and time of use rates making the matter even more complicated.

In the case of state of Victoria in Australia, Bruce Mountain, who is also featured in a chapter in this volume, points out that the typical customer, depending on their location, load profile, and existing loads and solar, may face as many as 140 competing offers from about 25 different retailers. To find the best deal, he says, is "phenomenally complex."[13]

Mountain points to a competent acquaintance who spent considerable time and effort using a spreadsheet to find the optimal deal, but apparently ended up with one that would have cost him $700/year more than the best available option. He says, "Customers have no chance of buying effectively in the market," adding that a typical customer, on average, pays about $500/year more than s/he should simply by failing to find the best available offer.

Mountain, who has examined retail markets in other countries, including Texas, which has the most competitive retail electricity market in the United States, says the same problem exists virtually everywhere where retail markets have been fully deregulated.

Not surprisingly, a number of businesses have emerged to assist clueless consumers to make better decisions. One, Energy Ogre in Texas, offers a service to find the best available option and reportedly has attracted 50,000 customers over the past 3 years and is growing.[14] In Britain Flipper offers similar services and it too is on an upward trajectory.[15] In Australia Mountain's own company, MI Retail Energy, provides a similar service through CHOICE TRANSFORMER.[16]

As the preceding examples illustrate, the migration of consumers to prosumers to prosumagers and the more sophisticated varieties is complicated and the emergence of more behind-the-meter options, considerable innovation is needed to ensure that customers make good choices while the societal interests of fairness and equity are not compromised.

[13]For further details refer to Mountain's article in The Conversation https://theconversation.com/if-you-need-a-phd-to-read-your-power-bill-buying-wisely-is-all-but-impossible-98617.
[14]Refer to www.energyogre.com.
[15]Refer to https://flipper.community who claims on its website "Flipper saves you time and money by seamlessly auto switching you onto the best energy deals. Join tens of thousands of Flipper customers saving an average of £385/year."
[16]Refer to www.choice.com.au/transformer.

existing grid already serves virtually everyone and self-selection and consumer stratification is likely to be driven by customers who wish to take advantage of even better, cheaper, more convenient, more customized, or more environmentally responsible options.

The story is rather different in the developing world, where millions of customers do not have access to a reliable grid and/or commercial services. In some remote and isolated areas without existing service, small-scale micro-grids are emerging offering limited services at affordable prices for highly value-added applications such as charging mobile phones, lighting and limited refrigeration, and entertainment. Successful models of pay-as-you-go have emerged in some places[17] and are likely to proliferate. These small-scale schemes may eventually expand to become larger micro-grids and/or join the super-grid when and if it eventually reaches these areas.

Ironically, the model for some remote or developing regions may initially start with a prosumager model, then gradually move toward prosumer and perhaps eventually consumer model as the range of services offered catches up with the demands of the customer base.

This book is primarily focused on the possible evolution of electricity services, the changing role of the distribution network and incumbent service providers over time assuming that customers will in fact be stratified into prosumers, prosumagers and more exotic types as outlined in the preceding narrative.

This book, which consists of 19 chapters, is organized into 3 parts as outlined below.

In the book's **Foreword, Jean-Michel Glachant** points out that electricity sector is facing a new wave of radical changes because the three pillars of the industry – generation resources, the consumption patterns, and the trading arrangements – are simultaneously changing. Many consumers, for example, have become small-scale producers, of a kW size, compared to the time when the efficient size of generation was in the hundreds of MWs.

He asks what could be the future role of the grid, the operations of the system, or the products exchanged in the wholesale and retail markets, as more prosumers become active in fine tuning their consumption, self-generation, storage while potentially trading with their peers.

Glachant says that over time people will come to perceive all behind-the-meter assets as valuable local resources in need of a community

[17]Refer to Chapter 14 by Couture et al.

approach and governance, hence the rising role of intermediaries, aggregators, and trading platforms. The new European Commission energy legislation, he says, has already introduced the role of "*energy communities*" as a new category of players in the market.

In the book's **Preface**, **Ron Ben-David** points out that competitive electricity markets offer a rather unhappy experience for many customers especially those who are not able, willing, or interested enough to shop around – leaving them with higher prices. This explains why many are distrustful and angry about the retail electricity markets.

Ben-David acknowledges that the challenges faced by regulators – he knows since he is one – are mounting while the regulatory models and solutions that worked so well for decades are struggling to keep pace with new service options and business models.

Moreover, he asserts that the distinction between retailer, distributor, and generator is blurring – asking how will customers be supplied in the future, who will supply them, who will own the assets, and what will be the services they receive? Ben-David contends that increasingly regulators' effectiveness will be judged by the outcomes customers experience and not by service providers' mechanical compliance with a checklist of rules.

Part 1 of the book is focused on how service innovations are leading to consumer stratification and disruption.

In **Chapter 1**, **Digitalization of energy**, **Mostyn Brown**, **Stephen Woodhouse**, and **Fereidoon Sioshansi** point to many indications that the electric power sector is – at last – on the verge of a digital revolution which can facilitate a more integrated, highly flexible, distributed, and customer-centric energy system. They examine what this may mean in new and innovative products and services, cost reductions, increased consumer engagement, and/or productivity gains.

Rather than the incremental cost-cutting efficiency measures characteristic of digitalization efforts to date, the next wave of change will be driven by data-savvy organizations that manage to establish direct relationships with consumers, resulting in the provision of new services with new revenue streams.

The chapter's main insight is to suggest that many offerings will focus on the intelligent management of demand and supply, leading to the proliferation of new business models while concluding that most of the innovations are likely to come from newcomers rather than the incumbents.

In **Chapter 2**, **Peer-to-peer trading and blockchains: Enabling regional energy markets and platforms for energy transactions,**

David Shipworth, Christoph Burger, Jens Weinmann, and **Fereidoon Sioshansi** examine the emergence of distributed energy resources and the proliferation of alternative service options available to consumers. This, it is argued, is rapidly changing how electricity services are delivered to end-users, how they are consumed, stored, and/or potentially shared with others on the same network.

Unsurprisingly, there is tremendous interest in the concept of peer-to-peer (P2P) trading, which allows future consumers, prosumers, prosumagers to potentially exchange excess energy at times of surplus and retrieve it at times of deficit, relying on enabling technology including blockchains to keep track of transactions.

The chapter's main contribution is to examine the technical, regulatory, and institutional context including an assessment of the risks, challenges, and barriers that arise in bringing such a transformative technology into practice.

In **Chapter 3, Integrated energy services, load aggregation, and intelligent storage, Jim Baak** and **Fereidoon Sioshansi** describe the holy grail of distributed energy resources (DERs), namely, the interface of intelligent management of distributed generation and storage enabled by remote sensing, monitoring, and optimization.

The authors explain how value can be created and – more important – monetized by aggregating large numbers of residential, commercial, and industrial assets and managing them with little input from or inconvenience to customers. A myriad of start-ups and existing players are striving to successfully master the art of adding intelligence to otherwise dumb behind-the-meter resources including distributed generation and storage.

The chapter's main insight is that tremendous value resides in intelligent management, control, and optimization of hardware and assets, and those who manage to aggregate and control customer loads and DERs stand to be the big winners in the transformation of the energy sector.

In **Chapter 4, Service innovation and disruption in the Australian contestable retail market, Stephanie Bashir, Aleks Smits,** and **Tim Nelson** point out that Australia's electricity market is undergoing a significant transformation as the once linear and one-way supply chain is becoming increasingly decentralized and bidirectional – offering both opportunities and challenges as customers exercise choice.

In the competitive retail market, customer options are proliferating from who sold them energy to a plethora of choices including self-generation, distributed storage and schemes enabling monitoring and management of time and volume of usage – and increasingly options on how energy may be shared, traded, and its value enhanced through sophisticated stacking, aggregation, and monetization.

The chapter, describing the strategies and challenges facing traditional energy service providers and the opportunities for service providers that have adopted the digital and innovation trends and culture. The chapter takes a customer perspective of this transformation and explores customer drivers, service innovation, and disruption trends, and how existing companies are responding to these disruptions.

In **Chapter 5, Do I have a deal for you? Buying well in Australia's contestable retail electricity markets, Bruce Mountain** argues that to promote efficient operation and development of electricity assets economists often suggest and regulators mostly agree that retail prices should reflect industry cost structures. In practice, however, customers might not always choose the price structures that regulators and economists prefer. In contestable markets retailers have an incentive to respond to customers' rather than economists' or regulators' preferences.

Drawing on the author's personal and professional experience, the chapter examines how customers actually interact in Australia's retail electricity market by focusing on the disconnect between the way retail customers actually engage with the market which may have little bearing with what the regulators and economists think they do.

The chapter encourages regulators to put themselves in customers' shoes particularly as distributed production and storage increasingly complicates the way that customers interact with their suppliers.

In **Chapter 6, Platforms to support nonwire alternatives and DSO flexibility trading, Rachel Stanley, James Johnston,** and **Fereidoon Sioshansi** describe the challenges imposed on an aging distribution network designed to handle one-directional flows increasingly facing distributed generation, storage, electric vehicle charging and discharging, bidirectional flows, and complex tariffs.

The authors examine the pressures on distribution system operators (DSOs) who must accommodate the plethora of new behind-the-meter devices and support new services offered by demand response aggregators, virtual power plants, and others without impacting the reliability of the grid or increasing customer bills.

The chapter features services developed by Piclo, an innovative start-up providing a platform that enables DSOs to procure flexibility services from demand response aggregators as an alternative to conventional reinforcement in congested networks.

In **Chapter 7, Consumer-centric service innovations in an era of self-selecting customers, Emi Minghui Gui** and **Iain MacGill** describe how the growing choice of electricity products and services, from customized home energy solutions to aggregated community based options, creates greater opportunities for electricity consumers to make meaningful decisions about what is best for them.

The authors analyzes the consumer decision making process and how it may be influenced by behavioral factors and external stimuli, such as information sensitivity, individuality, biases, as well as marketing and social influences. Key categories and examples of emerging consumer-centric in-novative services, their opportunities and challenges are discussed.

The chapter's main contribution is to highlight the evolving nature of modern electricity services, from universal provision of standardized, undifferentiated products to provision of value-added, customized and integrated customer solutions. This provides insights to energy service providers and policy makers in facilitating customer choices when shifting to a more services-based electricity sector.

Part 2 of the book is focused on how regulatory policy will impact the evolution of services and the speed and spread of disruptions in the power sector.

In **Chapter 8, Fair, equitable, and efficient tariffs in the presence of distributed energy resources, Scott Burger, Ian Schneider, Audun Botterud,** and **Ignacio Pérez-Arriaga** point out that distributed energy resources and digital technologies are enabling demand flexibility and creat-ing new means of meeting customer demands. This new dynamic requires tariffs, historically designed to recover costs within acceptable social and regu-latory goals of equity, understandability, and volatility, to serve a new purpose: engaging demand to help the system achieve an efficient mix of resources.

To do this, efficient tariffs are required. Regulators, utilities, and con-sumer advocates have historically viewed equity and efficiency as conflict-ing concepts. However, this chapter highlights that novel tariff structures can, in fact, improve both economic efficiency and certain aspects of equity. The inequities present in today's tariffs are likely going to be exacerbated in a DER-heavy future.

The chapter explores trade-offs between equity and economically effi-cient tariffs that underscore the complexity of the decisions that regulators and utilities face.

In **Chapter 9, New distribution network charges for new inte-grated network services, Ibtihal Abdelmotteleb, Tomás Gómez,** and **José Pablo Chaves Ávila** describe the emerging need for designing efficient distribution network charges that well accounts for the integration of distributed energy resources (DERs) and end-users' flexibility services.

The authors discuss how distribution-level flexibility mechanisms should be designed to align with preestablished tariff signals to efficiently integrate DERs and utilize end-users' flexibility services in the short- and long-run. The flexibility mechanisms aim to procure necessary energy services to economically enhance network's performance.

The chapter's main contribution is to demonstrate how future-looking distribution charges integrated with flexibility mechanisms would lead to efficient end-user responses, integration of new energy services, and consequently lower total system costs.

In **Chapter 10, Community energy storage: Governance and business models, Binod Prasad Koirala, Rudi A. Hakvoort, Ellen C. van Oost,** and **Henny J. van der Windt** conceptualize community energy storage (CES) as complex sociotechnical schemes deploying a variety of technologies, stakeholders, and transactions. The chapter explores the most important issues affecting the deployment of CES.

Two dominant options for implementing CES, local and virtual, are identified and elaborated. The chapter also discusses economic and noneconomic value streams as well as regulatory and policy implications for both options.

The chapter demonstrates the need for new regulations, governance, as well as the business models for the emergence of community energy storage. CES has potential to engage and transform local communities from consumers to prosumagers and eventually to nonsumers.

In **Chapter 11, Challenges to the promotion of distributed energy resources in Latin America: A Brazilian case study, Lucas Noura Guimarães** examines the pace and the regulatory conditions under which distributed energy resources are penetrating in Latin America, specifically looking at how this phenomenon is disrupting the distribution utilities' traditional business model while introducing a paradigm shift in the relation between consumers and utilities.

The author examines the regulatory framework including legal constraints and financial impediments that effectively result in the slow-paced development of DER, especially distributed generation, focusing on Brazil as a case study.

The chapter's main contribution is to offer a clearer insight about the consequences and influences of a regulatory framework on the development of distributed generation, including solutions to unblock the growth of this disruptive technology.

Part 3 of the book is focused on how the business models and strategies of incumbent distribution companies and newcomers will evolve in transformation of the power sector and vice versa.

In **Chapter 12, The future of electricity distribution: A California case study, Fereidoon Sioshansi** describes how the rise of variable renewable generation, distributed generation, zero net energy building codes, and community choice aggregation are beginning to change the traditional role of regulated utilities in California.

The chapter examines the intended and some of the unintended consequences of the regulations in the past, which has resulted in a host of service options that were not traditionally available. Moving forward, the regulators are grappling to keep pace with multiples of challenges unleashed by their own initiatives over the years.

The chapter also examines the evolving role of the state's three large private utilities may lose as much as 85% of their "customers" – turning them into regulated distribution-only companies no longer responsible for power procurement and largely devoid of generation assets. With all these changes, what will distribution business in California look like?

In **Chapter 13, Using flexibility resources to optimize distribution grids: A French case study, Pierre Germain** and **Etienne Jan** analyze how flexibility resources such as demand response, storage capacity, and so on, could be used to avoid or postpone DSO's investments and reduce operational costs. The chapter presents the results of a study conducted for the French energy regulator, CRE.

The authors assess the nationwide value of flexibility resources in serving electrical distribution grids, the appropriate activation schemes of flexibility at the local scale, and the coordination issues between local and national mechanisms.

The chapter demonstrates that local flexibility is valuable for the French distribution grids and analyzes the paradigm shift that it represents. The flexibility concept changes the traditional role of CAPEX for OPEX – pointing out that although DSO was historically "paid" for CAPEX, they must increasingly focus on optimizing capacity expansion, potentially exposing the DSO to greater risks.

In **Chapter 14, Off-grid prosumers: Electrifying the next billion with PAYGO solar, Toby Couture, Setu Pelz, Catherina Cader,** and **Philipp Blechinger** describe the dynamic growth of pay-as-you-go (PAYGO) solar companies and their success in establishing newer, smarter infrastructure free from the constraints of a centralized electricity distribution system.

The authors describe how these new PAYGO business models work and highlight how they are transforming the way electricity services are provided in countries throughout sub-Saharan Africa and Asia.

The main contribution of the chapter is to describe how these new business models are bringing technology, an innovative delivery model, and targeted consumer finance to areas, and customers, that have long been beyond the reach of traditional utilities. In the process, these business models are helping turn the estimated 1.1 billion citizens around the world without electricity access into off-grid prosumers, unleashing endless possibilities for economic, social, and educational development and redefining the way electricity is delivered and financed.

In **Chapter 15, Customer stratification and different concepts of decentralization, Dierk Bauknecht, Joß Bracker, Franziska Flachsbarth, Christoph Heinemann, Dominik Seebach,** and **Moritz Vogel** disentangle the debate on decentralization – examining what is meant by decentralization in different contexts – using Germany as the case study.

The authors examine different technical dimensions of decentralization, such as distributed generation close to demand as well as concepts to balance generation and demand locally. The motivation for these concepts can be wide ranging, from economic advantages, increased system resilience to better participation in the energy system. The chapter presents insights into the actual effects of decentralization on these objectives. Depending on the type of decentralization and the objective that is to be achieved, there are also different regulatory requirements.

The chapter's main insight is to highlight how decentralization interacts with new roles for consumers in the transformation of the energy system.

In **Chapter 16, Designing markets for innovative electricity services in the EU: The roles of policy, technology, and utility capabilities, Guillermo Ivan Pereira, Patrícia Pereira da Silva,** and **Deborah Soule** examine how new distribution utility business models are being supported in the European Union through policy adaptation, technological innovation, and organizational capabilities.

The authors provide an in-depth review of policy developments enabling new markets. This is complemented with novel empirical data from over 100 EU electricity distribution utilities, on adaptation and operational capabilities, providing a perspective on adaptation to a rapidly changing electricity sector.

The chapter provides policy makers and the utility industry a comprehensive perspective on the dynamics of market transformation and offers insight into the different dimensions that contribute to business model innovation. Moreover, the findings position incumbent utilities as relevant players in enabling innovative services.

In **Chapter 17, How incumbents are adjusting to the changing business environment: A German case study, Florian Weiss, Richard Groß, Sarah Linowski, Christian von Hirschhausen, Ben Wealer,** and **Timon Zimmermann** analyze disruptive changes affecting the German utilities over the past decade while speculating how they may evolve moving forward. In particular, the chapter examines the industry's traditional focus on conventional energy generation and business models, which were radically challenged by the global trends toward low-carbon energy mix as well as the specific dynamics of the German *energiewende*.

The authors point out that the combination of the *energiewende* and the 3Ds has resulted in substantial structural change, not only within the electric sector but spilling into others including electrified transportation.

In addition to an analysis of changing utility business strategies, the chapter examines the restructuring of the two major German utilities, RWE and E.on, and innovative strategies taking place at the electricity-transportation nexus.

In **Chapter 18, Who will fuel your electric vehicle in the future? You or your utility? Jeremy Webb, Jake Whitehead,** and **Clevo Wilson** explore the impact of the impending electrification of the world's automotive fleet and its impact on utility distribution networks. Of critical interest is the extent to which EVs will be charged from distributed generation or from the network.

The authors examine a survey of Australian EV owners and their charging habits as well as the potential of residential rooftop solar to charge them.

The chapter concludes that EV ownership and residential rooftop solar are likely to be common attributes of many suburban while stand-alone batteries for storage are likely to become a common addition. However, retail electricity prices, feed-in-tariffs, and availability of workplace charging will be key issues in determining which regime might prevail in charging EVs and the extent to which they are charged on or off-grid.

In **Chapter 19, Distributed energy resources in the US wholesale markets: Recent trends, new models, and forecasts, Udi Helman** examines recent trends including federal regulatory policies intended to further facilitate the participation of distributed energy resource in the US organized wholesale markets.

The author reviews the long history of distributed resource participation on both the supply and the demand side, and how the newer technologies, notably distributed generation and storage, are rapidly changing the electric power landscape against the backdrop of continued wholesale market price depression due to low natural gas prices and expansion of grid-connected renewables.

The chapter suggests that within a decade or two, the DER expansion may account for 20–30% of the renewable energy produced in some regions as well as about half of the forecast storage installations, measured by capacity. Hence, the impact of distributed resources on wholesale markets will be significant.

In the book's **Epilogue, Jean Laurent Lastelle** and **Dominique Jamme** agree that the innovation will create a new world of opportunities for energy consumers and change the way distribution networks are managed while self-consumption, local energy communities, and micro-grids will challenge traditional business models.

Self-consumers are likely to pay less for energy and for the network than the cost they impose on the system, which is not be a good outcome on either efficiency or equity grounds – cautioning regulators to remain vigilant.

The incumbents, in particular former monopolies, will be forced to make bold strategic decisions, as has been the case recently in Germany. At the same time, there will be many newcomers, from the simplest low-cost retailers to the most sophisticated offering customized services using platforms and new business models. This initial phase will most probably be followed by consolidation leading to more viable business models – perhaps the topic of a sequel volume?

Fereidoon Sioshansi
Menlo Energy Economics, Walnut Creek, CA, United States

PART 1

How Service Innovations Are Leading to Consumer Stratification and Disruption

CHAPTER 1

Digitalization of Energy

Mostyn Brown*, **Stephen Woodhouse***, **Fereidoon Sioshansi†**
*Pöyry Management Consulting, Oxford, United Kingdom
†Menlo Energy Economics, Walnut Creek, CA, United States

1. INTRODUCTION

In recent years, growing numbers of businesses and industries, notably banking, communication, entertainment, publishing, and many others, have embraced the potential of modernization, automation, and digitalization, with varying degrees of commercial success. Publishing, for example, has moved inexorably toward digitalization as more newspapers, magazines, journals, and books are published electronically – this book being no exception. In the case of Netflix®, the company has single-handedly transformed the movie and entertainment industry by moving its delivery channel to wireless Internet, in the process disrupting incumbent movie studios, television, and cable services.

But digitalization is not simply the process of moving from analogue to digital, from print to electronic or wireless delivery. It is the use of digital tools to change the underlying business model.

In particular, platform businesses, as further described in chapter by Stanley et al., are emerging that connect large numbers of suppliers and consumers, but do not own the underlying energy infrastructure. Many utilities meanwhile are making concerted efforts to join the digital revolution through acquisition of start-ups while competition is fierce from forward-thinking Internet and communication technology (ICT) and automotive companies built on a "trial fast/fail fast/learn fast" culture. The real pay-offs will take time as forging a new digitally enhanced relationship requires change on both sides, and consumer attitudes to existing brands are slow to change. Players unable to establish – or patient enough to wait for – these data-orientated customer relationships will be forced further upstream, focusing on the lower margin work of owning generation assets and selling electricity as a commodity as further described in chapter by Weiss et al.

This chapter explores how the digital revolution in the electricity sector may play out: what are the impacts of digitalization, how will future digital energy companies make their money, and which are the likely organizations to succeed.

The chapter is structured as follows:

- Section 2 describes what digitalization means when applied to the electricity sector;
- Section 3 explains how digitalization will impact the electricity value chain and why the retail sector will see the most disruption;
- Section 4 explores how the various digital business models may emerge and how they may operate; and
- Section 5 examines who is likely to thrive in this new energy arena followed by the chapter's conclusions.

2. DIGITALIZATION IN THE ELECTRICITY SECTOR

First order of business is to define what is meant by "digitalization" in the electricity sector, followed by how it may emerge, what its benefits may be, and who are likely to gain the most from the digital transformation.

In the case of publishing — which has largely embraced the transition to digital — it can be said that the traditional business model is increasingly being eroded by new models; electronic publications are sold online, leased through subscription, or provided for free in return for exposing the reader to advertising. This is a response to two developments brought about by digitalization, namely:

- The new economics of (near) zero marginal-cost supply; and
- The disruption of the conventional linear value chain brought about by the proliferation of authors — anyone can now publish their writing and/or opinion to the world for free on social media and other channels.

Similar characteristics apply to the electricity sector through increasing supplies of essentially zero marginal cost renewables and the growing role of distributed generation, where millions of small-scale generators are now feeding the network rather than a few central power plants. However, the energy sector as a whole, and the electricity sector in particular, has not made the transition to digital yet (Box 1.1). Products and services are still largely sold in the same way they always have.

However over the last few years, electric utilities have become much more open to the idea that the new business models will crowd out the old, and are proactively exploring new ideas, powered by new digital approaches as further explained in chapters by Shipworth et al., Baak and Sioshansi, and

Box 1.1 What Is "Digitalization"?

Broadly speaking, digitalization can be defined as the use of digital technologies to improve efficiency by reducing costs and risks; or to change the underlying business model by engaging with customers to understand and influence their preferences while creating new sources of revenue.

Digital technologies include all types of electronic equipment and applications that use information in the form of numeric code – usually binary code consisting of two numeric characters, 0 and 1. These "digital technologies" are not new: most of today's workforce started employment in the age of desktop computers, and digital information and processing has been mainstream for several decades. But the pace of change is accelerating, as both data and communication become increasingly accessible.

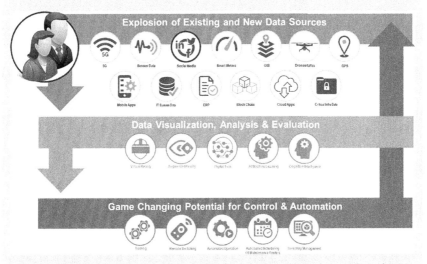

Digital technologies in the energy industry. *(Source: Pöyry Management Consulting.)*

These technologies can be grouped into three categories:
- Access to new sources of data and communications;
- Decision-support systems based on improved analysis and visualization tools; and
- Automation and control.

The future digitalized system will allow decisions to be taken and executed autonomously based on a wide range of uncontrolled data sources while cybersecurity protocols must adapt to this new decentralized and autonomous reality. Digitalization also allows companies to interact directly with people through social media, assessing people's real needs and preferences – potentially influencing their preferences.

Stanley et al. The key is to establish direct relationships with end consumers without necessarily having ownership of the underlying assets, as testified by the likes of Amazon®, Uber®, Airbnb®, and so on.

While digitalization in the electricity sector spans the entire value chain, the front line in this battle for the customer is taking place at the *grid's edge*, generally defined as where the distribution network meets the customers' premises and what takes place on the customer side of the meter – the so-called *behind-the-meter* (BTM) space.

3. HOW WILL DIGITALIZATION IMPACT THE ELECTRICITY VALUE CHAIN AND WHY WILL RETAIL FACE THE MOST DISRUPTION?

To date, the digitalization of the power sector has mostly focused on more efficient, secure, and sustainable electricity systems. The main benefits have been reduced operations and maintenance (O&M) costs, improved efficiencies, increased reliability, and extension of operational lifetimes of critical assets. While these are critical components in delivering services to end customers, further opportunities are spread across the value chain as illustrated in Fig. 1.1. As accompanying chapters in this volume explain, many unexplored opportunities exist in trading, distribution, and retail space, the last three boxes in Fig. 1.1.

Some of the significant potential impacts of digitalization on the various parts of the electricity value chain include:

- Gains in generation asset management mainly focused on the optimization of plant maintenance, fuel, and spare parts. Technologies used will include remote sensing and digital monitors, new control systems with automatic predictive and remote maintenance/control – perhaps linked

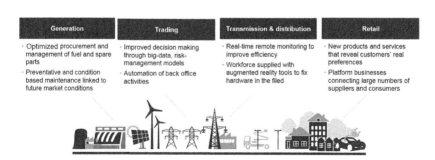

FIGURE 1.1 Digitalization opportunities across the value chain. *(Source: Pöyry Management Consulting.)*

to projected market conditions – augmented intelligence for decision making, and machine learning for better short-term forecasts for balancing and trading;

- Digitalization could improve decision making in trading and scheduling of generation by utilizing strategies based on big data, new risk-management models, and new trading products, based on more rapid decision-making and algo-trading including optimization of short-term generation operations;

- Reduced losses, reduced labor costs, and predictive maintenance in transmission and distribution networks through real-time remote monitoring, real-time sensor data to aid forecasting, at data hubs compiling smart meter data, and augmented intelligence for network management. Furthermore, digitalization and smart switching at lower voltage networks can facilitate deferred/avoided network investment and the transition to active distribution network management. New regulatory approaches could emerge based on shared data, which could narrow the information asymmetry between companies and regulators; and

- Finally, digitalization of the retail sector, where the truly revolutionary and transformative aspects of digitalization comes in. Establishing direct relationships with customers will lead to provision of new products and services, lower prices, more customer differentiation through digital marketing, electronic billing/settlement, charging for access to the grid, bundling of other services with energy and/or its delivery, peer-to-peer trading and other topics further described in the following chapters of this volume.

In addition to impacting the linear value chain as described here, digitalization will also facilitate the move to a more integrated, highly flexible decentralized energy system as conceptually illustrated in Fig. 1.2 and further explained in Box 1.2.

The truly transformative benefits of digitalization will be achieved by organizations who will manage to establish direct and lasting digital relationships with customers, leading to new service offerings and associated revenues. Currently, most electricity retailers know extremely little about their customers. Digitalization will make it possible to offer more personalized services and one-on-one relationships. In the near future, energy companies digitally interacting with their customers could, for example, know which rooms and appliances customers use the most and at what times, detect when the customer is not home or on holiday – perhaps even being

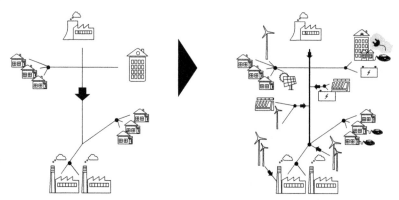

FIGURE 1.2 Digitalization will accelerate the transition to a highly flexible and decentralized energy system. *(Source: Pöyry Management Consulting.)*

Box 1.2 Digitalization Will Facilitate the Move to a Decentralized Energy System

The most significant and untapped cost reduction opportunities are expected to come from unlocking customers' demand-side flexibility and similar opportunities in behind-the-meter assets. This is because it is a very large value pool that remains largely untapped using existing technology.

Digitalization can provide the information flows required to make this complex and disparate system viable, alongside nondigital drivers such as the electrification of transport and growth in decentralized and variable generation. In a report published in 2017, the International Energy Agency (IEA)[1] characterizes three inter-related elements that digitalization can make possible, notably

- Smart demand response;
- The integration of variable renewables; and
- Smart charging for electric vehicles (EVs).

These are briefly outlined as follows.

Smart Demand Response

Demand response (DR) refers to the process of consumers – or their appliances – responding flexibly to price signals from the market, e.g., by shifting consumption to those hours with a surplus of electricity supply, or responding to system needs for real-time frequency control. DR today is – in the main – unsophisticated and is largely restricted to energy-intensive industrial consumers who are offered financial incentives in return for accepting the possibility of their supply being interrupted but with very little expectation that such response will actually be required.

---

[1]Digitalization & Energy, IEA (2017).

Box 1.2 Digitalization Will Facilitate the Move to a Decentralized Energy System—cont'd

It is estimated that currently only 1% of global demand flexibility is able to directly respond to shortages or excess supply.[2] Clearly, the untapped potential is enormous and with the rising variability of increasing amounts of renewable generation the value of DR will further increase.

Numerous digitalization technologies can help achieve vastly greater DR penetration, not just in the commercial and industrial (C&I) sectors but eventually in the residential sector. For instance, automated Internet of Things (IoT) devices in the residential and commercial sector, e.g., smart thermostats directly connected to the wholesale electricity market prices and to weather forecast providers – which in turn may be made from other distributed sensors – are among the viable options to be explored.

Most of the global DR potential lies in the buildings sector, especially in space and water heating and cooling. The thermal inertia in these systems means that heating and cooling can be shifted over a certain number of hours without a noticeable impact on the end consumer. Most of the remaining potential in buildings is related to electricity used for large domestic appliances such as washing machines, fridge/freezers, dishwashers, clothes dryers, and so on. Another promising application can be expected from the rising numbers of EVs over the years. Large commercial buildings, such as supermarkets, hotels, hospitals, shopping malls, and offices, also offer significant potential for DR as do certain types of industrial loads.

The benefits of increased DR are estimated to be substantial. According to the IEA, for example, the technical potential of demand response could be of the order of 6900 TWhs and may results in about 185 GW of *additional* flexibility for the electricity system globally by 2040.

This amount of flexibility, if successfully captured, would avoid a cumulative $270 billion (in 2016 dollars) of investment in new electricity infrastructure including new power-generation capacity and transmission and distribution expansions. With today's technology and resources, the IEA estimates that as many as a billion households and 11 billion smart appliances may be remotely monitored and managed. Clearly, DR and various forms of integrated energy services such as those covered in the following chapters of this book would fit the bill.

Currently this enormous potential of DR has remained untapped because the financial rewards to consumers or the market enablers have not been sufficient to cover the costs including the initial investments plus the costs of managing and implementing DR. With implementation costs expected to falling dramatically in the coming years, a much larger share of the DR benefits may be captured.

[2] Market data: Demand Response, Navigant Research (2017).

Box 1.2   Digitalization Will Facilitate the Move to a Decentralized Energy System—cont'd

As an illustration of the remaining obstacles to unleashing this potential, at Pöyry/EURELECTRIC's #ENERGY4.0 conference[3] roughly 60% of the audience thought it will be harder to unlock the value in *flexibility* relative to *energy efficiency*, which itself has proved rather intractable. The situation has not been helped by the introduction of capacity arrangements in some markets, which have the effect of dampening wholesale price volatility. Similarly, in most markets, consumers and their retailers are not yet fully exposed to real-time prices arising from their actual consumption. Future innovators in this space must make the business model work by removing some of the regulatory constraints.

Integration of Variable Renewables

Another clear source of value will be through improved integration of variable renewable energy resources. The IEA study found that by 2040, renewable curtailment in the EU could be cut from 7% of wind/solar generation to 1.6%, representing a saving of 67 TWh; roughly 27 TWhs from DR and another 45 TWhs by using storage technologies. This will improve returns for renewable generators, save costs through less ramping up and down of conventional energy sources, and impact how infrastructure is planned and how well it is utilized.

Although the IEA report does not dwell on the impact of better management of distributed renewable generation such as rooftop solar PVs, digitalization could offer significant savings in utilization of such behind-the-meter DER resources.

Smart Charging for EVs

Through "smart charging," price signals provide incentives for connected EVs to charge when there is abundant production of low-cost electricity or to stand by/discharge when the network is congested as further described in chapter by Webb et al. This requires digital infrastructure to permit communication between charging points and control systems and to allow parties to send requests to increase or reduce demand at certain times. With growing fleets of EVs expected over the next decade, managing when the cars are charged and at what price will be crucial to their commercial success.

There is, however, considerable uncertainty over the volume of EVs that may be deployed over the next two decades. The IEA estimates that in a scenario where 150 million EVs are deployed by 2040, EV charging capacity would need to reach 140 GW. With smart charging, the required charging requirement would drop to 75 GW – roughly half as much as might be needed under a business-as-usual – or not fully digitalized – case. Under a scenario

[3]#ENERGY4.0 – when Internet meets energy. Pöyry and EURELECTRIC joint conference, London, November 2017.

Box 1.2   Digitalization Will Facilitate the Move to a Decentralized Energy System— cont'd

where there may be as many as 500 million EVs globally by 2040, the respective figures are 300 vs. 190 GW, respectively. In either case, the value of a fully digitalized and sophisticated EV charging infrastructure is evident from these illustrative numbers.

The IEA estimates the flexibility provided by smart charging could avoid as much as a $100 billion of investment in electricity infrastructure including new power generation capacity and transmission and distribution, which would otherwise be required to cover the peak in electricity demand from EVs. Of course, one would have to account for the extra cost of investing in the smart charging infrastructure to come up with the net savings. These numbers are based on the assumption that the future EVs will be operating in a similar way as they are today.

Digitalization of EV charging infrastructure, however, could have other important implications, for example, leading to drastic change in ownership patterns. If *shared* automated vehicles, for example, became widespread, the flexibility outlined would arguably diminish since the vehicles would operate at much higher load factors. On the other hand, in this case, batteries could be charged at dedicated high-voltage charging stations, perhaps with battery swap technology.

able to detect if the customer is *thinking* about going on holiday, just as Facebook®, Google®, and other data-savvy companies currently do.

Such intelligence, of course, raises issues about privacy and access to data – which has become highly sensitive and controversial in view of the widespread perceived breach of trust at Facebook® and others with access to consumer data in recent years.

A new relationship with energy customers could, for example, unlock and reveal a different degree of "willingness-to-pay" for what are perceived as premium value services or combinations of services. Such intelligence and customization could enable retailers to offer a wider range of quality and brand differentiators, e.g., customers could choose their own level of service reliability, engage in peer-to-peer trading, manage the operation of their "virtual battery"[4] and possibly select other, nonenergy products to be bundled with their energy supply. This requires the customers to change

---

[4]Based on an E.ON offering in which customers inject their own self-generated energy surplus into a virtual tank, and may draw it out in a range of ways including their daughter at university, their EV away from home, and so on.

their perceptions and attitudes on how they buy energy and how they interface with their energy supplier.

Many such customized services and individualized relationships, of course, are unexplored territory with uncertain risks and rewards. For example, it is not clear if consumers' perception of values will change, and if retailers who are offering new bundled retail offerings can determine and capture the added values. Equally unclear are questions about which brands or which types of organizations will be capable of taking customers on this transition.

One area of product differentiation that has started already is the rise of the *prosumers* and the proliferation of behind-the-meter assets, extensively discussed in accompanying chapters of this volume. As the cost of solar PVs and distributed batteries continues to decrease, more consumers can produce and manage their own energy supply independently from the electricity retailers.

Total grid defection, however, is expected to be rare to limited, especially in places with cold winters, which requires seasonal storage. Moreover, in most developed countries, the fact that the existing grid is already built, and its ongoing operating costs are low compared to the value it brings in terms of reliability, diversity, shared backup, and so on, suggests that nearly all prosumers and prosumagers would remain connected to the grid. Off-grid solutions – further described in chapter by Couture et al. – only make sense where new grid is required or where there are very great distances between electricity clusters, such as Oceana or remote parts of Africa, where isolated mini-grids could proliferate in the next decade or so.

In developed countries, therefore, it is hard to justify going totally off grid while maintaining high level of reliability. Instead, some customers may decide to operate in a grid-assisted or grid-parallel mode, which means they remain connected to the main grid but rely on it in a limited or minimal way, mostly for reliability and back-up services. Many micro-grids, for example, coexist with the super-grid operating in parallel but with the ability to "island" in emergencies or in cases when the super-grid may go down.

In this context, the underlying motivation for consumers to go "off-grid" is driven by a desire to be independent or, in rare cases, because a higher level of reliability is required than the super-grid can currently provide. For those who wish to be independent, they may be willing to invest in assets at low or even negative rates of return for reasons that may be hard to justify economically.

This line of reasoning also applies to branded electricity, which have been suitably differentiated from competitors. At the #ENERGY4.0 conference,[4] for example, roughly 40% of the audience said they would be willing to pay a 10% premium for electricity that was from a local and/or renewable source.

Those that doubt the ability of firms to create brands around a homogeneous, undifferentiated, commodity product like electricity should note the success of bottled water brands where sales have now surpassed carbonated soft drinks to become the largest beverage category by volume in the US. Rather than relying on a standard commodity that comes down a pipe or wire, consumers are apparently willing to pay more for something they believe is superior. Unfortunately estimating the size of this value pool is exceedingly hard.

As an extreme example, digital energy consumers of the future could be supplied with branded batteries, differentiated by generation technology, location, and possibly other characteristics. Digitalization already provides the means to track renewable or locally generated electricity at a much more granular level than was possible before. Furthermore through peer-to-peer trading, digitalization will allow communities of prosumers to optimize the supply and demand of their electricity. The next section will further explore the various business models that may emerge to unleash and monetize these sources of value.

4. HOW WILL FUTURE DIGITAL ENERGY COMPANIES MAKE MONEY?

Utilities have begun to accept that digitalization will disrupt the industry while questions remain on exactly how and how soon. At the #ENERGY4.0 conference[4] a leading European utility executive boldly claimed that

> *By 2025, the largest global energy company (by market cap) will not have any generation or network assets.*

While this statement could not be construed as a matter of corporate policy, it was nevertheless an astonishing claim. If true, the question is, if not by investing in assets, then how will digital energy companies of the future make money?

This is a crucial issue since regulated utilities have traditionally made money primarily, if not exclusively, by investing in assets, which in turn, are allowed a reasonable rate of return by the regulator. If energy sales flatten or decline due to the rise of prosumers and prosumagers and utilities no longer own many (or any) generation or network assets, as claimed, then how would they survive, or what new forms and organizations will they evolve into?

Three broad business models come to mind for the digitalized utilities of the future:

- First, they could charge for access to the grid, perhaps based on capacity rather than volumetric consumption. This approach suggests that prosumers and prosumagers would continue to pay for the maintenance and upkeep of the network even if they buy few or no net kWhs from it;
- Second, they could bundle electricity with other services and/or products; and
- Third, they could charge for access to a platform, i.e., a virtual marketplace where a variety of useful products and services can be bought, sold, or traded.

These three options are briefly outlined here.

4.1 Charging for Access to the Grid

This business model represents a relatively small departure from the current ways of doing business. It does not require total digitalization or transformation of assets or a major overhaul of the existing infrastructure. It mainly changes how consumers, prosumers, and prosumagers of the future pay for the privilege of remaining connected to the existing network and the upstream assets and services provided. With digitalization, electricity business may finally be moving toward a "subscription" service as in other industries (Box 1.3).

While in its infancy, the subscription service business model is beginning to find applications in the utility space. An example is Green Mountain Power's (GMP) energy storage offering where customers can lease a Tesla Powerwall 2.0 battery for $15 a month provided that they allow GMP to manage when the batteries are charged and discharged. The basics of this business model are further described in Box 1.4.

As the preceding discussion illustrates, there are many challenges and opportunities in transitioning to a capacity-based access fee to the network and much speculation on how fast it may happen, how profitable it may be and – most important – how access charges may be determined.

Box 1.3 From Products to Subscription Services

In his book *Subscribed: Why subscription model will be your company's future – and what to do about it*, author Tien Tzuo points out that

> *The world is moving from products to services. Subscriptions are exploding because billions of digital customers are increasingly favoring access over ownership, but most companies are still built to sell products.*

While electricity has traditionally been sold as a *service*, albeit an undifferentiated, unexciting commodity, digitalization offers challenges and opportunities to redefine how the service will be delivered and how it will be charged.

In the case of prosumers and prosumagers, in particular, who may not be buying very many, if any, net kWhs, the subscription business model, where they are charged a flat monthly fee, makes good sense. Amazon® Prime, Netflix®, iTunes, or Spotify, for example, charge their members a flat monthly fee for the privilege of being able to order and/or download services to which they are entitled. In the process, these companies get to know their customers much better by following their shopping/buying habits – which in turn – allows them to offer more targeted and personalized services.

In his book, Tzuo is convinced that many industries historically focused on manufacturing and selling products need to migrate to innovative business models based on leasing and services – whether through a basic subscription service or a pay-as-you-go fee. For example, automakers may move to a mostly lease option where all costs including maintenance, insurance, taxes – perhaps even the gas or electricity to power the car – may be included in a fixed monthly fee.

Box 1.4 Charging for Access to the Grid[5]

Tariffs designed for the one-directional networks of the past century with passive consumers – which are still prevalent nearly everywhere in the world – are clearly outdated. Volumetric tariffs no longer capture the emerging value proposition offered by the grid – which offers connectivity, balancing services, frequency control, voltage stability, and 24/7 reliability – services most coveted by increasingly sophisticated prosumers or prosumagers rather than delivering a large volume of kWhs, especially as zero-marginal cost generation erodes the value of each kWh.

This suggests that the power sector is on a path not unlike that of mobile phone industry where most users pay a fixed monthly fee based on a term

[5]This box is based on Innovation and disruption at the grid's edge, S. Woodhouse & S. Bradbury, in Innovation & disruption at the grid's edge, F. Sioshansi (Ed.), Academic Press, 2017.

Continued

Box 1.4 Charging for Access to the Grid—cont'd

contract (e.g., 1–2 years) with a network service provider. Note although in this example even though the price is *fixed*, when choosing the product, the consumer can select a tariff that suits their volume requirements. In the case of electricity, there is a strong case to have a capacity-based fee – the thickness of the copper wire – rather than a kWh volumetric fee. In this case, customers who need more capacity – either to export or import electrons to/from the network – pay a higher subscription fee for more capacity.

While the mobile phone analogy is not perfect – e.g., currently electrons cannot be delivered without copper wires – it is clear that mobile phone service is increasingly about *connectivity* and *access* to the network rather than the volume or frequency of calls. Subscribers choose a provider on the basis of the ubiquity and reliability of its network access, the strength of the signal, bandwidth, and speed. They are rarely charged on a per-call or per-minute basis. The cost of service is much better reflected, and collected, through a fixed fee almost regardless of the volume of calls. The same goes for garbage collection and many other services where the fixed costs account for the overwhelming percentage of cost of service. This is not yet true in electricity, but as zero marginal cost renewables increase in market share, it is clearly coming.

Furthermore, as the commodity portion of the service continues to fall, charging based on volume will become unsustainable as a means of covering the cost of the delivery network. Furthermore, digitalization could help schedule microgeneration and controllable loads, allowing users to mitigate their use of the network. To some degree, this avoids the need to increase network capacity – a good thing from a system perspective – and the benefits can be shared among all consumers. However, it may also allow users to time their consumption based on whatever charging regime is in place in such a way that they avoid their share of the costs of provision of the network, backup, stability, and so on – which is not a good thing, except for those who benefit.

The emerging digitalization arms race could be summed up by the statement: digitalization of your home will allow you to avoid paying for the network, and your less digitally enabled neighbors can pay instead.[6]

[6]Which explains why regulators can be expected to support a transition to cost-reflective capacity-related network tariffs.

4.2 Bundling Electricity With Other Services and/or Products

A second business model would be focused on bundling electricity with other products or services that consumers want and need – presumably in synergistic ways.

Bundling plays an increasingly important role in many industries including banking, insurance, software, and automotive. Through the economies of scale of bundling, companies can sell a package or set of goods or services for a lower price than they would charge if the customer bought them separately. They also provide an opportunity to "lock-in" consumers although this can cause disputes as in the infamous example of Microsoft's attempt to bundle its flagship Internet Explorer browser software with the sale of its operating system.

Successful bundled services can be found in other industries, say insurance, where by combining car insurance with home and/or life insurance, the customer is offered a lower total premium than buying three separate policies, three bills, and the extra effort to interface with three different agents. The transactions and marketing costs are significantly reduced – and the bundled service becomes "sticky" in the sense that it takes a lot of effort to unbundle once it has been bundled.

The variety of bundled solutions is growing across the energy spectrum. For example, Centrica sells the Hive smart thermostat and tools to detect boiler breakdowns in the UK. Meanwhile, Ovo and Nissan have partnered together to create special tariffs to reward customers for control over their V2G charging. Many more examples of bundled products and service are expected to emerge.

At the #ENERGY4.0 conference,[4] roughly half of the audience expected that the majority of future EV sales will be bundled with an electricity supply contract by 2025. In addition to their V2G tariffs, Ovo and Nissan have launched a similar product for home battery storage to rival Tesla's plans for an integrated electricity package, further described in chapter by Baak & Sioshansi.

The next stage in this evolution could be the bundling of electricity with the sale of smart domestic appliances or other behind-the-meter (BTM) devices (Fig. 1.3). As with the Ovo-Nissan offering, the price of the electricity could be discounted in return for control over the appliance in a bundled package. In a crowded market for "white goods," which include washing machines, dryers, refrigerators, dish washers, etc. bundling electricity with a known brand, say LG or Samsung, could give both an advantage over unbundled rivals. EVs, PVs, and distributed storage devices – all expensive behind-the-meter investments – naturally lend themselves into being bundled in clever ways.

It is estimated that the volume of controllable smart appliances in the EU could be at least 60 GW by 2025. Controlling the pattern and energy use

£299 Hotpoint washing machine

☐ Express delivery

☐ Instant Energy Bundle - 5 year
£25/year, requires Amazon Prime subscription

☐ Green Managed Energy Bundle
£20/year, only available with Amazon Echo

FIGURE 1.3 Hypothetical offering: bundled electricity with smart appliances. *(Source: Pöyry Management Consulting.)*

of these devices could reduce peak demand by 10%.[7] Electricity-intensive EVs and appliances with large and easily controllable demand such as fridge/freezers and electric hot water heaters are likely to be first to be remotely monitored and controlled.

The end goal, however, is a fully connected smart home, where all the BTM devices and assets can be remotely monitored and managed through the optimization of all significant energy-consuming appliances, self-generation, and storage if applicable. Amazon® and Google® both have made inroads into this space – through Echo and Nest, respectively – and are currently in prime position to lead further developments. Tesla, Sonnen, and a number of other major players are also interested. Many existing players may end up merging and/or acquiring other smaller players in the process.

Currently there are many regulatory obstacles, which prevent such bundled offerings from materializing in many markets, but regulators are under growing pressure to give customers more choice in how they buy – and potentially sell or trade – their energy. In the UK, for instance, it is currently not possible for end consumers to buy power from multiple providers, but Elexon has outlined proposals to adapt the Balancing and Settlement Code to allow this to happen, potentially as early as 2020.[8] Similar provisions are already allowed in the Netherlands, which introduced them in early 2018.[9]

---

[7]Best practices on renewable energy self-consumption. European Commission, 2015.
[8]Enabling customers to buy power from multiple providers. ELEXON, 2018.
[9]Meerdere leveranciers op een aansluiting (Multiple suppliers on a single connection). ACM, 2017.

4.3 Platform Business Models

Arguably, this is the most disruptive of three digitalized business models and potentially the most profitable. Platform businesses connect large numbers of suppliers and consumers without owning the underlying infrastructure or – necessarily – taking title to the product or service being delivered. As further described in chapter by Stanley et al., they can be thought of as virtual marketplaces. Uber® and Airbnb® are particularly pertinent examples (Fig. 1.4).

Platform providers may charge the energy companies for access, as is presently the case for switching sites, or take a fee for each transaction – most likely a % cut on the value of each transaction performed using the platform, which is the common practice in other industries. Alternatively, the customers may pay the platform operator for allowing them to find the best deals and switch them for a fee. This type of service, for example, could be connected to smart home/auto DR offerings, combining the two business models described earlier in this section.

Clearly, we are in the midst of an explosion of platform offerings attempting to harness the flexibility value pools identified in the previous section. Broadly speaking, BTM platform applications may be grouped into three areas:
- Distributed storage;
- E-mobility; and
- Peer-to-peer energy trading, a topic that is further explored in the following chapter.

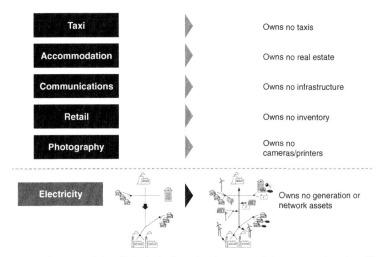

FIGURE 1.4 The rise of the digital platform business model across industries. *(Source: Pöyry Management Consulting.)*

There is also lots of activity in the commercial and industrial (C&I) space including the examples in chapter by Baak and Sioshansi and in offering price visibility and/or relieving congestion on the distributed networks as described in chapter by Stanley et al.

The storage sector is mainly made up of battery manufacturers like Tesla (USA) and Sonnen (Germany) and numerous others entering the business. These and their peers are in the process of establishing platforms, which aggregate the capacity of multiple distributed batteries to create a virtual power plant, which can deliver services on demand to the system operator, local electricity networks, and utilities. The ambition of these companies appears to be able to expand the existing platforms to manage a wider range of third-party home batteries, EV batteries, and IoT batteries – and potentially other devices or assets. As the cost of ICT declines and more BTM devices can be remotely monitored and controlled, the business model can be expanded to include smaller commercial and eventually even residential customers.

Platform business models are also emerging in the e-mobility space. For instance, Motionwerk's Share&Charge platform, based on Ethereum, an open-source public blockchain, enables users to find parking spots or smart charging solutions and processes the billing and handles the settlement process with multiples of providers in the value chain. The value of an offering that allows an EV driver to charge from multiple providers at different times and locations across an entire country or continent becomes overwhelming as more people migrate to EVs over the next two decades.

Toyota is developing a Mobility Services Platform to make use of flexible, purpose-built autonomous vehicles. Launch partners include Amazon®, DiDi®, Mazda®, Pizza Hut®, and UBER®, who will collaborate on vehicle planning, application concepts, and vehicle verification activities. Meanwhile battery specialist Blue Solutions has launched America's largest fully electric car-sharing service, which continues to blur the lines between public and private transport.

The expected rapid growth of EVs suggests that there will be room for multiples of platforms and players – at least initially – before winning business models emerge to dominate the space.

The peer-to-peer energy trading sector is also currently receiving lots of attention, some of which is simply enthusiasm for the vision rather than reflecting the mechanics and economics that underpins the concept given the many obstacles and challenges that remain to be resolved – the topic of the following chapter.

For instance, at the #ENERGY4.0 conference,[4] roughly 70% of the audience expected peer-to-peer platforms to deliver energy that is cheaper than conventional alternatives by 2025, despite the fact that representatives of the peer-to-peer trading organizations themselves acknowledged this would be overambitious. Many with the knowledge of the business believe that among the main selling point of peer-to-peer energy trading is the perceived value to customers for knowing the source of their energy rather than a significant reduction in delivery cost. Some P2P models may circumvent network charges, but as noted earlier this is not a sustainable model.

There are numerous peer-to-peer energy trading initiatives that have appeared over the last few years with many others to follow. Some are algorithm based, such as Powerpeers in the Netherlands and Open Utility (now called Piclo Flex) in the UK, as described in chapter by Stanley et al. Others are based on Distributed Ledger Technologies (DLTs), of which Blockchain is one form. These protocols record transactions across many computers so that the record cannot be altered retroactively without collusion of the network. The attraction of this approach is that because the peer-to-peer network is self-regulating, there is no need for a central administrator resulting in a more efficient system – at least in theory.

Of course one of the downsides of this approach is that the governance is intractable, making it harder to adapt the system as circumstances change, which explains the reason for the various blockchain "forks" or alternatives that have occurred. One of the front-runners in this area is LO3 Energy who rose to fame in April 2016 when they facilitated a blockchain-based trade between neighbors on a micro-grid in Brooklyn, New York.

Despite the enthusiasm, however there are concerns that the current generation blockchain technologies may not be sufficiently scalable or low cost to allow widespread peer-to-peer transactions. IOTA's DLT, which uses a protocol called the Tangle, has been designed to address these limitations and is intended for IOT volume transactions. Users of the Tangle validate two previous transactions, via proof of work, to be able to conduct one of their own. No one receives a reward and no one has to pay transaction fees. These initiatives are at a very early stage but one of IOTA's potential strengths is that the peer-to-peer energy trading is part of a larger system attempting to facilitate machine-to-machine transactions more generally.[10]

---

[10]Refer to https://www.iota.org/.

5. WHO WILL THRIVE IN THIS NEW ENERGY ARENA? WHERE WILL THE MAJOR THREATS COME FROM?

The nature of the changes unleashed through digitalization opens up parts of the value chain to new actors, by removing natural synergies or barriers to entry. This disruption, in turn, forces existing companies to reposition themselves, either through adopting the new technologies – including acquiring the new companies if they are small enough – or ceding territory and moving out of parts of the value chain. The key question is which scenario is more likely.

Already, some of the European majors are adapting their strategies away from the conventional generation, which has been their core business for many years – as further described in chapter by Weiss et al. – and are using media channels and new tools to build meaningful relationships with their customers. Other companies are continuing to focus on the core business of asset ownership, asset management, and asset operation, lubricated by trading and risk management in the wholesale markets. In some markets, notably Australia, those with generation assets have combined with retail to form powerful *gentailer* business models, while other retailers are experimenting with innovative services, further described in chapter by Bashir et al. Many other companies are following an active "hybrid strategy," or just act passively.

For either strategy to succeed, the companies need to become more effective in their chosen areas of focus. This is where the digitalization story becomes relevant.

Transformation to a digitalized operating model requires a realignment of companies' core values, internal organization, and long-term business model. Up to now, wholesale digital transformations in the energy sector have been extremely rare, and digital start-ups remain mostly small, niche players within the industry.

At the same time, incumbents are unearthing major inefficiencies in their existing operations, which are the low-hanging fruit to improve profitability, even without full adoption of digital technologies. On the customer side, for example, forging a new digitally enhanced relationship requires changes on both sides, and consumer attitudes to existing brands are slow to change. End-to-end digital transformation, on the other hand, faces challenges from the conservative nature of the business and its staff, and the ponderous IT systems built to handle – certainly by the standards of previous decades – large volumes of data. Indeed, the energy utility industry has historically exhibited significantly lower levels of innovation relative to other industries.

Among the many reasons for the slow pace of change is the acknowledgment that most "major" transformations are complex, expensive, and fail, and strong leadership and effective change management is a prerequisite to successful adaptation. Nonetheless, there is a significant threat from ICT and automotive companies built on a "trial fast/fail fast/learn fast" culture forcing utilities to move forward with more ambitious digitalization efforts.

Moreover, established companies like Facebook®, Apple®, Amazon®, Netflix®, and Google®, collectively known as FAANG, which already have well-established relationships with end consumers and business models built around utilizing data pose a significant threat, particularly in the connected home space. The FAANGs may soon be joined alongside, automotive companies with strong brands and experience in managing physical, rather than purely digital, relationships with end consumers.

The real threat is likely to materialize if a powerful player with established links to large numbers of consumers can develop products and/or services that make use of cross-sectoral linkages – say combining electric transport with electric heating, cooling, distributed storage, and so on. Tesla's integrated energy services model combining EVs, PVs, and distributed storage, described in chapter by Baak and Sioshansi, for example, may be one such cross-sectoral offering.

Another threat may come from independent start-ups, some of whom were mentioned in the section on platform business models and in chapter by Baak & Sioshansi, which are aiming to rewrite customer relationships in the energy sector.

The truly radical successes in the dotcom era came from a few highly able people working on problems they were obsessively passionate about. Often these individuals were driven by a desire to change and/or disrupt the world – with appropriate financial backing – with thoughts of commercialization only materializing as a secondary priority. Several of the initiatives currently in the making, particularly ones relying on DLTs such as IOTA, are not-for-profit; a structure that may attract the world's best talent who are intrinsically motivated around a common vision.

Taken together, these indicators suggest that much of the new and transformative innovations in digitalization space may be expected from *outside* the traditional utility industry. At the #ENERGY4.0 conference[4] less than 50% of the audience thought that the existing electricity companies will be in the driving seat in the digitalization space within a decade. The real stumbling block for utilities is the difficulty in transitioning to a corporate culture that embraces innovation, risk taking, and moving fast. The major threats are likely to come from the likes of forward-thinking FAANGs, ICT, and automotive companies, with a few wild cards from independent start-ups.

6. CONCLUSIONS

Digitalization was defined as the use of digital technologies to improve efficiency by reducing costs and risks; or to change the underlying business model by engaging with customers to understand and influence their preferences – in the process creating new products and services *and* new sources of revenue. In the short run, the immediate impact of digitalization on the linear value chain will be significant mainly around efficiency gains and cost savings. For instance, the intelligent management of demand, and supply, from electrified buildings and vehicles could reduce the need for new generation/network assets to be built, as well as reducing renewable curtailment.

But the much larger longer-term impacts of digitalization is likely to come from its ability that enables retailers to understand their customers better by establishing direct and lasting personalized or customized relationships. Such new relationships with energy customers could unlock a different degree of "willingness-to-pay" for what are perceived as premium value services or combinations of bundled services.

These developments, alongside other changes like ever-increasing deployment of zero marginal-cost renewables, will provide opportunities for companies to shift their business model away from selling kilowatt-hours as a commodity. Alternatives include charging for access to the grid based on capacity rather than volume of kWhs delivered, bundling electricity with other services/products like smart appliances; and charging for access to a platform, i.e., virtual marketplaces for storage, e-mobility, or peer-to-peer energy. Platform businesses are particularly disruptive – and potentially profitable – because they connect large numbers of suppliers and consumers without the burden of owning the underlying infrastructure or handling the products.

Many utilities are making concerted efforts to join the digital revolution through acquisition of start-ups. However, there are not likely to be very many quick or easy wins at scale, because the process of building new relationships with customers, bundling with other sectors and finding higher value services which customers are willing to pay for will take time. The unspoken fear remains that if the FAANGs or automotive giants turn their attention toward the marketing of energy, in whatever form, they will be able to attract customers and unlock data value in ways, which the traditional energy companies cannot reach. In such a world, despite the various bold statements of intent, utilities may be forced to retreat away from the customer, concentrating on managing their generation and distribution assets instead.

CHAPTER 2

Peer-to-Peer Trading and Blockchains: Enabling Regional Energy Markets and Platforms for Energy Transactions ☆

David Shipworth*, Christoph Burger†, Jens Weinmann†, Fereidoon Sioshansi‡
*UCL, London, United Kingdom
†ESMT, Berlin, Germany
‡Menlo Energy Economics, Walnut Creek, CA, United States

1. INTRODUCTION

As we move toward increased reliance on renewable, distributed, and intermittent energy sources, the successful integration of these resources into conventional centralized energy systems becomes increasingly challenging. To provide a functioning energy system in this context requires distributing balancing services close to the distributed generation to minimize bidirectional flows of energy over the distribution network. Doing so reduces network congestion, avoids expensive infrastructure upgrading, and increases network resilience as well as providing a range of other benefits further described in accompanying chapters in this volume.

Peer-to-peer energy trading provides one solution to this grid-edge management problem. This approach sees "prosumers" buying and selling energy directly from each other. This is frequently facilitated by local energy storage and building energy management systems, such as those described in chapter by Baak and Sioshansi. These mechanisms require little or no intermediary support from traditional actors in the energy system such as energy suppliers. Increasingly, such trading mechanisms are seen not only as providing a necessary balancing service in the energy transition, but also

---

☆ This chapter draws on material originally published by Shipworth in the December 2017 and March 2018 editions of "DSM Spotlight" – the newsletter of the International Energy Agency Demand-Side Management Technology Collaboration Programme.

Consumer, Prosumer, Prosumager
https://doi.org/10.1016/B978-0-12-816835-6.00002-4

27

as a way of re-engaging consumers and placing them at the heart of the decentralized energy system.

One class of technology facilitating such a vision is distributed ledgers, also called "blockchains." It is argued that these can securely account for, and settle, transactions of energy over either local or long-distance networks in ways that reduce transaction costs and increase trust between parties. These create both opportunities and challenges for the energy system, and while it is tempting to think that there may be a rapid transition to such a diverse and collaborative energy ecosystem, in practice this is unlikely for regulatory, technical, and social reasons as explained here.

This chapter walks through the fundamentals of peer-to-peer energy trading via blockchains, assessing the impact on different existing actors within the energy ecosystem, and highlighting opportunities and challenges that such a system presents for policy makers and regulators.

The chapter is organized as follows:

- Section 2 examines the evolution of P2P trading and its context in the energy transition;
- Section 3 describes the potential role of blockchain as an enabling technology for P2P trading;
- Section 4 explains the elements of P2P trading and elaborates on applications for regional energy markets and platforms for energy transactions respectively; and
- Section 5 examines some key risks, challenges, and barriers to adoption of Blockchain-based P2P trading followed by the chapter's conclusions.

2. THE EVOLUTION OF PEER-TO-PEER ENERGY TRADING AND ITS CONTEXT IN THE ENERGY TRANSFORMATION

Peer-to-peer energy trading is not new. It has been done on a limited scale over private wire networks for decades. It is, however, only very recently that it has become scalable over public distribution networks and is seen as part of the wider trends in energy transition which include decarbonization, decentralization, democratization, and digitalization.

The more recent rise of awareness and interest in peer-to-peer trading may be traced to a number of factors including three key technologies highlighted in the IEA's report, *Tracking Clean Energy Progress: 2017,*[1] which

---

[1] IEA (2017), Tracking Clean Energy Progress 2017, OECD/IEA, Paris, France. URL: http:// www.iea.org/etp/tracking2017.

aims to deliver the 2°C goal of the Paris climate accord. The three enabling technologies are:

- Electric vehicles (EVs) and electrification of transport;
- Energy storage; and
- Solar PVs.

As it happens, all three technologies enable consumers to become pro-active participants in the future decentralized energy ecosystem.

The interest in peer-to-peer may also be traced to the trend toward digitalization – further described in chapter by Brown et al. – which is becoming so much more feasible with the rollout of smart meters and the need to connect and control above mentioned technologies across the distribution network.

Peer-to-peer first came to prominence in the US under the title of "Transactive" energy, publicized by, among others, Barrager and Cazalet who described its purported merits in 2014[2] and by the US led GridWise Architecture Council under the auspices of the US Department of Energy in 2015. Over the years, others have examined the benefits of transactive energy in different context and using different definition of the term. Chen and Liu (2017), for example, note that "*[Transactive energy] aims to balance supply and demand in a real-time, autonomous, and decentralized manner*" in such a way that

"…distributed flexible resources are directly controlled by their owners" and that "transaction mechanisms are designed to align individual behaviors with the system's interests.[3]"

Transactive energy is technically similar to what in Europe goes under a variety of titles including "Community self-consumption" (France), and "Tenant self-consumption" (Germany). France, in April 2017, made changes to Article D of its Energy Code to support electricity self-consumption at the grid's edge. Germany has likewise recently amended the German Renewable Energy Sources Act (EEG 2017) to explicitly include self-consumption of PV electricity by buildings' tenants. Both of these anticipated changes foreshadowed in the proposed fourth EU Electricity Directive, which substantially enhances measures to proactively support consumer participation in the energy system (Butenko, 2017).[4]

---

[2] S. Barrager & E. Cazalet, Transactive Energy: A Sustainable Business and Regulatory Model for Electricity, 2014.

[3] Chen, S. and C.-C. Liu (2017). "From demand response to transactive energy: state of the art." Journal of Modern Power Systems and Clean Energy 5(1): 10-19.

[4] Butenko, A. (2017). 'User-centered Innovation in EU Energy Law: Market Access for Electricity Prosumers in the Proposed Electricity Directive', Oil, Gas & Energy Law Intelligence, October 2017.

In alignment with the proposed fourth EU Electricity Directive, on Jun 14, 2018, the European Council amended the Renewable Energy Directive to enshrine the right of European citizens to renewable self-consumption including peer-to-peer energy trading[5] – a significant regulatory milestone. The draft Directive defines peer-to-peer trading as follows:

"Peer-to-peer trading" of renewable energy means the sale of renewable energy between market participants by means of a contract with pre-determined conditions governing the automated execution and settlement of the transaction directly between participants or indirectly through a certified third party market participant, such as an aggregator. (p.55)

Moreover, Article 21 of the same draft Directive says:

Member States shall ensure that renewable self-consumers, individually or through aggregators, are entitled to generate renewable energy, including for their own consumption, store and sell their excess production of renewable electricity, including through power purchase agreements, electricity suppliers and peer-to-peer trading arrangements… (p.94)

At the time of this writing the draft Directive is still subject to ratification; however, substantive changes are unlikely at this stage, making this a substantial legislative step to making peer-to-peer energy trading a reality for the European Union's 500 million citizens. Clearly, similar regulatory and policy measures are needed in the US and elsewhere to further promote peer-to-peer trading, as described in Section 5.

3. DISTRIBUTED LEDGERS AS AN ENABLING TECHNOLOGY FOR P2P TRADING

Distributed ledgers, of which Blockchains are one type, are a type of distributed database in which all holders of the database see the same set of data at all times and agree to any changes by consensus. They are essentially a version of double-entry book keeping updated for the information age. Distributed ledgers have four axiomatic properties:
1. Distributed nature: This feature leads to three forms of system resilience:
    a. social resilience through distribution of political/economic control;
    b. cybersecurity resilience through avoiding a central point of failure; and
    c. energy system resilience through distributed asset control and subsystem independence.

---

[5] https://eur-lex.europa.eu/legal-content/EN/TXT/PDF/?uri=CONSIL:ST_10308_2018_INIT&from=EN.

2. Moving trust from actors to a "trusted by design" system: This feature is important for trading between unknown parties; fair trading between parties of unequal knowledge/power; and system action transparency.
3. Immutable accountability: This feature is critical for guarantees of origin, evidencing and authenticating Demand Side Response (DSR).
4. Digital asset scarcity: This feature is important for trading in a zero-sum pooled resource system.

Stemming from these primary properties, distributed ledgers have a range of secondary properties that make them of particular value to the decentralized energy system including:

- Elimination of counterparty risk, a feature that eliminates the need for vetting and risk of default;
- Automation, a feature that allows smart contracts and Internet of Every Things (IoET) control architectures;
- Transaction cost minimization, a feature that enables new grid-edge energy and flexibility markets to evolve;
- Pseudonymity, a feature that helps with data protection and compliance;
- Account transparency, a feature that allows all parties to see/share the contents of the common ledger – which is critical to building trust among the traders; and
- Process transparency, a feature that allows all parties to see the rules and to verify that they are applied fairly and consistently.

Collectively, the preceding features make it possible for participants in trading to trust the outcome of the transactions and to conduct business without a central bank or an intermediary, as further described in Box 2.1.

Box 2.1 A Primer on Blockchain[6]

A growing number of experts working on blockchain technology are convinced it has great potential. They claim it will revolutionize trading of virtually anything among any two parties virtually anywhere they may be. It is expected to be secure, inexpensive, and instantaneous. Its applications are expected to revolutionize many industries, including peer-to-peer (P2P) electricity trading and much more. Yet nobody is really sure exactly how, when or why?

RMI Outlet
[6] *Original article appeared in April 2017 issue of EEnergy Informer, available at: http://www.eenergyinformer.com.*

Continued

Box 2.1 A Primer on Blockchain—cont'd

If the claims about its tremendous potential and the uncertainties about the means to its fulfillment sound contradictory, that is as things currently stand. Like the Internet in its early days, one can speculate about all the great applications but uncertain about how and when it may materialize.

What is clear is that Distributed Ledger Technologies (DLTs), in general, have the potential to make transactions among unlimited users, or possibly devices, seamless, virtually costless, secure, and instantaneous – just as PayPal made it easy for people to buy and sell items on, say eBay, and pay for it. The problem with public blockchains is that (for now) the transaction costs are high and the transaction process is slow. It is not yet clear that public blockchains can overcome this scalability problem. Other types of DLT, e.g., the "Tangle" and perhaps private blockchains may be scalable and have greater application to peer-to-peer transactions.

Today, most transactions among parties require one or more intermediaries, for example a bank, a financial institution, or a broker, and these intermediaries – which typically facilitate trade and provide back office services, charge fees for their services. Blockchain technology offers an opportunity to cut out these intermediaries and their associated transaction costs.

A Feb 23, 2017 article by the Rocky Mountain Institute at *RMI Outlet* says,

… we believe that blockchain technology has the potential to play a significant, potentially game-changing role in the global electricity system's transition to a more secure, resilient, cost-effective, and low-carbon grid.

RMI points out that with the rapid "… growth in distributed energy resources (DERs)—such as rooftop solar, demand response, and electric vehicles—governments, utilities, and other stakeholders from across the globe are experimenting with new ways to better regulate and manage the electricity grid. These experiments currently face four main issues regardless of their geography:

- Controlling demand is difficult: Customers are concerned about privacy and sometimes loathe to share data—let alone allow third parties to control DERs that they own.
- Tracking flows of energy is imperfect: Energy markets and markets for the attributes of energy (e.g., renewable energy credits) can be expensive to run, can be subject to double spending, and can usually be accessed only via intermediaries.
- Not everyone can participate in the grid's evolution: In developed economies, only large, sophisticated businesses are able to enter into off-site power purchase agreements for renewables. In emerging economies, access to capital is a major barrier to accessing DERs and renewable energy, even if these technologies are capable of generating cost savings.

Box 2.1 A Primer on Blockchain—cont'd

- Putting customers and DERs first is challenging: The entire grid was originally designed from the top down, making it challenging to put customers and DERs first."

RMI goes on to say that, "Although it is not yet 100% clear *how*, blockchain technology may be capable of solving these challenges:

- Blockchains provide privacy, enhance cybersecurity, and are a low-cost way of managing DER-focused transactions at the edge of the distribution grid.
- Blockchains provide a more transparent and, at the same time, a more secure way of tracking energy flows than the status quo.
- Blockchains enable small-scale and low-credit customers to participate in business models focused on DERs and renewable energy.
- Blockchains are a key enabler of balancing and managing the grid from the bottom up versus today's top-down approach."

Which explains why RMI and Grid Singularity, an Austrian start-up, have joined forces to launch Energy Web Foundation (EWF) to unleash the potential of the blockchain technology in the energy sector.

When technologists connected individual computers via phone lines to exchange packets of information in the late 1960s, no one knew exactly what that technology—which would eventually become the Internet—was capable of. Sending digitally signed messages, or "e-mail," was immediately seen as a clear and interesting application, but not much else. In other words, the beginnings of the Internet looked intriguing, but nobody quite knew the extent of what it could do.

Not surprisingly, EWF believes that blockchain technology in the energy sector is at a similar early stage with many uncertainties about its future evolution and applications. According to the *RMI Outlet* article,

We understand, at pilot scale, how to connect electricity loads, generators, and everything in between (e.g., distribution lines and batteries) to a blockchain ecosystem ... to track flows of energy and value while allowing multiple parties to transact.

Which explains the rapid proliferation of numerous DLT pilot demonstration projects to test the feasibility and basic functionality of, say, rooftop solar PV customers exchanging their excess generation with others in Brooklyn, New York, or Sydney, Australia.

According to experts working in this area, however, small-scale peer-to-peer trading such as these is just the tip of the iceberg. For example, Christoph Burger and Jens Weinmann at the European School of Management and Technology (ESMT) in Berlin point out:

Continued

Box 2.1 A Primer on Blockchain—cont'd

Within the energy transition we can distinguish between Energiewende 1.0 (German energy transformation) where the focus is on pushing renewables versus fossils. Some countries have now reached a high share of renewables, Energiewende 2.0, where the focus of the grid operator is to balance variable supply and demand. In this environment, blockchain offers a powerful alternative to traditional solutions by enabling active participation of large numbers of distributed resources without an intermediary.

The real disruptive potential of blockchain in the energy market, however, is realized in the context of an off-grid or micro-grid environment where blockchain technology operating on an open platform manages multitudes of small distributed generators, loads, EVs, and energy storage devices on the network by facilitating trades among its members. In such an environment, the function of the distributed network would be automated.

Among the challenges facing experts working in the emerging field is to identify exactly where the technology's value proposition lies and how to commercialize and monetize it. This is among the priorities of EWF, which intends to conduct studies on several hundred potential applications already identified. Multiple stakeholders including utilities, regulators, and customers have to be convinced of the value of the applications and their benefits before DLT can be successfully implemented on wide scale.

The development of common, open-source DLT platform that multiples of users can use for multiples of applications creates other challenges, e.g., speed, transaction cost, scalability, and security. Once such a platform is in place, utilities, traders, customers, and financial institutions can build specific applications that deliver value.

Burger and Weinmann, however, acknowledge that there might be *not* one open source blockchain platform given the many alternatives competing for widespread acceptance. ESMT offers a blockchain program further described at their website.

The foregoing set of properties leads to hundreds of potential practical applications of distributed ledgers in the energy system. Burger et al. (2016)[7] divide these applications into two broad categories:
- Those providing trading *platforms*; and
- Those supporting the trading *processes*.

---

[7]Burger, C., et al. (2016). 'Blockchain in the energy transition: A survey among decision-makers in the German energy industry', European School of Management and Technology GmbH Deutsche Energie-Agentur GmbH (dena) - German Energy Agency.

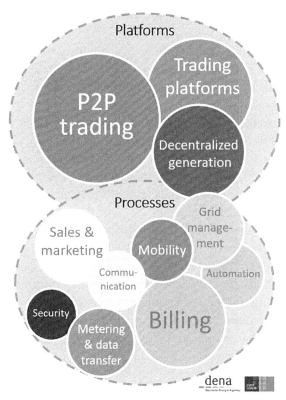

FIGURE 2.1 Potential applications of Blockchain in the energy sector. *(Source: Blockchain in the energy transition, European School of Management & Technology (ESMT), Berlin, Nov 2016, p. 20.)*

Fig. 2.1 illustrates the potential practical applications of blockchain in the energy sector, where the size of the circles corresponds to the significance of the potential applications. The visual indicates that the highest potential applications of the technology are expected to be in security, followed by decentralized generation, P2P trading, mobility, metering and data transfer, and in trading platforms.

Considering the fact that current behind-the-meter distributed generation and storage assets come in small sizes, the cost to monitor, manage, and integrate these into the network becomes important. Consequently, Blockchain-based process solutions might help to reduce these "transaction" costs – for example, by reducing billing and collection costs by avoiding or reducing the fees normally charged by an intermediary such as a commercial bank or a payment provider. The implication is that the disruptive potential is likely to be greater in new markets and new applications rather than in existing ones.

Platform applications include those that support/facilitate peer-to-peer trading including those supporting decentralized generation. *Processes* include a range of back-office services and applications including verification, billing, and settlements – the types of services that are essential to any successful trading platform such as the one described in chapter by Stanley et al. This chapter focuses only on peer-to-peer energy trading, which, while far reaching, is certainly not the easiest use-case to implement, nor the one most likely to yield the most immediate return on investment.

Any type of trading contemplated for the electricity network has to meet two fundamental requirements:

- Firstly, it must meet the physical requirements of the electricity transmission and distribution network, sometimes referred to as the "grid"; and
- Secondly, it must be consistent with the existing information, accounting, and billing systems for keeping track of who generated the energy, how it was transmitted and distributed, who has used it and that they've paid for it – the complicated legacy balancing, settlement, and billing systems.

The latter breaks down into the following components:

- a meter for measuring exported electricity;
- a data structure for recording the amount exported;
- a mechanism for matching and contracting between buyers and sellers;
- a meter for measuring imported electricity by the buyer; and
- a way to financially settle the transaction.

The fundamentals of the electricity business – like all others – dictate that accurate records be kept of who supplied and who consumed electrons in real time among an ever-larger pool of stakeholders with a variety of trading options as illustrated in Fig. 2.2. Keeping track of these transactions and their settlement becomes too cumbersome using traditional approaches.

These functions exist and are routinely performed in the current energy system, but at a considerable cost, and with a system designed for unidirectional flows of energy from centralized generators to consumers.

With old technology, trading small amounts of energy at the grid's edge is cumbersome and uneconomic – not unlike the limitations described in trading flexibility services described in chapter by Stanley et al. The costs of operating and managing the centralized system have been tolerable to date because the number of parties to the transactions has been limited and

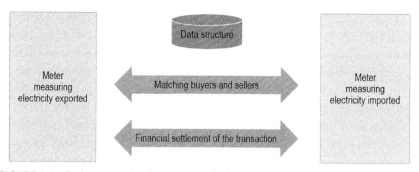

FIGURE 2.2 Blockchain technology is regarded central to facilitating complex transactions among multiple stakeholders. *(Source: Burger and Weinmann, ESMT.)*

technical alternatives for balancing and settlement have not been available. However, as the number of transactions and the number of transacting parties are expected to grow exponentially with the decentralization of the energy system, the traditional ways of handling transactions are not going to be sustainable. This is particularly true as generation and balancing is increasingly pushed to the grids' edge and to the behind-the-meter, the topic of multiple chapters in this volume.

Clearly, to make the system balance, both electrically and financially, the producer can't sell the same unit of energy to more than one buyer, so a system is needed that prevents this from happening. Normally, this is done through some centralized trusted authority that records and balances all exchanges.[8] Moving to distributed ledgers, the records will be shared among multiple trading parties, and they must be automatically and simultaneously updated every time a transaction takes place.

With this distributed, constantly updated, and cryptographically secure ledger, a trusted central authority is no longer needed – thus saving the costs of maintaining one – the "cost of trust" needed to resolve disputes. With a distributed ledger, each party can check their copy of the ledger to see that the seller has units of energy for sale, and that the buyer has funds to cover the sale. Thus, in the energy context, a distributed ledger is simply a record of all transactions – production, consumption, and sales – open to all market participants and all updating simultaneously by consensus in a secure and unhackable manner. This sounds wonderful, but clearly requires massive computational power for each trading party – which, as will be further described, could potentially consume voracious amounts of power.

---

[8]All centralized wholesale markets, for example, currently operate in such fashion.

There is one additional important feature of some distributed ledgers of use in the energy system, namely, the capacity to offer and manage "smart contracts." These are pieces of code that automate trading between parties. Buyers and sellers may set strategies for offering and bidding, and when terms match, a trade is automatically executed. Such smart contracts reduce costs and speed up the settlement processes making trading smaller amounts of energy economically viable. The addition of "smart contracts" powerfully extends the capacity and applicability of distributed ledgers in domains such as energy trading, especially when extended to thousands or potentially millions of small parties, say in a decentralized energy future – the types of applications that are likely to emerge as described in accompanying chapters on digitalization, trading, and platforms.

Another important distinction in the taxonomy of blockchains is who can hold – and therefore view – a copy of the ledger. The archetypal application of blockchain is "Bitcoin" – the crypto currency for which they were originally developed. In the case of crypto currency, everybody who mines Bitcoin holds a copy of the ledger, which contains every transaction that has ever occurred by all parties since its inception. This is an example of a "public" ledger open to all. Consequently, it is open to anybody to attack, and therefore challenging to secure. The ingenious system to do this, called "proof of work," is highly secure – but makes transactions slow, and the system very energy intensive to run.[9] This makes it unsuited for energy trading applications.

There are multiple ways to simplify things, to increase the speed of transactions, and to reduce the energy use in processing and verification of transactions. One promising solution is the use of so-called *private* or *permissioned* blockchains, where the identities of all parties trading on the network are known and previously verified. In such a network, increased scalability can be reached via proof of stake where network members with the highest stake validate transactions or proof of authority, where selected members validate the transactions. A number of other ways to reach consensus among all members are being tested to increase the scalability of blockchains, whether open or private, with the aim of lowering energy consumption and speeding the number of transactions that can be processed per second.[10]

While distributed ledgers are pseudonymous,[11] it has been shown possible to reidentify individuals through their pattern of transactions, thus

---

[9]https://digiconomist.net/bitcoin-energy-consumption.

[10]For example, Chalaemwongwan, N. and Kurutach, W., State of the Art and Challenges Facing Consensus Protocols on Blockchain, ICOIN 2018.

[11]Trading is typically done under a pseudonym, disguising the identity of the trader.

effectively making public, data deemed as private in many data protection jurisdictions. This is compounded by the fact that, for carbon accounting purposes, most governments will want to register renewable energy generation assets to specific meters to create a "chain of custody" of low carbon energy entering the system and for supporting trading of Renewable Energy Guarantees of Origin (REGOs).

To support such Proof of Origin applications would require encoding each meter's unique identification number into the ledger, thus linking reidentified energy trading data to a physical asset of known address. Such chain of custody applications of distributed ledgers are important and valuable, but create further challenges under data protection legislation. For these, and other reasons, many in the energy area view "permissioned" or "consortium" blockchains as a more viable option. These are where access is governed by a consortium that complies with regulation or where the regulator itself acts as a validator of smart contract transactions. Because in either case access is vetted, securing such ledgers from outside attack is easier, and energy cost of securing them is lower.

Additionally, because access is restricted, issues of accessing personal data are easier to manage, and additional information can be encoded into the blockchain without compromising consumers' privacy. The use of public, versus permissioned ledgers is a contentious one in the field, with many believing that permissioned ledgers are antithetical to the spirit of openness and collaboration that underlies technologies such as Bitcoin. In practice, systems are now emerging that use hybrid structure containing both public and permission ledgers at different levels. In the energy field, it seems likely that pragmatics will prevail given the necessarily highly regulated nature of critical national infrastructure systems like electricity grids.[12]

While the terms blockchain and distributed ledger are used interchangeably in this chapter such use is not, strictly speaking, correct. Blockchains are one type of distributed ledger – one in which the ledger is held in a series of encrypted blocks of data each containing data from tens to thousands of trades. Each of these blocks is then linked like a chain where changing the encrypted data in *any* block in the chain, corrupts that *entire copy* of the chain. However, because there are thousands of copies of the blockchain distributed on thousands of computers, these corrupted copies are easily identified as being wrong by comparing them with the others, and the

---

[12]https://energyweb.org/beyond-bitcoin-as-blockchain-adoption-accelerates-a-need-to-manage-energy-and-climate-emerges-by-sam-hartnett/.

corrupted chain can then be replaced through a consensus process. This linear chain of blocks is, however, only one form of distributed ledger.

Others are based on complex networks or meshes of blocks. The best known of these are IOTA[13] – a ledger built for the Internet of Things, and Hedera[14] by Hashgraph – a powerful new ledger architecture that addresses many of the challenges facing conventional blockchain structures. This is just one example of what are becoming a rapidly growing family of distributed ledger architectures tailored around specific applications. There is an increasing consensus that there will ultimately be a plethora of different ledger structures with systems to support interoperability. Polkadot[15] from Parity or Cosmos[16] from Tendermint are examples of such initiatives.

4. ELEMENTS OF PEER-TO-PEER TRADING, REGIONAL ENERGY MARKETS, AND PLATFORMS FOR ENERGY TRANSACTIONS

Peer-to-peer trading can be realized in many ways – this section describes one approach, which is applicable to many liberalized and distributed energy markets. This entails treating the peer-to-peer participants as a "balance group" as illustrated in Fig. 2.3. This balance group estimates its net position for the following day in the form of a "balance schedule" – a 24-hour profile of net demand in time periods corresponding to the wholesale market. It then purchases enough energy from the wholesale market in each period to cover their estimated requirements. Any imbalances – that is differences between projected and actual demand – are then settled through the wholesale market.

Alternative market structures such as peer-to-peer could potentially threaten the role of traditional energy suppliers. While the extent of the threat is probably exaggerated, it could certainly change both their size and role in the energy system. The rate of such changes will ultimately be governed by the rate of regulatory reform, and thus rests with regulators as much as with other market actors.

On the question of how soon blockchain technology might find useful applications in the electricity sector, opinions differ. According to a survey of attendees at the EventHorizon Conference in Vienna in 2017,[17] roughly

[13]https://www.iota.org/.
[14]https://www.hederahashgraph.com/.
[15]https://polkadot.network/.
[16]https://cosmos.network/.
[17]The Global Summit on Blockchain Technology in the Energy Sector, 14. - 15. February 2017, Hofburg Wien at https://www.ait.ac.at/en/news-events/single-view/detail/4591/?no_cache=1.

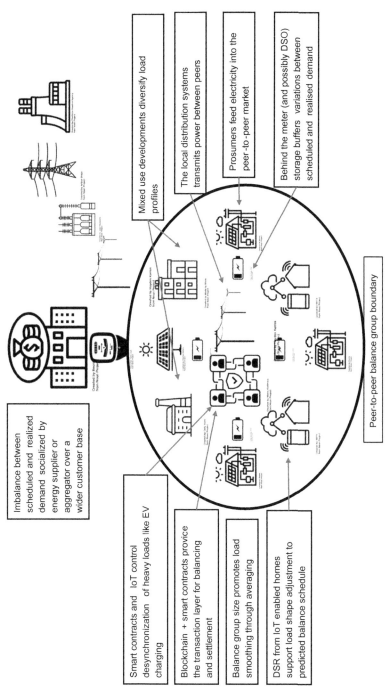

Mixed use developments diversify load profiles

The local distribution systems transmits power between peers

Prosumers feed electricity into the peer-to-peer market

Behind the meter (and possibly DSO) storage buffers variations between scheduled and realised demand

Peer-to-peer balance group boundary

Imbalance between scheduled and realized demand socialized by energy supplier or aggregator over a wider customer base

Smart contracts and IoT control desynchronization of heavy loads like EV charging

Blockchain + smart contracts provice the transaction layer for balancing and settlement

Balance group size promotes load smoothing through averaging

DSR from IoT enabled homes support load shape adjustment to predicted balance schedule

FIGURE 2.3 Peer-to-peer balance group and balancing mechanisms. *(Source: Shipworth.)*

2/3rd of the respondents said they expect the share of P2P trading to be below 20% of all electricity traded in Europe by 2025, while 1/3rd said they expect it to be more than 20%.

The primary economic function of energy suppliers in a deregulated energy market is to mitigate counterparty risk between the wholesale market and consumers. There is therefore likely to be an ongoing role for suppliers in mitigating the financial risk of settling imbalances on the wholesale market faced by smaller peer-to-peer markets. This is particularly the case where the peer-to-peer trading is occurring within a local community, which may only have a few tens or hundreds of participants. Likewise, participants in the wholesale market are not going to want the cost, administrative complexities, and financial risk of default arising from dealing with large numbers of consumers and peer-to-peer balance groups. In this context, a supplier provides the legal framework, financial risk mitigation, and interface to the services of the wider energy system.

Over time, however, there are factors intrinsic to distributed ledgers and the energy transition that are likely to reduce imbalances and the risk of financial default. Imbalances can be reduced through a number of mechanisms including the following:

- *Improving day ahead prediction of demand.* Such predictions are likely to improve at the individual property level as penetration of smart metering increases, and the data are combined with high spatial and temporal resolution data on buildings, weather and consumer lifestyles. This will allow application of machine learning methods to construct more precise house-level demand forecasts.
- *Integrating energy storage on the consumer side of the meter.* This will allow buffering of supply and demand over hours or days to match predicted and actual demand more closely. Such storage may come from electric vehicles or home battery systems.
- *Increasing penetration of smart home appliances.* Linked to integrated home management systems, IoT-enabled smart appliances will increasingly offer control over the timing and settings of appliances for comfort, convenience, and energy management.
- *Dynamic time of use tariffs.* Supported by smart metering, dynamic time of use tariffs will help communicate larger-scale energy system and network level constraints to the peer-to-peer groups level.
- *Coordinated scheduling of demand over time.* Desynchronization of demand across *participating properties in the peer-to-peer network can both control and increase network* diversity factors thus reducing peak congestion. This can

be coordinated by smart contracts executed on the blockchain trading platform and can make the collective profile match the day ahead balance schedule submitted to the system operator.

- Finally, scaling both the number and type of participants – residential, commercial and industrial – can both reduce statistical fluctuations from small numbers, and square the balance schedule profile, to make attractive and stable blocks of energy to buy from the wholesale market at least cost.

Thus, the emerging technologies that make peer-to-peer work – be it in generation, storage, smart metering – enabled by blockchains can themselves work to minimize imbalances and thus reduce the cost to participants, be that before or behind the meter. On the financial risk side, near-instant settlement of accounts using smart contracts, where supply is conditional on availability of credit on the ledger system, can vitally eliminate financial default risk much as prepayment meters do presently. In such a system, the role of suppliers could be radically diminished for those customers participating in peer-to-peer markets.

The other important roles of suppliers, however, may continue for the foreseeable future. These include that of providing a near-universal service of an essential good, and in many countries delivering policy objectives related to energy poverty and maintaining priority services registers for those for whom loss of energy may be life threatening.

As will be further explained, peer-to-peer trading schemes carry potential wider social risks that regulators will need to address. One such risk is that of creating "energy gated communities" of affluent, technology-literate consumers for whom trading-off capital costs against operating costs is viable. In such circumstances, those with access to financial capital for purchasing generation assets (such as photovoltaic arrays), storage assets (such as electric vehicles), and control assets (such as home energy management systems) could form peer-to-peer trading networks in affluent areas. Such a collection of assets would allow those in the network to manage their generation and demand to minimize their purchases from the grid, and to structure any such purchases into highly predictable parcels of energy ("squared clips") that can be purchased at low cost on wholesale markets.

Through minimizing their purchase of energy outside the peer-to-peer group, they would pay less network taxes and charges, thus contributing comparatively little to overall network upkeep. As such communities grow, they could potentially defect from the grid entirely, leaving those less able to generate and manage their energy paying for the provision of the national energy infrastructure. This could lead to adverse social distributional effects whereby those least well off may be forced to pay increasing amounts for their energy, topics explored elsewhere in this volume. This presents important challenges for policy makers and regulators that will need to be addressed as the technology develops.

5. RISKS, BARRIERS, AND CHALLENGES OF BLOCKCHAIN-BASED P2P TRADING

Distributed ledger technologies are still in their infancy. Open chains such as Bitcoin or Ethereum are governed by democratic peer processes where majorities are needed to change rules. This takes time. If no agreement can be reached, chains split via a hard fork into different chains such as, e.g., Bitcoin with a 1-MB block size and Bitcoin cash with an 8-MB block size. At the same time, current regulation is trying to find ways to allow the nascent technology and associated business models to evolve and fit within the existing rules and practices while finding better ways to amend existing protocols and/or simplify and streamline them (Box 2.2). The challenges are not limited to technological issues but also stem from the complex regulatory, policy and privacy environment they operate in. These range from issues such as revision of energy codes around balancing and settlement, to broader social issues around data privacy.

This section provides an overview of the challenges, grouped under technological, legal, policy, and social categories.

5.1 Technological Challenges

The technological challenges associated with distributed ledger technologies may be grouped under three categories, further described
- Performance;
- Security/privacy; and
- Usability and standards.

5.1.1 Performance

For distributed ledgers to be useful in the complex evolving energy ecosystem, they must perform and produce value. In this context, performance can be measured along three key dimensions:

Throughput and Scaling

That is transactions per second. This is an area that has long been identified as a challenge, but in which considerable progress has and continues to be made. The Bitcoin blockchain is slow, processing at around seven

Box 2.2 Rapid Progress Expected

Despite the many remaining challenges and obstacles, there is continuing progress in blockchain, Bitcoin, Ethereum, and Initial Coin Offerings (ICOs) as exemplified in press coverings. Blockchain remains in the spotlight and is sought after by myriad of stakeholders in a variety of markets thanks to its purported benefits and numerous applications including those in electricity markets. The technology is widely seen as central to establishing a new form of digital trust that traders can use to replace the current cumbersome and labor-intensive processes that have traditionally been used to verify transactions and settle.

As further described in this chapter, to unblock its full potential in the electricity sector, a number of key issues need to be addressed including:

- What is behind this innovative technology;
- How can it actually create added value for individual companies;
- Which application possibilities exist and can be exploited in the near term; and
- How can the implementation of blockchain technology work within the company?

The blockchain payment network Bitcoin showcased that it is possible to perform high-value transactions, that is, send money around the world as simply as an email, without the need for a commercial intermediary to handle settlement and clearing processes typically run by banks and payment processors. The past few years have seen significant applications of the technology with a number of universities, research institutions, and others concentrating on developing useful, practical, near-term applications. The European School for Management and Technology (ESMT), for example, is focused on examining near-term practical applications of blockchain technology across all industries primarily to understand its disruptive potential.[18]

The ESMT program allows executives across industries to get an introduction to the cutting edge, digitalized technologies including blockchain to understand its potential for disruption, and how they can harness the technology to the benefit of their businesses including issues such as:

- Understanding blockchain and its characteristics;
- Value creation and business models;
- Technology stack and smart contracts; and
- Implementing blockchain solutions.

Similar research, innovation, experimentation and education are taking place in numerous other places such as universities, startups, and a number of academic and research institutions including the Energy Web Foundation.

---

[18] https://www.esmt.org/executive-education/executive-development-programs/managing-technology-and-strategy/blockchain-using-its-potential-benefit-your-business.

transactions per second (tps). By comparison VISA has processing speeds of around 24,000 tps. Work done for the Bank of England on permissioned ledgers has achieved speeds of more than 5000 tps, and Ethereum, the most widely applied blockchain technology in the energy area, is testing a "Proof of Authority" consensus mechanism capable of processing over one million transactions per second (http://netstats.energyweb.org/).

Latency

That is time to verify a transaction. Along with throughput, latency is frequently identified as being a limitation of blockchains. In the case of Bitcoin, each block on the chain takes around 10 minutes to create ("mine"), and depending on how secure you want your transaction to be, you may want to wait for up to six blocks to be mined before being completely sure the transition has gone through. That's an hour to fully confirm a transaction. Ethereum, by contrast, takes around 20 seconds per block making transactions quite secure after around 2 minutes. Most major credit cards (e.g., Visa) take around 3 seconds. Much research is going into reducing transaction times on blockchains down to seconds and considerable progress is being made. This is unlikely to significantly constrain energy-trading applications.

Energy Intensity

That is how much energy is used to power the transactions. Bitcoin is famously energy intensive, currently consuming between 2.5–4 GW of power. This is driven by the "proof of work" consensus algorithm that rewards miners for solving the cryptographic puzzles that secure the blockchain. The total energy broadly follows price, with investments in computing resources reflecting the return on investment to miners. It is important to stress that energy demand is dependent on the consensus mechanism and whether the blockchain is public or permissioned. This is why platforms like the Ethereum are testing Proof of Authority[19] consensus mechanisms, which radically reduces energy use (https://www.greentechmedia.com/articles/read/energy-web-foundation-fix-blockchain-biggest-problem#gs.1R98HpU).

5.1.2 Security/Privacy Challenges

Security and privacy issues are equally paramount for obvious reasons.

Security

Blockchains have proven to be very secure. That is not to say they are foolproof. To date, the most substantial problems have arisen from vulnerabilities

[19]http://kovan-stats.parity.io.

in the code of the blockchains or smart contracts with companies rushing to get products to market. This has resulted in some well-publicized security breaches and financial losses. The second substantive problem is loss of individuals' "private keys." Blockchains are secured using a method called "asymmetric" or "public-key" encryption. This relies on individuals holding one cryptographic key private, and making the other public. If you lose your private key all your value, be that in energy units or crypto currencies, is lost forever. If someone steals your private key, by hacking into your computer or the server it's stored on, they can control all your value on the blockchain. While other forms of attack are possible (such as 51% "double spending" attacks), the probability of these is so low, and the attention on them so great, that they are a comparatively low risk to any individual on the system.

Privacy

As noted earlier, data on blockchains, while encrypted, can be reidentified through construction of transaction network graphs. Where the data encode information linked to a physical address, such as a smart meter unique identifier, this could violate data protection regulations in many regions. This suggests that fully public networks will face problems under things like the EU General Data Protection Regulations (the GDPR). Other criteria of the GDPR, such as the "right to be forgotten," present more fundamental challenges to an immutable ledger like a blockchain. Privacy is an area of considerable current research interest in blockchains, with advances in cryptography such as homomorphic encryption and zero knowledge proofs offering the potential for preserving individual privacy while still providing the benefits of collective data analysis to support innovation in products and services.

5.1.3 Usability/Standards

The final challenges in adopting blockchain technology include

Usability

There are two areas where usability is limiting rapid scaling and uptake of these technologies. The first is at the application developer level. Coding applications to run on platforms such as Ethereum or IOTA are currently substantially more technically challenging than writing applications to run on a smart phone. Some environments, like HyperLedger-fabric from the Linux foundation, are substantially improving usability, but widespread application development will require making such platforms very accessible to mainstream developers. This will, in turn, lead to the development of consumer interfaces that are much more intuitive for participants in peer-to-peer energy trading. It is likely that such interfaces will not be complex trading screens tracking energy prices on multiple markets – but very simple interfaces allowing consumers to express binary or sliding preferences between settings such as "maximize savings," "share with family," or "donate to school."

Governance of Platforms and Token Systems

An emerging area throughout the blockchain community is agreeing the processes of governance over platforms and token systems. To date, this is mostly handled through the establishment of "foundations" that are not-for-profit bodies seeking to prove arms-length governance over how these blockchain platform address issues that affect all the users of that platform. Defining the governance processes at the inception is increasingly seen as important for the long-term viability of blockchain platforms. Organizations like Decred; e.os and others are working on this issue.

Standard

A plethora of blockchain architectures, platforms, and middleware applications are emerging from start-ups and foundations targeting energy trading using distributed ledgers. Each of these offers different functionality for different applications. In this environment, development of standards is becoming increasingly important. Some bodies such as the Energy Web Foundation are looking to establish consensus positions across the sector, but built on specific blockchain platforms (in this case Ethereum). Standards will be essential to ensure interoperability, ensure integration with legacy energy systems, and ensure consistency where the physical energy infrastructure spans jurisdictions. There are now bodies in the European Commission addressing such issues in the crypto currency field, but this has yet to be developed in energy.

While still in nascent state, there are currently many actors promoting the application of distributed ledger technologies in the energy arena – including for peer-to-peer energy trading and community self-consumption. Increasingly, the dominant actor in this sector is the Energy Web Foundation. The EWF has drawn together both energy market incumbents and innovators to support development of an underlying set of software tools, protocols, and standards based on the Ethereum blockchain.

While Ethereum is the underlying distributed ledger technology of choice for the majority in the energy industry, it is not the only viable architecture. The linear structure of blockchains presents problems that are proving challenging to resolve while retaining the original strengths of the system. Alternative, graphical architectures such as used by IOTA and Hashgraph offer alternative solutions that address some of the limitations of the linear architecture of blockchains. Both IOTA and Hashgraph are exploring applications in the energy domain, albeit without the early mover advantage of the Energy Web Foundation.

5.2 Legal, Policy, and Social Challenges

Besides the technological challenges, outlined here, blockchain technology must overcome a number of legal, policy, regulatory, and social challenges before it can successfully be applied for P2P trading on a large scale as is generally envisioned.

The legal challenges may be grouped under two broad categories:

Smart contracts. Much of the benefits of blockchains comes from execution of trades based on smart contracts. Such contracts pose challenges in terms of determining the jurisdiction any legal dispute would be resolved in, determining the legal status of such contracts, and who would be at fault if they failed. A validation of smart contracts by the regulator in charge might be a solution to this issue. Again, this is an ongoing area of research in which there are more questions than answers at this stage.

Financing. In 2017, the US Securities and Exchange Commission (SEC) made a test-case advisory ruling that Initial Coin Offerings, or ICOs, could fail the Howey test of securities and investments.[20] This meant that SEC regarded the ICO as equivalent to an IPO in that the tokens offered by the Distributed Autonomous Organisation (DAO) to be securities under US law. This ruling has very substantially increased the financial and administrative cost and complexity of raising funds through ICOs in the US, slowing the boom in the sector. While unpopular among start-ups, this may be a good mechanism for improving confidence in an otherwise largely unregulated sector.

The policy challenges may be grouped under three broad categories:

Delivering policy/industry objectives. The architecture of a peer-to-peer energy-trading scheme fundamentally determines the policy

---

[20] https://www.thesecuritiesedge.com/2018/02/is-your-initial-coin-offering-a-securities-offering/.

outcomes delivered. This, in part, is what drives the diversity of peer-to-peer schemes emerging from different providers. Systems can be designed to provide balancing at the grid edge to promote grid asset utilization and efficient network management, or systems can be designed to drive uptake of PV and storage irrespective of their geographic location on the network. Over time, the desired outcomes will change as the physical and sociodemographic composition of different geographic areas evolves. This will unlimitedly require incentive systems able to adapt as PV, EV, or battery penetration increases, or as social expectations change around economic collaboration.

Consumer protection and data privacy policies. A challenge to success of Blockchain-based P2P trading lies in the unintended consequences of consumer protection and data privacy policies. These are frequently reflected in legislation that explicitly embodies assumptions about energy consumers as passive actors in the system with limited choice over a homogeneous product.

This impedes the development of new models of consumers as engaging, either directly or indirectly, in multiple markets serving differentiated social values. A challenge of success is managing the distributional impacts arising from widespread uptake of peer-to-peer schemes. Uptake could lead to grid defection by energy-gated communities, this would push the costs of maintaining the network on those without the resources (financial, social, and intellectual capital) to participate in such schemes.

Regulatory challenges. A challenge to success is prescriptive regulatory environments that stipulate actions rather than outcomes to deliver policy ends. Such systems are prevalent, are frequently structured around an assumed one supplier per customer model, and have evolved into extensive and complicated networks of regulations and codes that are often highly constraining of innovation.

Another challenge to success will be responding to pressure from peer-to-peer prosumers and others who prefer to apply a scheme where "user pays" for distribution service charges on the network. Currently consumers pay a flat fee for such services as a component of their electricity bills, usually a percentage of the kWhs used. But as the proportion of kWhs bought from the network diminishes – due to self-generation and improved efficiency – pressure will rise to increase fixed monthly fees and/or connection charges to reflect this trend. Moreover, if average network traffic distances shorten – due to the increased localization and balancing of self-generation, distributed storage and more flexible demand, future prosumers, prosumagers, and traders will contribute less to the upkeep of the distribution network while imposing higher costs on it. This will require balancing against the wider social benefits of national network infrastructure maintenance, topics further described elsewhere in this volume.

Social value stacking. Analysis from early peer-to-peer trials indicates that "social value stacking," the addition of financial and nonfinancial consumer value propositions, is likely to be an important driver of consumer uptake for peer-to-peer trading schemes.

Social value stacking entails identifying and tokenizing the social, psychological, and financial value to consumers from participating in peer-to-peer schemes. Such social values include environmental value from local renewable energy consumption, creating opportunities for donating energy to local energy poverty charities, and setting differential prices for friends and family over providing frequency response services to the grid. Psychological values include increasing personal control, and a sense of autonomy from national infrastructure.

Wider economic values include supporting the local economy by keeping value within the community, and identifying local synergies between social and commercial enterprises (say schools and local supermarkets) with complementary load and generation profiles. Maximizing the social value stack requires tailoring peer-to-peer markets to individual communities by differentiating the value of energy and the services it provides, and identifying combinations of values that drive uptake in each area.

These challenges are not only known at the blockchain startup community but also among existing players, regulators, and governments. While time to resolve these issues is delaying the implementation and is frustrating to the eventual applications of blockchain technology, a race to the top on blockchain applications and legislation is taking place including countries who would like to establish new markets, infrastructure, legislation, and exchanges for what could turn into lucrative business opportunities.[21] Solving the challenges will provide a more reliable framework for blockchain to develop and exploit its full potential.

---

[21]Dubai, for example, has developed a Blockchain strategy under its leader Sheikh Mohammed bin Rashid Al Maktoum, to create the future of Dubai, and make it the happiest city on earth (https://smartdubai.ae/en/Initiatives/Pages/DubaiBlockchainStrategy. aspx). Likewise, Malta has enacted the world's first comprehensive DLT legislation with three bills regulating DLT & Blockchain, Crypto & Service Providers (https://www. ccmalta.com/news/malta-blockchain-crypto-legislation).

6. CONCLUSIONS

The energy system is undergoing an unprecedented period of change. For decades, policies driving renewable energy have driven research and development into new forms of generation that are decarbonized and decentralized. This is driving generation to the grid's edge and making it intermittent. To manage this requires digitalization of control/balancing systems leading to development of smart grids and a shift to prioritization of flexibility and local balancing services to maximize grid asset utilization and accommodate greater renewables penetration, both utility scale and distributed.

As generation scale drops to kilowatts, and generation moves to rooftops, transaction costs must fall to near zero to make balancing and settlement economically viable at the grid's edge. And with the promise of lower-cost decentralized storage, aggregation, intermediation, and virtual power plants, the demands placed on the distribution network are increasing rapidly, with complicated flows and emerging business models, topics extensively covered in other chapters of this volume.

In this context, peer-to-peer energy trading on blockchains provides one mechanism to make such markets viable and to integrate prosumers as owners in potentially autonomous or partially autonomous local energy communities. Alternatively, blockchain solutions provide the transaction layer that may partially disintermediate energy suppliers and almost entirely disintermediate financial institutions and serve as platforms for energy services.

While blockchain-based P2P trading platforms promise a huge potential to deal with the complex characteristics of the emerging energy ecosystem, it currently faces a number of technological, legal, policy, and social challenges. Due to the disruptive nature of the enabling technology, it will take some time for viable business models to emerge. Given the interest of the players involved, it seems that the decision to test and expand the concept is imminent. The question remains which country, which business model, and which innovative players will be able to drive this transformation and which will learn from the mistakes of the frontrunners and leapfrog the nascent technology to its ultimate potential.

CHAPTER 3

Integrated Energy Services, Load Aggregation, and Intelligent Storage

Jim Baak[*,a], **Fereidoon Sioshansi**[†]
*Stem, Inc., Millbrae, CA, United States
†Menlo Energy Economics, Walnut Creek, CA, United States

1. INTRODUCTION

The rapid proliferation of distributed energy resources (DERs) is no longer in dispute. As more consumers become prosumers – and by adding storage – become prosumagers, the traditional role of the distribution network and the utilities' relationship with the customers radically changes. Many prosumers and prosumagers no longer get all or most of their kWhs from the distribution grid. Some may become net exporters of kWhs during certain parts of the day or month, certainly true for customers with solar PVs who may generate more power than they consume during the sunny hours of the day. This results in two-way flows on a distribution network originally designed to be a one-way conveyor of electrons to the customers. And this creates challenges for the network operators who must increasingly deal with more unpredictable energy flows and potentially localized congestion on the distribution network while maintaining reliability, power quality, and frequency.

Other challenges to the traditional operation and management of the grid are coming from the even more rapid rise of variable renewable generation – both utility scale and distributed. The result is more frequent episodes when renewable generation exceeds load on the network resulting in negative wholesale prices exacerbated due to inflexible conventional generation, legacy agreements for imported power as well as inadequate transmission and storage capacity to absorb the excess renewable generation. These challenges are well documented and considerable

---

[a]The authors acknowledge the assistance of Polly Shaw, Vice President of Regulatory Affairs and Communications at Stem, who reviewed and contributed to an earlier draft of this chapter.

resources are devoted to resolving them, including efforts to make customer loads more flexible and more responsive to prices.

This chapter is primarily focused on efforts to aggregate and intelligently manage customer loads, distributed generation, and storage assets primarily on the customer side of the distribution network. With so much variable renewable generation expected in the coming years, the traditional means of keeping generation and load in balance are becoming impractical. The time has arrived for flexible load to more actively tango with the variable generation in real time in an increasingly decentralized and complex environment.

The chapter illustrates how significant value can be created and monetized by aggregating large numbers of residential, commercial, and industrial assets and managing their generation, flexible loads, and storage using artificial intelligence and machine learning. As will be shown through some examples, this can be achieved largely through automation with little input from, or inconvenience to, customers. A myriad of startups as well as traditional stakeholders are striving to successfully master the art of adding intelligence to otherwise "dumb" resources especially distributed generation and storage – resources that have hitherto been operating as passive assets, unresponsive to price signals.

The chapter is organized as follows:

- Section 2 provides a primer on integrated energy services, load aggregation, and intelligent storage;
- Section 3 describes a case study of Stem, Inc. a successful energy storage enterprise focused on a profitable niche in this expanding space; and
- Section 4 features additional case studies of a handful of other noteworthy companies engaged in similar services, each filling a particular need in given markets followed by the chapter's conclusions.

2. A PRIMER ON INTEGRATED ENERGY SERVICES, LOAD AGGREGATION, AND INTELLIGENT STORAGE

Customers, as everyone knows, do not consume energy for the sake of using energy. They consume energy to meet their *energy services needs* – to keep the buildings cool or hot, to run machinery, to pump, lift, crush, melt, freeze, or whatever they need to do to manage the business needs and operations. Since energy costs money, customers are motivated to use less energy, and to apply it productively and efficiently. The higher the retail tariffs, the stronger the incentive, which explains why many large, energy-consuming commercial and industrial (C&I) customers have energy managers whose job is to minimize energy bills while maintaining operational requirements.

In this context, many are investing in distributed energy resources (DERs), and more recently in energy storage systems (ESS), so long as such investments reduce their energy bills. Even though the size of the customers and their energy bills varies greatly, the fundamentals are the same: Customers invest in DERs, ESS, and other energy using/saving devices to the extent that the reduced bills over a reasonable period of time more than offset the initial investments.

Given the desire to minimize energy bills and – more recently – the environmental footprint, many existing and new companies now offer integrated energy services. As further explained later, in the past few years, a new generation of energy service companies (ESCOs) has emerged with load aggregation and intelligent storage as their core competency and value proposition.

Despite the growing consumer interest, creating a profitable enterprise based on saving customers' energy bills is challenging for a number of reasons:

- First is the fact that regulation on retail tariffs is in state of flux, introducing uncertainties in estimating the revenue potential;
- Another challenge is that the savings or gains from individual interventions tend to be modest, which means that multiple sources of revenues must be captured to make it truly worthwhile. This practice, referred to as *value stacking*, is central to many enterprises in this field.
- Even with value stacking, the profit margins may be modest – which means significant volume is required to make it worthwhile. Most successful firms therefore scale up by aggregating large number of assets from multiples of customers as soon as they develop a working solution; and
- Finally, with massive aggregated assets, there are simply too many moving parts, which means that managing – let alone optimizing – becomes impossible rather quickly. The solution is two-way communication to multiples of devices using sophisticated software, artificial intelligence, and machine learning.

It is another example of how the digitalization of the power sector is transforming the industry and how trading and transactions among multiples of customers are being managed, the topic of Chapters 1 and 2.

The result is a proliferation of assets on the customer side of the meter, also called behind-the-meter (BTM), that need to be individually managed and controlled. While large C&I customers may have the resources to optimize their use to manage demand charges, they often lack the expertise and the time to optimize for the multiple value stacking opportunities, which make storage worthwhile. Consequently, many customers do not get the full value of the investments they have made in DERs and/or ESS, leaving a lot of value on the table.

As the market becomes more complicated along with the introduction of temporally and locationally granular retail tariffs and new products and services, there are growing opportunities for intermediaries to step in, aggregate large number of customer loads and resources, and capture value across the entire value chain, further described in the following sections.

3. CASE STUDY: STEM[1]

In the past few years, a growing number of companies have emerged to master the art of aggregation and intermediation in the DER and ESS space. Each has adopted a different focus and has developed a unique business model to capture and deliver value, while many of the fundamentals are the same.

Stem, based in Millbrae, California, is among a handful of established businesses with plans to expand its footprint as it finetunes its business model. The company's forte is minimizing customers' energy bills – including demand charges – by improved management of when and how much energy is consumed. This is accomplished by adding intelligent storage to the equation. Stem describes itself as follows[2]:

Stem creates innovative technology services that transform the way energy is distributed and consumed

The company's software product, Athena™, named after goddess of wisdom

… is the first AI (artificial intelligence) for energy storage and virtual power plants. It optimizes the timing of energy use and facilitates consumers' participation in energy markets, yielding economic and societal benefits while decarbonizing the grid.

The company's mission is to build and operate the smartest and largest digitally-connected energy storage network for our customers.

---

[1]Visit www.stem.com for more information.
[2]http://www.businesswire.com.

In examining typical C&I customer bills, Stem recognized that for many, maximum demand charges – usually measured in 15 minute intervals – account for a significant portion of the bill for the entire month. This means that a spike in demand, even if for a few minutes, could have significant financial consequences.[3] Unsurprisingly, managing peak demand and associated demand charges is among the valuable services provided by Stem.

stem

By managing the charging and dispatching of the ESS to minimize maximum monthly demand charges, customers' bills can be reduced. And since batteries have limited life span and wear out with repeated cycles of charging and discharging, maximizing their lifetime value becomes critical.

But what may seem rather trivial at first, can get quite complicated in practice. Imagine, for example, a large industrial customer with multiples of energy-intensive assets, distributed generation, and ESS spread across a plant. There are too many moving parts to monitor and manage. And the pattern of consumption, generation, and storage changes from day to day and from hour to hour based on variables such as production targets, operational levels, temperature, solar generation, and variable prices at the retail and wholesale levels.

Describing the many intricacies of Stem's business model to Peter Kelly Detwiler, who wrote an article on the subject in Feb 8, 2018 issue of *Forbes*,[4] CEO John Carrington said Stem spent a good deal of time with its counterparts thinking these issues through and identifying what would be necessary to take the problem to the next level, "and all of it was data-related."

---

[3]Another consideration, and an increasing focus of Stem's service offerings, is the recognition of the fact that many C&I customers can reduce their energy bills by investing in distributed generation *and* storage. The more they generated on site means the less they would have to buy from the grid. Moreover, on-site storage, adds flexibility – for example allowing them to store some of the excess generation for use at other times. Since many large C&I customers are on time-of-use or variable tariffs, the added flexibility of distributed generation *plus* storage allows them to adjust *net* consumption from the grid, say to times when prices are low. During such periods, the on-site ESS can be charged. This is another example of value stacking: avoiding high demand charges, reducing net kWh consumption from the grid, and taking advantage of arbitrage opportunities provided by storage.

[4]Stem Adding Artificial Intelligence To Storage And Branching Out To New Markets by Peter Kelly Detwiler, Forbes, 8 Jan 2018 available at https://www.forbes.com/sites/peterdetwiler/2018/01/08/stem-adding-artificial-intelligence-to-storage-and-branching-out-to-new-markets/#278be65a74b9.

Which explains the critical function of Athena, the software tool that turns data into value by making "dumb" assets such as distributed generation and storage into intelligent, proactive devices. Stem uses its artificial intelligence (AI) platform to aggregate its sites, when unused, into large networks that act as "Virtual Power Plants," providing capacity or grid services for additional revenue opportunities, such as in an 85-MW Local Capacity Requirement contract for Southern California Edison.

As the preceding discussion indicates, the critical factor in success of Stem, and its counterparts, is the mastery of "value stacking," which refers to the fact that – by relying on artificial intelligence and machine learning – one can add value from a broad range of assets in a typical setting. As described in the *Forbes* article, storage can:

- Store or release energy into the grid to stabilize the frequency;
- Provide energy during peak demand periods or assume the role of a peaking plant; or
- Be used behind the customer meter to reduce maximum demand and lower the monthly demand charges.

These are among roughly a dozen useful functions that can be performed by having an intelligent ESS.

Maximizing the value of a customer's multitude of assets, devices, distributed generation, and storage – however – is not trivial because delivering more of one reduces the value of others. Some of the most desirable functions of storage, for example, may compromise the battery's longevity or performance. As described in the *Forbes* article,

> … if you are deploying a battery at a specific moment for managing a customer's demand charge, you might not be able to use it for grid frequency regulation. That might be OK, unless the frequency regulation event pays more than the demand management function, in which case one gets a sub-optimal result.

That is where Athena becomes useful since it can simultaneously monitor and assess the monetary value of multiple functions, including:

- The state of charge in the ESS;
- How fast to cycle;
- How deep to discharge while mindful of the longer-term impacts of such decisions on battery life;
- Anticipate grid or utility capacity calls and associated revenues; and
- Keeping track of facility's own tariff options, in particular maximum demand charges.

Athena calculates those factors against the anticipated building demand and local grid congestion learned from one-second data capture and predictive analytics, relying on machine learning from terabytes of data stored to Stem's "cloud." Athena must decide in real-time how to optimize real-time data it collects from multiple sources against multiples of scenarios while making sure the customers' critical loads and operational requirements are met.

The problem gets even more interesting when dealing with an aggregation of customers with distributed assets spread around a city or state and beyond using different suppliers' battery and inverter technologies, and across vast differences in load shapes, tariffs, and customer requirements. Stem and its counterparts are increasingly managing aggregated assets of multiple clients as described in the *Forbes* article,

> With all of these installed systems and diverse technologies across multiple locations, this would be utterly impossible for humans to orchestrate. It is, in short, a complex multi-variable task that is perfectly suited to artificial intelligence.

And that is precisely where value is added and where managing distributed assets becomes interesting.

In the interview with *Forbes*, Carrington is quoted:

> What's so exciting to me are the attributes that you can bring to the grid, to the customer and the utility…Just putting a storage device at the customer to manage demand charge reduction is analogous to buying an iPhone and just using it as a telephone. We have multiple applications we can drop into a storage device to open up and monetize many components that may or may not be useful today, but will be useful going forward.

Needless to say, as with any enterprise in this space, the key is to add intelligence to otherwise dumb devices, be it solar PV systems or storage. In the case of Stem, Athena's machine-learning algorithms are constantly collecting, analyzing, and applying useful patterns to manage the energy usage, distributed generation, and storage of devices at customers' premises.

According to Carrington, Stem's capabilities to maximize value have increased over time:

> Our data set is really remarkable – we have billions of data points and have battery companies interested in acquiring our data. We think it's the biggest data set in the C/I space.

Unsurprisingly, Stem has ambitious expansion plans for 2019 and beyond. The company plans to engage in more partnerships with more clients over time while expanding its footprint overseas. The company is betting on continuous improvements in storage technology and lower costs – neither of which is unreasonable.

The company, which currently has 8 utility contracts and 860 systems under management for 280 customers totaling 225 MWh, primarily operates in California, Hawaii, Massachusetts, New York, and Texas. In 2017, Stem dispatched its VPPs in over 600 executions into the CAISO wholesale market, with the majority on real-time (5-minute) calls. Stem is also already active in Japan and Ontario, Canada, with plans to enter other attractive markets. Its early backers include Constellation, GE, Mitsui, and RWE.[5]

4. OTHER BUSINESSES, OTHER BUSINESS MODELS

Clearly, there is a lot of interest in integrated energy services, load aggregation, and intelligent storage. Unsurprisingly, new and old companies are emerging to develop products and services in what is viewed as a promising field. Stem, featured in the preceding section, is among many. While each company is focused on a part of the value chain with a different value proposition, all are essentially chasing the same pie – how to aggregate assets, manage loads, distributed generation and storage, and how to generate and monetize value through multiple streams.

There have been a number of mergers and acquisitions as established companies and investors with deep pockets buy promising start-ups or invest in them. There is even an Energy Storage Association (ESA) solely focused on the emerging field, which is at the center of much attention.

This section highlights a few notable and/or promising companies – there are too many to mention – not in any particular order.

4.1 Advanced Microgrid Solutions (AMS)[6]

AMS is among the pioneers in the field of combining loads, distributed generation and storage, and managing the lot using sophisticated software. The company has scaled up quickly and plans to expand. As is usually the case, it has developed Armada, its proprietary software tool in house, and it has been successful in raising funding from a number of strategically important investors in the US as well as overseas. Moreover, the company was founded and is managed by Susan Kennedy, a veteran of California energy scene and extremely well connected to the who's who in the electric power sector.

What it does is not fundamentally dissimilar to Stem and others featured in this chapter as further described in Box 3.1.

---

[5]Stem is funded by a consortium of leading investors including Activate Capital, Angeleno Group, Constellation Technology Ventures, Iberdrola (Inversiones Financieras Perseo), GE Ventures, Mithril Capital Management, Mitsui & Co. LTD., Ontario Teachers' Pension Plan, RWE Supply & Trading, Temasek, and Total Energy Ventures.
[6]http://advmicrogrid.com.

Box 3.1 AMS: What Makes it Tick? What Sets it Apart?[7]

San Francisco-based Advanced Microgrid Solutions (AMS) is a startup with a fleet of behind-the-meter batteries that can shape load to help meet building and grid energy needs. The company has successfully raised several rounds of investments with funding from key utilities and corporate investors in the US and overseas.[8] It is among a handful of companies trying to break into the distributed energy resources (DER) business by managing loads, generation, and behind-the-meter storage.

AMS is using its funding to expand into new markets outside California, and to scale up its Armada software, the "building-to-grid DER optimization platform" that it uses to design, implement, and operate its current fleet of battery-equipped buildings.

AMS, one of the larger behind-the-meter battery operators in California, signed a 50-MW contract with Southern California Edison Company (SCE) in 2014, adding another 40 MW and 4 MW with SCE and San Diego Gas & Electric Company (SDG&E), respectively, as well as numerous others. It also has multiple large commercial buildings in Irvine, CA, Walmart superstores and other major commercial property owners. It has major expansion plans for the rest of the US and possibly Australia.

As is the case for all start-ups in this space, its main asset – aside from its staff and contracts – is its proprietary software Armada. According to CEO Susan Kennedy, Armada is "a key differentiator between AMS and the other distributed energy resource management system (DERMS) providers." Kennedy is quoted in the gtm article saying, "What we have that is different, that they don't have, is the economic optimization at the portfolio level to provide grid services."

"If you want to turn things on and off, there are a lot of players to do that," add-ing, AMS focuses on "the algorithms that perform the economic optimization of distributed energy resources, using energy storage as the key technology that allows load control."

According to Kennedy, the "… combination of flexibility and dispatchability, properly analyzed and utilized, can yield a lot more revenues than just using batteries for backup power, demand charge management, or other single-purpose functions."

[7]This box is based on Advanced Microgrid Solutions Raises $34M Series B From a Who's Who of Strategic Investors by Jeff St. John, which appeared in GreenTech Media (gtm) on Jul 10, 2017, available at https://www.greentechmedia.com/articles/read/advanced-microgrid-solutions-raises-34m-from-a-whos-who-of-strategic-invest#gs.6qnE_As.
[8]Its funders include Energy Impact Partners (EIP), and Southern Company, Macquarie Capital, GE Ventures and Australian utility AGL, among others.

Continued

Box 3.1 AMS: What Makes it Tick? What Sets it Apart?—cont'd

"We use the battery to completely reshape the customer's load, so you get maximum savings," adding, "There are 10 different ways you can create savings on the customer side of the meter, from demand-charge management and price-responsive load shaping, to offering load flexibility to meet local or system-wide grid needs."

Recognizing that one size does not fit all, AMS offers flexible arrangements in how it structures the financing and ownership models for the different distributed energy resources (DERs). Kennedy said AMS can finance solar or storage or rely on customer-owned assets including backup generators or building energy management systems.

"There's a pretty broad range of models for financing and ownership structures," adding, "We're working with a number of energy services companies to tap into those savings, and it's extremely valuable for our end-use customers."

As more C&I customers invest in energy efficiency, distributed solar, battery and advanced energy management systems, AMS and its counterparts must find ways to remotely monitor, manage, and optimize the load, generation, and storage assets without disrupting customers' key operational requirements or inconveniencing commercial property occupants.

Office parks, shopping malls, and warehouse are among AMS' major clients as are major distribution companies within congested localized load centers that are hard to serve. The sudden closure of SCE's San Onofre Nuclear Generating Station (SONGS) left parts of Orange County and San Diego poorly served with the existing transmission and distribution network. AMS filled some of the void with its distributed model.

With its direct data links to customers' "assets," AMS can monitor every critical variable remotely. According to Kennedy,

… If I've sized the battery appropriately, I can tell the utility, 'This customer, this service account, has this much load if you need it' – in real time.

Since there are others going after the same clients, offering similar services, a key driver of success is product and service differentiation. Kennedy says "one important difference between AMS and many of the "other" behind-the-meter (BTM) battery companies is that AMS hasn't built its business around designing and selling a particular combination of technology to its customers."[9] She adds,

Moreover, "We're designing systems to take advantage of future opportunities," Kennedy said. That's an important consideration in California, where DERs

---

[9] In a fiercely competitive environment with firms jockeying for advantage, statements and press releases such as this should be taken with "a grain of salt" – a dose of skepticism.

Box 3.1 AMS: What Makes it Tick? What Sets it Apart?—cont'd

are starting to gain access to grid markets run by state's grid operator CAISO while taking a more active role in distribution utilities' multi-billion dollar distribution grid investment plans.[10]

> *"If I can respond in two minutes – if I can respond in two seconds – I can provide a full range of ancillary services that's not here today, but coming tomorrow,"* adding, *"If I put in the wrong telemetry, I'm locked out of a lot of future revenues."*

[10]It should be noted that Stem is already extensively involved in utility DER and CAISO opportunities.

4.2 Sonnen[11]

Sonnen, a German company with an expanding footprint across Europe, North America, and Australia, is among the more established energy storage companies with – it claims – a powerful software that adds value to ESS and DERs in distributed markets. According to Christoph Ostermann, the company's CEO:

> *Our goal is a world in which everyone is able to cover his energy needs with decentralized and clean energy source. Everyone can connect with each other to share energy where and when it's needed. This will emancipate our world from the dependence on fossil fuels and anonymous energy corporations.*

According to its website:

> *… Sonnen's signature accomplishment is the deployment of the largest distributed network of energy storage systems in the world, the sonnenCommunity, deployed in Europe and most recently Australia.*

> *The sonnenCommunity in Germany acts as both a VPP as well as a peer-to-peer clean energy trading platform … with over 21,000 installed and working systems.*

> *Additionally, sonnen offers amongst the longest lasting, robust and safest energy storage systems available….*

Sonnen's innovative projects include a few more-or-less self sufficient "clean energy communities" where the loads, distributed generation, and storage of the entire community is aggregated, monitored, and optimized in a fashion similar to the one described in Box 3.2.

Further details on Sonnen's clean energy community in Prescott Valley, AZ[12] may be found at company's website. Most important is that each of the 2,900 homes will have 8 kW and 16 kWh of storage system, which adds up to a total of 11.6 MW and 23 MWhs of energy storage capacity for the community.

---

[11]https://www.sonnen-batterie.com/en-us/vision.
[12]Text based on press release on 12 Oct 2017 available at company website.

Box 3.2 Sonnen to Synergize the Power of Aggregation[13]

Intelligent storage is the centerpiece of a proposed scheme in Arizona.

In mid-October 2017, German-based **Sonnen** announced it was embarking on an ambitious project with an American homebuilder in sunny **Prescott, Arizona**. The aim is to build a community of 2,900 homes capable to generate, store, and share electricity in collaboration with **Mandalay Homes**. While the initial press release (PR) was rather short on specifics, it is not hard to read between the lines, so to speak. According to the PR, each home in the new community will have solar PVs on the roof plus a battery in the garage enabling every household to produce, consume and/or store most of its own electricity.

But in an added twist, that is common to others in this emerging field including **Tesla Energy** and **Stem**, the **energy storage systems** (ESS) in the homes will be *interconnected* and able to communicate with each other using the same technology that has already been used in similar experiments for power sharing in Germany.

Sonnen calls it "sonnenCommunity." Think of it as an intelligent aggregated and enabled **peer-to-peer (P2P) trading** scheme where the participants are entirely passive. And that is the beauty of the idea: it does *not* require individual households to mess around with their thermostats, PVs, batteries or, for that matter, anything else. Sonnen will manage the whole thing for them.

What is the advantage of this clever twist? It turns the community of 2,900 homes into a **virtual power plant** (VPP) with an aggregated capacity of 11.6 MW and potential output of 23 MWh, according to Sonnen.

The batteries, collectively, can store energy during peak production times – say sunny days of summer – and feed it back into the grid after the sun has set – and when peak demand typically happens these days. In **California**, for example, the utilities have redefined the peak demand to be between 6 and 9 pm, not noon to 2 pm, as it used to be in presolar days. What is more, the VPP can offer services to the **distribution network** or the **grid operator**, relieving stress at times of peak demand. Schemes such as this will be sorely needed to cure the **California's Duck Curve** problem (refer to Fig. 12.4 in Sioshansi's Chapter 12) or its equivalents now appearing elsewhere.

Such schemes typically include a smart **home energy management** system, which optimizes solar power generation, storage, and consumption while communicating with the network all the time. There are significant synergies when the load, generation, and storage of 3,000 homes are pooled together and collectively managed, optimized, and ultimately *monetized*.

In announcing the venture, **Philipp Schröder**, Managing Director of Sales and Marketing at Sonnen said, "This is the city of the future, a place where all residents produce, store and share their own energy." Setting the PR aside, it is a brilliant idea whose time has arrived. Moreover, with the expected emergence of **digitalization** and big data, the business model is ripe for implementation and scaling up.

[13]Excerpted from EEnergy Informer, Dec 2017.

Box 3.2 Sonnen to Synergize the Power of Aggregation—cont'd

While Sonnen's community in Arizona is not unique, it clearly shows the growing role of storage in an **integrated energy management system**. And if you think aggregating the load, generation, and storage of 3,000 homes is a good idea, think how much more can be done with a community of 30,000, or 300,000 or 3 million homes?

The state-of-the-art homes will have the latest features in insulation, energy-efficient lighting, HVAC, pool pumps, appliances, and demand control offering comfort coupled with extremely low-energy costs for the homeowners.

Each of the homes will be capable of communicating with others to form an intelligent network, which can operate as a *Virtual Power Plant* (VPP) capable of dynamically interacting with the needs of the distribution grid in real time. This will allow the system to flatten the load of the entire community, minimize grid stress and reducing costs. Over time such *sonnenCommunities* can operate more or less on their own, by relying on thousands of distributed energy resources as opposed to a handful of central power plants.

According to press release at company's website.

The … sonnen energy storage system harnesses excess solar energy generated during the daytime, storing it in a smart battery. Later in the day, when the sun is no longer shining, the sonnen energy storage system is calibrated to discharge and meet the specific load of the home, running the home on stored sunshine in the evening.

Essentially, the sonnen system will pull energy from the grid, partially charging its batteries… The first load shift will be during the middle of the night (2-5 am), pulling otherwise wasted excess energy that is being produced and unused … The second load shift will occur during the early high solar production hours of approximately 10 am-2 pm. During this late morning/early afternoon timeframe, the electricity grid in Arizona has a tremendous excess of solar generated energy that is pumped into it from thousands of rooftop solar arrays, creating a highly inefficient usage pattern and even negative impact, increasing stress on the grid.

The sonnenCommunity in Jasper will act as a giant receptacle for this excess solar generated energy from around the region, taking it off the grid and "time shifting" it to discharge during a peak period, dramatically increasing the effectiveness of solar power throughout the grid. The Sonnen system will store this cheaper and far cleaner energy from both load shifts and discharge it to flood the morning and evening peak periods.

Describing the main features of the experiment, Christoph Ostermann, CEO of sonnen says:

Self-Consuming locally harvested sunlight energy, while collaborating with your neighbors and with the grid, to create a clean energy community, represents a transformational design concept for the US homebuilding industry.

Clearly, Sonnen is pushing the envelope by integrating distributed energy generation and storage, aggregating it across a large community of homes and manages and optimizes the entire system more or less as a virtual microgrid. It is among the first to experiment on such a massive scale in the residential sector, where few others are currently focused.

4.3 Tesla Energy[14]

Tesla, with its powerful brand, has also been engaged in integrated energy services. As described in Box 3.3, its CEO Elon Musk has been talking about his vision as early as 2016 when he wrote a blog explaining how he thinks the future will, or should, look like.

Integrated energy services, according to Tesla. (Source: https://www.tesla.com/tesla_theme/assets/img/solar/panels/section-hero.jpg?20180104.)

Storage and solar: increasingly popular. (Source: https://www.tesla.com/tesla_theme/assets/img/energy/utilities/section-centralized_power_generation.jpg?20170331.)

[14]Excerpted from EEnergy Informer, Dec 2016. https://www.tesla.com/solarpanels?utm_expid=.36XSKMxWSxerIeL8zEtw6g.1&utm_referrer=https%3A%2F%2Fwww.google.com%2F.

Box 3.3 Elon Musk of Tesla Energy Unveils His Integrated Mobility, Solar, and Battery Solution Under One Roof[15]

In late October 2016, **Elon Musk**, the CEO of **Tesla**, unveiled what his integrated mobility, solar roof, and battery storage solution might look like – literally all under the same roof – that is an elegant solar roof integrated into the design of the house. It is a **building-integrated PV** or BIPV. In his characteristic hyperbole style, Musk claimed the new roof will cost less "than a normal roof plus cost of electricity" without further clarifications.

The cost of electricity, of course, varies from place to place, and so does how much solar energy one can get from the roof. Hence, it is fair to assume that the new system would make sense in sunny places with high retail tariffs, say California or Hawaii.

In the meantime, Musk acquired Tesla's sister company, **SolarCity**, the biggest US distributed solar installer with the intention of integrating mobility – **Tesla car** – distributed solar – **SolarCity** rooftop PVs – and storage – **Powerwall** – into a single company under **Tesla Energy** brand. And what a powerful brand that would be, if he can pull it off. With too many balls to juggle – all his companies are burning cash at fast pace – not everyone is convinced that he will be able to deliver on so many promises. Yet his ideas are simply too good to dismiss.

As Musk described in his blog, the new roof system would integrate with the Powerwall 2.0 battery system, which could power the refrigerator, sockets and lights of a four-bedroom house for a day. Add the rooftop solar system and the house becomes virtually self-sufficient – except on extended cloudy periods when it must rely on the network. Musk envisions a future where *every* household has an electric car – a Tesla, of course – a battery – a Powerwall, of course – and a solar roof – installed by Tesla Energy, of course, on their home.

According to Musk, however, incumbent electric utilities need not fear Tesla's new business model – there will be enough business to go around. The projected growth of electric vehicles would add to demand. In the long term, about one-third of the power needed for EVs will come from rooftop solar with the remaining supplied by the utilities, according to Musk.

Many agree with Musk that future buildings, residential, commercial and industrial, will rapidly migrate into the so-called **building integrated designs**, where **energy efficiency**, **solar self-generation**, sophisticated **energy management and control systems** plus **storage** will be integrated into the initial design of buildings, rather than added later – resulting in major operational cost savings over the long life of typical buildings.

California's **zero-net-energy** (ZNE) mandate, for example, requires *new* residential buildings to produce as much energy as they consume starting in 2020; the same would apply to commercial buildings starting in 2030.

Already, a growing number of manufacturers including **Onyx**, a Spanish company, are offering a host of new products such as transparent PV windows that can serve as roofing material for atriums, generating electricity while taking advantage of daylighting. The days of building a roof, and then adding solar panels on top of it are over.

Musk is among the entrepreneurs who are going to make a fortune offering such integrated solutions.

[15]Originally appeared in Dec 2016 issue of EEnergy Informer, page 8.

Not only is Tesla working on the residential sector, it has been active with utility-scale applications. Its Powerwall batteries are increasingly used alongside utility-scale solar and wind farms in the US (photo) and Australia.

Tesla recently built the world's largest battery, a 100-MW facility in South Australia, which has been operating successfully (photo).

Tesla's 100 MW/120 MWh battery went into service in Dec 2017 in South Australia. *(Source: Tesla.)*

Tesla is building a factory in Buffalo, New York, to manufacture solar tiles, which it intends to offer as part of its integrated energy services package to residential and commercial customers. As Elon Musk has repeatedly said, his vision is to make future prosumagers virtually independent of the distribution utilities and to make oil and traditional automobile companies obsolete.

Musk cannot always be taken too seriously. At the same time, he cannot be entirely dismissed. He is building a new EV factory near Shanghai expected to produce as many as 500,000 EVs when completed. In the next 2 years, one will be able to say how successful Tesla is in electric mobility, in distributed storage, in solar tiles and – potentially – in offering fully integrated energy services.

4.4 Engie Storage[16] (Previously Green Charge)

French company Engie has been an active player in the DER space with a number of important acquisitions including acquiring Green Charge, now called Engie Storage. According to its website

[16]http://www.engiestorage.com.

ENGIE Storage provides turnkey and collaborative energy storage solutions serving producers and consumers on both sides of the meter.

Like its counterparts in this space, Engie believes the future of variable renewable generation will rest on ESS – utility scale, distributed, or most likely both.

As your energy storage partner, ENGIE Storage will help ensure that the energy generated by your solar systems will be available when customers and energy providers need it, to offset spiky loads and reduce grid power use during peak time-of-use periods.

Engie says it will address its customers' performance concerns through:

- System design process with performance projections;
- Supplier-backed performance warranties;
- Energy storage operation and monitoring; and
- Performance guarantee options.

Prior to being acquired by Engie in Apr 2018, Green Charge spent considerable effort on its GridSynergy™ energy storage solution to help commercial customers reduce their energy costs while partnering with solar providers and EV charging companies to supply the needs of clients more efficiently.

As distributed energy resources became increasingly important to utilities and other grid operators, we aggregated our customer-sited storage systems to help those operators manage the demands of an increasingly complex energy ecosystem.

Following the acquisition, ENGIE's financial resources makes Engie Storage a powerful player – giving its clients, "… even greater confidence that we would follow through on our projects, and that we would be around to operate and support their systems for the full term of their contracts."

As part of the ENGIE family of companies, Engie Storage is well positioned to offer a broader range of services including energy efficiency, energy management, and energy-as-a-service (EaaS) solutions.

4.5 EnerNOC[17]

The company's motto is "Tackle Your Biggest Challenges with Better Energy Intelligence." EnerNOC was acquired by Italy's Enel in Aug 2017, incorporating EnerNOC's more than 8,000 customers, 14,000 sites under management, and a total of 6 GW of demand response capacity.[18]

---

[17]https://www.enernoc.com.
[18]https://globenewswire.com/news-release/2017/08/07/1081096/0/en/Enel-Group-Completes-Acquisition-of-Leading-Us-Based-Provider-of-Smart-Energy-Management-Services-EnerNOC.html.

According to the company's website

"Whether you need a focused solution to a specific problem or a broad solution to a range of issues, our technology-enabled solutions ... can help ... address ... key energy management challenges," including:

- Energy intelligence software that boost facility efficiency, simplify utility bill management, and ease reporting burdens;
- Demand response services generating revenue; and
- Energy procurement services that help buying energy more strategically, manage risk, and deliver lower bills.

4.6 CPower[19]

Campbell, CA-based CPower is an energy management company, which "helps businesses streamline how they use energy." According to the company website

At CPower ... we take the time to learn about the intricacies of your business. Then we sharpen your energy management strategy with the optimal combination of demand response and demand management programs.

Similar to Stem[20] and AMS, CPower has a contract with SCE to provide 35 MW of DR capacity under demand response auction mechanism or DRAM. It is part of the effort in California to integrated DERs and storage with other resources in the California Independent System Operator's (CAISO) markets.

According to Jennifer Chamberlin, CPower's Executive Director for California, CPower is positioned to help the state achieve its clean energy and grid reliability goals with the DRAM program while helping organizations earn revenue through curtailment.

"The DRAM Pilot is an exciting way for customers to participate directly in the CAISO markets," Chamberlin said. "Our customers offer load curtailment that can be used to meet grid needs instead of turning on a power plant, helping to support the CAISO grid with a carbon-free resource attained by allowing customers to respond to market prices and reduce energy consumption when the system needs it most."[21]

---

[19]https://cpowerenergymanagement.com.

[20]Stem and CPower have a partnership agreement to provide customers with both conventional DR and energy storage, currently mainly focused in Southern California. this represents a pairing of traditional DR and energy storage to achieve greater savings and demand reductions during times of critical grid needs.

[21]7 Nov 2017 Press release at CPower website.

4.7 Enphase Energy[22]

Among those focused on integrated energy services, Enphase claims to offer the "total solution" for homes and commercial clients (visual). According to the company's website

Only the Enphase Home Energy Solution brings you solar, storage, and powerful monitoring software, all from one company. It's built to work together, with continuous, seamless communication, for a fully integrated system that's far more than solar – it's truly a smart home.

Schematic of Enphase's integrated energy service solution. *(Source: https://enphase. com/sites/default/files/content/HES_Flat_Illustration_House_1440w.jpg.)*

4.8 Charge Point[23]

Electric vehicles are expected to grow exponentially over the next couple of decades especially in California, currently home to roughly half of all EVs in the US with a target to get as many as 5 million by 2030.

Naturally how, when, and where EVs are charged, and at what price, will matter a lot as further described in Chapter 18 by Webb et al. in this volume. And this has led to the rise of number of companies narrowly focused on this particular kind of energy storage, including Charge Point.

At its website, the company claims that it "operate the world's largest and most open electric vehicle (EV) charging network. Our mission is to get everyone behind the wheel of an EV, and provide them a place to charge wherever they go. As our network grows, it makes it easier for people to adopt EVs and driving an EV makes even more sense."

[22]https://enphase.com/en-us.
[23]https://www.chargepoint.com.

It says: "The future of transportation Is here. Are you ready?"

Over 763,000 EVs have been sold in the US as of 2017, we expect one million EVs will be on the road within the next two years and more than half of all car sales will be electric by 2040. It's clear that driving electric is going mainstream, but what does the growth in e-mobility mean for you? Get an understanding of where this industry is headed and how you can be a part of it.

4.9 eMotorWerks[24]

Based in San Carlos, CA, eMotorWerks is another start-up in the EV-charging business, and like many others, it was acquired by Enel in Oct 2017. According to its website

Our solution is to build the largest network of distributed load control devices, used to provide grid stabilization services to Independent System Operators (ISOs), utilities, and large commercial electricity consumers. Our company's current initial offering is a line of SmartGrid-ready EV charging stations with world-class grid management and user-facing control features, managed through our cloud-based platform.

eMotorWerks provides valuable grid management services - such as demand response, frequency regulation, peak shaving, local load balancing, and many others - that help utilities and ISOs better manage the grid volatility and prepare for and fully leverage accelerating EV adoption. Low manufacturing and operating costs of our company's networked assets support high ROI and short payback periods on initial capital investments.

These examples, of course, are a small sample of many start-ups and incumbents who are entering into the rapidly expanding space of behind-the-meter space.

5. CONCLUSIONS

As the preceding discussion makes clear, the time has arrived for a new breed of "integrated energy service companies" to take advantage of the emerging opportunities made possible by the rise of distributed generation *and* storage. These newcomers are increasingly enabled with advances in digitalization, remote monitoring, and two-way communication – not just with individual customers through their smart meters but multiple behind-the-meter (BTM) energy-consuming and/or storing devices. The range of services they can offer and the value proposition is enhanced with

---

[24]https://emotorwerks.com.

advances in artificial intelligence (AI) and machine learning (ML) – which allows automated monitoring and optimization of aggregated bundles of load, generation, and storage distributed across a network.

What has been experienced to date is not even the tip of the iceberg. There is a lot more to come in a range of applications including in electric transport sector – a giant opportunity that is yet to be tapped.

CHAPTER 4

Service Innovation and Disruption in the Australian Contestable Retail Market

Stephanie Bashir*, Aleks Smits†, Tim Nelson†
*Nexa Advisory, Melbourne, VIC, Australia
†AGL, Melbourne, VIC, Australia

1. INTRODUCTION

Australia's electricity needs are primarily met by the National Electricity Market (NEM). The NEM comprises around 40,000 km of transmission lines and cables and supplies around 19 million people through 9 million connections. It stretches over 5000 km from far north Queensland to the south of Tasmania and west to Adelaide and is the longest alternating current system in the world. The NEM has a total electricity generating capacity of almost 55,000 MW, and over 200 TWh of energy (or AUD$16bn) was dispatched and delivered in 2016–17.

The NEM has historically offered electricity supply via a linear value chain made up of three components: contestable generation, deregulated and competitive retail services, and regulated monopoly transmission and distribution networks. Key to the original design of the NEM is the underlying design of financial markets through which retailers purchase energy from the wholesale market.

The NEM is an energy-only market where generators are only paid for the energy they dispatch to the market, and not the capacity they make available. Generators bid into a market within a range[1] that is centrally cleared and dispatched by the Australian Energy Market Operator (AEMO). Additionally, ancillary markets exist to value frequency control and system restart capabilities.[2] The NEM wholesale price is extremely volatile and can increase from an average weighted volume price of around AUD$80/MWh to the market price cap of $14,200/MWh within a very short period

[1]Generators may bid at any range from the market floor, −$1000/MWh, to the market price cap (MPC), currently set at $14,200/MWh.
[2]Frequency control ancillary service (FCAS) and system restart ancillary service (SRAS).

Consumer, Prosumer, Prosumager
https://doi.org/10.1016/B978-0-12-816835-6.00004-8

of time when temperatures increase in summer or when the system loses generation as a result of unexpected events.

The traditional role of the energy retailer in the Australian context has been to mitigate this price risk for customers by hedging against the volatility of the wholesale price, either through utilizing a range of energy market derivatives such as swaps and caps,[3] or by investing directly in generation facilities. Retail electricity markets are deregulated, and through minimizing their risk in wholesale markets and procuring energy through competitive markets, retailers provide a range of offers to customers at different prices. This highly deregulated retail market makes Australia unique and responsive to a decentralized customer-driven value proposition and innovative business models.

In a market with steadily increasing demand, investments in large-scale thermal generation, such as coal-fired power stations, have traditionally been effective at providing the majority of Australia's energy needs.[4] However, these thermal assets are reaching the end of their design life and soon will need replacing. At the same time, conditions across the NEM have changed. Overall system demand since the mid-2000s has decreased, subsidized small-scale and large-scale renewable assets have entered the market on a significant scale, and low-emissions generation technologies such as solar and wind are increasingly becoming the cheapest replacement generation source.

Both wholesale and network prices have increased dramatically over the last 10 years, with real electricity prices increasing 63% between 2007–08 and 2015–16 (ACCC, 2017), making self-generation, storage, and energy optimization and efficiency products and services more attractive to customers. At the same time, the NEM has also changed at a more micro level, as customers are increasingly looking to utilize emerging technologies to take control of their energy use and meet their unique needs and comfort.

These technological developments in large-scale renewables and distributed energy technologies, as well as a global focus on reducing greenhouse gas emissions, are transforming Australia's electricity industry. This chapter explores these new technology developments and key trends in how con-

[3]Energy market futures and standardized products are traded through the Australian Stock Exchange (ASX), where financial services companies participate as well as energy market participants.
[4]Installed generation capacity increased in a linear fashion from around 3 GW in 1955 to 30 GW in the mid-1990s, supported mostly by the development of a number of coal-fired power stations in the 1980s, funded by State-owned electricity commissions.

sumers are interacting with and to some extent driving the electricity market transformation. The chapter also considers the policy reforms needed to facilitate the emergence of new products and services that build on new distributed technology capabilities in ways that respond to customer preferences. The chapter is structured as follows:

- Section 1 outlines the Australian context to disruption;
- Section 2 discusses the imperatives for change within this context;
- Section 3 outlines key trends in the Australian electricity market transformation;
- Section 4 outlines the response of traditional energy players and nontraditional new entrants to technology disruption followed by the chapter's conclusions.

2. IMPERATIVES FOR CHANGE

Irrespective of the direction of technological advancements that enable change, there are two fundamental imperatives driving the future of energy generation in Australia: decarbonization, and the centricity of customers' unique preferences and expectations.

The electricity sector has an important role to play in meeting Australia's emissions reduction targets and its long-term international commitments under the Paris Agreement: a 26–28% reduction in emissions by 2030 relative to 2005 levels.[5] While electricity generation currently accounts for approximately one-third of Australia's greenhouse gas emissions inventory and represents the single largest source of domestic emissions, technological substitutes to fossil fuels are available and are increasingly cost effective. For example, Fig. 4.1 shows that in Australia the lowest cost form of new energy generation technology is wind. Decarbonization of the electricity generation also has the potential to facilitate emissions reductions in other sectors, most notably transport, with electrification powered by renewable energy.

Decarbonization of the electricity generation sector, however, is not the only driver to market transformation. As described elsewhere in this volume, customers are also playing a critical role in the energy market transformation, driving a shift away from the traditional linear electricity supply chain, to a more decentralized and bidirectional market. New distributed

---

[5]This figure represents Australia's current Nationally Determined Contribution (NDC) to reduce national emissions and adapt to climate change under the framework of the 2015 Paris Agreement.

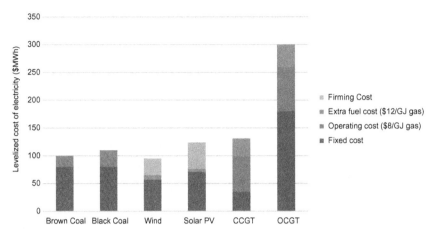

Figure 4.1 Levelized cost of generation projects. *(Source: AGL estimates; assumes capacity factors of 40% for wind, 25% for solar, 75% for CCGT and 10% for OCGT; heat rates of 8 for CCGT and 10 for OCGT.)*

generation and storage technologies are offering new opportunities for customers to actively manage their energy use and to share in value beyond the home, whether by trading energy with peers, or participating in programs that support the operation of the network or the wholesale market. The digitalization of services experienced in other sectors is driving an expectation of more choice and increased competition in the energy sector as well. More importantly, customers are seeking comfort, and energy is essential in that it enables comfort of our everyday lives.

This emerging role of the active customer driving change in the energy industry is significant. Whereas the retail market traditionally provided a homogeneous good, with price the only significant differential between products, increasingly, a spectrum of customers with different needs is emerging that businesses need to respond to (see Nelson et al., 2018a,b).

Not only do retailers still need to compete for the provision of electricity at the cheapest available price, they also need to respond to customers that have concerns with the emissions component of their energy, provide options for customers that want to utilize technological opportunities to participate actively in the market, and manage energy flows for customers who want to generate and export their own electricity.

These developments are disrupting the existing roles of generators and traditional retailers, affecting grid utilization, and fundamentally changing the way in which consumers interact with electricity markets.

3. KEY TRENDS IN THE ELECTRICITY MARKET TRANSFORMATION

Advancing technology, falling costs, and ubiquitous connectivity are opening the door to new models of producing and consuming energy. These present opportunities with the potential to build new architectures of interconnected energy ecosystems, but also the breaking down of traditional boundaries between demand and supply. The electricity sector is at the heart of this transformation, where digitalization is blurring the distinction between generation and consumption.

Chapter 3 of this book explains how value can be monetized by adding intelligence to distributed energy resources to control and optimize hardware and assets. While these trends are not necessarily unique to Australia, there are localized impacts in Australia due to the bespoke characteristics of the NEM.

The NEM is a vast grid with limited interconnection, containing regions of high demand traditionally supplied by a relatively small number of thermal generators. The NEM has recently experienced declining demand, and aging thermal assets that have also provided grid stability services (such as inertia and frequency control) have exited the market, being replaced by renewables. Technological disruption is magnifying impacts on grid security and reliability, posing serious concerns for policy makers on how to incentivize new investment and reduce costs while maintaining reliability.

3.1 Distributed Generation

Australia leads the world with small-scale solar photovoltaic (PV) installations on a per capita basis. Across the country, approximately 17% of households have a solar PV system installed, and in some regions this number exceeds 25%. The vast uptake of solar PV since 2009 was initially driven by significant subsidies from Government, both in terms of savings related to upfront costs for installation and premium rates for energy exported to the grid.[6]

However, even with the closure of most solar incentive schemes, solar PV installations are approaching a cumulative capacity of 7500 MW (Fig. 4.2) and are expected to continue to remain on a stable growth rate

---

[6]For example, feed-in tariff subsidies meant that some customers in New South Wales were eligible to receive a rate for exported energy of 60c/kWh, compared to the average volume weighted wholesale price of electricity, which at the time was more like 5c/kWh.

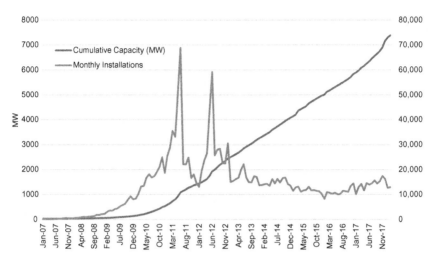

Figure 4.2 Growth in Solar PV in Australia. *(Source: Australian PV Institute, Australian PV market since April 2001, available at: http://pv-map.apvi.org.au/analyses.)*

for some time. According to a Jacobs report for AEMO, uptake rates for solar PV will continue on a linear trend until 2027 before slowing down due to declining retail price offsets and penetration reaching assumed saturation levels in some regions. Even so, by the end of 2037, the total capacity of residential PV systems may be over 12,000 MW (AEMO, 2017). Some studies (Climate Council, 2017) place this figure even higher, toward 20,000 MW.

The expansion of solar PV has had a significant impact on the profile of overall system load. Within a few years, some states within the NEM are forecast to become net exporters of energy during the middle of the day when solar PV and other renewables will meet the generation needs of an entire region. In fact, by 2027–28, AEMO forecasts negative minimum demand for South Australia under certain conditions. For 90% Probability of Exceedance (POE) minimum demand days, continued uptake of rooftop PV is forecast to offset 100% of demand in South Australia during the middle of the day.

However, despite the significant uptake, solar PV has done little to reduce peak system demand, which in most Australian regions occurs early in the evenings when solar PV generation is minimal. With a hot summer climate, Australia's peak electricity demand occurs on hot summer evenings, when there can also be a risk of low wind due to extended high pressure conditions. This effect is similar to the California "duck curve" referenced elsewhere in this volume. There is also some growing concern that continued uptake of solar PV and electric vehicle charging at residential properties

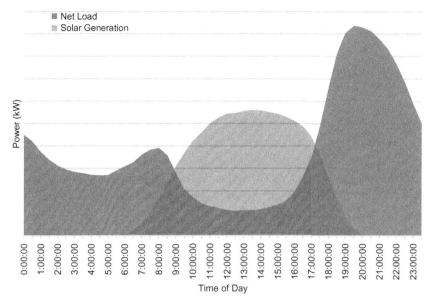

Figure 4.3 Indicative customer load profile after solar PV self-consumption in South Australia. *(Source: AGL data.)*

during the evening peak may, without planning to mitigate such effects, contribute to an increase in network peaks at these times (Fig. 4.3).

Chapter 6 of this book further examines these pressures on distribution system operators who must accommodate shifting load patterns, as well as changes to grid parameters such as frequency, voltage, and localized capacity limits. Policy makers in Australia are also reviewing how best to optimize distributed resources in the context of these operational constraints, including how markets for these services will drive their utilization and efficiency.

Increasing network peak demand in the context of declining overall volumes is also problematic for the cost recovery of energy market participants under current price settings. Electricity generators operate in an energy-only market, and so must be efficiently utilized and regularly dispatched to recover their costs. Similarly, network prices and retail products in Australia are generally based on volumetric rather than demand characteristics, which means that increasing network costs must be recovered through less volume.

The continued growth in distributed energy resources and shifting load pattern is therefore likely to have significant implications for price and bill dispersion among customer demographic cohorts, and already there are concerns regarding the equitability of prices for different types of customers under current tariff settings (Simshauser, 2016). This is covered in considerably more detail by Bruce Mountain in Chapter 5 of this volume regarding demand tariff uptake in Australia. Chapter 9 also discusses how network tariffs may need to be redesigned to more efficiently account for the integration of DER.

Digitalization of Distributed Energy Resources (DER)[7] can create better incentives and make it easier for customers to store and sell surplus electricity to the grid. New tools such as blockchain technology will help to facilitate peer-to-peer electricity trading or sharing within local energy communities. Smart demand response is also emerging as an increasingly useful option to avoid peaks in demand that cannot easily be offset by capacity increases. Demand response can be cheaper and more efficient than new generation build, especially at managing extremely low-probability but high-consequence events. Technology is now also available that allows small customers to participate in demand response at their homes, and some energy market participants are providing products and services that enable customers to switch off their energy in exchange for payment during peak periods.[8]

While these changes have resulted in intense price competition among Australian electricity retailers, with increasing price dispersion, some customers are beginning to heavily weight emerging energy services over unit prices alone when considering the best options for their supply of electricity. These services the ability to participate in peer-to-peer electricity sharing, contributing through demand response products, or the opportunity to be rewarded for provision of network and wholesale support services back to the system.

While connected smart appliances, home management systems, smart inverters, and battery software may be able to mitigate the impacts on load profiles by optimizing localized usage or shifting periods of usage, underlying incentives to efficiently utilize this technology must be in place for those services to be offered to customers and for price discrimination impacts to be mitigated.

---

[7] At a high level, DER is a term that refers to electricity assets behind a customer's meter, such as solar PV and battery storage, and any associated technologies that regulate the operation of these assets.

[8] For example, Energex Network's PeakSmart program in Queensland, and Powershop's Curb Your Power program in Victoria.

3.2 Battery Storage and Electric Vehicles

The intermittency of solar PV and its inability to effectively address evening peak demand has led to discussions regarding the value of intermittent distributed generation.[9] Indeed, electricity in an energy-only market such as the NEM is more valuable at peak times, and storage is therefore increasingly a compelling value proposition for customers as well as aggregators of energy to choose when to draw energy from the grid and when to consume energy that they have generated themselves.

While battery storage uptake has begun slowly, with only 20,789 battery storage systems comprising a total of 135 MWh installed nationally in 2017 (Sunwiz, 2018), a report for AEMO has forecast that it will accelerate sharply after 2020 in both the residential and the commercial sectors. As capital costs decline and more cost-reflective pricing structures incentivize load shifting, more storage is forecast to be adopted resulting in a total of over 11,000 MWh of battery storage across both commercial and residential sectors by 2037 (AEMO, 2017).

As well as residential and business storage systems, substantial increases in the electrification of the passenger vehicle fleet is likely to occur (see Chapter 18 by Webb et al.). The widespread uptake of electric vehicles (EVs), when coupled with the decarbonization of the electricity grid, presents a substantial opportunity to deliver emissions reductions consistent with Australia's long-term commitments under the Paris Agreement. For example, complete electrification of the transport sector could unlock almost 100 Mt of emissions representing 17.7% of Australia's total emissions inventory (Fig. 4.4).

Today, less than 1% of new car sales in Australia are EVs (ClimateWorks Australia, 2017); however, under AEMO's forecasts, EV sales within the NEM are forecast to reach 431,000 vehicles per annum by 2036, or a total of 36.5% of new vehicle sales, increasing to 90% of new vehicle sales by 2050. As a result, total EVs on the road are forecast to reach over 2.5 million by 2036 (Energeia, 2017).

Indeed, the transition toward automated and zero emission technology vehicles could have substantial implications for Australia's electricity grid with flow-on effects for infrastructure. Smart EVs in effect will be able to operate as a portable smart battery, interacting with the electricity grid to

---

[9]See for example, the Essential Services Commission of Victoria's report: Essential Services Commission of Victoria, *The Energy Value of Distributed Generation, Distributed Generation Inquiry Stage 1 Final Report*, August 2016.

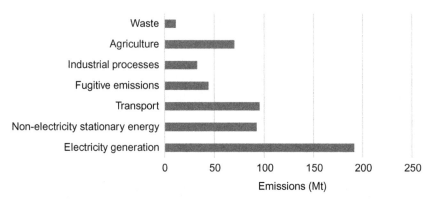

Figure 4.4 Australia's National Greenhouse Gas Inventory, "unadjusted" emissions by sector, year to Dec 2016. *(Source: Australian Government Department of Environment and Energy, Quarterly Update of Australia's National Greenhouse Gas Inventory: December 2016, May 2017.)*

provide optimized services at the right location and time. This and other characteristics of Electric Vehicles are covered in more detail in Webb et al.'s Chapter 18 in this volume.

Automation and the ability to integrate EVs into the grid will enable further opportunities for system-wide optimization. This could be enabled through technology platforms that enable EVs and EV supply equipment to connect to various nodes allowing energy service providers to proactively manage charging activity to assist with a variety of grid services. An example of this is the Electric Power Institute's Open Vehicle-Grid Integration Platform (OVGIP), which aims to allow equipment manufacturers to use existing on-vehicle communication technologies and energy service providers' standard interface protocols.

However, the transition will require careful consideration of generation to support charging. System optimization and charging management must progress to address the risks of wholesale market distortion in order to realize the full benefits of an efficient EV uptake. Network infrastructure to support EVs must be developed in an efficient manner, enabling EVs without resulting in excessive costs on customers. Tariffs in particular may need to be redesigned to optimize EV charging and reduce impacts on system load shape (see also Chapter 9 by Abdelmotteleb et al.).

All of these trends are customer driven, meaning customers are choosing to invest in technologies and services to meet their comfort needs and provide them with transparency. This requires careful thought and design of the regulatory environment by policy makers that ensures customer centricity, a level playing field and modernized grid.

3.3 Digitization of Services: Smart Meters and the Connected Home

Changes to the way that customers interact with energy are not merely limited to generation and storage. In 2006, to replace basic accumulation meters, the Victorian Government mandated a rollout of 2.6 million digital interval meters capable of measuring energy use at 30-minute intervals and remotely sending that meter information back to energy businesses.

Since December 2017, in other NEM jurisdictions, new metering regulation requires that all new and replacement meters must be smart meters, and retailers have also been given the responsibility to manage customers' old meters and arrange installation of new smart meters through the newly created role of a "metering coordinator." Importantly, a key principle of this reform is that customers, rather than energy companies, are the key decision makers in whether a digital technology solution is adopted within their home or business.

This increased digitalization of energy data, further explained in Chapter 1 by Brown et al., through meters and other smart devices is a trend that is likely to continue. The connected device ecosystem is likely to grow rapidly over the next 5 years, with increased monitoring of homes at the device and appliance level. Customers will have increased visibility over the efficiency of their homes and will have greater ability to automate and optimize their energy usage. Fig. 4.5 shows that in Australia, household penetration of smart home technologies is at 19.1% in 2018 but is expected to hit 37.6% by 2022 (Statista, 2018).[10]

There will be continued growth in the world of home energy monitoring using a range of devices including submeters, power sensors, and current transformer clamps. The number of internet connected devices in Australian households is forecast to more than double by 2021 to 31 devices per home, resulting in over 300 million devices in Australia homes by 2021, while the total revenue from these devices is estimated to reach almost $5 billion (Telsyte, 2017). Globally, the number of connected IoT[11] devices is forecast to grow from 8.4 billion in 2017 to over 20 billion by 2020 (IEA, 2017). Baak and Sioshansi discuss these trends further in Chapter 3.

---

[10] This figure includes digitally connected or controlled devices within a house that can be remote controlled; for example, sensors, actuators, and cloud services that support automation but does not include connected home appliances such as smart TVs or audio devices.

[11] IoT, or Internet of Things, is the concept of connecting everyday objects to networks to provide a range of advanced services or applications.

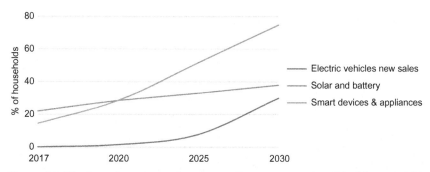

Figure 4.5 Distributed energy and smart appliance penetration (% of households). *(Source: Statista, Smart Home Market Report 2018.)*

Growth in smart device monitoring is likely to expand concurrently with appliance monitoring as smart devices are relatively inexpensive. These include devices such as smart plugs, internet connected locks, sensors, cameras, and security alarms. Lighting will also become smarter with smart light bulbs connected to hub platforms becoming widely available at increasingly affordable prices.

The nexus between smart home and energy will change how customers experience and interact with energy. Smart home–connected appliances already provide customers with data insights that allow them to understand their energy usage and enable them to make informed choices. These devices will increasingly provide subsecond data readings available in near real time, allowing not only customers but third parties to utilize data to optimize the energy experience. Even so, the trend of major appliance loads becoming connected to the internet and remotely controlled is at an early stage. While white goods and electronic appliances contribute to almost half of the electricity use of an average Australian household, very few of these appliances are currently internet connected or remotely controlled. The uptake of smarter large appliances (such as air conditioning, white goods, water heating, and pool pumps) is therefore likely to grow more slowly than smart devices, as the replacement capital commitment cycle for these appliances is longer at 5–15 years.

Nevertheless, even without access to load data from individual appliances, service providers may still be able to provide innovative services utilizing improved data analytics. For example, AGL has recently developed an Energy Insights platform where data including a customer's smart meter data, home profile information, and weather, are run through algorithms to approximate energy usage and costs by appliance category including lighting, cooling, heating, entertainment, pool pumps, and refrigerators (Fig. 4.6).

Your estimated energy breakdown

We estimate that 30% of your usage went towards
heating your home.*

🏠 **Heating** (incl. electricity to run fans in ducted gas systems) $55

▲ 4% more than your last bill

🛁 Pool pump $35

🧊 Fridges & freezers $19

🏠 Cooling $18

🚿 Electric hot water $14

🧺 Laundry & dishwasher $9

📺 Home entertainment $8

⚫ Anything else $7

💡 Lighting $2

⏻ Standby & always on $2

🍳 Cooking $2

Supply Charge $10.91 ($0.97 per day)
This is the cost of getting energy to your home

Discounts & Concessions-$12.00
These are your energy plan discounts or government concessions

Learn more

We use your smart meter data, home profile info, weather and other data to
approximate your energy breakdown. The energy breakdown is not 100% accurate,
and appliance usage may differ from acual consumption. You can learn more about
each appliance category and how they're calculated.

Figure 4.6 AGL Energy Insights approximates energy usage and costs at an appliance
level based on smart meter data. *(Source: Energy Insights, AGL.)*

The extraordinary growth in data generation and usability, fueled by developments in digital transformation and internet connectivity, has enabled a series of new business models, products, and insights to emerge. Individuals, businesses, governments, and the broader community have all benefited from these changes. However, in the energy sector, recent reviews and inquiries into access to data in Australia have identified that we are still behind in establishing robust framework to manage the data. The frameworks and protections that were developed for data collection and access prior to sweeping digitization now need reform.

The substantive argument in favor of making data more available is that opportunities to use it are largely unknown until the data sources themselves are better known, and until data users have been able to undertake discovery of data. However, lack of trust and numerous technological and regulatory barriers to sharing and releasing data are stymieing the use and value of customers' data.

Further developments as well as improvements in regulatory frameworks for access to standardized customer data will enable customers to receive device-level notifications and insights as well as increased service optimization, allowing customers to participate in emerging services that provide them with control over their energy bills and allow their third-party agents to find innovative ways for them to save on their energy.

3.4 Sharing Economy and Other Emerging Retail Services

Increased technological expansion has also led to increased opportunities for new entrants and businesses to develop new products and services for customers. The evolution of technology, digitalization of services, and increased product innovation and competition means more choice for customers than ever before.

Customers may choose to combine grid supplied and distributed energy sources and expect to be able to trade energy and share in value streams beyond the home, such as network and wholesale values. Improved technology capabilities and potential for aggregated and dynamic response offers an abundance of innovation potential, from enabling peer-to-peer energy trading and the participation in large-scale Virtual Power Plants (VPP), to the development of highly dynamic and efficient embedded networks or microgrid systems.

These product and service models represent emerging trends in sharing services that are not unique to energy. Economy wide, nearly two-thirds of Australians are using a sharing economy service. More than a third of

Australians now spend at least $50 per month on P2P goods or services, while over 20% are earning the same amount each month through these sharing economy services (Ratesetter, 2016). Indeed, the proliferation of disruptive peer-to-peer sharing platforms seems to have been slower in energy than it has been in other industries. The emergence of P2P trading as well as technological, regulatory, and institutional barriers that explain these trends are further considered in Chapter 2 of this volume.

Despite a slower uptake in the utilities sector, the growth of these different customer services in other sectors has led to the emergence of new retail models to service those requirements in the energy industry as well. For example, alongside the 36 traditional licensed retailers operating in Victoria and the 59 operating across the remainder of the NEM, the number of alternative energy sellers, exempt from the requirements to hold an authorized retail license, has increased dramatically.

A prime example of a model for these alternative sellers is firms selling energy to customers from a solar PV system installed behind-the-meter at the customer's own premises, under what is known as a power purchase agreement (PPA). Another common form is firms reselling energy within an embedded network. Over 3000 current license exemptions have been granted by the Australian Energy Regulator (AER),[12] a figure which under-represents those in place across the NEM since Victoria operates its own licensing and exemption system, and networks that have not applied for an exemption but still operate behind the meter.

Increasingly, customers are also looking to act in a unified way to meet their energy needs. For example, community energy is an emerging trend where groups of individuals are grouping together to develop, deliver, and benefit from clean energy under a range of different models. Such projects could include community-owned wind or solar farms, community demand management initiatives or energy efficiency programs, or the emergence of a new energy retailer providing specific localize energy solutions.

Currently, there are approximately 70 community energy projects across Australia, with around two-thirds of them in regional centers or edge-of-grid locations. The first project was a 4.1-MW wind farm, comprising just two turbines, established in 2011 near Daylesford in Victoria. This wind farm is owned by the local community through the cooperative Hepburn

---

[12]See, for example: Australian Energy Regulator, *Public register of retail exemptions* (accessed 2 May 2018) https://www.aer.gov.au/retail-markets/retail-exemptions/public-register-of-retail-exemptions.

Wind, which also provides financial returns to its members. Almost 2,000 cooperative members (or local shareholders) contributed $9.8 million toward the construction of the turbines, which have the capacity to power around 2,000 households.

Koirala et al. cover in detail the pathways to developing community energy storage. In the Australian context, rural and regional communities are at the forefront of these developments, not only because they often face higher network charges and lower reliability as a result of long transmission and distribution services with little or no redundancy, but also because within these communities there is often have more engagement in community issues, more development options, and more accessible natural resources such as wind and solar.

As the cost of renewable generation and storage displaces network augmentation and asset replacement, more and more communities at the edge of the grid will seek non-network solutions to deliver their energy requirements. Some of these systems as well as regulatory and market barriers to their uptake are explained in further detail by Germain et al.

4. RESPONSE TO TECHNOLOGY DISRUPTION: "DISRUPTING THE DISRUPTORS"

Over the last decade, exponential technology advances, greater customer power and increased competition has been breaking down the traditional boundaries between demand and supply and blurring the distinction between generation and consumption. The ongoing digitization of everything is a step change and the impact on traditional utilities is significant.

New entrants with novel business models that do not fit the traditional utility model of an energy retailer have entered the energy market with new service models that range from remote storage or embedded generation to monitoring and optimizing the usage of appliances via direct connectivity solutions behind the meter creating an ecosystem of digital services and connectivity. As technology creates more options and customer data become richer, there are opportunities for increased levels of optionality and control for customers, using data to personalize interactions and provide bespoke services.

For example, small retailers such as Mojo and Energy Locals have developed a model whereby customers pay a fixed monthly subscription and are then billed all their energy consumption at a wholesale "cost pass through" rate. Power Ledger has developed a blockchain-based peer-to-peer energy-trading platform to enable consumers and businesses to sell their surplus solar power to their neighbors without an intermediary energy provider or retailer, settling energy trades on predetermined terms and conditions in near real time. Enosi is an open-source blockchain-based platform that supports community energy programs and allows new entrants to compete effectively with large players, by separating wholesale market access from customer facing functions, and without needing microgrids or incumbent grid partners. Enova is the first Australian community-owned energy retailer whose customers have access to energy efficiency services, community energy products, and competitive solar tariffs. Reposit have developed software that assists customers with solar PV and battery energy systems to optimize energy use and earn credits for power exported back to the grid at times of high demand. GreenSync is trialing a decentralized energy exchange through which retail customers are remunerated for grid services provided to the network using their own behind-the-meter installations. Powershop offers customers forward purchase discounts and is also trialing a peer-to-peer trading platform.

In addition to these, there are many more emerging companies. A decade ago, the choice for customers was simply "who?" sold them energy. Now the choice is "who?" and "how?": how they will be supported by online services and flexible payment options, how they will combine grid supplied and distributed energy sources, how they expect to be able to monitor and control usage, and how they will share energy and share in value streams available beyond the home (such as network and wholesale value).

5. DISRUPTING THE REGULATORY LANDSCAPE

These emerging responses to technological disruption require changes to the regulatory landscape. The future of the grid will be as a gateway to multiple competitive platforms that enable a range of markets for customers, and change may need to occur to enable this direction. Effectively managing uncertain system impacts of new technologies (and maximizing their efficient deployment) is likely to require commitment to several principles including:

- Customer centricity and choice: Ensuring that customers are embedded within the broader energy ecosystem and act as participants in multifaceted energy communities such as virtual power plants, energy-sharing programs, and intelligent microgrids and communities.

- Promoting competitive platforms and innovation: Competition and innovation in technology and business models are the primary means for allying the needs and interest of customers with their energy service providers.
- System security and reliability: Decarbonization and modernization of the power system both in the wholesale market and at the grid level to support and optimize adaptive and modular distributed generation and associated services. This includes allocating risks to parties that are best able to manage them to enable an equal playing field.
- Establishing appropriate technology standards that enable interoperability and encourage economies of scale.

Keeping these principles as a guidepost improves the predictability of modifications to existing regulatory and market frameworks when it becomes evident they are required. Open competitive markets and technology neutrality provides firms the impetus and latitude to pursue technology and service delivery innovations that meet system needs at efficient cost.

The distribution network will increasingly become the platform across which customers expect to be able to connect and transact. Rather than simply enabling the consumption of electricity delivered from centralized plant, the modernized grid will have an increasingly important role as the facilitator of a range of other service markets. These include markets for grid stability services (frequency and voltage), markets for services which support the network in constraint conditions, markets for wholesale demand response at times of tight supply, and peer-to-peer energy trading.

A network support or grid stability service might only be required on a limited number of occasions per year, and this is similarly the case with demand response to meet a wholesale supply constraint. The remainder and majority of the time, customer-owned DER is likely to be employed directly for meeting the comfort and consumption needs of the customer. Accordingly, an efficient deployment and use of DER will enable co-optimization across these multiple uses and value streams. It will also recognize that it is ultimately a customer's choice as to how their behind-the-meter resources are deployed and what compensation or reward they expect for participating in different service markets (including providing network support).

The wholesale market will also need to accommodate new firming contracts and services delivered from customer investments behind the meter. This may require a new market mechanism that ensures an equal playing field in the competitive market between the traditional and nontraditional players coming into the market to meet certain customer needs and gaps (see Nelson et al., 2018a,b).

Networks operate monopoly infrastructure and are currently the monopoly purchasers of demand response and other non-network solutions. Therefore, it will be critical to maintain a clear focus on the role of distribution businesses through the grid modernization process. There will need to be a gradual shift toward demand response and non-network solutions to grid requirements being met by contestable markets. Network businesses should be required to test the competitive market for the provision of demand response and other non-network solutions before developing their own programs or directly investing in distributed energy technologies and including such expenditure in the regulated asset base.

Further, network businesses must demonstrate greater value to customers prior to proceeding with network-based solutions. To facilitate the development of viable competitive products, which address network needs, network businesses should also make available sufficient and useful data about the characteristics and location of those network needs and the costs of alternative network investments.

Care in the design of network cost recovery and pricing frameworks is key to driving efficient network utilization, efficient adoption of distributed energy technologies, and mitigating potential equity issues that arise where those without the ability to adopt distributed generation technologies are left to bear a disproportionate share of remaining network costs (see Simshauser, 2016). Distribution businesses are currently introducing more cost-reflective network tariffs to support the achievement of these outcomes. However, with overall declining grid utilization and spare capacity in many networks, there is a question as to whether the policy intent behind the introduction of cost-reflective pricing can be achieved without a clear policy on the treatment of the existing regulated asset base and considering write-downs or revaluations of those assets (see Simshauser, 2017; Grattan Institute, 2018).

While the competitive market is already delivering products and services to overcome some of these obstacles (for example, virtual solar products for customers that are unable to have their own solar PV installation), there will also remain customers who do not actively engage with the retail energy services market, whether through disinterest or difficulty in doing so. For these customers, competition on traditional elements such as unit pricing and customer service remains very important.

Further policy interventions may depend on the reasons for customer nonengagement, and measures to make engagement, at least at a basic level, simple and achievable are important for all customers. Vulnerable customers may require a more proactive form of assistance to engage and realize the benefits of a competitive market. As an essential service, innovation and disruption will only be embraced by regulators if all customers benefit from the energy market transformation.

6. CONCLUSIONS

This chapter has, at a glance, highlighted how Australia's electricity system is undergoing a significant transformation through the lens of the customer. Where the uptake of customer DER and digitalization is blurring the distinction between generation and consumption. The proliferation of digital channels and devices gives consumers greater control and access to information, and the means for communication and collaboration. The physical world of energy is being replicated in the digital world through energy communities, virtual products, and energy sharing between homes, businesses, and communities, fundamentally changing the way consumers engage with their energy providers demanding transparency and high levels of personalization. A new kind of customer means a new way of doing business and this is not limited to the energy sector. But while traditional energy retailers are responding to this transformation with new products and services, new entrants are also responding with new business models utilizing digital technologies and emerging frameworks. Ultimately, the companies that are the most successful will be those that accurately gauge and predict consumer preferences and adopt the digital transformation, as it is the consumer that is in the driving seat.

REFERENCES

AEMO, 2017. Jacobs report: projections of uptake of small-scale systems. 9 June 2017.
Australian Competition & Consumer Commission, 2017. Retail electricity pricing enquiry preliminary report. 22 September 2017.
Climate Council, 2017. State of Solar 2016: Globally and in Australia by Petra Stock. Andrew Stock and Greg Bourne.
ClimateWorks Australia, 2017. The state of electric vehicles in Australia. June 2017.
Energeia, 2017. Electric vehicles insights: prepared by Energeia for the Australian Energy Market Operator's 2017 electricity forecast insights. September 2017.
International Energy Agency, 2017. Digitalization and energy. 5 November 2017.
Nelson, T., McCracken-Hewson, E., Whish-Wilson, P., Bashir, S., 2018a. Price dispersion in Australian retail electricity markets. Energy Econ. 70, 158–169.
Nelson, T., Orton, F., Chappel, T., 2018b. Decarbonisation and wholesale electricity market design. Aust. J. Agric. Resour. Econ. 62 (4), 654–675.
RateSetter, 2016. Sharing Economy Trust Index (SETI): winter 2016. August 2016.

Simshauser, P., 2016. Distribution network prices and solar PV: Resolving rate instability and wealth transfers through demand tariffs. Energy Econ. 54, 108–122.

Simshauser, P., 2017. Monopoly regulation, discontinuity & stranded assets. Energy Econ. 66 (C).

Statista, 2018. Smart Home market report 2018. Available at: https://www.statista.com/outlook/279/107/smart-home/australia.

Sunwiz, 2018. Australian battery market report for 2018. March 2018.

Telsyte, 2017. Australian Internet of Things @ Home Market Study 2017.

Wood, T., Blowers, D., Griffiths, K., 2018. Down to the Wire: A Sustainable Electricity Network for Australia. Grattan Institute.

CHAPTER 5

Do I Have a Deal for You? Buying Well in Australia's Contestable Retail Electricity Markets

Bruce Mountain
Director, Victoria Energy Policy Centre, Melbourne, VIC, Australia

1. INTRODUCTION

In Australia, a combination of high retail electricity prices and declining solar PV costs has seen the rapid adoption of rooftop solar PV by households. Similar expansion of rooftop PV is also taking place among commercial, industrial, and agricultural electricity users. Combined with improvements in consumption efficiency has led to a persistent decline in per capita demand for grid-supplied electricity. The prospect of significant uptake of distributed batteries is likely to improve the economics of distributed production even more and accelerate this decline.

This is of interest elsewhere even where the rate of rooftop PV penetration does not yet match that in Australia. The design of network tariffs often has a significant impact on retail tariffs structures and the prospects for consumers, prosumers, and prosumagers. The specification of such price structures is of course a focus of most chapters in this book.

In this context policy makers, regulators, the industry, and consumers have debated changes to the ways the monopoly distribution network service providers charge small customers. In the contestable Victorian electricity market, tariffs with demand charges have been implemented. However, consumers have shown no desire to be supplied on these tariffs and only a small number of Victoria's competing retailers have chosen to offer tariffs with demand charges. The main thrust of the network tariff reform has failed. This chapter examines why this has occurred and what might be learned from it.

The chapter is organized as follows:
- Section 2 sets the context by providing background on the industry, its institutions, distributed resources, and the network and retail pricing arrangements;

Consumer, Prosumer, Prosumager
https://doi.org/10.1016/B978-0-12-816835-6.00005-X

- Section 3 surveys the literature;
- Section 4 describes the outcomes in Victoria followed with the chapter's conclusions.

2. BACKGROUND

This section provides relevant background on industry structure and institutional arrangements, information on distributed energy resources, network tariffs, retail offers, and network tariff regulation.

2.1 Industry Structure and Institutional Arrangements

The National Electricity Market (the NEM) in Australia covers the south and eastern states and territories (South Australia, Tasmania, Victoria, New South Wales, the Australian Capital Territory, and Queensland). It is an interconnected power system whose high-voltage transmission back bone apparently stretches further from one end to the other, longer than in any other country. The market serves a population of 20.5 million with a little over 9.6 million connections.[1] Bashir et al. and Gui & McGill also present useful information on the retail sector in Australia.

Networks were separated from generators and retailers and a wholesale market was introduced in 1999. Retail markets have been progressively deregulated with one regional market, Victoria, fully contestable since 2009 and the most recent addition, South East Queensland, fully contestable since July 1, 2017. In all the fully deregulated markets, distribution network service providers ("distributors") are separately owned and distributors are prohibited from selling electricity. There is one distributor in Queensland, one in South Australia, three in New South Wales, and five in Victoria.

The Australian Energy Markets Commission (AEMC) establishes and maintains rules that distributors are required to follow in establishing their regulated tariffs. The Australian Energy Regulator (AER) authorizes the tariffs that the distributors propose pursuant to those rules. In Victoria, the Government also oversees network tariffs and requires that customers who purchase less than 40 MWh per year should have the flexibility to opt-in to the tariffs, rather than being forced onto them with the option to then opt-out. Customers above this size have the choice to opt out of newly introduced peak demand tariffs.

---

[1]For general information on the industry, the websites of the regulators and power system operators are helpful. See www.aemc.gov.au, www.aer.gov.au, and www.aemo.com.au.

2.2 Distributed Energy Resources

One in five of the households in this market (1.5 million) have installed rooftop solar capacity, typically of around 3.5 kW per household. System sizes continue to expand. In some regions (South Australia), rooftop solar penetration has risen to 1.3. Rooftop solar Photo-Voltaics (PV) continues to expand rapidly at the rate of around 1,000 MW per year. Rooftop and distributed ground-based PV systems are also expanding rapidly.[2]

Electricity prices in the NEM are high by comparison to those in other countries, as shown in Fig. 5.1.

Solar insolation is also high across the market ranging from 1.2 MWh per kW per year in Tasmania and southern Victoria to 1.65 MWh per kW per year in most of South Australia, New South Wales, and Queensland. Average production costs for rooftop solar are around 6 cents per kWh, compared to variables charges for grid supply that are seldom less than 20 cents per kWh. Capital subsidies that are worth around 2 cents per kWh of solar energy produced are paid for the installation of rooftop solar up to system sizes of 100 kW. Worked out over their effective life, large-scale solar installations (bigger than 100 kW) currently receive approximately similar subsidies although paid as a production credit rather than capital sum.[3]

FIGURE 5.1   Comparison of residential electricity prices (before and after tax) (Australian cents per kWh) (May 2017 prices in Australia, 2015 prices in European countries). *(Source: Mountain, 2017, p. 44.)*

[2]See www.cleanenergyregulator.com.au.

[3]For information on capital and production subsidies, see http://www.cleanenergyregulator. gov.au/RET.

2.3 Network Tariffs

The network service providers publish tariffs for the usage of the network and that are approved by the AER and according to rules established by the AEMC. The most commonly used tariff structure in all regions in the NEM is either a two-part (daily charge and cents per kWh usage charge) or a slightly declining block rate tariff with a daily charge and typically two block rates, the second very slightly lower than the first. However, the network providers also publish tariffs that have time of use variation (peak/off-peak or increasingly also peak/shoulder/off-peak).[4]

In Victoria in 2016, one of the five distributors introduced network tariffs with charges for the highest hourly average demand incurred from 3 pm to 9 pm on weekdays. The remaining four introduced such network tariffs in 2017. Demand measured this way attracts a cents per kW per day charge that is charged for all the days in the billing period (which is typically a month). Additional daily (cents per day) and usage charges (cents per kWh) apply in these tariffs.[5]

2.4 Retail Offers

In all the regions within the NEM except Tasmania, the Australian Capital Territory, and Queensland (except the populous south east corner), customers are able to choose their supplier (often known as "retailers" in Australia). In April 2018, in the New South Wales, there were 26 competing retailers, the Victoria market had 23, South Australia 19, and Queensland 21 retailers. In these four markets on 2 April 2018, the retailers made 3,273 different offers[6] publicly available through the two official price comparison websites. In each distribution region, this averages around 400 offers in New South Wales and Victoria, 291 in Queensland, and 121 in South Australia.[7]

However, the number of competing offers reduces when you limit it to offers of the same tariff structure. This means that there are around 150–170 competing offers in each of the subregional markets in New South Wales and Victoria to just 6 (for customers wishing to choose a time of use tariff structure in South Australia). While some retailers allow customers to choose a tariff structure different from their current structure (for example

[4]The Australian Energy Regulator provides the network tariffs published by all network service providers. See www.aer.gov.au.
[5]Ibid.
[6]This information is publicly available on www.miretailenergy.com.au.
[7]Ibid.

moving from a two-part tariff to a time of use tariff) this is not common, and retailers often charges additional fees for customers that wish to select a tariff with a structure that is different to their existing tariff.

In Victoria in 2016, after demand-based network tariffs were introduced, some retailers also introduced retail tariffs with a demand charge component. This has not grown however. By April 2018, just five of the 23 retailers publish tariffs on the official price comparison websites, with demand components. In one distribution area (Ausnet Services) there is just one demand tariff on offer, in two areas (Citipower and Powercor) just two retailers offer demand tariffs, in the distribution area of United Energy, there are three retailers while in the distribution area of Jemena there are four retailers that make offers with demand charges. Bashir et al. and Gui & MacGill cover similar ground elsewhere in this volume.

Retail offers with demand charges usually include a price (cents per kW per day) based on the highest demand (measured as the highest consumption in any half hour) between 3 pm and 9 pm on a weekday, the demand rates are also seasonal. Daily charges (cents per day) and consumption charges (cents per kWh) also apply.

Even leaving demand charges to one side, customers find it hard to find the best deals in the market or know whether they are better off on those deals. One reasons for this is the complexity of discounts. From our analysis of many thousands of individual bills, we find a wide diversity of approaches to discounts in customers' bills:

- some retailers' discounts are worked out as a percentage of usage charges while others are on the total bill;
- some discounts are before the receipt of concessions, others after;
- some discounts are before solar feed-in receipts, others after;
- few bills actually clearly state the discount rate, some don't state the rate at all;
- some discounts are only received on subsequent bills (so that if the customer leaves, the retailer avoids discounting their last bill);
- some retailers offer several discounts in the bill but sometimes some apply after other discounts are taken off first;
- some will discount controlled load consumption, others not;
- some discounts are payable as rebates when the customer transfers to the retailer; other rebates are paid out over months and even years
- some offer discounted amounts, which are contingent on advance purchases of electricity, but the discount is not achieved unless purchases exceed the contingent amounts;

- some discounts in bills are not actually calculated in customers' bills as the retailers say they are calculated;
- some retailers take upfront payments from customers and then feed those payments back to customers on each subsequent bill as if they are discounts;
- most discounts are conditional on customers doing something (usually paying the bill on time), but some are unconditional. Some bills have both conditional and unconditional discounts; others just one or the other.

Besides the complexity associated with discounts, electricity tariffs in Australia are in fact stunningly complex commercial arrangements.[8] They have daily charges, a wide range of methods for charging for consumption (flat rates, daily, monthly or quarterly block rates, time of use rates with two or three bands, combinations of time of use and block rates, separate rates for controlled loads of different types, consumptions rates that are seasonal, and now even some bills with peak demand charges). Solar feed-in rates often (but not always) vary depending on the receipt of a subsidy in addition to the payment that retailers choose to offer. Most recently, some retailers offer block rates for solar feed-in, with higher rates for the first tranche of solar power feed-in.

2.5 Network Tariff Regulation

Network tariffs have been the subject of considerable regulatory discussion (what the AER describes as "a long process of reform"[9]) following changes recommended by the AEMC in 2012. The main purpose of the changes was to establish tariffs that better reflect costs incurred by electricity networks in response to customer decisions to use electricity at specific times or locations. The network service providers argued, and the AER agreed, that marginal network costs are primarily driven by peak demand, not by usage outside of peak demand periods. Distributors' "cost-reflective" tariffs, it was argued, will send a signal to retailers about the cost of using the network. Retailers will then determine if, and how, their retail offerings to customers will reflect these signals.

The implementation of network tariffs with demand charges was proposed by the distributors and enthusiastically supported by the AER and

---

[8]For more context, see https://theconversation.com/if-you-need-a-phd-to-read-your-power-bill-buying-wisely-is-all-but-impossible-98617.
[9]Australia Energy Regulator (2016, p. 12).

AEMC as fulfillment of their wish for tariffs that are more cost reflective. The AER suggested tariffs with demand charges are "more cost reflective" than time of use tariffs (tariffs with time-variant consumption rates) While some customer groups preferred tariffs with time-variant energy charges, most seemed to share the regulators' enthusiasm for network tariffs with demand charges. The largest retailers generally supported the introduction of network tariffs with demand charges (in addition to the other network tariffs), though two retailers raised concerns about complexity associated with seasonal demand charges and that it was likely that customers would struggle to understand the new tariff structure.

3. RELEVANT LITERATURE

The theory of electricity pricing has a long and illustrious history having been the focus of the work of many eminent economists over the last 130 years. The strand of this literature relevant to this chapter is the question of whether, and if so how, to relate the prices charged for network services to the simultaneous demands on the networks.

The practice of differentiating prices on the basis of time of use and by implication demand, predates the key theoretical works in monopoly network pricing. For example, Hausman and Neufeld (1984) describe time of day pricing by nascent electricity providers in the United States in the 1890s when electricity first became widely distributed. Similarly, Chick (2002) describes price elasticity-differentiated tariffs in various parts of Paris prior to 1946, applied by the then privately owned companies.

In one of the earliest major theoretical contributions, Hotelling (1938) argued that monopoly utility prices should be based on marginal rather than average costs. However, he also allowed for a rental to be charged to customers that demand services when the system is at its capacity. Subsequent major theoretical contributions (Boiteux, 1949; Houthakker, 1951; Steiner, 1957; Turvey, 1968; Williamson, 1966) argued to various extents for some form of demand charge (for large customers) or time of use differentiation (or time-controlled tariffs) for smaller customers (for whom the cost of meters to record peak demand were not then a viable proposition).

More recently, abundant literature on the merits of demand tariffs for smaller customers, and motivated particularly by the rise of distributed energy can be found, for example (Azarova et al., 2018; Bartusch et al., 2011; Borenstein, 2016; Hledik, 2014; Johnson et al., 2017; Langlois-Bertrand and Pineau, 2018; McLaren et al., 2015; Nijhuis et al., 2017; Picciariello et al., 2015;

Simshauser, 2016). In Australia's debate, Passey et al. (2017) argued that if a demand charge is desired then the demand charges proposed by the networks, and agreed to by the AER, were quite a long way from being "cost-reflective" as the networks and AER had suggested.

There is a much more limited literature that examines consumer preferences in relation to demand tariffs. Dutschke and Paetz (2013) examine a form of demand pricing and conclude that individual and societal advantages are not obvious to consumers. In Australia, Hall et al. (2016) survey 53 households and find that there was no clear preference for peak demand tariffs.

4. COMPLEXITY OF RETAIL TARIFFS

We discuss here the issue of tariff complexity, particularly in the context of demand charges in residential tariffs. Before embarking on that discussion, it should be noted that the underlying problem of complexity undermining the effective operation of retail markets exists already, particularly in those retail markets that are most open to competition. In the Preface, Ron Ben-David discusses nonsumers who simply give up in the face of such complexity, to the benefit of their suppliers.

In Victoria, the implementation of networks tariffs with demand charges followed a long process of regulatory deliberation, consultation, and then implementation. The approach enjoyed (and continues to enjoy) enthusiastic support by the Australian Energy Regulator. While some customer groups expressed reservations, and some retailers expressed concern about tariff complexity, the official customer groups strongly supported the approach.

However, almost 2 years after retailer offers with demand charges were introduced, it is understood there are almost no customers that have selected such tariffs. As discussed, none of the retailers promote their demand tariffs; only a small number of the 23 retailers even offer tariffs with demand charges. The official price comparison website (www.switchon.vic.gov.au) does not price the demand charge component in these tariffs, but instead refers prospective customers to the retailers to explore this further themselves. None of the commercial price comparison websites include tariffs with demand charges in the offers that they compare. In their regulatory reporting, the network service providers do not identify any residential customers having selected offers with demand charges.

It is not difficult to see why customers have rejected the demand offers: they have no easy way of estimating whether they would be better off on those offers compared to their existing offer or the other alternatives.

For a customer to estimate how much they would pay each year on tariffs with demand charges, they would need to be able to estimate their peak demand during any single hour from 3 pm to 9 pm during a week day for each month of the year. This is obviously difficult: customers would need to access their half-hourly smart meter data and then analyze those data to find the two consecutive half hours of maximum consumption and then apply the demand charge to the demand for those two consecutive half hours. It can be no surprise that customers do not do this.

Other features of the demand tariff are also likely to explain customers' rejection. Demand charges encourage customers to avoid the simultaneous use of high-consumption appliances, such as water heaters, space conditioners, ovens, pool pumps, washing machines, and dishwashers. While in many cases there may be no great loss of utility to achieve this, there might be times when simultaneous operation of various high-consumption appliances cannot be avoided. Confidence that this is a tariff structure that serves customers' interests will be undermined if this results in higher charges in the absence of convincing evidence that this will have imposed additional costs on distributors. With such a wide window during which peak demand is measured – 3 pm to 9 pm on weekdays – it is quite possible that individual customers will record peak demands at times that are poorly correlated to simultaneous peak demands on the networks. Customers would then rightly question whether the arrangement is designed in their interests.

These issues received little attention in the regulatory processes that led to the development of demand tariffs in Victoria. Indeed the AEMC pointed toward demand-based tariffs without considering the actual operation of the retail market and mechanisms by which customers are able to compare competing offers. In its review of distributors' proposals, the AER encouraged the adoption of demand tariffs on the basis that they are more cost reflective, and saw no problem in the complexity they presented to customers. As noted, while some customer advocates raised concern about complexity, the official customer group supported the promotion of tariffs with demand charges. Environmental advocates supported the introduction of demand tariffs on the basis that it would provide an opportunity for households with solar and/or batteries to reduce their bills.[10]

---

[10]Those wishing to examine the views expressed by stakeholders during the consultation on tariff structure statements, can find copies of the submissions on the AER's website. Further relevant submissions can be found on the AEMC's website by searching under the "Power of Customer Choice" program.

In the Australian tariff reform debate, the concept of "cost-reflective" tariffs is often frequently referred to, and commonly understood to, be the main priority. Perhaps regulators considered that even if customers didn't select them it would nonetheless be beneficial for networks to promote "cost-reflective" tariffs. Evidence for this can be seen for example in the AER's approval of network proposals on the basis of the AER's wish " … *to see movement towards more cost reflective tariffs*" and because " … *cost reflective tariffs will send a signal to retailers about the cost of using the network. Retailers will then determine if, and how, their retail offerings to customers will reflect these signals.*"[11] But, although there is no regulatory obligation on retailers to base the structure of their retail offers on the structure of the underlying network tariff, retailers typically do design retail offers that reflect the structure of the underlying network tariffs. As a result, if customers do not select a retail tariff that has a demand charge, the distributors' "cost-reflective" demand tariff is not used by the retailer. In other words, the "*signal to retailers about the cost of using the network*" is not sent. This is what has occurred and prompts the question: to what end the "*long process of reform*"?[12]

The academic literature on demand tariffs specifically, and tariff structures more generally, typically steers clear of issues associated with tariff implementation in the context of contestable retail markets where customers are free to choose tariffs with demand charges or tariffs without such charges. In the literature, tariff theory is considered typically from the perspective of the choices available to a monopoly service provider where those choices can be imposed by regulation. In many cases – for example among others (Azarova et al., 2018; Passey et al., 2017; Simshauser, 2016) – the literature examines issues of tariff structure that appear to be motivated mainly by the search for efficient and fair ways to restore the otherwise diminishing revenues for the network monopolies as customers increasingly produce and now also store the electricity that they consume. In this context, cross subsidies between consumers with PV and those without are assumed to arise under the assumption that the aggregate regulated revenue will be held constant and so revenue reductions from households with distributed energy and/or storage will have to be offset by commensurately higher revenues from the remaining captive customers.

An alternative approach is to recognize the declining usage of networks as electricity production (and storage) is increasingly distributed

---

[11]Australia Energy Regulator (2016, p. 12).
[12]Ibid.

and as consumption efficiency improves. This approach begs the question of the valuation of regulated network assets in the context of declining demand. In this instance, it is useful to remember Hotelling's advice as railroads in the United States became increasingly stranded by private transport in the 1930s,

… the fact is that we now have the railroads, and in the main are likely to have them with us for a considerable time in the future. It will be better to operate the railroads for the benefit of living human beings, while letting dead men and dead investments rest quietly in their graves.

(Hotelling, 1938, p. 269)

5. CONCLUSIONS

In 2016, network tariffs with demand charges were introduced in Victoria following a long process of reform. Policy makers, regulators, the regulated industry, and the official customer groups supported the approach. There is substantial literature, built on the rationale that tariffs that better reflect costs will help to avoid unnecessary network expansion and hence improve efficiency that supports the approach. The rationale has a long history that predates debates about the merits of demand charges for small customers. Application of the idea to the justification for demand tariffs for small customers has been renewed in response to the rise of distributed generation and also in response to improvements in consumption efficiency that is leading to sharply declining per capita network usage.

There is a much smaller literature on customer preferences in regards to demand-based tariffs. The available literature suggests customers generally have little interest in tariffs with such charges. The experience in Victoria where almost no consumers have chosen tariffs with demand charges and only a small number of retailers offer plans with these charges is consistent with this literature.

This outcome is not hard to explain: customers need to engage in sophisticated data analysis to work out if they are likely to be better off on tariffs with demand charges than they currently are on their existing plans or other competing plans. In addition, it is difficult for customers to predict how changes in their consumption patterns will impact their bills: customers on demand tariffs lose utility by having to change the pattern of their consumption but are unable to assess how they will be compensated for this loss. Customers' disinterest in demand tariffs, and retailers disinterest in providing them seems to be well explained by these search and transaction costs.

In the Australian tariff debate, demand-side search cost and transaction cost issues did not feature in the debate on the introduction of demand tariffs. The regulated networks, the regulators, or even the main customer groups did not raise concern about these costs. Only a couple of retailers alluded to them in their submissions. Privately, regulatory officials, some in industry and even some customer advocates, bemoan the Victorian Government's decision to require customers to opt-in to demand tariffs rather than their preferred position that customers be required to opt-out of them. This suggests a mindset that customers just don't know what's good for them – hospitals would work better if it wasn't for the patients! But the evidence that without coercion almost no customers have chosen demand tariffs, and very few retailers offer them, vindicates the Government's decision.

Technology changes – and specifically distributed production and increasingly also distributed batteries – create opportunity for transformative innovation in the relationship between customers and the electricity grid. The Australian experience with demand tariffs for small customers suggests that those promoting new commercial arrangements in contestable markets would benefit by directing greater effort into trying to understand what customers value and how, in practice, customers will engage with the commercial arrangements they propose.

REFERENCES

Australia Energy Regulator, 2016. Final decision tariff structure statement proposals: Victorian Electricity Distribution Network Service Providers—Citipower, Powercor, AusNet Services, Jemena Electricity Networks and United Energy.

Azarova, V., Engel, D., Ferner, C., Kollmann, A., Reichl, J., 2018. Exploring the impact of network tariffs on household electricity expenditures using load profiles and socio-economic characteristics. Nat. Energy 3, 317–325.

Bartusch, C., Wallin, F., Odlare, M., Vassileva, I., Wester, L., 2011. Introducing a demand-based electricity distribution tariff in the residential sector: demand response and customer perception. Energy J. 39 (9).

Boiteux, M., 1949. Peak-load pricing. (Translated by H.W. Izzard in 1960) J. Bus. 33 (2), 157–179.

Borenstein, S., 2016. The economics of fixed cost recovery by utilities. Electr. J. 29, 5–12.

Chick, M., 2002. Le Tarif Vert Retrouvé: the marginal cost concept and the pricing of electricity in Britain and France, 1945-1970. Energy J. 23 (1), 97–116.

Dutschke, E., Paetz, A.-G., 2013. Dynamic electricity pricing—which programs do consumers prefer? Energy Policy 59, 226–234.

Hall, N.L., Jeannert, T.D., Rai, A., 2016. Cost-reflective electricity pricing: consumer preferences and perceptions. Energy Policy 95, 62–72.

Hausman, W.J., Neufeld, J.L., 1984. Engineers and economists: historical perspectives on the pricing of electricity. Technol. Cult. 30 (1), 83–104.

Hledik, R., 2014. Rediscovering residential demand charges. Electr. J. 27, 82–96.

Hotelling, H., 1938. The general welfare in relation to problems of taxation and of railway and utility rates. Econometrica 6 (3), 242–269.

Houthakker, H.S., 1951. Electricity tariffs in theory and practice. Econ. J. 61 (241), 1–25.

Johnson, E., Beppler, R., Blackburn, C., Staver, B., Brown, M., Matiso, D., 2017. Peak shifting and cross-class subsidisation: the impact of solar PV on changes in electricity costs. Energy Policy 106, 436–444.

Langlois-Bertrand, S., Pineau, P.-O., 2018. Pricing the transition: empirical evidence on the evolution of electricity rate structures in North America. Energy Policy 117, 184–197.

McLaren, J., Davidson, C., Miller, J., Bird, L., 2015. Impact of rate design alternatives on residential solar customer bills: increased fixed charges, minimum bills and demand-based rates. Electr. J. 28, 43–58.

Mountain, B.R., 2017. The retail electricity market for households and small businesses in Victoria. A report prepared for the Independent Review Panel, Melbourne.

Nijhuis, M., Gibescu, M., Cobben, J.F.G., 2017. Analysis of reflectivity & predictability of electricity network tariff structures for household consumers. Energy Policy 109, 631–641.

Passey, R., Haghdadi, N., Bruce, A., MacGill, I., 2017. Designing more cost reflective electricity network tariffs with demand charges. Energy Policy 109, 642–649.

Picciariello, A., Vergara, C., Reneses, J., Frias, P., Soder, L., 2015. Electricity distribution tariffs and distributed generation: quantifying cross-subsidies to consumers to prosumers. Util. Policy 37, 23–33.

Simshauser, P., 2016. Distribution network prices and solar PV: resolving rate instability and wealth transfers through demand tariffs. Energy Econ. 54, 108–122.

Steiner, P.O., 1957. Peaks loads and efficient pricing. Q. J. Econ. 71 (4), 585–610.

Turvey, R., 1968. Peak-load pricing. J. Polit. Econ. 76 (1), 101–113.

Williamson, O.E., 1966. Peak-load pricing and optimal capacity under indivisibility constraints. Am. Econ. Rev. 56 (4), 810–827.

CHAPTER 6

Platforms to Support Nonwire Alternatives and DSO Flexibility Trading

Rachel Stanley*, James Johnston*, Fereidoon Sioshansi[†]
*Piclo, London, United Kingdom
[†]Menlo Energy Economics, Walnut Creek, CA, United States

1. INTRODUCTION

The challenges imposed on the current aging distribution network designed to handle one-directional flows are well known and extensively covered in other chapters of this volume. These include increasing numbers of consumers with distributed generation, storage, electric vehicles charging and discharging, and other behind-the-meter (BTM) assets collectively resulting in bidirectional flows in increasingly congested distribution networks. In the meantime, regulators are contemplating the introduction of complex tariffs that could conceivably vary by time and location as well as the changing nature of congestion on the distribution network.

In this context, there are rising pressures on distribution system operators (DSOs) who must accommodate the plethora of new devices and support new services offered by demand response aggregators, virtual power plants, and other intermediaries without impacting the reliability of the grid or increasing customer bills.

Making matters worse, in many parts of the world, prosumers are paying little to its upkeep – certainly in places where the bulk of the revenues are derived from flat or declining volumetric consumption, as further described elsewhere in this volume.

At the same time, as regulators introduce more complex granular tariffs that better reflect the cost causality of services rendered by the DSOs along with other more market-based pricing methods – say for fast charging electric vehicles or feeding the excess distributed generation into the network – there is no telling if these will relieve congestion or put additional stress on the distribution network.

Consumer, Prosumer, Prosumager
https://doi.org/10.1016/B978-0-12-816835-6.00006-1

Additionally, many prosumers and prosumagers may wish to trade with one another – the so-called peer-to-peer (P2P) trading as further described in Chapter 2 by Shipworth et al. – and/or allow intermediaries to aggregate their load, generation and storage with those of others and optimize the entire portfolio of assets as described in Chapter 3 by Baak and Sioshansi. In the last few years, various forms of virtual power plants (VPPs) have emerged to offer such innovative products and services.

To be feasible, many of these services require much more granular and temporal price transparency across the distribution network. Currently, such price transparency is totally or mostly lacking even in markets with nodal pricing at the wholesale level. Important price signals virtually reach a cul-de-sac at the interface between the high- and low-voltage network, which handicaps entrepreneurs who wish to offer flexibility services, voltage or regulation support, demand response, or similar types of services at the distribution network.

This chapter focuses on a number of services currently offered or being explored by Piclo, formerly known as Open Utility, an innovative start-up developing platforms that offer visibility and transparency to real-time prices on the network and flexibility services facilitating bilateral trading between buyers and sellers. While Piclo is not alone in this space, it offers a window to how the future of price visibility on open platforms may evolve and the range of innovative services it can support.

The chapter is organized as follows:
- Section 2 outlines the value of and some of the key barriers to the distribution networks transition;
- Section 3 introduces the evolution of distribution networks; and
- Section 4 introduces a case study of the Piclo Flex platform followed by the chapter's conclusions.

2. THE VALUE OF AND BARRIERS TO DISTRIBUTION NETWORKS TRANSITION

Technological breakthroughs and the increasingly favorable economics of renewable energy have helped pave the way for distributed energy resources (DER) such as solar PVs, next-generation batteries, and electric vehicles. This is leading to an increasingly volatile demand on the networks and making future network needs increasingly complex and uncertain.

At the same time advances in monitoring, communications, and control technology enable the networks to be operated in an increasingly smart manner. This means that the way the networks are planned and operate must change to be as cost effective as possible. The historical reliance on having sufficient network capacity – poles and wires – to always meet peak demand anywhere on the network will become increasingly expensive and – as will be demonstrated – unnecessary. This trend is already evident as regulators seek "nonwires" solutions when distribution companies seek approval for multibillion dollar grid modernization investments, further described here.

2.1 The Value of Running a Smarter Grid

Take the case of Western Power Distribution (WPD) – a UK distribution network operator – which has put the cost of upgrading its own network at £224.5 million (roughly $300 million) over the next 5 years. WPD estimates that it can experience significant savings by implementing initiatives to encourage distributed resources to help relieve constraints and other distribution network issues (WPD, 2017).

Further savings can be made from reduced system losses due to reduced flows at peak times through network assets. Preliminary research by WPD has indicated that if just 10% of demand from half-hourly metered end-users in the WPD area was matched with local generation, these customers could make combined annual savings of £1 million ($1.3 m) on avoided generation through reduced losses plus additional gains from avoided carbon emissions. These types of savings, of course, are not limited to WPD or the UK, but apply universally on stressed and aging networks across the globe.

The transition from network operators to system optimizers has begun across the globe. Often areas with the biggest challenges on the distribution networks are most advanced. However, having a need and opportunity for transformation is not enough. Network operators are heavily regulated, and have very clear regulatory responsibilities for maintaining reliability and cost management.

At the same time, their revenues are highly regulated and can be collected in prescribed ways and for specific investments. In this sense, changes in how networks are managed, maintained, upgraded, and operated can be either helped or hindered by the regulatory incentives and the prevailing practices, topics that are further covered in other chapters of this book.

2.2 Incentivizing Nonwire Alternatives

The UK provides illustrative examples of regulation, which are beginning to encourage the introduction of innovative "nonwires" alternatives to traditional network reinforcement and management. Presently, there are three mechanisms that encourage it:

- The first is through clear signposting of intent. All UK DNOs are required to develop, and are beginning the first steps to implement, a DSO transition plan. And the Energy Networks Association, the trade body of the UK network operators, has been tasked by Ofgem, the regulator, to develop a national plan of transition through the Open Networks Project (ENA, 2018);
- The second is through establishing Innovation funds, which have allowed DNOs to test out potential innovative technologies and business models through agreed funding streams without affecting the business as usual network services they provide;
- And the third is through the method for calculating the regulated income of the network operators. Ofgem's RIIO framework[1] attempts to consider a full-cost price cap, so if it is cost effective on a total cost basis to increase operational costs to reduce capital costs then there is a financial incentive on the network operators to do this (Ofgem/ RIIO, 2018).

The regulation in the UK, as virtually everywhere else, is in transition. Ofgem has highlighted the areas of improvement still needed to be truly fit for purpose. In a recent consultation, Ofgem is seeking views from the industry on how it should address network charges in the future (Ofgem/ Consultation, 2018).

By contrast, under current German regulation, the majority of the price cap calculation is based on the capital costs of the network operator and is retroactively raised or lowered depending on actual capital costs. So any usage of more market-based network management, which decreases capital costs leads directly to a decrease in revenue for the network operators.

There are a number of examples from other jurisdictions where these issues have been recognized, and there are a number of examples of proposals under consideration on regulation to encourage changes in approach. For example, in the US, many state regulators now routinely ask for "nonwire" alternatives to distribution grid expansion investment plans submitted by distribution companies for approval. These initiatives are following a similar approach to the ones taken in the UK.

Moreover, in a few states, including New York, the regulator is literally stepping outside the proverbial regulatory "box" by imagining alternative

---

[1]RIIO refers to Revenue = Incentives + Innovation + Outputs.

scenarios for the fundamental role and function of the distribution network of the future and the nature of innovative services provided by newcomers and incumbents. Details of this innovative approach to regulation of distribution network, referred to as Reforming the Energy Vision or REV, are further described at the website of the New York Public Service Commission.[2]

Chapters 9 and 13 by Abdelmotteleb et al. and by Germain and Jan also provide examples of regulatory reforms and treatment of distribution network charges for Spain and France, respectively.

Clearly, regulators in different parts of the world are beginning to realize the need for innovative approaches to how monopoly distribution networks of the future will function and how they should be paid for given the dramatic changes taking place in how, when, and where electricity is generated, used, stored, and potentially traded.

3. EVOLUTION OF DISTRIBUTION NETWORKS

Advances in intelligent metering and improved communications and control technology are opening the door to new demand and supply models that carry the potential to fundamentally change the relationship between customers and their energy suppliers and networks as further described in the book's introduction.

In the following content, a few key areas where the nature of services delivered by the distribution networks of the future is changing are briefly highlighted.

3.1 Local Peer-to-Peer (P2P) Trading

Trading is one such model attracting the attention of a wide range of energy stakeholders as a way to maximize value from local networks and DERs by taking advantage of the changing energy landscape and emerging digital capabilities that can match generation and load profiles of different types of customers with local energy generators as further explained in Chapter 2 by Shipworth et al.

Many applications of P2P trading rely on enhanced price transparency on the local distribution networks as well as open platforms that can serve as marketplace for buyers and sellers of services to trade.

---

[2]Refer to http://www3.dps.ny.gov/W/PSCWeb.nsf/All/CC4F2EFA3A23551585257 DEA007DCFE2?OpenDocument.

As it happens, Piclo, formerly Open Utility, has developed a peer-to-peer trading system for energy suppliers and DSOs to transact. The Piclo platform offers sophisticated algorithms to match end-users' electricity demand with those of a nearby generator[3] – among other things.

One critical requirement of such platforms, of course, is that they be open to all buyers and sellers, neutral in the sense that they don't take positions on the trading taking place on the platform and transparent in the sense that everyone can see the prices and transactions taking place on the platform.

The key benefit of the local matching of supply and demand facilitated by the Piclo peer-to-peer platform is that it encourages peer-to-peer trading that minimizes the distance the power has to travel between typical buyer and seller. In doing so, it also typically reduces power flows at higher-voltage levels on the grid, thus potentially removing the need for costly future enhancement and upgrading to create additional network capacity to meet increased peak demand flows.

Another important benefit of a peer-to-peer trading system is that it provides provenance or increased visibility to the *source* and *location* of each kWh of energy being traded, which helps underwrite an energy system based on principles of transparency and openness.

Unsurprisingly, many environmentally conscious consumers – say those who are willing to pay a premium to get 100% renewable energy – typically want to know where their electrons are actually coming from in real time. In many cases, they prefer local renewable generators to more distant ones.

Trading platforms that offer enhanced visibility in real time allow retailers to differentiate themselves from their peers. Piclo has been working with innovative retailers in the highly contestable UK retail electricity market by offering such enhanced services with initial success.

With the advance of peer-to-peer trading, similar preferences will become important as consumers, prosumers, and prosumagers are enabled to begin to interact with one another using the common distribution network.

3.2 Missing Incentives

Despite the proven capabilities for local matching and the vast potential savings it affords, P2P trading in local energy markets remains a niche sector.

---

[3]Open Utility's business model was included in chapter by Johnston in Innovation and disruption at the grid's, also edited by this volume's editor. The company has evolved over time and is now called Piclo, after its platform of the same name. Refer to https://piclo.energy.

The reason for this is that, while logic might dictate that there should be cost savings for using energy close to where it is produced, there are currently no financial incentives for all but the biggest businesses to locally match their electricity supplies. And this is because the current approach to pricing assumes that the grid is still a centralized, fossil-fuel-fed energy system with unlimited capacity to serve consumer, prosumer, and prosumager demands at all times regardless of where they are on the network, and regardless of whether they are feeding the network or taking energy from the network (Fig. 6.1).

Such outdated assumptions along with the prevailing undifferentiated tariffs mean that today's networks and their regulation are no longer suitable in view of the changing energy scene.

This means that existing P2P energy customers are signing up primarily as a demonstration of their support for local, low-carbon energy producers, which means that under current regulatory and market conditions P2P will remain niche. To take the P2P trading model to scale, it is vital to make the traditional, money-driven business case. One way of doing this is through

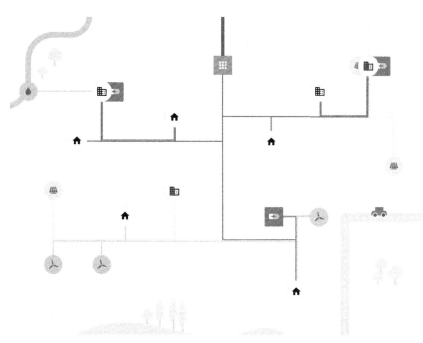

FIGURE 6.1 A visualization showing increasing complexities of local power flows. *(© Piclo, 2018.)*

updating the regulated network charging methodology so customers are incentivized to match their consumption profile with nearby generators: improving the economics of local trading and helping balance the local grid.

3.3 Incentivizing More Efficient Local Balancing Through Network Charges

Network charges are needed to cover the costs of operating and expanding the network as needed, and cover both the costs of new connections and the ongoing operations and maintenance (O&M) costs of the network. Naturally, how the network charges are structured affects the behaviors of the consumers, prosumers, prosumagers, traders, aggregators, and intermediaries that are connected to the network and rely on its essential services. And, of course, regulators must be conscious of the allocative efficiency and fairness of the network tariffs and the inherent cross subsidies that emerge – and exacerbated – as some consumers migrate to become prosumers, prosumagers and change their usage profiles, topics that are further described by Burger et al.

Certain methods of covering costs can encourage users to act in ways that reduce total costs on the network. Firstly through encouraging network customers to shift their energy use or generation to different times of the day so that local supply and demand is more aligned. Secondly by encouraging end users or generators to connect to parts of the network currently dominated by supply or demand as applicable, thereby increasing the scope for additional local matching.

Historically, network charges did not assume or allow for such local flexibility, nor assumed localized self-generation or storage, let alone trading or other forms of transaction.

There are a number of charging mechanisms that can encourage these types of behaviors:

1. **Time-dependent mechanisms**: Regulators are increasing looking into schemes such as time-of-use (TOU), real-time pricing (RTP), critical peak pricing (CPP), and peak time rebates precisely to incentivize consumers to modify their behavior, load, generation, and storage profiles in order to manage peak load periods.

2. **Location-based mechanisms**: Going a step further, moving toward location-based pricing signals can further encourage loads and behind-the-meter distributed resources to modify their profiles based on where they are on the network. This can be achieved through nodal and local pricing methods, which can allow network operators to consider local constraints in the pricing structures.

3. **Virtual microgrids**: pricing structures that encourage groups of network customers to entirely balance their supply and demand in clusters on the grid, effectively creating virtual microgrids that mimic the power flows of real microgrids, without the need for any hardware interventions.

One challenge that needs to be overcome through the design of any such granular pricing methodology is to ensure that there is not an increased cost burden on customers who are not able to control their usage of the network or participate in such schemes. That explains why regulators are interested in revenue-neutral solutions when introducing new tariffs. In a report prepared by Piclo, WPD, and other partners a number of models have been explored (Piclo, 2018).

3.4 Solving Networks Constraints Through DSO Contracts for Flexibility

Granular network charging will go some way toward encouraging behaviors that reduce network costs, and to enabling innovative, local-energy business models. However, to allow more targeted and tighter control of grid needs, DSOs are increasingly interested in procuring flexibility directly from aggregators and prosumagers to relieve congestion on the network. Among the early schemes to do so are competitive auctions where, for example, the DSO can identify and publish congestion zones on the network and choose the flexibility providers that meet their requirements at lowest cost.

This can be targeted to specific locations and the level of contracted flexible load can vary over time depending on the needs of the system. In principle, this makes it a very agile option with payments only being made in areas and at times when they are needed.

Until recently, contracting for local flexibility has been a resource-intensive process, where each stage has been manual, and hence was only used in extreme situations. Piclo believe that the development of marketplaces for flexibility that can automate and standardize trading will be crucial in normalizing and scaling up DSO flexibility schemes.

4. CASE STUDY: PICLO FLEX

This section introduces a case study of the Piclo Flex platform, a project funded by UK Department of Business, Energy & Industrial Strategy (BEIS) and developed in partnership with three of the six distribution network operators in Great Britain – UK Power Networks, Scottish and Southern Electricity Networks, and Electricity North West (Grimwood, 2018; Pratt, 2018).

The discussion first describes what the Piclo Flex platform is, followed by examples of services that can be supported by the platform and future applications and enhancements.

4.1 Why Flexibility Platforms?

Interest in procurement of location-specific flexibility services has been steadily growing over the last couple of years for the reasons mentioned in the earlier sections, further discussed in Chapter 19 by Helman describing the increasing importance of DSO and DNOs coordinating their localized distribution-level management and operational practices with those of TSOs and RTOs who operate at the high-voltage level and at the wholesale markets.

Fundamentally, in any market, there are a variety of buyers and sellers who – given the opportunity – would like to trade in flexibility services as illustrated in Fig. 6.2. Obvious examples of sellers include aggregators, energy suppliers, community-based groups, battery storage service providers, electric vehicle charging providers, and so on – on the left side of the visual. Obvious examples of buyers include the TSO as well as DSOs – on the right side of the visual.

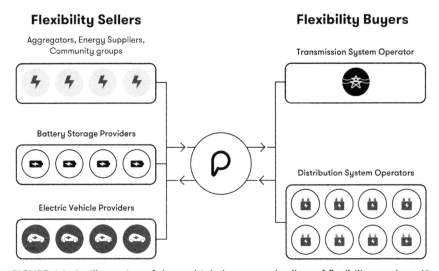

FIGURE 6.2 An illustration of the multiple buyers and sellers of flexibility services. (© *Piclo, 2018.*)

However, until now, the process of allowing such trades to take place has been highly manual and time consuming due to the low transparency that surrounds the market and need for bespoke tendering, bilateral discussions, and agreements.

Consequently, traditional contracts for flexibility services has been a painstakingly laborious and slow process, which limits the scale to which a service can be rolled out, and sets arbitrary limits on the minimum size thresholds of flexibility assets that can be considered.

The complexity, time, and costs also make it less practical for aggregators and suppliers with distributed flexibility to participate in any procurement process. Increasingly, the aggregators of distributed flexibility and DER resources act across whole states, provinces and, in the future, across borders. They therefore not only have multiple loads and resources to manage but have to interface with multiple DNOs with different processes, interfaces, systems, and preferences. Furthermore, there are additional challenges, as location-specific DER flexibility needs to be coordinated with DER flexibility procured by the Transmission System Operator (TSO) to ensure conflicts are minimized and handled appropriately.

Needless to say, in order to make it more easy and practical to trade flexibility services, the following are important:
- to bring the parties together onto a common platform where they can transact in an open and fair way;
- to offer price transparency & visibility in real time;
- to facilitate competitive auctions, so buyers and sellers can bid, buy, and sell in liquid and transparent markets;
- to verify that transactions agreed were in fact executed, delivered, and received; and
- to provide back-office settlement services to compensate those who delivered flexibility services.

4.2 What Functions do Flexibility Platforms Perform?

The basic mechanics of trading flexibility services is illustrated in Fig. 6.3.

Broadly speaking, it consists of nine steps starting with analysis of where congestion may be a problem on the network followed by the intermediate steps. Of the nine steps,
- The first, network analysis to forecast needs, is the responsibility of the DSO;
- The next three are the functions of an online marketplace, open to all buyers and sellers;

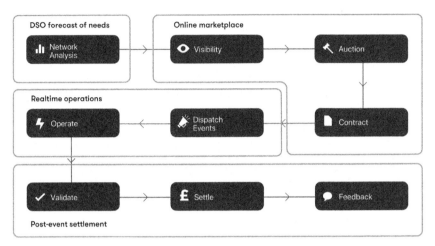

FIGURE 6.3   A schematic of sequence of steps required to handle transactions for offering flexibility services. *(© Piclo, 2018.)*

- The following two steps require physical dispatching and operations performed in real time;
- This is followed by validation, settlement, and feedback – referred to as post-event settlement process.

A cloud-based platform like Piclo Flex can facilitate each of these steps of the process.

4.2.1 Step 1: Online Marketplace

The first function developed by Piclo is the online marketplace. This provides a trusted and independent marketplace where buyers and sellers can assemble to trade efficiently, at low cost, with speed and price transparency. Like any marketplace, a key role is providing visibility to the participants of each other; so sellers of flexibility services understand the needs of those who will procure the services, and buyers can see the amount of potential flexibility that is available.

As schematically shown in Fig. 6.4, Piclo Flex provides DSOs with visibility on where flexibility assets are located and how these correspond with their congested areas of need.

A common interface across DNOs increases reach, transparency, speed, and efficiency, thus increasing the potential success of the trading and procurement processes. Platform automation also reduces the costs of transactions while increasing the scale of transactions by significantly decreasing the time and effort required to trade.

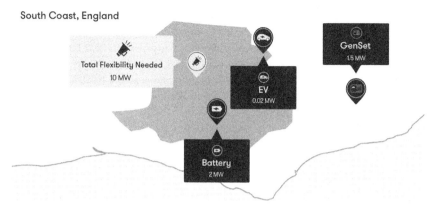

FIGURE 6.4 Matching the flexibility need on the network with flexibility resources in real time. (© Piclo, 2018.)

4.2.2 Step 2: Real-Time Operations

The real-time operations can be facilitated by an online platform by enabling dispatch signals to be automated. With the results of procurement stored on the marketplace platform, all that is needed from the DNO is one dispatch signal to the platform, which can then automatically allocate to the appropriate providers and communicate via agreed channels.

4.2.3 Step 3: Post-Event Settlement

The post-event settlement steps can be facilitated by automating the data communications as well as validation and settlement calculations, as well as providing a common platform for feedback.

4.3 The Value of Piclo Flex

Piclo's main innovation is providing an efficient online marketplace for local flexibility by cutting through the complex barriers and the multiple steps required. In doing so, it helps DSOs to tender for local DER capacity while improving coordination and avoiding conflicts with the TSO.

The primary impact of the innovation is in facilitating faster deployment of local flexibility and unlocking the value of local balancing of loads and DER resources at scale as described in Box 6.1.

The online marketplace is also intended to be used by other participants who want to buy location-specific flexibility. Licensed electricity suppliers who purchase their power from distributed renewable generators have higher than average imbalance risk, as the forecasting of distributed renewables is more complex than demand alone. Timely access to regional

Box 6.1 Platform for Flexibility Services[4]

Among newcomers in the platform space in the electricity sector is **Piclo Flex**, an on-line marketplace in the UK for **Distribution Network Operators** (DNOs) who wish to procure **demand-side flexibility** to reduce **congestion on the electricity grid**.

Research by **Imperial College** and **Carbon Trust** found that a smart and flexible grid could save UK customers £17–40 billion by 2050.

UK Power Networks, one of UK's DNOs, were the first to add their areas of need onto Piclo Flex to signpost where they are looking for **flexible services** to better manage the network. They were also the first to use Piclo Flex in 2018.

Sotiris Georgiopoulos, Head of Smart Grid Development at UK Power Networks, said:

We are interested in working with Piclo because we want to develop a flexibility market that is accessible to DERs, providers, industry, communities and all other market participants.

UK Power Networks have been joined by **Scottish and Southern Electricity Networks** and **Electricity North West**, two other UK DNOs who have now signed up to trial the platform.

Cara Blockley, Central Services Manager at Electricity North West, said:

We are delighted to join the Piclo Flex consortium. An online platform could lower barriers and increase participation in this important new service needed by the industry.

Our energy landscape is evolving at a rapid pace and as an organization, we are absolutely committed to the transition to a low carbon economy and as such, it's vital that we play a central role in facilitating this transition both in the North West and across the UK.

James Johnston, CEO and cofounder of Piclo, said:

*We hope to demonstrate how better visibility of **flexible assets** and streamlining of procurement processes through our platform can lead to better outcomes and more efficient operation of the grid.*

[4]Excerpted from Piclo Press Release 11 July 2018. A longer version appeared in Aug 2018 issue of EEnergy Informer, p.20.

flexibility capacity can help these suppliers reduce their imbalance risk, meaning they can supply renewable power at lower cost to customers.

A core value of Piclo is that it is an independent and neutral marketplace open and accessible to all. By maximizing participation from as many buyers and sellers of flexibility as possible, Piclo can create a "liquid market" where anyone can find opportunities to buy or sell in any area, at any time.

As is true of all platforms, Piclo's flexibility marketplace will gain from the network effects for growth. The more buyers and sellers who use the platform, the more popular it will be, the more services and features it can support and the lower the costs of services it can offer.

Once proven in the UK, Piclo intends to replicate the model in new markets including, potentially, Australia, New York, and across the EU. As more DSOs express interest to procure flexibility or "nonwire alternatives," Piclo's platform could be a good candidate for future trials.

5. CONCLUSIONS

As further described in the preceding discussion, ongoing research has identified a number of key challenges that need to be addressed to significantly increase the prevalence of localized matching of buyers and sellers, for facilitating peer-to-peer trade, for offering flexibility and other services sought by aggregators and intermediaries at the distribution level.

The first consideration is the incentive structure for DSOs. In the UK, the RIIO (Revenue = Incentives + Innovation + Outputs) price control framework introduced by Ofgem is very helpful in rewarding the network companies in an agnostic manner. There is a level playing field for making decisions on whether to reinforce networks or use smarter nonwire alternatives.

The second consideration is the incentive structure for participants. Currently in the UK (which broadly reflects the global situation), there are no financial incentives for local trading. The economic signals were generally designed for an era of centralized production and unidirectional transportation, and no longer reflect reality. A more reflective tariff would better represent the value and cost of connecting and using the grid – however, regulatory conditions mean any progress toward this is slow.

An alternative solution, and one that is free of regulatory burdens, is that DSOs can set up direct contracts with providers of flexibility – aggregators of flexibility, other intermediaries, or even the prosumeragers themselves. The contract terms can be very targeted in time and space, and enable the DSOs to avoid specific reinforcement works by contracting providers to be more flexible in their use of energy.

Thus far, these nonwire alternatives have been a very manual, slow, and expensive process, which is a significant barrier to their adoption and usefulness. A UK company, Piclo, is attempting to streamline this process by developing a platform called Piclo Flex that enables buyers (DSOs) and sellers (aggregators) to trade and setup these arrangements quickly and cheaply.

Key functions of this platform include visibility of buyer needs and seller assets; auctions that enable competitive bidding; real-time operations to facilitate better dispatch; and settlement functions for validating performance and paying providers accordingly.

Platforms like Piclo Flex have great potential for scaling up flexibility trading with DSOs. The network effects could enable rapid growth and could unlock a whole new trading paradigm for the energy sector globally.

If successful, the value that platforms can offer distribution network companies and society is enormous. Not just saving billions of dollars in unnecessary reinforcement costs but also acting as an enabler for a decarbonized and democratized energy system.

REFERENCES

ENA, 2018. Energy Networks Association—Open Networks Project website. http://www.energynetworks.org/electricity/futures/open-networks-project/open-networks-project-overview/. [(Accessed July 2018)].

Grimwood, T., 2018. Electricity north west joins local flexibility marketplace Online article: https://utilityweek.co.uk/electricity-north-west-joins-online-trial-local-flexibility/. [(Accessed July 2018)].

Ofgem/Consultation, 2018. Getting more out of our electricity networks through reforming access and forward-looking charging arrangements https://www.ofgem.gov.uk/publications-and-updates/getting-more-out-our-electricity-networks-through-reforming-access-and-forward-looking-charging-arrangements. [(Accessed July 2018)].

Ofgem/RIIO, 2018. Network regulation—the 'RIIO' model. Website https://www.ofgem.gov.uk/network-regulation-riio-model. [(Accessed July 2018)].

Piclo, 2018. Local grid charging whitepaper. http://bit.ly/local-grid-charging. [(Accessed July 2018)].

Pratt, D., 2018. UKPN's second flexibility tender to launch under 'Online Dating' Piclo Flex platform. Online article: https://www.current-news.co.uk/news/ukpns-second-flexibility-tender-to-launch-under-online-dating-piclo-flex-platform. [(Accessed July 2018)].

WPD, 2017. Comparison of price incentive models for locally matched electricity networks. Published online https://www.westernpower.co.uk/docs/Innovation/Other/Location-signals-report-18-12-17.aspx. [(Accessed July 2018)].

CHAPTER 7

Consumer-Centric Service Innovations in an Era of Self-Selecting Customers

Emi Minghui Gui, Iain MacGill
UNSW, Sydney, NSW, Australia

1. INTRODUCTION

As explained in other chapters of this volume, the development of distributed and smart grid technologies in recent decades has led to a new paradigm where consumers can become professional consumers that are actively engaged in their energy supply including potentially demand response, producer-consumers or prosumers, prosumagers who also have storage, as the title of this book suggests. Behind all of these consumer possibilities lie new technology options, and growing consumer interest in greater participation in their energy service provision. As noted by the CEO of the Australian Energy Market Operator (AEMO) Audrey Zibelman (Parkinson, 2018),

> In 10 years time, the influence of distributed energy – rooftop solar, battery storage and smart software – would mean smart homes and consumers who understood their appliances, such as pool pumps, rooftop solar, fridges, would respond to price signals.

This phenomenon reflects the underlying economic benefits with greater consumer participation, yet also presents commercial retail "market" and wider societal imperatives for improved energy sector outcomes. On one side, varied technology and service providers are "pushing" a growing range of clean energy and energy-efficient technologies, products, and associated services to "market." On the other side, rising electricity costs, governments' policy incentives on clean energy and energy efficiency, and consumer awareness and commitments to renewable energy and sustainability, are all driving market "pull" for these new products and services (Gui and MacGill, 2018).

The strong growth in household investments in energy efficient and distributed energy products and services seen in many parts of the world is shifting the entire equipment vendor and service provider ecosystem, with significant implications for utilities and other energy products and services providers, old and new. In particular, some of the existing players are finding that the "consumers" that they once served are now selecting to be "customers" – customers whose business they need to win, and may perhaps lose.

All participants, therefore, need to better understand the consumer decision-making and behavioral processes that lie behind them choosing whether to engage in their energy service provision, and what such engagement will involve:

- what choices do energy consumers really have in view of the proliferation of new energy products and services, yet existing institutional and "market" arrangements?
- how do they make energy-related decisions in the context of the potential costs and benefits involved, yet also their demographic, personal, and financial resources, and social networks, and indeed interest or otherwise in energy service provision?
- what "consumer-centric" service innovations will allow providers to build business models for improving consumer outcomes taking into account consumer options and their decision making processes?

Some of these aspects have been discussed in the introduction of this book and previous chapters. In particular, Mountain's Chapter 5 discusses some of the challenges of meaningful end-user engagement in present retail markets, with a focus on the Australian National Electricity Market (NEM) – a jurisdiction that features in this chapter. Stanley et al.'s Chapter 6 reviews new platforms for service trading, and Weiss et al.'s description of how the large German utilities have responded to these and other disruptions to their traditional business model are also very relevant.

Our contribution in this chapter focuses on the three questions identified – in summary, what are the key behavioral factors of engaged consumer decision making in an energy future full of complex and interacting choices, and what business models and strategies are emerging to better facilitate such consumer decision making.

This chapter is organized as follows: Section 2 reviews three key groups of choices of energy products and services that are available to energy consumers in today's electricity sector; Section 3 analyzes the process of consumers' decision making and behavior, as well as the external and psychological factors influencing their decisions; while Section 4 provides some case studies of utilities and new players developing consumer-centric service models, and discusses their value proposition and potential.

2. WIDENING SET OF ENERGY CHOICES

Technology innovation in home energy management, home automation, distributed energy, and smart grids is creating an ever-widening set of energy choices for consumers, provided by an expanding set of providers. Based on their functional characteristics, three key opportunities for consumer energy products and services can be identified, as illustrated in Fig. 7.1.

I "off-the-shelf" physical products that customers can purchase, such as LED lighting, energy-efficient electrical appliances and water heaters, thermostat, home energy management devices and systems, solar PV panels, battery storage, electric vehicles; in general, products that are typically modular and address specific demand or supply side needs;

II "add-on" services on top of the first group of products that change the nature of service provision such as more cost-reflective dynamic electricity tariffs, demand response, energy efficiency, virtual power plants, and peer-to-peer trading. Although requiring no or little extra capital investments, they involve greater customer interaction and management of their electricity–derived service activities; and

III community-based energy solutions or community-invested energy projects that can be managed by either communities themselves or third parties, such as community energy projects, community microgrids, integrated energy systems; in general, activities that require community-level planning and governance.

The first two groups involve primarily individual decisions, and these choices are typically not mutual exclusive; for example, consumers can purchase appliances and systems they desire, while still participating in different service arrangements. The third type is community based, hence requires a certain level of community consensus and involvement, and the choices tend to be mutually exclusive, customers may need to choose to engage in one solution or the other.

In general, the first and third groups require considerable upfront investments, thus are subject to consumers' willingness-to-pay for these products and services, and budgetary constraints. These choices can be competing with each other, for example, a budget-constrained consumer may choose to invest in energy-efficient appliances and participate in a time-based

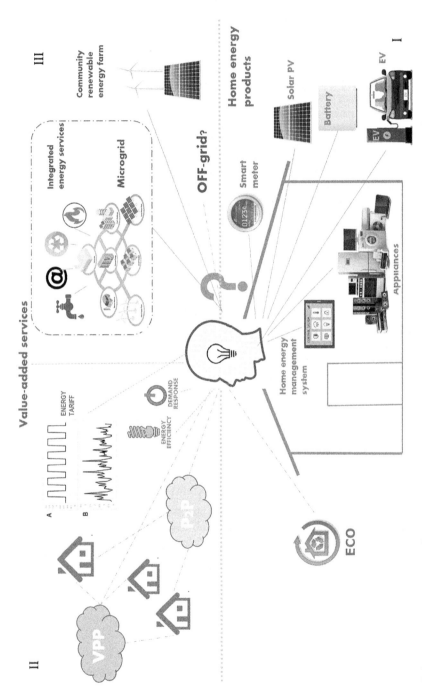

FIGURE 7.1 Key categories of consumer energy products and services. (*Source: Authors' own illustration (some images from Shutterstock.com).*)

electricity tariff, rather than purchasing solar PV and battery storage. In contrast, others may invest more on the supply-side technologies by installing solar PV and battery storage in order to gain savings and rewards from greater self sufficiency as well supply to the grid.

The focus of this book chapter is on consumer-based products and services described in groups I and II. Further discussion on community-based solutions can be found elsewhere in this book; for instance, Chapter 10 by Koirala et al. examines the sociotechnical, economic, and institutional requirements for the development of community energy storage, while Couture et al. discuss decentralized energy systems in the context of off-grid electrification applications.

Our chapter also focuses, of course, on potential "customers" for such products and services; that is, those self-selected consumers who are ready, willing, and able to engage in their energy service provision. However, it needs to be kept in mind that even with all the exciting new products and services, and emerging business models to provide them, electricity industry arrangements still need to cater for those consumers who "self-select" not to be customers, as discussed further in Section 3.4.

2.1 Consumer Energy Products

Consumer energy products are mostly modular products around homes or small businesses that typically allow consumers to self-generate own electricity and/or self-manage their consumption to achieve private goals, whether these are to lower energy bills, to gain financial rewards, to use home appliances more efficiently, or to reduce their carbon footprint. For example, with the investment of around A\$15,000 for a solar and battery energy storage system, an average Australian family might in some circumstances be able to reduce their electricity bills to below A\$10 per month, instead of paying a A\$200–A\$300 monthly bill without this equipment installed (Mayoh, 2017). The family's carbon footprint will also be markedly reduced given the high emissions intensity of the present Australian electricity generation mix.

On the demand side, products such as smart meters and home energy management equipment and systems (HEMS), as well as more energy efficient appliances, can all aid consumers in self-regulating their consumption in terms of both timing and overall consumption. More recently, the next generation of smart home energy management devices enabled by Internet of Things (IoT), cloud computing, data analytics, and advanced device interconnectivity, allows households and businesses to precisely control key energy equipment including air conditioners, computers, television, and other appliances with advanced automated scheduling as well as "just-in-time" responses, all enabled through their smartphones to realize real-time energy management.

Some key components and communication technology players at the forefront of the HEMS market at present include Aclara, Energate, Trilliant, Honeywell, Nest, Logitech, Energyhub, GE, Panasonic, etc. (Market Research Future, 2018). According to Navigant Research, the HEMS market is projected to grow from $2.3 billion in 2016 to $7.8 billion by 2025 (Navigant Research, 2018).

The evolution of HEMS is moving away from HEMS1.0 technology mostly deployed by utilities through point solution devices such as direct load control and thermostat programs, to HEM3.0 offering bundled residential services through holistic cloud-based platforms by blue chip and start-up service providers (Saadeh, 2015). As noted by GTM Research (Hill, 2015),

"Blue chip vendors, such as Apple®, ADT, Google® (after its acquisition of Nest), Samsung, Verizon, and Wal-Mart are all partnering with incumbent hardware and software providers to develop home internet-of-things ecosystems to usher in a new phase of home energy management solutions."

"Venture-backed startups are positioning themselves to take advantage of the new and competitive era of energy management in the connected home that is driven by the proliferation of consumer interest in smart devices and increasing efforts to reduce home energy bills," "market growth is creating opportunities for companies on both sides of the meter."

2.2 "Value-Added" Services

The second and third groups are services that can be supplied by both utilities and third-party providers as "value-added services," that can be defined as *"energy services beyond electricity supply and energy grid services that may include customized or bespoke energy products/services that meet customer demand for renewable energy, integrated energy management solutions, energy storage, microgrids, electric vehicle charging, private or community solar, energy efficiency, or other services"* (Blansfield et al., 2017).

Many of these services require specialized support systems, dedicated infrastructure, and large investments, and are therefore primarily provider-dependent, with mostly voluntary participation by interested consumers. They allow joint value creation to increase utilization of assets and exchange of services, while offering secondary economic, environmental, and societal value to households and communities (Gui et al., 2017). Key categories of value-added services and their rationale are listed in Sioshansi's Introduction for this book, including cost-reflective tariffs, demand response, energy efficiency, VPPs, P2P, community microgrids, and community-scale energy projects.

There is still debate on whether the incumbent utilities should be restricted in the provision of such value-added services. After all, they have the advantages of an established customer base, technical capability in network design, grid operation and management, and often ample financial resources. Nonetheless, many of them are facing competition from numerous niche providers that can offer specialized and customized services for residential customers and communities, such as residential demand response (DR), P2P trading, VPP, and community microgrids.

Benefiting from a new generation of distributed technologies and home energy products, and the plethora of energy data and communication options for devices and customer messaging, these new businesses can quickly emerge to fill needs in the residential sector that are traditionally underserviced by utilities, often due to lack of enabling technologies and the traditionally large transaction costs related to serving a large number of small customers. For instance, the residential DR market is rapidly developing with the aid of new hardware and software offerings by many startup companies such as Whisker Labs, EnergyHub, AutoGrid, and Nest (Wokutch, 2011). As noted earlier, P2P trading, VPP, and community microgrids are discussed in depth in a number of Chapters in this book.

Further, nonutility service providers can now interact directly with consumers by bypassing a consumer's electric utility and providing smart grid products and services directly to the consumers. Their services can assist consumers in managing their electricity activities on a real-time basis, using electric efficiency analysis and energy management interfaces via advanced metering devices, web portals, software, and home area networks (Blansfield et al., 2017).

Meanwhile, for many incumbent utilities, the development of new service offerings is seen as a way to recoup eroded revenue base as a result of more energy-efficient and self-sufficient consumers, or simply to stay relevant. As noted in Chapter 1 by Brown et al., many new innovations are expected to come from outside the industry not from within. Unsurprisingly, the PwC's 13th global utilities CEO survey result indicates that more than a quarter of respondents agreed that the biggest competitive threat could come from companies with strong brands outside the sector (PwC, 2014).

3. CONSUMER DECISION-MAKING PROCESS

The proliferation of energy products and services brought about by the distributed and smart home technology advancements creates new opportunities yet challenges for consumers. As note earlier, many consumers may not wish to engage, and arrangements must continue to work for them. For those consumers ready, willing, and able to engage, it does require them to make important, yet complex decisions regarding their energy service provision, including:

- What new electric appliances to purchase, and with what features?
- Whether to deploy smart metering, monitoring, and load management?
- Whether to install solar rooftop PV panels and battery energy storage?
- Which electricity retailer and type of tariff plan to select?
- What other possible service providers might they engage with, for which services?
- Whether to participate in a community energy project?
- To stay on-grid or off-the-grid?

These individual consumer decisions, not only affect their own energy situation, but also influence the market development of new technologies, products, and services as well as, in aggregate, potentially driving broader energy industry changes. Thus, understanding the consumer decision-making process is indispensable for utilities and other product and service providers for effective long-term engagement of their customers.

3.1 Five Stages of Consumer Decision Making

A five-stage consumer decision-making process (Dudovskiy, 2013) for a household facing energy-related decisions might involve the following steps (Fig. 7.2):

- needs recognition,
- search for information,
- evaluation of alternatives,
- purchase, and
- post purchase evaluation.

As many energy-related consumer decisions are complex, technical, unfamiliar, and novel, only a small number of sophisticated consumers may be able to gather and process all required information and perform reasonably rational decisions. Worse, many separate but interrelated decisions need to be made progressively over an extended period of time while one decision can affect subsequent decisions. Therefore, the process of evaluation of alternatives

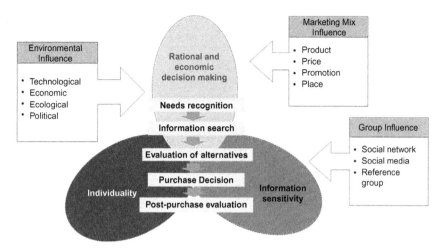

FIGURE 7.2 Consumer decision process, external influences, and behavioral factors (Kanagal, 2016; Kotler, 1997). *(Source: Adapted from Kanagal, 2016; Kotler, 1997.)*

can be difficult, time consuming and potentially pressured (Ha et al., 2010) even for an energy expert, let alone an average "mum and dad" consumer.

Considerable upfront capital requirements and long replacement life cycles for many of these products and services add additional complexity and the decision making often requires professional knowledge and skills. For example, working with a budget of $5000 and desire to lower heating and cooling bills, a household may consider to either purchase a reverse cycle air conditioner, or install a 2.5-kW solar system. Although both can arrive at a lower heating and cooling bill, the choice is not readily straightforward, particularly given future uncertainties.

The adaptation of energy behaviors and solutions is often necessary post acquisition of energy products and services in order to achieve best outcomes. For instance, a case study in the Netherlands on TOU pricing and home energy management systems found that changed customer behavior to achieve savings may be maintained for only a short period, after which the rebound effect takes hold and benefits are not sustained for the long term as a significant number of customers revert to their traditional patterns of electricity consumption (Hu et al., 2015).

The decision-making process is further complicated by consumer behavioral processes bounded by information sensitivity, individuality, and rational and economic decision making, and influenced by environmental, marketing, and group influences, as illustrated in Fig. 7.2.

3.2　External Stimuli

The consumer decision-making process may be influenced by external stimuli (Engel et al., 1995), including environmental influences, such as economic, technological, political, and social/culture aspects, marketing influences, such as product, price, promotion, and place, and group influences, such as "word-of-mouth" and peer groups.

As widely acknowledged, technological, political, and social environments are particularly significant in the context of energy market and climate change, as consumers' choices of products and services are primarily driven by technological advancements, and consumer decisions largely respond to policy incentives yet also broader market and social settings. The marketing and group influences on the consumer decision-making process are clearly worthy of further consideration. They are discussed in more detail here.

3.2.1　Marketing Influences

In a competitive marketing environment, home energy products are evaluated and selected based on price, promotion, and a varied set of product parameters such as quality, functionality, design, and energy efficiency. Some innovative products have been introduced to Australian households and consumers to support more efficient use of electricity and better experiences, for example, Redback Hybrid System, offering intelligent technology that can store, monitor, and manage solar energy around consumers' home in a compact and elegant unit, controlled from your smartphone (RedBackTech, 2018). To help reduce barriers to adoption, including high upfront costs and uncertainty regarding product performance for some home energy products, many innovative financing schemes such as leasing options and zero interest loans are being offered by providers. As one recent example, an innovative startup ShineHub has released a "fixed rate, free access" product in Australia to get solar panels and battery energy storage installed without any upfront costs. Households also get free hardware, free installation, a reduced electricity tariff, and can save between 14–50% on their electricity bill (Chang, 2018).

Research on European and US consumer preferences for energy-efficient products highlights that the final consumer buying decision is strongly influenced by point-of-purchase promotions and information from all channels including state efficiency programs. These decisions are indirectly affected by the availability of efficient products as determined by the manufacturer and the stocking practices of the retailers since customers cannot buy what is not offered in the market (Attali et al., 2009; McNary, 2008). Governments can also play a direct role in promoting products and services, through targeted government programs and information portals. For example, the Victorian government in Australia offers a A$50 cash incentive for each household, which visits an energy comparison website during a specified period to encourage people to find better power deals. It is claimed that the website has clear impacts on consumer decisions and can result in savings of $330 on energy bills of a typical household in the first year alone (Edwards, 2018). The challenges of comparison shopping in the Victorian retail electricity market within the Australian NEM are discussed at length in Chapter 5 by Bruce Mountain.

3.2.2 Group Influences

Consumers acquire their knowledge and experience through a process of learning and usage of the products and services under consideration, which is heavily influenced by the group and business environment around the consumer. This environment is, of course, impacted in the longer-term by the aggregate outcomes of consumer decision-making processes. Informal and formal discussion groups and forums on Facebook®, Twitter®, etc., including more professional channels and moderated sites by expert organizations, such as the Alternative Technology Association and consumer advocacy group CHOICE in Australia, can be set up to engage targeted groups to share knowledge and experiences. Some, such as "My Efficient Electric Home" discussion forums created by Melbourne Energy Institute, provide a platform not only for information sharing, but also for members to lobby governments toward more progressive policies and regulations removing disincentives for certain products and technologies, for example, heat pumps. It is estimated that the discussions on this particular platform may have influenced more than A$400,000 worth of member purchases to date (Forcey, 2017).

Social influences, such as "word of mouth," reference groups, and interaction in mass media that allow for social interactions, can all have spillover effects on energy consumer decision processes and encourage behavior change. This has proven to be so effective that part of Sonnen's sales strategy for their solar and battery energy storage product hinges on the "cluster" or "contagion" effect – people who buy cutting-edge "cool" products, such as solar battery, solar panels, electric vehicles, like to tell their neighbors and peers about it, some then follow suit, and further spread the message (Kelly-Detwiler, 2017).

These groups thus can play an important intermediary role as knowledge brokers to foster social learning and innovation by recombining and transferring knowledge among members and communities. These intermediaries not only facilitate exchanges of knowledge and ideas, among close-knit communities, but also geographically dispersed communities, with some also offering commercial, technical, and financial advice, policy advocacy, and policy support. In community-based projects, their role is even more prominent through linking individual project and isolated initiatives and discussing common pathways for development, through to sharing an increasingly coherent identity and more networked activities (Smith et al., 2016). This experience generates important social and technical know-how, and hopefully supports the more complex energy activities required in community-based initiatives, such as applying for grants, seeking loans, raising money, planning and building permissions, insurance and marketing strategies (Hargreaves et al., 2013).

3.3 Behavioral Process

In theory at least, energy-related consumer decisions are made through choices for customized electricity products and solutions best attending to individual preferences (time and trust), behavior (knowledge and information, convenience), and economic circumstances (financial). These mostly relate to consumers allocating resources as they see fit, among the options that are available to them, to acquire their "choice of products," "choice of services," or "choice of investments." It is, however, a bounded exercise for reasons including those outlined here, specifically information sensitivity, individuality, and rational and economic decision making (Kanagal, 2016).

3.3.1 Information Sensitivity

Nowadays, there exist numerous information outlets, providing information on relevant government initiatives and incentives, smart homes and home automation, home energy ratings, advice on how to choose solar products and energy-efficient appliances, as well as on how to adjust consumption patterns for more efficient use of consumers' solar systems and other technologies. These often require consumers to possess certain degree of proficiency to understand adequately the products and services they require, administering technologies involved, market and policy information, and their combined effects. Or else, consumers can make economically disadvantageous decisions. From this perspective, appropriate communication strategies from "expert advisors" such as policy makers, utilities, and other providers, through education, marketing, advertising, and regulation, will help overcome inertia or information barriers, and facilitate appropriate consumer choices and thus more efficient marketplace outcomes.

As one example of efforts to induce consumers to make better informed decisions, the energy regulator in the UK has recently trialed an auction process in an attempt to find better energy deals for "sticky" customers who failed to shop around in the last 3 years. The customers can decline the chance to opt-in to the switch. In this case, government intervention acts as a "nudge"[1] (Thaler and Sunstein, 2008), which is carefully selected and helps to minimize the decision costs and individual error costs. The results are yet to be seen in overcoming the inertia of not acting, thus leading to more satisfied consumers and improved consumer welfare.

3.3.2 Individuality

In at least part, self-interest drives people to consider different energy plans and options for economic optimization or personal satisfaction. Consumer decision making is often closely related to their willingness-to-pay that is not only exhibited in economic terms, but also in people's perception of satisfaction such as comforts and habits, and time value. Some research highlights that energy behavior is strongly linked to households' financial situation (Pongiglione, 2011). For example, people with low incomes may be more willing to make life style changes such as taking up time-of-use tariffs or forgoing air conditioning at peak demand times. People with higher incomes can be more willing to pay extra for low-energy electrical appliances, and new technology products such as solar PV, battery storage, and electric vehicles. They are however more reluctant to constrain their personal freedom and give up habits and lifestyle, therefore less inclined to participate in recycling programs (Huhtala, 2010), and are more willing to drive than taking public transport.

The trust and credibility of service providers is also an important determinant of residential energy-related choices and behavior, as well as acceptance of energy innovation and technology. Distrust reduces the likelihood of consumers to take up products and services offered by utilities. Evidently, electricity bill shocks and lack of trust in Australian electricity retailers are pushing householders increasingly toward generating their own power on their rooftops (Orchison, 2018). In another instance, when a distribution

---

[1] A nudge alters people's behavior in a predictable way without forbidding any options or significantly changing their economic incentives.

network company in Victoria asked its customers who should pay for investments for network reliability due to the increased uptake of rooftop solar on its networks: (a) All customers, (b) Customers with solar panels who export, the unanimous response was clear (Vorrath, 2018):

> *None of the above!! … Power company invest own money so to get returns..,*
>
> *we have paid over and over for your infrastructure, it's part of your expense, it's the solar panel owners who are supplementing your grid thus avoiding upgrades we are told,*
>
> *If you start charging me more, SIMPLE I will just disconnect and install batteries.*

3.3.3 Rational and Economic Decision Making

The rational and economic decision-making process serves to maximize utility for the consumption basket at the least cost, given budget constraints. In order to behave rationally in the economic sense, as this approach suggests, a consumer would have to be aware of all the available consumption options, be capable of correctly rating each alternative, and be available to select the optimum course of action (Schiffman and Kanuk, 2007). Many product providers facilitate this process by offering online evaluation tools or quotes, tips, and product/service comparisons to facilitate consumers decision making, for example, solar calculators/estimators to determine how many solar panels a household needs, payback periods, based on roof space, household appliances, products, and more.

The complexity of the decision-making process increases significantly for value-added services categories as most require active management that involve an exchange of personal comfort and convenience for economic benefits. For solution-based services, such as microgrids, community-scale energy projects, rational and economic decision making will require even more complex and professional planning, ideally treated as "investment" decisions. These often imply opportunity costs in decision making, as consumers need to decide how to allocate their limited budget to energy assets and options that often have much longer replacement life cycles.

3.4 Decision-Making Biases

In practice, a consumer's actual decision is often not made rationally by assessing their individual situation for the best long-term benefits. Instead, household decision makers are prone to systematic errors in judging the benefits and costs of their energy choices. Sometimes, consumers choose one option over another because they misestimate its value to them.

For example, research shows that despite the push from the government and utilities toward the time-of-use (TOU) electricity tariff, NSW families who have moved from a single rate to a TOU electricity plan in an effort to cut costs may actually end up paying $370 more each year if their demand cannot be reduced in the peak pricing period[2] (Han, 2017).

Some may be incapable or unwilling to choose for various reasons, referred to as "nonsumers" by Ben-David in the Preface of this book. Chapter 5 by Bruce Mountain also discusses why consumers in Victoria, Australia, have shunned away from electricity tariffs with demand charges for reasons including the difficulties in assessing potential benefits, and lack of product information and promotion from retailers.

Some consumers may delay choice due to "status quo bias"[3] or "inertia." For instance, it is observed that switching energy provider to a more efficient one or substituting old household appliances with more energy-efficient ones are not the easy and linear decision that one could expect (McNamara and Grubb, 2011; Pongiglione, 2011). As a result, many consumers may prefer simple rather than complicated alternatives, and be open to default options.

Human beings also discount future benefits by instinct, are therefore inclined to shy away from more capital intensive upfront investment solutions even though they may yield medium/long-term savings as the cash flow from these investments will be more uncertain and difficult to forecast. This aspect has created a major barrier for the commercial development of community-based long-term energy solutions, such as community microgrids, and integrated community energy systems (Gui et al., 2017). When visible immediate benefits are not achieved, this can also lead to limited incentives to adopt more efficient energy products and services, or change individual behavior.

In summary, energy consumers' decisions are mostly limited by accessibility of information, marketing, and promotion activities, and significantly impacted by common cognitive and psychological factors, including individual knowledge and network effects. All these aspects of consumer decision making present huge challenges to providers in customer acquisition and retention, yet present opportunities for innovative providers to gain a foothold in a traditionally utility-dominated business environment.

---

[2]The peak period, in this context, typically refers to be between 2 pm and 8 pm on weekdays.
[3]That is, consumers tend to resist change, and often reluctant to alter their habits and comforts, and instead favor the status quo or "default" setting.

4. CUSTOMER ENGAGEMENT AS A KEY FOCUS FOR UTILITIES

As noted earlier, electricity utilities around the world are facing ever more demanding customers, stagnant on-grid load demand, and competition from nonutility providers to deliver value-added services. Consequently, utility partnerships and cooperation with innovative nonutility providers have become increasingly common. As an example, Greensync, an Australia's home-grown demand-side management (DSM) provider, provides a range of products and interfaces to help manage virtual power plant, demand side resources, and network constraints, for utilities, retailers, energy markets, commercial and industrial businesses. It also offers a decentralized energy exchange (deX) platform that creates open market places for local energy to be generated, controlled or stored, and then traded between households, businesses, utilities, and the larger market operators (GreenSync, 2018).

The growing pressure for better utility services from customers, competitors, and the broader marketplace requires a shift of business strategy from performance-based to customer-centric models, and the increase of offerings from the universal provision of standardized and undifferentiated products to the provision of personalized and customized solutions. These new products and services can help to engage and retain customers, and establish new revenue streams and areas for growth for utilities or, if they fail to do so, new competitors.

On the other hand, individual traits and characteristics of consumer decision making and behavior allow them to self-select into different energy options and solutions, which provides information for providers to design more targeted services. To better satisfy customers' needs, these additional programs and services should aim to help remove key constraints and hindrances in the consumer decision process, such as time, money, information barriers, and decision complexity.

Deepening customer engagements demands providers and utilities better understand the science and art of consumer decision making and behavior, and embrace value-added services and solutions that are simple and easy to use, customized to individual needs, and integrated services to cater for multiple needs. In this section, we review three key consumer-centric service models working with utilities or employed by utilities, simple and fast services, personalized and customized services, and integrated utility services, as illustrated in Fig. 7.3. These are drawn from around the world and only represent a small part of the growing activities being seen in the electricity sector.

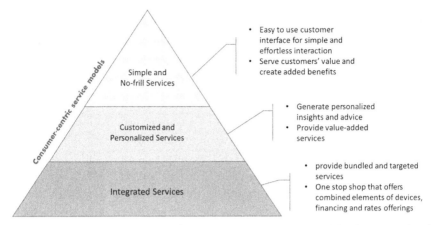

FIGURE 7.3 Three key categories of consumer-centric service models. *(Source: Authors' own illustration.)*

4.1 Simple and Fast Services – Ohmconnect

Ohmconnect is a start-up based in California that claims to be the first to help residential consumers to save energy and get paid for it. It covers the area in between from San Diego to Buffalo serving 300,000 small customers, and reports to have helped its customers save around $4 million to date (Ohmconnect, 2018). Customers typically earn between $50–150 per year, depending on how much electricity they typically use.

It works in three simple steps for customers:

1. Connect – customers first sign up for *Ohmconnect* and authorize the company to access their homes' smart meter and any supported internet-connected devices.
2. Save – the company will alert customers to energy spikes a few times a week, and ask them to cut back power consumption for the periods.
3. Cash out – The customer then get paid for the energy they don't use.

It is even simpler for customers who have the right thermostat, smart switches, or a *Tesla* electric vehicle since *Ohmconnect* can automatically manage their power consumption on behalf of the customers. The service includes an interactive map of where the electricity is coming from, to help customers better appreciate the emissions they reduced by using less electricity. After the designated hour is over, the company compares how much customers used with what they usually use to determine the payments to customers (Finley, 2015).

Ohmconnect provides added value to small customers by helping them to extract more value from their electricity usage, and to utilities better connecting to their customers. Further, its appeal to customers also lies in its easy-to-use interface and fast interaction with them. Therefore, the company can help significantly lower transaction costs for a large number of residential customers to participate in the wholesale market as a bundle.

A big challenge to the company, however, is how to effectively grow its customer base with minimum customer acquisition costs (EEnergy Informer, 2018), and encourage greater customer participation. Given the small savings it generally offers, its revenue generation currently relies heavily on voluntary demand response (VDR)[4] behavior (Gyamfi and Krumdieck, 2011) or proenvironmental charitable contributions by customers. For the long-term sustainability and growth of the business, the company needs to expand its customer base and revenue streams, for example to more effectively identify and raise awareness among potential customers, to target customers with right equipment, or joint promotion of its services through utilities and equipment retailers. All this requires deeper understanding of potential customers behavior and decision-making process.

4.2 Personalized and Customized Services – Wattcost, Opower, Bidgely

The digital transformation of the electricity system now makes personalized and customized services to households a real prospect, when these services have not been considered as economically viable for residential customers to date due to technology and transaction costs.

Wattcost, an Australian startup, offers a smart product with a wireless sensor that listens to every appliance from electricity meter and captures real-time energy use to create personal intelligent home. It also helps to identify potential electricity cost savings, reveal the lowest cost electricity plans to match customer's actual home energy use, and even send real-time alerts for appliance and home protection, and offer features for experience sharing with communities (Wattcost, 2017).

Opower, now part of Oracle, provides cloud-based software to the utility industry. Its software uses statistical algorithms to perform pattern recognition analysis from energy data and presents personalized insights to consumers in order to motivate reductions in energy consumption. Without any devices installed in the home, the platform can perform usage-disaggregation analysis, to generate recommendations about specific types of energy use such as

---

[4]It is defined as external signals or information changing normal electricity usage patterns for a certain period of time.

heating or cooling usage, and to present marketplace suite, a utility-branded product recommendation engine, which enables the customer to search and sort products based on personalized estimates. It is reported that the average customer receiving the *Opower* platform has cut energy usage by more than 2.5% (Leuschner, 2017).

Bidgely (Bidgely, 2018) offers a white-label platform to utilities called HomeBeat Energy monitor that uses customer data to disaggregate energy use among household devices to help utility customers prioritize energy-savings efforts. The platform includes a mobile app and web portal that has features for personalized energy-saving insights, neighborhood comparisons, alerts and notifications, and social media channels.

The huge market potential in smart home space, unsurprisingly, also invites entries from tech giants, such as Google®, Apple®, Amazon®, who can easily leverage their existing relationship with customers, their connectivity, data and analytics capacity to lead the market development, as alluded by Woodhouse et al. All three companies have launched to market their smart home hub services – Google® Home, Apple® HomeKit, and Amazon® Alexa, enabling customers connect and automate control of various smart home devices and set preprogrammed actions, from switching on and off lights, regulating room temperature through thermostats, to locking doors.

These technologies may well provide these tech giants with far greater insights about customer homes and their energy consumption behavior than the utilities that actually provide them electricity. These companies can exploit their direct close relationship with their customers in a number of ways:

- offering customized and personalized home energy solutions by understanding their needs around customers' homes through data aggregation, data mining, and AI;
- leveraging data from customers' online searches, purchases, social media likes and shares, to suggest services based on their previous behavior with least information search costs, thus offering a range of new services such as more efficient devices, equipment such as solar cells, battery storage, rainwater tanks;
- offering retail services through digital metering, advanced communications and big data analytics, to reduce peak demand and prices through timely feedback of data and appliance control;
- offering more itemized customer data to utilities so to better optimize electricity grids.

4.3 Integrated Utility Services – Powershop, Green Mountain Power (GMP)

Powershop is an online electricity retailer in Australia, New Zealand, and UK that seeks to differentiate itself from the conventional retailers, focusing on customer experience improvement, care for environment, and support for renewable energy. *Powershop* offers innovative yet integrated products and services that help to make electricity usage and bills more transparent, to help customers save, and options to participate in community energy. The company provides a mobile app to help customers control and understand their electricity account, to pay for power on the go, monitor their electricity usage and to get credit by providing referrals (Powershop, 2018).

Green Mountain Power (GMP) is an investor-owned utility in Vermont, serving approximately 265,000 residential and customers (Green Mountain Power, 2018). In the face of disruptive DER technologies and declining energy sales, GMP is going through the business transformation, focusing on a new way of doing business to meet the needs of customers with integrated energy services that help people use less energy and save money, while continuing to generate clean, cost-effective, and reliable power. As stated by *GMP* CEO Mary Powell, "*This is so important as we partner with customers on a new energy future that is home-, business-, and community-based and leverages the latest innovations in grid modernization to drive down costs and provide value for all customers.*"

GMP offers customers a suite of new products to meet their energy needs with new and efficient technologies, and financing options to reduce or eliminate up-front costs to the *customer.*

- Its eHome program offers free smart control to manage electric water heaters and heat pump from customer's smart phone for a home energy management and energy efficiency overhaul.
- Customers can upgrade their space and water heating with efficient electric heat pumps while also enrolling these devices in demand response to support the grid.
- *GMP* offers free home electric-vehicle chargers and discounted off-peak charging.
- Customers can install a *Tesla* Powerwall battery system for backup energy at reduced cost in return for enabling GMP to dispatch the battery to lower grid costs.
- Its new "Bring Your Own Device" program allows home battery storage owners to share their surplus power to reduce energy costs for all customers.
- Rural customers wishing to go off-grid can get *GMP's* support to plan and manage their very own independent energy system.

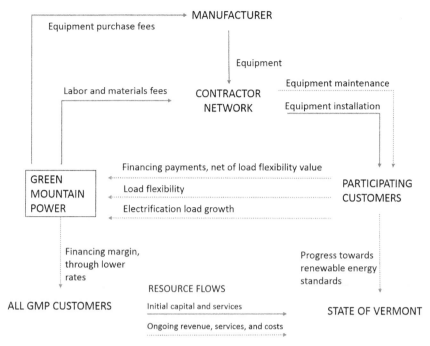

FIGURE 7.4 Illustration of resources flow in GMP's innovative pilots (RMI, 2018). *(Source: Adapted from Customer-Centric Energy transformation: A Case Study of the Opportunity with Green Mountain Power. Rocky Mountain Institute (RMI), 2018.)*

Its new financing business model as illustrated in Fig. 7.4, works as follows: GMP provides finance and procures the heat pumps to replace fossil-fuel heating systems for participating customers. Local contractors are responsible for installation. The up-front cost of the heat pumps is captured in GMP's rate base alongside other utility investments. The financing payments from participants return to the broader customer base by offsetting a portion of GMP's annual revenue requirement. These payments are structured to return a net benefit to nonparticipating customers. These new energy sales can help spread the fixed costs of the grid and keep bills affordable, particularly when the devices are managed to shift load to low-cost times of day.

GMP argues that it can deepen its business transformation through more bundled and targeted programs, combining elements of devices, financing, and rates offerings to encourage active energy management and demand flexibility, adopt renewable energy and energy efficiency products, and fuel switching from fossil-fuel based to electric products. The success in this transformation will be rooted in its ability to understand customer needs so to provide added value to its customers.

Looking beyond Vermont, the role of future utilities will inarguably be all of these:

- As an "energy conductor" to help create a more efficient and optimized electric system, leveraging customer-sited resources to the benefit of all customers (Blansfield et al., 2017).
- As an Energy-as-a-Service company that applies innovative technology and data management in ways that give customers more control of electricity consumption through customizable pricing and cutting-edge energy management options (Warwick, 2017).
- As an "energy enabler" that enables "energy solutions" and in many cases "home solutions" – enable customers to optimize their energy positions (PwC, 2014)
- As a combination of supplier, integrator, enabler, and optimizer, to address customers' needs through proactive engagement and integrated products and services.

Table 7.1 lists the key value proposition, customer benefits, opportunities, and barriers to the adoption of these models.

5. CONCLUSIONS

In a new era of choice and energy consumer engagement, this chapter first summarizes and classifies the growing range of products and services available to consumers. It then presents some possible models for the process of consumer decision making toward improving their energy service provision, given these opportunities, yet also their complexities, uncertainties, and hence risks. Through this self-selection process, we now see growing diversity across energy consumers, from professional consumers, prosumers, and prosumagers, and perhaps more, through to nonsumers at the other end of the "engagement" spectrum.

The consumer challenges presented have also inspired a new generation of service providers that strive to better facilitate consumer decision and choice making, and hence capture the value that such consumer engagement can create, than existing industry players have achieved to date. The provision of these products and services requires an intimate understanding of individual customer needs and their decision making process, to assist in acquiring information and resources, removing barriers, thus reaching a solution that is mutually beneficial. Those businesses who can innovate to offer value-added products and services that allow simple and fast interaction, personalized and customized services, and integrated

Table 7.1 Value proposition, customer benefits, opportunities, and barriers to adoption of consumer-centric service models

	Simple and no frills, e.g., OhmConnect	Customized and personalized, e.g., Wattcost, Opower, Bidgely	Integrated services, e.g., Powershop, GMP
Value proposition	Simple and easy-to-use interface, fast services; Reduced transaction costs to serve a large number of small customers as a bundle; Engagement of customers and utilities as the cocreator of value	Personalized and customized services; Leverage with companies' other products and services; Insights into customer consumption behavior and even decision-making process; Low customer acquisition costs	Integrated and hassle-free services; Bundled services combining home energy management, transport, rates and financing; Engagement of customers and utilities to cocreate value; Reduce asset investment costs
Benefits to customers	Save electricity and earn; Contribution to reduce emission; Satisfaction from being responsible users	Full control of smart and automated homes; Personalized and customized services; More comfort and convenience	One-stop shop for financing, installation, maintenance; Bundled and integrated services
Opportunities	Considerable market potential to engage more energy consumers; replicate business model to expand to other regions	Leverage with existing user base and user data; Lock-in potential; potential multiple service offerings to customers and utilities	Leverage with existing customer base and user data; Increased revenue stream; Early mover in utility transformation
Barriers to adoption	Small savings to customers; Relying on voluntary participation	Costs to hardware and systems; lack of compatibility among providers	Competition from other providers; trial-and-error process

solutions for consumers seem best placed to succeed in an increasingly competitive distributed energy future.

To conclude, utilities, potential new product and service providers, and regulators and policy makers will all need to take into consideration the psychological and behavioral characteristics of consumers when establishing business strategies and policies to assist consumers to maximize their personal as well as larger social outcomes.

REFERENCES

Attali, S., Bush, E., Michel, A., 2009. Factors Influencing the Penetration of Energy Efficient Electrical Appliances Into National Markets in Europe. Market Transformation Programme, Defra.

Bidgely, 2018. Bidgely Solutions to Attract and Retain Customers. Bidgely, Inc.

Blansfield, J., Wood, L., Katofsky, R., Stafford, B., Waggoner, D., Givens, S., Mork, R., 2017. Value-added electricity services: new roles for utilities and third-party providers. In: Schwartz, L. (Ed.), Future Electric Utility Regulation. Lawrence Berkeley National Laboratory.

Chang, C., 2018. ShineHub offers 'fixed rate, free access' solar and battery plan. News.com.au.

Dudovskiy, J., 2013. Consumer decision making process: a detailed analysis.

Edwards, J., 2018. Victorian government offers cash incentive to help households get better energy deal. ABC News.

EEnergy Informer, 2018. New Business Models at the Grid's Edge and Beyond, p. 18. Fereidoon P. Sioshansi, PhD, Walnut Creek, CA.

Engel, J., Blackwell, R., Miniard, P., 1995. Consumer Behaviour. Dryden, Florida.

Finley, K., 2015. The internet of anything: the system that pays you to use less electricity. Wired.

Forcey, T., 2017. Can Facebook help you make your home more sustainable? The Conversation.

Green Mountain Power, 2018. Products to help you use less energy and save. Green Mountain Power.

GreenSync, 2018. Creating markets through the decentralised energy exchange. GreenSync.

Gui, E.M., MacGill, I., 2018. Typology of future clean energy communities: an exploratory structure, opportunities, and challenges. Energy Res. Soc. Sci. 35, 94–107.

Gui, E.M., Diesendorf, M., MacGill, I., 2017. Distributed energy infrastructure paradigm: community micorgrids in a new institutional economics context. Renew. Sust. Energ. Rev. 72, 1355–1365.

Gyamfi, S., Krumdieck, S., 2011. Price, environment and security: exploring multi-modal motivation in voluntary residential peak demand response. Energy Policy 39, 2993–3004.

Ha, H., Janda, S., Muthaly, S., 2010. Development of brand equity: evaluation of four alternative models. Serv. Ind. J. 30, 911–928.

Han, E., 2017. NSW families paying $400 more under 'time of use' electricity plans, new research shows. The Sydney Morning Herald.

Hargreaves, T., Hielscher, S., Seyfang, G., 2013. Grassroots innovations in community energy: the role of intermediaries in niche development. Glob. Environ. Chang. 23, 868–880.

Hill, J.S., 2015. GTM identifies 120 major home energy players. Gleantechnica.

Hu, Z., Kim, J.-h., Wang, J., Byrne, J., 2015. Review of dynamic pricing programs in the U.S. and Europe: status quo and policy recommendations. Renew. Sust. Energ. Rev. 42, 743–751.

Huhtala, A., 2010. Income effects and the inconvenience of private provision of public goods for bads: the case of recycling in Finland. Ecol. Econ. 69, 1675–1681.

Kanagal, N.B., 2016. An extended model of behhavioral process in consumer decision making. Int. J. Mark. Stud. 8, 87–93.

Kelly-Detwiler, P., 2017. Sonnen: changing the way we buy, store, and well electricity. Forbes.

Kotler, P., 1997. Marketing Management: Analysis, Planning, Implementation and Control. Prentice Hall, India.

Leuschner, P., 2017. Utilities must proactively engage their customers-here's how. Smart Energy International. Spintelligent (Pty) Ltd.

Market Research Future, 2018. Smart home energy management device market research report—global forecast 2023. Market Research Future.

Mayoh, L., 2017. Using solar power to reduce your electricity bill. News Corp.

McNamara, S., Grubb, M., 2011. The pyschlogical underpinning of the consumer role in energy demand and carbon abatement. Electricity Policy Research Group Working Paper 1110 Cambridge.

McNary, B., 2008. Market penetration of ENERGY STAR qualified appliances: an analysis of various predictor variables. In: ACEEE Summer Study on Energy Efficiency in Buildings. D&R International.

Navigant Research, 2018. Home Energy Reports, Digital Tools, Standalone HEM, and Networked HEM, Market Data: Home Energy Management. Navigant Research.

Ohmconnect, 2018. Small changes add up to a big difference.

Orchison, K., 2018. Coolibah commentary. Coolibah.

Parkinson, G., 2018. Zibelman: old market rules make no sense. RenewEconomy.

Pongiglione, F., 2011. Climate Change and Individual Decision Making: An Examination of Knowledge, Risk Perception, Self-Interest, and Their Interplay. Universita di Bologna.

Powershop, 2018. 2018 Powershop Australia Pty Ltd.

PwC, 2014. Utility of the Future a Customer-Led Shift in the Electricity Sector. An Australian Context. PwC.

RedBackTech, 2018. Powering Your Future. Redback Technologies.

RMI, 2018. From Customer-Centric Energy Transformation: A Case Study of the Opportunity With Green Mountain Power. Rocky Mountain Institute.

Saadeh, O., 2015. Energy in the Connected Home 2015: Technology Evolution, Landscape and Distribution Strategies. Grid Edge. GTM Research.

Schiffman, L.G., Kanuk, L.L., 2007. Consumer Behavior, ninth ed. Prentice Hall, New Jersey.

Smith, A., Hargreaves, T., Hielscher, S., Martiskainen, M., Seyfang, G., 2016. Making the most of community energies: three perspectives on grassroots innovation. Environ. Plan. A 48, 407–432.

Thaler, R.H., Sunstein, C.R., 2008. Nudge: Improving Decisions About Health, Wealth, and Happiness. Yale University Press, New Haven, CT.

Vorrath, S., 2018. Victoria networks ask if solar households should pay for grid upgrades. This was the response…. One Step Off the Grid.

Warwick, M., 2017. Introduction as Energy as a Service (EaaS). Pacific Northwest National Laboratory, Tampa, FL.

Wattcost, 2017. New technology to make your home energy intelligent so you always pay less. Wattcost.

Wokutch, A.S.V., 2011. The role of non-utility service providers in smart grid development. J. Telecommun. High Technol. Law 9, 532–571.

PART 2

How Regulatory Policy Will Impact the Evolution of Services and the Speed and Spread of Disruptions

Fair, Equitable, and Efficient Tariffs in the Presence of Distributed Energy Resources

Scott Burger*, Ian Schneider[†], Audun Botterud[†],
Ignacio Pérez-Arriaga*[,‡,§]
*MIT Energy Initiative, Massachusetts Institute of Technology, Cambridge, MA, United States
[†]Laboratory for Information and Decision Systems, Massachusetts Institute of Technology, Cambridge, MA, United States
[‡]Florence School of Regulation, Florence, Italy
[§]Institute for Research in Technology, Comillas University, Madrid, Spain

1. INTRODUCTION

Utilities, regulators, and academics no longer debate whether or not distributed energy resources (DERs) will reshape the power sector; they now debate what form this transformation will take and when it will take place. At the center of the new vision for the power sector is the consumer. As highlighted in the introduction to this book, DERs give consumers new options for how to source and manage their electricity and offer utilities and service providers new means to provide better services to their customers. This trend can potentially deliver significant benefits to electricity consumers by lowering costs, increasing reliability, lowering emissions, and enhancing customer choice. However, if integrated poorly, DERs can substantially increase power system costs and emissions (Fares and Webber, 2017; Pérez-Arriaga et al., 2016; Schmalensee et al., 2015).

Regulators, policy makers, consumer advocates, and utilities are searching for solutions to ensure that DER integration increases – rather than decreases – the social net benefits of the power system. While many regulatory and market changes will be required to efficiently integrate DERs, changes to tariff design are one of the primary tools for increasing the benefits of customer engagement and DER adoption (Pérez-Arriaga et al., 2016, chap. 4). The New York Department of Public Service concluded that value-driven DER adoption requires "more precise price signals for these new products and services that will, over time, convey increasingly granular system value further enabling increasingly accurate compensation and driving

Consumer, Prosumer, Prosumager
https://doi.org/10.1016/B978-0-12-816835-6.00008-5

155

informed and therefore effective investment decisions" (NYDPS, 2016). New York is not alone. In 2017, regulators in 45 of 50 U.S. states and the District of Columbia opened dockets related to tariff design or made changes to tariff design to better enable socially beneficial DER integration (North Carolina Clean Energy Technology Center, 2018). Similarly, in November 2016, the European Commission issued a sweeping set of rulings designed to put consumers at the center of the European power system, and tariff design was central to the new rulings (European Commission, 2016).

Of course, economics is not the only consideration in tariff design. In order for regulators to adopt more efficient tariff designs, these tariffs must be socially and politically acceptable. The perception of the fairness and equity of a tariff are critical aspects of whether or not the tariff will be accepted, and fairness considerations have historically been critical components of regulatory decision making (Jones and Mann, 2001). For example, both the Massachusetts Department of Public Utilities (DPU) and the New York Department of Public Service list fairness as a core principle for tariff design, and the Massachusetts DPU recently cited fairness in a recent ruling denying a utility's petition for an increase in fixed charges (Massachusetts DPU, 2016; New York DPS, 2016). Similarly, the Nevada Public Utilities Commission recently overturned a previously approved increase in fixed charges, citing, fairness considerations (Nevada PUC, 2017). These anecdotes are supported by the fact that equity is central to commonly cited tariff design principles (Bonbright, 1961; Pérez-Arriaga et al., 2013, chap. 8).

This chapter builds on existing literature to examine the issue of whether or not efficient tariffs are fair and equitable.[1] While many scholars have considered the economic and emissions implications of efficient tariffs and their relationship to DER adoption, comparatively few have examined fairness and equity considerations. This chapter aims to fill this gap, with a special focus on the equity and fairness of efficient and inefficient tariffs in the presence of DERs.

This chapter provides a clear definition of several key equity and fairness considerations in the context of electricity rate design and proposes distinct mechanisms for improving each consideration. Different groups and individuals often have different views of what is fair and equitable, and these views are sometimes grouped together or blurred in discussion regarding fairness and equity. The clear boundaries around the considerations we describe

---

[1]Pérez-Arriaga et al. (2013, p. 402) define equity as meaning that "equal power consumption should be charged equally, regardless of the nature of the user or the use to which the energy is put." Section 4 highlights a number of aspects of the debate on fairness and expands upon how fairness and equity are used in this chapter.

enable a better understanding of how efficient tariffs will impact equity and fairness. This chapter uses illustrative examples to highlight how properly designed, efficient tariffs can improve equity and fairness along many dimensions in the presence of DER adoption. Moving to more efficient tariff designs is critical to ensuring that customer choice and the resulting customer stratification benefit society as a whole, rather than a single customer or set of customers at the expense of others. As this chapter highlights, in many cases, tariffs can be made more efficient without compromising equity and fairness.

The chapter is organized into eight sections:

- Section 2 summarizes the existing literature on the equity and fairness of electricity tariffs.
- Section 3 provides a brief overview of the economic theory of efficient tariff design.
- Section 4 outlines three key aspects of equity and fairness in the power system context. While the three considerations outlined are not novel, they provide clear boundaries between commonly discussed ideas of equity and fairness in the context of tariff design.
- Section 5 highlights how one particular aspect of equity – what we term "allocative equity" – is always improved by improving economic efficiency.
- Section 6 discusses how efficient tariffs often improve distributional equity with respect to key vulnerable customer groups. Section 6 highlights the fact that, while efficient tariffs may have "unfair" impacts on some vulnerable customers, there are many mechanisms for alleviating these distributional concerns that are superior to today's tariffs.
- Section 7 discusses the fairness and equity challenges that must be overcome in transitioning from one tariff structure to another.
- Section 8 concludes.

2. LITERATURE REVIEW

The existing literature on the fairness and equity of tariffs has focused on three primary issues. First, some stakeholders have argued that more efficient tariff designs are inequitable or unfair. Second, an alternative set of scholars – primarily academics and economists – have taken an opposing stance, generally arguing that efficient tariffs are indeed more equitable and fair. Finally, in response to the rapidly increasing penetration of rooftop solar photovoltaics (PV), some scholars have examined the extent to which policy support for rooftop solar PV is fair or equitable. This has also been a primary focus of regulatory proceedings in recent years.

Some power sector stakeholders – primarily select consumer advocates and trade groups – have advocated for maintaining today's largely time-invariant and volumetric[2] tariffs. These stakeholders argue that efficient prices will be fundamentally unfair and/or inequitable, arguing that efficient tariffs will have undesirable bill impacts for certain classes of consumers (e.g., low-income, fixed-income, or rural customers) (AARP et al., 2010; Southern Environmental Law Center et al., 2015; Solar Energy Industries Association et al., 2017; Alexander, 2010). These stakeholders argue that today's temporal and locationally invariant tariffs protect vulnerable customer groups. Moreover, they argue that at-risk customer groups will not be able to respond to efficient prices and would face higher and more volatile bills as a result (Alexander, 2010). Others take a more precautionary approach, noting that, because real-time pricing may harm some vulnerable customers, real-time pricing should be offered with caution and only to certain groups (Horowitz and Lave, 2014).

Focusing primarily on time-varying versus flat[3] rates, many scholars have noted that today's flat tariffs are inequitable, as they imbed cross subsidies between customers that consume more power during high price hours and those that consume less (Simshauser and Downer, 2016; Faruqui, 2012; Hogan, 2010; Faruqui et al., 2010). In the short term, these "expensive" customers pay less than their cost of service, while other customers pay more. In the long term, customers that tend to consume at times of high system demand drive greater need for investment in system infrastructure, which drives up costs for all users. Further, they argue that concerns over the distributional impacts of efficient tariffs are exaggerated, as, depending on the local circumstances, vulnerable customers will not be harmed on average by time-varying rates (Simshauser and Downer, 2016; Faruqui, 2012). For example, Hledik and Greenstein (2016) highlight how demand charges do not systematically harm low income customers in the dataset they examined. Similarly, Borenstein (2012, 2016) shows that volume of electricity consumption is imperfectly correlated with income, and argues that, as a result, increasing fixed charges[4] won't necessarily increase bills for low-income customers. Borenstein (2013) discusses an opt-in time-varying tariff design, showing how the introduction of this option is unlikely to

[2]Volumetric refers to charges that are based on the volume of energy consumed. That is, the charges are primarily in a dollar-per-kilowatt-hour form.
[3]Flat rates refer to time and locationally invariant tariffs.
[4]That is, a charge on a customer's bill that does not scale with quantity of energy consumed or peak demand.

significantly impact those that do not opt-in. Pérez-Arriaga et al. (2016) and Convery et al. (2017), among others, argue that economic efficiency should be the guiding principle for tariff design in the face of distributed resources, as efficient tariffs are likely to minimize cross subsidies between customers with and without distributed resources. Neuteleers et al. (2017) take a broader view, outlining different theoretical definitions of fairness and different consumer perceptions of fairness. Neuteleers et al. (2017) present a strong overview of different concepts of fairness and conclude that dynamic tariffs may be perceived as more or less fair than flat tariffs and other tariff designs, depending on the context and implementation.

The increasing penetration of rooftop solar PV has led many researchers to examine the distributional impacts of this adoption. Nelson et al. (2011, 2012) argue that the mechanism for supporting rooftop solar PV in Australia is regressive, benefitting high-income customers at the expense of low-income customers. Also focusing on Australia, Simpson and Clifton (2016) use surveys to explore sentiments of Western Australians surrounding the "justice" of rooftop solar support policies; they show that many Western Australians support rooftop solar despite concerns about the inequity of these policies. In the U.S., utilities have repeatedly argued that current subsidy policies for rooftop solar are unfair and inequitable (Rule, 2015). This stems from a host of economic analyses highlighting the potential for cost shifts from solar owners to nonsolar owners (Kassakian et al., 2011; Schmalensee et al., 2015; Borenstein, 2017).

This chapter expands upon this body of literature on equity considerations of electricity tariffs in two ways. First, this chapter clearly articulates three component parts (allocative, distributional, and transitional equity) of the equity and fairness discussion. By breaking down the discussion into these three parts, this chapter is able to propose more targeted solutions to the identified challenges. Second, this chapter extends the discussion of previous authors to account for the impact of DERs beyond solar PV and pricing structures beyond time-varying pricing. Specifically, this chapter expands the conversation by explaining how three key features of more efficient rates – time and location varying, and higher fixed charges – impact equity and fairness.

3. A REVIEW OF ECONOMICALLY EFFICIENT ELECTRICITY TARIFFS

Tariffs recover four broad classes of costs from customers: energy, capacity and ancillary services, networks, and policy and regulatory costs. Energy costs vary over time and space due to the changing marginal cost of power generation, the physical laws that govern the flow of power over transmission and distribution networks, and the need to keep electricity supply and demand balanced at all times and locations (Schweppe et al., 1988). At any given point in time and location in the power system, the efficient energy price is the short run marginal cost of delivering power to that point, adjusted for losses, congestions, and the potential for scarcity (Rivier and Pérez-Arriaga, 1993; Hogan, 2013).[5]

Capacity and ancillary services[6] costs stem from various forms of forward commitments to enhance the reliability of energy supply. Generation capacity costs are driven by the desired margin of available generation capacity over power demand required over a period of time.[7] Under certain conditions, short run marginal energy prices can cover the full operating and investment costs of the generating plants in a given power system. However, these conditions are rarely met in practice for a variety of reasons (Read et al., 1999; Vázquez et al., 2002; Joskow, 2008). As a result, in many locations throughout the world, regulators have implemented some form of capacity remuneration mechanism. These mechanisms pay generators to maintain a desired margin of available capacity above demand. These capacity mechanisms have the effect of suppressing short run marginal energy prices below the level necessary to support the level of installed firm capacity in the system. Where capacity remuneration mechanisms are in place, an efficient tariff would include a charge that reflects the impacts that a customer's consumption or production decisions during times of generation scarcity have on future capacity procurement costs (Joskow and Tirole, 2007; Pérez-Arriaga et al., 2016; Mays and Klabjan, 2017). This charge would resemble a peak-coincident demand charge.

[5]The nature of the efficient short-run energy price is clear, but questions remain regard default notification strategies for time-varying prices (Schneider and Sunstein, 2017). Transaction costs and behavioral biases impact the optimal type and frequency of price notifications.

[6]The costs of ancillary services, that is, short-term operating reserves and other services required for system security, typically make up less than 1% of a consumer's bill. This chapter therefore focuses primarily on capacity and largely ignores cost allocation for ancillary services.

[7]In most thermal-generation-dominated system, capacity requirements have historically been driven by peak demand. As variable renewable resources and energy-constrained resources gain market share in power systems globally, firm capacity requirements will increasingly be driven by the desired margin of generation capacity during periods of minimum available generation capacity margin over demand. Due to the variability of many renewable resources, these periods will not necessarily align with the periods of peak demand.

While network costs are driven in the long run by the need to develop network infrastructure to meet peak injections and/or withdrawals, the costs of existing network infrastructure largely do not change in the short term with the amount of energy consumed or produced (Borenstein, 2016; Pérez-Arriaga et al., 2016). Differences in energy prices at different locations in the network can recover only a small fraction of network costs due to the significant impact of a variety of nonconvex costs and constraints, including:

- regulatory, political, engineering, and environmental constraints on network investment decisions;
- the discrete nature of network investments; and
- economies of scale (Pérez-Arriaga et al., 1995).

In areas of growing demand, peak-coincident demand-based charges, that is, charges as a function of a network user's demand during times of peak network utilization, can improve economic efficiency by signaling a network user's contribution to future network costs (Pérez-Arriaga et al., 2016). It is critical to distinguish these forward-looking charges from more generic demand-based charges. Many argue that, because networks are developed to meet peak demand, demand-based charges are "cost reflective" and efficient. This is a common misconception. Residual costs do not change with respect to peak demand; if peak demand is not growing or driving new network investments, peak demand-based charges do not improve efficiency. In locations in which forward-looking, peak-coincident charges are in place, these charges will recover some, but not all, network costs.

All network costs that are not recovered through differences in energy charges and through forward-looking peak-coincident network charges are referred to as "residual" costs. Designing efficiency maximizing charges for residual network cost recovery is extremely challenging. Depending on the adopted assumptions made, different methods for residual cost allocation vary.[8] Some of the key assumptions are:

1. the benefits that customers receive from connecting to the system;
2. the wealth elasticity of electricity demand for different customers;
3. the ability of customers to avoid paying for residual costs by self-generating or defecting from the grid; and
4. the information available to the regulator regarding assumptions 1, 2, and 3.

[8]See Joskow (2007) for a discussion of the impacts of several of these assumptions.

For a wide range of reasonable assumptions, fixed charges are the most efficient mechanism of residual cost recovery. This chapter assumes that the utility must serve all customers in its service territory that desire service and that customers can't avoid paying for residual network costs by defecting from the grid.[9] The latter assumption is generally true in practice today, as the costs of grid defection are prohibitively large for the vast majority of customers (Khalilpour and Vassallo, 2015; Hittinger and Siddiqui, 2017); for a wide range of fixed charges, the benefits of connection are still greater than the costs for essentially all customers. Under these assumptions, the welfare maximizing method of residual cost allocation is through "Ramsey-like"[10] fixed charges, in which residual costs are allocated in inverse proportion to elasticity of demand.

Any residual cost allocation method that has no effect on marginal consumption or production decisions can be considered equally economically efficient (Borenstein, 2016). Critically, however, wealth effects mean that fixed charges for some customers may impact marginal consumption decisions; that is, an efficient allocation would account for the fact that higher fixed charges may reduce total electricity consumption and welfare more for poor customers than for wealthy ones. In practice, wealth and/or income effects can be substantial. For example, the European Commission estimates that at least 50 million Europeans struggle to pay their energy bills or heat their homes (Csiba et al., 2016). However, these effects are also very challenging to measure in practice.

Finally, policy and regulatory costs are any taxes or charges designed to recover costs associated with programs like energy efficiency, renewables support, or general taxation. While some policy costs scale directly with the amount of energy consumed or produced,[11] the majority of policy costs are independent of the energy that a customer consumes or produces. Any essentially fixed policy costs are also best recovered through a nondistortive, fixed, per-customer charge following "Ramsey-like" principles.

In sum, an economically efficient customer bill would look approximately like the bill in Fig. 8.1.

The possibility of self-generation and grid defection (or "prosuming," "prosumaging," or "nonsuming") challenges much of the existing economic literature on efficient tariff design. The ability for customers to defect from the grid gives electricity provision many characteristics of "club goods" in

[9]This could be the case, for instance, if residual costs are recovered through taxation. It could also occur if utilities use disconnection fees to recover residual costs.
[10]Following from Frank Ramsey's seminal work on taxation (Ramsey, 1927).
[11]For example, the costs of renewable portfolio standards.

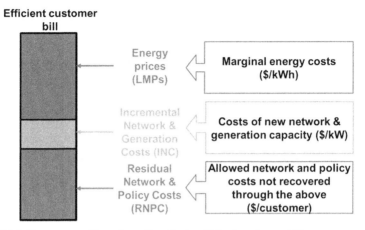

FIGURE 8.1 The composition of an allocatively efficient customer bill.

economic literature. However, there are limits to drawing upon club goods literature, and the presence of DERs creates many interesting challenges that must be explored in future work.

While the exact details of an efficient tariff will vary across systems, certain recommendations are robust to all systems. These are:

1. Volumetric prices should closely mirror marginal energy prices and should vary throughout time and across locations.
2. Fixed charges should be utilized to recover network and policy costs that are not recovered through efficient, cost-reflective short run charges (that is, residual costs).

This chapter takes these recommendations – that efficient tariffs should feature time- and location-varying volumetric prices and non-negligible fixed charges – as a starting point. It then examines certain equity considerations associated with their implementation.

In order to explore the fairness and equity of efficient tariffs and DER adoption, we must first define these concepts in the context of this paper. Drawing from economic theory and the existing literature on equity and fairness, we define certain aspects of these concepts in the context of electricity tariff design in Section 4.

4. ALLOCATIVE EQUITY, DISTRIBUTIONAL EQUITY, AND TRANSITIONAL EQUITY

Different stakeholders in the power sector may have dramatically different views of what is fair or equitable (Harvey and Braun, 1996). Indeed, there are a multitude of ways to define fairness and equity with respect to tariffs

(Neuteleers et al., 2017). In general, regulators must attempt to balance these varying views to achieve an acceptable design at least economic cost. For example, some may consider that a tariff in which all customers within a service territory pay the same per-kilowatt-hour (kWh) charge – regardless of when or where they consume – to be equitable. Many scholars have noted that tariffs of this nature benefit some customers at the expense of others (that is, some customer pay less than the costs that they drive, while others pay more) and, relatedly, that meeting this definition of equity comes at a significant societal cost.[12] Of course, others may consider tariffs of this nature to be inequitable for these reasons and others. Making informed tariff design decisions requires understanding these various tradeoffs.

The purpose of this chapter is not to definitively define equity and fairness. Rather, this chapter examines the potential tradeoffs between economically efficient tariffs and certain key aspects of equity and fairness. This chapter explores three equity considerations with respect to electricity tariff designs: allocative equity, distributional equity, and transitional equity.

In this chapter, we define an **allocatively equitable** tariff as a tariff that treats identical customers equally. Our definition of allocative equity therefore aligns with common definitions of equality (Isaac et al., 1991) and, in particular, those of Bonbright (1961) and Pérez-Arriaga et al. (2013, chap. 8). In practice, this has two key implications:

1. Marginal consumption or production decisions are charged or paid according to the marginal costs or values they create.
2. Residual costs are allocated according to customer characteristics that are not impacted by their short-term electricity consumption or production decisions. In other words, one customer's behavior cannot cause another customer to pay more or less residual costs.

Because customers located in different areas of a given network or consuming at different times are not electrically identical, this definition does not mean that all customers pay the same rate for electricity. This implies that two customers connected at the same location and consuming at the same times would pay the same marginal rates for electricity, and that no cross-subsidies of marginal costs between customers exist.[13] Many previous scholars have assessed how time-invariant tariffs create cross-subsidies between customers and thus violate this concept of equity (see, for example, Faruqui et al., 2010).

[12]See the many citations in the Literature Review section.
[13]That is, if one customer drives a cost, no other customer pays for that cost. This eliminates, for example, cross-subsidies between peaky and nonpeaky customers.

Of course, as noted in Section 3, marginal cost-based charging does not recover residual costs. By definition, residual costs aren't caused by the actions of any one customer and therefore can't be charged to those who cause them. Identical customers would, according to this definition, have an identical allocation of residual costs; this meets definitions of distributive justice or equality based on equal starting points (Rawls, 2001; Dworkin, 2000). If a tariff allows a customer to alter their contribution to residual cost recovery by changing their consumption or production, the tariff would not be charging or paying according to marginal costs or values. Therefore, the second implication follows from the first. Tariffs that allow customers to alter their contribution to residual costs based on consumption or production decisions allow customers to deviate from the equal starting point allocation based on factors other than cost or value.

This definition of equity provides regulators leeway to define which customers are identical. For instance, regulators could use wealth or other customer characteristics to determine residual cost allocations. Section 5 delves into this issue in more detail, and highlights how improving economic efficiency always improves allocative equity.

This chapter defines a tariff structure as **distributionally equitable or fair** if it meets locally defined standards of social justice[14] with respect to the distribution of goods between vulnerable and nonvulnerable customers.[15] Of course, as noted, other definitions of fairness exist; nonetheless, here we focus on the issue of whether or not vulnerable customer groups pay an acceptable amount for electricity service, as this is a critical consideration for many regulators.

As Hogan (2010) and Neuteleers et al. (2017) describe, society's preferences for equitable distribution do not necessarily imply specific goals or preferences for how to distribute individual goods; for example, how to price electricity (Young, 1995). Practically, however, regulators and policy makers in many power systems explicitly or implicitly price electricity in such a way as to meet social justice outcomes. Indeed, scholars have long recognized that one of the key regulatory functions in electric power is to distribute benefits among members of society – a function typically associated with the government (Posner, 1971; Newbery, 2018). For example,

---

[14]Throughout this paper, fairness, social justice, and distributional equity are used interchangeably.

[15]Vulnerable customers in this context refer broadly to any customer group that has been defined as needing electricity price and/or bill protections in a given location. Low-income, fixed-income, and rural customers are the most common types of vulnerable customers.

the state of New York funds programs to ensure that low-income customers spend less than 6% of their total income on electricity (New York State, 2017), and the state of California offers discounts on electricity and gas prices to low-income customers (CPUC, 2018).

To the extent that a certain tariff scheme meets local and regional goals designed to achieve social justice, this chapter considers this scheme to be distributionally equitable or fair. Efficiency maximizing tariffs would, in theory, incorporate wealth effects into residual cost allocation, achieving some socially desirable and welfare enhancing redistribution. However, this does not imply that efficient, allocatively equitable tariffs will always meet local targets for a fair distribution of goods.

Finally, this chapter notes that in a transition from one tariff structure to another, there are also likely to be **transitional equity challenges**, as some consumers experience higher costs and others lower costs. In the context of electricity tariffs, the Pareto criterion[16] for a transition states that a transition should be made only if at least one customer will experience lower electricity bills while no customers experience higher bills. On the other extreme is the Kaldor-Hicks criterion,[17] which states that a transition should be made if it is net welfare improving, regardless of whether certain customers are worse off. In practice, tariff structure transitions will not satisfy the Pareto criterion. Tariff design changes may negatively impact the value of assets, and, in some cases, create stranded assets.[18] This may violate certain concepts of fairness to legitimate expectation and holds the potential to create political economy opposition to new tariff designs. To the extent that regulators or policy makers wish to address these transitional impacts, they should be addressed separately from allocative and distributional equity considerations.

Of course, these three equity considerations are not intended to cover the entire scope of possible definitions of equity. However, they are commonly discussed concepts, and thus deserve special attention.

Sections 5–7 provide more in-depth discussion of allocative equity, distributional equity, and transitional equity, respectively, in the context of electricity tariff reform.

---

[16]See Hochman and Rodgers (1969).

[17]See Hicks (1940) and Kaldor (1939).

[18]For example, the value of a home may decrease due to an increase in energy bills. Similarly, tariff design changes may render an investment in solar photovoltaics (PV) unprofitable, stranding the asset.

5. THE ALLOCATIVE EQUITY OF ELECTRICITY TARIFFS

The following subsections explore three examples to better understand the allocative equity of different tariff designs. In order to maintain consistency and provide more clarity, many examples draw on a common, hypothetical power system. For simplicity and without loss of generality, this paper assumes that the system is run by a vertically integrated utility, called Investor-Owned Utility, or IOU for short. The concepts described in this paper hold for all utility types (for example, municipal utilities or co-operative utilities), and are not specific to investor-owned utilities.

IOU's system is depicted in Fig. 8.2. IOU's system has three meshed nodes (nodes A, B, and C) in its distribution system and two radial distribution feeders (one connected to node A and one to node B). During both day and night, demand at node B is 30 megawatts (MW) and demand at node C is 50 MW. All customers within IOU's system are identical. For simplicity, IOU's meshed distribution power lines are lossless, and each line (i.e., lines A-B, B-C, and A-C) has equal impedance. Line B-C has a 20-MW

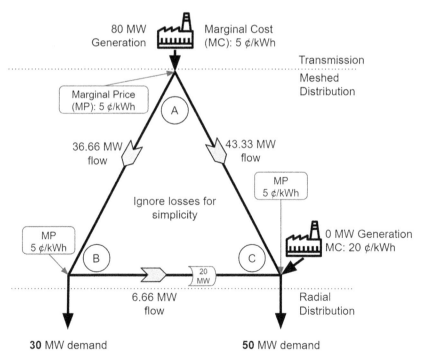

FIGURE 8.2 Investor-Owned Utility's (IOUs) system and power flows with no distributed generation.

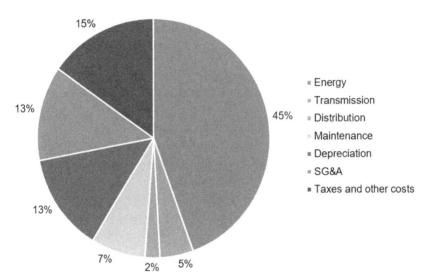

FIGURE 8.3 Cost structure of IOU. *(Data source: FERC (2017).)*

transfer capacity – that is, the line will become congested at 20 MW. The other lines each have 60-MW transfer capacities. The power flows are shown in Fig. 8.2. The marginal cost of generation coming from the transmission grid is 5 cents per kilowatt-hour (kWh). Because this transmission-connected generator serves all of IOU's customers day and night and because there are no losses or congestions, the marginal prices at nodes B and C are 5 ¢/kWh. There is an additional generator connected to node C with a high marginal cost of 20 ¢/kWh. Because of its high marginal cost, this generator is not currently producing any power.

In this example and those that follow in Section 5, all power flows and marginal costs are calculated using a simple direct current, lossless, linearized optimal power flow model. The formulation of this model is outside of the scope of this chapter.

It is assumed that IOU's cost structure is identical to the average investor-owned utility in the U.S., as depicted in Fig. 8.3.[19] 45% of IOU's costs are related to the production and procurement of energy; 27% are related to network asset investment, maintenance, and depreciation; 13% are related to sales, general, and administrative (SG&A) costs; finally, 15% are taxes and other policy and regulatory costs. For the sake of simplicity, this chapter assumes that all network and depreciation costs, SG&A costs, and taxes and

[19]Average investor-owned utility cost from FERC (2017).

other costs are essentially fixed in the short term.[20] Thus, 45% of costs vary in the short term with the quantity of energy consumed, while 55% do not.

The following sections explore the equity and fairness of efficient and inefficient tariffs in the presence of DERs.

To analyze the typical tariff structure today, Section 5 first examines a situation in which IOU's tariffs are volumetric. The energy price for IOU's customers is 5¢/kWh and the charge for all the remaining costs is 6¢/kWh.[21] IOU therefore recovers $96,000 in energy costs and $115,200 of residual costs per day, which will be assumed to be its regulated revenue requirement.[22] For the sake of simplicity, with the exception of one example, we assume that demand in IOU's system is not growing. This chapter thus ignores the forward-looking, peak-coincident charges for network and generation capacity expansion in most examples.

This type of volumetric tariff is very common. Despite broad agreement on the benefits of efficient tariffs and widespread deployment of the infrastructure needed to calculate and communicate these tariffs,[23] less than 0.5% of residential customers and less than 5% of commercial customers in the United States even have the option of being exposed to real-time prices today (EIA, 2017). Instead, the vast majority of electricity consumers are on time and locationally invariant ("flat") electricity prices that recover residual policy and network costs via volumetric (that is dollar per kilowatt-hour) charges.

5.1 Allocatively Equitable Tariffs Minimize Network Cost Shifts

Let us consider a situation in which customers at node B adopt solar. Fig. 8.4 depicts the flows and marginal prices at each node when customers at node B have adopted a moderate amount of solar (10 MW). For simplicity, the solar system produces an average of 10 MW for all 12 daylight hours.

---

[20]This is a reasonable assumption, although some costs are likely not entirely fixed. For example, certain taxes and maintenance costs may vary with the volume of energy consumption. Network and depreciation costs vary in the long term according to peak demand, but are invariant in the short term. Similarly, SG&A costs, taxes, and policy costs are related to the total size of the utility, and thus may vary in the long term but are not likely to vary in the short term.

[21]5¢/kWh covers 45% of IOU's costs, thus the remaining 55% of the costs are recovered through a 6¢/kWh charge.

[22]5¢/kWh for 80 MW during 24 hours for energy costs, and 6¢/kWh for 80 MW during 24 hours for residual costs.

[23]47% of American households and 45% of American commercial properties have advanced metering infrastructure (EIA, 2017)

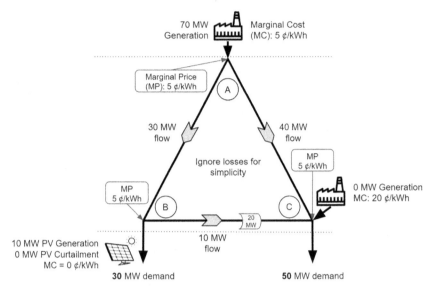

FIGURE 8.4 Moderate solar adoption at node B.

All solar produced at node B is consumed locally, and any additional power demand must be produced at node A. Thus, the marginal prices at nodes B and C are still 5 ¢/kWh.

An allocatively equitable tariff design would allocate IOU's residual costs through fixed, per customer charges. If these charges also accounted for each customer's wealth elasticity of demand, they would be economically efficient. In this example, this fixed charge would cover 55% of each customer's bill. Under an allocatively equitable tariff design, as customers increased solar production, they would be paid the marginal value of that production: 5 ¢/kWh.

Solar customers that reduce the need for future network investments should benefit from doing so. These benefits could come in the form of lower forward-looking charges in advance of a network investment and lower fixed charges in the future associated with lower levels of residual costs. Where distribution wires are constrained, this may also come in the form of payments for reducing demand during constrained network periods (Pérez–Arriaga et al., 2016). If these payments are fixed for any period of time, they are essentially residual and should be recovered as such.

With flat, volumetric tariffs, customers at node B are in effect paid 11 ¢/kWh for every kWh generated since their consumption is reduced by the amount of solar generated.[24] Customers at node B are offsetting 120 megawatt-hours (MWh)[25] of 5 ¢/kWh generation, thus reducing the system's costs by $6,000 during the day time period. Solar customers at node B also avoid paying $7,200 in residual network and policy charges (per day).

Solar at node B does not change the total amount of residual costs associated with existing infrastructure that must be recovered (Schmalensee et al., 2015; Borenstein, 2016). Some argue that distributed solar systems decrease future distribution system costs. Both modeling-based and empirical research efforts demonstrate that distributed solar rarely reduces and often increases future distribution system costs (Cohen et al., 2016; Schmalensee et al., 2015; Wolak, 2018). Where distributed solar does reduce future network costs, the costs of any remuneration mechanisms for providing this value should be recovered as a residual cost (as no near-term action can change the need to pay for this remuneration mechanism).[26]

In this example, under flat, volumetric tariffs, IOU does not fully recover its residual costs. IOU has two options: raise tariffs to recover these costs or write these costs off.

First, IOU can raise tariffs. This would require IOU to increase tariffs for all customers by 0.4 ¢/kWh, or a 3.6% increase; this impact is especially significant for nonsolar owners, because solar owners have low consumption of grid power. Citing the Faulhaber principle for cross-subsidization,[27] Wolak (2018) argues that this does not, in fact, create a cross-subsidy between customers, as solar owners are likely paying more than their incremental cost of service. Some stakeholders have used similar arguments to justify volumetric tariffs that enable customers with self-generation to contribute less to residual cost recovery. However, this idea violates both economic efficiency

---

[24]This example does not require that customers are net-metered; indeed, under most tariff designs, consuming energy produced on site reduces net consumption and thus total residual cost payments.

[25]10 MWh per hour for 12 hours.

[26]Distributed solar also provides emissions mitigation benefits (that is, avoided CO_2 and other pollutants). In some cases, the magnitude of these benefits exceeds the magnitude of residual network costs on a per-kWh basis (Borenstein and Bushnell, 2018). These benefits should be remunerated. However, remunerating these benefits via decreased residual cost payments simply results in a cost shift as described herein (as there is a revenue adequacy constraint on total residual cost payments). These benefits should ideally be remunerated through mechanisms independent of residual cost recovery (e.g., a carbon tax).

[27]The Faulhaber principle states that there are no cross-subsidies between customers if all customers are paying more than their incremental cost of service and less than their stand-alone cost of service. See Faulhaber (1975).

principles and the allocative equity principles outlined (as solar customers' marginal actions impact the residual cost payments for nonsolar customers). Second, IOU may write these assets off as stranded, and pass these losses on to IOU's shareholders. There is legal precedent for such action (Hempling, 2015). However, in most cases, regulators and utilities are hesitant to write off assets if regulators have approved cost recovery for these assets. In addition, writing off assets runs the risk of increasing IOU's cost of capital, as IOU's investments are now more risky. An increased cost of capital will have one of two effects. First, IOU may require a higher regulated rate of return, which will ultimately increase costs for all consumers. Second, IOU may slow investment in its network if the cost of capital increases closer to the allowed rate of return. This has the risk of causing deteriorating service for all network users (Baumol and Sidak, 1995).

This example demonstrates how tariffs that allocate sunk costs through volumetric charges are not allocatively equitable in the presence of rooftop solar. This example also highlights how allocatively equitable tariffs would eliminate this inefficient cost shift. The following example builds on this example and previous research, demonstrating how the inequities present in time and locationally invariant tariffs can be exacerbated by the presence of DERs like rooftop solar.

5.2 Allocatively Equitable Tariffs Minimize Energy Cost Shifts

Let us now consider another example in which solar at node B grows significantly. This section ignores residual cost allocation, as the previous section covered this topic. Fig. 8.5 depicts the flows and marginal prices at each node when customers at node B have adopted a large amount of solar. In this case, solar at node B meets all of the load at node B and 10 MW of the load at node C during the daylight period. Because of the line constraint between nodes B and C and because of the need for power to flow according to Kirchhoff's laws, any production greater than 40 MW must be curtailed. The marginal price at node B is $0 \not{c}/kWh$, as any additional demand will be met locally by zero marginal cost solar. The marginal price at node C, on the other hand, is $10 \not{c}/kWh$, as, in order to meet an increment of 1 megawatt-hour (MWh) of demand at node C, the generator at node A must increase production by 2 MWh and the solar system at node B must curtail production by 1 MWh.

If flat, locationally invariant prices are used, the energy price seen by customers at nodes B and C will be $5.625 \not{c}/kWh$: the average energy price. This is inefficient and problematic for several reasons.

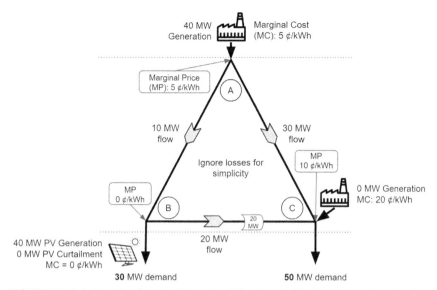

FIGURE 8.5 Substantial solar adoption at node B creates a binding network constraint.

First, customers at node B cross-subsidize customers at node C substantially during the day. Customers at node C pay less for energy than the marginal cost of service during the day, and customers at nodes B and C pay more than the marginal cost of production at night. Similarly, customers at node B pay more for energy during the day than necessary, underutilizing the zero marginal cost resource.

Second, if customers at node B are paid the average energy price for solar production, this sends a signal that power at this node is still valuable, despite the fact that any new solar production will simply be curtailed. This could drive further solar adoption at node B, exacerbating cost shifting problems. This also masks the value of power at node C.

Allocatively equitable tariffs would charge each customer the marginal cost of energy at each time and location (that is, the marginal price at each node). Hence, allocatively equitable tariffs would enhance social welfare by eliminating inefficient under- and overconsumption, and by providing better investment signals.

5.3 Allocatively Equitable Tariffs Improve Incentives for Efficient Network Utilization

The final example in this section highlights how forward-looking network charges can improve allocative equity over today's socialized, volumetric

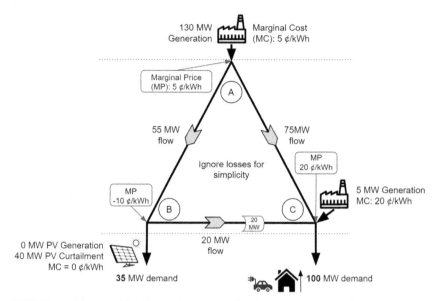

FIGURE 8.6 Substantial load growth at node C leads to dramatically different nodal energy prices.

network charges. In this example, substantial load growth at node C creates a binding constraint on the B-C line. Some load growth occurs at node B, but this load growth is not nearly as large. Due to the load growth at node C, the high marginal cost generator at node C must be dispatched to meet additional demand at node C. This drives the marginal price at node C to 20 ¢/kWh. In this case, consuming more at node B would actually lower the total system cost, as it would enable more demand at node C to be met by the generator at node A. This is reflected in the marginal energy price at node B, which is −10 ¢/kWh.[28] This scenario is depicted in Fig. 8.6.

In this example, if energy prices are averaged, customers at node B may pay significantly more than their cost of service, while customers at node C will pay significantly less than their cost of service.

Imagine that IOU found it welfare improving to expand the capacity of the B-C line by 5 MW. In this case, the beneficiaries of this investment are the generator(s) connected to node A, the generators connected to node B, and the consumers connected to node C. Generators at nodes A and B benefit by selling more power. Customers at node C benefit substantially, as the marginal price of energy falls 75% from 20 ¢/kWh to 5 ¢/kWh. Consumers

[28]That is, consumers would get paid for increasing consumption, and producers would pay for increasing production.

at node B pay higher prices, as the marginal cost of service increases to $0¢/$ kWh during daylight hours and $5¢/$kWh during night hours.

An allocatively efficient tariff design would charge customers at node C for their impact on future network costs, signaling the impact of customers at node C's behavior on future network costs and enabling IOU to recover the costs of the B-C line. Consumers at node B would not face such charges, as their behavior is not driving the investment. If the costs of this upgrade were socialized to all customers at nodes B and C, consumers at node B would pay substantially more than their benefits would justify, while customers at node C would pay substantially less. This is clearly not an allocatively equitable outcome.

Cost socialization could be considered allocatively equitable if all customers had similar benefits from electricity consumption and production and similar load and production profiles. However, as customers begin to stratify through DER investments and other services, the assumption of customer homogeneity will be increasingly problematic.

6. DISTRIBUTIONAL EQUITY

The previous section demonstrated that efficient tariffs improve allocative equity (that is, minimize the amount that one customer's actions negatively impact other customers). Efficient tariffs internalize the costs (or value) of consumers' (or producers') decisions, eliminating cost shifts from one customer to another. However, policy makers and regulators often use tariffs as a means to achieve distributional outcomes (Posner, 1971). Some power sector stakeholders insist that efficient tariffs will have undesirable distributional outcomes for some vulnerable customers, particularly customers with low and fixed income. Nevertheless, today's tariffs are allocatively inequitable and inefficient. Thus, this argument begs three key questions, further explored in this section:

1. Will efficient tariffs create undesirable distributional outcomes?
2. How do DERs affect the distributional impacts of today's tariffs?
3. Are there ways to achieve desired distributional outcomes without sacrificing allocative equity and efficiency?

The nature of residual cost recovery under efficient tariffs provides initial insight into the distributional impacts of efficient tariffs. Ramsey cost allocation allocates costs in inverse proportion to the demand elasticity of the customer. Given that residual costs under an efficient tariff are recovered through fixed charges, customers will only respond if, due to wealth effects, higher fixed charges lead to a reduction in total consumption. Thus, in short, efficient tariffs would allocate a higher proportion of residual costs to high-income customers relative to low-income customers.

6.1 Efficient Tariffs Likely Improve Distributional Equity on Average

The distributional outcomes of efficient tariffs will depend on the locational context, the demand patterns of vulnerable customers in the region, and the exact structure of the implemented tariffs. However, the bulk of the existing literature on efficient tariffs indicates that efficient prices neither harm low income or other vulnerable customers on average nor disproportionately harm these groups relative to high income customers (Allcott, 2011; Faruqui et al., 2010). On the contrary, by driving demand reductions and DER generation during high cost hours, efficient tariffs will reduce power system costs for all customers, including vulnerable groups. While efficient tariffs likely won't increase prices on average for vulnerable customers, efficient tariffs may increase costs for *some* vulnerable customers. Vulnerable customers whose demand is correlated with local and system-wide high price periods or who are located in high cost areas will likely see higher bills.

However, the fact that some vulnerable customers may be worse off under efficient tariffs – absent any intervention – should not dissuade regulators, policy makers, and consumer advocates from pursuing efficient tariffs for at least two reasons:

1. Today's tariffs are imperfect tools for socially desirable redistribution, and are therefore not inherently distributionally equitable compared to other tariff designs under consideration.
2. There are superior ways to support vulnerable customers than through flat, volumetric tariffs.

The argument that flat, volumetric tariffs aren't distributionally equitable follows directly from the fact that efficient tariffs do not harm vulnerable customers on average. That is, as demonstrated by Allcott (2011) and Faruqui et al. (2010), moving from flat to dynamic prices benefits low-income customers on average. Some research has indicated that certain volumetric tariff structures do benefit low-income customers on average (Borenstein, 2012). However, this research highlights that income and electricity consumption are imperfectly correlated, and that there are alternative mechanisms for improving distributional equity and efficiency simultaneously (Borenstein, 2012). Section 6.3 dives deeper into the argument that

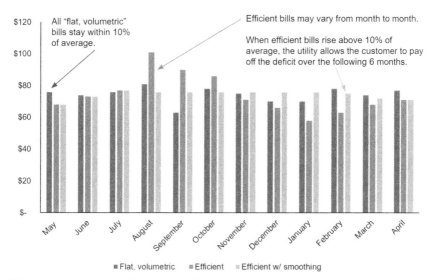

FIGURE 8.7 Illustration of customer bills under a simple volatility-smoothing payment plan (with synthetic data).

there are more efficient mechanisms for improving distributional outcomes in the following subsection.

While average bills for vulnerable customers may not increase under efficient tariffs, efficient tariffs may increase month-to-month bill volatility. Increased bill volatility can be a concern for all customers, but the challenge presented by bill volatility may be especially acute for low- and fixed-income customers. Borenstein (2006) examines the extent of that volatility and shows that simple hedging and payment plan options can mitigate the bulk of bill volatility. For example, utilities can automatically provide a payment plan that allows customers to pay off bills over many months when bills rise to a certain percent above average. This concept is demonstrated in Fig. 8.7. In each of the cases in Fig. 8.7 (that is, in flat, volumetric, efficient, and efficient w/ smoothing cases), the average bill is $74 per month. In the "efficient w/ smoothing" case, in any given month, if the customer's bill increases above 10% of his or her average bill, he or she automatically pays off the remainder of the bill over time.

6.2 DERs Create Distributional Inequity With Flat, Volumetric Tariffs

Under today's tariff designs, DER adoption and customer stratification is likely to drive greater distributional inequity. This stems from the fact that, under inefficient tariffs, DERs drive significant cost shifts as described in Section 5. The average DER adopter tends to be significantly higher income than non-DER adopters, so low-income customers are likely to pay higher bills as a result of these cost shifts.

In the largest review of solar owner income to date in the United States, the Lawrence Berkeley National Laboratory found that median income of solar adopting households is over 50% higher than the U.S. median (Barbose et al., 2018). This finding is consistent with other findings regarding the income of solar PV owners (Borenstein, 2017). EV owners also tend to be substantially wealthier than non-EV owners (Tal and Nicholas, 2014); in fact, as of 2015, the top income quintile had received 90% of electric vehicle tax credits in the U.S. (Borenstein and Davis, 2016). EV adoption is ultimately expected to drive significant investments in network infrastructure, especially if charging is poorly coordinated (Muratori, 2018; Fernandez et al., 2011). If the cost of this infrastructure is socialized (rather than paid for by the individuals driving the investments in this infrastructure), low-income customers will likely pay for network costs incurred for the benefit of high-income customers.

The distributional impacts of flat, volumetric tariffs[29] in the presence of rooftop solar are demonstrated in Fig. 8.8. The figure shows the changes

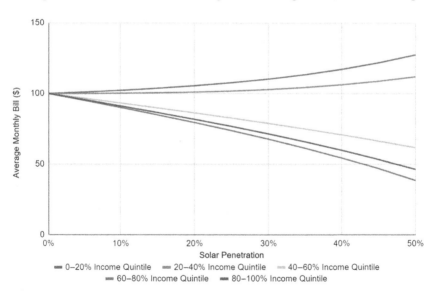

FIGURE 8.8 Changes in customer bills by income quintile as rooftop solar PV grows under flat, volumetric tariffs.

[29]The tariff structure in this example is initially identical to the tariff used in Section 5: 5 ¢/kWh for energy and 6 ¢/kWh for all residual network and policy costs. As solar penetration decreases net consumption, the utility must raise the rate for network and policy costs to fully recover residual costs.

in customer bills by income quintile as the penetration of rooftop solar increases. This analysis assumes that solar adoption in each income quintile remains at the average adoption by quintile in the U.S. as of 2016, as described in Barbose et al. (2018). That is, the 0% to 20% income quintile accounts for 7% of rooftop solar adoption; 20% to 40% accounts for 11%; 40% to 60% for 24%; 60% to 80% for 30%; and the top income quintile for 28%. This example also assumes that IOU's fixed costs remain the same under all solar PV penetration levels.[30] As solar PV penetration grows, all income quintiles offset some energy expenditures. However, given that solar PV adoption rates are highest among high-income quintiles, the average bill for the bottom two income quintiles ultimately increases, as these customers pay for the majority of residual costs. This stems from the fact that low-income customers now have higher average net consumption (household consumption minus PV production) versus customers in the higher-income quintiles.

By charging all residual costs to customers in the form of a fixed charge, efficient tariffs would eliminate cost shifts from wealthy to low-income customers, improving distributional outcomes. Similarly, tariff designs that charge future network investments to the beneficiaries of those investments improve distributional outcomes, as highlighted in Section 5.3.

6.3 Achieving Distributional and Allocative Equity

Sections 6.2 and 6.3 have demonstrated that efficient tariffs likely improve distributional outcomes on average and that today's tariffs are not distributionally equitable to begin with. However, Section 6.1 showed that moving from today's tariffs to more efficient designs may result in higher bills for *some* vulnerable customers. It is possible to support these vulnerable customers without sacrificing efficient marginal signals. As aforementioned, an efficient tariff structure would ideally allocate residual costs in such a way as to have the minimal impact on the utility of low-income customers. However, in practice, it is extremely challenging to measure the impacts of fixed charges on a customer's utility, and other measures may be necessary.

The optimal method would be to create means-tested bill rebates for vulnerable customers. In means-tested programs, the parameter of interest (e.g., income level) is directly measured and used to determine the level of bill support.[31] These types of program should be financed through fixed

---

[30]This is a generous assumption, as the bulk of existing research suggests that distributed solar PV more often increases rather than decreases distribution network costs (Wolak, 2018; Schmalensee et al., 2015; Vaishnav et al., 2017).

[31]One could conceive of a state-sponsored program whereby, when creating a utility account, customers are required to provide information that enables the utility to verify income levels without violating privacy.

charges levied on nonvulnerable customer bills. This mechanism would maintain allocatively efficient marginal price signals while achieving desired distributional outcomes. If regulators or consumer advocates are concerned with the feasibility of implementing means-tested programs, rebates provided to customers in predominately low-income geographies or alternative mechanisms are possible.

As the majority of customers are likely not vulnerable, small charges to the majority of customers could finance substantial bill reductions for the small set of vulnerable customers. Fig. 8.9 demonstrates this concept using synthetic data. In this hypothetical example, small fixed charges ($2.50 per customer) slightly increase the bill of the 80% of customers who do not qualify as vulnerable. Because vulnerable customers represent a minority (20% of customers), these customers' bills are reduced substantially (by $10 per month). These charges and rebates enable nearly all low-income customers to benefit from the transition to more efficient tariffs. So long as the increased fixed charges on nonvulnerable customers do not:

(1) drive costs above customers' incremental cost of service; and
(2) cause customers to consume below what their marginal value would dictate,

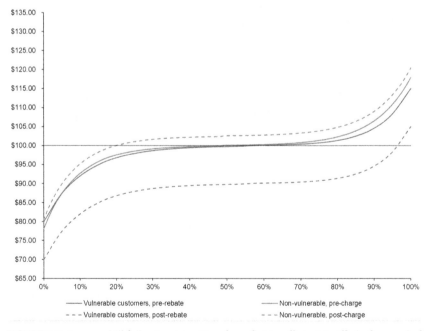

FIGURE 8.9 Average bill following transition from flat to efficient tariffs, before and after vulnerable customer support (synthetic data).

There is no loss of economic efficiency.

Some stakeholders have advocated for creating DER deployment mechanisms targeted at low-income customers. While such programs may lower bills for participating low-income customers, they solve none of the fundamental allocative or distributional equity problems described herein. A better mechanism would be to improve the allocative efficiency of tariffs, support low-income customers through means-tested rebates, *and* support targeted DER deployments for vulnerable customers if desired.

This section has demonstrated that flat, volumetric tariffs are distributionally inequitable, and that these inequities are likely going to be exacerbated as DER penetration grows. This section introduced mechanisms for managing the transition from today's tariff regime to more efficient tariffs for vulnerable customer groups. The next section introduces mechanisms for supporting all customers in the transition from today's tariff regimes to more efficient tariffs.

7. TRANSITIONAL EQUITY

A tariff design change that is net welfare improving will reduce average bills while potentially increasing bills for certain customers or customer groups (this meets the Kaldor-Hicks criteria for a beneficial transition, as introduced in Section 4). As prices become more temporally and spatially granular, customers who consume more than average in high price hours and areas will see higher bills. An increase in fixed charges to recover residual costs will mean a commensurate decrease in volumetric charges. This may raise bills for customers with relatively low net consumption (either due to low gross consumption or due to ownership of distributed generation). These bill increases may materially affect the value of long-lived assets with substantial fixed costs, like homes and solar PV plants.

Regulators and policy makers may wish to address these concerns, as, in general, customers cannot reasonably be expected to account for the potential for future tariff design changes in their investment decision-making processes. This is generally referred to in the natural justice literature as fairness to legitimate expectation (Rawls, 2001, p. 72). Customers may feel they have a right to compensation following the change, given their legitimate expectation of the continuation of a previously implemented tariff design. Such views also have grounds in behavioral economics; because customers often evaluate fairness based on changes relative to a baseline, tariff design changes that make some worse off may be viewed as unfair (Kahneman et al., 1986).

These transitional impacts are simply the result of prices becoming more aligned with costs or value. Nonetheless, they are often conflated with allocative equity or distributional fairness considerations.

While regulators and policy makers may wish to address these transitional challenges, these challenges are distinct from the allocative and distributional equity issues discussed here. Distinct problems call for distinct solutions. In many ways, the issues regulators will face in transitioning toward more efficient tariffs will mirror those faced in the transition from vertically integrated to restructured markets; however, in this case, customers, rather than utilities will own the sunk assets.

One of the key methods to alleviate transitional equity challenges is implementing changes gradually (this is commonly referred to as gradualism). Regulators may wish to educate customers (for example, through shadow billing) in the months or years preceding a tariff design change. Similarly, regulators could implement a tariff design change and fully hedge customers against the impact of that change. Over time, regulators could reduce and eventually eliminate the hedge. This hedge would effectively act as a transfer from customers who benefit from the change to those who lose under the change. These transfers would ideally take the form of lumpsum bill rebates, financed through nondistortive taxes or charges, as introduced in Section 6.3. Regulators may also wish to grandfather certain assets into existing programs (for example, solar PV systems into net metering programs). Finally, regulators may wish to maintain opt-out options. For example, if regulators changed default prices from flat, volumetric tariffs to a more efficient design, regulators could maintain the option to opt into the old design. This option would not guarantee that the magnitude of the flat, volumetric tariff would remain unchanged; it could be combined with the hedging option described earlier in order to reduce the rate of change.

In the long run, consumers can internalize the impacts of tariffs on their investment decisions. While this concept may seem far-fetched in the context of electric power, there is precedent for this type of cost internalization. Similarly, consumers buy cars and home appliances understanding the impact of fuel and electrical efficiency. Armed with appropriate information, consumers could make similar decisions regarding investments in a greater array of electricity-consuming or -producing goods. If companies design products that schedule energy usage to reduce energy costs, more efficient tariffs will help concentrate the benefits of the product in certain areas; companies can more effectively advertise to customers with high value of adoption, reducing acquisition costs. After a transition period, and with appropriate technological enablement and education, efficient tariffs could simply be another part of a consumer's investment decision-making process. Beyond the considerations of fairness with respect to legitimate expectation, regulators may seek to blunt transitional impacts in order to mitigate political economy issues that limit the viability of more equitable prices. People who would experience higher bills under a new tariff design might lobby to keep the current design in place, even when the current design is inefficient for society as a whole. Higher bills or other negative outcomes (for example, lower valuations for distributed solar) are likely to be concentrated, while the benefits of more efficient tariffs will likely be diffuse (assuming a net beneficial transition with relatively evenly distributed costs and benefits). The converse of this is that customers may not clamor for more efficient tariffs, as the benefits are often diffuse and opaque.

8. CONCLUSIONS

With improved tariff design, the transition to a more distributed power system holds great potential to produce a more equitable, reliable, low-carbon, and cost-effective power system. However, flawed tariff designs such as those in place today will enable customer stratification based on regulatory arbitrage. This outcome is neither equitable, sustainable, nor desirable.

This chapter demonstrates that the tariffs necessary to enable socially beneficial customer stratification are more equitable across many dimensions than today's flat, volumetric tariffs. By reducing cross-subsidies of marginal costs and cost shifts of residual costs between customers, efficient tariffs are more "allocatively" equitable. In addition, this chapter highlights that, within a set of reasonable assumptions, it is possible to improve the efficiency of electricity tariffs without sacrificing allocative equity. Should regulators or policy makers wish to mitigate all potential distributional impacts, means-tested, minimally distortionary rebate programs can protect vulnerable customers without sacrificing efficient signals for the remaining mass market customers. In other words, supporting vulnerable customers is not synonymous with creating rate designs that lead to inefficient and distortionary customer stratification and DER deployment. Finally, this chapter also demonstrated how tariff designs that improve equity may create negative outcomes for certain customers in the short term. These transitional concerns are distinct from distributional and allocative equity issues and deserve tailored solutions.

Contrary to commonly held beliefs, today's flat, volumetric tariffs are not inherently more equitable than efficient tariffs across many dimensions. The emergence of DERs will only exacerbate the allocative inequities present in today's tariffs. Transitioning from today's designs to more efficient and equitable tariffs will not be seamless. The benefits of efficient tariffs are diffuse, while the costs are often concentrated to certain companies, service providers, and customer groups.

However, as highlighted in the introduction to this book, the trend of customer stratification is likely to accelerate in the coming years. Technologies like solar PV panels, energy storage systems, and smart home devices might look more like consumer electronics than traditional power system infrastructure. Nonetheless, their aggregate impact on the grid could be massive. These technologies have the potential for major positive changes, creating a more efficient, low-carbon, and equitable system for all consumers. However, without bold regulatory action, this impact could be destructive, creating a power system that works for certain customer strata at the expense of others. Which future is realized depends on the ability of regulators and policy makers to align the benefits and costs of increased customer stratification and DER adoption. Fortunately, such actions will create a more equitable system for all customers.

REFERENCES

AARP, et al., 2010. The need for essential consumer protections: smart metering proposals and the move to time-based pricing. Available at: https://www.energy.gov/sites/prod/files/oeprod/DocumentsandMedia/NASUCA_Smart_Meter_White_Paper.pdf. (Accessed April 6, 2018).

Alexander, B.R., 2010. Dynamic pricing? Not so fast! A residential consumer perspective. Electr. J. 23 (6), 39–49. Available at: https://www.sciencedirect.com/science/article/pii/S1040619010001417. (Accessed April 6, 2018).

Allcott, H., 2011. Rethinking real-time electricity pricing. Resour. Energy Econ. 33 (4), 820–842. Available at: https://doi.org/10.1016/j.reseneeco.2011.06.003.

Barbose, G., et al., 2018. Income trends of residential PV adopters: an analysis of household-level income estimates. Berkeley, CA. Available at: http://eta-publications.lbl.gov/sites/default/files/income_trends_of_residential_pv_adopters_final_0.pdf.

Baumol, W.J., Sidak, J.G., 1995. Stranded costs. Harv. J. Law Public Policy 18 (3), 835–850. Available at: http://heinonline.org/HOL/Page?handle=hein.journals/hjlpp18&div=44&id=&page=&collection=journals.

Bonbright, J.C., 1961. Principles of Public Utility Rates. Columbia University Press, New York, NY.

Borenstein, S., 2006. Customer risk from real-time retail electricity pricing: bill volatility and hedgability. Cambridge, MA.

Borenstein, S., 2012. The redistributional impact of nonlinear electricity pricing. Am. Econ. J. Econ. Pol. 4 (3), 56–90.

Borenstein, S., 2013. Effective and equitable adoption of opt-in residential dynamic electricity pricing. Rev. Ind. Organ. 42 (2), 127–160.

Borenstein, S., 2016. The economics of fixed cost recovery by utilities. Electr. J. 29, 5–12.

Borenstein, S., 2017. Private net benefits of residential solar PV: the role of electricity tariffs, tax incentives, and rebates. J. Assoc. Environ. Resour. Econ. 4 (S1), S85–S122. Available at: https://doi.org/10.1086/691978.

Borenstein, S., Bushnell, J.B., 2018. Are residential electricity prices too high or too low? Or both? Berkeley, CA. Available at: http://www.nber.org/papers/w24756.

Borenstein, S., Davis, L.W., 2016. The distributional effects of US clean energy tax credits. Tax Policy Econ. 30 (1), 191–234. Available at: https://doi.org/10.1086/685597.

Cohen, M.A., Kauzmann, P.A., Callaway, D.S., 2016. Effects of distributed PV generation on California's distribution system, part 2: economic analysis. Sol. Energy 128, 139–152. Available at: https://www.sciencedirect.com/science/article/pii/S0038092X16000062. (Accessed April 6, 2018).

Convery, F.J., Mohlin, K., Spiller, E., 2017. Policy brief—designing electric utility rates: insights on achieving efficiency, equity, and environmental goals. Rev. Environ. Econ. Policy 11 (1), 156–164. Available at: https://doi.org/10.1093/reep/rew024.

CPUC, 2018. CARE/FERA programs: discounts on energy bills for income qualified households. Available at: http://www.cpuc.ca.gov/lowincomerates/.

Csiba, K., et al., 2016. In: Csiba, K., Bajomi, A., Goztonyi, A. (Eds.), Energy Poverty Handbook. European Union, Brussels.

Dworkin, R., 2000. Sovereign Virtue: The Theory and Practice of Equality. Harvard University Press.

EIA, 2017. Form EIA-861. . Washington, DC.

European Commission, 2016. COM(2016) 769 final: Report from the Commission to the European Parliament, the Council, the European Economic and Social Committee, and the Committee of the Regions: Energy prices and costs in Europe. Brussels, Belgium. Available at: https://ec.europa.eu/energy/sites/ener/files/documents/com_2016_769. en_.pdf.

Fares, R.L., Webber, M.E., 2017. The impacts of storing solar energy in the home to reduce reliance on the utility. Nat. Energy 2, 17001. Available at: https://doi.org/10.1038/nenergy.2017.1.

Faruqui, A., 2012. The ethics of dynamic pricing. In: Sioshansi, F.P. (Ed.), Smart Grid. Academic Press, Waltham, MA, pp. 61–83.

Faruqui, A., Sergici, S., Palmer, J., 2010. The Impact of Dynamic Pricing on Low Income Customers. Institute for Electric Efficiency Whitepaper.

Faulhaber, G.R., 1975. Cross-subsidization: pricing in public enterprises. Am. Econ. Rev. 65 (5), 966–977.

FERC, 2017. Form 1—Electric utility annual report. Washington, DC. Available at: https://www.ferc.gov/docs-filing/forms/form-1/data.asp.

Fernandez, L.P., et al., 2011. Assessment of the impact of plug-in electric vehicles on distribution networks. IEEE Trans. Power Syst. 26 (1), 206–213.

Harvey, D., Braun, B., 1996. Justice, Nature and the Geography of Difference. Wiley Online Library.

Hempling, S., 2015. From streetcars to solar panels: stranded cost policy in the United States. Energy Regul. Q. 3 (3). Available at: http://www.energyregulationquarterly.ca/articles/from-streetcars-to-solar-panels-stranded-cost-policy-in-the-united-states#sthash.85DYExTN.ZiRnkhbM.dpbs.

Hicks, J.R., 1940. The valuation of the social income. Economica 7 (26), 105–124.

Hittinger, E., Siddiqui, J., 2017. The challenging economics of US residential grid defection. Util. Policy 45, 27–35. Available at: https://www.sciencedirect.com/science/article/pii/S0957178716300066. (Accessed June 27, 2018).

Hledik, R., Greenstein, G., 2016. The distributional impacts of residential demand charges. Electr. J. 29 (6), 33–41. Available at: https://doi.org/10.1016/j.tej.2016.07.002.

Hochman, H.M., Rodgers, J.D., 1969. Pareto optimal redistribution. Am. Econ. Rev. 59 (4), 542–557.

Hogan, W.W., 2010. Fairness and dynamic pricing: comments. Electr. J. 23 (6), 28–35.

Hogan, W.W., 2013. Electricity scarcity pricing through operating reserves. Econ. Energy Environ. Policy 2 (2), 1–27. Available at: http://www.iaee.org/en/publications/eeeparticle.aspx?id=48.

Horowitz, S., Lave, L., 2014. Equity in residential electricity pricing. Energy J. 35 (2), 1–23.

Isaac, R.M., Mathieu, D., Zajac, E.E., 1991. Institutional framing and perceptions of fairness. Constit. Polit. Econ. 2 (3), 329–370.

Jones, D.N., Mann, P.C., 2001. The fairness criterion in public utility regulation: does fairness still matter? J. Econ. Issues 35 (1), 153–172. Available at: https://doi.org/10.1080/0021 3624.2001.11506345.

Joskow, P.L., 2007. Regulation of the natural monopoly. In: Polinsky, A.M., Shavell, S. (Eds.), Handbook of Law and Economics. vol. 2. Elsevier B.V.

Joskow, P.L., 2008. Capacity payments in imperfect electricity markets: need and design. Util. Policy 16 (3), 159–170.

Joskow, P., Tirole, J., 2007. Reliability and competitive electricity markets. RAND J. Econ. 38 (1), 60–84.

Kahneman, D., Knetsch, J.L., Thaler, R., 1986. Fairness as a constraint on profit seeking: entitlements in the market. Am. Econ. Rev. 728–741.

Kaldor, N., 1939. Welfare propositions of economics and interpersonal comparisons of utility. Econ. J. 49 (195), 549–552.

Kassakian, J., et al., 2011. The Future of the Electric Grid. Massachusetts Institute of Technology, Cambridge, MA.

Khalilpour, R., Vassallo, A., 2015. Leaving the grid: an ambition or a real choice? Energy Policy 82, 207–221. Available at: http://linkinghub.elsevier.com/retrieve/pii/S0301421515001111.

Massachusetts DPU, 2016. D.P.U. 15-155. Boston, MA. Available at: https://www.mass.gov/files/documents/2017/08/30/15-155.pdf.

Mays, J., Klabjan, D., 2017. Optimization of time-varying electricity rates. Energy J. 38 (5), 67–91.

Muratori, M., 2018. Impact of uncoordinated plug-in electric vehicle charging on residential power demand. Nat. Energy 3 (3), 193–201. Available at: https://doi.org/10.1038/s41560-017-0074-z.

Nelson, T., Simshauser, P., Kelley, S., 2011. Australian residential solar feed-in tariffs: industry stimulus or regressive form of taxation? Econ. Anal. Policy 41 (2), 113–129. Available at: https://www.sciencedirect.com/science/article/pii/S0313592611500153. (Accessed June 4, 2018).

Nelson, T., Simshauser, P., Nelson, J., 2012. Queensland solar feed-in tariffs and the merit-order effect: economic benefit, or regressive taxation and wealth transfers? Econ. Anal. Policy 42 (3), 277–301. Available at: https://www.sciencedirect.com/science/article/pii/S0313592612500305. (Accessed June 4, 2018).

Neuteleers, S., Mulder, M., Hindriks, F., 2017. Assessing fairness of dynamic grid tariffs. Energy Policy 108, 111–120. Available at: http://www.sciencedirect.com/science/article/pii/S0301421517303129.

Nevada, P.U.C., 2017. Docket No. 17-06003: order granting in part and denying in part general rate application by Nevada Power Company. Las Vegas, NV. Available at: http://pucweb1.state.nv.us/PDF/AxImages/DOCKETS_2015_THRU_PRESENT/2017-6/26509.pdf.

New York DPS, 2016. CASE 14-M-0101—Proceeding on Motion of the Commission in Regard to Reforming the Energy Vision: Order Adopting a Ratemaking and Utility Revenue Model Policy Framework. . Albany, NY.

New York State, 2017. Governor Cuomo announces expansion of financial benefits for low-income utility customers. Available at: https://www.governor.ny.gov/news/governor-cuomo-announces-expansion-financial-benefits-low-income-utility-customers. (Accessed April 6, 2018).

Newbery, D.M., 2018. What future(s) for liberalized electricity markets: efficient, equitable or innovative? Energy J. 39 (1), 1–27. Available at: http://www.iaee.org/en/publications/ejarticle.aspx?id=3025. (Accessed April 6, 2018).

North Carolina Clean Energy Technology Center, 2018. 50 states of solar: Q4 2017 quarterly report & 2017 annual review.

NYDPS, 2016. Case 15-E-0751—Staff report and recommendations in the value of distributed energy resources proceeding staff report and recommendations.. Albany, NY.

Pérez-Arriaga, I.J., et al., 1995. Marginal pricing of transmission services: an analysis of cost recovery. IEEE Trans. Power Syst. 10 (1), 65–72.

Pérez-Arriaga, I.J., et al., 2013. In: Pérez-Arriaga, I.J. (Ed.), Regulation of the Power Sector. first ed.. Springer-Verlag London, London. Available at: http://link.springer.com/10.1007/978-1-4471-5034-3.

Pérez-Arriaga, I.J., et al., 2016. Utility of the Future: An MIT Energy Initiative Response to an Industry in Transition. Massachusetts Institute of Technology, Cambridge, MA. Available at: http://energy.mit.edu/research/utility-future-study/.

Posner, R.A., 1971. Taxation by regulation. Bell J. Econ. Manag. Sci. 22–50.

Ramsey, F.P., 1927. A contribution to the theory of taxation. Econ. J. 37 (145), 47–61. Available at: http://www.jstor.org/stable/2222721.

Rawls, J., 2001. In: Kelly, E. (Ed.), Justice as Fairness: A Restatement. The Belknap Press of Harvard University Press, Cambridge, MA.

Read, W.S., et al., 1999. Reliability in the new market structure (Part 1). IEEE Power Eng. Rev. 19 (12), 4–14.

Rivier, M., Pérez-Arriaga, I.J., 1993. Computation and decomposition of spot prices for transmission pricing. In: 11th PSC Conference. Avignon, Francia. pp. 1–10.

Rule, T.A., 2015. Solar energy, utilities, and fairness. San Diego J. Clim. Energy Law 6 (2014–2015), 115–148.

Schmalensee, R., et al., 2015. The Future of Solar Energy. Massachusetts Institute of Technology, Cambridge, MA.

Schneider, I., Sunstein, C.R., 2017. Behavioral considerations for effective time-varying electricity prices. Behav. Public Policy 1 (2), 219–251.

Schweppe, F.C., et al., 1988. Spot Pricing of Electricity. Kluwer Academic Publishers, Boston, MA.

Simpson, G., Clifton, J., 2016. Subsidies for residential solar photovoltaic energy systems in Western Australia: distributional, procedural and outcome justice. Renew. Sust. Energ. Rev. 65, 262–273. Available at: http://linkinghub.elsevier.com/retrieve/pii/S1364032116302933. (Accessed June 4, 2018).

Simshauser, P., Downer, D., 2016. On the inequity of flat-rate electricity tariffs. Energy J. 37 (3), 199–229.

Solar Energy Industries Association, et al., 2017. Principle for the evolution of net energy metering and rate design. Available at: https://votesolar.org/files/6314/9623/9565/NEM_Future_Principles_Final_5-31-17.pdf. (Accessed April 6, 2018).

Southern Environmental Law Center, Golin, C., The Greenlink Group, 2015. A troubling trend in rate design: proposed rate design alternatives to harmful fixed charges. Available at: https://www.southernenvironment.org/uploads/news-feed/A_Troubling_Trend_in_Rate_Design.pdf. (Accessed April 6, 2018).

Tal, G., Nicholas, M.A., 2014. Studying the PEV market in California: comparing the PEV, PHEV and hybrid markets. In: 2013 World Electric Vehicle Symposium and Exhibition, EVS. pp. 1–10.

Vaishnav, P., Horner, N., Azevedo, I.L., 2017. Was it worthwhile? Where have the benefits of rooftop solar photovoltaic generation exceeded the cost? Environ. Res. Lett. 12. Available at: http://iopscience.iop.org/article/10.1088/1748-9326/aa815e/meta.

Vázquez, C., Rivier, M., Pérez-Arriaga, I.J., 2002. A market approach to long-term security of supply. IEEE Trans. Power Syst. 17 (2), 349–357.

Wolak, F.A., 2018. Evidence from California on the economic impact of inefficient distribution network pricing and a framework for a proposed solution. Stanford, CA.

Young, H.P., 1995. Equity: In Theory and Practice. Princeton University Press.

CHAPTER 9

New Distribution Network Charges for New Integrated Network Services

Ibtihal Abdelmotteleb, Tomás Gómez, José Pablo Chaves Ávila
Comillas Pontifical University, ICAI, Institute for Research in Technology, Madrid, Spain

1. INTRODUCTION

Distribution networks are currently departing from their traditional passive nature to an active one, mainly due to the increasing penetration of distributed energy resource (DERs). Moreover, as described in other chapters in this volume, end-users linked to the distribution network are being more active as they consume, produce, and store energy, in the process becoming prosumers, prosumagers, traders, and more. Distribution network charges that have been designed to serve in passive networks can no longer serve their purpose in active ones. Therefore, efficient distribution network charges need to be designed to provide three main objectives:

- ensure full cost recovery in the light of increasing penetration of DERs;
- incentivize end-user response through locational and/or temporal prices, promoting efficient utilization of the existing network; and
- defer/avoid network reinforcements when more economically efficient alternatives are available.

Although distribution network charges, if well designed, may incentivize efficient end-user behavior, yet they do not well coordinate end-users' short-term and long-term decisions. Thus, new tools are required to enable network charges in achieving their goals, engaging end-users efficiently and utilizing their flexibility.

Around the world, utilities[1] are encouraged to innovate in the way their networks are handled to increase the system's efficiency. Many of those in

---

[1]Utilities in North America have similar functions to DSOs in Europe.

Consumer, Prosumer, Prosumager
https://doi.org/10.1016/B978-0-12-816835-6.00009-7

© 2019 Elsevier Inc.
189

North America mandatorily file Integrated Resource Plans (IRPs)[2] with the commission showing the improved energy efficiency measure taken as well as their proposed future plans, which must consider DERs. For example, in Arizona[3] since April 2015, utilities are required to specifically include, or otherwise explain why they exclude, DERs into their IRPS, such as energy storage, expanded energy efficiency, and demand response. Similarly, in Colorado,[4] DERs in the form of approved Demand-Side Management programs should be included in their plans. In Arkansas,[5] the commission approved the "Resource Planning Guidelines for Electric Utilities," which specifies that for the case of additional capacity required, utilities should first efficiently consider available generation and demand resources, whether belonging to a utility or its customers, through means of energy efficiency and DSM encouragement. PacifiCorp files IRP on a biennial basis with the state utility commissions of Utah, Oregon, Washington, Wyoming, Idaho, and California. Their 2017 IRP action plan identifies specific resource actions that includes DSM (PacifiCorp, 2017).

Moreover, in Massachusetts, under the Green Communities Act utilities mandatorily should prioritize cost-effective energy efficient solutions before considering other resources. Utilities prepare 3-year plan for their annual budgets and goals taking in account available energy-efficient resources that are more economical than generation. Furthermore, in North America, the New York Reforming Energy Vision (REV) is a state initiative that calls for restructuring the way utilities and energy companies sell electricity. It aims to maximize the utilization of resources and reduce the need for new infrastructure through expanded demand management, energy efficiency, renewable energy, distributed generation, and energy storage programs. This requires regulated utilities to act as distributed system platform providers (DSPPs) that will own the distribution networks as well as create markets, tariffs, and operational systems to enable behind-the-meter resource providers (Bigliani et al., 2015).

In line with the emerging need of recognizing the benefits of DERs and correctly deploying it and utilizing its flexibility potential, this chapter focuses on the need of distribution-level market-based coordination mechanisms that complement efficient cost-reflective distribution network charges. Such mechanisms aim to maximize the value of flexibility, employing it in

---

[2]Provided by American Council for an Energy-Efficient Economy (ACEEE) in database. aceee.org/state/energy-efficiency-resource.
[3]According to Docket No. E-00000V-13-0070 and Decision No. 75068.
[4]According to Docket No. 07A-447E and Decision No. C08-0929.
[5]According to Docket No. 06-028-R.

a way that enhances the system's total economic efficiency, while rewarding those that provide it. In addition, it discusses distribution-level mechanisms designed to procure end-user flexibility to provide network services.

The chapter is organized as follows:

- Section 2 discusses why traditionally designed distribution network charges can no longer serve in current networks with active end-users, requiring new cost-reflective charges;
- Section 3 discusses the emerging need of distribution-level coordination to complement distribution network charges, and to create means for DSOs to efficiently make use of end-users' flexibility services;
- Section 4 presents short- and long-term flexibility mechanisms that could be implemented to achieve the required distribution-level coordination and utilization of end-users' flexibility, followed by the chapter's conclusions.

2. THE NEED FOR DESIGNING EFFICIENT DISTRIBUTION NETWORK CHARGES

For decades, distribution network charges were designed to be as consistent as possible with tariff design principles,[6] focusing mainly on allocating costs to end-users in a fair and equitable manner to recover network costs. Since historically end-users had similar consumption patterns, it allowed utilities to average costs among them. Generally, averaging costs would follow one of two approaches:

- either full averaging of all distribution network costs into a single kWh charge- i.e., volumetric charge, or
- averaging losses plus a portion of distribution network costs into a kWh charge, and the remaining distribution network costs into a kW charge- i.e., demand charge on peak coincidence, individual peak, or contracted demand basis.

A fixed charge may be also included to recover administrative costs such as the costs of electric meters. Overall, although the distribution network charges did not seek efficiency, as it was not crucial with passive end-users, it fit well for the purpose and has been socially accepted. Chapter 8 of Burger et al. further discusses equity issues in tariff design.

Nowadays, however, such network charges are no longer able to serve active distribution networks with increasing penetrations of DERs driven

---

[6]Tariff design principles include sustainability/sufficiency, equity/nondiscriminatory, economic efficiency, additivity, simplicity, consistency, stability, and transparency. Further discussion available in Berg and Tschirhart (1989) and Rodríguez Ortega et al. (2008).

by decarbonization objectives and other policies. End-users are no longer only withdrawing energy from the network, but they are also injecting and storing as they become prosumers as further described in other chapters. They are rational and are driven by financial benefits they can gain through inappropriate volumetric charges.[7] Hence, inefficient DERs investment may be taken by end-users as a way of reducing their share of network costs. These decisions may lead to less network usage and causing network cost recovery deficits, or may stress network assets, particularly due to bidirectional power flows, and leading to network reinforcements. In extreme cases, it may lead to death spiral or even grid defection. The costs included in the network charges along with the way it is allocated to end-users highly affects end-users' choices and decisions. As they gradually reduce their network usage, the higher the residual costs[8] becomes, and as they serve their energy needs independently from the network, fewer end-users will bear these costs, and soon the case may progress into death spiral (Felder and Athawale, 2014; Costello and Hemphill, 2014).

Currently, for instance, in Spain, end-users receive a three-component electricity bill[9] that reflects network, energy, and policy costs as illustrated in Fig. 9.1. The access tariff covers costs that include both the network and policy costs, which is recovered through demand and energy charges. Demand charges mainly target the network costs and are based on the

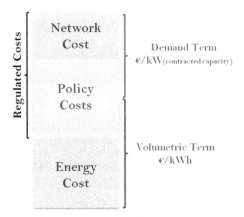

FIGURE 9.1 Spanish electricity bill components.

---

[7]Through DERs end-users can reduce their energy consumption, and consequently their share of network charges. A discussion on this can be found in Abdelmotteleb et al. (2018a,b).
[8]Residual costs include network costs and may include policy costs as well.
[9]Discussed in www.iea.org/media/workshops/2015/esapworkshopiv/Laveron.pdf.

end-user's contracted peak capacity. Whereas policy costs are partially recovered through demand charges, and the rest are recovered through volumetric charges. This tariff incentivizes end-users to reduce their peaks rather than their energy consumption. However, depending on the portion of policy costs within the electricity bill, which is currently approximately a third of the electricity bill on average, end-users may be encouraged to more economically meet their energy needs.

Hence, the challenge is to allocate distribution network costs to end-users in a way that encourages efficient end-users' responses and promotes short- and long-term efficiency. The charging methodology should comply with tariff design principles enabling full network costs recovery as well as leading to system economic efficiency.

Ultimately, the aim is to engage end-users' participation to provide flexibility services to the network, along with an efficient mechanism for coordination and utilization of their flexibility. Thus, end-users need to receive clear and effective economic signals upon which they can react and respond to. For that, cost-reflective network charges that vary by time and location reflecting costs incurred by end-users due to their injections/withdrawals are most efficient in obtaining these goals.

With this in mind, in 2017 a pilot project was implemented in Portugal to assess end-users' engagement to dynamic cost-reflective network charges. Dynamic time of use tariffs (ToU) were introduced to replace static ToU which have been in place for a long time (CEER, 2017). This is because static ToU tariffs incentivizes end-users to permanently shift their load from peak to off-peak periods and discourages them to respond to short-term flexibility signals. The dynamic ToU proposal aims to promote demand side flexibility that will in turn encourage end-users to participate in mechanisms that more efficiently utilize existing network assets and reduce network withdrawal during network peaks. Thus, it would postpone network investments and minimize costs. The pilot project will last for 1 year and is targeting industrial end-users to confirm the preliminary cost benefit analysis carried out before putting the dynamic cost-reflective network charge into place.

A number of elements contribute to an efficient cost-reflective network charge.

Firstly, since network investments are driven by the network's peaks, a peak-coincidence network charge (PCNC) would more effectively reflect end-users' contributions to those network's peaks than individual peak network charges. A PCNC is a forward-looking component of the network charge that aims to capture and reflect the incremental costs of utilizing distribution network assets. The inclusion of forward-looking distribution network charges sends economic signals to end-users that reflect prevailing network conditions. These economic signals transmit the value of network reinforcements driven by increasing network utilization. Hence, the economic signals would influence end-users' behavior regarding whether to produce, store, or consume electricity. Consequently, end-users' behavior will efficiently affect the network's short-term operation and long-term investment decisions taken by the distribution system operator (DSO) and end-users. Case studies were carried out in Abdelmotteleb et al. (2018a,b) showed that network charges based on individual peaks encourage end-users to reduce their peaks further than what is actually required. Meanwhile, network charges based on network's peak (PCNC), with a predefined network capacity threshold, limited end-users' peak reduction and investments in DER capacities to what is optimally economical from the system's perspective.

Secondly, when to/not to send economic signals is another important element. The economic signals transmitted through dynamic network charges are sent to end-users to convey messages regarding network's status. Chapter 6 by Stanley et al. covers price visibility and transparency on the network. Hence, when networks are underutilized, no economic signals should be transmitted, as it may result in further reduction of network usage. Too many signals may lead to end-users' confusion. Signals should be transmitted only during critical periods when action is required. Otherwise, end-users are allowed to freely use the network without any restrictions. Therefore, EVs or storage are incentivized to charge when networks are not highly utilized and when energy prices are attractive.[10]

However, when network's utilization level is high and expected to increase further requiring additional network investments, then economic signals should be transmitted to alert end-users. These signals should reflect the cost of network upgrades required, through which end-user can compare with other alternatives, leading to higher system economic efficiency. Hence, a PCNC should only be applied when a certain level of network utilization is achieved, and network upgrades are expected to meet future needs.

---

[10]It is important for end-users to consider both charges; network and energy to optimally schedule their demand and DERs' profiles. Local network congestions may conflict with low energy prices, and consequently both charges are necessary to encourage overall end-users efficient reaction.

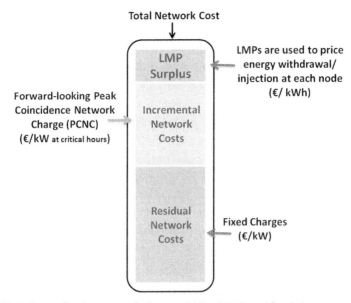

FIGURE 9.2 Cost-reflective network charges: LMPs, PCNC, and fixed charges.

It should be noted that the PCNC may only recover part of the network costs, whereas the rest of network costs, the residual costs, that are not recovered through cost-reflective charges (PCNC) should be recovered in a minimally distortive manner, for example through fixed charges.[11] Furthermore, locational marginal prices (LMPs) may be employed for energy prices to reflect temporal and spatial variations at the distribution level. The surplus obtained through LMPs account for network losses – and congestions if any – and covers a portion of network costs[12] as illustrated in Fig. 9.2, and further described in Chapter 8 of Burger et al.

Thirdly, network charges should be symmetrical in the sense that they do not discriminate between generator, consumer, prosumer, or prosumager. Depending on the condition of the network, whether high network utilization level is due to excess withdrawal or injection, network charges should be allocated to those increasing the utilization level, and those reducing it should be compensated. This would act as an incentive for end-users to curtail/store their energy injections or increase their energy withdrawals when local generation exceeds local demand, and vice versa.

DSOs and utilities around the world are adapting their charging methodologies to accommodate the changes taking place in the distribution network.

[11]Examples for proxies to apply fixed costs are presented in MIT (2016).
[12]Further discussion on distribution-level LMPs is available in MIT (2016).

An individual peak capacity charge component is used rather than a volumetric charge to better reflect end-users' contribution to network costs. For example, in Spain and Netherlands, demand charges are applied according to the installed fuse size at end-users, limiting individual peak capacity.[13] Whereas recently in Australia, new distribution network charges have been introduced, where peak-coincidence demand charges are applied based on the highest 30-min consumed power during peak periods. The peak-coincidence charge is based on the Long-Run Marginal Cost, which is a forward-looking component of the network tariff that recovers part of the network costs, while the rest is recovered through fixed and energy charges (AER, 2016).

Network charges that include the aforementioned elements would incentivize end-users to use, store, and export energy at times that are most beneficial or least costly to the network. Moreover, it will encourage end-users to be flexible and provide services to the network. This may lead to network reinforcement's deferral, as well as bill savings for flexible end-users. Besides receiving efficient economic signals through the network charges, end-users will need to find it easy and appealing to participate and offer their flexibility services. They need to be aware of the opportunities available, be clearly informed about what their participation will entail, and have a clear choice about how they can participate. Thus, in order for them to access the benefits of cost-reflective charges, new markets/mechanisms need to develop, in which end-users can offer their flexibility services. As shown in Fig. 9.3, this chapter proposes Local Flexibility Mechanism (LFM) that complements distribution network charges to enhance end-users' reaction and consequently reducing future network costs. LFM is further discussed later in the chapter.

3. WHY DISTRIBUTION-LEVEL COORDINATION?

Dynamic cost-reflective network charges play a major role in incentivizing end-users' response, yet the complexity of their design increases the uncertainty of end-users' engagement, and thus it is difficult for distribution system operators or DSOs to fully involve them within their short-term operational and long-term planning decision-making processes. In order for DSOs to account for end-users' flexibility, which includes load and generation shifting/curtailment, as a real and effective alternative to grid investments, DSOs need to be able to count on the availability of these resources when needed.

---

[13] A review on distribution network charges implemented in different European countries is available in CEER (2017).

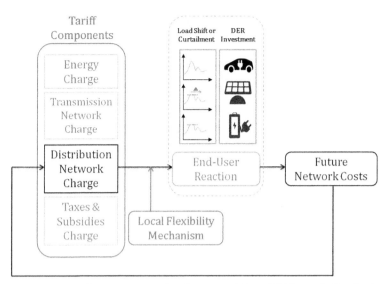

FIGURE 9.3 Cost-reflective network charges: LMPs, PCNC, and fixed charges (Abdelmotteleb et al., 2018a,b).

Recent researches have tackled the issue of uncertainty in end-users' engagement (Esmat et al., 2017; Vallés et al., 2018). In Esmat et al. (2017), the authors presented what they called "uncertainty in commitment" method, which accounts for deviations resulting from uncommitted end-users. The proposed method takes into account end-users' historical data, and according to it the DSO assigns a commitment probability for each end-user, which is then taken into account during the decision-making process of end-user flexibility activation. Moreover, in Vallés et al. (2018), uncertainty in end-users' engagement is considered through an empirical methodology that accounts for human behavior through a probabilistic characterization of end-users' flexibility following Quantile Regression (QR).

The mentioned approaches are based on probabilistic methods, which may provide an approximate estimation of power flows in the network, but not necessarily the actual ones. Lack of knowledge regarding actual power flows makes it difficult for DSOs to predict where and how often network challenges may occur.[14] Thus, some means of distribution-level coordination are required to effectively integrate and coordinate end-users' flexibility into the planning and operation of electricity networks. This coordination

---

[14]Further discussion on this topic is available in CEER (2017).

would firstly complement cost-reflective network charges, compensating its implementation shortages and allowing it to be more stable, predictable, and socially accepted. Secondly, it would utilize end-users' flexibility in the short-term reducing network operational costs, and in the long-term, to promote efficient end-user DER investments, ensuring an optimal mix between network reinforcements and other solutions.

3.1 Complement Cost-Reflective Distribution Network Charges

As previously mentioned, the most efficient designs of network charges are those that are demand-based and particularly those that consider network peak-coincidence, rather than individual peaks. They act as a driver to influence the way end-users manage their energy needs. Network peak-coincidence charges send economic signals to end-users reflecting the network's status when network reinforcements are needed and its associated incremental costs. End-users may respond to these price signals in four different ways to meet their electricity demand:

* continue purchasing energy from the network;
* produce energy through DERs;
* shift load; and
* curtail load/generation injections.

Although well-designed network charges may lead to efficient end-user responses by revealing their flexibility potentials, some unintended consequences may result including the following:

1. Since network peaks are difficult to predict ex-ante, PCNC are applied ex-post. Thus, there is high uncertainty in the value of the PCNC and when it is expected.

2. When end-users are engaged and respond to the network charges, uncoordinated responses might generate new challenges. For instance, creating unexpected network peaks as a consequence of avoiding the expected ones.

3. End-users' might over- or underinvest in DERs. Some may overinvest to insure themselves against high network charges (PCNC), or underinvest due to financial risk. On the one hand, DSOs and the society[15] may miss the opportunity of more cost-efficient solutions to replace network investments as end-users decide to underinvest in DERs. On the other

---

[15]Network reinforcement costs are recovered through the network charges. Therefore, replacing them with less costly solutions will increase the system's economic efficiency, benefiting the society.

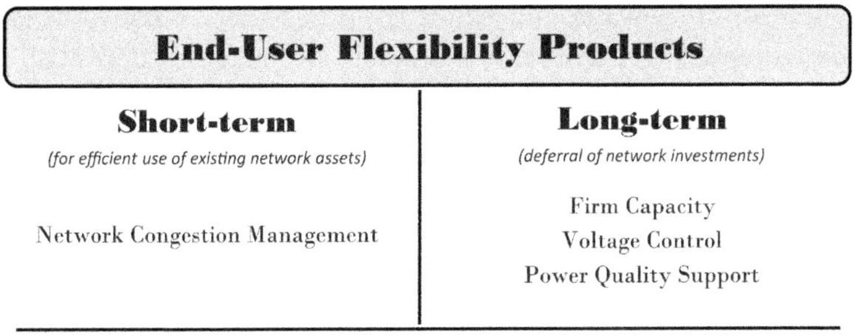

End-User Flexibility Products

Short-term	**Long-term**
(for efficient use of existing network assets)	*(deferral of network investments)*
Network Congestion Management	Firm Capacity Voltage Control Power Quality Support

FIGURE 9.4 Distribution-level Flexibility services.

hand, overinvestment in DERs may cause technical conflicts within the network related to the network's operation, control, and stability. In addition, it may result in less network usage and increase network costs, leading to network cost recovery deficits. Thus, end-users' DER investment decisions should be well guided and linked to the network needs. For example, regarding DER investments, California has established what they call a "loading order"[16] for additional capacity procurement[17] (PacifiCorp, 2017).

3.2 Utilize End-Users' Flexibility

End-users' flexibility, which may be obtained for example through DSM, provides opportunities to utilities and/or DSOs to manage their networks in a more efficient and flexible manner in the short- and long term. The use of end-user flexibility may be employed to assist the network through a range of services[18] as shown in Fig. 9.4.

Flexibility products that could be linked to network charges include:

- *Network congestion management:* this is a short-term flexibility product that is related to network's operation and management. End-users' flexibility is used to efficiently utilize existing network assets and DERs.
- *Firm Capacity:* this is a long-term flexibility product. This is different from network capacity management, as it aims to provide a long-term solution to network congestions that require network reinforcements. A more viable and less costly solution to network reinforcements could be offered by DERs. Instead of upgrading the network to accommodate

---

[16]As authorized under California Public Utility Code § 454.55-56, which established aggressive targets and associated funding for energy efficiency programs (PacifiCorp, 2017).

[17]It prioritizes cost-effective renewable resources and cost-effective efficiency resources over conventional energy sources.

[18]A discussion on distribution-level flexibility services is provided in EDSO (2018).

an increase in network utilization level, end-users' flexibility may be used to replace it. Network investments are linked to network's peak utilization periods that generally occur few times a year. Through end-users' commitment to provide firm capacity as a flexibility product during those periods, an optimal mix between network reinforcements and other cost-efficient solutions could be implemented.

- **Voltage control/Power quality support:** this is a long-term flexibility product. Voltage and power-quality network problems are commonly caused by increase in local injections or withdrawals, requiring network reinforcements. A more efficient substitute could be offered through DERs. For example, smart PV inverters could contribute in enhancing the network's voltage profile through volt-var control.[19]

For DSOs to consider local flexibility as an alternative to network reinforcements, they should be able to supervise, coordinate, and utilize it when needed. This requires engaging end-users through well-designed distribution-level flexibility mechanisms that enable extraction and management of their flexibility while correctly valuing it. End-users will benefit most from a system of network charges, mechanisms, and markets that are aligned with network's needs, providing solutions that are economically optimal, in both the short- and long term. Thus, innovation in new distribution-level market designs that facilitates end-user's participation and coordinates them in an efficient way will enhance the system's economic efficiency. These markets/mechanisms should ensure a level playing field for all types of DERs to compete transparently, and correctly compensating flexibility providers.[20]

4. DISTRIBUTION-LEVEL SHORT- AND LONG-TERM FLEXIBILITY UTILIZATION

New distribution-level instruments need to develop to achieve the required coordination and utilize end-users' flexibility, such as efficient local mechanisms that encourage end-user engagement. These instruments should be applicable in a decentralized way, allowing end-users' responses

---

[19]Smart PV inverters can provide efficient operational management opportunities such as increasing network transfer capabilities. A discussion on this topic is available in Abdelmotteleb et al. (2017).

[20]Piclo platform where end-users' flexibility services may be auctioned is discussed in Chapter 6 by Stanley et al., is an example of distribution-level mechanism that facilitates end-users' participation. Moreover, nine different mechanisms for the use and valuation of flexibility are investigated for the French case and presented in Germain and Jan' Chapter 13.

to be applied in a more localized manner to efficiently influence the utilization of network assets. Their design should follow a market-based approach to enable the system to access its available physical flexibility, and when existing flexibility is insufficient, invest in additional flexibility. In addition, these instruments should not distort the economic signals pre-established through cost-reflective network charges.

The instruments allow end-users' flexibility services to be traded through predefined flexibility products. Clear flexibility product definition and standardization of products allow investment security for end-users. These products serve the network through either the short term, to assist the DSO during network operational decisions, or in the long term to assist in the network planning phase, providing alternative solutions to network reinforcements. Therefore, two flexibility mechanisms could be implemented within the distribution network for these purposes as shown in Fig. 9.5: the Short-term Local Flexibility Mechanism (LFM) and the Long-term LFM.

Combined, they aim to influence the efficient utilization of network assets in the short-term, and coordinate end-users' DER investment decisions with network planning in the long-term. First, short-term LFM is implemented during network peak hours. End-users are called 24 hours ahead to participate voluntarily in local distribution-level auctions to book their network capacities in advance. Then, based on their responses, the need for additional network capacity is predicted. Long-term LFM is then implemented to procure the additional network capacity required through DERs if they are more cost efficient in comparison to conventional network investments.

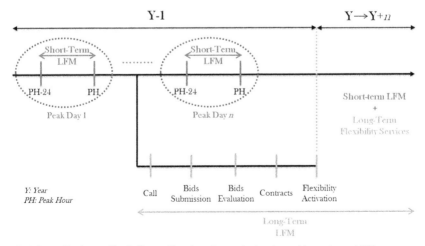

FIGURE 9.5 End-user flexibility utilization through short- and long-term LFM.

The objective is to ensure optimal reactions and efficient DER investment decisions are conducted from the end-users' side, as well as efficient network reinforcement decisions are executed from the DSO's side as further described below.

4.1 Short-Term Local Flexibility Mechanism

The first mechanism is the Short-term LFM, which complements distribution network charges discussed earlier. Within the short-term LFM, flexibility services are traded in the form of network capacity reservation, offering DSOs network capacity management. It is a preventive approach in line with PCNC to avoid network congestions. Network capacity is offered in advance to be reserved for expected peak network utilization hours, which could be due to excess power injection or withdrawal. End-users are given the opportunity to manage their network utilization profile, shift their injections to nonpeak hours, and book their network capacity needs during peak hours and pay accordingly. On one hand, this allows end-users to hedge against high PCNC in the short term. Since end-users are probably risk averse, they need to be insured against high bill risks due to the volatility of network charges. Therefore, the Short-term LFM provides them with an approach that allows them to hedge against PCNC, while they are able to provide flexibility services to the network. On the other hand, DSOs are able to utilize the available end-users' flexibility to manage the network more efficiently, as well as retrieve more accurate information regarding expected power flows during peaks hours.

Since end-users receive the PCNC during peak hours, which account for the costs of future network investments required, the short-term LFM auctions are designed to align with these signals and coordinate end-users to reduce their network usage during these hours or shift it to other nonpeak hours. End-users may participate in the auction to reserve network capacity in advance, for example a day in advance. Flexible end-users would shift part of their load/generation to nonpeak hours, and book network capacity equivalent to their inflexible load. Whereas inflexible end-users would book their full capacity needs. End-users pay for their booked capacity according to the auction clearing price, which is lower than PCNC. In the event of peak hours, following the network charges design, PCNC will be allocated to unreserved capacities.

Short-term LFMs could be implemented through dynamic auctions, where multiple auctions are held simultaneously for expected peak hours within the same day. Dynamic auctions with simultaneous rounds are designed for auctioning simultaneously for multiple units, i.e., network capacity, of different products, i.e., hours, that act substitutes for each other.[21] Hence, end-users are encouraged to shift part of their load or injections to hours when PCNC are not expected. The auctions are held to allocate network scarce capacity that is not yet absolute, to reveal end-users' preferences whether the local network should be upgraded to accommodate extra capacity, or other more economical solutions could be held from the end-users' side, such as load shifting or distributed generation (DG) dispatching.

4.2 Long-Term Local Flexibility Mechanism

The second mechanism is the Long-term LFM, which is implemented to procure end-users' flexibility services in a competitive and transparent way. Through a market-based approach, such as requests for proposals, end-users make a forward commitment to provide future network services upon being called. Such network services are related to network operation management during critical hours to reduce losses or resolve congestions through providing firm capacity or voltage compensation services. These flexibility services are procured to replace costly network reinforcements, thus ensuring end-users' commitment is vital.

Long-term LFM is implemented when existing flexibility is insufficient to alleviate the need for network reinforcements. As shown in Fig. 9.5, existing flexibility is utilized through short-term LFM. Then, when network reinforcements remain needed, Long-term LFM is implemented. It aims to optimally mix between long-term end-user flexibility and network reinforcements to enhance the system's economic efficiency. Calls for flexibility procurement are announced a year ahead to allow end-users of accepted bids a reasonable period of time to invest in DERs. The link between short- and long-term LFM is further illustrated in Fig. 9.6.

End-user flexibility commitment is guaranteed through contracts that allows DSOs either the intervention during network critical hours to constrain their injections/withdrawals, or signaling them to provide a predefined flexibility service. The contracts will include terms related to the predefined flexibility product to be traded, the level of DSO intervention, notification period in advance, remuneration rate, and noncompliance penalties to ensure end-users' commitment. Then, in the following year, involved end-users would provide their flexibility services during peak network hours upon being called.

---

[21]Detailed discussion on Short-term LFM is available in Abdelmotteleb et al. (2018a,b).

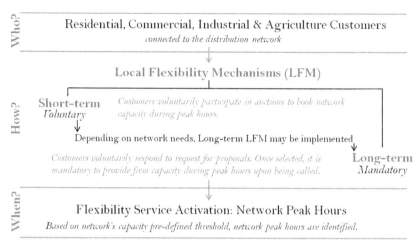

FIGURE 9.6 Short- and long-term LFM.

A number of pilot projects have been carried out in different countries presenting different ways of utilizing end-users' flexibility. For examples, in Finland, two Finnish companies offered a locally and remotely controlled flexibility solution. OptiWatti[22] offered domestic heating flexibility solutions based on optimizing the heating of individual rooms/spaces depending on the user's needs, electricity prices, and weather forecast. Multiple sensors are combined with the end-user's preferences in a learning control system that operates on end-user's behalf. Whereas Fortum offered a remotely optimizing flexibility solution by installing additional equipment. The system is also able to alternate between oil and electrical heating depending on the electricity price (Nordic Energy Regulators, 2016). Another example is the Smart Grid Vendée project in France. It is a 5-year project carried out to develop the use of DER flexibility services through market models. It includes testing market designs, active management of the medium voltage grid, increases in grid hosting capacity, and new demand response mechanisms (Bigliani et al., 2015).

Furthermore, in Germany, a demonstration project ended in 2017 implemented a traffic light system, where the distribution network's status is identified through the traffic light colors (Wiedemann, 2017; BDEW, 2015). The green color indicates that the network is the normal condition, facing no congestions, and end-users may use it freely. The yellow light indicates emerging network congestions, where the end-users' flexibility services are

[22]www.optiwatti.fi.

required to maintain the system's stability. The red light indicates emergency network conditions, where the DSO along with the transmission system operator (TSO) coordinates to solve network congestions. Moreover, recently in the Netherlands, a common DSO-TSO energy-trading platform has been created to manage local congestions (ETPA, 2018).

As discussed earlier in Stanley et al.'s Chapter 6, local flexibility services may be considered as a nonwire alternative to network investments. An important aspect of utilizing flexibility services as a long-term solution to replace network investments is that most flexibility products are location specific. Therefore, the market-based procurement approach should consider the location as an essential factor in the selection process. It would also incentivize end-users to optimally locate their DERs, and allow DSOs to gain access to necessary flexibility resources at locations with network constraints.

Hence, locating DERs in specific locations would promote several advantages to the distribution network, depending on the type and location of the DER. For example, the installation of small-scale DG close to a load can reduce losses as well as postpone network investments. Moreover, certain types of DERs may also have the ability to offer different network ancillary services to DSO and TSO, through DSO-TSO cooperation and flexibility utilization (Hadush and Meeus, 2017). Thus, coordinating end-users' response to optimally allocate most efficient DER types depending on network needs will generate many benefits for the network operation and eventually achieve network cost reductions.

The analysis carried out in Abdelmotteleb et al. (2017) and MIT (2016) showed that introducing DERs efficiently to the distribution network may increase its capabilities. For example, smart PV inverters can provide volt-var control; voltage support by changing the reactive power injection/absorption levels depending on the active power output of the PV system. Voltage can be maintained within permissible operational limits by optimizing reference set points for local PV inverter controllers, and consequently energy losses are reduced, while line transfer capacities and the loadability[23] of networks could be significantly increased.

4.3 Short- and Long-Term LFM: Why Both?

Through the two mechanisms mentioned, the DSO may efficiently make use of end-users' flexibility while providing coordination to end-users' response. The Short-term LFM is designed for network operation and is

---

[23]Loadability is the maximum load that can be supplied at peak hours.

concerned with energy coincidence with peak demand as a product for flexibility, targeting peak shifting to optimize network usage. Whereas the long-term LFM is designed to assist the long-term network planning and targets efficient investment in DERs that would replace costly network reinforcements, providing network support when needed. It is important to distinguish between end-users being flexible and efficiently managing their network usage during network peaks to hedge against high network charges, and those that provide a flexibility service to the network when being called, such as firm capacity or voltage control. The formers are voluntarily utilizing their flexibility when it is convenient to them to reduce their total costs. Whereas the others are providing a future commitment that replaces network reinforcements, which they are financially compensated for and penalized when they fail to comply.

Although the Short-term and the Long-term LFM are complementary and both aim to extract end-users' flexibility through financial incentives to more efficiently operate the network and defer network reinforcements, yet they are different in a number of aspects as illustrated in Fig. 9.7.

- Firstly, although both contribute to network cost recovery, the long-term LFM is designed uncoupled from network charges, whereas the

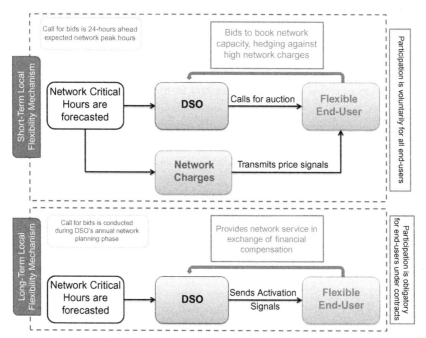

FIGURE 9.7 Comparison between the Short- and Long-term LFM.

short-term LFM is designed to be aligned with dynamic PCNC; hence, it follows the economic signals already established through the cost-reflective tariff.

- Secondly, the traded flexibility product in the long-term LFM is the end-user's flexibility services to provide congestion management, voltage control, or power quality support. Whereas in the short-term LFM end-users' flexibility is utilized to manage network capacity.
- Thirdly, opposing to the long-term LFM, in the short-term LFM end-users are not remunerated for their flexibility services through payments. Instead, end-users gain financial benefits by avoiding PCNC.
- Finally, the Short-term LFM complements cost-reflective network charges that are based on PCNC, whereas the Long-term LFM could be implemented by itself without the short-term LFM or with other network charge designs. However, linking it to efficient cost-reflective network charges and the Short-term LFM would lead to higher economic efficiency.

5. CONCLUSIONS

Well-designed distribution-level mechanisms that enable end-users' participation and facilitate market-driven investment and the efficient utilization of flexible resources are critical to support a smart and flexible electricity system. However, this requires first correct economic signals to be received by end-users through efficient distribution network charges. Then, flexibility mechanisms are needed within the distribution level to coordinate end-users' responses, embracing and well valuing their flexibility, while guiding them through efficient short-term and long-term decisions.

The main objectives of the presented local flexibility mechanisms are to extract available flexibility from end-users, recognize its value, and coordinate it to increase the system's overall economic efficiency. In other words, they are designed in a way that encourages end-users to be flexible, correctly valuing their flexibility, and efficiently manage it to reduce system's total costs. The short-term LFM is used first to extract and utilize existing flexibility. Then, if this flexibility is insufficient, Long-term LFM procures extra flexibility to replace network reinforcements when it is cost efficient.

This requires institutional, governance, and market arrangements, which enable flexible solutions to compete based on their value to the whole system. It should be noted that the utilization of end-users' flexibility in the distribution-level affects higher parts of the system, transmission, and centralized generation. Flexibility mechanisms should well recognize and consider the energy adjustments consequently taking place in other parts of the system. Their design should be well coordinated with existing wholesale balancing and congestion markets.

REFERENCES

Abdelmotteleb, I., Gómez, T., Chaves Avila, J.P., 2017. Benefits of PV inverter volt-var control on distribution network operation. In: 2017 IEEE Manchester PowerTech, pp. 1–6. https://doi.org/10.1109/PTC.2017.7981098.

Abdelmotteleb, I., Gómez, T., Chaves Ávila, J.P., Reneses, J., 2018a. Designing efficient distribution network charges in the context of active customers. Appl. Energy 210, 815–826. https://doi.org/10.1016/j.apenergy.2017.08.103.

Abdelmotteleb, I., Gómez, T., Chaves Avila, J.P., de Vries, L., Reneses, J., 2018b. A framework for electricity distribution-level coordination through local flexibility mechanisms. . Working paper in IIT.

AER, 2016. Final Decision Tariff Structure Statement Proposals: Victorian Electricity Distribution Network Service Providers. Australian Energy Regulator, Australia.

BDEW, 2015. Smart Grid Traffic Light Concept: Design of the Amber Phase. BDEW, German Association of Energy and Water Industries, Berlin.

Berg, S.V., Tschirhart, J., 1989. Natural Monopoly Regulation: Principles and Practice. Cambridge University Press, Cambridge.

Bigliani, R., Eastman, R., Segalotto, J.-F., Feblowitz, J., Gallotti, G., 2015. Designing the New Utility Business Models. White Paper IDC Energy Insights.

CEER, 2017. CEER guidelines of good practice for distribution network tariffs. C16-DS-27–03.

Costello, K.W., Hemphill, R.C., 2014. Electric utilities' 'death spiral': hyperbole or reality? Electr. J. 27 (10), 7–26. https://doi.org/10.1016/j.tej.2014.09.011.

EDSO, 2018. Flexibility in the energy transition a toolbox for electricity DSOs.

Esmat, A., Pinson, P., Usaola, J., 2017. Decision support program for congestion management using demand side flexibility. In: 2017 IEEE Manchester PowerTech, pp. 1–6. https://doi.org/10.1109/PTC.2017.7980976.

ETPA, 2018. Energy Trading Platform Amsterdam. ETPA. https://www.etpa.nl.

Felder, F.A., Athawale, R., 2014. The life and death of the utility death spiral. Electr. J. 27 (6), 9–16. https://doi.org/10.1016/j.tej.2014.06.008.

Hadush, S.Y., Meeus, L., 2017. DSO-TSO Cooperation Issues and Solutions for Distribution Grid Congestion Management. EUI Working Paper RSCAS 2017/65 European University Institute.

MIT, 2016. Utility of the Future. An MIT Energy Initiative Response to an Industry in Transition. Massachusetts Institute of Technology.

Nordic Energy Regulators, 2016. Status report on regulatory aspects of demand side flexibility.

PacifiCorp, 2017. 2017 Integrated Resource Plan. vol. I. . Portland, Oregon https://www.pacificorp.com/content/dam/pacificorp/doc/Energy_Sources/Integrated_Resource_Plan/2017_IRP/2017_IRP_VolumeI_IRP_Final.pdf.

Rodríguez Ortega, M.P., Ignacio Pérez-Arriaga, J., Abbad, J.R., González, J.P., 2008. Distribution network tariffs: a closed question? Energy Policy 36 (5), 1712–1725. https://doi.org/10.1016/j.enpol.2008.01.025.

Vallés, M., Bello, A., Reneses, J., Frías, P., 2018. Probabilistic characterization of electricity consumer responsiveness to economic incentives. Appl. Energy 216, 296–310. https://doi.org/10.1016/j.apenergy.2018.02.058.

Wiedemann, T., 2017. The proactive distribution grid: traffic light concept for more efficient distribution grids.

CHAPTER 10

Community Energy Storage: Governance and Business Models

Binod Prasad Koirala*, Rudi A. Hakvoort†, Ellen C. van Oost*,
Henny J. van der Windt‡

*Department of Science, Technology and Policy Studies, Faculty of Behavioral, Management and Social Sciences, University of Twente, Enschede, The Netherlands
†Faculty of Technology, Policy and Management, Delft University of Technology, Delft, The Netherlands
‡Science and Society Group, Faculty of Science and Engineering, University of Groningen, Groningen, The Netherlands

1. INTRODUCTION

As further described in accompanying chapters of this volume, the energy sector worldwide is facing increased innovation and disruption (Sioshansi, 2017). The ongoing changes in the energy sectors such as higher penetration of intermittent renewables, local energy initiatives, increasing electrification of transport and heating sector, and decreasing costs of energy storage for stationary and electric mobility applications as well as the need to balance of system is leading to an increased attention on energy storage systems (Barbour et al., 2018; Parra et al., 2017b; van der Stelt et al., 2018). Energy storage can enable effective energy system integration and get maximum benefits of local generation leading to flexible and resilient energy supply systems (Lund et al., 2015). In this way, energy storage can play an important role in achieving renewable energy and climate policy objectives such as higher penetration of renewables, decarbonization, energy security, and competitiveness as well as market and energy system integration (Koirala, 2017). Recent studies show that energy storage has a similar learning curve and cost reduction as the renewables such as solar photovoltaics (IRENA, 2017; Kittner et al., 2017). A central question is which policies and regulations will continue to keep energy storage in similar pathways as renewables.

The ongoing energy transition is driving the demand for energy storage. Energy storage can be implemented across the energy value chain as illustrated in Fig. 10.1. There are several ways and scales energy storage can be implemented in the energy systems such as residential energy storage, community energy storage (CES), distributed energy storage as well as large-scale energy storage (Next Kraftwerke, 2018; Parra et al., 2017b;

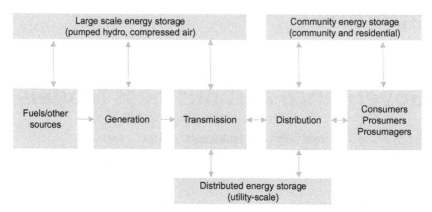

FIGURE 10.1 Positioning energy storage in energy system value chain.

SonnenCommunity, 2016). The need for CES is expected to grow in the future in line with the increasing local energy initiatives and distributed energy resources (DERs) penetration as well as to meet increasing demand for flexibility and self-sufficiency (DGRV, 2016; HierOpgewekt, 2017; IRENA, 2017).

Local communities are increasingly taking active roles in the energy system as evident from the increasing number of local energy initiatives (DGRV, 2016; HierOpgewekt, 2017; REN21, 2016; RESCOOP, 2016; van der Schoor et al., 2016; van der Schoor and Scholtens, 2015). Accordingly, the role of end-users in the energy system is changing from passive consumers to active prosumers and prosumagers, referring to their role in local energy production and storage, respectively (Schill et al., 2017; Sioshansi, 2017). In addition to individual behavioral change, collective action through community engagement is needed for wider energy system transformation (Koirala and Hakvoort, 2017; Koirala et al., 2018). These developments provide opportunities for further social and technical innovation toward smarter, decentralized, flexible, and inclusive energy system.

This chapter is focused on CES rather than the utility-scale energy storage. CES refers to a local energy storage unit or cluster of storage units with community ownership and governance, which can be grouped together to operate as a single unit to generate collective benefits such as higher penetration and self-consumption of renewables, reduced dependence on fossil fuels, reduced energy bills as well as revenue generation through multiple energy services. This definition excludes purely residential and utility-scale application. Actually, CES in terms of scope lies between these two applications. The key issues are aggregation of smaller storage units and energy sharing among the members. Intelligence through the digitalization facilitates clustering of residential energy storage as well as energy sharing among members and aims to make CES predictable and manageable. The community or microgrid organization of energy storage is increasingly making sense and becoming financially viable.

If more CES as well as community engagement therein is desired, not only the energy system as a whole but also the related business models, regulation, and governance should be transformed. Yet, pathways for such transition as well as changing roles and responsibilities of different actors therein are not yet clear. In this chapter, different options for such pathways are explored.

The chapter is organized as follows:
- Section 2 introduces CES and its prominent pathways;
- Section 3 discusses values streams and business models requirements for CES;
- Section 4 explains new types of regulation and governance required to make new business model for CES possible such as division of responsibilities and new revenue streams, followed by the chapter's conclusions.

2. COMMUNITY ENERGY STORAGE IN CHANGING ENERGY LANDSCAPE

In this section, first of all CES is conceptualized. Then, the main developments regarding energy transition, in particular community energy, will be explained. The problems, in particular concerning CES, are outlined.

2.1 Community Energy Storage: A Complex Sociotechnical System

The definition of CES varies among the scholars (Arghandeh et al., 2014; Barbour et al., 2018; Parra et al., 2015, 2016, 2017a; Roberts and Sandberg, 2011; van der Stelt et al., 2018). Roberts and Sandberg (2011) suggest CES as intermediate local energy storage solutions between residential and utility scale (Roberts and Sandberg, 2011). Residential energy storage are typically installed behind the meter in consumer premises and CES are shared by group of consumers. Several scholars have demonstrated the added benefits of CES over residential energy storage (Barbour et al., 2018; Marczinkowski and Østergaard, 2018; van der Stelt et al., 2018). This could be attributed to the size, economy of scale of CES as well as its potential applications in the energy systems. With the digitalization of the energy sector, residential energy storage can also be shared among the community members and used as CES (Lombardi and Schwabe, 2017; Next Kraftwerke, 2018; Rahbar et al., 2016; SonnenCommunity, 2016; Wang et al., 2018).

Parra et al. (2016) and van der Stelt et al. (2018) refer it as energy storage located at the consumption level with several potential applications and impacts to both end users and network operator (Parra et al., 2016; van der Stelt et al., 2018). According to these definitions, the interesting dynamics of CES is that the energy systems actors such as system operators as well as program responsible parties who are not the owner still might get the benefits. However, these definitions are limited to the location of energy storage and do not cover important issues such as virtual communities, community engagement, governance, ownership as well as business models. Alternatively, Barbour et al. (2018) define it as energy storage introduced for the community that can be shared between members who are typically but not exclusively located in the local community, opening up the possibilities for virtual CES (Barbour et al., 2018).

2.1.1 Technologies

CES consists of storage technologies, the energy storage management systems, energy converters as well as cloud services. Often they are embedded in the community energy system consisting of distributed energy resources and physical energy networks. Table 10.1 presents different technical components of the CES systems.

The energy storage technologies and balance of the systems such as charge controllers, inverters, and energy management systems as well as energy exchange platforms need to be compatible and interoperable with each other. This demands for standardization as several different technology developers are engaged in research and development of different energy storage system components. For example, Modular energy storage architecture (MESA) standards are being developed by consortium of electric

Table 10.1 Technical components of community energy storage

Components	Descriptions
Energy storage device	Residential energy storage technologies CES technologies
Balance of systems	Bidirectional inverters, charge controllers
Energy management systems	Energy storage management systems
Energy exchange platforms	Energy exchange platforms to enable peer-to-peer exchange, local balancing

utilities and technology suppliers worldwide to ensure interoperability, scalability, safety, quality, availability, and affordability of the energy storage components and systems (MESA, 2018).

As the technologies for CES such as energy storage technologies, bidirectional inverters, charge controllers, cloud services, and energy management systems are gaining maturity, it is important that simultaneously an enabling environment is created for business model innovation, community ownership, and participation as well as governance through flexibility in regulation as well as energy policy (Burger and Luke, 2017; Koirala and Hakvoort, 2017).

2.1.2 Actors

CES involves multiple actors, which includes households, local communities, energy co-operatives, housing corporations, local municipalities, national government, energy suppliers, intermediaries or aggregators, system operators, energy service and technology providers, regulators as well as local energy market operators. The intermediaries or aggregators are new actors with a role to organize a physical or virtual community, which can then be monitored, optimized, and managed.

These actors have different roles and responsibilities with variety of interests, expectations, and functionalities. For example, CES can be used for local balancing through the physical network of distribution system operators. At the same time, local congestion in an energy network can be managed through CES. The surplus energy can often be traded to the energy market through the aggregators. Yet, the actors are interdependent in the realization of their goals and different actors might have different expectations from the CES. For instance, households may want low-cost and local energy at their disposal while aggregators seek to maximize the value of their flexibility in the various energy markets. There are methods such as value-sensitive design and value case method to manage these conflicting interests and expectations (Berkers et al., 2015; Correljé et al., 2015).

2.2 Pathways for Community Energy Storage

Based on the current developments, two pathways for CES, namely, local and virtual, can be identified. A local CES is location specific, mainly within a distribution transformer. A virtual CES is often commercial with no location specificity and can expand to a national level and beyond.

2.2.1 Physical Local Community Energy Storage

In this case, there is a coherence between local community and a specific physical territory (Moroni et al., 2018; Walker et al., 2010). Local CES refers to shared residential as well as shared energy storage in a localized community. The members have shared goals such as energy independence, resiliency, autonomy as well as energy security and self-govern and own the CES. Shared local energy storage is emerging in the energy landscape.

Feldheim CES in Germany is a pioneering example for the local CES in which a 10-MWh energy storage not only provides local balancing services but also frequency regulation for a transmission system operators (NEFF, 2016). Often local CES are developed in co-operation and collaboration with different societal and energy system actors with the aim of maximizing self-consumption of local generation as well as identifying suitable conditions for sustainable operation of local energy storage (Enexis, 2012; Liander, 2017). For example, the pilots of CES in the Netherlands in Ettenleur, Rijsenhout, and Heeten are developed in collaboration with distribution system operators as well as energy storage and information technology developers (Enexis, 2012; Gridflex, 2018).

There is a huge potential for local CES in Island energy systems (Blechinger et al., 2014). Few examples of local CES being implemented in the islands are Pampus island near Amsterdam and Samso Island in Denmark (Pampus, 2018; SMILE, 2018).

2.2.2 Virtual Community Energy Storage

In this case, there is a no coherence between the community and a specific physical territory (Moroni et al., 2018). The community need not to be an actual neighborhood or physical community but a collection of participants or members who form a virtual community, typically through intermediaries. Due to liberalization and restructuring of the energy sector, there are enabling conditions for virtual CES. Accordingly, virtual CES networks are being developed worldwide (ARENA, 2018; IERC, 2018; LichtBlick Schwarmbatterie, 2018; Next Kraftwerke, 2018; SonnenCommunity, 2016).

For example, in Germany, there are already few commercial practices in virtual energy storage enabled by intermediaries such as SonnenCommunity®, Lichtblick – Schwarmbatterie® and Nextkraftwerke® (LichtBlick Schwarmbatterie, 2018; Next Kraftwerke, 2018; SonnenCommunity, 2016). Nextkraftwerke® digitally aggregates distributed energy resources as well as storage units and valorize the power and flexibility smartly in different energy markets and grid balancing services. Currently, Nextkraftwerke® has total networked capacity of 4200 MW and can even balance frequency fluctuations of the grid (Next Kraftwerke, 2018).

Similarly, the SonnenCommunity® is a growing network of above 10,000 end-users in Germany who produce, store, use, and share energy, Fig. 10.2 (SonnenCommunity, 2016). Distributed generation, energy storage technologies, and digital networking are the three basic building blocks of the SonnenCommunity®. In fact, SonnenCommunity functions as a

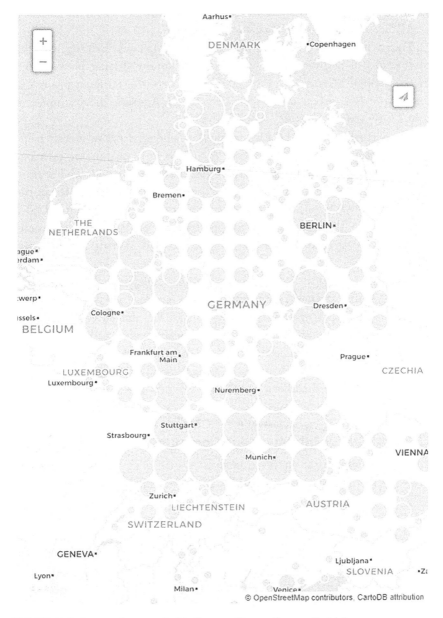

FIGURE 10.2 SonnenCommunity® in Europe. *(Source: Sonnen Gmbh.)*

shadow utility ensuring optimal energy balance within virtual network and minimizing the balance responsibility. Recently, the SonnenCommunity® is being realized beyond Germany to Austria, Italy, Switzerland, United Kingdom, The Netherlands, USA, and Australia. For example, An off-grid SonnenCommunity® is recently implemented in Puerto Rico and the Prescott valley in Arizona is building SonnenCommunity® with PV storage systems in 2900 new homes which will integrate 11.6 MW of solar and 23 MWh of energy storage (Spector, 2017).

The Schwarmbatterie® consist of interconnected batteries via the smart platform Schwarmdirigent®, enabling energy sharing between users (LichtBlick Schwarmbatterie, 2018). Similarly, the Storenet project in Ireland and the virtual power plant project in Adelaide are examples of virtual CES (ARENA, 2018; IERC, 2018).

The virtual CES can be used to provide energy services to other energy communities and system operators such as transmission and distribution system operators as well as balance responsible parties. Flexibility from CES can be aggregated and offered to a distribution system operator or the balance responsible party through a separate market for flexibility (USEF, 2016). Virtual CES can provide grid support functions such as voltage control, power factor correction, load leveling, and peak shaving as well as ancillary services.

Favorable regulatory conditions as well as sufficient grid capacity for exchange within virtual communities are prerequisite for this option. For example, SonnenCommunity® is emerging in EU due to enabling regulatory conditions, whereas in US, the European model could not be implemented as such due to different regulatory conditions. Moreover, this pathway does not necessarily defer the need for grid reinforcements entirely but do benefit from the liberalized energy markets and digitalization of the energy sector.

2.3 Local Energy Initiatives and Community Energy Storage

Existing and new local energy initiatives can offer a platform for the deployment of the CES systems (NEFF, 2016). As CES is still in its infancy, very few local energy initiatives are engaged with CES (DGRV, 2016; HierOpgewekt, 2017). Yet, the increasing number of local energy initiatives signifies huge potential for CES. For example, some of the local energy initiatives in the Netherlands are starting to engage with pilot projects in CES in collaboration with distribution system operators and technology developers (Enexis, 2012; Gridflex, 2018). In USA, Brooklyn microgrid consisting of 400-kW Solar PV, 400-kW fuel cell, and 300-kW/1.2-MWh lithium ion batteries provides added benefits of economic incentives through demand charge reduction, grid relief, and grid services as well as energy security and resiliency (Brooklyn Microgrid, 2016).

CES may have an important role in creating a more efficient energy system (Koohi-Kamali et al., 2013; Lund et al., 2015). It can increase the self-consumption of local generation and decrease the energy import and network costs for local communities (van der Stelt et al., 2018). Other contributions of CES for the local communities are economic incentives, flexibility, reliability, resiliency, efficiency, sustainability, local circular economy, community engagement as well as sense of community (Koirala, 2017). Moreover, CES are important building blocks toward achieving community objectives such as energy autonomy, independence, and energy security. Table 10.2 provides examples of CES.

3. VALUE STREAMS AND BUSINESS MODELS FOR COMMUNITY ENERGY STORAGE

In this Section, an array of economic and noneconomic value streams for CES for different actors will be demonstrated and discussed. CES offers a range of technical, economic, environmental, and institutional values to its actors, as summarized in Fig. 10.3.

These values can be monetized differently by households, local communities, and the wider society. For example, these values are affected by community objectives such as costs reduction, emissions reduction, and resiliency as well as other geopolitical and socioeconomic factors (Koirala et al., 2018). Moreover, CES is expected to have interaction and co-ordination such as local balancing and strategic exchanges with member households, community as well as the larger energy system, leading to wider applications. Through the aggregation of individual households and shared energy storage, CES can have new roles of "flexibility provider" in the future energy system. The flexibility from CES can provide different technoeconomic value to the different actors in the energy system such as system operators, aggregators, and balance responsible parties. In addition, CES can curtail both demand and supply peaks and defer the need for the grid reinforcement.

However, it is a significant challenge to address different value expectations of different actors and combine these values into a meaningful business case (Berkers et al., 2015; D'Souza et al., 2015). Often, CES might

Table 10.2 Examples of community energy storage value streams

Examples	Technical specifications	Value streams (Technoeconomic)	References
Feldheim CES, Germany	10 MWh	Local balancing, network service (primary reserve)	NEFF (2016)
SENSIBLE project The meadows, Nottingham, UK	40 houses with residential energy storage and a CES	Peak shaving, higher self-consumption, hedging against price fluctuations	SENSIBLE (2018)
SMILE project, marina in Ballen, SAMSO Island	Linking renewables (solar and wind) to energy storage (thermal and electric)	Local balancing, higher renewables penetration, local circular economy	SMILE (2018)
Roding CES, Canada	500-kW/250-kWh Li-ion batteries	Higher renewable penetration, network services, peak shaving	eCAMION (2013)
Alkimos CES, Australia	250-kW/1.1-MWh lithium ion batteries	Network reinforcement deferrals, local balancing, higher renewables penetration	ARENA (2016)
SonnenCommunity®, virtual CES, Germany	Virtual community of 2–16kWh energy storage and renewables in 10,000 households	Hedging against price fluctuations, peak shaving, reduced network costs, network services	SonnenCommunity (2018)

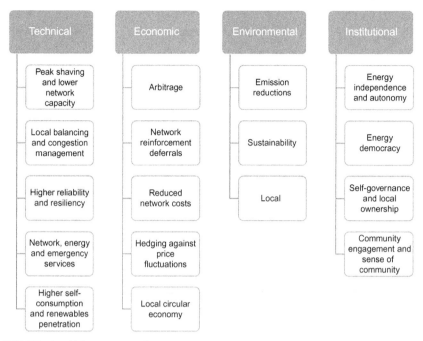

FIGURE 10.3 Value streams of community energy storage.

need to stack multiple of these value streams simultaneously to improve its economic feasibility, to minimize risk of single revenue streams, and to address multiple community objectives to improve its social acceptability (IEA, 2014; Stadler et al., 2016; Van Melven et al., 2018; Wolsink, 2012). The stacking of value is covered in Chapter 3 by Baak and Sioshansi in this volume. The environmental and institutional values are difficult to monetize but are often in line with the normative positions of local communities and might lead to wider societal benefits as well as acceptability. Table 10.2 provides an overview of different technoeconomic value streams captured by existing CES projects.

3.1 Business Model Developments

The business case for CES is not always straightforward and we have to deal with rapidly changing environments (D'Souza et al., 2015, 2018). Despite the falling costs, energy storage still requires very high upfront investment costs (IRENA, 2015). Several other factors such as availability of energy resources, existing energy mixes, conditions of physical infrastructures, market structures, regulatory framework, as well as demand and supply patterns affect the deployment of CES. At the same time, the traditional utility business models are being affected through changing ownership structures, increasing local generation as well as energy storage (Energy Post, 2013; EON, 2014; Morris and Pehnt, 2016). These developments have forced several energy utilities to develop new customer-centered business models for managing energy (Burger and Weinmann, 2013, 2016; Energy Post, 2013; EON, 2014). Accordingly, the incumbents such as EON and RWE in Germany are also changing their roles and strategies in the energy system and starting to focus on renewables, energy storage, distribution as well as customer solutions (Energy Post, 2013; EON, 2014). In this context, CES might have to compete with the utility-scale storage with economies of scale, highlighting the need for location-specific and robust business models.

If CES is desired to be scalable and successful, economic and noneconomic values need to be aligned through innovative business models. Moreover, business models for CES need to be dynamic with time, technology, and policy (Burger and Luke, 2017). Financial tunnel vision, existing regulation of energy storage and market design as well as involvement of multiple actors also challenges the business models development in CES (Berkers et al., 2015). At the same time, there are lot of uncertainties in CES emergence and its potential impact, in particular regarding technological adoption, energy services, and consumer preferences.

Business models are often seen as effective instruments to analyze, identify, and communicate the innovation potentials and it is all about how value is created, captured, and delivered (Osterwalder and Pigneur, 2010). Different perspectives and definitions of business models have been developed over the time (Casadesus-Masanell and Ricart, 2011; Dilger et al., 2017; D'Souza et al., 2015). However, existing business models concepts based on traditional profit-driven concepts of business economics are not appropriate for collective action-oriented systems such as CES (Dilger et al., 2017). People and actors are the missing links as they are being neglected in most concepts and definitions of traditional business models (Berkers et al., 2015; Dilger et al., 2017; Stähler, 2014). The sustainability of business models, however, depends on internal structure and capabilities of different actors (Stubbs and Cocklin, 2008). For the CES to be viable, the value must exceed the costs.

In this context, new business model developments methods to include people and social actors are emerging such as value case method and business model canvas (Berkers et al., 2015; Osterwalder and Pigneur, 2010). Value case method helps align economic and noneconomic values of multiactor

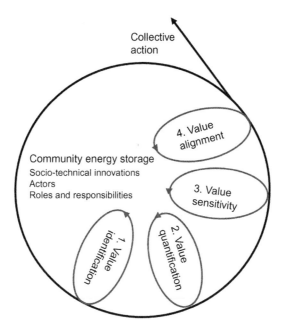

FIGURE 10.4 Operationalization of the value case method for community energy storage. *(Source: TNO, Adapted from Berkers et al., 2015.)*

and multivalue system and is being developed by TNO in the Netherlands (Berkers et al., 2015). It is implemented in four iterative steps, namely, value identification, value quantification, value sensitivity, and value alignment, Fig. 10.4 (Berkers et al., 2015). The ultimate outcome is a decision for collective action in which multiple values of different actors are adequately addressed. Business model canvas (BMC) is widely used in practice and academia due to its easy-to-follow visual representation and building blocks as illustrated in Fig. 10.4 (Osterwalder and Pigneur, 2010). BMC is used to develop business models in several research projects such as CITYOPT and IDEAS (CityOpt, 2018; IDEAS, 2018). Recently, the BMC concept has also been applied to the community energy systems by several scholars (Dilger et al., 2017; Herbes et al., 2017; Juntunen and Hyysalo, 2015; Koirala et al., 2016; Rodríguez-Molina et al., 2014). In the rest of this section, BMC is applied for local and virtual CES.

3.1.1 Business Model Canvas (BMC)

BMC might help to develop clear, concise, and focused business model for CES and to identify new value propositions that evolve with the changing energy landscape. Tables 10.3 and 10.4 illustrate the nine key elements of

Table 10.3 Business model canvas of the local community energy storage

Elements	Description	Example: Feldheim CES
Key partners	Local community member households, local communities, aggregators, energy suppliers, system operators, municipalities, regulators, technology and energy service providers	Wind turbine manufacturer (Enercon), Wind developer (Energiequelle), Transmission system operator (50 Hz), Feldheim regional regulating power station and Feldheim energy community
Key activities	Charging and discharging, storing, energy sharing, peak shaving, local balancing, congestion management as well as energy, network and emergency services, balancing and ancillary services, self-governance	Storing, load balancing, supplying, frequency regulation
Value propositions	Economic incentives, network reinforcement deferrals, local circular economy, higher self-consumption and renewables penetration, higher reliability and resiliency, autonomy, community engagement, self-governance and local ownership, sense of community, energy democracy	Grid stabilization, load balancing, network services, higher renewable penetration, local balancing, lower network capacity and grid reinforcement deferrals
Customer relations	Energy and network service providers, CES operators	Network service providers
Customer segments	Local community members, neighboring energy communities, system operators, aggregators, energy suppliers	Transmission system operator
Key resources	Energy storage technologies, physical grid, energy management system, energy exchange platforms	3360 li-ion batteries modules developed by LG chem (10 MW/10.79 MWh)
Channels	Energy exchange platforms, physical energy and communication networks	Energy network, energy community
Cost structures	Installation as well as operation and maintenance costs	Total investment cost of 13 million euros of which 5 million euros was subsidy of European regional development fund
Revenue structures	Avoided energy import costs, reduced network tariffs, revenue from flexibility provision as well as energy, network and emergency services, revenue from providing balancing and ancillary services	Primary balancing power to transmission system operator 50 Hz, avoided wind and solar curtailments

Table 10.4 Business model canvas representation of virtual community energy storage

Elements	Description	Example: SonnenCommunity
Key partners	Virtual community member households, energy storage and digital platform technology providers, energy service providers, system operators	Shareholders, installers, specialized dealers, energy storage associations, battery and technology suppliers
Key activities	Charging and discharging, storing, energy sharing, energy balancing in virtual community, valorize power and flexibility in different energy markets, balancing and ancillary services	Design, engineering, production, manufacturing, operation, marketing, installation, projects, sales and customer service
Value propositions	Economic incentives, clean and affordable energy, sustainability, energy independence, higher self-consumptions and renewables penetration	Reduction in energy costs, decentralized and clean energy
Customer relations	Digital platform providers,	Collaborative, cocreation, energy sharing, clean and affordable energy, analyze and control supply and demand of households, warranty of 10 years
Customer segments	virtual community members, System operators	Households and small businesses
Key resources	Energy storage technologies, energy management systems, digital platforms	Digital technologies, intelligent batteries, 10,000 existing members of SonnenCommunity, prizes and awards
Channels	Digital energy exchange platform enabled through energy grid, communication networks	Website, sonnenapp, SonnenCommunity, emails, telecommunications
Cost structures	Investment and operating costs for energy storage technologies, balance of the systems, energy exchange platforms	Research and development, raw materials, components, software, machinery costs, office space and human resources costs, logistics, taxes
Revenue structures	Avoided energy import costs, flexibility provision, avoided balance responsibility costs, revenue from providing balancing and ancillary services	Monthly fee from SonnenCommunity members, sales of sonnenbatterie, revenues from members, avoided program responsibility

business model canvas and its applicability in business model development of both local and virtual CES with the aid of specific case examples of Feldheim CES and SonnenCommunity®, respectively.

4. REGULATION AND GOVERNANCE OF COMMUNITY ENERGY STORAGE

In this section, the new forms of regulation and governance required to enable new business models maximizing the benefits and minimizing the costs for CES will be discussed. This involves changing roles and responsibilities as well as creating enabling conditions for the emergence of CES. The regulation and governance requirements may differ in local and virtual pathways. For example, the liberalized energy markets provide enabling conditions for virtual CES as evident by the emergence of virtual energy storage communities in Germany such as SonnenCommunity® and Nextkraftwerke® (Next Kraftwerke, 2018; SonnenCommunity, 2018). The regulators and policy makers also need to consider system and distributional effects of CES (Schill et al., 2017). In the rest of this section, we review current regulatory conditions and provide some recommendation for regulation and governance of CES.

4.1 New Regulations for Energy Storage

The current regulatory and governance arrangements were made for the traditional energy systems and do not provide the same level playing field for the CES, as they were not designed with collective action in the form of local energy initiatives, distributed energy resources (DERs) such as energy storage in mind. For example, the existing regulatory arrangements in most of the countries still treat energy storage as regular generation unit, which is the most important barrier for its deployment (Castagneto Gissey et al., 2018). On the other hand, in Germany it is still regulated as demand unit (GTAI, 2018). However, the technical characteristics of energy storage such as rate of charging and discharging, storage capacity, and energy losses as well as time decoupling of supply and demand are very distinct from those of generation and demand units. Moreover, current regulation does not fully recognize innovative products as well as services from CES such as ancillary and capacity-related services. In other words, there are regulatory barriers for realizing multiple energy services of energy storage. For example, a stable market or pricing signals does not exist for different energy services provided by the energy storage, hindering its investment.

With response to the changing energy landscape and increasing penetration of DERs such as energy storage, new regulations are being developed around the world, as summarized by four countries examples in Table 10.5. Some of these new regulation such as Spanish self-consumption regulation hinder implementation of CES, whereas other new regulations provide

Table 10.5 New regulations for energy storage

Country	Regulation	Implications
Italy	Decree no. 28/2011	TSO and DSOs to develop and manage distributed energy storage in order to increase the dispatch of intermittent generation. Recently, Italian energy agency has also published technical rules for the integration of energy storage (GSE, 2018).
Spain	Regulation on self-consumption, royal decree (900/2015) (MIET, 2015)	Ensure the same contribution from consumers with onsite generation to system costs as the consumers without DERs through "self-generated energy charge." The installation of energy storage is only possible with hourly energy generation and consumption meters so that the network and other regulated costs cannot be avoided. The regulation strictly forbids interconnection and energy exchange among group of consumers.
Germany	Renewables Act (EEG) 2017 (EEG, 2017)	According to EEG 2017, energy storage benefits from the connection privilege similar to renewables to the public grid. Energy storage also qualifies for the feed-in premium for the electricity fed to the public grid. EEG surcharge is only charged to the electricity fed to the public grid, provided that the metering requirements are fulfilled. However, energy storage is still regulated as consumers and subjects to different taxes and levies.
USA	FERC, RM 16-23 (FERC, 2018)	Recently, federal regulatory energy commission (FERC) of USA has enabled energy storage to participate in capacity, energy and ancillary service markets. The new rules adequately consider physical and operational characteristics of energy storage. The minimum size requirement is set to 100 kW.

enabling conditions for the emergence of CES such as in Germany and USA (EEG, 2017; FERC, 2018; MIET, 2015). For example, in Germany, every second rooftop solar PV is now combined with energy storage (GTAI, 2018). At the same time, countries like the Netherlands are lagging behind as local communities are not allowed to own and operate energy storage for the purpose other than pilot projects and experimental regulation (*experimentenregeling*).

4.2 Self-Governance and Ownership

CES has the advantage of collective organization and independent operation (Dilger et al., 2017). It shifts the energy governance from state and market to local energy initiatives in the form of self-regulation and self-governance. Yet, the CES governance has to coexist with state and market governance. Therefore, self-governance of CES depends on communities' abilities to be adaptive to co-ordinate with different governance circles (Cayford and Scholten, 2014). Self-governance of local and virtual CES might differ based on their social and technical complexity.

The ownership of CES is affected by financing requirements, operational requirements, social welfare issues as well as risk perceptions (Haney and Pollitt, 2013; Walker, 2008). The ownership of energy storage by system operators is unlikely due to the unbundling requirements (Energy Union, 2016). Accordingly, the ownership can be purely community based or shared with utility and public-private parties. Yet, the significant ownership and control need to be with local communities to qualify as CES (Table 10.6).

Table 10.6 Few examples of ownership and operation of community energy storage

Examples	Ownership	Operation
Feldheim CES (Local)	Third-party owned (joint venture by energiequelle, enercon, and local community)	Regional transmission system operator (50 Hz)
SonnenCommunity® energy storage (virtual)	Energy storage units owned by individual households and the software, which pools these storage units, is owned by SonnenCommunity®	Both home energy management system and SonnenCommunity in tandem

4.3 Flexibility, Energy Price Signals, and Future Role of Grid

With the increasing penetration of intermittent renewables, flexibility provision is becoming increasingly important as further explored in accompanying chapters in this volume. Currently, there are program responsible parties and metering responsible parties in the energy systems (ACM, 2018). In future, flexibility responsible parties also need to be defined and the flexibility provision needs to incorporate different actors of the energy system (USEF, 2016). Regulation needs to create enabling conditions to make flexibility potential of both local and virtual CES available to the energy system.

Market design needs to be inclusive of emerging technologies such as energy storage as they have potential to reduce the system costs. Both local and virtual CES need to receive appropriate price signals from different energy markets (Schill et al., 2017).

The role of electricity grid is also changing with the energy transition. Currently, the public grid extends till the metering point of each household. With decreasing costs of distributed energy resources and increasing willingness of local communities to take control of the energy systems, local communities in the future might be able to own a community microgrid. Local energy communities might even take over the ownership of part of the grid (Energy Union, 2016). In such case, the public grid will extend only until the distribution transformer and bidirectional power flows will be measured at the point of common coupling. In such a scenario, local CES will have important role in local balancing and avoiding peak network and energy tariffs. Behind the transformer microgrid concept is being tested in the Gridflex pilot project in the Netherlands (Gridflex, 2018).

Sometimes CES can be exchangeable to further reinforcement of the grid. In case of local congestion, CES might be used even when its costs are higher. Moreover, community energy systems need to be provided with right incentives to collaborate with system operators on energy management and grid issues.

4.4 Local Energy Market, Exchange Platforms, and Locational Net Metering

The energy exchange in both pathways of CES could take different form such as peer-to-peer exchange further enabled by innovative and transactive blockchain-based technologies (Brooklyn Microgrid, 2016; Giotitsas et al., 2015). There are already some platforms, which enable peer-to-peer energy trading, further described in Chapter 3 by Shipworth et al. For example, the Dutch platform Vandebron® allows Dutch consumers to buy their electricity directly from the independent renewable energy producers (Vandebron, 2017). Other examples for the peer-to-peer trading are OpenUtility® in the United Kingdom as described in Chapter 6 by Johnston, Stanley & Sioshansi and SonnenCommunity® in Germany. Using blockchain-based transactive solutions, a local market for energy is created in Brooklyn microgrid for transacting energy across existing energy infrastructures (Brooklyn Microgrid, 2016). These platforms create enabling conditions for the emergence of both pathways of CES.

Although *time-based energy balance or net-metering (saldering)* of the local generation has proven beneficial in increasing penetration of Solar PV in Dutch households, it has been counterproductive for the adoption of energy storage. In fact, net-metering is hindering the emergence of residential and CES in the Netherlands. *Location-based net metering* promotes co-operation among households through local energy exchange and might prove beneficial for the emergence of CES.

5. CONCLUSIONS

Community energy storage (CES) is emerging as another form of decentralized solution in the changing energy landscape to confront with technoeconomic, environmental, and societal challenges of the present energy systems. Based on current developments, the two dominant options for CES, namely, local and virtual can be identified. Several pilot and commercial projects are being developed to demonstrate the business case and viability of CES, as discussed in Section 2.3 of this chapter. These projects are crucial to show how CES works in practice, learn on new business and governance models as well to improve its public perception, acceptance, and boarder participation. CES is emerging as means to transform local communities from consumers to prosumagers and nonsumers.

CES brings along economic and noneconomic values and often multiple economic values needs to be stacked to have a viable business case. Some of the economic value streams are increased self-consumption of local generation, grid relief through peak shaving of both generation and demand, emergency services for critical infrastructures, short- and long-term decoupling of energy supply and demand, energy and network services as well as costs saving through grid reinforcement deferrals. The noneconomic value streams of CES such as sustainability, community engagement, energy democracy, sense of community, energy security as well as resiliency are in line with normative position of the local communities. CES has the potential to enhance the transformative role of the local communities, leading to the transition toward clean, sustainable, decarbonized, decentralized, and inclusive local energy system.

The business model canvas is a useful tool in documenting and visualizing key elements for both virtual and local options of CES. The virtual CES takes advantage of liberalized energy markets, whereas local CES exploit wider values through higher self-consumption, grid relief, local balancing as well as local congestion management. Current energy regulation seems to be more favorable for virtual pathways of CES as demonstrated by the emergence of intermediaries such as SonnenCommunity® in Germany. The existing regime needs to change to uptake these developments, consequently, the regulation, governance, and market structures.

The technical, operational as well as social characteristics of community energy storage needs to be adequately considered in new regulations. For local CES, the necessary preconditions are location-based net metering, community grid and local energy markets. Both local and virtual CES might benefit from the flexibility and responsibility provisioning, appropriate price signals as well as opportunities to participate in capacity, energy, and ancillary services markets. Enabling technical, regulatory, policy and market environment, innovative business models and governance structures, suitable conditions for collaboration between social and energy system actors combined with the intelligent energy management system will determine the emergence of CES bringing along the transformative impacts on the energy system.

ACKNOWLEDGMENT

This research funded through the social responsible innovation program of The Netherlands Organization for Scientific Research (NWO-MVI 2016 [313-99-304]).

REFERENCES

ACM, 2018. Energy codes. [WWW Document]. URL, https://www.acm.nl/nl/onderwerpen/energie/de-energiemarkt/codes-energie/actuele-codes-energie. (Accessed April 26, 2018).

ARENA, 2016. Projects. Australian Renewable Energy Agency. [WWW Document]. URL, https://arena.gov.au/projects/solar-and-storage-trial-at-alkimos-beach-residential-development/. (Accessed May 16, 2018).

ARENA, 2018. Virtual Power Plants. Aust. Renew. Energy Agency. [WWW Document]. URL, https://arena.gov.au/projects/agl-virtual-power-plant/. (Accessed March 26, 2018).

Arghandeh, R., Woyak, J., Onen, A., Jung, J., Broadwater, R.P., 2014. Economic optimal operation of community energy storage systems in competitive energy markets. Appl. Energy 135, 71–80. https://doi.org/10.1016/j.apenergy.2014.08.066.

Barbour, E., Parra, D., Awwad, Z., González, M.C., 2018. Community energy storage: a smart choice for the smart grid? Appl. Energy 212, 489–497. https://doi.org/10.1016/j.apenergy.2017.12.056.

Berkers, F., Blankers, I., van Dijk, W., Liebregts, W., van Weelden, M., 2015. Value Case Methodology (No. TNO 2015 R10148). TNO, Delft, Netherlands.

Blechinger, P., Seguin, R., Cader, C., Bertheau, P., Breyer, C., 2014. Assessment of the global potential for renewable energy storage systems on Small Islands. Energy Procedia 46, 325–331. https://doi.org/10.1016/j.egypro.2015.01.071.

Brooklyn Microgrid, 2016. Brooklyn Microgrid.

Burger, S.P., Luke, M., 2017. Business models for distributed energy resources: a review and empirical analysis. Energy Policy 109, 230–248. https://doi.org/10.1016/j.enpol.2017.07.007.

Burger, C., Weinmann, J., 2013. The Decentralized Energy Revolution. Palgrave Macmillan UK, London.

Burger, C., Weinmann, J., 2016. European utilities: strategic choices and cultural prerequisites for the future A2. In: Sioshansi, F.P. (Ed.), Future of Utilities—Utilities of the Future. Academic Press, Boston, MA, pp. 303–322 (Chapter 16).

Casadesus-Masanell, R., Ricart, J.E., 2011. How to Design a Winning Business Model.

Castagneto Gissey, G., Dodds, P.E., Radcliffe, J., 2018. Market and regulatory barriers to electrical energy storage innovation. Renew. Sust. Energ. Rev. 82, 781–790. https://doi.org/10.1016/j.rser.2017.09.079.

Cayford, T., Scholten, D., 2014. Viability of self-governance in community energy systems: structuring an approach for assessment. In: Proceeding of 5th Ostrom Workshop. Presented at the Ostrom Workshop, Bloomington, USA. pp. 1–28.

CityOpt, 2018. CityOpt. [WWW Document]. URL, http://www.cityopt.eu/. (Accessed June 14, 2018).

Correljé, A., Cuppen, E., Dignum, M., Pesch, U., Taebi, B., 2015. Responsible innovation in energy projects: values in the design of technologies, institutions and stakeholder interactions. In: Koops, B.-J., Oosterlaken, I., Romijn, H., Swierstra, T., van den Hoven, J. (Eds.), Responsible Innovation 2. Springer International Publishing, Cham, pp. 183–200. https://doi.org/10.1007/978-3-319-17308-5_10.

D'Souza, A., Wortmann, H., Huitema, G., Velthuijsen, H., 2015. A business model design framework for viability; a business ecosystem approach. J. Bus. Models https://doi.org/10.5278/ojs.jbm.v3i2.1216. Aalborg Universitetsforlag.

D'Souza, A., Wortmann, J., Rijksuniversiteit Groningen, Onderzoekschool Systemen, O. en M. (Groningen), 2018. A Business Model Design Framework for the Viability of Energy Enterprises in a Business Ecosystem. University of Groningen, Groningen.

DGRV, 2016. Cooperatives in Germany. Die Genossenschaften—DGRV. [WWW Document]. URL, https://www.dgrv.de/en/cooperatives.html. (Accessed December 5, 2017).

Dilger, M.G., Konter, M., Voigt, K.-I., 2017. Introducing a co-operative-specific business model: the poles of profit and community and their impact on organizational models of energy co-operatives. J. Co-op. Organ. Manag. 5, 28–38. https://doi.org/10.1016/j.jcom.2017.03.002.

eCAMION, 2013. Community Energy Storage (CES).

EEG, 2017. EEG 2017—Renewables Act. [WWW Document]. URL, https://www.gesetze-im-internet.de/eeg_2014/BJNR106610014.html. (Accessed April 26, 2018).

Energy Post, 2013. Exclusive: RWE Sheds Old Business Model, Embraces Transition. EnergyPost.eu.

Energy Union, 2016. Commission Proposes New Rules for Consumer Centred Clean Energy Transition. Energy—European Commission. [WWW Document]. Energy. URL, https://ec.europa.eu/energy/en/news/commission-proposes-new-rules-consumer-centred-clean-energy-transition. (Accessed December 5, 2016).

Enexis, 2012. Enexis installs smart storage unit in Etten-Leur. [WWW Document]. URL, https://www.enexis.nl/zakelijk/nieuws/enexis-installeert-smart-storage-unit-in-etten-leur. (Accessed February 8, 2018).

EON, 2014. Strategy. E.ON SE. [WWW Document]. URL, http://www.eon.com/en/about-us/strategie.html. (Accessed October 27, 2015).

FERC, 2018. FERC issues final rule on electric storage participation in regional markets. [WWW Document]. URL, https://www.ferc.gov/media/news-releases/2018/2018-1/02-15-18-E-1.asp#.WuG7eZexVaR. (Accessed April 26, 2018).

Giotitsas, C., Pazaitis, A., Kostakis, V., 2015. A peer-to-peer approach to energy production. Technol. Soc. 42, 28–38. https://doi.org/10.1016/j.techsoc.2015.02.002.

Gridflex, 2018. GridFlex.

GSE, 2018. Italian Energy Agency (GSE). [WWW Document]. URL, https://www.gse.it/en/. (Accessed April 26, 2018).

GTAI, 2018. Energy storage. [WWW Document]. URL, http://www.gtai.de/GTAI/Navigation/EN/Invest/Industries/Energy/energy-storage.html. (Accessed March 19, 2018).

Haney, M.A.B., Pollitt, M.G., 2013. New models of public ownership in energy. Int. Rev. Appl. Econ. 27, 174–192. https://doi.org/10.1080/02692171.2012.734790.

Herbes, C., Brummer, V., Rognli, J., Blazejewski, S., Gericke, N., 2017. Responding to policy change: new business models for renewable energy cooperatives—barriers perceived by cooperatives' members. Energy Policy 109, 82–95. https://doi.org/10.1016/j.enpol.2017.06.051.

HierOpgewekt, 2017. Lokale Energie Monitor 2017: Samen energie opwekken onverminderd populair. HIER Opgewekt. [WWW Document]. URL, https://www.hieropgewekt.nl/nieuws/lokale-energie-monitor-2017-samen-energie-opwekken-onverminderd-populair. (Accessed December 5, 2017).

IDEAS, 2018. IDEAS Project. [WWW Document]. URL, http://www.ideasproject.eu/. (Accessed June 14, 2018).

IEA, 2014. Technology Roadmap Energy Storage. International Energy Agency, Paris, France.

IERC, 2018. Storenet Project. IERC. [WWW Document]. URL, http://www.ierc.ie/current-research-portfolio/. (Accessed March 26, 2018).

IRENA, 2015. IRENA battery storage report 2015.

IRENA, 2017. Electricity Storage and Renewables: Costs and Markets to 2030. International Renewable Energy Agency, Abu Dhabi/Bonn.

Juntunen, J.K., Hyysalo, S., 2015. Renewable micro-generation of heat and electricity—review on common and missing socio-technical configurations. Renew. Sust. Energ. Rev. 49, 857–870. https://doi.org/10.1016/j.rser.2015.04.040.

Kittner, N., Lill, F., Kammen, D.M., 2017. Energy storage deployment and innovation for the clean energy transition. Nat. Energy 2, 17125 https://doi.org/10.1038/nenergy.2017.125.

Koirala, B.P., 2017. Integrated Community Energy Systems. Delft University of Technology https://doi.org/10.4233/uuid:10d555dd-8f03-4986-b5bf-ef09a63c92e1.

Koirala, B., Hakvoort, R., 2017. Integrated community-based energy systems: aligning technology, incentives, and regulations. In: Innovation and Disruption at the Grid's Edge. Elsevier, pp. 363–387. https://doi.org/10.1016/B978-0-12-811758-3.00018-8.

Koirala, B.P., Koliou, E., Friege, J., Hakvoort, R.A., Herder, P.M., 2016. Energetic communities for community energy: a review of key issues and trends shaping integrated community energy systems. Renew. Sust. Energ. Rev. 56, 722–744. https://doi.org/10.1016/j.rser.2015.11.080.

Koirala, B.P., Araghi, Y., Kroesen, M., Ghorbani, A., Hakvoort, R.A., Herder, P.M., 2018. Trust, awareness, and independence: insights from a socio-psychological factor analysis of citizen knowledge and participation in community energy systems. Energy Res. Soc. Sci. 38, 33–40. https://doi.org/10.1016/j.erss.2018.01.009.

Koohi-Kamali, S., Tyagi, V.V., Rahim, N.A., Panwar, N.L., Mokhlis, H., 2013. Emergence of energy storage technologies as the solution for reliable operation of smart power systems: a review. Renew. Sust. Energ. Rev. 25, 135–165. https://doi.org/10.1016/j.rser.2013.03.056.

Liander, 2017. Neighbours store local solar energy in community energy storage. [WWW Document]. URL, https://www.liander.nl/nieuws/2017/11/23/buren-slaan-lokale-zonnestroom-op-buurtbatterij. (Accessed February 8, 2018).

LichtBlick Schwarmbatterie, 2018. SchwarmBatterie®—LichtBlick. [WWW Document]. URL, https://www.lichtblick.de/schwarmenergie/schwarmbatterie/. (Accessed March 26, 2018).

Lombardi, P., Schwabe, F., 2017. Sharing economy as a new business model for energy storage systems. Appl. Energy 188, 485–496. https://doi.org/10.1016/j.apenergy.2016.12.016.

Lund, P.D., Lindgren, J., Mikkola, J., Salpakari, J., 2015. Review of energy system flexibility measures to enable high levels of variable renewable electricity. Renew. Sust. Energ. Rev. 45, 785–807. https://doi.org/10.1016/j.rser.2015.01.057.

Marczinkowski, H.M., Østergaard, P.A., 2018. Residential versus communal combination of photovoltaic and battery in smart energy systems. Energy https://doi.org/10.1016/j.energy.2018.03.153.

MESA, 2018. MESA standards—open standards for energy storage. [WWW Document]. URL, http://mesastandards.org/. (Accessed May 7, 2018).

MIET, 2015. New Spanish self-consumption regulation, Royal decree 900/2015.

Moroni, S., Alberti, V., Antoniucci, V., Bisello, A., 2018. Energy communities in a distributed-energy scenario: four different kinds of community arrangements. In: Bisello, A., Vettorato, D., Laconte, P., Costa, S. (Eds.), Smart and Sustainable Planning for Cities and Regions. Springer International Publishing, Cham, pp. 429–437. https://doi.org/10.1007/978-3-319-75774-2_29.

Morris, C., Pehnt, M., 2016. Energy Transition: The German Energiewende. The Heinrich Boell Foundation.

NEFF, 2016. New Energies Forum Feldheim. [WWW Document]. URL, http://nef-feldheim.info/?lang=en. (Accessed August 17, 2016).

Next Kraftwerke, 2018. Next Kraftwerke | Virtual Power Plant & Power Trading. [WWW Document]. URL, https://www.next-kraftwerke.com/. (Accessed March 26, 2018).

Osterwalder, A., Pigneur, Y., 2010. Business Model Generation: A Handbook for Visionaries, Game Changers, and Challengers. Nachdr.ed Flash Reproductions, Toronto.

Pampus, 2018. Self-Sufficient Pampus. Amst. Smart City. [WWW Document]. URL, https://amsterdamsmartcity.com/projects/self-sufficient-pampus. (Accessed May 7, 2018).

Parra, D., Gillott, M., Norman, S.A., Walker, G.S., 2015. Optimum community energy storage system for PV energy time-shift. Appl. Energy 137, 576–587. https://doi.org/10.1016/j.apenergy.2014.08.060.

Parra, D., Norman, S.A., Walker, G.S., Gillott, M., 2016. Optimum community energy storage system for demand load shifting. Appl. Energy 174, 130–143. https://doi.org/10.1016/j.apenergy.2016.04.082.

Parra, D., Norman, S.A., Walker, G.S., Gillott, M., 2017a. Optimum community energy storage for renewable energy and demand load management. Appl. Energy 200, 358–369. https://doi.org/10.1016/j.apenergy.2017.05.048.

Parra, D., Swierczynski, M., Stroe, D.I., Norman, S.A., Abdon, A., Worlitschek, J., O'Doherty, T., Rodrigues, L., Gillott, M., Zhang, X., Bauer, C., Patel, M.K., 2017b. An interdisciplinary review of energy storage for communities: challenges and perspectives. Renew. Sust. Energ. Rev. 79, 730–749. https://doi.org/10.1016/j.rser.2017.05.003.

Rahbar, K., Moghadam, M.R.V., Panda, S.K., Reindl, T., 2016. Shared energy storage management for renewable energy integration in smart grid. In: IEEE. pp. 1–5. https://doi.org/10.1109/ISGT.2016.7781230.

REN21, 2016. Renewables 2016 global status report.

RESCOOP, 2016. REScoop.eu | European Federation of Renewable Energy Cooperatives. [WWW Document]. URL, https://rescoop.eu/. (Accessed November 1, 2016).

Roberts, B.P., Sandberg, C., 2011. The role of energy storage in development of smart grids. Proc. IEEE 99, 1139–1144. https://doi.org/10.1109/JPROC.2011.2116752.

Rodríguez-Molina, J., Martínez-Núez, M., Martínez, J.-F., Pérez-Aguiar, W., 2014. Business models in the smart grid: challenges, opportunities and proposals for prosumer profitability. Energies 7, 6142–6171. https://doi.org/10.3390/en7096142.

Schill, W.-P., Zerrahn, A., Kunz, F., 2017. Prosumage of solar electricity: pros, cons, and the system perspective. Econ. Energy Environ. Policy 6. https://doi.org/10.5547/2160-5890.6.1.wsch.

SENSIBLE, 2018. SENSIBLE Project. Proj. Sensib. [WWW Document]. URL, https://www.projectsensible.eu/. (Accessed May 16, 2018).

Sioshansi, F.P., 2017. Innovation and Disruption at the Grid's Edge: How Distributed Energy Resources Are Disrupting the Utility Business Model, first ed. Academic Press, Elsevier.

SMILE, 2018. Samsø, Denmark | SMILE.

SonnenCommunity, 2016. sonnenCommunity. sonnen. [WWW Document]. URL, https://www.sonnenbatterie.de/en/sonnenCommunity. (Accessed July 21, 2017).

SonnenCommunity, 2018. sonnenCommunity. sonnen. [WWW Document]. URL, https://www.sonnenbatterie.de/en/sonnenCommunity. (Accessed July 21, 2017).

Spector, J., 2017. Sonnen brings its virtual power plant to the US with a 2,900-home project. [WWW Document]. URL, https://www.greentechmedia.com/articles/read/sonnen-virtual-power-plant-us-2900-home-project. (Accessed May 8, 2018).

Stadler, M., Cardoso, G., Mashayekh, S., Forget, T., DeForest, N., Agarwal, A., Schönbein, A., 2016. Value streams in microgrids: a literature review. Appl. Energy 162, 980–989. https://doi.org/10.1016/j.apenergy.2015.10.081.

Stähler, P., 2014. Geschäftsmodellinnovationen oder sein Geschäft radikal neudenken. In: Kompendium Geschäftsmodell-Innovation. Springer Gabler, Wiesbaden, pp. 109–136. https://doi.org/10.1007/978-3-658-04459-6_5.

Stubbs, W., Cocklin, C., 2008. Conceptualizing a "sustainability business model". Organ. Environ. 21, 103–127. https://doi.org/10.1177/1086026608318042.

USEF, 2016. Universal smart energy framework: a solid foundation for smart energy futures. [WWW Document]. URL, https://www.usef.energy/Home.aspx. (Accessed December 18, 2016).

van der Schoor, T., Scholtens, B., 2015. Power to the people: local community initiatives and the transition to sustainable energy. Renew. Sust. Energ. Rev. 43, 666–675. https://doi.org/10.1016/j.rser.2014.10.089.

van der Schoor, T., van Lente, H., Scholtens, B., Peine, A., 2016. Challenging obduracy: how local communities transform the energy system. Energy Res. Soc. Sci. 13, 94–105. https://doi.org/10.1016/j.erss.2015.12.009.

van der Stelt, S., AlSkaif, T., van Sark, W., 2018. Techno-economic analysis of household and community energy storage for residential prosumers with smart appliances. Appl. Energy 209, 266–276. https://doi.org/10.1016/j.apenergy.2017.10.096.

Van Melven, M., van der Vegte, H., Huibers, M., 2018. DNV GL-Led Consortium Finds Viable Business Case for Community Energy Storage (No. 18–0126). DNV-GL, Arnehm, The Netherlands.

Vandebron, 2017. Vandebron—marktplaats voor duurzame energie. [WWW Document]. URL, https://vandebron.nl. (Accessed August 3, 2017).

Walker, G., 2008. What are the barriers and incentives for community-owned means of energy production and use? Energy Policy 36, 4401–4405.

Walker, G., Devine-Wright, P., Hunter, S., High, H., Evans, B., 2010. Trust and community: exploring the meanings, contexts and dynamics of community renewable energy. Energy Policy 38, 2655–2663.

Wang, Z., Gu, C., Li, F., 2018. Flexible operation of shared energy storage at households to facilitate PV penetration. Renew. Energy 116, 438–446. https://doi.org/10.1016/j.renene.2017.10.005.

Wolsink, M., 2012. The research agenda on social acceptance of distributed generation in smart grids: renewable as common pool resources. Renew. Sust. Energ. Rev. 16, 822–835.

CHAPTER 11

Challenges to the Promotion of Distributed Energy Resources in Latin America: A Brazilian Case Study

Lucas Noura Guimarães
Madrona Law, São Paulo, Brazil

1. INTRODUCTION

Energy power systems are facing a historical paradigm shift regarding how electricity is generated, transmitted, and supplied to consumers. As further described in other chapters of this book, power systems were designed to transmit electricity unidirectionally in high voltage from big power plants to consumers. In such a configuration, (few) large power plants are located far away from the load center, requiring high-voltage transmission lines to take energy to distribution networks, which delivered it in lower voltage to consumers. Within this scenario, consumers are passive, distribution utilities are only responsible to forecast load and make investments according to demand expansion (fit-and-forget approach), and power production is centralized.

While enjoying economies of scale, this centralized configuration has some problems, including:
- high transmission losses & costs;
- environmental side effects;
- consumer dependency from profit-driven companies;
- exposure to fossil fuel price volatility;
- need for proper regulatory oversight to avoid rising tariffs, cross-subsidies, and excessive profits due to the concentration of power among a limited number of large stakeholders.

Considering its potential to counteract these issues, together with the rising interest to move toward a low carbon future while taking advantage of lower cost distributed options, the implementation of distributed generation (DG) has been gaining momentum in the last decade in

Consumer, Prosumer, Prosumager
https://doi.org/10.1016/B978-0-12-816835-6.00011-5

Latin American and the Caribbean (LAC), with the appearance of legal frameworks and policy instruments.

Distributed energy resources (DERs) include DG, energy storage, energy efficiency, and demand response management (DRM). Since thus far in LAC, DG is the most prominent form of DER, this chapter will focus on DG development.

A possible explanation for the low development of DER in LAC countries lies in the fact that undertakings can still explore plenty of available resources in LAC under the traditional business model. Furthermore, there is not enough environmental pressure to force LAC countries to adopt disruptive technologies, since in many LAC countries, the GHG emissions are relatively low due to heavy reliance on hydro resources. Besides that, DER is often interpreted by policy planners as a source of uncertainty, due to the lower predictability of prosumption behavior, and a risk for the system reliability.[1]

Moving forward, however, many countries in the region, including Brazil, are trying to encourage other forms of DER, especially DRM. Having adopted policies to encourage DG, many countries now recognize that DER is an indispensable component of the future's energy market.[2]

This chapter offers insight about the importance of a regulatory framework for DG as well as describing the major legal and policy-related constraining its further adoption, including the major remaining challenges that need to be addressed to establish a legally safe and trustworthy environment for future investments. The expectancy is that DG will pave the way toward the introduction of other DERs in LAC.

The chapter is organized as follows:

- Section 2 introduces several definitions for DG and typical conceptual misunderstandings;
- Section 3 analyzes how some LAC countries[3] regulated DG and incorporated it into their legal frameworks, including examples from Argentina and Colombia;
- Section 4 provides an in-depth analysis of DERs in Brazil followed by the chapter's conclusions.

---

[1]EMPRESA DE PESQUISA ENERGÉTICA. *Distributed Energy Resources*. Rio de Janeiro: EPE, 2018, p. 4.
[2]WORLD ECONOMIC FORUM. *Fostering effective energy transition – A fact-based framework to support decision-making*. 2018, p. 12.
[3]Considering the impossibility to fully cover all regulatory aspects of each LAC country – that would exceed the scope and length of this chapter – only the main aspects and singularities of each chosen country are highlighted.

2. WHAT IS DG?

There is lack of consensus as to what constitutes DG, also known as distributed energy or decentralized energy. Literally speaking, DG means electricity generation that is injected directly into the distribution utility's network. A source of DG could be a power generation source connected directly to the distribution network, regardless of generation capacity.[4]

Considering that, the concept itself has no limitation as to *which* energy source fits the concept – renewable or not – nor as to *how big* is the installed capacity or the energy input into the network. Hence, the environment-friendly appeal that DG lately acquired does not derive directly from the DG concept. The modulation of the concept – small-scale renewable energy systems, as commonly seen – is a *construction*, varying from a myriad of factors, such as the network location, the voltage level, the resource and technology used to generate electricity, the installed capacity, the environmental impact, or the person entitled to explore DG.

For example, DG can be defined as power generated by facilities that are sufficiently smaller than central power plants to allow interconnection at nearly any point of an energy system.[5] "Sufficiently smaller" delivers no accurate answer to the concept,[6] since "small" can range from less than a kW to tens of MW.

One can also understand DG as the power produced by small energy sources distributed throughout the cities.[7] It is also broadly defined as "small generation units of 30 MW or less, sited at or near customer sites to meet specific customer needs, to support the economic operation of the distribution grid, or both."[8] IEA, on the other hand, does not even refer to the generation capacity level, defining DG as "units producing power on a customer's site or within local distribution utilities, and supplying power directly to the local distribution network."[9]

[4]ACKERMANN, T; ANDERSSON, G.; SÖDER, L. *Distributed generation: a definition.* In: Electric Power Systems Research, vol. 57, 2001, pp. 195-2041.

[5]DONDI, P.; BAYOUMI, D.; HAEDERLI, C.; JULIAN, D.; SUTER, M. *Network integration of distributed power generation.* In: Journal of Power Sources, vol. 106, 2002, pp. 1-9.

[6]PEPERMANS, G.; DRIESEN, J.; HAESELDONCKX, D.; BELMANS, R.; D'HAESELLER, W. *Distributed generation: definition, benefits and issues.* In: Energy Policy, vol. 33, 2005, p. 796.

[7]PORCELLI, Adriana Margarita; MARTÍNEZ, Adriana Norma. *Una inevitable transición energética: el prosumidor y la generación de energías renovables en forma distribuida en la legislación argentina nacional y provincial.* In: Actualidad Jurídica Ambiental, n. 75, 2018, p. 7.

[8]CHAMBERS, A. *Distributed generation: a nontechnical guide.* PennWell, Tulsa, OK, 2001, p. 283.

[9]INTERNATIONAL ENERGY AGENCY. *Distributed generation in liberalized electricity markets.* IEA: Paris, 2002.

Some legislations limit DG to relying on renewable sources. That is the case in the Argentinean Law,[10] which defines DG as power generated from RES by energy consumers connected to the utility's network and that fulfill the legal requirements to inject their energy surpluses.

The Brazilian legislation offers a broader concept, defining DG as the production of electricity from undertakings connected directly to the distribution utility's network. Excluded from the concept are (i) hydropower projects with an installed capacity of over 30 MW and (ii) thermoelectric projects, including cogeneration, with energy efficiency level lower than 75%, according to the regulatory body's regulation.

Considering the consumer side, DG can be regarded as the possibility given to power consumers to generate their own electricity from RES, not only for self-consumption, but also to inject it into the distribution utility's network, receiving for it either a financial compensation or a credit to be used in the next energy bills.

No definition can adequately capture the range of power plants that can be subsumed under the heading of DG, nor do they provide a satisfying description of their common characteristic.[11] Due to the concept's high variability, DG cannot be more specifically defined as "power produced by generation units installed close to the load, connected to the distribution grid."[12]

3. EXAMPLES OF DG IN LAC COUNTRIES

Although DG implementation undergoes a general rationale, there are some specific reasons why DG is beneficial in LAC:

- Reduction of the electricity cost for consumers.[13] Not only PV panels and other renewable-related components should be commercially viable, but also the power produced from renewables should be cheaper than power produced by thermal power plants, after accounting for the transmission cost savings and environmental benefits;

---

[10]Law 27,424, art. 3, "h".

[11]BAUKNECHT, D.; BRUNEKREEFT, G. Distributed Generation and the Regulation of Electricity Networks. In: SIOSHANSI, Fereidoon P. (org.). *Competitive Electricity Markets: Design, Implementation, Performance.* United Kingdom: Elsevier, 2008.

[12]The legal definition of transmission or distribution line, according to the voltage, will also vary from country to country, or from region to region within one country, PEPERMANS, G.; DRIESEN, J.; HAESELDONCKX, D.; BELMANS, R.; D'HAESELLER, W. *Distributed generation: definition, benefits and issues.* In: Energy Policy, vol. 33, 2005, p. 796.

[13]GISCHLER, Christiaan; JANSON, Nils. *Perspectives for distributed generation with renewable energy in Latin America and the Caribbean - Analysis of case studies for Jamaica, Barbados, Mexico, and Chile.* IDB Discussion Paper 208, 2011, p.14.

- For fossil-fuel-dependent countries,[14] RES-DG would increase energy security, making them less vulnerable to geopolitical risks and fossil-fuel price volatility;
- DG expansion would save environmental costs in hydrodependent countries, like Brazil and Peru by avoiding or at least postponing the construction of transmission lines;
- The possibility to develop a green economy, promoting domestic manufacturing, installation, and maintenance of equipment.[15]

3.1 DG Policy Overview in Argentina

The Argentinean National Congress passed in September 2015 Law 27,191, altering Law 26,190, which established the legal framework for the promotion of RES. It set the goal to have, by 2018, consumers receiving at least 8% of the electricity produced by RES.

Although the 2015 Law propelled the development of centralized renewable energy projects,[16] there was no nation-wide Law regarding DG until recently. While the absence of a national Law could be considered an obstacle to DG development, the Argentinean Constitution establishes that power distribution is the competence of the *provincias* (municipalities).[17] Since the prosumer is connected to the distribution utility's network, the regulation of DG would fall into the *provincias'* competence.[18]

---

[14]The Caribbean countries (around 85%), for instance, KEMA. *CARILEC Position Paper on Energy Policy.* Caribbean Association of Electric Utilities, 2008.

[15]GISCHLER, Christiaan; JANSON, Nils. *Perspectives for distributed generation with renewable energy in Latin America and the Caribbean - Analysis of case studies for Jamaica, Barbados, Mexico, and Chile.* IDB Discussion Paper 208, 2011, p.15.

[16]For an explanation of how the development of renewables should take place among big consumers and a summary of the latest tendering process for renewable projects, see PORCELLI, Adriana Margarita; MARTÍNEZ, Adriana Norma. *Una inevitable transición energética: el prosumidor y la generación de energías renovables en forma distribuida en la legislación argentina nacional y provincial.* In: Actualidad Jurídica Ambiental, n. 75, 2018, p. 16-20.

[17]ELIASCHEV, Nicolás. *Autogeneración distribuida y balance neto. Introducción a su regulación jurídica.* In: Revista Jurídica de la Universidad de San Andrés, vol. 3, 2016, p. 10.

[18]From the 23 Argentinean *provincias*, 8 of them have a legislation of their own, while 2 others are on their way to regulate DG. The *provincia* of Santa Fe adopted NEM for RES-DG, allowing energy systems with installed capacity of less than 1.5 kW. The energy injected into the utility's network by the prosumer and compensated with the energy taken from the network is calculated considering a promotional tariff that will last for 8 years (estimated payback time). The government of Salta *provincia* established that only consumers with a nominal power of up to 30 kW and industries of up to 100 kW are allowed to connect their power systems to the distribution utility's network.

Still, the Argentinean government published in December 2017, Law 27,424, establishing a framework for the promotion of DG-RES, supported by four pillars:

(i) prosumers are any consumer connected to the utility's network, with a demand of up to 300 kW;

(ii) adoption of NEM, where the energy injected turns into credits that can be used within 6 months;

(iii) there is no installed capacity limitation for a DG project;

(iv) establishment of a public fund for RES-DG,[19] with the goal of financing incentive tariffs for DG adoption and of subsidizing credit lines for the acquisition of RES-related equipment.

Argentina has kickstarted its project to change the energy matrix into a more renewable and democratic one, offering legal and financial conditions to allow DG to flourish. Some limitations need addressing:

- the impossibility for prosumers to sell their electricity surpluses to power traders, aggregators, and/or outside the utility's zone;
- lack of sufficient attractiveness, if the prosumers are to be remunerated according to the *precio estacional* – a subsidized tariff established during the Argentinean 2002 crisis, which does not reflect anymore the energy production cost;
- lack of financing alternatives[20];
- lack of a mechanism to prevent the "death spiral."[21]

---

[19] *Fondo para la Generación Distribuida de Energías Renovables (FODIS).*

[20] The stimulus for consumers to use DG was not achieved by the provincial legislation, since the payback amounted to 20 years, QUINTERO, Sandra Ximena Carvajal; JIMÉNEZ, Juan David Marín. *Impacto de la generación distribuida en el sistema eléctrico de potencia colombiano: un enfoque dinámico.* In: Tecnura, vol. 17, 2013, p. 79.

[21] While for some part of the literature the death spiral is a serious issue, with high disruptive potential, that can only be properly addressed with long-term policy measures, CASTANEDA, Monica; JIMENEZ, Maritza; ZAPATA, Sebastian; FRANCO, Carlos J.; DYNER, Isaac. *Myths and facts of the utility death spiral.* In: Energy Policy, vol. 110, 2017, p. 105-116, for others it is doubtful to what extent a migration from consumption to prosumption can really harm the financial health of the utility. When analyzing the Brazilian energy market, its regulatory agency came to the conclusion that the total average tariff impact within the period from 2017 to 2024 would be as little as 1.1%, AGÊNCIA NACIONAL DE ENERGIA ELÉTRICA. *Nota Técnica n° 0056/2017-SRD/ANEEL.* Brasília: ANEEL, 2017, p. 11. For some part of the literature, the death spiral is unlikely to occur, COSTELLO, K.W.; HEMPHILL, R. C. *Electric utilities' "death spiral": hyperbole or reality?* In: Electricity Journal, vol. 27, 2014, p. 7-26; SATCHWELL, A.; MILLS, A.; BARBOSE, G. *Quantifying the financial impacts of net-metered PV on utilities and ratepayers.* In: Energy Policy, vol. 80, 2015, p. 133-144, MUAAFA, Mohammed; ADJALI, Iqbal; BEAN, Patrick; FUENTES, Rolando; KIMBROUGH, Steven O.; MURPHY, Frederic H. *Can adoption of rooftop solar panels trigger a utility death spiral? A tale of two U.S. cities.* In: Energy Research & Social Science, vol. 34, 2017, p. 154-162.

3.2 DG Policy Overview in Colombia

To balance energy security, sustainability, and price fairness, Law 1,715/2014 introduced DG in the Colombian energy landscape,[22] regulating "non-conventional" RES[23] and seeking to improve energy efficiency and demand response.

Small-scale self-generators[24] that use "nonconventional" renewables can receive energy credits correspondent to the energy produced and offered to the distribution utility's network. Aggregators can buy those credits and their related rights. There is no limitation as to how much energy can be injected into the system, relative to the energy consumed from the distribution utility.

An important feature of Colombian DG is the obligation,[25] set by the Colombian Energy and Gas Regulation Commission (CREG)[26] for each network operator, to make available in their website a georeferenced information system. Before accepting the connection request, the consumer has to check if the network is available to receive the new load.

Regarding the legal treatment given to the commercialization of energy surpluses, the legal framework sets different rules:

- For *distributed generators* with an installed capacity of up to 100 kW, the surpluses:
  - ○ can be sold to energy traders operating in the regulated market, to big energy users and other power generators or to the power trade company integrated to the network operator, according to a price formula, which considers the energy price in the market and the network restriction costs.
- In the case of *small-scale self-generators* with an installed capacity of up to 1 MW, the surpluses:
  - ○ are sold as established for distributed generators, if the self-generator does not use unconventional RES;
  - ○ are recognized as credits and cleared considering the energy price traded in the market, for self-generators that use unconventional RES.

---

[22]QUINTERO, Sandra Ximena Carvajal; JIMÉNEZ, Juan David Marín. *Impacto de la generación distribuida en el sistema eléctrico de potencia colombiano: un enfoque dinámico*. In: Tecnura, vol. 17, 2013, p. 79.

[23]Wind, geothermal, solar, marine, and small hydro.

[24]According to art. 1 of the Resolution 281, from 2015, of the *Unidad de Planeación Minero Energética – UPME*, the maximum limit for small-scale self-generators should not be over 1 MW installed capacity.

[25]Resolution n. 121, in 2017.

[26]*Comisión de Regulación de Energía y Gas.*

In comparison with other DG frameworks, the Colombian legislation adopted a more cautious approach to DG expansion, setting a modest limit for the installed capacity of the projects. On the other hand, it allows for the trade of energy surpluses generated by *small-scale self-generators*, a feature not often seen in other LAC countries' legal frameworks.

Table 11.1 summarizes the main regulatory aspects of DG in some LAC countries.

4. DER IN BRAZIL: A PARADIGM SHIFT TAKING SHAPE

Despite being the 5th biggest country, with some remote regions, historically Brazil has never benefited from decentralized energy systems and chose to construct big hydropower plants and stretch long transmission lines.

Only recently, with the environmental pressure – be it to reduce GHG emissions, be it regarding the impossibility to construct big dams in the Amazon® – is the Brazilian Government turning its attention to DER, regulating DG and promoting a pilot project in DRM. Nevertheless, a lot has yet to be achieved, especially in promoting research and innovation[27] and in encouraging the development and adoption of new business models.[28]

Although having an essentially clean energy matrix[29] (Figs. 11.1 and 11.2, as of 2017), Brazil has set ambitious targets within the scope of the Paris Agreement.[30]

Brazil was one of the first countries to introduce DG in its legal framework. After the privatization wave and policy reform of the 90s, along with an energy rationing in 2001, a new market design was implemented in 2004, featured by State presence and power capacity auctions.[31] Within this scope, while making mandatory for distribution utilities to have 100% of their

---

[27]Among 137 countries, Brazil is only the 85th when it comes to innovation, according to The Global Competitiveness Index 2017-2018. WORLD ECONOMIC FORUM. *The Global Competitiveness Report 2017-2018.* Geneva: WEF, 2017, p. 70.

[28]RESENDE, Joana; AQUINO, Thereza. New Business Models with Diffusion of Distributed Generation. In: CASTRO, Nivalde de; DANTAS, Guilherme (orgs.). *Distributed Generation: international experiences and comparative analyses.* Rio de Janeiro: Publit, 2017, P. 156.

[29]IEA. *World energy outlook special report: energy and climate change.* Paris: International Energy Agency, 2015.

[30]In the Paris Agreement, Brazil obliged – Intended Nationally Determined Contributions – itself to reduce in 37% its gas emissions by 2025. Enforcing the implementation of the Climate Change National Policy, approved by Law 12,187/2009, together with the National Energy Policy (Law 9,478/97), Brazil intends to achieve 45% of renewables in the energy mix by 2030, which includes mitigation and adaptation measures in transport and electricity sectors. As of 2016, that number was already in 41.5%, but it was of 48.1% in 2007, EMPRESA DE PESQUISA ENERGÉTICA. *Brazilian Energy Balance 2017.* Rio de Janeiro: EPE, 2017, p. 22.

[31]GUIMARÃES, Lucas Noura de Moraes Rêgo. *Regulação da exploração da eletricidade: compatibilidade com as leis da natureza e com a ordem econômica constitucional.* Brazil: Editora CRV, 2013.

Table 11.1 Regulatory aspects of distributed generation in some Latin American countries

Country/feature	Legal acts	DG system adopted	Energy sources	Power limits	Energy surpluses' legal treatment	Time required for DG project authorization[a]
Argentina[b]	Law 27,424/17	NEM + tariff incentive	Nonconventional renewables and cogeneration	Pending regulation[c]	Energy credits (6 months rollover)	Varies according to each *provincia*
Brazil	Law 10,848/04 and ANEEL's Resolution 482/12	NEM (mini- and microgeneration)	Renewables and cogeneration	<5 MW (mini- and microgeneration)	Energy credits (60 months rollover)	15 days for microgeneration 30 days for minigeneration
Chile	Law 20,571/14 and Decree 71/14	NEM	Nonconventional renewables and cogeneration	<100 kW	Energy credits (noncompensated credits are paid by utilities)	20 days (or 30, for rural zones)
Colombia	Law 1,715/14 and CREG Resolution 121/17	NEM	Nonconventional renewables	<100 kW	Energy surpluses are traded	7 days
Costa Rica	Decree 39,220-MINAE[d]	NEM	Renewables	<1 MW	Energy credits (12 months rollover) or trade of energy surpluses	N/A
Guatemala	Resolution CNEE 227/14	NEM	Renewables	<5 MW	Energy credits	30 days
Uruguay	Decree 173/10	FiT	Nonconventional renewables	<150 kW	Energy surpluses are bought by ISO	N/A

[a]Time considered between the connection request and the acceptation by the distribution utility, not taking into consideration time taken to amend requests, verify installation in loco or execution of work, such as meter change, network repairs, and improvements.

[b]Considering the national legal framework. Regulation from municipality to municipality may change.

[c]Art. 6 of Law 27,424/17 left to further Decree to establish the installed capacity of DG projects. Still, each *provincia* is allowed to set different installed capacity limits.

[d]Ministry for Environment and Energy (MINAE in its Spanish acronym).

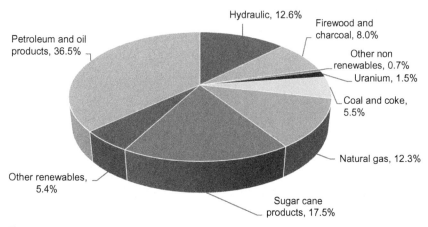

Figure 11.1 Domestic energy supply. Includes electricity imports originated from hydraulic sources. 1 kWh = 860 kcal. *(Source: Empresa de Pesquisa Energética (EPE/Brazil).)*

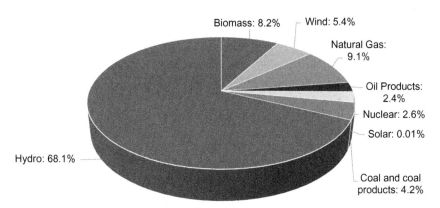

Figure 11.2 Domestic electricity supply by source. *(Source: Empresa de Pesquisa Energética (EPE/Brazil).)*

demand contracted through those auctions, Law 10,848/2004 also provided for distribution utilities to take into account power produced from DG.

4.1 The Brazilian Way of DG Regulation: Prosumers Only Lately Included

Although having kickstarted the DG deployment, Brazil still has great untapped potential for DG.[32] While finishing 2016 with a fourfold DG increase, amounting for 81 MW of installed capacity spread among 7.7 thousand

[32]Especially PV, GOMES, P.Vilaça et. al. *Technical-economic analysis for the integration of PV systems in Brazil considering policy and regulatory issues*. In: Energy Policy, vol. 115, 2018, pp. 199-206.

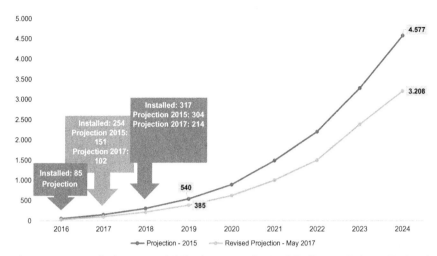

Figure 11.3 Installed capacity (MW) of micro and mini DG. *(Source: Agência Nacional de Energia Elétrica. Nota Técnica n° 0062/2018-SRD/SCG/SRM/SGT/SMA/ANEEL. Brasília: ANEEL, 2018.)*

consumption units, projections for 2026 expect PV to hit 3.3 GWp of installed capacity in 770,000 units, which would be sufficient to supply 0.6% of the total national energy demand.[33,34]

Fig. 11.3 (as of April 2018) depicts the expected growth in mini- and microgeneration, showing that Brazil has still a long way to go to make DG a significant component of its power system.

In Brazilian Energy Law, at first, DG did not focus on prosumers, but rather to power generation made available by *undertakings* connected directly to the distribution utility's network. The consideration of prosumers within the concept of DG occurred in 2012 within the scope of the Program for the Development of Distributed Generation.[35] The legislation divided DG into two groups:

---

[33]EMPRESA DE PESQUISA ENERGÉTICA. *Brazilian Energy Balance 2017*. Rio de Janeiro: EPE, 2017, p. 221.

[34]To demonstrate how late is Brazil and how big is the potential being missed, it is worth comparing that as of 2018, California, which has a population one-fifth smaller than Brazil's, has 700,000 units with PV panels, while Australia has around 1 million homes equipped with solar roofs.

[35]*Programa de Desenvolvimento da Geração Distribuída de Energia Elétrica* (ProGD in its Portuguese acronym), established by the Ministerial Ordinance 538, of December 15th 2015, from the Ministry of Mines and Energy.

- DG, as defined in Law 10,848/04, with undertakings with up to 30 MW of installed capacity;
- Distributed micro- and minigeneration, as defined in ANEEL's[36] Resolution 482/12, focused on prosumers with up to 75 kW and from 75 kW to 5 MW installed capacity, respectively.

Regarding DG by undertakings, Decree 5,163/04 imposed the obligation of distribution utilities interested in contracting power produced by DG projects to launch a *public call for interest*. Power produced from DG can cover a maximum of 10% of the utility's load.

Despite the legal provision related to DG projects, this contracting configuration did not evolve as expected, because the distribution utilities, when launching public calls, were only allowed to pass to the consumers' tariff the Annual Reference Value (VR), based on the average price of the regulated public auctions. The main problem of applying the VR to DG is that it does not take into account the inherent advantages of DG, such as generation near the load and environment friendliness.

In 2015,[37] the Brazilian government introduced a different policy, determining the Energy Research Office[38] as the public body responsible for calculating and setting the Specific Reference Values (VRES)[39] of each renewable energy source, considering the technical conditions and specificities of DG projects.

Still, only 2 years later, with the publication of the Ministerial Ordinance 65/2018, the VRES were set.[40] As for now, there is hope that DG by undertakings will find room in Brazil. Concrete results are still expected.

4.2 Regulation of Small-Scale Prosumption

In 2012, ANEEL enacted Normative Resolution n. 482, establishing the general rules for distributed micro- and minigeneration. The Law prohibits energy trade by consumers with demand lower than 500 kW. Brazil adopted NEM system, according to which prosumers cannot sell the power

---

[36] *Agência Nacional de Energia Elétrica* (ANEEL in its Portuguese acronym).
[37] Law 13,203/15.
[38] *Empresa de Pesquisa Energética* (EPE in its Portuguese acronym) is a state-owned think tank, supporting the Brazilian Ministry of Mines and Energy with studies and research on energy planning.
[39] *Valores Anuais de Referência Específicos* (VRES in its Portuguese acronym).
[40] VRES for each renewable energy source are: biogas, US$ 114.00/MWh; dedicated biomass, US$ 158.00/MWh; residual biomass US$ 102.00/MWh; gas-fired cogeneration, US$ 132.00/MWh; wind, US$ 87.00/MWh; small hydro, US$ 105.00/MWh; waste, US$ 165.00/MWh; PV, US$ 131.00/MWh.

produced to the distribution utility – nor to aggregators nor in the spot market – but rather obtain a credit that compensates, in future energy bills, the amount of electricity taken from the network.

When published, the Resolution did not attract the interest of power consumers for some reasons:

- economic crisis Brazil was facing;
- lack of financial incentives and credit lines for individuals to install solar panels in their homes,[41] leading to extensive payback time;
- erroneous interpretation of the NEM's logic by the National Council of Financial Policy, which established the calculation basis for ICMS[42] considering the totality of the energy taken from the distribution utility's network, without any compensation with the energy produced by the prosumer[43];
- time-consuming procedures and bureaucracy from distribution utilities to accept DG requests (but delays on the side of consumers were also significant)[44];
- unattractive validity time for energy credits accumulated.

In 2015, Normative Resolution n. 687 amended Normative Resolution n. 482, changing the definitions for distributed micro- and minigeneration, creating other legal configurations for prosumers to produce their electricity ("undertaking with multiple consumption units,"[45] "shared generation,"[46] and "remote self-consumption"[47]) and increasing the credits validity period

---

[41]HOLDERMANN, Claudius; KISSEL, Johannes; BEIGEL, Jürgen. *Distributed photovoltaic generation in Brazil: An economic viability analysis of small-scale photovoltaic systems in the residential and commercial sectors*. In: Energy Policy, vol. 67, 2014, p. 617.

[42]ICMS is a federal tax on circulation of goods and services and it is applicable to energy distribution.

[43]AGÊNCIA NACIONAL DE ENERGIA ELÉTRICA. *Nota Técnica n° 0017/2015-SRD/ ANEEL*. Brasília: ANEEL, 2015, p. 1.

[44]AGÊNCIA NACIONAL DE ENERGIA ELÉTRICA. *Nota Técnica n° 0017/2015-SRD/ ANEEL*. Brasília: ANEEL, 2015, p. 11-12.

[45]"Undertaking with multiple consumption units" is a form of DG, in which several individual consumption units share the electricity produced by the DG Project. The consumption units need to be located within the same property or in an adjoining property, like a residential condominium, for example.

[46]"Shared generation" is the reunion of consumers, inside the same concession zone, by means of a cooperative or consortium, which owns a distributed mini- or microgeneration unit and shares the energy surpluses injected into the network.

[47]"Remote self-consumption" is characterized by consumption units owned by the same individual person or legal person that have a DG unit, located within the same concession zone. As an example, there are summerhouses, which are not quite often used but can generate energy credits to be compensated with the energy consumption of a city apartment (considering both properties are owned by the same individual person, within the same concession zone).

from 36 to 60 months. Those amendments led to a DG boom, mainly solar driven[48] (Fig. 11.4), which can still be seen in 2018, as depicted in Figs. 11.5 and 11.6 (as of 2017).

On the fiscal side, the National Council of Financial Policy published the ICMS Agreement 16/15, granting exemption of the tax on the circulation of goods and services on the electricity supplied to prosumers, within the scope of NEM.

Considering the legal improvements, Normative Resolution 482/12 defined distributed microgeneration as a power generation unit with an installed capacity of up to 75 kW and that uses qualified cogeneration or renewable energy sources, connected to the distribution utility's network through a consumption unit. Distributed minigeneration are units with an installed capacity ranging from 75 kW to 5 MW.

The same regulation established the Energy Compensation System, according to which energy generated by a distributed mini- and microgeneration unit compensates[49] energy consumed in this unit. That compensation is done monthly, either by two unidirectional meters or a bidirectional meter. If, in any given month, a surplus is verified, that is, if more energy is produced as taken from the network, a credit is given to the prosumer, to be used within the next 60 months, compensating future energy consumption.

There are reasons to believe that DG will continue to grow in Brazil, especially due to new financing possibilities, considered the biggest bottleneck of the solar market. Several banks – Banco do Brasil, BNDES, Banco do Nordeste, Santander, Banco Votorantim, BV Financeira, BDMG – have opened credit lines for individuals to buy and install solar panels, with reasonable interest rates and long-term access to capital. The expected payback lies around 5 years.

On the other hand, prosumers are still not allowed to choose their power supplier nor are they allowed to freely trade electricity, despite the

---

[48]For an analysis of the development of solar energy in Brazil, see SILVA, Solange Teles da; DUTRA, Carolina; GUIMARÃES, Lucas Noura de Moraes Rêgo. Solar energy and the dawn of 'solar cities' in Brazil. In: COSTA, José Augusto Fontoura; RIBEIRO, Marilda Rosado de Sá; XAVIER JÚNIOR, Ely Caetano; GABRIEL, Vivian Daniele Rocha. *Energy Law and Regulation in Brazil*. Springer, 2018.
[49]The compensation occurs by means of a "free loan", legal figure adopted to circumvent the prohibition for residential consumers to trade energy.

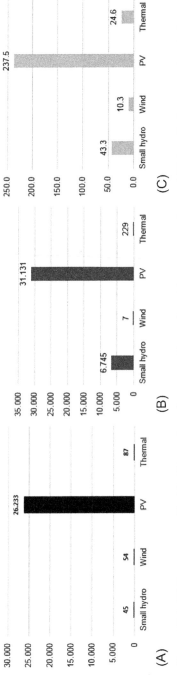

Figure 11.4 (A) Consumers with DG, (B) number of consumption units with energy credits, and (C) installed capacity (MW). (*Source: Agência Nacional de Energia Elétrica. Nota Técnica n° 0056/2017-SRD/ANEEL. Brasília: ANEEL, 2017.*)

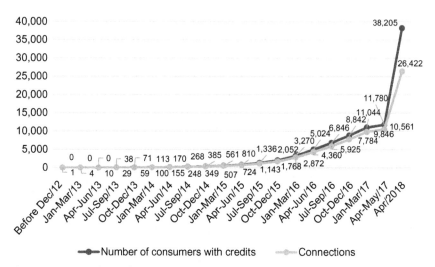

Number of consumers with credits   Connections

Figure 11.5 Number of consumers with credits × number of connections. *(Source: Agência Nacional de Energia Elétrica. Nota Técnica n° 0056/2017-SRD/ANEEL. Brasília: ANEEL, 2017.)*

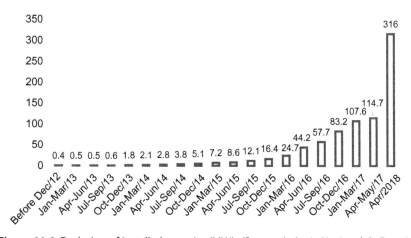

Figure 11.6 Evolution of installed capacity (MW). *(Source: Agência Nacional de Energia Elétrica. Nota Técnica n° 0056/2017-SRD/ANEEL. Brasília: ANEEL, 2017.)*

discussion whether a free market is advantageous or not to residential consumers.[50] Besides that, the existence of concession zones limits the application of the NEM. That last point could be improved in 2019, when the Normative Resolution 482/12 undergoes a revision.

Lastly, a new market reform is in progress, with a Draft Bill addressed to implement hourly prices in the spot market, introduce peak/off-peak prices, and implement the binomial tariff for residential consumers, which could be necessary to counteract the "death spiral." Even if the argument is sound and the problem of cross-subsidies between consumers and prosumers urges for a solution, the new legislation must be cautious so that it does not result in a disincentive for DG.

With a view on the need to keep offering a safe regulatory framework for investments in DG projects, it is paramount that the new reform establishes incentives, such as the implementation of a locational signal for DG – prosumers that generate near the load should be duly awarded for avoiding the use of power lines – and take into account the sustainability gains obtained by the diffusion of DG. Given the distribution utility's side, there is an urgency to recognize – to pass the costs to the tariff – investments made by the utilities in digitalization and network improvements related to DG expansion.

4.3 Pilot Project on DRM

The DRM in Brazil has a potential market of more than 14.5 GW (as of 2013) and it could avoid ca. 370 million dollars in costs between 2008 and 2013 (considering a 5% reward over the spot price). Besides that, as of 2013, 621 hours of demand response from all potential market would have been necessary to avoid the dispatch of fossil-fuel-fired power plants.[51]

On November 2017, ANEEL approved[52] an 18-month pilot project on DRM for industrial consumers. The project allows those consumers to bid load reductions to the Brazilian ISO and receive a reward for load relief.

[50] HORTAÇSU, Ali; MADANIZADEH, Seyed Ali; PULLER, Steven L. *Power to Choose? An Analysis of Consumer Inertia in the Residential Electricity Market.* NBER Working Paper N° 20988, 2015; BRENNAN, Timothy J. *Consumer preference not to choose: methodological and policy implications.* In: Energy Policy, vol. 35, 2007, p. 1616-1627; YANG, Yingkui. *Understanding household switching behavior in the retail electricity market.* In: Energy Policy, vol. 69, 2014, p. 406-414; AUSTRALIAN ENERGY MARKET COMMISSION. *2017 AEMC Retail Energy Competition Review.* Final Report, 2017.

[51] SOUSA, Helder Wilson Amade. *Utilização de programas de reação da demanda como alternativa à necessidade de geração termelétrica complementar para garanti do suprimento de energia elétrica.* Brasília: UnB, 2013, pp. 53-57.

[52] Normative Resolution n. 792/2017.

Like energy efficiency measures, the demand response management seeks to stimulate consumers to reduce their energy consumption. They are different, though, because the former is targeted to a structural decrease in demand, while the latter aims for a change in consumer's behavior, encouraging the partial relocation of power consumption.[53] Demand response divides itself into load shifting – when consumption is shifted from a critical period, like peak hours, to off-peak hours, without a decrease in the monthly average consumption – and load shedding – when a consumption decrease is not later compensated.

With the demand response project, it will be possible to make demand more flexible and to couple it with RES intermittency and avoid the dispatch of pollutant and expensive thermal power plants. The mechanism will determine what is more convenient at a given moment: reward consumers to decrease their demand or dispatch non-RES.

The Brazilian ISO can contract ancillary services for demand decrease for periods varying from 1 to 7 hours, with at least 5-MW load, divided into 1-MW blocks. The volumes required must be defined the day before dispatch, for the day-ahead operation, and until the early morning of the dispatch day, for the intraday operation.

Since Brazil is still testing the demand response management, this form of DER has great potential to enhance grid reliability, contribute to tariff affordability, and allow for a high penetration of RES other than hydro, helping deconstruct the baseload generation myth[54] and maintain the Brazilian electricity matrix mainly clean and avoid the use of gas-fired power plants as backup generation.

4.4 Energy Storage and Electric Vehicles in Brazil

To fulfill the temporal gap between a continuous and widespread demand, on one side, and an intermittent supply, on the other, energy storage systems play a fundamental role. Energy storage systems are technology or system, in which electric energy is loaded in and, by necessity, can lately be discharged into the network.[55] Examples of different storage technologies

---

[53]FGV ENERGIA. *Recursos energéticos distribuídos*. Rio de Janeiro: FGV Energia, 2016, p. 33.

[54]SOVACOOL, Benjamin K. *The intermittency of wind, solar and renewable electricity generators: technical barrier or rhetorical excuse?* In: Utilities Policy, vol. 17, 2009.

[55]MAHNKE, Eva; MÜHLENHOFF, Jörg. Strom speichern. In: *Agentur für Erneuerbare Energien* (org.). Renews Spezial, Edition 57, 2012, p. 6; SCHILL, Wolf-Peter. *Systemintegration erneuerbarer Energien: Die Rolle von Speichern für die Energiewende*. DIW Berlin. Vierteljahrshefte zur Wirtschaftsforschung. 82. Jahrgang, 2013, p. 71.

are water reservoirs, compressed air reservoirs, flywheels,[56] thermal energy storage systems, condensers, superconductive magnetic energy storage system, batteries,[57] and hydrogen.[58]

The storage technology finds itself still in the invention and innovation phase and it is still unclear, how much flexibility in future energy systems will be necessary and which mix of flexibility options is optimal, so that more time and financial means will be required, until the energy storage systems find a place in the energy markets.[59]

Regarding its relation with DG, energy storage systems can be implemented near the consumption units – consumer-sited storage or consumer-located storage – allowing for short-term benefits in remote areas not fully connected to the grid.

The vehicle-2-grid (V2G) solutions offer another aspect of this relation, where batteries from automobiles can be "dispatched" when cars are parked, supplying the network, or can be called to take electricity from the network, in moments of network stress.[60]

DRM is very helpful when addressing V2G solutions since the network can overload if many consumers charge their electric vehicles at the same time. To avoid a suboptimal signal for investment in network expansion, the "charging demand" for electric vehicles can be steered. For example, for a worker who parks his car at home (equipped with an individual charging station) after work it might be irrelevant when exactly is his car going to be charged again, as long as, by the time he wakes up to go to work the following day, his car is charged.

In Brazil, regulatory authorities and undertakings are starting to explore the potential for energy storage solutions. Within the scope of ANEEL's

[56]Flywheels are storage devices used for maintaining power quality and to provide black start capacity. Unless they are able to store more energy, they may not be a primary technology choice for peak-shifting applications needed to integrate intermittent renewables, PIERPOINT, Lara M. *Harnessing electricity storage for systems with intermittent sources of power: Policy and R&D needs.* In: Energy Policy, vol. 96, 2016, p. 753.

[57]A detailed description of different types of batteries is found in SUBERU, Mohammed Yekini; MUSTAFA, Mohd Wazir; BASHIR, Nouruddeen. *Energy storage systems for renewable energy power sector integration and mitigation of intermittency.* In: Renewable and Sustainable Energy Reviews, vol. 35, 2014, p. 502-506.

[58]FUCHS, Georg; LUNZ, Benedikt; LEUTHOLD, Matthias; SAUER, Dirk Uwe. *Overview on the potential and on the deployment perspectives of electricity storage technologies.* On behalf of Smart Energy for Europe Platform Ltd., 2012, p. 17.

[59]PIERPOINT, Lara M. *Harnessing electricity storage for systems with intermittent sources of power: Policy and R&D needs.* In: Energy Policy, vol. 96, 2016, p. 755; SCHUMACHER, Pascal. *Innovationsregulierung im Recht der netzgebundenen Elektrizitätswirtschaft.* Baden-Baden: Nomos, 2009, p. 168.

[60]See Chapter 18 for an analysis of EVs.

Public Call n. 21/16, undertakings are developing strategic R&D,[61] but no concrete incentive or policy framework has been launched (the first results of the R&D Program for energy storage are to be presented only in 2021). The Energy Research Office considers that there is a low degree of economic viability for the immediate application of energy storage systems in Brazil, especially to supply additional power to the system. Although acknowledging the potential of energy storage solutions, the Energy Research Office concludes that the insertion of this technology will highly depend on further studies and the identification of additional features for energy storage, while expecting the prices to fall within the next 5 years.[62]

Despite this scenario, the country has seen some private-driven initiatives. For example, in May 2018 came into operation in Brazil the first DG (PV mini-generation) with energy storage (300 kW installed capacity plus 1-MW energy storage capacity).

Regarding electric vehicles, the Energy Research Office is also skeptic, mainly due to:

- high prices for hybrid or electric vehicles (Brazil has only 3.5 thousand of these vehicles in its fleet, out of a 41.5 million cars fleet), even with 100% import tax exemption for fully electric models with a range of at least 80 km[63];
- Brazilian consumers have a preference for sedans, SUVs, and midlevel luxury cars, whose features are distinct from electric vehicles;
- lack of regulatory solutions regarding the location of charging stations, the forms of charge payment;
- lack of forecasts for additional load and network investments;
- lack of adequate legal treatment for environmental protection in the battery recycling and disposal;
- current budgetary restrictions on the Government's side, hindering any policy investments;
- competition with ethanol-fired vehicles.[64]

While some of these arguments may sound reasonable, others are not. Taking forecasts, for example, a study by a Brazilian thinktank showed that in a scenario where EV represents 20% of the fleet and cover 8,000 km per year, with consumption of 6 kWh/km, these vehicles would demand less than

[61]FGV ENERGIA. *Recursos energéticos distribuídos*. Rio de Janeiro: FGV Energia, 2016, p. 21.
[62]EMPRESA DE PESQUISA ENERGÉTICA. *Brazilian Energy Balance 2017*. Rio de Janeiro: EPE, 2017, p. 68-69.
[63]FGV ENERGIA. *Electric vehicles*. Rio de Janeiro: FGV Energia, 2017, p. 72.
[64]EMPRESA DE PESQUISA ENERGÉTICA. *Brazilian Energy Balance 2017*. Rio de Janeiro: EPE, 2017, p. 33-34.

2% of all electricity consumed in the country in 2011. Regarding power, the increase would be 10% if vehicle charging occurred after 6:00 p.m.[65] Likewise, a distribution utility (CPFL) also conducted simulations, demonstrating that considering a share in total vehicle fleet from 4% to 10% by 2030, the additional electricity consumption caused by these vehicles would increase from 0.6% to 1.6%, which would be completely manageable by the Brazilian electricity grid.[66]

There is some hope that the Brazilian EV industry will flourish with the help of the Draft Bill n. 65/14, which determines the installation of charging stations for EVs in public roads and residential and commercial locations. The Draft Bill is currently passing through the Senate.

Besides that, the Emotive Initiative, of a distribution utility (CPFL), implemented 10 charging stations in the city of Campinas (São Paulo State), within an R&D project. Another utility, in the State of Paraná (COPEL), inaugurated in March 2018, its electric highway, installing the first of eight 50-kVA charging stations, with three types of plugs, which take between 30 minutes to 1 hour to charge 80% of the EV battery. CELESC, the distribution utility in the State of Santa Catarina, also installed seven charging stations, forming a 150-km-long electric highway. The 430 km separating São Paulo and Rio de Janeiro can be done with EVs thanks to a cooperative effort from BMW and EDP, which installed six charging stations along the highway.

5. CONCLUSIONS

While in some countries, like Chile and Brazil, the improvements in the regulatory framework have led to an initial – but small, when compared to California, for example – DG boom, concrete results in other jurisdictions are not considerable, despite spectacular irradiation levels in LAC countries. The maximum installed capacity for a DG project in some LAC countries is too low – ranging, on average, from 1 MW to 100 kW. Besides that, it is paramount that the Government sets public policies and financial incentives targeted to prosumption.

Regarding Brazil, small-scale DG only flourished when the regulatory authority creatively decided to establish other legal configurations, enabling DG cooperatives and consortia, extending the energy surpluses' monthly rollover and solving the taxation issue. That legal scenario, together with new credit lines and finance arrangements for prosumers, constitute a successful formula for an initial DG expansion.

[65]GESEL. *Mobilidade elétrica: relatório técnico.* 2014.
[66]FGV ENERGIA. *Electric vehicles.* Rio de Janeiro: FGV Energia, 2017, p. 79.

Nevertheless, long-term regulatory issues will have to be properly addressed in the near future, like whether prosumers will be allowed to trade electricity; how to properly recognize, in the energy tariff, investments in the network made by utilities to safely accommodate large amounts of DG-produced energy; and how to adequately price the benefits of DG for the system operation and reliability.

The possibility for prosumers to arrange themselves into other configurations, beyond cooperatives and consortia, as well as forms to limit the consumer's financial risk, as the leasing scheme in California has shown, are part of the solution.

Regarding other DER, like DRM, energy storage solutions and EVs, Brazil has still a long way to go. To overcome the pilot-project stage and individual initiatives, the Government should adopt some measures:

- massive investments in smart grids, especially in digitalization and smart metering;
- systematic public policy incentives, like tax exemptions on DER-related components, products, and devices;
- comprehensive regulatory framework, providing adequate remuneration for service providers and aggregators – recognition of locational signal and environmental benefits and allocating risks adequately.

REFERENCES

Ackermann, T., Andersson, G., Söder, L., 2001. Distributed generation: a definition. Electric Power Syst. Res. 57.

Agência Nacional de Energia Elétrica, 2015. Nota Técnica n° 0017/2015-SRD/ANEEL. ANEEL, Brasília.

Agência Nacional de Energia Elétrica, 2017. Nota Técnica n° 0056/2017-SRD/ANEEL. ANEEL, Brasília.

Agência Nacional de Energia Elétrica, 2018. Nota Técnica n° 0062/2018-SRD/SCG/SRM/SRG/SGT/SMA/ANEEL. Brasília, ANEEL.

Australian Energy Market Commission, 2017. 2017 AEMC Retail Energy Competition Review. Final Report.

Bauknecht, D., Brunekreeft, G., 2008. Distributed generation and the regulation of electricity networks. In: Sioshansi, F.P. (Ed.), Competitive Electricity Markets: Design, Implementation, Performance. Elsevier, United Kingdom.

Brennan, T.J., 2007. Consumer preference not to choose: methodological and policy implications. Energy Policy 35, 1616–1627.

Cámara Argentina de Energías Renovables, 2015. Aportes para un sistema eléctrico eficiente y sustentable. Desarrollo industrial y de las economías regionales. CADER, Buenos Aires.

Castaneda, M., Jimenez, M., Zapata, S., Franco, C.J., Dyner, I., 2017. Myths and facts of the utility death spiral. Energy Policy 110.

Chambers, A., 2001. Distributed generation: a nontechnical guide. PennWell, Tulsa, OK.

Costello, K.W., Hemphill, R.C., 2014. Electric utilities' "death spiral": hyperbole or reality? Electr. J. 27.

da Silva, S.T., Dutra, C., Guimarães, L.N.d.M.R., 2018. Solar energy and the dawn of 'solar cities' in Brazil. In: Costa, J.A.F., Ribeiro, M.R.d.S., Xavier Júnior, E.C. (Eds.), Energy Law and Regulation in Brazil. Springer.

Dondi, P., Bayoumi, D., Haederli, C., Julian, D., Suter, M., 2002. Network integration of distributed power generation. J. Power Sources 106.

Eliaschev, N., 2016. Autogeneración distribuida y balance neto. Introducción a su regulación jurídica. Revista Jurídica de la Universidad de San Andrés 3.

Empresa de Pesquisa Energética, 2017. Brazilian Energy Balance 2017. EPE, Rio de Janeiro.

Empresa De Pesquisa Energética, 2018. Distributed Energy Resources. EPE, Rio de Janeiro.

FGV Energia, 2016. Recursos energéticos distribuídos. FGV Energia, Rio de Janeiro.

FGV Energia, 2017. Electric vehicles. FGV Energia, Rio de Janeiro.

Fuchs, G., Lunz, B., Leuthold, M., Sauer, D.U., 2012. Overview on the potential and on the deployment perspectives of electricity storage technologies. On behalf of Smart Energy for Europe Platform Ltd.

Gesel, 2014. Mobilidade elétrica: relatório técnico.

Gischler, C., Janson, N., 2011. Perspectives for distributed generation with renewable energy in Latin America and the Caribbean—analysis of case studies for Jamaica, Barbados, Mexico, and Chile. IDB Discussion Paper 208.

Gomes, P.V., et al., 2018. Technical-economic analysis for the integration of PV systems in Brazil considering policy and regulatory issues. Energy Policy 115.

Guimarães, L.N.d.M.R., 2013. Regulação da exploração da eletricidade: compatibilidade com as leis da natureza e com a ordem econômica constitucional. Editora CRV, Brazil.

Holdermann, C., KISSEL, J., BEIGEL, J., 2014. Distributed photovoltaic generation in Brazil: an economic viability analysis of small-scale photovoltaic systems in the residential and commercial sectors. Energy Policy 67.

Hortaçsu, A., Madanizadeh, S.A., Puller, S.L., 2015. Power to choose? An analysis of consumer inertia in the residential electricity market. NBER working paper N° 20988.

International Energy Agency, 2002. Distributed generation in liberalized electricity markets. IEA, Paris.

KEMA, 2008. CARILEC Position Paper on Energy Policy. Caribbean Association of Electric Utilities.

Mahnke, E., Mühlenhoff, J., 2012. Strom speichern. In: Agentur für Erneuerbare Energien. Renews Spezial, Edition 57.

Muaafa, M., Adjali, I., Bean, P., Fuentes, R., Kimbrough, S.O., Murphy, F.H., 2017. Can adoption of rooftop solar panels trigger a utility death spiral? A tale of two U.S. cities. Energy Res. Social Sci. 34.

Pepermans, G., Driesen, J., Haeseldonckx, D., Belmans, R., D'Haeseller, W., 2005. Distributed generation: definition, benefits and issues. Energy Policy 33.

Pierpoint, L.M., 2016. Harnessing electricity storage for systems with intermittent sources of power: policy and R&D needs. Energy Policy 96.

Porcelli, A.M., Martínez, A.N., 2018. Una inevitable transición energética: el prosumidor y la generación de energías renovables en forma distribuida en la legislación argentina nacional y provincial. Actualidad Jurídica Ambiental 75.

Quintero, S.X.C., Jiménez, J.D.M., 2013. Impacto de la generación distribuida en el sistema eléctrico de potencia colombiano: un enfoque dinámico. Tecnura 17.

Resende, J., Aquino, T., Dantas, G., 2017. New business models with diffusion of distributed generation. In: Castro, N.d. (Ed.), Distributed Generation: International Experiences and Comparative Analyses. Publit, Rio de Janeiro.

Satchwell, A., Mills, A., Barbose, G., 2015. Quantifying the financial impacts of net-metered PV on utilities and ratepayers. Energy Policy 80.

Schill, W.-P., 2013. Systemintegration erneuerbarer Energien: Die Rolle von Speichern für die Energiewende. DIW Berlin.

Schumacher, P., 2009. Innovationsregulierung im Recht der netzgebundenen Elektrizitätswirtschaft. Nomos, Baden-Baden.

Sousa, H.W.A., 2013. Utilizaçõo de programas de reação da demanda como alternativa à necessidade de geração termelétrica complementar para garanti do suprimento de energia elétrica. UnB, Brasília.

Sovacool, B.K., 2009. The intermittency of wind, solar and renewable electricity generators: technical barrier or rhetorical excuse? Util. Policy 17.

Suberu, M.Y., Mustafa, M.W., Bashir, N., 2014. Energy storage systems for renewable energy power sector integration and mitigation of intermittency. Renew. Sustain. Energy Rev. 35.

World Economic Forum, 2017. The Global Competitiveness Report 2017-2018. WEF, Geneva.

World Economic Forum, 2018. Fostering Effective Energy Transition—A Fact-Based Framework to Support Decision-Making. WEF, Geneva.

Yang, Y., 2014. Understanding household switching behavior in the retail electricity market. Energy Policy 69.

How Will the Emerging Business Models of Incumbent Distribution Companies and Newcomers Transform the Electric Power Sector

CHAPTER 12

The Future of Electricity Distribution: A California Case Study

Fereidoon Sioshansi[a]
Menlo Energy Economics, Walnut Creek, CA, United States

1. INTRODUCTION

California is among a handful of states pushing the envelope on multiple fronts while firing on multiple cylinders, both literally and figuratively speaking. Following a tumultuous electricity crisis in 2000–01[1] – which nobody wants to repeat – the state's regulators abandoned retail choice or direct access[2] while implementing a number of emergency measures to restore a resemblance of normalcy to the dysfunctional wholesale and retail markets.

Fast forward to 2019. By most measures, the grid operator, the California Independent System Operator (CAISO), has restored confidence to the wholesale market, which has been functioning without major reliability issues. The retail market, while no longer competitive – except for those who already switched while they could – also appears to be functioning. Adequate capacity is maintained through a mandatory resource adequacy mechanism overseen by the regulator, the California Public Utility Commission (CPUC).

Superficially, at least, one can say that all is well in California's electricity market. The lights stay on, the bills get paid, and the state is making measurable progress on a number of regulatory and policy fronts notably:

- Meeting or exceeding the target mandated by the renewable portfolio standard (RPS) – currently 33% by 2020, 50% by 2030, and 100% by 2045;
- Reducing the state's greenhouse gas (GHG) emissions to 1990 level in 2020[3] and further reductions by 2030 and 2050; and

---

[a]The author acknowledges Scott Murtishaw and Rafael Friedmann for their comments on earlier drafts of this chapter.
[1]The California Electricity Crisis, James Sweeney, Stanford Univ. Press, 2002.
[2]Terms referring to option to select a retailer other than the incumbent monopoly poles and wires company.
[3]California, in fact, has met both of the 2020 targets 2 years ahead of schedule.

261

- Expanding the state's electric vehicle (EVs) charging infrastructure to allow 5 million EVs to be on the roads by 2030 as envisioned by Governor Jerry Brown.

This chapter examines the cumulative impact of the myriad of environmental, regulatory, and policy-driven initiatives, which have resulted in the rise of variable renewable energy generation, distributed energy resources (DERs), and community choice aggregation (CCAs).[4] These, in turn, are beginning to impact the day-to-day operations of the CAISO and the traditional role of the incumbents, in particular the three large regulated distribution utilities in California. The CAISO is increasingly challenged to integrate more variable generation while maintaining the grid's reliability. The incumbent distribution utilities are trying to reposition themselves in view of the rapidly changing landscape. According to some projections, the state's three large private utilities – which historically served virtually all customers within their monopoly franchise service areas – may lose as much as 85% of their customers over time to the CCAs.[5]

The chapter is primarily focused on the intended, and some of the unintended, consequences of California's prevailing energy and environmental policies and regulations, which have resulted in a host of new service options that were not traditionally available to customers. Specifically, the chapter examines the evolving role of the state's three large private utilities who are fast turning into regulated distribution-only companies, no longer responsible for power procurement and largely devoid of generation assets. Moving forward, the regulators are grappling to keep pace with multiples of challenges mostly unleashed by their own initiatives as well as the fast-moving pace of technological innovations that are transforming the electric power sector, particularly in the behind-the-meter space.

The experience of California, the most populous state in America, is relevant to the rest of the US and is, in many ways, similar to developments taking place in other parts of the world where decarbonization, decentralization, and digitalization are changing the traditional electric sector business imperatives.

---

[4] It must be noted that it is difficult to cover so many aspects of a complex story in a single chapter since the implications of retail choice/CCAs and DERs on the distribution utilities – of which there are many – are inherently different and distinct.

[5] CPUC Green Paper, 3 May 2018 http://www.cpuc.ca.gov/uploadedFiles/CPUC_Public_Website/Content/Utilities_and_Industries/Energy_-_Electricity_and_Natural_Gas/CCC%20FAQs.pdf and the proceedings from the En Banc hearing on 22 June 2018.

The chapter is organized as follows:

- Section 2 provides a synopsis of the challenges facing California's power sector;
- Section 3 focuses on the impact of DERs, net energy metering (NEM), zero net energy (ZNE) building codes and appliance energy efficiency standards, which collectively impact demand for kWhs;
- Section 4 examines the impact of CCAs, which by some estimates may render the incumbent utilities into predominantly distribution-only enterprises over time[6]; and
- Section 5 speculates how the cumulative effect of the preceding plus the state's ambitious climate law, energy storage, and electric transportation initiatives are likely to reshape California's electricity landscape followed by the chapter's conclusions.

2. CHALLENGES FACING CALIFORNIA'S POWER SECTOR

As already noted, a casual observer might conclude that all is well in California's power sector. Retail tariffs may be a bit above national average, but given the state's relatively mild climate and stringent building codes, average electricity bills are tolerable.[7] With little energy-intensive industry, California spends less on electricity compared to other major states with heavy industry.[8]

On some dimensions, California may in fact seem like a leader or role model. Among the populous states, for example, it has one of the highest mandatory targets for renewable generation in its resource mix – currently 50% by 2030 – and that does not count existing hydro and other renewable generation. In Sep 2018, California passed a new law mandating that by 2045 100% of electricity used in the state must come from noncarbon resources plus an executive order to make the entire state into a carbon neutral economy by the same date.

California leads the country in installed solar capacity – both utility scale and distributed – far exceeding other populous sunny states such as Florida or Texas (refer to Fig. 3 in Introduction). It has more distributed

---

[6]The impact of CCAs, as will be further explained, may not apply to all customers or cover all parts of California.

[7]Residential customers living along the coast, enjoy mostly Mediterranean weather, which means little heating or cooling.

[8]California spends less on electricity as a percentage of its GDP than other major states such as Texas, Florida, or New York – partly because of mild climate and partly due to the lack of energy-intensive industry.

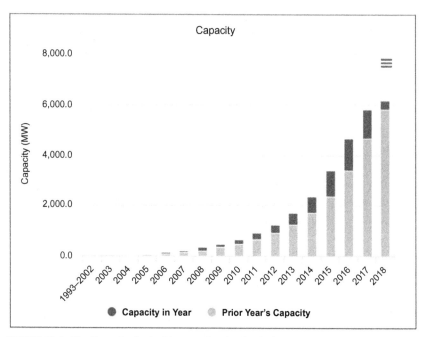

FIGURE 12.1 Distributed solar in CA exceeds 6 GW (Includes solar PV net energy metering (NEM) applications in PG&, SCE, and SDG&E service territories – serving roughly 80% of customers; excludes others.). *(Source: https://www.californiadgstats.ca.gov/charts/.)*

solar, roughly 6 GW and growing (Fig. 12.1). It is home to roughly half of all electric vehicles on the US roads at the present, with a target to get as many as 5 million by 2030. California's per capita electricity consumption is the lowest among the states – and has remained flat since 1978 while the rest of the US has experienced rising per capita electricity consumption overtime. The state is routinely ranked among the top three in the US in terms of energy efficiency.[9]

The state's climate bill,[10] passed in 2006, calls for statewide greenhouse gas (GHG) emissions to fall to 1990 levels by 2020, 40% below 1990 level by 2030, and 80% below 1990 level by 2050 (Fig. 12.2). A myriad of environmental policies, including a cap-and-trade scheme and stringent auto efficiency and fuel standards, are expected to contribute to achieving to future targets despite a growing population and economy.[11]

---

[9]Latest ACEEE survey at http://aceee.org/state-policy/scorecard, ranks CA #2 in USA.

[10]The California Global Warming Solutions Act of 2006, also known as Assembly Bill 32 may be found at https://www.arb.ca.gov/cc/ab32/ab32.htm.

[11]Refer to AB 398 (2017), which codifies the 40% target by 2030 goal.

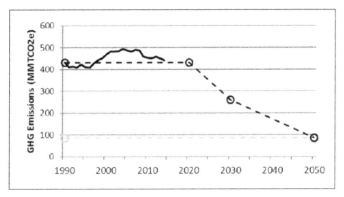

FIGURE 12.2 California climate bill targets for 2020, 2030, and 2050. *(Source: Deep decarbonization is a high renewable future, for CEC, E3, June 2018.)*

The climate bill is, by far, the most ambitious of all targets and is the main driver of many of the other policies including the RPS target, stringent building codes, and appliance energy efficiency standards, EV targets and other measures further described in Section 3.[12]

As a consequence of having so many targets, mandates, and policies – which may be duplicative, overlapping, and not necessarily coordinated – California is now facing a multitude of challenges, some more pressing than others, including:

- Rising utility-scale variable renewable generation;
- Growing distributed solar;
- Evolving – and some might say uncertain – role of distribution network and distribution utilities;
- Retail tariffs that are unfit for the changing times; and
- Inadequate EV charging infrastructure to meet the intended targets.

The first two, the rapid rise of variable renewable generation, particularly solar, are manifested in the famous "California duck" curve[13] (Fig. 12.3), resulting in too much generation during the sunny mid-day hours of the year, particularly in the spring and the fall when temperatures are mild and there is little or no air conditioning load to speak of.

As described in Box 12.1, on many cool, sunny spring days, utility-scale solar meets half of the load on the CAISO network – and that does *not*

---

[12]Climate change has already resulted in hotter, longer, and drier summers with more frequent and extensive forest fires, less hydro resources in the Summer/early Fall. The IOUs are potentially facing multibillion dollar losses from the 2018 fire season, which are likely to get worse.

[13]Chapter 18 by Webb includes a similar duck curve for Queensland, Australia.

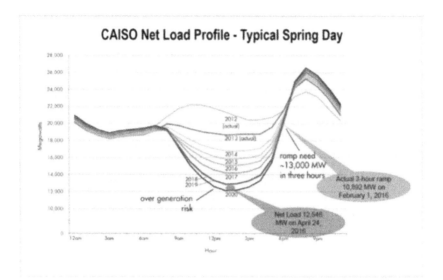

FIGURE 12.3   California "duck curve." *(Source: CAISO.)*

Box 12.1   Solar Hits 50% of Demand in California[14]

The arrival of spring brings cool and exceptionally sunny days in California, which causes the **California Independent System Operator** (CAISO) huge headaches due to the prevalence of solar generation when there is virtually no air-conditioning load.

On two consecutive days in early March 2018, solar generation approached and exceeded 50% of load on CAISO system with challenging ramping requirements when the sun sets.

According to CAISO, at around 1 pm on Sunday 4 Mar – a cool, clear day – large-scale solar supplied nearly 50% of demand, beating the prior record of 47% set in May 2017.

Explaining the new record, **Anne Gonzales**, a spokesperson for CAISO, said, "The escalating integration of solar power has created a new operating paradigm for our system operators." Translated to plain English, the growing ramp-down and ramp-ups in the morning and evening, respectively, are becoming harder to manage. She added, "Our operators are skilled at handling these ramps, and we expect them to continue."

On a cool, sunny day, especially on weekends, there is little load – the minimum load was 18,800 MW while solar production was 9,400 MW. This does not include distributed solar, for which the CAISO has virtually no visibility. It merely sees the **net load**.

[14] *Excerpted from April 2018 issue of EEnergy Informer.*

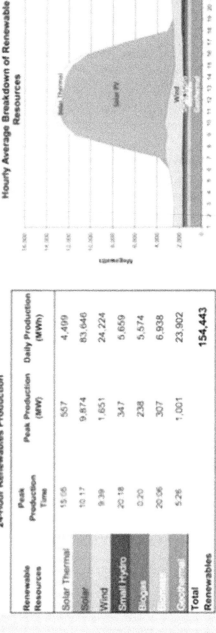

Hourly Average Breakdown of Renewable Resources

This graph shows the production of various types of renewable generation across the day.

System Peak Demand (MW)   28,378
*one-minute average
Time: 18:40

24-Hour Renewables Production

Renewable Resources	Peak Production Time	Peak Production (MW)	Daily Production (MWh)
Solar Thermal	15:06	557	4,499
Solar	10:17	9,874	83,646
Wind	9:39	1,651	24,224
Small Hydro	20:18	347	5,659
Biogas	0:20	238	5,574
Biomass	20:06	307	6,938
Geothermal	5:26	1,001	23,902
Total Renewables			**154,443**

Total 24-Hour System Demand (MWh):   570,183

This table gives numeric values related to the production from the various types of renewable resources for the reporting day. All values are hourly average unless otherwise stated. Peak Production is an average over one minute. The total renewable production in megawatt-hours is compared to the total energy demand for the ISO system for the day.

Utility-scale solar supplied 50% of demand. (Source: CAISO.)

include the behind-the-meter (BTM) solar – which is currently around 6 GW and rising as illustrated in Fig. 12.1.

A CAISO analysis in 2012 not only predicted a progressively worsening "California duck" problem, but also identified more frequent episodes of "overgeneration," negative wholesale prices and challenging ramping issues in the morning – when the sun rises – and in the late afternoon – when it sets. While CAISO should be given credit for accurately predicting the arrival of the "duck," it underestimated the speed at which it would arrive. The deep belly of the "duck" illustrated in Fig. 12.3, which was originally predicted to arrive by 2020 actually materialized 4 years earlier in 2016.

Not surprisingly, CAISO is working on multiple fronts to manage the daily ramping requirements of the "California Duck" including efforts to expand the energy imbalance market (EIM[15]). Longer term, CAISO would like an expanded geographical footprint, which will allow a more diverse generation portfolio of generation from out of state to better balance the state's variable generation and load (Fig. 12.4). This vision, however, faces many political hurdles and institutional challenges that are likely to take significant time and effort to overcome.

In the mean time, to assist CAISO in managing the daily ramping issues, California regulators have introduced mandatory storage requirements – 1.325 GW by 2024[16] – which may offer some short-term relief but will most likely have to be expanded beyond the current scale. Storage is among a number of options pursued by CAISO to address a worsening "California Duck" problem.

Ultimately, however, price-responsive demand has to play a much more pronounced role as further described in several chapters in this volume including Chapters 3 and 6 by Baak and Sioshansi and Stanley et al., respectively.

The next two challenges are closely intertwined. The rise of DERs and the proliferation of behind-the-meter options mean that the distribution network is increasingly turning into a two-way conduit that has to work much harder and in ways that it was not originally designed to perform. This problem will only get worse as millions of EVs are expected to be added to the network over the next decade. The problem becomes quite acute in neighborhoods with high concentration of EVs – and PVs – especially if EVs are all plugged in at about the same time to be charged. If charging takes place predominantly at home and at the end of commute day, then it will

---

[15]CAISO website covers the inception of EIM, its evolution over time, and plans for future expansion.

[16]https://www.energy.gov/sites/prod/files/2014/06/f17/EACJune2014-3Charles.pdf.

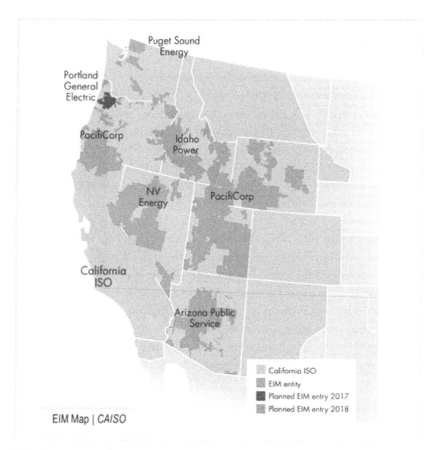

FIGURE 12.4 Map of CAISO's Energy Imbalance Market (EIM), 2018. *(Source: CAISO.)*

further raise the neck of the California Duck curve, making the evening's ramping requirements even more challenging.

Ironically, just as the need to upgrade and modernize the aging distribution network increases, the revenues of the distribution utilities are being eroded by the combined effect of more distributed generation and improvements in the energy efficiency of buildings and appliances.

As long as the retail tariffs remain mostly if not totally based on volumetric consumption, the rising numbers of prosumers and prosumagers will be contributing relatively little to the upkeep of the distribution network. Under current net energy metering (NEM) regulation, expected to be modified in 2019, a prosumer who feeds the network more than it takes from it can essentially reduce the monthly bill to zero, or potentially receive a payment from the utility – as described in the book's introduction.

This explains the rising pressure on the CPUC to introduce more fixed charges as well as granular tariffs, which could potentially vary not only by time but also location and direction of the flow of the electrons. In the face of requests by the distribution utilities for approval for additional investment to upgrade the network, the CPUC and its counterparts in other parts of the US are increasingly asking for "nonwire" solutions – which include smarter ways of relieving stress and congestion given the fact that the network is generally not stressed or congested everywhere or all of the time. Chapters 3 and 6 by Baak and Sioshansi and by Stanley et al., for example, offer clever ways of dealing with localized congestion rather than indiscriminately gold plating the entire network.

Regulators in California are not alone in facing the pressing need to redefine the future role of the distribution network while redefining and redesigning retail tariffs that better capture the cost causality of prosumers and prosumagers while remaining mindful of the needs of the remaining *consumers* who rely on traditional regulated bundled retail tariffs. As described in Chapter 8 by Burger et al., keeping the playing field level – that is avoiding unsustainable cross-subsidies among consumers, prosumers, and prosumagers – never easy, has become far more complicated. It is among the many vexing issues facing regulators, and not just in California.

3. FACTORS AFFECTING SALES AND UTILITY COST RECOVERY

Given the preceding discussion, there is much to cover in a chapter on the future of utility distribution business in California. This section and the balance of the chapter, however, will primarily focus on factors that may result in erosion of electricity sales and revenues and their impact on cost recovery through regulated tariffs.

To start off, California has a complicated distribution landscape consisting of three large investor-owned utilities (IOUs), two large municipal utilities (Munis), and a number of smaller utilities (Fig. 12.5). These are referred to as distribution companies, load-serving entities or LSEs, or electric service providers or ESPs. Making matters more complicated is a rapidly growing number of CCAs, further described in the following section.

Of these, only the three major IOUs are subject to rate regulation by the CPUC. The rates charged by the CCAs are governed by internal boards, city councils, and so on – depending on the organization of the CCA – not by the CPUC. The CCAs, however, are subject to certain reliability regulations promulgated by the CPUC, such as the resource adequacy requirements.

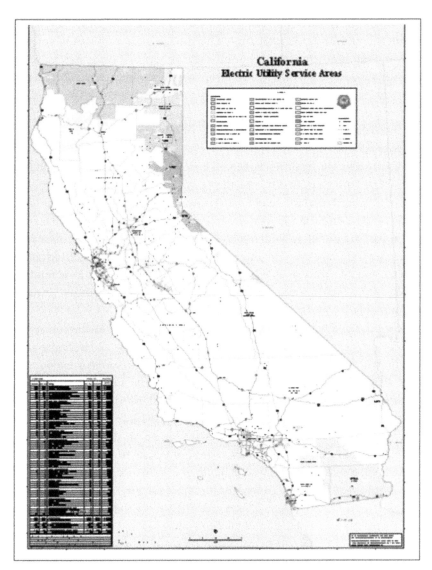

FIGURE 12.5 Map of CA with service areas of three major IOUs and others. *(Source: CEC.)*

Focusing on the changing role of distribution utilities, a few key trends are particularly relevant:

- First is the continued growth of DERs and/or behind-the meter (BTM) devices in multiple forms and shapes;
- Second is the current net energy metering (NEM) law; and
- Third is a new zero net energy (ZNE) building code and appliance energy efficiency standards that goes into effect starting in 2020.

These and other trends have been gradually cutting into customers' volumetric consumption over time. The fundamental problem is not just that the volume of net consumption may be flat or falling but more to do with the way in which distribution costs are allocated and revenues collected. Against this background, there are expectations that the rapid penetration of EVs will boost electricity sales, possibly compensating for, or potentially exceeding, any loss of sales due to the growth of DERs and BTM devices.[17]

Historically, the utilities collected revenues by applying a regulated multiplier – the cents/kWh – to the volume consumed, resulting in the allowed "revenue requirements" – the amount that would make the IOU whole by covering the O&M costs and leave extra to cover financial costs and to pay shareholder dividends, taxes, insurance, and so on. In the past, there was little attention, or incentive, to distinguish between covering fixed vs. variable costs or even which class of customers paid how much – so long as the total amount collected from all equaled the utility's "revenue requirements."

Since the overwhelming portion of costs of a typical distribution utility is fixed – namely, maintenance of poles and wires – flat or declining sales volume has the effect of pushing retail tariffs upward. And that encourages more customers to invest in DERs, resulting in the so-called *death spiral* scenario, further described – among others – in an Edison Electric Institute report,[18] which publicized the phenomenon in 2013.

The growth of DERs, of course, is no longer in dispute (Box 12.2), while its impact on utility revenues varies from place to place.

As further explained in Box 12.3, net energy metering (NEM), which allows customers with self-generation to inject their excess supply into the local distribution network and get a credit for every net kWh exported, is another reason for the erosion of sales in California and elsewhere.

The full impact of NEM on California utility sales is hard to measure. Neither utilities nor CAISO can tell with any certainty how much of the drop in sales may be due to distributed generation, energy efficiency, self-generation, weather-related, behavioral factors, or the result of an intervention by an intermediary who may remotely adjust a customer's thermostat – the types of intervention further described in Chapter 3 by Baak and Sioshansi.

---

[17] As reflected in Chapter 18 by Webb et al. and others, EVs can be a cure or a curse depending on when, where, and how they are charged. A recent study by the CEC, for example, suggested that they may add 1 GW to California's peak – which could in fact make the "duck problem" even worse.

[18] Peter Kind, Disruptive Challenges: Financial Implications and Strategic Responses to a Changing Retail Electric Business, EEI, 2013.

Box 12.2 DERs Projected to Reach 530 GW by 2026

A recent report by Navigant Research says the global market for distributed energy resources (DERs) can be expected to reach 530 GW by 2026. As a point of reference, total installed capacity in the US is around 1,000 GW.
According to Navigant:

Technology advances, business model innovation, changing regulations, and sustainability and resilience concerns have brought DER into the core of the future deployment of energy infrastructure.
...... the global proliferation of DER has begun to have a significant, and at times controversial, influence on the electricity industry.

Not surprisingly, the influence of increasing DER deployments will vary in different countries based on the prevailing retail tariffs and other policies favoring or discouraging DERs. Despite these regional variations, it is fair to say that the rapid rise of investment in DERs not only represents a major shift in the traditional centralized, one-way electrical grid but a major substitute for it. In the mean time, the industry, its regulators, and grid operators are struggling to "understand the evolving landscape that is redefining the relationship between utilities and customers," according to Navigant.

Box 12.3 How Net Energy Metering (NEM) Cuts into California Utility Sales

First introduced in 1996 in California, when solar PVs were an expensive novelty for the environmentally committed, the NEM regulation was intended to encourage the early adopters by lessening its cost. The scheme allowed customers to get a credit for each net kWh fed into the network equal to the full retail cost of electricity purchased from the network.

This allowed customers to "spin the meters backward" during the sunny parts of the day, thus reducing their net kWhs purchased from the network. Depending on the size and number of panels and load, customers could zero out the net purchase from the network, and some apparently did. In some cases, the customers could get a rebate if their kWh injection over the course of the year exceeded kWhs taken off the grid.

The original law placed a limit on the size of distributed solar capacity, which were not expected to be reached for quite a while. But the uptake of solar PVs shot up due to the combination of three factors:

- The top retail rates – which at one time had five tiers – rose significantly[19] making NEM so much more attractive to consumers with big monthly bills, such as those living in hot interior climate with big air conditioning load;

[19] The number of tiers has been reduced to two over time.

Continued

Box 12.3 How Net Energy Metering (NEM) Cuts into California Utility Sales—cont'd

- The cost of solar PV panels began to plummet,[20] making their installation far less costly; and perhaps more important
- Solar PV installers began offering lease options with little or no money down[21] – which made self-generation a no-brainer for anyone with big monthly bills.

  By 2018, California has acquired over 6 GW of distributed solar capacity, by far the biggest among the US states.

[20] The price of panels – without the installation and balance of system costs – has dropped to around 40 cents/W.
[21] SolarCity, now part of Tesla Energy, was among the first to offer leasing options in the residential sector.

In the case of CAISO, it essentially is flying in the cloud. It only sees the *net* load – that is total demand minus behind-the-meter generation, storage, or whatever. There had been claims that if the current trends continue, the net revenue loss for the three IOUs would balloon into millions and billions. These estimates have been scaled back because of the recent modifications in NEM regulations as well as the fact that most residential customers are now billed on only two tiers – which means that the disparity between the top and the bottom tier is not as substantial as it used to be.

A back-of-the-envelope 2018 estimate by Lucas Davis, a professor at Univ. of California at Berkeley, puts the number of California solar roofs around 700,000 and says the revenue loss may be as much as $840 million per annum,[22] roughly 5% of the industry's annual revenues.

Since the distribution utilities operate on an essentially "cost-plus" basis, any revenue loss due to NEM, DERs, energy efficiency measures such as building codes or appliance energy efficiency standards, climate related, or behavioral effects is recovered through upward adjustments in retail tariffs. This mechanism, while reducing the immediate pain on the IOUs, is clearly not a viable long-term strategy, as explained by the death spiral scenario.

[22]Why Am I Paying $65/year for Your Solar Panels? Lucas Davis Blog, 26 Mar 2018 at https://energyathaas.wordpress.com/2018/03/26/why-am-i-paying-65-year-for-your-solar-panels/.

As more consumers become prosumers and buy less from the regulated network, the remaining consumers have to pay more – given the fact that the cost of maintaining the network is mostly fixed.[23] This has led to controversies about unsustainable and unfair cross-subsidization among solar vs. nonsolar customers. Most studies looking into the matter have concluded that, broadly speaking:

- More affluent customers are more likely to install solar panels;
- These same customers typically tend to be on top tiers – which suggests that any decline in their contributions disproportionately impacts utility revenues[24];
- Less affluent customers, including many who live in inner cities and/or apartments, are less likely to install solar panels; and consequently
- Nonsolar customers, as a class, end up subsidizing the solar customers under prevailing tariffs – broadly considered unfair and inequitable, hence politically unpopular.

While there are many ifs and buts to these "general" conclusions and the existence of alternative studies, which suggest that solar customers are *not* being subsidized, but in fact may be *subsidizing* the nonsolar ones, the controversies about the longer-term unsustainability of the original NEM regulations – generally regarded to be overly generous – have prompted the CPUC to gradually modify them in stages.[25]

The expected modifications in NEM regulations are clearly overdue. They will certainly help reduce the revenue losses that the utilities claim they are, and will be, suffering in the coming years. For its part, however, the CPUC has not changed its support for self-generation or solar PV panels; it is merely taking the necessary steps to "level the uneven playing field."

Across the US and in other parts of the world, regulators are making, or have already made, similar adjustments in how much is paid for the excess generation fed into the grid. There is a growing acceptance that the price of a kWh, flowing in either direction across the meter, should no longer be fixed but should vary based on time, location, and direction of the flow.

---

[23]Davis estimates the current cross-subsidy at around $65 for each nonsolar customer to solar customers.

[24]As already stated, this is less of an issue since the number of tiers and the price disparity among them has been significantly reduced.

[25]The ongoing debate on whether, when, and how to modify existing NEM regulation basically boils down to IOUs claiming large and growing cross-subsidies from nonsolar to solar customers vs. the solar lobby and its supporters who claim that DERs, broadly speaking, and solar PVs specifically, are actually good for nonsolar customers and reduce bills. Further details may be found at CPUC website under NEM proceedings.

As a case in point, a kWh injected into a distribution network already flooded with excess solar generation from other prosumers and at a time when there is an excess of supply from utility-scale solar plants in the wholesale market is not worth much if any. The Energy Services Commission (ESC), the energy regulator in state of Victoria in Australia, for example, recently completed a study examining the value of kWhs injected into the network based on time and location.[26]

Subsequently, ESC introduced a new variable price for feeding excess distributed generation into the grid,[27] considered among the first in the world. It sets a precedence, which says all kWhs are not worth the same, whether they are feeding the network or taking energy away from the network.

Another factor impacting utility revenues has to do with building codes, appliance energy efficiency standards, and mandatory energy efficiency programs implemented by utilities and third parties – all of which are focused on reducing energy consumption in general, and electricity consumption in particular. All three are areas in which the state of California excels.

A new building code to take effect in 2020 requires virtually all *new* residential buildings to meet zero net energy (ZNE) standard – in effect generating as much energy as they consume, schematically illustrated in Fig. 12.6.

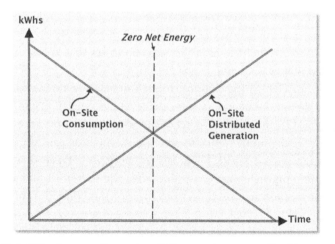

FIGURE 12.6 ZNE schematic illustrating CEC's recently approved building code, which applies to all new residential buildings starting in 2020 and is expected to be extended to new commercial buildings by 2030.

[26]Reference to ESC study may be found in Feb 2018 issue of EEnergy Informer.
[27]ESC: Time has arrived for variable pricing for feeding into the grid, EEnergy Informer April 2018.

To achieve such a target, residential building shells must be properly insulated and lighting and appliances must be ultra efficient. By adding solar PV panels and other types of self-generation, such a building, or collection of buildings, can meet the ZNE definition.[28]

California also has some of the most stringent energy efficiency standards for appliances as well as mandatory utility-sponsored energy efficiency programs. The state is frequently ranked among the top 1–2 among all states in terms of its energy efficiency programs.[29]

The net effect of the growth of behind-the-meter generation plus the impact of energy efficiency gains is two-fold:

* First, electricity consumption falls over time relative to the business as usual or reference scenario; and
* Second, consumption projections deviate from kWh sales as more consumers generate some of their own.

Prosumers, in other words, are becoming noticeable, as reflected in the projections of the California Energy Commission, where "consumption" figures are higher relative to kWh "sales," – that is how many kWhs are consumed vs. how many are bought from the grid. Once the effect of self-generation is taken into account, the sales projections to 2028 are as shown in Fig. 12.7.[30]

Needless to say, over time, forecasting consumption and sales becomes even more complicated due to conflicting trends that point in different directions, namely,

* Distributed solar and energy efficiency improvements reducing net kWh consumption; and
* Electric vehicles and gradual electrification of the transport and industrial sectors increasing kWh consumption.

As described in Chapter 18 by Webb et al., if a significant number of EV owners are also PV owners – as is quite possible – and if the EVs are primarily charged from the PVs, then the impact on sales and peak demand would be quite different than under other scenarios. In short, everything, including forecasting future demand growth and peak, becomes more complicated given the fast pace of behind-the-meter technological innovations and new service options.[31]

[28]Refer to zero net energy ordinance in May 2017 issue of EEnergy Informer, p. 22.
[29]According to ACEEE's 2017 rankings, CA is number 2 behind MA. Details at http://aceee. org/research-report/u1710.
[30]Reference found at CEC website.
[31]How these conflicting drivers may evolve over time, of course, is largely dependent on how regulators at the CPUC and/or the policymakers at the CEC influence the outcome. For example, if they allow/encourage the IOUs to invest in the DER space or in EV charging infrastructure, it could lead to a radically different outcome for the IOUs.

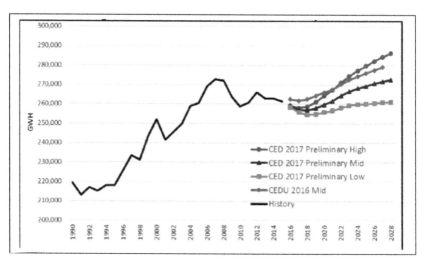

FIGURE 12.7 CEC kwh sales projections are below total consumption figures reflecting the impact of self-generation. *(Source: CEC.)*

4. IMPACT OF COMMUNITY CHOICE AGGREGATION (CCA)

Another development, with potential consequences for the incumbent distribution utilities, is the rapid growth of community choice aggregation or CCAs.[32]

The basic idea behind a CCA is to switch a community of customers – a city, county, or group of cities and counties – en masse to a new retailer or supplier without changing any of the underlying generation or delivery infrastructure. The transition to CCA leaves all of the functions of the existing energy delivery system essentially unaffected including the meter reading, billing, and collection, which will continue to be the responsibility of the existing incumbent regulated distribution company. The CCA's role is limited to *procuring energy* on behalf of its newly acquired customers – which shows up as a line item on the bill delivered and collected by the incumbent distribution company and passed on to the CCAs.[33]

These newcomers – which may be referred to as retailers – have been successfully expanding their footprint in the past few years[34] taking customers away from the incumbent distribution utilities.

---

[32]CCAs were enabled by Assembly Bill 117 in 2002 with the goal of allowing communities to deliver green power, sooner and cheaper than the incumbents were prepared to deliver.
[33]For further details on the history of CCAs, consult CPUC website at http://www.cpuc.ca.gov/general.aspx?id=2567.
[34]Refer to EEnergy Informer, June 2017, p.9.

The relentless migration of customers to CCAs raises a number of questions, not all of which can be definitely answered at this point in their evolution including the following:

- How much further will the migration of customers to CCAs continue?
- Will the remaining customers of the incumbent distribution utilities be worse off, better off, or virtually indifferent[35] following the exit?
- Will the new CCAs ultimately prove to be successful in procuring more renewable energy than the incumbents and at about the same or at lower costs?
- Can the reliability of the distribution network be maintained over time given the growth of CCAs?
- How well will the CCAs deliver on the provision of the social goods – such as implementation of energy efficiency programs[36] – traditionally provided by the incumbents[37]?
- Will the incumbents be able to continue more or less on "business-as-usual" basis or will their business model be radically altered, and if so in what ways?
- Since power procurement is already treated as a strict pass-through cost item – i.e., with no profit margin – will it ultimately matter who procures the energy?
- How will the role of the CPUC change given the expected migration of large numbers of customers to the CCAs?
- How will the CPUC's erosion of rate setting affect the implementation of time-of-use, dynamic rates, and other regulatory proceedings such as integrated resource planning?

---

[35]The CPUC has attempted to make sure the remaining IOU customers are not saddled with stranded costs, mostly through an exist fee on customers acquired by the CCAs.

[36]A likely scenario is that CCAs may end up balkanizing the energy efficiency programs, which are currently predominantly administered by the three large IOUs. This will result in many much smaller programs managed by multiple CCAs potentially making it harder for both vendors of products and services as well as customers to embrace. The same happens in power procurement where multiple CCAs have to compete for low-cost generation resources – with lots of duplicative effort in administrating, contracting, recording, and reporting to the CPUC. Clearly, each CCA – regardless of size or resources – must set up its own administrative structure that mimics that of the IOUs. This is likely to make compliance and overall integration of energy efficiency programs and coordination with efforts by IOUs even harder. For those who are unhappy with the current bureaucracy of the IOU handling such programs, things are likely to get much worse.

[37]There are efforts to move energy efficiency programs to third parties.

- Will CCAs be more or less proactive than the CPUC and the IOUs in promoting more advanced rate designs and/or more innovative service options?
- Will the CCAs adhere to resource adequacy requirements as do the current IOUs?

On the question of how much further can the customer migration to CCAs continue, one answer may be that CCAs will go as far as there are cities and communities where a viable business case for forming a CCA can be made.

Based on current and planned developments, it seems likely that CCAs will eventually cover the most populous parts of the state – primarily along the more urbanized and affluent coast – while leaving some of the more remote and sparsely populated areas – primarily rural, agricultural, and forest or desert – for the incumbents to serve. If CCAs cherry-pick the "best" – that is the easiest to serve and/or the most affluent urban areas – as seems to be the pattern, the remaining customers may be, on average, more expensive to serve.[38]

There is already evidence that as communities in the more temperate zones along the coast form CCAs, inland communities with peakier summer loads will have to bear the higher costs associated with serving these loads and this, in turn, may accelerate the introduction of time-of-use rates.

In Feb 2018, for example, the newly formed Los Angeles Clean Choice Energy (LACCE) began the first phase of its operations by serving county buildings in the Southern California Edison territory. The new CCA, to be called the Clean Power Alliance[39] (CPA) of Southern California, is expected to grow in size over time, eventually serving cities with population of 2.4 million across greater Los Angeles County.

According to Ted Bardacke, the Executive Director of the Clean Power Alliance (CPA), nearly 50% of the county's 88 cities have expressed interest to join, making this one of the biggest CCAs not just in California but in the US.

On the question of what happens to the remaining customers of the incumbent utilities, the answer is not entirely clear.[40]

---

[38]These customers may also have more-expensive-to-serve load shapes – for example those in hot interior or hot dry deserts. The sparsely populated north-eastern third of the state, for example, has a much lower population density requiring many miles of distribution network per customer.

[39]For further details visit http://www.cleanpoweralliance.org.

[40]For those concerned about how energy efficiency programs will be administered in the future, there is the additional issue of how best to avoid confusion among customers and product and service providers who may face myriad different rules and protocols for each CCA, and disjointed service territories.

At the request of the incumbents who are concerned about being left with stranded costs – for example for procured renewable contracts that will no longer be needed – the CPUC introduced a mechanism called Power Charge Indifference Adjustment (PCIA).[41] The regulator's intent is to acknowledge the legitimate stranded costs and other cost burdens associated with the departing customers by introducing a mechanism that would essentially make the customers of the incumbent utilities indifferent. PCIA, in other words, basically charges an *exit fee* for each departing customer acquired by a CCA.

As one might expect, what seemed like a simple idea in principle, was soon bogged down in controversy and heated debate. The incumbents, to varying degrees, did their best to make it painful for CCAs to take their customers away by arguing for higher exit fees. In contrast, the CCAs made counter arguments that the proposed PCIA's were excessive and punitive.[42]

Much attention is paid to arriving at a fair and reasonable exit fee given the high stakes.[43]

The remaining questions on the list of questions posed earlier are difficult to answer partly because

- The eventual fate of the exit fee will influence how many more customers may leave the incumbents; and
- How well or poorly the newly formed CCAs manage to operate and deliver high renewable energy mix at reasonable cost.[44]

On the surface, one might ask: "so what?" Since the energy component of the bill of existing incumbents is a mere pass through, what difference does it make if the utility or the CCA procures the power on behalf of the customers? But in practice, things are never that simple.[45]

---

[41]For further details of recent PCIAs refer to https://www.mcecleanenergy.org/wp-content/uploads/2015/11/PCIA_FF_Fees-Residential.pdf or visit CPUC website at http://www.cpuc.ca.gov/uploadedfiles/cpuc_public_website/content/news_room/fact_sheets/english/pciafactsheet010917.pdf.

[42]Some of the arguments & counter arguments may be found at http://www.cpuc.ca.gov/uploadedfiles/cpuc_public_website/content/news_room/fact_sheets/english/pciafactsheet010917.pdf.

[43]CPUC opened a proceeding in June of 2018 (R.17-06-026) with further details available at http://www.cpuc.ca.gov/PCIA/ , including presentations from a January 2018 workshop.

[44]For a discussion refer to http://ecomotion.us/white-paper-on-community-choice-aggregation-the-opportunity-and-its-status-nationally/.

[45]Does customer defection matter? EEnergy Informer, Sept 2017, p. 12.

The issues surrounding the expected expansion of CCAs have been among the thorny issues on CPUC's agenda. The regulator released a White Paper in May 2018[46] stating its main concerns and held an *En Banc* hearing in June 2018[47] where many of the issues were debated and discussed with the stakeholders.

While many uncertainties remain, few things are reasonably clear:

- First, there is little disagreement that the CPUC is gradually losing influence over setting retail rates in California as more customers are served by the CCAs;
- Second is the implications of contested degree of control over CCAs and ESPs in the procurement process and portfolio content of their generation resources – big item of contention in the CPUC's integrated resource planning (IRP) proceeding, where the regulator traditionally exercised considerable direct control over IOU's investment decisions[48];
- Third, it is fair to say that the three large IOUs are gradually turning into regulated distribution-only companies. This is not necessarily bad.[49] It merely means a different type of business and different relationship with customers; and
- Finally, the CPUC is concerned about lack of control in how the CCAs will meet their obligations for resource adequacy requirements – a critical mechanism in making sure there are sufficient resources available to meet customers' peak load.

The CCAs contend that, except for the first item, the others are not problems, hence dismissing CPUC's concerns as unjustified and unsupported. Only time will tell if these concerns are well founded.

While opinions on the subject vary, most observers agree that the CCAs' financial impact on the IOUs will be negligible at most. This is because energy procurement is a strict pass through. These people point out that while most savvy investors recognize that the rise of CCAs does not impact IOU profits, perhaps some bondholders may not react favorably to the fact that the revenues collected by the IOU are shrinking over time. It is not

---

[46]http://www.cpuc.ca.gov/uploadedFiles/CPUC_Public_Website/Content/Utilities_and_Industries/Energy_-_Electricity_and_Natural_Gas/CCC%20FAQs.pdf.

[47]https://www.utilitydive.com/news/as-california-customer-choice-expands-are-reliability-and-affordability-at/526906/.

[48]Among the concerns is the erosion of CPUC clout in how many of the current proceedings and directives – for example the mandates to increase storage or invest in charging stations and others – will be carried out in a balkanized future with multiples of CCAs.

[49]In states and countries with retail competition, this has already happened.

entirely clear if this will really matter at the end unless the IOUs' credit rating suffers or the cost of capital rises – neither of which appear likely. Once the dust is settled, the most visible impact may be that the IOUs will not have as many personnel in power procurement or in administrating energy efficiency programs.

5. RESHAPING CALIFORNIA'S ELECTRICITY LANDSCAPE

As the preceding discussion illustrates, California's electricity landscape is undergoing fundamental and rapid transformation driven by a plethora of ambitious environmental targets and regulatory policies with significant challenges for the incumbents and opportunities for newcomers who can take advantage of new technologies to deliver a host of products and services.

- The climate bill is the main driver of many of the other mandates and policies offering perils and opportunities – depending on the specifics;
- The electric transportation initiatives are likely to reshape the future of transport in the state and beyond[50];
- The renewable portfolio standards will continue to create demand for more variable renewable generation and more challenges for the CAISO;
- The building codes, zero net energy regulations, and appliance energy efficiency standards will dampen the demand for electricity consumption;
- The net energy metering law and similar initiatives will encourage further DER developments;
- The variability of renewable generation will create opportunities for storage and demand response;
- The emergence of aggregators and intermediaries is virtually guaranteed by the emerging opportunities for price responsive demand and virtual power plants; and
- The introduction of more granular tariffs will increase the need for price transparency on the distribution network.

---

[50]This chapter skips a discussion of how increasing sales from EVs and electrifying other end uses would offset losses due to the other trends highlighted in the preceding coverage. Some of sales erosion attributed to DERs, EE, and CCAs, for example, may be partially compensated through increased sales for electrification of the transport sector and electrification of the industrial and commercial loads.

Not surprisingly, with so much upheaval and so many moving parts, the regulators in California, like their counterparts elsewhere, are examining their *own* future role and function.[51]

In the state of New York, for example, the regulators have introduced an ambitious new vision for the distribution companies called Reinventing the Energy Vision or REV – which attempts to fundamentally redefine the contours of the business and the roles, responsibilities, and functions of the stakeholders moving forward.[52]

Equally important is the future role of the distribution utilities. Despite all the talk about prosumers, prosumagers – and potentially nonsumers – a significant number of customers are likely to remain as full-service, bundled tariff consumers for the foreseeable future, relying on the existing poles and wires, bundled services and rates with which they are accustomed. Many customers live in apartments in city centers or don't have properly shaped or directed roofs to make the prosumer model universal.

Moreover, even for those who migrate away from the regulated bundled tariff and traditional full-service business model, the overwhelming majority are expected to remain connected to the grid and rely on myriad of services it offers. In most cases, prosumers and prosumagers will continue to rely on the super grid for backup, balancing and reliability services and pay for them. In some cases, the reverse may happen – that is the microgrid may provide services to the super grid and get paid for it.

In either case, the two will maintain a symbiotic relationship, helping one another as the specifics of the case dictates. The number of prosumers and prosumagers who may go *off-grid* by literally cutting the cord, will remain rare. Simply said, there is so much to be gained from remaining connected relative to going off grid.

Unsurprisingly, the incumbents in California, like their counterparts elsewhere, are beginning to ask the questions that need to be asked and making some of the adjustments that need to be made.[53]

---

[51]California regulators examine rapidly changing retail landscape, EEnergy Informer, Jul 2017, p. 21.
[52]For further details visit https://rev.ny.gov.
[53]The future of incumbent "utilities" in flux, EEnergy Informer, Sept 2017, p. 9.

For the time being, the three IOUs in California appear resigned to the fact that their future will be mostly devoid of generation[54] – with the exception of hydro assets – and with far fewer "customers" in the standard sense of the word. The remaining customers – once the current CCA expansion comes to an end – are likely to be rather different than the current average in terms of their load shapes and how much energy they will feed into or take from the distribution network.

The biggest uncertainty confronting the IOUs – and others – in California and elsewhere is the speed and impact of electrified transportation and other behind-the-meter devices and services on their network – a topic further explored in Chapter 18 by Webb et al.

6. CONCLUSIONS

Challenges facing the state of California are not unique or isolated. Many similarities exist in other states and countries who are experiencing or expecting similar behind-the-meter developments.

In the case of California, three broad trends are already evident:

- First, utilities are experiencing declining revenues due to the rise of DERs, namely, energy efficiency gains *and* distributed self-generation, both of which result in reduced net consumption from the distribution network;
- Second, the continued growth of customer choice aggregation (CCA) – a trend currently pronounced in California – is turning the incumbent utilities in the direction of becoming distribution-only utilities as in many other parts of the world with competitive retail; and
- Third, the likely growth of EVs in the coming decade is expected to boost electricity consumption, but it is not clear how, when, and where these EVs will be charged and potentially discharged.

Each is significant. Combined, they are transformative.

---

[54]CA IOUs divested most of their conventional generation assets during the failed restructuring process keeping primarily the hydro and nuclear plants. Of the four operating reactors, two have already been shut down and PG&E is phasing out of Diablo Canyon by 2025. With the expected growth of CCAs, they will turn into distribution only regulated utilities.

It must be noted that other jurisdictions in the US, and elsewhere, have similar or even higher shares of distributed solar and/or utility-scale renewable generation. What sets California apart is

- The state's strong commitment to storage – with several passed and pending bills that authorize the utilities to procure more storage; and
- The degree to which California regulators and policymakers are trying to include equity considerations in how the combination of renewables, distributed solar, storage, and EVs will contribute to broader goals, in particular the climate targets.

Forced to venture an educated guess as to the impact of these and other developments leads to the following observations:

- The expected rise of DERs and behind-the-meter (BTM) devices and services including load aggregation, peer-to-peer trading (P2P) and intermediation will most likely result in complicated flows of power among and between customers in ways, times, locations, and magnitudes that exceed the original design of the distribution network – in California and many other places;
- This is likely to lead to localized congestion at certain circuits at certain times, which will require novel solutions – such as localized flexibility services as described in Chapter 6 by Stanley et al.;
- The expected growth of EVs, virtually guaranteed in places such as California, could be a blessing or a curse depending on how and when the EVs are charged or potentially discharged;
- The interface between the distribution company and prosumers, prosumagers and nonsumers will be minimally or radically different than those of full-service consumers who remain totally dependent on regulated bundled tariffs;
- Regulations and tariffs must ultimately reflect these changing relationships and charge each group of customers based on the costs they impose on the network and services received in such a way that minimizes massive cross-subsidies among them; and
- The ultimate challenge facing regulators is to keep the playing field level without discouraging or favoring one form of innovation over another – and this can be achieved by keeping the tariffs fair, reasonable and equitable, as further described in Chapter 8 by Burger et al.

CHAPTER 13

Using Flexibility Resources to Optimize Distribution Grids: A French Case Study

Pierre Germain, Etienne Jan
E-CUBE Strategy Consultants, Paris, France

1. INTRODUCTION

Electrical distribution grids in all European countries face a surge in electrical connections of renewable power generation units, and a radical change in the demand profile with the proliferation of all sorts of behind-the-meter assets. Devices, including EVs and heat pumps, are generating a growth rate in peak demand higher than the consumption. The French distribution grid is a typical example, with an additional 13 GW of renewable generation connected to the distribution network over the last 7 years, representing an annual growth rate of 12% and doubling renewable generation. The surge in electrical connections and the evolution of the peak demand are likely to increase the physical constraints on this distribution network and thereby the need for network reinforcement.[1]

In parallel, European consumers are increasingly stratified: prosumers (in France) and prosumagers (in Germany, UK, Italy) are more and more numerous: the recent achievement of grid parity in Europe has led to the development of self-consumption with PV generation. More prosumers are likely to became prosumagers thanks to tariffs that encourage a higher rate of self-consumption, and due to the decreasing cost of batteries. This stratification leads to two consequences for the distribution networks operators:

- First, prosumers and prosumagers do not use the network the same way as traditional consumers: their energy withdrawal from the network is lower, whereas their peak usage remains mostly unchanged, especially for prosumers; and

---

[1]Investment in hardware to increase the injection or withdrawal capacity of the network, in the present case high/medium voltage transformers (63 kV–15/20 kV), and medium/low voltage transformers (15/20 kV–400V).

Consumer, Prosumer, Prosumager
https://doi.org/10.1016/B978-0-12-816835-6.00013-9

- Second, prosumers, and even more so prosumagers, can provide new services such as demand response and flexibility to the distribution network by shifting their time of consumption.

This allows distribution system operators new opportunities in areas such as network reinforcement as a result of the decreasing costs of specific technologies – e.g., energy storage, IoT, electric vehicles – and in the development of decentralized flexibility capacity[2] – which is boosted by mechanisms implemented in recent years to serve the Transmission System Operator, e.g., supply-demand balancing and management of constraints. This chapter examines the value of local flexibility, mostly provided by prosumers and prosumagers for the distribution grid, using France as a case study.

The chapter is organized as follows:

- Section 2 provides an assessment of the national net value that could be expected out a systematic roll-out of flexibility in France;
- Section 3 covers the appropriate mechanisms for the activation of flexibility on a local scale for the most interesting situations identified in Section 1;
- Section 4 examines the options in terms of governance to coordinate local flexibility services (serving DSOs) with the existing national mechanisms (serving the TSO), followed by the chapter's conclusions.

2. VALUE OF FLEXIBILITY FOR PUBLIC ELECTRICAL DISTRIBUTION GRIDS IN CONTINENTAL FRANCE

The French distribution grid, schematically illustrated in Fig. 13.1, includes ~2,300 HV/LV substations,[3] ~23,500 MV lines, and more than 770,000 MV/LV transformers. This network delivered ~390 TWh of consumption and ~40 TWh of electricity generation in 2016. The French grid, like its counterparts in other countries, is designed to meet the maximum demand projected and to provide high levels of reliability and service quality. When the grid confronts demand that is higher than its nominal capacity, e.g., when there is too much consumption or too much generation locally, there is a "constraint." Historically, the DSOs would invest in new capacity to cope with the extra demand and the new constraints. However, local

---

[2]In this study, flexibility is defined as a temporary increase or decrease of the amount of energy exchanged with the grid, which is dispatched in real time (automatically or manually) based on the needs of grid operators and to local variables.

[3]In France, the distribution grids perimeter starts at the high (>50 kV) to low (<50 kV) transformers.

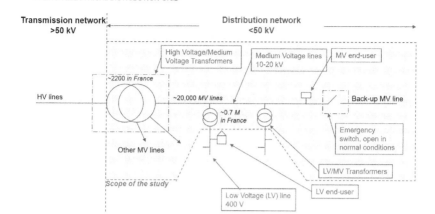

FIGURE 13.1 French electrical distribution network. *(© E-CUBE Strategy Consultants.)*

flexibility is also able to eliminate emerging constraints on the network by reducing the local load and/or the local generation. In many cases, providing local flexibility may be a more efficient solution than added investment since it offers a less expensive way to relieve congestion while creating value for the DSO and the community.

There are at least two ways for local flexibility to create economic value for the distribution grid:

- By temporarily relieving constraints on a piece of hardware or a portion of the network by postponing or avoiding reinforcement. This can be referred to as the *value for planning* – the deferral or avoidance of investment; and
- By enabling the reconnection of customers faster after an outage, or reducing outages due to work on the grid or incidents. This is referred to as the *value for operation* – the reduced cost of lost load.

For local flexibility to result in tangible value, two key conditions must apply:

- First, real constraints must exist, that is, the network must be locally undersized; and
- Second, flexibility to relieve congestion or constraint must be available locally.

By definition, local flexibility is decentralized, available in small quantities in particular areas and not everywhere or across the network. This characteristic is also true for constraints: each year, only a small part of the network is constrained, and the location of the constraints typically changes over time. Constraints appear locally due to new generation assets, demand increase, or new connections. Conversely, constraints disappear as a result of reinforcements made by the DSO and/or due to changes in the pattern or level of demand. This makes it difficult to assess the potential value of flexibility on a large scale. Constraints are also temporal and occur only during specific times of the year or during specific weather conditions.

In 2016,[4] a first study commissioned by French Energy Regulator (CRE[5]) on several illustrative cases of local network constraints demonstrated that in some instances, local flexibility could have a positive net value for the management of distribution grids (CRE, 2017).

Following this first study, a second study was commissioned by CRE to identify the best options to deploy local flexibility to local constraints (CRE, 2015), which is directly relevant to this chapter.[6]

For purposes of discussion, the *gross* value of local flexibility is defined as the benefit from using flexibility to postpone or avoid an investment, through faster reconnection after outages or from lower probability of occurrence of outages. The *net* value of flexibility is the gross less the costs as noted here:

Net value = gross value − cost of flexibility.

The net value generated is strongly dependent on the local configuration of the network. To represent this diversity within the study, five different configurations[7] were defined and analyzed in the study. Each configuration is defined by a particular type of constraint addressed in the network such as a piece of network hardware and/or a particular type of flexibility need as identified below and schematically shown in Fig. 13.2[8,9]:

1. Injection constraints on high/medium-voltage transformers, such as those caused by too much local generation;

[4] *Etude sur la valeur des flexibilités pour la gestion et le dimensionnement des réseaux de distribution*, CRE, January 2016.
[5] *Commission de Régulation de l'Energie.*
[6] *E-CUBE Strategy Consultants has supported the French Regulator for these two studies. This chapter introduces the main results of the second study.*
[7] Defined as the combination of a cause for the constraint (injection or withdrawal) and an impacted piece of hardware (transformer, grid…). In each configuration, a method was defined to assess the local value of flexibility.
[8] The study was not extended to hardware located on the low-voltage network (below-medium/low-voltage transformers), mainly for two reasons: because aggregated generation and consumption values are more volatile, the ability to predict, anticipate, and study constraints is still limited to date; there are few data available.
[9] The configuration where withdrawal from the medium-voltage grid is constrained is not presented in this study. Indeed, according to DSOs, such occurrences are very rare under normal circumstances, and they are difficult to anticipate under degraded circumstances (because there are a large number of possible incidents), while sources of flexibility are useful only if in the right location on the grid.

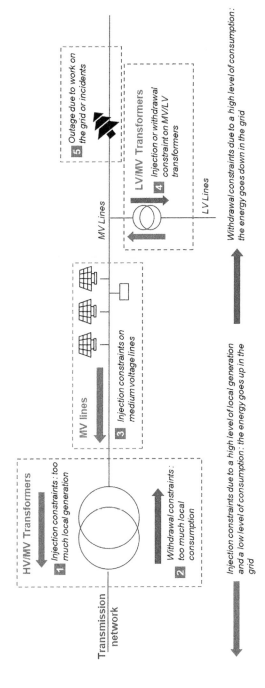

FIGURE 13.2 The five assessed configurations to value local flexibility. (© E-CUBE Strategy Consultants.)

2. Withdrawal constraints on high/medium-voltage transformers such as too much local consumption;
3. Injection constraints on the medium-voltage grid;
4. Injection and withdrawal constraints on medium/low-voltage transformers; and
5. Outages due to work on the grid or incidents.

Of the five configurations identified, the value of local flexibility in the first four primarily lies in planning of network investments. In these cases, local flexibility helps to avoid or defer network investments. The value of local flexibility in the last configuration primarily lies in real-time operations – by reducing the frequency and/or severity of electricity outages on the network and reduced costs associated with the loss of load.

The value of local flexibility for a piece of the distribution network may be derived from two main variables: the cost of reinforcement avoided or deferred, expressed in euros, and the amount of constraints, measured in kW, and kWh, that the local flexibility will have to provide. The main difficulty of this analysis is the wide variety of local configurations: each piece of the distribution network is specifically adapted to the local "history" of a local area: an MV line may be 1 km or 10 km, an LV/MV transformer may be 50 kW or 500 kW, depending on what was required historically. This is also the case for generation units and load connected to the network: locally, there may be PV, Wind, CHP, supermarket, hospitals, offices, or only residential units. Each of these network customers uses differently the network, creates different constraints, and has different flexibility potential.

In the CRE study, for each configuration, the gross and the net value of local flexibility were assessed based on a specific methodology, and developed with the French DSO and the French regulator:

- For configuration n° 1 and 3, a statistical analysis of the current and expected constraints, and of current and planned reinforcements, was realized on all equipment in France, to characterize typical constraints and reinforcement costs on this equipment. To assess the flexibility value by 2030, generation and load growth scenarios were modeled at a regional level to identify the number of constraints and the flexibility potential that would appear. By crossing the statistical analysis and the scenarios, it was possible to derive the gross and net value of local flexibility;
- For configuration n° 2 and 4, data were available only for a sample of cases. Therefore, the value of investment deferral and the cost of flexibility were calculated specifically in these cases, and then extrapolated to France thanks to adequate extrapolation variables – size of the

equipment, local typology, number of subequipments, etc. The current frequency of reinforcement in France was taken into account to assess the frequency of constraints' apparition;

- Finally, for configuration n° 5, a statistical analysis of all outages that occurred in recent years was realized to assess the cost of the outages and the capacity of local flexibility to limit them. This depends mostly on the response delay of flexibility and the predictability of the outage. The available gross value of the outages was derived from the value of loss load used in France on the distribution network (9–20 k€/MWh).

These calculations quantified the unit value (value per occurrence of configuration), the frequency of occurrence of constraints in each configuration at the perimeter of continental France, and the cost of the flexibility able to manage the constraint. The detailed methodology of the calculations is not described here, but the results are presented in Fig. 13.3 and are discussed now.[10]

Across France, the annual gross value of flexibility for the distribution grid is between €20M/year and €60M/year – summing all configurations, and taking into account uncertainties due to the extrapolations. In comparison to the €1.5B invested each year in new connections (€1.2B) and reinforcement (€300M). This demonstrates that local flexibility may optimize 10–20% of reinforcement costs. However, it also highlights the reduced volume of annual reinforcements in a mature network, where the grid is already well sized and partly resilient to load/generation evolutions.

However, after including the costs associated with implementing flexibility, the net value lies between €11M/year and €18M/year,[11] which represents only 1% of total network investments, and up to 6% of investments dedicated to network reinforcement (excluding connection investments). Therefore, local flexibility is a 2nd-order optimization of network costs. However, the value of local flexibility is likely to grow with its deployment: in early stages of local flexibility deployment, the network is well sized, if not oversized. The use of flexibility pushes network operators to reduce their capacity margins, accept and deal with constraints.

---

[10]Full study available from "Etude sur les mécanismes de valorisation des flexibilités pour la gestion et le dimensionnement des réseaux publics de distribution d'électricité" – https://www.cre.fr/Documents/Publications/Etudes/etude-sur-les-mecanismes-de-valorisation-des-flexibilites-pour-la-gestion-et-le-dimensionnement-des-reseaux-publics-de-distribution-d-electricite.

[11]These estimates are for the medium run (2020 or 2030, depending on cases) for continental France.

Analyzed configurations	Gross value	Net value	Occurrences	Level of interest for flexibility
1 Injection constraints on high/medium voltage transformers	5–10 M€/yr	1–3 M€/yr	15–30 occ./yr	• Significant net value • Limited number of local cases • Priority configuration for the implementation of a market design
2 Withdrawal constraints on high/medium voltage transformers	0–18 M€/yr *Middle hypothesis at 8M€/yr* → 1–5–4 M€/yr	~15 occ./yr	• Net value subject to high uncertainty • High unit value • Need to assess the maturity of flexibility on other cases before going into this configuration
3 Injection constraints on medium-voltage network	> 5M€/yr	~5 M€/yr (2030 outlook)	~15–20 occ./yr	• Significant net value • Limited number of local cases • Priority field for the implementation of a market design
4 Constraints on medium/low voltage transformers	9–20 M€/an *(maximum)*	~0 M€/yr →Positive value only under specific conditions	Potential of ~2000 occ./yr →Unknown portion of cases with positive net value	• Close to zero net value • Profitability subject to specific conditions • High number of cases • Least priority configuration
5 Incidents	~3M€/yr	~3M€/yr	~1000 occ./yr	• High total net value but low unit value because of the high number of cases • Opportunistic approach could be developed on cases with low unit value • Way to experiment on cases with low unit value with lower risk than if differing investment
Outages due to: Work on the grid	1–5 M€/yr	1–3 M€/yr	2000–6000 occ./yr	

FIGURE 13.3 Gross and net values of flexibility for the management of electrical distribution grids on the five analyzed configurations in France. (© E-CUBE Strategy Consultants.)

This suggests that the frequency of such constraints could increase with the use of flexibility, as the network becomes less and less oversized. Therefore, flexibility value could grow in the long run. On the contrary, if flexibility is never used and if network operators keep using large capacity margins to limit future works and compensate the lack of accurate data, flexibility value will be limited.

The current value is highly concentrated on a few cases: it can be estimated that up to 50% of the value of local flexibility is concentrated on the HV/MV transformers (configurations #1 and #2), the biggest and most expensive equipment. Moreover, the value for local flexibility on this equipment is limited to a few number of cases per year: less than ~5% of the HV/MV transformers are concerned by constraints each year in France and therefore may require local flexibility. It means that up to 50% of the gross value of local flexibility that appears each year is concentrated on less than 60 pieces of equipment each year across France. The remaining gross value is widely spread over a high number of cases. More precisely, for each of the configurations, the following results have been found during the analysis (Fig. 13.3):

Using flexibility to address injection constraints on high/medium-voltage transformers (configuration #1) or on the medium-voltage grid (configuration #3) represent:

- 45–55% of the total net value of local flexibility in France. It is the most valuable configurations of the study, due to the high cost of HV/MV transformers; and
- This value is concentrated in a limited number of occurrences per year (~15–30 per year). It means that with a limited deployment of local flexibility, a significant share of the local flexibility value assessed for France may be obtained.

Based on these estimates, it can be concluded that local flexibility should be developed for these two configurations as a priority, for several reasons:

- First, because local flexibility is guaranteed to be available locally in these configurations: it may be provided by the source of the constraint itself. Indeed, if a new PV plant creates a local constraint on the network for a few hours per day, the same PV plant can be curtailed during those few hours at a small cost – the value of energy, i.e., 0–200 €/MWh most of the time. In configurations where the constraint is caused by too much consumption, the cost is only capped by the loss of load value – 9,200–20,000 €/MWh in France, if no one wants to realize some demand response;

- Secondly, because the implementation of local flexibility mechanisms could essentially be limited to simply compensating producers for the amount of energy curtailed, as there is no collateral damage to the curtailment than a financial loss for the producer; and
- Thirdly, as the value of local flexibility for each case is significant, the cost of implementation of a mechanism for local flexibility is unproblematic. The DSO will be able to study each case specifically and set up a specific mechanism for each one, making it easy to implement.

In the short term, configurations #1 and #3 are the prime candidates for the first mechanism on local flexibility, as these configurations are more valuable and suitable for preliminary local flexibility developments.

The net value of the configuration with withdrawal constraints on high/medium voltage transformers (configuration #2) represents:

- 15–25% of the total net value of local flexibility in France;
- However, both the gross and net values are subject to significant uncertainties for this configuration, due to the methodology of extrapolating data from a small sample, whereas flexibility value depends strongly on the location of constraints and sources of flexibility. A larger sample would have limited the uncertainties; and
- As for configurations #1 and #3, this value is concentrated in a limited number of occurrences per year (~15–30 per year);

Withdrawal constraints (configuration #2) are more complex to address than injection constraints (configurations #1 and #3). Indeed, they appear mostly when the grid is not fully operational:

- In France, the grid is designed to deliver electricity even if part of the grid is malfunctioning, as a result of redundancy of the grid;
- Therefore, when the grid is fully operational, it is highly uncommon that withdrawal constraints appear, as the grid is designed to manage extra load;
- As a result, the withdrawal constraints strongly depend on the type of malfunction – e.g., when a tree falls on a power line.

This is not the case for injection constraints: when local grid is malfunctioning, it is not expected to absorb all energy generated locally.

Despite these difficulties and the high uncertainties on the net value for this configuration, it remains interesting to implement a market design to leverage local flexibility for this configuration: the value of each case is around tens of thousands of euros per case, which is high, and the number of occurrences in France is low (streamlining the implementation). It gives an opportunity to the DSO to study precisely the value of local flexibility in each case that arises, without being too time consuming.

The net value of the configuration with outages due to work on the grid or incidents (configuration #5) represent:

- Between 30–35% of the total net value of local flexibility in France;
- The number of occurrences where flexibility could be used is higher than for the other configurations, in the thousands. This is due to a very large number of small outages that happen in France each year, especially in rural areas;
- However, the unit value of each occurrence is low compared to other configurations. It raises the question of the interest of such configuration for local flexibility.

The net value is close to zero in the last configuration (#4) with medium/low-voltage transformers. Indeed, this configuration refers to inexpensive (less than 50,000 €) but numerous (more than 700,000) equipment in France. As a result, local flexibility is not cost effective with today's technology compared to reinvestment. Therefore, this configuration is set aside for the time being and is not addressed in the remainder of the chapter. In the long run, technology breakthroughs may improve the economics of this configuration, especially through cheaper flexibility instrumentation and controls.

3. MECHANISMS FOR THE USE AND VALUATION OF FLEXIBILITY ON A LOCAL SCALE

Flexibility solutions are assets with the ability to increase or decrease their electricity generation or their electricity consumption on demand at short notice. Currently, flexibility solutions are mainly used at the level of the transmission or system operation. To use flexibility solutions, mechanisms have been designed to find, contract, value, and activate flexibility when required by the system operator.

Until now, most flexibility mechanisms have been designed to operate at the scale of a state or a country, managing terawatt hours of energy or gigawatt of power. They provide ancillary and balancing services, and optimize flexible asset values on energy or capacity markets. Thus, at a local level, flexibility mechanisms have traditionally been very rare. They are limited to Time-of-Use (TOU) Tariffs,[12] which are not

---

[12]In France, only residential TOU are set up by the distribution grids

"local flexibility mechanisms" *per se*.[13] The goal of this section is to define and select mechanisms that could provide and value flexibility on a local scale, on the medium- or low-voltage network. These mechanisms define possible terms of agreement between flexibility providers and distribution system operators.

These mechanisms have three objectives:

(1)   To source a flexibility in the required area;

(2)   To activate it when necessary; and

(3)   To set its value.

A list of nine mechanisms has been set up (Fig. 13.4). All of the mechanisms have been assessed and ranked with the French regulator and the main French DSO. This assessment used technoeconomic and operational efficiency criteria including the following:

- Large technoeconomic flexibility potential: the mechanism should encourage the participation of the greatest volume of locally available flexibility, in order to encourage competition, reduce costs, and thus maximize economic efficiency;

- Low transaction costs: local flexibility is, by definition, a small market restricted to a small perimeter. Therefore, these mechanisms cannot afford to have transaction costs higher than the market value, which is always below 100,000 euros a year;

- Control of the risk of failure: contrary to system-wide mechanisms, if a local flexibility fails to provide the required service, the probability to find a replacement solution is very low (due to the limited local flexibility potential), and therefore the risk of a power outage is high. This characteristic of local flexibility requires a calibration of the mechanisms in order to guarantee the availability of assets providing flexibility, while avoiding making it prohibitive (the cost of a loss of load may exceed the value of local flexibility); and

- Criteria less specific to local flexibility: visibility for stakeholders (including the DSO), ease of implementation, controllability, compliance and impartiality of mechanisms.

A flexibility mechanism must be adapted to the size, the frequency, and the geographical perimeter of the local flexibility sought:

- A mechanism that requires a transaction cost of €10,000 to be set up – e.g., a large tender process, with complex technical specifications, is not adapted to a case where flexibility would represent only €1,000/year

---

[13]TOU tariffs do not adapt to real-time constraints, neither geographically (on assets downstream of the constraint) nor over time (peak hours are not dynamically adapted to real constraints).

INJECTION CONSTRAINT	WITHDRAWAL CONSTRAINT
Smart grid connection contracts – *injection*	**Smart grid connection contracts – *withdrawal***
Alternative grid connection solution including an option for the DSO to restrict injection during a set number of hours per year in exchange for lower grid connection costs	*Alternative grid connection solution including an option for the DSO to activate the flexibility during a set number of hours per year in exchange for lower grid connection costs*
Alternative regional connection fee	
Lower (or even negative) regional fee to be connected to the distribution or transmission network in exchange for flexibility services	
Local Critical Peak Pricing	
Price signal activated by the DSO, according to terms defined in the "TURPE pointe mobile" tariff (frequency, duration, location)	
Direct contracting of flexibility by the DSO	**Opportunistic use of flexibility by the DSO ("DSO option")**
DSO contracts flexibility from the market. Various patterns are possible: tender, competitive dialogue, call for expression of interest	*Call for existing flexibility to participate in network management, without commitment.*
Regulated feed-in tariff for flexibility	
Regulated (and flat) feed-in tariffs to remunerate flexibility for as long as it is activated	
Local intraday/day-ahead market	
Equivalent to a balancing mechanism on a local scale	
Investment and management of flexibilities by the DSO	

FIGURE 13.4 Mechanisms for the use and valuation of flexibility to address injection and withdrawal constraints (TURPE: Tariff of public electrical grids). (© *E-CUBE Strategy Consultants.*)

configuration #3. Also, it is unrealistic to expect to launch such tender process hundreds of time per year: it will be limited to flexibility cases with high value and low frequency. The configuration #1 and 2 are typical cases that meet these criteria;

- However, for configuration #3, a standardized solution – e.g., a standard price for a standard service, valid at the scale of France and limiting transaction costs to a few hundred euros – thanks to automation, is far more adapted; and

- There is a tradeoff between the customization of the mechanism, that makes local flexibility efficient, and the cost of the mechanism. The level of customization will therefore depend on the local configuration.

Some of the mechanisms, especially concerning network tariffs such as the local Critical Peak Pricing, are discussed more extensively in other chapters of the book including Chapter 5 by Mountain, which discusses customer preference for a mechanism based on network tariffs and demand charges, and Chapter 8 by Burger et al., which discusses the fairness and equity issues associated with tariffs. Based on criteria described, three mechanisms stand out and cover all previously described positive-value configurations:

The "smart grid connection contracts," which would correspond to a connection contract with limited network usage rights. Historically, a new asset that requires a new grid connection invests in a connection to, and obtains the right to use, a certain amount of power at his discretion. However, in a situation where such connection would require an investment to reinforce the network, a more innovative connection contract could provide a modular right to use the local network. Such connection contract would allow the distribution grid operator to limit temporarily the capacity of the connection to the asset for a determined amount of time, whenever it needs it. In compensation for this service, the end user would pay a reduced cost for the connection,[14] and the grid operator could avoid expensive reinforcement costs, upstream of the connection. All stakeholders would be better off with lower connection costs for the end user and lower socialized reinforcement investments for the community.

This solution has several advantages: it uses an existing framework, the connection contract; it has low transaction costs; it targets the root of the constraints (i.e., newly connected asset, which generates the new constraint

---

[14]In France part of the reinforcement costs are paid by the owner of the connection, the remaining part is paid by the community.

on the local network). However, the mechanism does not offer the largest technoeconomic flexibility potential, as only newly developed assets may participate. For instance, if the new asset does not want to provide flexibility, but its neighbor does, this mechanism will not be able to source the neighbor's flexibility. Indeed, the neighbor will have already paid for full rights to use the local network. Moreover, for regulatory reasons specific to France,[15] only injection constraints will be managed by this mechanism (e.g., new PV plant, wind power, etc.).

The "direct contracting": this mechanism lets DSO directly find and contract the flexibility required with a flexibility provider through a tender process or a competitive dialogue. Under this scheme, the DSO must identify and characterize its need for flexibility locally (volume, frequency, technical requirements), and then set up the requirements of the tender. This mechanism enables all sources of local flexibility to compete to the tender process, therefore offering a large technoeconomic flexibility potential. However, this mechanism is cumbersome to implement because it requires the DSO to run an analysis and issue specifications, to interact with flexibility providers, and to tightly monitor and verify the offered flexibility (for withdrawal constraints). Hence, this mechanism should be earmarked for cases and areas with high unit values and where it is relevant to introduce competition (i.e., supply must be sufficient). This makes it suitable mainly for constraints on high/medium-voltage transformers.

The opportunistic use of flexibility by the DSO ("DSO option"): this mechanism is specifically designed for the purpose of handling grid operation in an agile manner under unforeseen circumstances. This mechanism consists in the prior identification of sources of flexibility, to be able, if appropriate, to activate them in real time during a problem on the network (such as a breakdown). This identification would be done without any commitment from flexibility suppliers to offer flexibility, or from DSOs to use it. It allows the DSO to curtail collaborative customers instead of choosing arbitrarily customers, and therefore minimize the cost of loss load. It is easy to implement and does not generate any risk for stakeholders. However, it is strictly limited to grid operation (and not planning) because DSOs do not have any guarantee regarding the availability of flexibility, which is the tradeoff for flexibility.

---

[15]The French DSO is not allowed to activate or realized demand response by itself, excluding specific conditions.

On the contrary, several mechanisms have not emerged as effective for local flexibility (Fig. 13.5). Among them are critical peak pricing and the implementation of a local electricity market (similar to spot market, but within a smaller perimeter). They are not adapted for different reasons: prohibitive transaction costs in relation to available value, technoeconomic efficiency, and visibility (i.e., certainty) for the DSO.

For instance, Critical Peak Pricing (CPP), currently used efficiently for decreasing energy cost at the scale of a state, is not adapted for the local level. Indeed, it does not target sufficiently the local assets that are able to bring value locally, but instead it targets all its customers. Moreover, it does not provide sufficient guarantees to the DSO that there will be sufficient flexibility activated during the Peak Pricing. This is true especially in the first years, when the number of customers and their reaction to the peak pricing are unknown. This uncertainty prevents the DSO from avoiding any reinforcement of the network and therefore from capturing the value. This is debated in Chapter 5, where it is discussed that demand charges tariffs (a way to optimize network costs) in Australia are not successful.

Local flexibility markets, such as Piclo described in Chapter 6 by Stanley et al., were analyzed. However, local flexibility markets were not considered as a primary solution for the French grid. This highlights the criteria used in this study to select mechanisms for France: a solution targeting medium/low-voltage constraints that can provide flexibility with a guarantee similar to network reinforcement, and adapted to the current planning rules of the French distribution network. Such local markets, at a small scale (below HV/MV transformers), were not considered liquid or competitive enough and could not provide a sufficiently advanced guarantee that flexibility would be available to postpone network reinforcements.

In conclusion, for each identified configuration bringing value to the community, there is an appropriate mechanism that allows the DSO to find and activate local flexibility: from a specific tender ("direct contracting") for large projects, to standardized solutions ("smart grid connection contracts") and opportunistic mechanisms, without commitment from the parties, for unpredictable situations ("DSO Option").

4. COORDINATION OF LOCAL FLEXIBILITY SERVICES WITH THE EXISTING NATIONAL MECHANISMS, AND POSSIBLE WINDFALLS FROM THOSE SERVICES

The operational implementation of the local flexibility within an electric system already valuing flexibility at an ISO/TSO scale is complex. Indeed, future local flexibility is a matter for the Distribution System Operator,

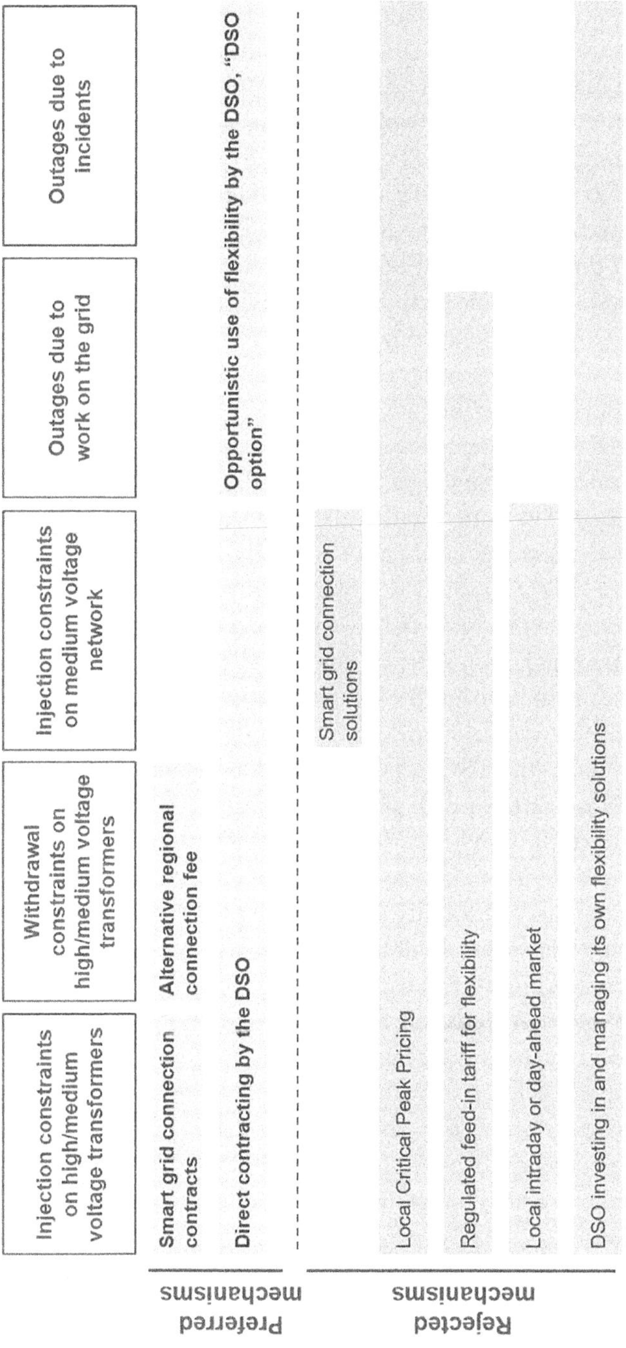

FIGURE 13.5 Mechanisms for flexibility use and valuation on a local scale. (© *E-CUBE Strategy Consultants.*)

whereas current flexibility mechanisms are managed by the ISO or the TSO. However, these mechanisms are not entirely disjointed: on one hand, the activation of a local mechanism can modify the national balance (and conversely); and on the other hand, existing flexibilities should be able to respond to the different mechanisms provided it creates value, in order to maximize community value. The subject is also discussed in Chapter 9 by Abdelmotteleb et al., where the value of the integration of network tariffs and flexibility mechanisms for the grid is assessed. This section focuses on the issues of the coordination between the different flexibility signals and markets. It results from bilateral discussions with the French TSO, the main French DSO, and the French regulator.

The most challenging issues examined in collaboration with the French DSO and TSO were the following:

(1) The collateral effect of local flexibility activation at the national level (and conversely): any flexibility activation on the local grid, if not compensated or anticipated at the national level, will cause an imbalance at the national level (and conversely). For instance, if a battery is activated locally by the DSO to reduce a peak consumption on a local network, it will increase the level of generation at the national level. If not anticipated, such increase could lead to the activation of national mechanism to manage the overgeneration of electricity. Conversely, flexibility activation on national mechanisms (e.g., dispatch of Demand Response by the TSO) can intensify the constraints on a local grid (e.g., if there is too much generation locally);

(2) The activation conflicts due to the overlapping of different mechanisms: in order to maximize the value of an asset for the community, it is essential that a flexibility asset has the possibility to combine different sources of valuation (local, national mechanisms). This has already been studied during experimental projects with batteries, which were valued simultaneously on frequency reserves, on self-consumption, on capacity markets, etc. The combination of value sources minimizes the cost of assets for each flexibility mechanism and maximizes social benefits. However, such combination creates activation conflicts, due to the possibility that over a given period, the flexibility asset receives orders that are not compatible between them, or are even opposed. For instance:

   • Simultaneous and conflicting activations on two distinct mechanisms – e.g., one order to consume more electricity, one order to consume less – of one source of flexibility may happen;

- The management of flexibility resources with a limited energy stock, such as battery or demand response, can generate conflicts between mechanisms: a battery activated on one mechanism, it could be impaired for an activation closely afterwards on another mechanism.

(3) The management of a subset of sources of flexibility within a portfolio: to participate to the flexibility markets of the ISO/TSO, flexibility providers aggregate various and numerous flexibility sources within a unified "portfolio." This methodology allows small assets (e.g., an electric heater) to participate in large markets within a larger entity. Most of the time, the portfolio is aggregated at the national level, with flexibilities from all over the perimeter of the ISO/TSO. However, for local use, it may be necessary to activate only a subset of sources of flexibility, which are concentrated in a local area. Local activation of a subset of these portfolios would interfere with the current business of aggregators, which main value was to build and manage these portfolios, comprising multiple sources of generation and flexibility. Thus, if a new integrated system was able to directly manage small entities, it may not be as efficient as when it is realized by aggregators. On the other hand, activation restricted to a local subset of the portfolio would enable sources of flexibility to participate on both the local and the national scale while minimizing conflicts.

Among these three issues, the latter two – activation conflicts and the management of a subset of sources of flexibility within an aggregated portfolio – are more critical. Indeed, the collateral effect of one mechanism over another (1) has a low probability to occur, as it would require a strong desynchronization between local and national needs, which is possible but deemed rare in a context where local flexibility is emerging. On the contrary, the (2) and (3) have a higher probability of occurrence and the resulting consequences in case of failure are more important.

Moreover, all the local flexibility mechanisms identified in Section 3 do not have the same exposure to these conflicts. Indeed, depending on the requirements of a mechanism, the issues identified here may apply or not. A flexibility participating in a mechanism that does not require a firm availability commitment (such as the "DSO option") does not face the "critical" conflicts arising from participation in several mechanisms with commitment: it was clear to all parties that the flexibility could be available or not.

On the contrary, the mechanism that causes the most issues is the direct contracting of sources of flexibility by DSOs. It is the strictest in terms of availability requirements and commitment from flexibility sources. If the flexibility is not available due to another mechanism, the DSO may have to curtail customers in order to counterbalance the flexibility's unavailability, as the DSO may have no backup plan. This is why contracting is the mechanism with the highest potential for conflicts, whereas the "DSO option" on existing sources of flexibility minimizes this risk.

There are two approaches to address these issues:

(a) explicit rules, which should dictate the priority between mechanisms but also penalties that should guide asset behavior in the face of conflict; and

(b) coordination between players, and pre-established protocol to manage these conflicts when they arise.

In either case, the ultimate aim is to:

- Enable each source of flexibility to participate in several mechanisms, provided it contributes to social welfare, and makes it possible to split the costs between mechanisms;

- Minimize the social cost of conflicts: conflicts can be addressed in different ways, and the selected solution must be optimal with respect to social costs;

- Define and allocate the extra costs generated by these conflicts: conflicts create extra costs, hence the need to clearly define which stakeholders are to bear them. The aim of efficient coordination is to avoid these extra costs; and

- Limit transaction costs for flexibility providers: the participation in several mechanisms generates additional transaction costs.

These two options to implement these rules are currently being investigated in France and differ in the level of governance between the DSO and the TSO. Either a central platform is created for both local and national levels; or the DSO and the TSO operate their own platform, under predefined governance between them.

The French balancing mechanism, currently managed by the TSO, was designed to address both balancing needs and constraints on the transmission grid. Because of this latter purpose, it structurally considers the location of sources of flexibility. Thus, one option would be to extend this platform to resources and constraints on the distribution grid. However, there are several hurdles to this project. For the time being, the platform is not able to integrate distribution-level constraints and sources of flexibility.[16]

---

[16]Information at the scale of the distribution grid is not needed to manage constraints on the transmission grid.

Besides, such an integration would require the implementation of business rules regarding local activations and restrictions by DSOs. Finally, governance issues would have to be solved to allow DSO to participate to the design of the mechanism.

Alternatively, an *ad hoc* mechanism for local sources of flexibility, coordinated with the transmission system, could be implemented and operated by DSOs. This option would limit conflicts and the associated consequences, but would require flexibility providers to use two distinct mechanisms, possibly making their work more complicated. However, it would bring greater agility to the management of local flexibility and ensure that the interests of each grid operator are clear.

No matter the governance and the level of integration eventually selected, the priority measures to prevent and solve potential conflicts between local and national mechanisms have to include:

- Efficient communication between flexibility providers and distribution and transmission grid operators to prevent conflicts or make their resolution easier;
- Priority rules in case of conflict to opt for the best option in terms of social cost;
- Well-calibrated penalties to prevent fraud without deterring players from participating and to direct choices toward the social optimum;
- Monitoring and verification of registered sources of flexibility by the TSO (regular flexibility tests, verification of actual load variation, …); and
- Efficient governance.

In France, discussions are in progress between DSOs and the TSO regarding the coordination of flexibility mechanisms. However, the debate on these issues is still ongoing. Participants will have to define the governance, to define and enforce coordination rules, and how deeply TSO and DSO operational systems are to be integrated. In the US and UK, there is a greater degree of freedom between ISOs and utilities, facilitating possible combinations (and local flexibility development) at the expense of conflict reduction (which shall be negligible at first). Given the very low volumes of local flexibility that should be activated in the coming years, the potential theoretical conflicts should not unduly hinder the development of local flexibility in the first instance, even if this means strengthening the rules as difficulties arise.

5. CONCLUSIONS

In this chapter, the services that local flexibility could provide to the distribution network have been studied to assess their value and the practical ways to capture it. The chapter's six main conclusions may be summarized as follows:

1. Local flexibility has value for the distribution grid. In France, the gross value of local flexibility could represent up to 20% of reinforcement costs. Once the cost of flexibility reimbursed, the net gain for the community would represent 6% of the annual reinforcement costs;

2. Although this value is currently limited compared to the overall investments, it should be expected to grow in the future: the deployment of local flexibility will lead to a change of approach when dealing with network constraints. The more local flexibility is used, the lower the capacity margins will be, the more flexibility will become necessary to manage the network;

3. The most promising configurations for local flexibility are the constraints on HV/MV transformers, which concentrate 50% of the total value on the distribution network and where mechanisms could easily be implemented, especially for constraints due to an excess of local generation;

4. For each constraint on the network, a mechanism to source, contract, value, and activate local flexibility efficiently can be implemented. These best mechanisms are from direct contracts with the DSO ("direct contracting"), connection contracts evolution, or on an optional basis, based on real-time conditions ("opportunistic option");

5. To let prosumers and prosumagers participate to the best of their ability to the local flexibility, the key element will be the opportunity to combine the different markets (local, national). These two strata will grow if they are able to participate to the various electricity markets, from the European to the local markets, from energy to capacity markets; and

6. Although a number of issues were identified in order to allow such combination, volumes and probabilities of occurrence will be low, as long as local flexibility is emergent. The solutions to all of these issues could be gradually improved using feedback from implementation, by developing a progressive and coherent prosumagers participation framework.

Local flexibility differs in many ways from its older brother, the flexibility at a national scale. It is a change of paradigm for the DSO, for the ISO/RTO, and also for the prosumers/prosumagers – at a local level, their impact and responsibility is direct and visible.

The small volumes of local flexibility that should be deployed at first shall push the public authorities to favor a "test & learn" approach, by deploying adaptable market designs for local flexibility, in order to allow the prosumers/prosumagers to move forward in the services they offer to the electric system.

REFERENCES

The full text of E-CUBE Strategy Consultants's study for the French Regulatory Commission (CRE). Etude sur les mécanismes de valorisation des flexibilités pour la gestion et le dimensionnement des réseaux publics de distribution d'électricité, 2017, may be found at: https://www.cre.fr/en/content/download/16510/204074.

A preliminary study was realized in 2015 by E-CUBE Strategy Consultants for the French Regulatory Commission (CRE). It focused on assessing the value of local flexibility in specific use cases depending on the constraint and highlighted the economic rationale for this valuation - Etude sur la valeur des flexibilités pour la gestion et le dimensionnement des réseaux de distribution, 2016, may be found at https://www.cre.fr/content/download/14045/168027.

CHAPTER 14

Off-Grid Prosumers: Electrifying the Next Billion With PAYGO Solar

Toby Couture*, Setu Pelz[†], Catherina Cader[†], Philipp Blechinger[†]
*E3 Analytics, Berlin, Germany
[†]RLI, Berlin, Germany

1. INTRODUCTION

While the other chapters of this volume are mostly focused on new technologies and business models that give traditional consumers options to become prosumers and engage in peer-to-peer trading and interact with each other in new and innovative ways, in some parts of the world, a different but equally fundamental revolution is underway.

The convergence of solar, storage, high-efficiency appliances, and mobile payment technologies is enabling millions of low- and middle-income households that previously lacked access to reliable electricity to become "off-grid prosumers," owning their own distributed power supply and meeting their own electricity needs. This trend has been widely covered in major news outlets, including in the *Economist* (Economist, 2016), the *Guardian* (Guardian, 2016), Reuters (Reuters, 2018), and the *New York Times* (New York Times, 2016).

In the process, millions of households have begun leapfrogging traditional, centralized grid infrastructure and adopting standalone solar home systems equipped with storage to meet their electricity needs, often financing them on a pay-as-you-go (PAYGO) basis.[1]

In the past three decades, the number of people without access to electricity has only slightly decreased from 1.3 billion in 1990 to currently approximately 1.1 billion (World Bank, 2018). While more than 2.5 billion people have gained access to electricity mostly via grid extension and densification since that time, rapid population growth has more than offset progress on electrification in many countries. Put simply, the rate of population growth in many countries, particularly in sub-Saharan Africa, has been greater than the rate of growth of electrification.

[1]Note that in practice, "pay-as-you-go" often means "rent-to-own," since customers typically become owners of the systems once the loan is paid off.

Consumer, Prosumer, Prosumager
https://doi.org/10.1016/B978-0-12-816835-6.00014-0
311

Across Africa, for instance, the average rate of electrification in 2015 was estimated at 39% (PwC, 2015), while in some countries the percentage of the population with access to electricity remains below 20% (SEforALL, 2017a,b).

A key factor behind the slow increase in the rate of electricity access is the failure of centralized grid expansion efforts to scale-up on the time-frames and at the pace required. The slow rate of progress in centralized grid expansion is driven by a number of factors (Attia and Shirley, 2018):

- First, investments in extending the central grid are often not econom-ically viable as the tariffs that can be collected from residents in rural and remote areas are often insufficient to recover the high capital costs of transmission and distribution infrastructure. Retail tariffs are often set artificially low due to social and political considerations, making it dif-ficult for utilities (whether public or private) to recover their costs, even when grid connection fees are in place.

- As a result of this first challenge, some utilities resort to connection charges, but many customers in rural and remote areas cannot afford the connection fees on offer: such fees can be two or more times higher than an average household's monthly income and still only cover a frac-tion of the overall connection costs of grid extension, which are esti-mated at between 2,000 and 2,500 USD.

- Third, many developing countries lack the financial capability to cross-subsidize grid extension to rural areas, resulting in chronic under-investment and high disparities between the rates of electricity access in urban vs. in rural areas.

- Fourth, many developing countries with low rates of electricity ac-cess also have underdeveloped banking and capital markets and often lack the ability to borrow internationally, making them highly depen-dent on international development organizations and philanthropy to extend electricity access; this significantly reduces the pool of capital available.

- Finally, a further constraint on centralized grid expansion efforts is that local utilities are often highly indebted, making it difficult for them to invest on the scale required. This hinders local and international in-vestments in central power generation and infrastructure and makes it difficult for local utilities to scale-up electrification efforts. Under the current paradigm, off-grid electrification frequently increases utility losses, as connecting new, largely rural customers by extending central-ized grid infrastructure is simply not profitable.

Despite the many challenges facing centralized electrification initiatives, many governments remain committed to a largely centralized paradigm. The need for new solutions is clear.

This chapter argues that in many cases, small-scale solar home systems provide a quicker, more cost-effective, and lower-risk approach to off-grid electrification than either mini-grids or the extension of traditional transmission and distribution infrastructure. Such a solution offers a potential way to break through the vicious circle of weak on-grid infrastructure, low electrification rates, and increasing utility losses.

These new business models open up the possibility not only of accelerating national electrification efforts and helping achieve the SDG 7 targets, but also of putting electrification as a whole on a more financially sustainable footing.

This chapter describes the dynamic growth of off-grid solutions for enabling energy access and establishing newer, smarter infrastructure in greenfield environments free from the constraints of a centralized electricity distribution system. As will be illustrated, off-grid solutions allow a quick and demand-driven local supply of energy needs, turning consumers in rural and remote areas into prosumers, or alternatively, into "nonsumers."

The chapter is organized as follows:

- Section 2 provides an overview of the off-grid market worldwide;
- Section 3 analyzes the PAYGO business model;
- Section 4 looks at how decentralized solutions like PAYGO solar can help reach the 1.1 billion people around the world without access to electricity;
- Section 5 looks at some of the challenges that remain for the sector to continue growing and delivering onsite power at scale and at a price point that customers can afford, followed by the chapter's conclusions.

2. THE OFF-GRID MARKET: A SNAPSHOT

There are four main options used around the world to provide electricity service to areas lacking it: Pico-solar systems, solar home systems (SHS), mini-grids, and grid extension as outlined in Table 14.1.

This chapter focuses on the second market segment, namely, solar home system business models with a particular focus on those operating on the PAYGO or "rent-to-own" basis. This option is rapidly emerging as the most promising solution to overcome some of the challenges of traditional, grid-based electrification efforts while still providing life-changing energy

Table 14.1 Off-grid electricity service technologies

Electrification option	Brief description	Service level MTF
Pico-solar	Pico-solar systems are very small independent PV-powered systems up to 11W usually providing lighting services or simple cell phone charging.	Tier 1
SHS	SHS stands for solar-home-systems. These are small independent supply systems powered by solar PV. Combined with battery storage and control devices, they are usually designed to directly serve DC loads for lighting, cell phone charging, but also larger appliances such as TVs or fridges. Recent SHS combine the system with smart meter or pay-as-you-go (PAYG) solutions to enable microfinancing or leasing. They can be in a range of 12–300W.	Tier 1–3
Mini-grids	Mini-grids are small power stations powering local low distribution grids serving specific settlements, which can be off-grid or interconnected to the central grid. Mini-grids are generally deployed in rural areas with a higher population density to serve reliable AC power also to commercial loads.	Tier 2–5
Grid extension	This refers to the extension of the medium voltage (MV) and low voltage (LV) distribution grid to connect households or other customers to the central energy supply system. This central system includes power generation, transmission, and distribution.	Tier 4–5

Source: Authors' own depiction, based on Bhatia and Angelou (2015).

service for citizens in periurban, rural, and remote areas. SHS can be individually purchased, financed, implemented, and operated. This level of independence and flexibility allows rapid market growth without the need of extensive regulatory frameworks or policy support.

It is estimated that independent off-grid systems provided electricity access to approximately 73 million households, or over 360 million people, in 2017 (Dalberg, 2018). The total sales value generated by the off-grid sector has reached more than 3.9 billion USD for pico-solar systems and SHS (Ibid). This attracted substantial capital investments in related companies of approximately 500 million USD in 2016 and 2017 alone, underscoring the growth potential and attractiveness of these new business models.

3. PAY-AS-YOU-GO SOLAR: UNDERSTANDING THE BUSINESS

This section describes these pay-as-you-go business models, how they work, and why they've managed to be successful in delivering energy solutions to low- and middle-income customers around the world. This section outlines the business model, its growth, as well as its "hotspots" to give the reader a good understanding of where the action is and what this rapid and exciting new development looks like in practice.

Solar home system companies providing "rent-to-own" or "pay-as-you-go" (PAYGO) solar + storage solutions are now providing reliable, affordable electricity access at a fraction of the upfront cost of traditional electrification options, and often in a fraction of the time.

The main advantage of solar home systems is that they can be dimensioned based on each individual household's needs and ability to pay, thereby avoiding significant over- and/or underinvestment, all while avoiding the need for costly distribution infrastructure. Due to their rapid scalability and low implementation barriers, local and international companies active in countries such as Kenya, Rwanda, Tanzania, and Nigeria are setting out what is rapidly becoming a new paradigm off-grid electrification, one based on a "rent-to-own" concept according to which the customer pays off their solar + storage system in a series of installments and then assumes ownership of the system.

In countries like Kenya, Rwanda, and Tanzania, these companies are combining the core technologies of solar PV systems and battery storage with sophisticated real-time analytics, large networks of on-the-ground sales representatives, customized consumer finance solutions, all while leveraging the power of mobile money. Taken together, these solutions enable companies to deliver electricity services to households at a cost and scale that they can afford.

The success of these business models has been greatest in markets with a simple but powerful combination of factors:
- A light-touch regulatory framework;
- An active mobile money market enabling quick and efficient transfers of small sums of money;
- A relatively stable currency; and
- Simplified import procedures for solar home system components – generally consisting of PV panels, batteries, wiring, and efficient appliances.

Fig. 14.1 provides an overview of the standard PAYGO solar offering:

Although the business models differ somewhat from one company and country to the next, the majority of the companies active in this rapidly

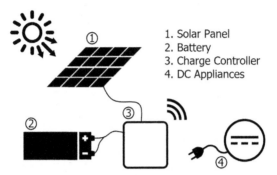

1. Solar Panel
2. Battery
3. Charge Controller
4. DC Appliances

FIGURE 14.1 A standard PAYGO solar home system. *(Source: Authors' own depiction.)*

growing sector provides on-going maintenance and troubleshooting support and remain on-call to supply replacement parts as well as to upgrade a given household's system and battery bank when needed.

By providing an electricity access solution that is carefully dimensioned based on each household's needs and can be accessed with a much smaller up-front payment than traditional grid connection fees, a far greater number of households can afford getting on the electricity access ladder than under traditional electrification options.

The entry point for a standard household system is often a simple 30–40W solar PV panel equipped with a small battery unit, a mobile phone charger, and a few high-efficiency light bulbs. For households with a greater ability to pay, larger systems are available up to 200W or more that come equipped with a small television, a radio, and a range of other appliances. By starting at a lower level of energy access and building upward from there, small-scale solar home systems like this are in the process of revolutionizing electrification in many parts of the world.

Globally, there are several countries that have significant electricity access gaps, where 20 million or more inhabitants lack access to reliable electricity (Fig. 14.2).

The main solar PAYGO companies are working on providing electricity to customers in periurban, rural, and remote regions using different forms of the basic rent-to-own concept. The initial down-payment often differs depending on the system size and the customer's credit score, as does the number and size of each monthly payment. Companies also differ in terms of the service platform they use, which mobile money providers are eligible, as well as in terms of the variety of their products, the warranties available, as well as the pricing offered for different system sizes (Mangoo, 2018).

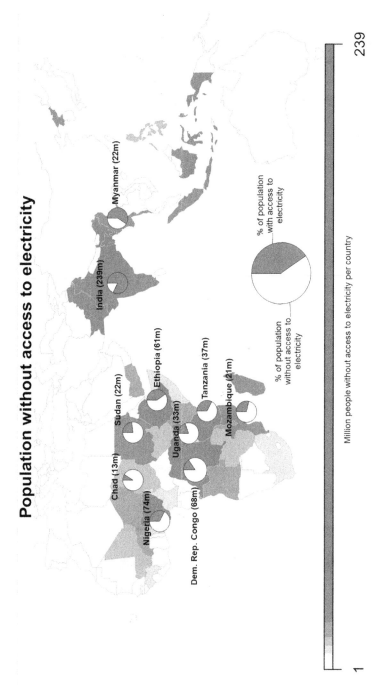

FIGURE 14.2 Overview of key markets – countries with more than 20 million people without access to electricity. (*Source: Authors' own depiction; data drawn from Dalberg (2018, p. 29).*)

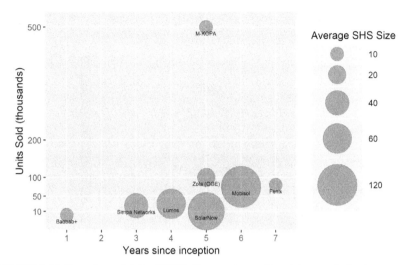

FIGURE 14.3 Overview of Solar PAYGO Companies: units sold, years in business, and average SHS size in Wp. *(Source: Authors' own depiction, data drawn from Hystra (2017).)*

Each of these companies has a slightly different approach to the market, with some targeting the smaller SHS systems (10–20Wp), while other companies have preferred targeting larger households and business customers (80–120Wp) (Fig. 14.3).

In recent years, several PAYGO companies, notably in East Africa, but also in parts of West Africa such as Nigeria, are beginning to diversify their operations. These companies are now starting to build on their growing customer base and the relationship of trust that has been forged to start to sell appliances, productive use technologies such as pumps and refrigeration, mobile phones, as well as residential and commercial cooking solutions. This diversification is already helping accelerate the sector's growth as it helps improve company cash flow and offers greater flexibility to adapt to changing market needs.

Moreover, spreading high customer acquisition costs, which remain one of the industry's main challenges, over a larger total volume of receivables or customer payments can strengthen the business case for operating in rural and remote regions, where the financial return on investment is often modest due to high transaction costs and low per-customer sales volumes. Diversification makes it possible to change this by unlocking more economic activity, and actively contributing to more business formation and job creation in rural areas.

Indeed, these cobenefits are real and well documented: Mobisol – one of the leading companies active mainly in Tanzania and Rwanda – for example, has published data showing that 40% of their customers are now using their SHS to run a small business, such as a small store, a barber shop, or an office. As a result, many SHS system owners are now using their systems to increase their earning power: this additional income can then be used to facilitate the PAYGO loan repayment (Acumen, 2017). A growing number of PAYGO companies are actively encouraging business formation in this way as it contributes to local economic development, increases local income levels, and increase the likelihood that loans will be paid back on time (USAID, 2017).

The convergence of several technologies, including improved cell phone coverage, enabled remote monitoring, and activation of solar home systems, and facilitated mobile payments through mobile money platforms have helped reduce the costs of processing small customer payments dramatically.

Another key development that has helped bring SHS into the range of affordability for many rural and remote households in Africa and Asia is the increasing efficiency of end-use appliances – thus far mainly DC appliances – including LED light bulbs, efficient television sets, and laptops, as well as a range of other appliances. By shrinking the amount of electricity actually needed to deliver a certain "level" of electricity access (Bhatia and Angelou, 2015), higher efficiency appliances have helped scale down the total size of both the solar panel and the battery bank required. This development has been supported by the decline in the cost of Li-ion batteries, as well as the costs of solar PV modules (Fig. 14.4):

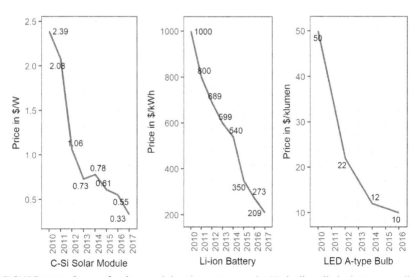

FIGURE 14.4 Costs of solar modules, batteries, and LED bulbs all declining rapidly. *(Source: Authors' own depiction, based on Dalberg (2018, p. 68).)*

By scaling down the PV array and battery bank, the full system cost has been dramatically reduced. Taken together, these technological changes have now made it possible to electrify households at a fraction of the cost of electrifying them only 7–8 years ago. By comparison, the costs of building transmission and distribution lines have remained broadly flat, and even increased in some cases due to increasing copper and other metal prices.

Despite decades of effort in expanding transmission and distribution infrastructure as the leading pathway to off-grid electrification, the economics now squarely favor decentralized solutions.

The revolution started in Kenya in 2009 with the establishment of M-Kopa, one of the early pioneers and still one of the market leaders in PAYGO solar. In the years since, several other companies have entered the market, bringing innovations to M-Kopa's business model, including the type and size of energy systems; available appliances; the design of payment plans and ownership models; as well as options in the duration of the payment term – usually ranging from 3 to 36 months. It is estimated that there are now approximately 1 million Kenyan households that have obtained an SHS through a rent-to-own agreement.

In contrast to typical microfinance schemes, it is in the interest of PAYGO operators to encourage early repayment in order to both recover capital necessary for growth and to enable consumers to continue to expand their systems beyond the initial investment (Winiecki and Kumar, 2014). The typical price of a PAYGO system covers leasing costs and risk, providing the end user with an attractive down payment and monthly fee combination alongside incentives for early repayment, while ensuring necessary returns for the operator.

Table 14.2 provides an overview of some of the standard solar PAYGO systems offered by a few of the leading providers; it outlines the capacity of the system, the initial down payment that customers have to make, as well as the weekly price (in USD) they are expected to make.

Table 14.2 Typical PAYGO system price breakdown

	Azuri Indigo Duo	M-KOPA III	Simpa Spark	Mobisol SHS
Solar PV capacity	2.5Wp	8Wp	40Wp	80Wp
Initial payment[a]	10	34	33	45
Weekly price[a]	1.5	3.22	2.33	5.25
Total cost[a]	135	201	368	801

[a]in 2014 USD.
Source: Winiecki and Kumar (2014).

Most businesses operating in this space include remote-satellite-enabled monitoring capabilities into their systems that enable them to monitor performance, system output, as well as any technical issues that emerge – for example, a nonfunctioning mobile phone charger, a defect in the battery storage unit, etc. These remote-monitoring capabilities also enable companies to deactivate systems in the case of nonpayment.

In addition, most systems are designed to be tamper-proof: attempts to open the electronic box deactivate the system. Interestingly, tampering with the systems has not been a major issue, perhaps partly due to the knowledge that the customer will eventually become owners of the system once the loan has been paid off (Clean Energy Finance Forum, 2014).

Importantly, a significant share of customers who buy an SHS system proceed to upgrade their system as their household electricity demand increases, or as they begin to add on business-related activities such as mobile phone charging, refrigeration, or other services. Fig. 14.5 provides an overview of the typical trajectory for an SHS solar customer who buys an entry-level SHS and gradually expands both his system and adds new appliances over time as income levels rise. This flexibility and scalability is at the heart of the success of PAYGO solar:

As illustrated in Fig. 14.4, the energy infrastructure can grow incrementally as customer needs grow, reducing the risks of "overdimensioning" that

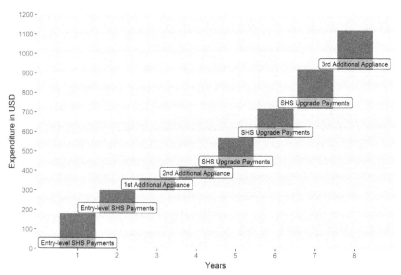

FIGURE 14.5 Overview of the evolution of a PAYGO customer. *(Source: Authors' own depiction, adapted from Dalberg (2018, p. 24).)*

mini-grids and distribution line extension often face. In that sense, PAYGO solar home systems represent a more efficient allocation of capital, as they are dimensioned according to each household's individual electricity needs and income level.

As a testament to these new business models' success, a growing number are successfully mobilizing private capital to continue to scale their operations. As the technologies and overall platforms have become tried, tested, and improved in recent years, the underlying business models have become more sophisticated; in turn, several such companies have begun to be able to mobilize significant volumes of capital.

Although the majority of finance continues to come from international investors, there are a few deals in recent months that have successfully involved local financial institutions providing local currency to support – and partially derisk – the overall project.

Recent analysis from SEforAll indicates that only 34% of the finance flowing for energy access are currently flowing to residential electricity access, and that the majority of that is on grid-based electrification (SEforALL, 2017a,b).

Given that the greatest electricity access need is at the household level, with some countries having over 85% of their residents without electricity, this underscores the sheer size of the challenge as well as the urgency of scaling up finance to household electricity access.

Although the majority of the off-grid solar market remains financed by equity, debt is beginning to be mobilized at a greater scale (SEforALL, 2017a,b). In fact, a few recent transactions in the PAYGO sector have even been able to mobilize local currency debt from local banks, a significant milestone for a sector that has long been heavily reliant on international capital (PV-Tech, 2017; M-Kopa, 2017).

As this brief snapshot of the PAYGO sector shows, the sector as a whole is growing rapidly, and is beginning to mobilize capital from a wide range of different sources to provide electricity access to millions around the world. In the process, these new decentralized business models are transforming the landscape of off-grid electrification, turning potential utility or mini-grid consumers into off-grid prosumers.

4. ELECTRIFYING THE NEXT BILLION

Currently, SHS business models have reached somewhere on the order of 2–4 million households (or 10–20 million citizens worldwide). When pico-solar products are added, over 300 million citizens worldwide have

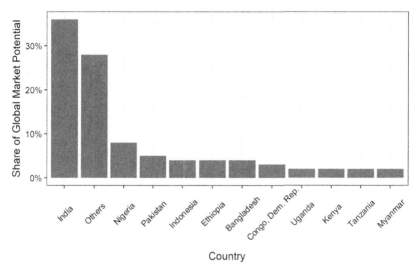

FIGURE 14.6 Total global market potential of 434 million households and related shares for largest countries. *(Source: adapted from Dalberg (2018, p. 57).)*

benefited from solar-powered lighting and electrification solutions. And yet, with an estimated global total of 1.1 billion without access, there is still much work to be done.

Fig. 14.6 provides an overview of the market potential.

The IEA estimates in its *new policy scenario* that under the expansion at current pace still more than 600 million people (or roughly 130 million households) will lack access in 2030. This is despite average investments of 24 billion USD per year into energy access or roughly 1.5% of the global annual energy investment (IEA and World Bank, 2017).

Closing this gap will require significant additional investments, particularly in rural and remote regions; in fact, the majority of the electricity access gap is found in these areas, with as much as 88% of the 119TWh of additional demand occurring there. To achieve access to sustainable energy for all by 2030, the IEA estimates that an additional 391 billion USD investments will be needed over that timeframe.

However, like many national governments and international organizations, the IEA arguably continues to underestimate the potential of decentralized SHS-based solutions for meeting energy access needs. In their most recent analysis, they estimate that only 23% of total financing would go into SHS businesses, while fully 48% would be allocated to mini-grids, with the bulk of the remaining 29% being invested in centralized grid expansion.

Given the significant challenges associated with developing bankable mini-grids in rural and remote areas, it is conceivable (and perhaps even likely) that SHS-based business models will prove more successful at mobilizing capital in the years ahead than mini-grids (IFC, 2017a,b; Schnitze et al., 2014; Salau, 2017). Indeed, SHS business models have thus far proved themselves more bankable than mini-grids and less reliant on government support and donor subsidies; also, they have been able to scale much more rapidly. In the absence of massive government and donor-led support for mini-grids and traditional grid expansion efforts, the market share of decentralized, SHS-based business models is likely to continue to grow, driven by favorable economics, continued improvements in storage technologies, more favorable import procedures, as well as economies of scale.

Thus, given sufficient capital, there is little doubt that PAYGO solar can make a significant contribution toward electrifying the 1.1 billion people around the world who still lack access to clean and affordable electricity. With the right combination of leadership and strategic vision, including a better recognition of the role of decentralized solutions such as SHS in national electricity sector planning, it is conceivable that SHS could even become the leading technology to provide new electricity access to households around the world in the years ahead.

These innovative new business models in the off-grid solar sector are demonstrating that a deeply distributed, "nonsumer" future is not only possible: in parts of Africa and Asia, it is already emerging.

5. PAYGO SOLAR: KEY CHALLENGES

Despite the remarkable success of PAYGO solar in recent years, a number of key challenges remain. Indeed, some businesses active in the sector have already started to adjust their business models to new market realities (for instance by focusing more on higher-income households in periurban areas rather than those in remote areas, or by evolving more into consumer finance companies providing customized financial services to unbanked customers rather than strictly energy-based services).

Another evolution that is underway is that a growing number of PAYGO companies are starting to form wide-reaching industry partnerships, often leveraging country presence and expertise in order to improve scale (Climatescope, 2017). Meanwhile, some investors have begun to express concerns over the amount of international capital (in particular venture capital) flowing into the sector, arguing that the sector may even be overheating, or headed for a bubble (Ceniarth, 2017).

Although most researchers and analysts remain optimistic about the sector's long-term potential, it is helpful to consider some of the challenges and risks that remain for the rent-to-own SHS sector (IFC, 2017a,b; Persistent Energy Capital LLC, 2017):

- **Ensuring user affordability**, particularly in lowest-income regions: despite the small system sizes and the customized offerings, some users in the lowest-income regions of sub-Saharan Africa are still unable to afford the entry-level solar home systems. In such cases, there may still be a case for targeted government or donor support, for instance via results-based financing schemes that provide a per-household subsidy for each household that obtains electricity access.

- **Maintaining quality across the loan portfolio:** SHS companies are growing rapidly and as a result, competition between companies is beginning to accelerate. In the process, there is a risk that lending standards across the sector start to deteriorate as companies compete for new customers. This could result in a decrease in the quality of the loan portfolio, and in higher rates of nonperforming loans (NPLs) as a growing number of new customers fail to meet their new financial obligations. If sufficiently widespread, such a deterioration in lending standards could spark broader concerns about the sustainability of the sector.

- **Securing and training skilled labor:** for many SHS companies, one of the biggest challenges is finding, training, and *retaining* skilled employees and installers, particularly in rural and remote regions where the bulk of their sales are located.

- **Managing competition with mini-grid providers:** In some countries, particularly those with ambitious mini-grid expansion plans, there is a risk that SHS companies come to be perceived as undermining the business model of mini-grid operators by tapping into the higher income customers first and reducing the residual load that remains to be served by the mini-grid. By decreasing the overall load that a mini-grid has to serve, SHS companies are likely to find themselves in direct conflict with mini-grid providers who need every last kWh sale in order to break even, let alone turn a profit. This conflict could increase the overall market and operational risks that SHS companies face.

- **Mobilizing sufficient patient capital:** although SHS companies are starting to become profitable, much of their working capital is currently being plowed back into the business. However, if an SHS company were to be financed largely by venture capital or private equity investors, for instance, the underlying investors are likely to want to cash out within the next few years, putting strain on the company's working capital and potentially undermining the overall sustainability of the business. As such, identifying and mobilizing sufficient quantities of so-called patient capital is likely to prove critical as SHS companies continue to scale.

- **Dealing with regulatory risk:** SHS companies are in many cases effectively becoming small financial services providers, providing unsecured loans to customers in the form of a solar system in exchange for a regular stream of monthly payments. As such, existing regulations on financial institutions could hinder the growth of certain SHS companies if they start to be regulated as financial services providers.
- **Entering new markets:** expanding from one established market into another carries a host of challenges. Cultures often differ widely from one region to the next, and local customs may make it difficult to simply copy a particular business model in another country, or even within another region of the same country.
- **Increasing the flow of local currency financing**, including local debt: in many cases, SHS companies are financed largely in hard currencies such as US dollars. On one level, this is logical, as many solar home system components (including PV modules, batteries, wiring, and appliances) are often purchased in dollars. However, the revenues generated by the company are typically collected in local currency. This gives rise to substantial currency risk. Without reliable instruments such as currency hedging tools, or more local currency financing from local banks, the risks that a significant currency devaluation in a country with a large SHS market could wipe out certain market players remains real.
- **Recycling of old SHS systems:** recycling of SHS remains critical to the long-term sustainability of the industry. In many cases, SHS companies continue to rely on lead-acid batteries as these are lower in cost and enable them to reach a wider range of customers by keeping their products affordable. However, lead-acid batteries raise a number of environmental, health-related, and waste management issues.
- **Overcoming the perception of being a "second-best" solution:** in many jurisdictions, the perception remains that SHS are a second-best option to either a mini-grid connection or a connection to the national system. This perception may make it difficult for governments to integrate SHS fully into their national electrification plans, as inequities (whether real or perceived) are likely to emerge between different

regions that have obtained electricity access via different means. The perception of preferential treatment could undermine public support not only for SHS, but for any option that is not full integration into the national electricity grid.

While it is unlikely that SHS companies will be able to overcome *all* of the above-mentioned challenges and risks, by being mindful of them and by continuing their focus providing quality, affordable electricity service to their customers, they can ensure that SHS play a leading role in lifting hundreds of millions of people out of poverty.

Whether these small-scale solar home systems will ever be networked with one another, pooling their storage capabilities to enable the usage of higher capacity appliances, or whether they remain as reliable, distributed, unconnected systems remains unclear. Moving from an individual ownership model toward a more communal model (especially once customers have already seen the benefits and reliability of their own solar home system) is likely to be challenging and may raise new issues, not least with regard to financing as well as technical interoperability.

For the time being, SHS often provide more reliable power than minigrids, facing fewer "outages" and less down-time due to maintenance (Climatescope, 2017). Convincing PAYGO customers to join a mini-grid (particularly once their SHS is paid off) and start paying for power from another company, particularly if it is less reliable than what they have known, is likely to prove challenging.

However, as mini-grids become more reliable and more widespread, it may be possible for these two business models to collide in more productive and synergistic ways; exactly how remains unclear.

6. CONCLUSIONS

As the physicist Niels Bohr once said, forecasting is tough, especially when it is about the future. The energy sector is no exception, as hundreds of different technological, economic, political, social, cultural, and other factors ultimately determine the unique trajectory a particular country takes. In some countries, a top-down, centralized electrification approach has worked quite well, as seen in US and much of Europe while in other places, such as Rwanda and Tanzania, a more decentralized approach is now bearing fruit.

In places that have existing grid infrastructure, there is a clear trend toward consumers moving away from the traditional bundled/regulated service options offered by regulated utilities toward more autonomous or semiautonomous options; this has given rise to the "nonsumer," "prosumer," and "prosumager" covered in other chapters of the book.

In a similar way, in some lower-income countries that still lack broad grid coverage, customers are beginning to turn to a range of autonomous and semiautonomous options, although from a different starting point: indeed, many of these "off-grid prosumers" have never had a grid connection before.

As this chapter has attempted to show, decentralized solutions such as solar home systems provided to customers on a rent-to-own basis can be a powerful vehicle for providing quality, affordable electricity service in off-grid and near-grid regions around the world.

Innovations in business models combined with rapidly declining technology costs are making it possible that autonomous or semiautonomous users become the norm, rather than the exception, in electricity markets worldwide.

REFERENCES

Acumen, 2017. An Evidence Review: How affordable is off-grid energy access in Africa? Acumen.

Attia, B., Shirley, R., 2018, June 13. Distributed models for grid extension could save African utilities billions of dollars. Retrieved from greentechmedia: https://www.greentechmedia.com/amp/article/grid-extension-done-right-for-sub-saharan-africas-utilities.

Bhatia, M., Angelou, N., 2015. Beyond Connections: Energy Access Redefined. World Bank.

Ceniarth, 2017, December 22. Retrieved from nextbillion.net: https://nextbillion.net/an-impact-investor-urges-caution-on-the-energy-access-hype-cycle/.

Clean Energy Finance Forum, 2014, October 4. Retrieved from cleanenergyfinanceforum.com: https://www.cleanenergyfinanceforum.com/2014/10/04/pay-as-you-go-solar-lights-up-india-and-africa.

Climatescope, 2017. Off-grid and mini-grid market outlook. http://global-climatescope.org/en/off-grid-quarterly/q3-2017/.

Dalberg, 2018. Off-Grid Solar Market Trends Report 2018. World Bank.

Hystra, 2017. Reaching scale in access to energy. Lessons from practitioners.

IEA & World Bank, 2017. Sustainable Energy for All 2017 — Progress Toward Sustainable Energy. World Bank.

IFC, 2017a, December 22. Retrieved from nextbillion.net: https://nextbillion.net/there-is-such-a-thing-as-too-much-too-fast-avoiding-mismatched-expectations-in-off-grid-energy-investing/.

IFC, 2017b. Operational and Financial Performance of Mini-Grid DESCOs. World Bank.

Mangoo, 2018. Solar products for Africa and Asia. Retrieved from: https://www.mangoo.org/product-catalogue/systems/.

M-Kopa. 2017, October 10. Retrieved from: m-kopa.org: http://www.m-kopa.com/breaking-records-in-financing-off-grid/.

New York Times, 2016. Electrifying India, with the Sun and Small Loans. Written by Max Bearak. Published January 2 2016.

Persistent Energy Capital LLC, 2017, December 22. Retrieved from nextbillion.net: https://nextbillion.net/hype-in-the-energy-access-sector-finally/.

PV-Tech, 2017, October 23. Retrieved from pv-tech.org: https://www.pv-tech.org/news/ bboxx-claims-first-of-its-kind-trilateral-financing-for-off-grid-power-in-r.

PwC, 2015. A new Africa energy world. A more positive power utilities outlook. PwC.

Reuters, 2018. Off-grid power pioneers pour into West Africa. Written by Joe Bavier. Published February 20 2018.

Salau, I., 2017. Today's Challenge: E&S Risks in Mini-Grid Development. Environmental Accord Limited.

Schnitze, D., Lounsbury, D.S., Carvallo, J.P., Deshmukh, R., Apt, J., Kammen, D.M., 2014. Microgrids for Rural Electrification: A Critical Review of Practices Based on Seven Case Studies. United Nations Foundation.

SEforALL, 2017a. High-Impact Countries Report. SEforALL.

SEforALL, 2017b. Taking the Pulse. Understanding Energy Access Market Needs in Five High-Impact Countries. SEforALL.

The Economist, 2016. Africa unplugged: small-scale solar power is surging ahead. Print Edition October 29 2016.

The Guardian, 2016. Investing in off-grid renewables in the developing world: what you need to know. Written by Tess Riley. Published August 24 2016.

USAID, 2017. Rapid Assessment Framework: Pay-As-You-Go Solar as a Driver of Financial Inclusion. USAID Global Development Lab.

Winiecki, J., Kumar, K., 2014. Access to Energy via Digital Finance: Overview of Models and Prospects for Innovation. CGAP.

World Bank, 2018. Sustainable Energy for All (SE4ALL) database from the SE4ALL Global Tracking Framework led jointly by the World Bank, International Energy Agency, and the Energy Sector Management Assistance Program.

CHAPTER 15

Customer Stratification and Different Concepts of Decentralization

Dierk Bauknecht, Joß Bracker, Franziska Flachsbarth, Christoph Heinemann, Dominik Seebach, Moritz Vogel
Oeko-Institut, Freiburg, Germany

1. INTRODUCTION[1]

A changing and more diverse role for consumers as described by the concept of customer stratification implies that the conventional top-down structure of the power system is increasingly complemented by more decentralized business models. One important driver for this is the rising share of renewables in the electricity sector. This not only leads to a changing generation mix, but together with other developments such as digitalization – further described in Chapter 1 by Brown et al. – can entail far-reaching structural changes beyond generation. Many of these changes are often labeled as "decentralization." Decentralization can mean, for example, increasing numbers of distributed generation plants with flexibility options connected to the distribution network, "behind-the-meter" devices and assets, the geographical distribution of plants, or the way generation and demand are balanced.

This chapter disentangles the multifaceted debate on decentralization and examines how this relates to new consumer roles. It uses Germany as a case study, which is also covered by other authors in this volume. The starting point for discussion is the "standard model of liberalized electricity markets" with a centralized market and a "copper-plate" network that enables all market transactions and where consumers are located at the end of the supply chain.

The focus here is on new concepts that affect the way in which generation and consumption are aligned and which deviate from the model

[1]This chapter is based on work carried out in the projects ENSURE, funded by the German Federal Ministry of Education and Research (project reference 03SFK1TO) and C/sells, funded by the German Federal Ministry for Economic Affairs and Energy (project reference 03SIN102).

Consumer, Prosumer, Prosumager
https://doi.org/10.1016/B978-0-12-816835-6.00015-2

of a centralized market, albeit in various ways and for different reasons in different parts of the world. These concepts offer new choices and entail potentially new roles for consumers. The motivation for these concepts can include economic advantages or improved participation of citizens and consumers in the energy system. The chapter focuses on a systemic perspective rather than on how decentralization affects individual business models. Depending on the type of decentralization and the objective that is to be achieved, there are different regulatory requirements.

The chapter is organized as outlined:

- Section 2 provides a brief overview of different concepts of decentralization. The following four chapters then focus on four different concepts of decentralization in more detail;
- Section 3 looks at concepts that challenge central markets with regional products and peer-to-peer approaches;
- Section 4 discusses concepts that use regional flexibility options for network management;
- Section 5 presents the most far-reaching concept, whereby the centralized market is broken down in decentralized markets that are used to balance generation and demand even when there is no network constraint; and
- Section 6 looks at the regional distribution of renewables that influences the other concepts of decentralization as well as the role consumers and citizens can play, followed by the chapter's conclusions.

2. DIFFERENT CONCEPTS OF DECENTRALIZATION: AN OVERVIEW

When talking about decentralization, people refer to a range of different concepts and developments. This includes technical as well as social dimensions. This section provides an overview and explains how these dimensions are related to new roles for consumers.

As for technical aspects of decentralization, Funcke and Bauknecht (2016) introduced a typology with four technological dimensions of the electricity infrastructure. Each of these dimensions can be designed in a centralized or decentralized way and, taken together, describe the corresponding infrastructure. Table 15.1 shows an overview of these technological dimensions and their possible configurations.

Besides these technical dimensions, there is also a debate on decentralization in the form of improved participation of citizens and consumers in designing and operating the power system. First, this refers to a broader

Table 15.1 Possible configuration of technological infrastructure dimensions

	Connectivity	Proximity	Flexibility	Controllability
Decentralized	Power plants are connected to the distribution grid level.	Power plants are located close to demand.	Flexibility is connected to the distribution grid.	Generation and demand are primarily balanced via distribution grid or prosumers.
Centralized	Power plants are connected to the transmission grid level.	Power plants are located at optimal locations, i.e., cost reducing or output maximizing.	Flexibility is connected to the transmission grid level.	Generation and demand are primarily balanced via centralized markets.

Source: Based on Funcke and Bauknecht (2016).

distribution of ownership, be it individual or collective, e.g., through cooperatives. Second, as consumers become prosumers and providers of flexibility, participation in electricity markets also becomes more widely spread.

In Germany, it is widely acknowledged that higher shares of renewables will increasingly lead to higher shares of generation and flexibility connected to the distribution grid – the first two dimensions in Table 15.1. However, the other two types of decentralization shown in the table are up for debate. As for regional distribution – *proximity* – a decision needs to be made as to whether renewables should be located in areas where they can be operated most efficiently or be more widely distributed. As for the way generation and demand are aligned – *controllability* – the question is whether a system with millions of small-scale renewable plants also requires a more decentralized balancing approach, moving away from the centralized market paradigm.

The focus of this chapter is on the controllability dimension. The regional distribution influences the control dimension and is strongly related to the possibility for consumers to participate in the development of renewables.

A centralized market paradigm assumes that plants should be located in areas and on sites with the lowest levelized costs of electricity and should be dispatched according to the merit order that is based on marginal costs, so that overall the most efficient generation can be achieved. This is achieved via centralized markets. Following market liberalization in the 1990s, a key objective has been to integrate separate markets, e.g., in the European internal electricity markets, further described in Chapter 16 by Pereira et al.

The developments presented in this chapter deviate from that paradigm in different ways. Regional distribution of plants not only relies on generation costs, but also takes into account other factors such as grid development as well as local participation and acceptance.

While the regional distribution of plants is a straightforward concept, decentralization of control can mean a range of different mechanisms. First, the development of renewables and the resulting changes in the regional distribution of generation can lead to grid bottlenecks that challenge the centralized markets. In Germany, this is currently solved via redispatch. While economists typically propose some form of nodal or zonal pricing, there are also concepts to develop markets for flexibility that can be used by the network operators to manage grid constraints. These would compete with the centralized electricity market for the use of flexibility.

A second development that challenges the centralized market is the rise of regional electricity products and peer-to-peer trading between prosumers. In contrast to the first concept, this does not react to network constraints. Rather, the rise of renewables and their regional distribution leads to a demand for regional electricity products. This can be met through regional products or direct peer-to-peer trading between prosumers that allows them to sell their surplus electricity without accessing the centralized market.

Finally, there are concepts to replace or complement the integrated market with so-called cells in which local balancing takes place. This has been proposed for example by VDE (2015). This is often presented mainly as a technical concept, but would have far-reaching implications for the market design. For consumers this could imply that they only have access to the cell market, while the centralized market is only used to balance residual load and generation between the cells. Therefore, while in the previous approach regional products would be an additional option for consumers, in the cell concept there would only be regional products.

Table 15.2 summarizes how these developments relate to the customer stratification model.

Table 15.2 Customer stratification and decentralization

Dimension of decentralization/section	Link to customer stratification level
Regional electricity marketing and peer-to-peer trading	**Prosumers and prosumagers** trade with each other via peer-to-peer trading. **Prosumer** model can be extended to residential blocks: Landlord-to-tenant electricity supply. **Consumers:** Even consumers without self-generation or storage may decide to buy specific products, such as green electricity or regional products and thus become active market players.
Using regional flexibility options for network management	**Prosumager** may not just use their flexibility (storage and DSM) to optimize their self-consumption, but also offer their flexibility to the market. These include new markets such as a TSO/DSO flexibility platform.
The cell concept as a new key structure of electricity systems	**Consumer, producers, prosumer, prosumager** could be bundled in regional markets. This would extend the prosumager model to regions. Compulsory participation in cells could limit the choice of consumers on the market.
Regional distribution of renewables	From a system perspective, the **prosumer** model implies a decentralization of renewables also in terms of a geographical distribution close to consumers.

3. REGIONAL ELECTRICITY MARKETING AND PEER-TO-PEER TRADING

This section presents concepts that challenge central markets with regional products and peer-to-peer approaches. The decentralization of energy systems has strong interdependencies with the way producers, utilities, and consumer interact in the energy market. Traditionally, the energy market has been characterized by a few utilities that operate large-scale generation capacities, trade electricity on centralized market places, and sell homogeneous "gray" electricity, i.e., electricity without any specific properties, to end consumers. The increasing number of small-scale generation units, prosumers and regional communities that strive for a self-sufficient renewable energy supply blurs the boundaries between producers and consumers. Furthermore, with renewables moving out of the niche market, the "traditional" market interactions are complemented by new forms of trading, different actor constellations, and greater differentiation in the electricity retail market.

In Germany, consumers have increasingly become interested in the characteristics of their power supply and a market for green and regional energy products has emerged (BEUC, 2016; Maaß et al., 2017). Furthermore, the digitalization of the energy market (e.g., smart meters) and new technologies (e.g., blockchain) allow for a strong differentiation of traded electricity, including the development of decentralized and regional market places.

It should be pointed out that these changes not only lead to a stronger role for prosumers and prosumagers, but also enable a stronger impact on traditional consumers. Producers with specific characteristics (e.g., regarding production technology, geographical location, or ownership structure) can gain extra revenues in a premium market segment, and high-interest consumers can now influence the production sector through their potentially specific and differentiated demand.

It is often assumed that the described new forms of trading, alternative actor constellations, and green electricity products positively influence the sustainability transition of the energy system. However, these developments are mostly driven by new technologies and individual interests of specific actors such as new business opportunities for local producers and preferences of consumers for local electricity supply. So far, the effects from an environmental, social, or economic perspective regarding these new markets and trading modes have not been fully assessed.

This section explores two examples of such new trading arrangements and market differentiation in Germany and how they have been framed by specific regulations.

3.1 Case 1: Local and Regional Electricity Products

Different marketing models for electricity are developing in Germany relating to the proximity of the production facilities on different levels. Many renewable producers strive to offer *regional products*, which are supplied from regional renewable plants that already operate or are to be developed.

However, the current regulatory framework in Germany stipulates that public support for RES-E include the sale of the "greenness" to those who pay for the support system. This means that all average household consumers, which are charged for the support scheme, get a share of some

45% "supported RES-E" in their electricity fuel mix disclosure in return (2017). Accordingly, this greenness, which is usually represented by a so-called guarantee of origin – GO – in Europe, is only available for use in a green electricity product in the rather rare case of unsupported RES-E.[2]

To meet the demand for regional products, so-called regional GOs have been legally introduced with the last revision of the Renewable Law in Germany in 2017 and are currently being implemented.[3] This instrument will allow substantiating claims about the regional sourcing of the 45% "supported RES-E" of a given electricity product but not for the remaining 55% share. In contrast to the use of GOs by suppliers, regional GOs may only be used if they are linked with a physical electricity supply contract between the electricity supplier and the respective RES-E plant, which is legally defined as "regional" if it is located within a range of 50 km from the consumer.

Currently, there is no regulation in place in Germany that covers the remaining 55% of electricity in terms of selling it as a "regional" product. In any case, it is possible for suppliers to source the remaining share of such a product from unsupported renewable production within a self-defined regional proximity, if GOs from these plants are acquired. However, for renewable plants, which are eligible for the public support scheme, this means that the level of public support defines a buy-out price, which is well above market price.

Another approach that enables a supply of electricity that is generated close to the consumer, albeit on a different scale, is the emerging landlord-to-tenant electricity supply. This model broadens the concept of self-consumption and includes a direct electricity supply from, e.g., a rooftop PV plant to tenants of the same building without using the public grid. Potentially, this also includes local storage behind the meter in order to increase the volume of on-site consumption.

In Germany, the last revision of the Renewables Law has clarified that public support for renewables is also applicable for such products. Under certain conditions, a market premium is given to the PV plant operator for electricity, which is used on-site by customers of the landlord-to-tenant

---

[2]In practice, this restriction to the free tradability of German GOs results in large imports of renewable GOs from Scandinavia and other European countries to Germany in order to supply German green electricity markets.

[3]The launch of the central electronic registry for regional GOs at the Federal Environment Agency (Umweltbundesamt – UBA) has been announced for the beginning of 2019.

supply contract. The former regulation required that the supported electricity had to be fed into the public grid. In combination with reduced grid charges for this on-site consumption, the additional market premium is supposed to give way to the increased use of this model and thereby also stimulate PV development, particularly in urban areas.

However, the landlord is required to fulfill all obligations of an electricity company to the participating tenant (while other tenants, who have not chosen to participate in this local supply model, are still supplied by a regular supply contract). In order to ensure a secure electricity supply for the consumer, the landlord therefore must also acquire electricity from the public grid. In many cases, a landlord would cooperate with a new electricity service provider or an established electricity supplier in order to handle the complex obligations. These administrative hurdles may explain why the uptake of this model is still low.[4]

The European Renewables Directive, which has been under revision since November 2016 and is supposed to be adopted by the end of 2018, will most probably encourage all EU Member States to assess the possibility to enable the active participation of all households, including tenants. It will also require the abolition of remaining unjustified regulatory barriers for renewable self-consumption, including for tenants (Council of the European Union, 2018).

Fig. 15.1 illustrates alternative arrangements for different types of producers and consumers in decentralized energy systems in differentiated and possibly regional markets. It also highlights how consumer and producer are connected to each other in the different models.

For the time being, it is hard to assess the degree to which such regional marketing approaches will actually have a relevant technical and economic influence on the electricity system. Generally, regional branding of RES-E is assumed to enhance public acceptance and therefore to reduce barriers for new renewable installations (Bundesministerium für Wirtschaft und Energie, 2016; Umweltbundesamt, 2017). This seems plausible, at least as long as there is still a low density of renewable installations in a region. It is argued that this effect is likely to be strengthened if a broad range of players can also financially participate in the regional added value (e.g., in

---

[4]While the German regulation defines a legal cap of registered PV plants of 500 MWp for the year 2018, the total capacity of registered PV plants in the period from July 2017 (the introduction of the landlord-to-tenant support in Germany) until May 2018 only adds up to 3.3 MWp (Bundesnetzagentur, 2018).

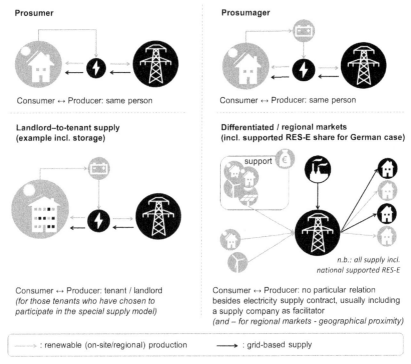

FIGURE 15.1 Grid situation for different production and consumption role models in a decentralized energy system. *(Source: Oeko-Institut e.V.)*

the form of energy cooperatives) (Bündnis Bürgerenergie e.V., 2015). The support system for the landlord-to-tenant electricity supply in combination with reduced grid charges in principle makes such supply contracts more attractive for both tenants and landlords. Thus, it also triggers additional PV installations on urban rooftops (close to the consumption) in contrast to large free-field PV.[5]

3.2 Case 2: New Trading Platforms/Peer-to-Peer Trading

The rise of smart meters, technologies like blockchain and growing numbers of prosumers have led to so-called P2P trading and regional market places, as further described in Chapter 2 by Shipworth et al. Examples of these new trading types in Germany are *Enyway* (enyway GmbH, 2018) and

---

[5]This is particularly relevant in Germany, which has a traditionally high share of rented housing in contrast to privately owned homes.

Tal.Markt (WSW Energie & Wasser AG, 2018). Both are trading platforms developed by electricity providers that connect individual renewable producers to consumers, either within a specific region or across Germany. The energy storage manufacturer *Sonnen* also offers its customers a possibility to connect their self-production and consumption with other customers or small-scale renewable production units. The *sonnencommunity* has already created a large network of 120,000 customers (KfW Bankengruppe, 2018). Chapter 6 by Stanley et al. also describes in more detail the features of a digital platform for "smart" local market places developed in England.

Ideally P2P trading allows renewable energy producers, including small prosumers or prosumagers (e.g., house owners with small-scale PV generation and a local storage unit), to directly sell their (excess) production to other consumers through the public grid without an intermediary. Through digital platforms, market actors find trading counterparts and conclude individual contracts. In many cases, these trading concepts are facilitated by blockchain technology that enables secure and instant settlement of payments between market actors. Fig. 15.2 depicts the different relationship between consumers, producers, and utilities in the traditional market setting and in P2P trading.

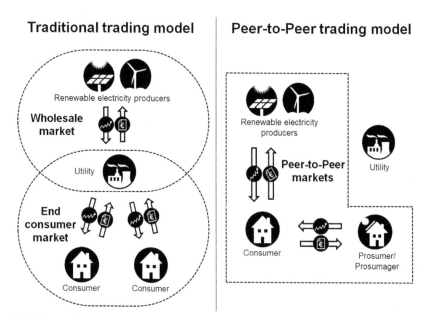

FIGURE 15.2 Peer-to-peer trading model. *(Source: Oeko-Institut e.V.)*

However, this kind of electricity trading is accompanied by numerous regulatory requirements originating from the "traditional" trading model (e.g., balancing management and metering). Therefore, consumers participating in the new trading platforms still have a "backup" contract with a standard utility that is responsible for the required regulatory processes. The P2P trading constitutes a second trading level besides the wholesale market that, at present, does not make traditional utilities redundant. However, the business model of utilities could change toward a service provider for P2P platforms.

For Germany, it is argued that P2P approaches have the potential to reduce the costs of renewables. In the case of regional market places, it could significantly reduce the usage of the public grid, even though it remains unclear to what extent this can actually reduce the required grid capacity (which is the main cost driver). It can also reduce electricity prices compared to self-consumption systems through a joint use of storage (Oppen et al., 2017). However, please note that a joint use of capacity is one the main rationales for having a centralized system in the first place.

The new trading platforms are still in a very early stage of commercial development and their impact on the electricity market and the energy transition in general have not yet been empirically evaluated. Most obviously, P2P platforms lead to greater interaction between consumers and renewable energy producers in comparison to the traditional consumer-supplier relationship. With more individual relationships to their market counterparts and possibly closer proximity, P2P trading could potentially increase the identification of consumers with renewable energy supply in their region (Wirth et al., 2018). As acceptance of renewable plants becomes a growing problem in Germany, positive social effects could occur.

However, it cannot automatically be assumed that this closer relationship between prosumers and consumers will also stimulate the expansion of small-scale renewable generation. These new revenue streams are not as reliable as support schemes and cannot provide the same investment security. Besides potential positive impacts on renewable energy development, intelligent connection of decentralized renewable production could also facilitate the stabilization of local distribution grids. First pilot and research projects are analyzing the potential benefits here (e.g., TenneT and Sonnen GmbH, 2018).

From an economic perspective, particularly the question of efficiency needs to be addressed. On the one hand, smaller markets with fewer trading counterparts decrease competition, which could in turn lead to higher prices. However, in general, allowing smaller actors to participate in electricity trade increases the competition and diversification of the market. The regulatory framework therefore should empower smaller producers to sell their electricity by removing disproportionate burdens for these new actors.

On a general level, it is plausible that an increased promotion of regional renewable products and P2P trading can lead to an increased identification of citizens and consumers with the deployment of regional electricity production, and thus reduce barriers for the further development of renewables. However, increased promotion of regional energy products and new trading concepts do not necessarily lead to a technical change of demand and supply. The actual environmental and economic effects depend on the specific context and are still subject to theoretical and empirical research. Potential positive effects include greater renewable electricity deployment and more renewable supply-oriented consumption through local price signals.

As a starting point, regulation should consider consumer preferences and technological possibilities by not imposing disproportionate administrative burdens on regional products and on new forms of trading. Whether such approaches should also be given active support, e.g., by creating exemptions from existing charges, fees and administrative expenses, has to be assessed on a more specific basis according to their social, economic, or environmental benefits.

4. PROVIDING LOCALIZED FLEXIBILITY FOR THE MARKET: THE EXAMPLE OF NETWORK MANAGEMENT

The role of electricity consumers is changing. This entails consumers increasingly taking care of their supply themselves and also a more active participation in electricity markets compared to today. Especially through the application of new technologies such as heat pumps, e-mobility, and batteries, consumers may offer flexibility in corresponding markets. This exceeds the consumer's classical role, which has already been extended by the introduction of decentralized renewable generation and provides new flexibility to the management of the electricity system.

Prosumagers can offer their flexibility in the market for network management. In this section, regulatory requirements for such markets and for an active role of consumers in these markets are highlighted.

As today's network infrastructure has developed with conventional load flows, it is not well suited to accommodate high shares of renewables. The rise of renewable generation entails grid bottlenecks and voltage fluctuations. Therefore, the demand for flexibility will rise. Grid bottlenecks themselves lead to some form of decentralization, as generation and demand need to be balanced locally in its presence. Distributed flexibility can help to solve this congestion. For a closer look at the future challenges of distribution grid operators, see Chapter 6.

From an economic perspective, nodal pricing would be the first best option to address network constraints and use flexibility in the market. In Germany, a zonal pricing approach, which represents a simplified form of nodal pricing, has been suggested for the North and South. It has been shown that zonal pricing would decrease liquidity and increase market power of individual market actors (see, e.g., DIW, 2015; Frontier Economics and Consentec, 2011). Also from a political point of view, such an approach is not feasible for the time being.

In Germany, the paradigm used to be that the grid should enable all market transactions. While this is still true, there are also attempts to enable flexibility for example from demand-side management for active grid management and in order to avoid grid extensions for integrating "the last kWh."

Today the primary flexibility option in network management is renewable curtailment. From an economic point of view, this can hardly be seen as the optimal solution: Renewable electricity is lost and corresponding demand has to be supplied by more expensive or emission-intensive generation. At the same time, renewable generators are compensated. Other options such as DSM, storage, or flexible generation could be part of an efficient solution by integrating renewable excess generation.

Various approaches are being researched to efficiently apply regional flexibility in active network management.[6] As opposed to the concepts outlined in the previous and following sections, these mechanisms are not about trading kWh, but rather trading flexibility to manage network constraints.

The coordination approaches that are suggested can make small-scale flexibilities available for network operators and comply with the unbundling

---

[6]For example, within the government-funded demonstration programme "Smart Energy Showcases – Digital Agenda for the Energy Transition" (SINTEG), https://www.bmwi.de/Redaktion/EN/Artikel/Energy/sinteg-funding-programme.html.

principle. Among others a decentralized, market-based coordination mechanism is suggested through which a network operator can contract regional flexibility that suits its needs. These markets are an additional option for flexibility operators to offer their services and have been suggested in Germany (see, e.g., Verband der Elektrotechnik Elektronik Informationstechnik e.V., 2014) as well as other European Member States (for a Dutch example see, e.g., USEF Foundation, 2015).

A drawback of these approaches could be the potentially low number of regional flexibility operators and a lack of competition that may lead to collusion and inefficiently high prices. It is thus all the more important that as many consumers as possible participate in these markets.

Centralized approaches integrate distributed flexibility options into existing central markets (see, e.g., research project enera (EWE, 2017)). Flexibility options can participate in the electricity market and at the same time offer regional flexibility products, which are accessible for the distribution system operator.

For these approaches, different regulatory changes are necessary, which are outlined in the following paragraphs.

From a consumer's perspective, the design of network fees is crucial when it comes to providing flexibility to the network. Network fees usually consist of a capacity fee depending on the highest capacity taken from the grid and a volumetric fee depending on the number of kWh. Especially the capacity fee that is typically charged on larger consumers prevents the use of flexibility. In situations that could be resolved by an increase of consumption, the capacity charge leads to an increase in costs as consumption becomes peakier.

This can be addressed by alternative grid fee designs. Especially variable volumetric and capacity fees that take the current state of the grid into account are discussed. Consumption in times of a stressed grid would lead to high costs for the consumer, who would then try to shift its consumption to times of low load and low grid fees (The Regulatory Assistance Project, 2014). For a closer look at distribution network charges, see also Chapter 9.

Also grid operators could offer different types of connectivity contracts with different maximum capacities. A consumer may choose the capacity that suits their needs, e.g., a high capacity to charge an electric vehicle over a short period of time. For average consumers, a regular contract with an average capacity might suffice. Consumers with a certain amount of flexibility might decide to reduce their maximum capacity, thereby reducing their costs and the stress they put on the grid. In terms of customer stratification, the possibility to choose between different capacity contracts may be necessary to fulfill consumers' needs. From a grid operator's point of view, this approach could reduce grid bottlenecks as the grid capacity could be limited a priori.

Moreover, the market-based use of flexibility options for network management has to be supported by regulatory changes for network operators. First, in Germany, the curtailment of renewable generation is the cheapest way for network operators to manage the network, as corresponding costs can be passed through to network customers via grid fees (see §11 ARegV (Bundesregierung, 2017)). Hence, from an economic point of view, there is no necessity for network operators to use other flexibility options to deal with bottlenecks or voltage fluctuations. A possible approach could be to abandon or reduce the share of curtailment costs that can be financed through grid fees and thereby incentivize the network operator to deal efficiently with these costs.

Second, in contrast to the costs for curtailing renewables or network expansion, the costs of procurement of market-based flexibility services will not necessarily be accepted by the regulator, as this is not yet a regular practice for network management. To support innovative flexibility solutions, the corresponding costs have to be regulated. At the moment, a reduction of generation or consumption in emergency situations can be realized without any cost for the distribution network operator as no compensation has to be paid. Similar to renewable curtailment, this does not lead to an efficient network management.

If the regulatory framework is put in place, a new role for consumers can emerge whereby the use of flexibility is not just limited to the consumer's premises, but is also offered to the network operator.

5. THE IMPACT OF THE CELL CONCEPT AS A NEW KEY STRUCTURE OF ELECTRICITY SYSTEMS, FROM A SYSTEM AS WELL AS CONSUMER PERSPECTIVE

A far-reaching decentralized concept under discussion in Germany is the so-called cell concept (Smart Grids-Plattform Baden-Württemberg e.V., 2017; VDE, 2015). In this concept, it is firstly proposed to subdivide the current electricity system into small-scale geographic cells, such as micro-grids or larger ones. This can provide certain functions to the overall system, although the approach emphasizes the principle of subsidiarity.

The concept implies that connections to other cells or the higher grid level should be used only if a cell cannot internally balance demand and supply. This concept would lead to a bottom-up cell-based electricity system, whereby consumers, producers, prosumers, and prosumagers are bundled together within one cell, jointly balancing its internal generation and demand. In contrast to the voluntary regional energy-marketing approach sketched out in Section 3, cells would be a compulsory structural element of the electricity system and would thus require a fundamental revision of the market design.

What are the main drivers behind the "cell" idea and which system effects can be expected? Various arguments in favor of the concept are discussed in the following paragraphs.

- If demand and supply are traded and balanced on the cell level, it can be expected that less electricity has to be transported via the transmission grid. As a consequence, demand will typically also be lower for grid expansion due to the increase of renewables. However, balancing demand and supply first and foremost on the cell level and irrespective of grid bottlenecks also implies that even the existing grid will not be used to its full potential. This applies even in situations where the centralized market result is not impeded by grid constraints. This represents an important difference to using flexibility to manage network constraints, as described in the previous section. The approach thus leads to a decrease of overall efficiency regarding costs but also CO_2 emissions. In addition, the grid may be the only option to cover demand in times of low solar radiation and wind. The following map of Germany shows administrative districts and their possible degree of self-supply. It can be concluded that especially urban areas show high deficits. Therefore, the electricity grid is important for transporting electricity from areas of generation to areas of high loads (Fig. 15.3).

  It is also important to assess the additional infrastructure needed for balancing primarily within the cell. If for example new storage options have to be implemented within the cell while existing flexibility options within the system are not used, costs will increase (Koch et al., 2017).

- Another challenge of energy system transformation is managing millions of decentralized renewable plants and flexibility options, which dramatically increase the complexity of the overall system. Therefore, subdividing the overall system into smaller units that manage demand

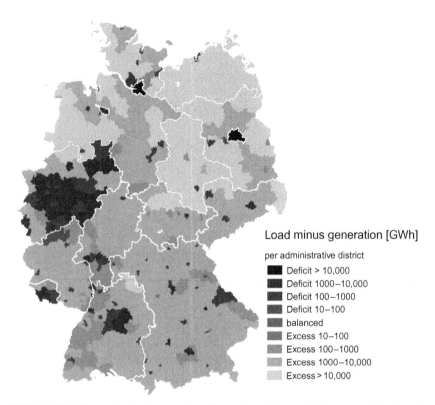

FIGURE 15.3 Theoretical degree of self-supply within administrative districts in Germany. *(Source: translated from Matthes et al. (2018).)*

and supply individually could increase overall system stability. However, there is so far not much scientific insight into the actual costs and benefits compared to a centralized approach. Moreover, data handling within IT systems needs to be distinguished from balancing the supply and demand of electricity. In order to address this issue and break down the system management, one alternative solution is to aggregate small-scale actors and to integrate them into the central market, for example as virtual power plants. In Germany, several new companies (e.g., Next Kraftwerke GmbH) as well as incumbent energy retailers specialize in aggregating supply and demand or even storage options and trading them as an aggregate on central markets.

- An additional argument for trading energy on a cell level is that it may result in higher participation of residents or at least an increased acceptance regarding renewables deployment. Again, detailed research is missing on the actual prerequisites for improved acceptance. Does acceptance require local balancing of demand and supply? Or is local production and ownership of renewable energy sufficient, including the option to buy regional products as described in Section 3?

Besides the drivers and the system effects of a compulsory cell structure, it is also important to discuss the possible effects on consumers and prosumers.

A compulsory cell structure does imply regional energy markets with regional **electricity prices**. The price for electricity, however, strongly depends on the geographical location of the cell and the natural options within the cell for cheap electricity generation. This is especially true if generation depends on variable renewable sources such as wind and radiation. Hence, for the consumer, the electricity price would highly depend on the location. This can lead to higher or lower prices compared to today's electricity prices. Also a cell structure would lead to markets with fewer generation units and market players compared to a country-wide market. This can lead to market power, its abuse, and as a result higher electricity prices.

On the one hand, the freedom of choice for consumers can be enlarged within a compulsory cell structure. Individuals have the option to engage in technology investments and participate in choosing the technology mix within the cell and its market. On the other hand, consumers are likely to be limited in their freedom of choice, as they have to participate in the cell that they are located in by default. Consumers would not be able to buy electricity from other markets. This could lead to a situation, which can be compared to heat-grid customers in Germany. In some cases, homeowners within a certain area are forced to consume heat from the local heat-grid and are stuck with a certain price.

The compulsory cell structure also impacts the level of complexity for the consumer. While the complexity of managing the system might be reduced due to smaller cells, the complexity for the consumer critically depends on the regulatory framework for the cell structure. If financial advantages for consumers within a cell are based on active participation within the cell such as investment in generation capacity or storage and its management, complexity for the individual consumer might rise. This issue also applies to peer-to-peer trading and providing flexibility to the network operator.

The cell concept has so far been mainly driven by technical considerations. However, it also implies various regulatory questions, which have yet to be addressed. First and foremost, compulsory cells within the energy system would also assign each generator and consumer to one specific cell. This would make investment decisions highly dependent on the expected regional energy prices. In addition, it can be questioned whether compulsory cells are in line with a liberalized market, such as the European internal electricity market. As opposed to regional marketing and peer-to-peer trading, both generators and consumers would be caught within one cell and would not have direct access to other markets.

Moreover, a new market role may be needed for managing the cell markets, including balancing. If a new market role has to be developed, how does this fit with the objective to reduce complexity? And last but not least: how will the borders of cells be defined and who decides on the structure of the cells? Would the definition of cells be aligned with the current grid infrastructure?

Overall this section has shown that the concept of subdividing the energy system into cells addresses several challenges of the system transition to higher shares of renewables. However, current concepts do not address important questions concerning markets, market roles, and overall system efficiency. These elements need to be further elaborated.

6. REGIONAL DISTRIBUTION OF RENEWABLES

An important dimension is the regional distribution of renewables, both in the debate on decentralization (including the role of consumers in general) and the implementation of the concepts described in the previous sections. The regional distribution as well as the technology mix of renewables influences the ability of people to participate regionally. The concepts described in the previous sections depend to a large degree on a regional distribution where generation and demand are geographically aligned. If there is only offshore wind, there is no real possibility for citizens to participate via regional energy cooperatives, to increase "self-generation" or to trade regional electricity products as described in Section 3. Regional flexibility markets for network management would not play an important role either.

Therefore, the development of decentralization along the lines discussed in the previous sections and changes to traditional business models is linked to mechanisms that influence the regional distribution of renewable energies.

The regional distribution in Germany is affected by the national support mechanism as well as the planning and permitting processes, which vary depending on the federal state.

The investment decision by wind developers based on a maximization of the electricity output and the resulting regional distribution can be questioned from a microeconomic perspective: Since the liberalization of the energy market, there has been no incentive for power plant operators to take grid constraints into account in their locational decision. As investments in the grid are paid by consumers, electricity prices can rise because of suboptimal location decisions. If there were a market-based or regulatory mechanism for locational decisions,[7] they would be likely to change.

An economically optimal model takes into account the energy system as a whole and includes annual variable costs as well as investment in new renewable power plants, storage capacities, and grid infrastructure for society. Models that do take into account these elements show results that are different from what can be observed due to the current Renewable Energy Law (Erneuerbare-Energien-Gesetz – EEG) financing mechanism for renewables.

Another method not only focuses on economic efficiency. Rather, starting from a given overall renewable capacity, it prioritizes generation that is close to demand. In this case, optimization involves looking at the optimal capacity of renewables and the optimal technology mix in specific regions to minimize the absolute level of residual demand for each region. As a result, this leads to a reduced need for grid extension. Such an approach is a prerequisite especially for a cell approach as outlined in Section 5.

The differences in the resulting regional distributions of the renewables can be examined in current energy market scenarios, for example in Matthes et al. (2018). In scenarios, which make assumptions based on the EEG such as the German network development plan (50Hertz Transmission GmbH et al., 2017, scenario B 2030), there is a high installed capacity of wind energy turbines in the north-eastern part of Germany, while the capacity is rather low in the South and West. Scenarios, which develop the distribution of wind turbines via an overall economic optimization, present a more equal regional distribution of the capacity, e.g., the "dezentral 2030" scenario developed by Rainer Lemoine Institut and BEE (2013). Finally, scenarios, which install the capacity of wind energy turbines in a decentralized, demand-orientated way, place a lot of wind energy turbines in regions with a high electricity demand, especially in the South and the West.

Different framework conditions can lead to different regional distributions, which could move from the North East to the South and West.

---

[7]Different possibilities of such mechanisms are discussed in Korte and Gawel (2018).

The definition of so-called grid extension regions in the current EEG may facilitate such a change.[8] Renewables closer to demand could be more efficient from a system perspective. At the same time, such a development is strongly linked to a new role for consumers and the concepts described in the previous sections.

7. CONCLUSIONS

The electricity system was historically characterized by top-down planning. This has been changed by the liberalization of electricity markets, but energy policy has maintained its pivotal role in designing the overall system framework. With the transformation toward renewables as a long-term political project, this role of policy has further increased.

At the same time, renewables and other developments challenge a top-down, centralized approach and decisions made by a surging number of prosumagers could transform the power system. However, a long-term political strategy to achieve long-term targets still seems paramount.

This chapter has shown various approaches that are currently being discussed and tested in the German market. They all challenge the centralized market paradigm, albeit in different ways. All these approaches depend on a regional distribution of renewables.

First, using regional flexibility for network management challenges the copper plate paradigm and can lead to new regional markets and can create new opportunities for flexibility providers including prosumagers. This complements the centralized market.

Second, regional energy marketing and peer-to-peer trading could transform the power market in a more fundamental and bottom-up way. The questions remain (1) whether there is a significantly higher willingness-to-pay for specific, e.g., regional products and (2) to what extent different regional and P2P markets will converge into more centralized markets.

Finally, the cell concept can only be implemented based on a top-down restructuring of the power market, as the cells would have to be defined centrally. This would lead to a completely different power market and leave the link to a centralized market still largely open.

Overall, power systems will become decentralized and new roles for consumers will emerge, although some of these developments are more valuable than others from an overall system perspective.

---

[8] In grid extension regions, there is a yearly cap on new wind energy turbines (EEG, §36c). This could lead to the installation of ca. 2.5 GW of wind energy turbines in the South.

REFERENCES

50Hertz Transmission GmbH, Amprion GmbH, TenneT TSO GmbH, TransnetBW GmbH, 2017. Netzentwicklungsplan Strom 2030 Szenariorahmen Version 2017: Ausführliche Fassung. 50Hertz Transmission GmbH; Amprion GmbH; TenneT TSO GmbH; TransnetBW GmbH. 66 pp.

BEUC, 2016. Current practices in consumer-driven renewable electricity markets. 184 pp. (Accessed 11 February 2016).

Bundesministerium für Wirtschaft und Energie, 2016. Regionale Grünstromkennzeichnung, Eckpunktepapier, 11. März 2016. 6 pp.

Bundesnetzagentur, 2018. Veröffentlichung der PV-Mieterstrom-Meldezahlen - Juli 2017 bis Mai 2018.

Bundesregierung, 2017. Anreizregulierungsverordnung: ARegV. 29 pp.

Bündnis Bürgerenergie e.V, 2015. Das bringt Bürgerenergie: 10 gute Gründe für eine breite Akteursvielfalt. 15 pp.

Council of the European Union, 2018. Proposal for a Directive of the European Parliament and of the Council on the promotion of the use of energy from renewable sources - Analysis of the final compromise text with a view to agreement Interinstitutional File: 2016/0382 (COD) Date: 21 June 2018. 269 pp.

DIW, 2015. Energiewende und Strommarktdesign: Zwei Preiszonen für Deutschland sind keine Lösung. DIW WOCHENBERICHT NR. 9/2015 VOM 25. FEBRUAR 2015.

enyway GmbH, 2018. Nicht einfach Ökostrom, sondern Ökostrom aus deiner Region!. https://www.enyway.com. (Accessed April 30, 2018).

EWE, 2017. enera. http://energie-vernetzen.de/en/project.

Frontier Economics, Consentec, 2011. Bedeutung von etablierten nationalen Gebotszonen für die Integration des europäischen Strommarkts ein Ansatz zur wohlfahrtsorientierten Beurteilung, Bonn. 144 pp. (Accessed 12 March 2018).

Funcke, S., Bauknecht, D., 2016. Typology of centralised and decentralised visions for electricity infrastructure. Util. Policy 40, 67–74. https://doi.org/10.1016/j.jup.2016.03.005.

KfW Bankengruppe, 2018. Solarkraft auf Abruf. https://www.kfw.de/stories/umwelt/erneuerbare-energien/sonnenbatterie-fuer-privathaushalte/. (Accessed June 26, 2018).

Koch, M., Flachsbarth, F., Bauknecht, D., Heinemann, C., Ritter, D., Winger, C., Timpe, C., Gandor, M., Klingenberg, T., Tröschel, M., 2017. Dispatch of flexibility options, grid infrastructure and integration of renewable energies within a decentralized electricity system. In: Bertsch, V., Fichtner, W., Heuveline, V., Leibfried, T. (Eds.), Advances in energy system optimization. Proceedings of the first International Symposium on Energy System Optimization. Birkhäuser, Cham, Switzerland. pp. 67–86.

Korte, K., Gawel, E., 2018. Räumliche Koordination im liberalisierten Strommarkt: angemessene Anreize für die Einspeisung. Analysen und Berichte Energiepolitik. ZBW - Leibnitz- Informationszentrum Wirtschaft, 8 pp. https://doi.org/10.1007/s10273-018-2242-6 (Accessed 16 April 2018).

Maaß, C., Güldenberg, J., Mundt, J., Werner, R., 2017. Theoretische Fundierung der regionalen Grünstromkennzeichnung in Deutschland. Endbericht. Climate Change 17/2017, Dessau, 73 pp. (Accessed 30 April 2018).

Matthes, F.C., Flachsbarth, F., Vogel, M., Cook, V., 2018. Dezentralität, Regionalisierung und Stromnetze: Meta-Studie über Annahmen, Erkenntnisse und Narrative. Oeko-Institut, Berlin. 87 pp. (Accessed 18 April 2018).

Oppen, M.V., Streitmayer, A., Huneke, F., 2017. A proposal for prosumer electricity trading, Berlin. 23 pp.

Reiner Lemoine Institut gGmbH, BEE, 2013. Vergleich und Optimierung von zentral und dezentral orientierten Ausbaupfaden zu einer Stromversorgung aus Erneuerbaren Energien in Deutschland. Studie im Auftrag von Haleakala-Stiftung, 100 prozent erneuerbar stiftung, Bundesverband mittelständische Wirtschaft (BVMW). Reiner Lemoine Institut, Berlin. 92 pp http://reiner-lemoine-institut.de/wp-content/publications/0_Vergleich_und_Optimierung_zentral_und_dezentral_071_100EE/Breyer2013.pdf. (Accessed February 5, 2018).

Smart Grids-Plattform Baden-Württemberg e.V, 2017. Die C/sells Leitidee: Zellularität, Partizipation und Vielfältigkeit. Smart Grids-Plattform Baden-Württemberg e.V. http://www.csells.net/ueber-c-sells/leitidee.html. (Accessed October 4, 2017).

TenneT, Sonnen GmbH, 2018. Europaweit erstes Blockchain-Projekt zur Stabilisierung des Stromnetzes startet: TenneT und sonnen erwarten Ergebnisse 2018. 2 pp.

The Regulatory Assistance Project, 2014. Netzentgelte in Deutschland, Berlin. 46 pp. (Accessed 9 April 2018).

Umweltbundesamt, 2017. Theoretische Fundierung der regionalen Grünstromkennzeichnung in Deutschland. Clim. Change. 17/2017, 73 pp.

USEF Foundation, 2015. USEF: The Framework Explained, Amsterdam. 55 pp. (Accessed 9 April 2018).

VDE, 2015. Der zellulare Ansatz: Grundlage einer erfolgreichen, regionenübergreifenden Energiewende. In: Verband der Elektrotechnik Elektronik Informationstechnik/Energietechnische Gesellschaft. Main, Frankfurt am. 96 pp. (Accessed 9 September 2015).

Verband der Elektrotechnik Elektronik Informationstechnik e.V, 2014. Regionale Flexibilitätsmärkte: Marktbasierte Nutzung von regionalen Flexibilitätsoptionen als Baustein zur erfolgreichen Integration von erneuerbaren Energien in die Verteilnetze. VDE-Studie 2014, Frankfurt a. M, 116 pp. (Accessed 30 September 2014).

Wirth, T. von, Gislason, L., Seidl, R., 2018. Distributed energy systems on a neighborhood scale: Reviewing drivers of and barriers to social acceptance. Renewable and Sustainable Energy Reviews 82, 2618–2628.

WSW Energie, Wasser, A.G., 2018. https://wsw-talmarkt.de. (Accessed April 30, 2018).

CHAPTER 16

Designing Markets for Innovative Electricity Services in the EU: The Roles of Policy, Technology, and Utility Capabilities

Guillermo Ivan Pereira*,†,§, **Patrícia Pereira da Silva***,†,‡, **Deborah Soule**§

*Energy for Sustainability Initiative, MIT Portugal Program in Sustainable Energy Systems, University of Coimbra, Coimbra, Portugal
†INESC Coimbra, Institute for Systems Engineering and Computers at Coimbra, Coimbra, Portugal
‡CeBER, Centre for Business and Economics Research, Faculty of Economics, University of Coimbra, Coimbra, Portugal
§Massachusetts Institute of Technology, Cambridge, MA, United States

1. INTRODUCTION

Traditional distribution network utilities, operating at the interface of large-scale generation and consumer electricity demand, are increasingly challenged to transition to a cleaner and more digital electricity sector (Pereira and Silva, 2017). The growth of decentralized generation, transportation electrification, and the evolving maturity of electricity storage technologies have contributed to establishing distributed energy resources as an important building block of a future electricity system (Castro and Dantas, 2017). These new resources, more variable and volatile than traditional generation technologies, are scattered throughout the grid. Their characteristics and integration in the grid create the need for utilities to access more granular and readily available data, enhance automation and control of the infrastructure, and reinforce their digital communication technologies (IEA, 2011; IRENA, 2015). The presence of these new energy resources on the grid also demands increased monitoring and management.

In this context, there is a virtuous cycle between the diffusion of smart grid and digital technologies and the deployment of distributed energy resources. As described in other chapters of the book, at the intersection of distributed energy resources and digital smart grid technologies, the role of electricity consumers is also evolving. Connected consumers, once passive participants in the electricity system, are now adopting technologies and behaviors that make them an important part of the future electricity sector and utilities. A new profile of consumer is evident as the use of smart grid and distributed energy resource technologies creates possibilities for consumers to be directly engaged in the provision of innovative energy services – especially those that rely on customer data, use consumer-owned energy generation assets, or require new consumer behaviors.

Innovative energy services can include those that directly improve energy provision by achieving greater electricity distribution flexibility. Such services might rely on distributed generation, electricity storage, electric vehicle charging management and coordination, and/or demand response actions and energy efficiency measures. Additionally, innovative services can also include those that indirectly improve energy provision by monetizing energy consumption data. Such services could support distribution utilities through the purchase of consumption data or the provision of new product and marketing insights from that data. Innovative services will likely involve companies beyond the current electricity value chain, such as data analytics and marketing firms.

This book examines how new energy services, resulting from an evolving policy and technology framework, are disrupting the traditional utility business and allowing for new customer interactions and relationships. The evolving transition to a clean and smart electricity sector is challenging existing distribution utilities' business models as well as legacy technologies and infrastructure. In addition, this transition also challenges existing market designs and the associated regulatory practices (Pereira et al., 2018a,b; Pérez-Arriaga, 2013).

This chapter contributes to this discussion by studying the ongoing market redesign efforts in the European Union (EU). This is achieved by describing recent policy and technology adaptation efforts contributing to enable distribution utilities to participate in the ongoing disruption of the electricity sector's status quo. Additionally, key indicators from a survey on business model adaptation from EU distribution utilities are presented as a proxy on business model innovation capabilities. The EU-level insights provided in this chapter give a complementary view to other regional perspectives offered in this volume.

Furthermore, this chapter and its insights on policy and technology adaptation governance, and the role of utilities' adaptation capabilities for business model innovation provide a complementary perspective to recent contributions focusing mostly on the regulatory aspects of the utilities of the future (Meeus and Glachant, 2018; Pérez-Arriaga et al., 2013;

Pérez-Arriaga and Knittel, 2016; Ruester et al., 2014). Our approach offers a better understanding of utilities' readiness for new business models designed for the emerging energy products and services driving the current shift in the utility paradigm.

The chapter is organized in five sections:

- Section 2 describes ongoing policy adaptation efforts in the EU intended to design a market supporting the transition of the electricity sector;
- Section 3 describes distribution utility efforts and progress in technological adaptation, particularly the development and integration of distributed energy resources and smart, digital, technologies; and
- Section 4 unveils the results of a EU survey measuring business model adaptation capabilities of electricity distribution utilities followed by the chapter's conclusions presented in Section 5.

2. EUROPEAN UNION MARKET DESIGN AND POLICY ADAPTATION

The ambition to deliver an internal electricity market for EU consumers has been a long-standing ambition of the European Commission and its Member States. The importance of delivering clean, affordable, and secure electricity has motivated the dedication of efforts and resources to adjust the existing liberalized electricity sector market design (European Commission, 2012). Specifically, distribution utilities' natural monopoly roles and responsibilities need to evolve to meet the challenges and embrace the opportunities of having more renewables and smart grid technologies connected to the grid.

To deliver on this ambition, the Energy Union policy package, introduced in 2015, set the priorities for delivering an integrated energy system, with consumers at its core as stated here (European Commission, 2015a):

> *[…] our vision is of an Energy Union with citizens at its core, where citizens take ownership of the energy transition, benefit from new technologies to reduce their bills, participate actively in the market, and where vulnerable consumers are protected. To reach our goal, we have to move away from an economy driven by fossil fuels, an economy where energy is based on a centralized, supply-side approach and which relies on old technologies and outdated business models. We have to empower consumers through providing them with information, choice and through creating flexibility to manage demand as well as supply. We have to move away from a fragmented system characterized by uncoordinated national policies, market barriers and energy-isolated areas.*

> *(European Commission, 2015a, p. 2)*

This vision highlights the importance of fundamentally transforming the electricity system and the role of adapting technologies and business models to enable new services and empower consumers. Moreover, this Energy Union proposes an integrated regulatory framework in lieu of the current arrangement in which 28 Member State–level regulatory approaches coexist under the European Union climate and energy policies (European Commission, 2015a). The scope of action of the Energy Union is wide ranging, targeting broad-based adaptation of the European energy system, Fig. 16.1. Nevertheless, within this broader ambition, it is possible to identify specific steps that focus on the transformation of the electricity system, directly affecting distribution utilities business models and electricity sector market designs.[1]

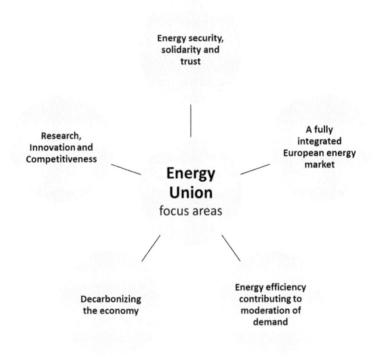

FIGURE 16.1 Energy Union focus areas. *(Source: Authors, adapted from European Commission (2015a).)*

[1]The approach and ambitions of the EU's Energy Union are comparable to the vision pushng forward the New York Reforming the Energy Vision strategy, supported by the New York State Energy Plan to build a clean, resilient, and affordable energy system for all New Yorkers (New York State, 2014).

The Energy Union focus area for a fully integrated European energy market has direct implications for the electricity sector. Its focus includes reforming both the sector's infrastructure and policies. In terms of infrastructure, it specifies the importance of increased interconnections among Member State's electricity systems. Only with an adequately interconnected electricity market can European citizens access and benefit from a common pool of increasingly clean energy resources. In this regard, an interconnection target of 10% of the installed electricity production capacity of each Member State has been set for 2020, and a target of 15% for 2030. The policy package also highlights the significant investments needed to update existing infrastructure and introduce smart grid and digital technologies.

Regarding the electricity sector's policy framework, the Energy Union aims to ensure the adequate implementation of existing policies – namely, the full implementation of the 3rd Electricity Sector Package, Directive 2009/72/EC. This will provide a strong foundation for introducing policy proposals that shape existing market designs. Electricity sector market redesign is driven by the increase in renewable energy sources connected to the grids, which requires greater levels of system flexibility management. Achieving the required demand and supply-side flexibilities will require infrastructure adaptation, but also an adjustment of the regulatory frameworks that ultimately shape the distribution utilities' business model.

Building on the momentum created by the Energy Union package, the European Commission is adapting the electricity sector market design, through the Clean Energy for All Europeans policy proposals (European Commission, 2016a). These proposals are motivated by the increased penetration of distributed renewables and digitalization of the electricity sector, which create new possibilities for businesses and households to use, generate, store, and trade electricity, a message repeated throughout this volume. Reforming existing utility roles and approaches to market design is therefore essential to enable these possibilities (European Commission, 2017b).

These policy proposals also specify roles for electricity distribution utilities – or "Distribution System Operators" (DSOs) in the EU context – including their involvement in system flexibility management, electric vehicle–charging infrastructure, data management, smart metering, and distributed generation management. The proposals for a new electricity directive – as a recast of Directive 2009/72/EC – give distribution utilities the responsibility to cost effectively integrate distributed generation from renewables, heat pumps, and electric vehicles. The proposals reflect the importance of enabling and incentivizing access and use of these new resources to the benefit of the grid's management and operational efficiency. They also suggest distribution utilities play a role in procuring services through distributed energy resources, demand response, and electricity storage technologies. Services should be accessed through market-based approaches, used to achieve greater efficiency in distribution network operation, and minimize expensive network reinforcements and expansions whenever possible.

These renewed electricity market design policies give Member States guidance on the steps necessary to implement this new distribution network reality. Each EU country is called to implement distribution network use guidelines, in the form of network codes, and market rules for the provision of new services and how distribution utilities can access these services. Network tariff redesign is also a key area of action, intended to reduce barriers to flexibility services, and enable the improvement of grid efficiency.[2] Additionally, European countries are now responsible for introducing distribution network development roadmaps. These roadmaps are expected to support the adequate integration of renewable distributed generation, the development of storage facilities, and the electrification of transport. Moreover, the roadmaps will allow system users to understand the future expansion and reinforcement plans of distribution grids. Roadmaps must be published at least every 2 years and provide information on the medium- and long-term flexibility services needed.

The ongoing market design policy proposals provide guidance for future EU distribution utilities by indicating that their responsibilities include the long-term capacity of the distribution system, in addition to the economically efficient operation of the networks, minimizing environmental impacts, and supporting energy efficiency improvements. Beside their core electricity distribution responsibilities, distribution utilities now have incentives to procure flexibility services, including congestion management services, to improve network infrastructure management and efficiency.

The policies highlight the need for a regulatory framework enabling these new services. This framework must ensure the nondiscriminatory participation of all market players in this new market for flexibility services, including the owners and managers of renewable energy generation units, electricity storage, demand response, and aggregators. Additionally, the

---

[2]Burger et al. in this volume explore the challenges of new tariff designs and associated trade-offs on an increasingly digital and decentralized electricity system. Furthermore, Abdelmotteleb et al., also in this volume, provide insights for enabling flexibility mechanisms through new tariff signals.

regulations to be implemented must consider the remuneration of the costs incurred by distribution utilities in procuring these new services, including digital technologies and infrastructure costs. Further, all electricity sector stakeholders must have nondiscriminatory access to relevant data. The future EU electricity market design promises distribution utilities access to the benefits of flexibility services, while generally prohibiting their ownership, development, management, and operation of electro mobility charging points and electricity storage (Table 16.1).

In sum, these market design proposals clarify the role of electricity distribution utilities in providing innovative services based on the growing share of distributed energy resources and digital technologies. Specifically, the policy framework argues for implementing and developing flexibility services through market-based mechanisms while ensuring that distribution grids can benefit by procuring these new services as a source of increased operational and investment efficiency.

3. TECHNOLOGICAL INNOVATION AND DEVELOPMENT

In addition to an updated electricity market policy framework, the evolution of the EU energy system also requires technological innovation and research to achieve a decentralized, decarbonized, and digital electricity sector – the 3Ds. The Energy Union addresses this challenge in the focus area on Research, Innovation, and Competitiveness (Fig. 16.1). It promotes an integrated innovation ecosystem in which academic-industrial collaborations can develop and market technologies effectively, putting the EU at the forefront of renewable energy, storage, and smart grid technologies (European Commission, 2015a).

The EU's strategic energy technologies plan – SET Plan – outlines priorities for research and technology adaptation in Europe's energy system (European Commission, 2015b). The reinforced SET Plan promotes the shift to a smarter, more flexible, and integrated approach to deliver energy to consumers. The plan includes (European Commission, 2015b, 2018):

- A set of focus areas including renewables, consumers at the center of the energy system, energy efficiency, sustainable transport, carbon capture and storage, and nuclear energy safety;
- An integrated innovation approach that prioritizes the identification of new opportunities to increase flexibility, and resilience; and
- A new technology innovation and development governance approach, more result oriented and with greater transparency.

Table 16.1 Distribution utility responsibilities in new market design

Activity	Distribution utility responsibility				
	Own	Develop	Manage	Operate	Exception
Integration of electromobility assets (recharging points)	No	No	No	No	– No other parties were granted this activity. – Is approved by the regulator. – The operation occurs in a nondiscriminatory manner.
Electricity storage facilities	No	No	No	No	– No other parties were granted this activity. – Is approved by the regulator. – The operation occurs in a nondiscriminatory manner. – When electricity storage facilities are fully integrated network components.

Source: Authors, adapted from Council of the European Union (2017) and European Commission (2017a).

Table 16.2 SET plan support to Energy Union priorities

Energy Union priority	Strategic Energy Technology plan action
- Global leadership in renewable energy technology - Smart energy systems with consumers at its core - Energy efficiency, with focus on the building stock - Sustainable transport technologies and services - Carbon capture innovation for storage and use - Safe operation of nuclear energy sources	- Develop low-cost renewables - Solutions for energy consumers - Flexible energy systems - Energy efficiency in buildings - Energy efficiency in energy intensive industries - Battery technology for electromobility and stationary use - Renewable fuels and bioenergy - Carbon capture and storage - Carbon capture and use - Nuclear safety

Sources: Authors, adapted from European Commission (2015a,b, 2016b).

The SET plan strives for a focused and efficient technological research and innovation adaptation process, by identifying areas of action that contribute to Energy Union priorities, Table 16.2. Additionally, it supports the coordination of low-carbon innovation at the EU and national levels (European Commission, 2018).

The Energy Union's emphasis on smart, consumer-centric energy systems, together with the SET plan for achieving smarter, more resilient, and secure energy systems, directly affect the electricity sector and distribution utilities. This action area targets the development and demonstration of innovative power system components, more flexible thermal generation, demand response and storage technologies and services, in addition to more efficient heat pumps and combined heat and power units. It also supports advances in electricity transmission technologies, techniques for physical and cyber security, and demand data analytics (European Commission, 2015b).

Delivering technological innovation in these areas will ultimately transform the electricity system and utilities' operations and business models. The European Technology and Innovation Platform on Smart Networks for the Energy Transition – ETIP SNET – brings together a diverse set of EU stakeholders to support this transformation. It aims to define a strategy for research and innovation, identify existing barriers to innovation, and effectively exploit research and innovation outputs (ETIP SNET, 2017).

The strategy of ETIP SNET considers the policy push for electricity markets and system transformation promoted by the Energy Union, which will impact electricity generation, transmission, and distribution networks, while calling for new ways of interaction between networks operators, integration of new technologies as well as greater system interconnection. It particularly aims to address upcoming network infrastructure challenges associated with the growing need for flexibility options. Changes challenging the role, planning, and management of network infrastructures include the following (ETIP SNET, 2016b):

- Variable generation connected to networks often located far from consumption areas;
- Changes in load characteristics partly due to the electrification of mobility and building energy efficiency measures;
- Integration of European electricity transmission networks and associated governance; and
- Expansion of the EU internal energy market, consequently increasing the scope of responsibilities and interaction of market makers – transmission and distribution utilities – with market players.

Considering these broader trends, specific challenges for distribution utilities have been identified[3] that contribute to the development of an adequate technological adaptation and innovation plan for distribution grids (ETIP SNET, 2016b). In this regard, electricity distribution utilities will have a key role in facilitating end-user participation in retail markets because of their involvement in shaping future market designs and regulations. Data management and analytical capabilities will be necessary at the distribution level. Possible applications may range from generation to consumer behavior forecasting to network infrastructure monitoring, maintenance, and planning. Distribution utilities will also need to plan for the necessary network reinforcement to accommodate both electrification of mobility and changes in building loads resulting from energy efficiency improvements. Additionally, they will need to deploy information and communication technologies, such as smart meters, in supporting a more engaged consumer base. Lastly, utilities should also ensure the necessary infrastructure and operational processes for the growing share of variable renewable generation connected to the distribution network (ETIP SNET, 2016b). To address these distribution-specific challenges, the planned research and

---

[3]Stanley et al., in this volume, provide a complementary perspective on the challenges for distribution utiltiies.

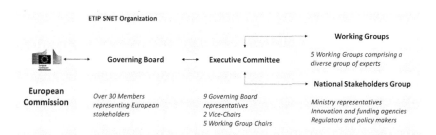

FIGURE 16.2 ETIP SNET platform organizational structure. *(Source: Authors, adapted from ETIP SNET (2017).)*

innovation actions focus on network upgrades, system flexibility and reliability, digitalization, market design, and regulation.

Recognizing the complexity of this innovation task, combined with the diversity across EU countries, the ETIP SNET proposes a structured governance approach, as shown in Fig. 16.2.

The existing Working Groups focus on the key priorities of innovation and technological adaptation, as follows:

- Reliable, economic, and efficient smart grid system: focusing on exploring disruptive business and technology opportunities that support energy system optimization through affordable investment and operational costs.
- Storage technologies and sector interfaces: targets new technology developments for storage applications that can increase system flexibility.
- Flexible generation: considers the technology and business model opportunities to support the delivery of the flexibility needs on an integrated power system.
- Digitalization of the electricity system and consumer participation: evaluates upgrading information and communication technologies across the entire value chain to enable new business models and services.
- Innovation implementation on the business environment: focuses on ensuring that the EU industry is engaging on the relevant research and innovation areas to deliver the electricity sector of the future.

Complementing the thematic Working Groups, the National Stakeholders Group ensures that the innovation and technological adaptation efforts match the needs and trends at the country level, by liaising with national governments and regulators. Fig. 16.3 illustrates the interactions of the different working groups across domains.

In addition to guiding innovation on the future power system, the ETIP SNET estimates the financial resources needed to deliver the

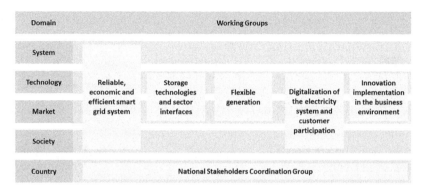

FIGURE 16.3 Working group interactions across domains. *(Source: Authors, adapted from ETIP SNET (2016a).)*

proposed innovations. Table 16.3 shows the estimated investment needs for the research and innovation areas related to electricity distribution, and which will influence distribution utility technology adaptation most directly. These estimates are the total investments expected from all relevant stakeholders from 2017 to 2026.

The future of electricity distribution utilities will depend to a significant extent on delivering the research and innovation roadmap set through the ETIP SNET and reaching the estimated investment needs. Aware of the complexity of its energy ambitions, in 2018 the European Commission and its Member States introduced a set of initiatives to accelerate technological adaptation and innovation, and complement the aforementioned efforts. The actions are introduced as an implementation plan for the ambition of the Strategic Energy Technologies Plan – SET Plan – focus area to increase the resilience, security, smartness of the energy system (European Commission, 2015b, 2018).

This implementation plan is wider in scope and complements ongoing efforts in transforming the power system infrastructure. In the collaborative process of structuring the implementation plan, the key European energy system stakeholders introduced two complementary flagship initiatives to ensure the necessary efforts for adapting electricity systems, and a crosscutting support imitative (European Commission, 2018).

The flagship initiative for optimized power systems aims to deliver an optimized European-level power system. Its ambitions include the delivery of the necessary technological innovation to support system reliability, and economic and operational efficiency, while increasingly being able to accommodate higher shares of variable renewables. This will include

Table 16.3 Investment needs for distribution system research and innovation priorities

Cluster	M€	%	Focus area	M€	%
Integration of smart customers and buildings	263	18%	Active demand response	124	8%
			Energy efficiency from integration with smart homes and buildings	139	9%
Integration of decentralized generation, demand, storage, and networks	622	42%	System integration of small DER	68	5%
			System integration of medium DER	79	5%
			Integration of storage in network management	100	7%
			Infrastructure to host EV/PHEV – Electrification of transport	100	7%
			Integration with other energy networks	150	10%
			Integration of flexible decentralized thermal power generation	125	8%
Network operations	442	30%	Monitoring and control of LV network	142	10%
			Automation and control of MV network	100	7%
			Smart metering data processing and other big data applications	100	7%
			Cyber security (system approach)	100	7%
Planning and asset management	148	10%	New planning approaches and tools	100	7%
			Asset management	48	3%
Total	1,475			1,475	

Source: Authors, adapted from ETIP SNET (2016b).

technologies that increase system flexibility and enable consumer participation. This initiative needs an estimated investment of 350 M€ per year until 2024.

The flagship initiative for local and regional energy systems aims to deliver integrated local and regional energy systems that enable the integration and efficient use of high shares of renewables. This will contribute to achieving local sustainability ambitions at the community level, while supporting the goal of reaching a fully integrated European energy system that fosters the sustainable use of clean energy sources across countries. This initiative needs an estimated investment of €250 M per year until 2025.

The ambitions of these initiatives are supported by a crosscutting action focused on innovation environments for smart devices and services. This action will address the digitalization of the sector and cybersecurity capability development, as well as new market models and regulatory options to support field experiments. This initiative needs an estimated investment of 100 M€ per year until 2022.

The technology adaptation and innovation efforts steered through the Energy Union demonstrate the intricate governance proposals to support innovation across 28 countries. The ambitious goals of both the ETIP SNET and the SET plan's flagship initiatives will require substantial investments and stakeholder engagement across EU countries. Thus, it is valuable to consider past EU engagement and investments in smart grid research and innovation as an indicator of European countries' abilities to deliver on these goals.

The European Commission Joint Research Centre, through its Smart Grid Observatory, provides an analysis of the evolution of smart grid investments across the EU. The latest available results include information from 950 projects, totaling almost 5 Billion Euros in investment, up until 2015. Fig. 16.4 shows the cumulative investments for both research and development and demonstration projects across the EU. The positive investment trend indicates the growing importance of smart grid innovations, as well as the ability of European countries to deliver such investments.

In this context, distribution utilities invest most heavily in demonstration projects, while universities lead investment in research and development projects (Gangale et al., 2017). Fig. 16.5 shows a breakdown of the cumulative investments by stakeholder and project category between 2004 and 2015.

These EU projects explore smart network management; demand-side management; integration of distributed generation and storage; electromobility; integration of large-scale renewable energy generation; and other applications

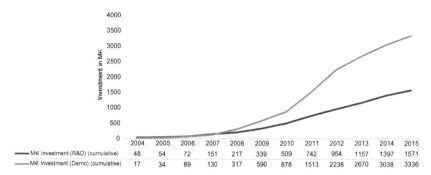

	2004	2005	2006	2007	2008	2009	2010	2011	2012	2013	2014	2015
M€ Investment (R&D) (cumulative)	48	54	72	151	217	339	509	742	954	1157	1397	1571
M€ Investment (Demo) (cumulative)	17	34	69	130	317	590	878	1513	2238	2670	3038	3336

FIGURE 16.4 Research and development investment on smart grid projects in the EU, M€. *(Source: Authors, adapted from Gangale et al. (2017).)*

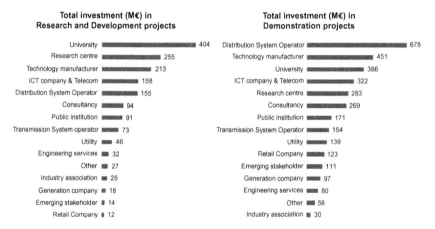

Total investment (M€) in Research and Development projects

University	404
Research centre	255
Technology manufacturer	213
ICT company & Telecom	158
Distribution System Operator	155
Consultancy	94
Public institution	91
Transmission System operator	73
Utility	46
Engineering services	32
Other	27
Industry association	25
Generation company	18
Emerging stakeholder	14
Retail Company	12

Total investment (M€) in Demonstration projects

Distribution System Operator	678
Technology manufacturer	451
University	386
ICT company & Telecom	322
Research centre	283
Consultancy	269
Public institution	171
Transmission System Operator	154
Utility	139
Retail Company	123
Emerging stakeholder	111
Generation company	97
Engineering services	80
Other	58
Industry association	30

FIGURE 16.5 Investments by stakeholder category, M€. *(Source: Authors, adapted from Gangale et al. (2017).)*

including market and regulatory models, cybersecurity, to name a few. Fig. 16.6 shows the investments in these areas between 2004 and 2015 per type of project.

Notably, private funds represent the majority of EU investment in smart grid innovation, as indicated in Fig. 16.7. However, European Commission and National funding, through support schemes, also play an important role. Only 15% of the 950 projects are exclusively supported through private funding. The remainder are sponsored by a combination of private, European Commission, and National funds.

In sum, the combination of ambitious but well-defined technological innovation plans and evidence of investment capacity necessary to advance these plans points to a positive outlook for building the future capabilities for distribution utilities.

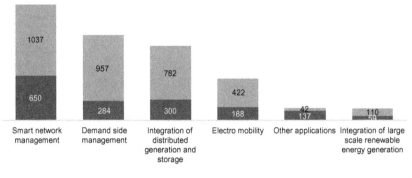

FIGURE 16.6 Investments by project focus area, M€. *(Source: Authors, adapted from Gangale et al. (2017).)*

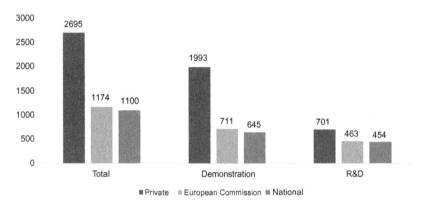

FIGURE 16.7 Investment funding sources, M€. *(Source: Authors, adapted from Gangale et al. (2017).)*

So far, this chapter has discussed both policy-driven and technology-focused efforts to transform the EU energy sector and, especially, its electricity distribution utilities. These efforts contribute to establishing a framework in which utilities are also given space to take potentially disruptive actions, therefore supporting the transformation of the electricity sector. The following section considers the industry's capacity for transformation by focusing on the EU distribution utilities' adaptation capabilities.

4. DISTRIBUTION UTILITIES BUSINESS MODEL ADAPTATION CAPABILITIES

As described in the previous sections, the EU is strengthening its governance structures to adapt policy and technology to support the transformation of distribution utilities. An enabling policy and technology framework is an essential support in adapting utilities to a rapidly changing electricity sector. Utility adaptation involves the ability to interact with new technologies and comply with new policies and regulatory frameworks. Such adaptation will subsequently support the emergence of innovative business models and new services, adding value for connected consumers and other stakeholders.

Although the need for distribution utility business model adaptation is clear, the ability of utilities to achieve this adaptation has received limited attention. To better understand business model innovation and adaptation by distribution utilities, the authors collected data about adaptation capabilities from 129 EU distribution utilities.[4]

Discussion of the future of utilities often focuses on resources such as their physical assets, e.g., grids, substations, or information and communication systems, their connected consumers, and their integration of a growing number of distributed energy resources. Utility capabilities are their abilities to organize and use their resources efficiently and effectively (Henkel et al., 2014).

Capabilities fall into two categories: operational and dynamic (Teece, 2017):

- Operational capabilities relate to core operations and include, for instance, technological capabilities corresponding to the extent to which a utility can best manage and use its technologies (i.e., grids, smart meters, automation systems)
- Dynamic capabilities are strategic and correspond to the extent to which utilities can adapt to a rapidly changing industry and, consequently, adjust not only their resources but also their operational capabilities. The existence of dynamic capabilities can ultimately influence the ability for an organization to design and adjust its business model, thereby impacting business model innovation (Teece, 2018).

In the ongoing discussion about utilities of the future, knowledge of the present capabilities of EU distribution utilities can complement the earlier policy and technology perspectives. The results presented next aim to contribute to developing this knowledge. The dataset represents a diverse sample of EU distribution utilities spanning 27 countries (Figure 16.8).

In addition, the dataset includes utilities operating across different scales and organizational characteristics (Table 16.4), and thus represents the diversity present in the European electricity distribution industry (Eurelectric, 2013).

Questionnaire items to measure adaptation capabilities used Teece (2007) framing of adaptation as the result of sensing, seizing, and transforming capabilities (Inigo et al., 2017). Sensing capabilities correspond to the ability to identify technological changes and disruption, potential regulatory

---

[4]Between May and December 2017, a questionnaire was sent to 1,733 EU distribution utilities; responses from 129 were obtained, operating in 27 countries.

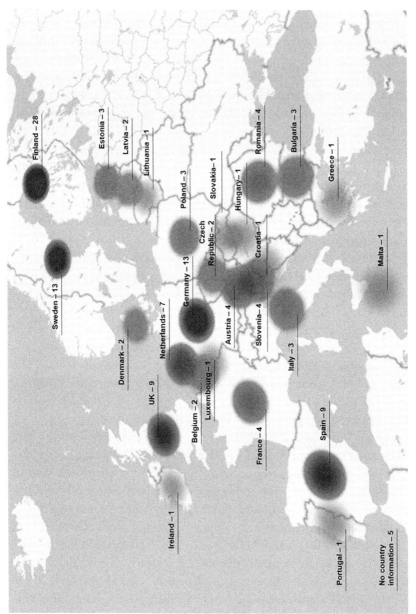

FIGURE 16.8 EU distribution utilities country of operation. (*Source: Authors.*)

Table 16.4 Distribution utilities sample characteristics (data for 2016)

Connected consumers	n	%	Age	n	%
1 to below 50,000	27	21	Up to 5	–	–
50,000 to below 150,000	10	8	5 to below 20	11	9
150,000 to below 350,000	8	6	20 to below 50	11	9
350,000 to below 1,000,000	53	41	Over 50	107	83
2,000,000 to below 5,000,000	11	9	Total	129	
Over 5,000,000	13	10			
Total	129				

measures, and current business model limitations. Seizing capabilities correspond to the ability to prepare for adaptation and transformation, for instance, by investing in new skills development, or acquiring and integrating new resources. Transforming capabilities correspond to the active ability to reorganize assets or drive other concrete business model changes. Analysis of the capability items,[5] using a Nonlinear Principal Components technique, yielded a set of three factors closely related to Teece's (2007) framework (Table 16.5).

The questionnaire also asked about electricity distribution performance (Table 16.6), innovation approaches (Table 16.7), and engagement in smart grid diffusion (Table 16.8).

Subsequent analyses examined the relationships between adaptation capabilities and electricity distribution performance, innovation approaches, and engagement in smart grid diffusion, respectively. Pearson's correlation coefficients[6] (r) were calculated to explore these associations (Pearson, 1920; Piovani, 2008).

The results indicate a positive association between sensing, learning, and transforming capabilities, and electricity distribution performance

---

[5]Participating distribution utilities rated their internal capabilities using ordinal Likert scales ranging from "1, not capable at all" to "6, extremely capable." We used a Nonlinear Principal Components Analysis technique, suited to identifying underlying dimensions from ordinal data (Linting et al., 2007; Linting and van der Kooij, 2012; Mori et al., 2016). In the analysis, Factors with Eigenvalues greater than 1 were retained (Ledesma and Valero-mora, 2007; Ruscio and Roche, 2012).
[6]Pearson's coefficients, or Pearson's r, provide a measure of linear correlation between variables. The coefficients obtained from the analyses range from −1 to 1, for which −1 represents a perfectly negative relationship, 0 represents no relationship, and 1 a perfectly positive relationship. We interpreted the results as follows: $1 < |r| < .3$ weak correlation; $.3 < |r| < .5$ moderate correlation, and $.5 < |r| < 1$ strong correlation.

Table 16.5 Factor analysis on adaptation capabilities

Questionnaire items	Identified dimensions		
	Sensing	Learning	Transforming
Identify technologies to improve the quality and efficiency of our operations	0.862[a]		
Identify new technologies (e.g., smart metering, electric vehicle charging infrastructure, flexibility management, etc.)	0.904		
Identify changes in policies and regulation to ensure the adequacy of our strategy	0.569		
Influence policies and regulation to be aligned with our business strategy		0.88	
Identify system changes (e.g., understanding the impact of distributed generation, the impact of the current DSO–TSO relationship, etc.)	0.66		
Identify the changing needs of grid users (e.g., accommodating the increasing number of smart homes, residential storage units, electric vehicles, etc.)	0.634		
Understand the implications of smart grid technologies			0.719
Learn to integrate new technologies			0.732
Understand the impact of policy and regulatory changes on our business		0.679	
Identify ways to adapt our business strategy to fit policy and regulatory requirements		0.734	
Identify the resources needed to adapt our business strategy			0.625
Identify the business areas that require adaptation			0.646
Adapt our organization to use new technologies (e.g., teams, responsibilities, departments, strategy; resource allocation, etc.)			0.826
Change our business to use new technologies			0.798
Adapt our activities and responsibilities given policy and regulatory changes			0.637
Implement business changes to explore opportunities from policy and regulatory changes			0.717
Analyze future strategies as we move toward a smarter grid environment			0.61
Develop organizational practices that adapt to our business model and strategy			0.804
Eigenvalue	1.021	1.076	12.19
% Explained variance	23.64%	23.99%	33.93%

[a]These are the loadings of each item into the latent capability dimensions. Factor loadings above 0.4 are considered as related to that specific dimension.
Source: Authors.

Table 16.6 Electricity distribution performance. "In the past 3 years our company…"

	Strongly disagree	Disagree	Somewhat disagree	Somewhat agree	Agree	Strongly agree
Improved cost efficiency	—	—	3.20%	26.90%	51.60%	18.30%
Improved service quality and reliability indicators (e.g., SAIFI, SAIDI)	—	2.20%	2.20%	21.50%	50.50%	23.70%
Improved general performance across departments	—	—	3.20%	32.30%	54.80%	9.70%

Source: Authors.

Table 16.7 Innovation approach. "In the past 3 years our company..."

	Strongly disagree	Disagree	Somewhat disagree	Somewhat agree	Agree	Strongly agree
Innovation exploration – through technologies and processes that are new to the utility industry.						
Introduced technologies, processes, or practices that are new to the electricity distribution sector	1.10%	4.50%	5.60%	20.20%	39.30%	29.20%
Started experimenting with innovative technologies in our operations	2.20%	6.70%	12.40%	16.90%	31.50%	30.30%
Innovation exploitation – through existing technologies and processes, already used by other utilities, but new to us.						
Improved our ability to increase quality of service	—	2.20%	5.60%	23.60%	44.90%	23.60%
Improved our ability to increase cost efficiency of our operations	—	2.20%	6.70%	22.50%	51.70%	16.90%

SOURCE: AUTHORS.

Table 16.8 Engagement in smart grid diffusion

Limited engagement	Moderate engagement	Extensive engagement
Smart grid infrastructure management		
We solve most of the grid challenges ...		
... at the planning stage	... at the operational stage	... across planning and operational stages
19.10%	14.60%	66.30%
Our main grid management practice is to ...		
... plan sufficient grid capacity to deal with changing system demands	... restrict distributed generation injections to manage grid congestion	... manage distribution system flexibilities
61.80%	16.90%	21.30%
Smart grid investments and operations		
Considering smarter distribution operations ...		
... we are aware of the opportunities	... we are experimenting with new processes, technologies, and practices	... we have integrated smart grid technologies (e.g., smart meters, electric vehicle charging infrastructure, distributed generation, automation devices)
11.20%	31.50%	57.30%
In terms of engagement in smart grids diffusion ...		
... we consider the possibilities for becoming more engaged in the deployment of smart grids	... we observed operational improvements from deploying a smarter distribution grid	... our processes, technologies, and practices reflect an extensive engagement in the deployment and facilitation of smart grids
27.00%	34.80%	38.20%
Our investments in a smarter distribution grid are ...		
... residual	... moderate	... substantial
7.90%	61.80%	30.30%

Source: Authors.

(Table 16.9). These findings indicate that greater adaptability is also associated with better operational performance.

A positive association between adaptation capabilities and innovation approaches is also identified (Table 16.10). These findings indicate

Table 16.9 Association between adaptation capabilities and electricity distribution performance

	Sensing capability	Learning capability	Transforming capability
Electricity distribution performance[a]	0.49★★★[,b]	0.43★★★	0.51★★★

[a]The measure for electricity distribution performance results from an average index of the items in Table 16.6.
[b]Statistical significance represented as ★★★ for p values ≤ 0.001, ★★ for $p \leq 0.01$, and ★ for $p \leq 0.05$.
Source: Authors.

Table 16.10 Association between adaptation capabilities and innovation approach

	Sensing capability	Learning capability	Transforming capability
Innovation exploration[a]	0.5114★★★[,b]	0.2844★★	0.4406★★★
Innovation exploitation[a]	0.536★★★	0.3954★★★	0.5173★★★

[a]These measures are the combinations of the items presented in Table 16.7 identified through Nonlinear Principal Components Analysis.
[b]Statistical significance represented as ★★★ for p values ≤ 0.001, ★★ for $p \leq 0.01$, and ★ for $p \leq 0.05$.
Source: Authors.

that greater adaptability is also associated with higher levels of innovation exploration and exploitation.

The results obtained indicate no statistically significant association between adaptation capabilities and smart grid infrastructure management. Nonetheless, a moderate positive association is observed for both sensing and transforming capabilities and smart grid investments and operations, while learning capabilities present a weak positive association (Table 16.11). These findings, similar to the previous, indicate also that utilities with greater adaptability show also greater level of smart grid diffusion engagement.

Table 16.11 Association between adaptation capabilities and engagement in smart grid diffusion

	Sensing capability	Learning capability	Transforming capability
Smart grid infrastructure management[a]	−0.0506	−0.0788	−0.0676
Smart grid investments and operations[a]	0.5712★★★[,b]	0.294★★	0.5207★★★

[a]These measures are the combinations of the items presented in Table 16.11 identified through Nonlinear Principal Components Analysis.
[b]Statistical significance represented as ★★★ for p values ≤ 0.001, ★★ for $p \leq 0.01$, and ★ for $p \leq 0.05$.
Source: Authors.

These results provide empirical evidence of the positive relationship between utility adaptation capabilities and electricity distribution performance, engagement in innovation, and smart grid diffusion. While correlation does not imply causation or directionality, these findings align with existing literature validating the positive impact of capabilities on both operational and innovation performance in companies (Janssen et al., 2016; Protogerou et al., 2012; Su et al., 2010).

These findings inform the ongoing discussion on the transformation of utilities, including their provision of innovative services, in a rapidly changing electricity sector. Specifically, the results obtained suggest that utilities' capabilities should be considered, alongside the regulatory and technological debates, in discussions of utility transformation.

Furthermore, the results showcased here bring a timely perspective on the value of supporting the creation of a supportive framework for utility business model innovation and adaptation. The assessment presented in this section validated that more adaptable utilities (i.e., those with greater adaptability capabilities) have a better operational performance, as well as greater levels of innovation exploration, exploitation, and smart grid diffusion engagement. This evidence can contribute also to affirm the relevance of utilities in adapting and being active participants in the disruption of the electricity sector, alongside contributions from new entrants.

5. CONCLUSIONS

In the transition to a more sustainable and digital electricity industry, there is increasing attention to the opportunities and challenges for utilities to deliver innovative services. This chapter offered a crosscutting perspective on the evolving dynamics of three key dimensions of market redesign and utility business model innovation, focusing on the EU.

The implementation of the Energy Union has been instrumental in driving efforts to adjust not only the policy framework, but also the electricity sector's technologies through detailed research and innovation action plans. A central goal of these efforts is the development of innovative services that offer greater distribution flexibility, which, in turn, can improve infrastructure management and reduce consumer costs. These grand visions, strategies, and investment roadmaps will require strong engagement from European countries to become a reality. With all the described strategies in place, it is now time to deliver and expectations are high. Granular actions across EU countries, and an actionable governance framework for monitoring, reporting, and ensuring accountability will be important building blocks to achieve the set goals. The analysis of distribution utility capabilities complements the analysis of EU policy and technology governance that often dominates the debate on the utility of the future. The findings obtained suggest that utility capabilities are an important driver of innovative services and should be further explored. Moreover, these findings indicate the value of adaptability to the benefit of operational performance, innovation, and smart grid engagement diffusion. Consequently, the results obtained position distribution utilities as contributors to the disruption of the electricity sector.

By focusing on policy, technology, and business adaptation, this chapter provided a perspective on the complexity and depth of market redesign efforts occurring in the EU electricity sector. These transformations will play a critical role in ensuring a level playing field for new services and business models, and thus providing consumers greater control and choice in their energy use.

ACKNOWLEDGMENTS

The authors acknowledge the Portuguese National Foundation for Science and Technology (FCT) for supporting this work through the Doctoral Grant PD/BD/105841/2014, awarded on the framework of the MIT Portugal Program funded through the POPH/FSE. Additionally, this work has been partially supported by FCT project grant: UID/MULTI/00308/2019, SAICTPAC/0004/2015-POCI-01-0145-FEDER-016434, and by the European Regional Development Fund through the COMPETE 2020 Programme and FCT project T4ENERTEC POCI-01-0145-FEDER-029820, as well as by the Energy for Sustainability Initiative of the University of Coimbra.

REFERENCES

Castro, N., Dantas, G., 2017. In: De Castro, N., Dantas, G. (Eds.), Distributed Generation: International Experiences and Comparative Analyses. PUBLIT, Rio de Janeiro.

Council of the European Union, 2017. Proposal for a directive of the European Parliament and of the Council on the Internal Market for Electricity - Annex I. Brussels. Retrieved from https://ec.europa.eu/energy/sites/ener/files/documents/1_en_annexe_proposition_part1_v6_864.pdf.

ETIP SNET, 2016a. ETIP SNET Working Groups Terms of Reference. European Technology & Innovation Platforms Smart Networks for Energy Transition, Brussels. Retrieved from https://www.etip-snet.eu/wp-content/uploads/2017/03/WG1.pdf.

ETIP SNET, 2016b. Final 10-year ETIP SNET R&I Roadmap Covering 2017-26. European Technology & Innovation Platforms Smart Networks for Energy Transition, Brussels. Retrieved from http://etip-snet.eu/pdf/Final_10_Year_ETIP-SNET_R&I_Roadmap.pdf.

ETIP SNET, 2017. Technologies and Methods for Making Europe's Energy Transition a Success Europe's. European Technology & Innovation Platforms Smart Networks for Energy Transition, Brussels. Retrieved from https://www.etip-snet.eu/wp-content/uploads/2017/04/ETIP-SNET_Brochure.pdf.

Eurelectric, 2013. Power distribution in Europe - facts and figures. Brussels. Retrieved from http://www.eurelectric.org/media/113155/dso_report-web_final-2013-030-0764-01-e.pdf.

European Commission, 2012. The European Union explained - energy. Brussels. Retrieved from http://europa.eu/pol/ener/flipbook/en/files/energy.pdf.

European Commission, 2015a. A framework strategy for a resilient energy union with a forward-looking climate change policy. Brussels. Retrieved from http://eur-lex.europa.eu/resource.html?uri=cellar:1bd46c90-bdd4-11e4-bbe1-01aa75ed71a1.0001.03/DOC_1&format=PDF.

European Commission, 2015b. Towards an Integrated Strategic Energy Technology (SET) plan: accelerating the European Energy System Transformation. Brussels. Retrieved from https://ec.europa.eu/energy/sites/ener/files/publication/Complete-A4-setplan.pdf.

European Commission, 2016a. Clean energy for all Europeans. Brussels. Retrieved from https://eur-lex.europa.eu/resource.html?uri=cellar:fa6ea15b-b7b0-11e6-9e3c-01aa75ed71a1.0001.02/DOC_1&format=PDF.

European Commission, 2016b. Integrated Strategic Energy Technology (SET) plan - progress in 2016. Brussels. Retrieved from https://ec.europa.eu/energy/sites/ener/files/documents/set-plan_progress_2016.pdf.

European Commission, 2017a. Proposal for a directive of the European Parliament and of the Council on the Internal Market for Electricity. Brussels. Retrieved from https://ec.europa.eu/energy/sites/ener/files/documents/1_en_act_part1_v7_864.pdf.

European Commission, 2017b. Proposal for a regulation of the European Parliament and of the Council on the Internal Market for Electricity. Retrieved from http://eur-lex.europa.eu/resource.html?uri=cellar:9b9d9035-fa9e-11e6-8a35-01aa75ed71a1.0012.02/DOC_1&format=PDF.

European Commission, 2018. Strategic energy technology plan implementation plan. Brussels. Retrieved from https://www.etip-snet.eu/wp-content/uploads/2018/03/set_plan_esystem_implementation_plan.pdf.

Gangale, F., Vasiljevska, J., Covrig, C.F., Mengolini, A., Fulli, G., 2017. Smart grid projects outlook 2017. EC JRC. Retrieved from https://ses.jrc.ec.europa.eu/sites/ses.jrc.ec.europa.eu/files/u24/2017/sgp_outlook_2017-online.pdf.

Henkel, M., Bider, I., Perjons, E., 2014. Capability-based business model transformation. In: Iliadis, L., Papazoglou, M., Pohl, K. (Eds.), Advanced Information Systems Engineering Workshops. Springer International Publishing, Thessaloniki.

IEA, 2011. Technology Roadmap - Smart Grids. Technology Roadmap - Smart Grids, Paris. Retrieved from https://www.iea.org/publications/freepublications/publication/smart-grids_roadmap.pdf.

Inigo, E.A., Albareda, L., Ritala, P., 2017. Business model innovation for sustainability: exploring evolutionary and radical approaches through dynamic capabilities. Ind. Innov. 24 (5), 515–542.

IRENA, 2015. Renewable energy integration in power grids. Retrieved from http://europeanpowertogas.com/wp-content/uploads/2018/05/Ngg1uITu.pdf.

Janssen, M.J., Castaldi, C., Alexiev, A., 2016. Dynamic capabilities for service innovation: conceptualization and measurement. R&D Manage. 46 (4), 797–811.

Ledesma, R.D., Valero-mora, P., 2007. Determining the number of factors to retain in EFA: an easy-to-use computer program for carrying out parallel analysis. Pract. Assess. Res. Eval. 12 (2), 2–11.

Linting, M., van der Kooij, A., 2012. Nonlinear principal components analysis with CATPCA: a tutorial. J. Pers. Assess. 94 (1), 12–25.

Linting, M., Meulman, J.J., Groenen, P.J.F., van der Kooij, A.J., 2007. Nonlinear principal components analysis: introduction and application. Psychol. Methods 12 (3), 336–358.

Meeus, L., Glachant, J.-M., 2018. In: Meeus, L., Glachant, J.-M. (Eds.), Electricity Network Regulation in the EU. Edward Elgar Publishing, Cheltenham, UK/Northampton, MA, USA.

Mori, Y., Kuroda, M., Makino, N., 2016. In: Mori, Y., Kuroda, M., Makino, N. (Eds.), Nonlinear Principal Component Analysis and its Applications. Springer.

New York State, 2014. Reforming the energy vision. New York. Retrieved from http://rev.ny.gov/.

Pearson, K., 1920. Notes on the history of correlation. Biometrika 13 (1), 25–45.

Pereira, G.I., Silva, P.P., 2017. The smart grid and distributed generation nexus. In: De Castro, N., Dantas, G. (Eds.), Distributed generation: international experiences and comparative analyses. PUBLIT, Rio de Janeiro.

Pereira, G.I., Silva, P.P., Soule, D., 2018a. Policy-adaptation for a smarter and more sustainable EU electricity distribution industry: a foresight analysis. Environ. Dev. Sustain. Retrieved from https://doi.org/10.1007/s10668-018-0119-x

Pereira, G.I., Silva, P.P., Soule, D., 2018b. Assessment of electricity distribution business model and market design alternatives: evidence for policy design. Energy Environ. .Retrieved from https://doi.org/10.1177/0958305X18758248

Pérez-Arriaga, I.J., 2013. Regulation of the power sector. In: Pérez-Arriaga, I.J. (Ed.), Power Systems. vol. 61. Springer London, London.

Pérez-Arriaga, I., Knittel, C., 2016. Utility of the future: an MIT energy initiative response to an industry in transition. Retrieved from energy.mit.edu/uof.

Pérez-Arriaga, I.J., Ruester, S., Schwenen, S., Battle, C., Glachant, J.M., 2013. From distribution networks to smart distribution systems: rethinking the regulation of European electricity DSOs. In: THINK project. Retrieved from https://www.eui.eu/projects/think/documents/thinktopic/topic12digital.pdf.

Piovani, J.I., 2008. The historical construction of correlation as a conceptual and operative instrument for empirical research. Qual. Quant. 42 (6), 757–777.

Protogerou, A., Caloghirou, Y., Lioukas, S., 2012. Dynamic capabilities and their indirect impact on firm performance. Ind. Corp. Change 21 (3), 615–647.

Ruester, S., Schwenen, S., Batlle, C., Pérez-Arriaga, I., 2014. From distribution networks to smart distribution systems: rethinking the regulation of European electricity DSOs. Util. Policy 31 (1), 229–237.

Ruscio, J., Roche, B., 2012. Determining the number of factors to retain in an exploratory factor analysis using comparison data of known factorial structure. Psychol. Assess. 24 (2), 282–292.

Su, Z., Xie, E., Peng, J., 2010. Impacts of environmental uncertainty and firms' capabilities on R&D investment: evidence from China. Innovation 12 (3), 269–282.

Teece, D.J., 2007. Exploring dynamic capabilities: the nature and microfoundations of sustainable enterprise performance. Strategic Manage. J. 28, 1319–1350.

Teece, D.J., 2017. A capability theory of the firm: an economics and (Strategic) management perspective. N. Z. Econ. Papers 9954, 1–43.

Teece, D.J., 2018. Business models and dynamic capabilities. Long Range Plann. 51, 40–49.

CHAPTER 17

How Incumbents Are Adjusting to the Changing Business Environment: A German Case Study

Florian Weiss, Richard Groß, Sarah Linowski, Christian von Hirschhausen, Ben Wealer, Timon Zimmermann
Berlin University of Technology, Berlin, Germany

1. INTRODUCTION

The new world of distributed electricity production, consumption, and storage, which in this book is referred to as the "prosumager-world," has important implications for the restructuring of incumbents, in particular (i) if they try to hang on to the old world of integrated utilities, and (ii) if the policy environment is rapidly moving to catch up with the new world. Both conditions were fulfilled in the case of the (former) Big-4 German utilities that have undergone creative destruction over the last 7 years, while at the same time new, decentral business models are emerging.

This chapter extends the main topic of this book, but focuses on the disruption of utility business models, brought about in the new world of electricity, applied to Germany, in the context of the energiewende, i.e., the low-carbon transformation process, and the specific policies pursued in this context. Combining the Schumpeterian "creative destruction" with the central theme of this book, i.e., disruption, we shall refer to this restructuring process as "creative disruption." In fact, not a single business unit, let alone company, of the early 2010s have survived the creative disruption. This also holds for the top management, even if some were able to survive or obtain other positions: "habits" underwent creative disruption, while new innovations were brought to the market by new actors. Thus, we combine a top-down perspective on the disruption of the utility business model, with a bottom-up case study on prosuming electric vehicles from scratch.

Consumer, Prosumer, Prosumager
https://doi.org/10.1016/B978-0-12-816835-6.00017-6
383

This chapter analyzes the drivers of this disruption, the process, and the current outcome and perspectives going forward. German utilities are going through an unprecedented period of disruptive change that has taken up the entire industry structure, reoriented the strategic choices, and left many opportunities, but also challenges to the future of what used to be the "Big 4." These previously "big" 4, let's call them E.ON-OldCo, RWE-OldCo, EnBW-OldCo, and Vattenfall-OldCo, used to be vertically integrated, and highly profitable incumbents. They have vanished during the process, fully disrupted, and none of them exists in the previous structure, or is pursuing the previous strategy, anymore. Disruptive change was both *endogenously* imposed by energy and climate policy instruments of the energiewende, e.g., the closure of nuclear power plants until 2022, and the gradual phasing out of coal plants, and *exogenously* imposed, e.g., the emergence of almost competitive renewables, emergence of storage solutions and prosumage (i.e., home production, consumption, and storage of energy), digitalization, and the emergence of coupling between the electricity, transport, and heating sectors.

At the same time, the disruption has opened up opportunities for new companies to enter the market, and for startups that seize these opportunities that the incumbents have ignored. The second case study, therefore, focuses on the "creative" part of creative destruction, where new forms of electric mobility were developed from scratch, by a combination of entrepreneurs and an unlikely energy firm, the German Postal Service.

The focus of this chapter is on emerging business models, which follows the theme of the book in particular the restructuring of incumbents implied by new forms of electricity distribution in California and other concepts of decentralization such as those covering Australia. However, the chapter adds an energiewende-flavor to the book by focusing on the specifics of the disruptive change in the context of the German energy and climate policy, moving away from conventional sources of electricity – fossil fuels and nuclear – to a largely renewables-based system. In addition, the discussion is focused on the structural changes of utility strategy, rather than on the consumer perspective.

The chapter is organized as follows:
- Section 2 presents the motivations, challenges, and opportunities of the German energiewende;
- Section 3 discusses the previous focus and strategic alignments of the incumbents;

- Sections 4 and 5 highlight this issue by the consultation of respective case studies followed by chapter's conclusions.[1]

2. BACKGROUND ON THE GERMAN ELECTRICITY SECTOR: FROM CONTINUITY TO DISRUPTION

For more than a century, German utilities were politically designed, but largely privately managed cash cows, benefitting from monopoly rents, and providing a high level of supply security and generation adequacy in exchange. This situation prevailed until recently, generating the Big 4, vertically integrated companies. However, this situation changed drastically about a decade ago – with two elements of disruptive change complementing each other – forcing new business models on the incumbents: The first one was the (unexpected) acceleration of policies in favor of renewables, and forcing the end of coal and nuclear plants; this bundle of policy instruments in now generally known as "energiewende." But on the other hand, the German incumbents also had underestimated the speed of technical change and digitization. This section provides a background for the strategy analysis that follows.

2.1 The Golden Age: Electricity Utilities as a "License to Print"

Since the establishments of big utilities, over a century ago, electricity was a very lucrative business, benefitting from the absence of competition, and a very favorable policy environment. Even the first round of restructuring, following the 1996/92 European Directive on liberalization, did not change the comfortable situation of the big oligopolists much. Deregulation was supposed to create more competition and allow consumers to choose between a wider choice of products and suppliers. This liberalization of the market was defined in 1998 by the law for the revision of the energy industry law in Germany and the minimum requirements of the EU single market directive were exceeded. The demarcation agreements were banned in concession contracts, territorial protection was lifted, and investment oversight was abolished. With this unbundling, a separate accounting of the energy supplying companies (ESC) in the areas of generation, transport,

---

[1] This chapter is based on a TU Berlin study project on the restructuring of the German utilities, which included visits and interviews to the headquarters of the major German utility companies, whose assistance is hereby acknowledged. Fereidoon Sioshansi's comments on an earlier version of the chapter are also acknowledged.

and trade was codified, in order to achieve a higher cost transparency.[2] Acceptance and reimbursement of renewable generation have thus been set by law. With the introduction of market liberalization, the EEX (European Energy Exchange) was established. Since then it has been dealing with electricity, coal, gas, and carbon dioxide.

The first decade of this century (2000s) will be remembered as the "golden age" of the Big 4: Liberalization had not really let to fierce competition, the shutdown of nuclear plants had been decided, but not enacted, and – as compensation for the nuclear deal – a power plant replacement program of about 20 GW of new coal plants has been agreed with the government, to fill a so-called capacity gap expected for post 2015. It was a decade in which political balance was maintained between coal (and some natural gas), nuclear, and renewables (von Hirschhausen et al., 2018, Chapter 2; Matthes, 2017).

Some underlying policy debates emerged, though, that would later be at the origin of the disruption. On the coal and climate policy front, conflicts intensified but thanks to the massive expansion of coal plants (and some natural gas plants), stable business was to be expected. With respect to nuclear, all Big 4 held considerable capacities, and lobbied hard to turn around the decision, taken in 2000, to close down the plants after a certain amount of energy had been produced. The idea of developing an "Energy Concept 2050" in the context of longer-term European energy and climate goals was seen as a means to bring the nuclear industry back into business. Last but almost least, the Big 4 had almost entirely neglected the opportunities offered by renewables, and the feed-in law of 1991, which was replaced by a more comprehensive Renewable Energy Act (*Erneuerbare-Energien-Gesetz*, EEG) in 2000. In fact, the EEG faced opposition mainly because the incumbent energy industry had realized that it might become a danger for conventional generation.

Thus, although some change was under way, the Big 4 were in a quite comfortable situation at the end of the last decade, and could afford to be "comfortably numb," stuck in the strategy of the 20th century.

---

[2]In addition, electricity from renewable energies and combined heat and power has been used since then, and the remuneration of renewable energies has been regulated by a power feed-in law. In 2000, the Electricity Feed Act was replaced by the Renewable Energy Sources Act. The aim was to promote further development of new sustainable technologies for the generation of electricity from renewable energies and to protect fossil energy resources. Deutscher Bundestag. 2013. Renewable Energy Sources Act. http://www.umweltbundesamt.de/themen/klima-energie/erneuerbare-energien/erneuerbare-energien-gesetz.

2.2 Eve of Disruption: The Energiewende and the Three Ds

2.2.1 The Energiewende

There had been a long tradition of public debates about a more sustainable energy mix, going back as far as 1980 with the publication of a book by Krause et al. (1980) entitled "energiewende." However, for the Big 4, the policy disruption occurred with the years 2010/2011 only: The combination of the government's Energy Concept 2050 of September 2010 (BMWi and BMU, 2010), including an ambitious climate and renewables target, and the decision of summer 2011 – following the Fukushima nuclear accident in Japan – to shut down nuclear power in Germany by 2022. Although the coal phase-out was not explicitly defined, it is a logical consequence of strict climate targets, broken down by sector, and thus hitting the CO_2-intensive, coal-based electricity sector particularly hard. The following elements make up the core of the energiewende, based on the Energy Concept 2050 and the 13th revision of the Law on Nuclear Energy (Table 17.1, for details see von Hirschhausen et al. (2018)):

- Greenhouse gases (GHG) are to be reduced by 40% (2020), 55% (2030), 70% (2040), and up to 80–95% by 2050 (basis: 1990). This longer-term perspective, in conjunction with a low probability of "clean coal," implies the full decarbonization of the power sector, and the phase-out of coal.
- Nuclear power plants are to be shut down between 2015 and 2022: The seven oldest remaining nuclear power plants shut down temporarily following the moratorium were not to restart operations, and a concrete timetable for the closure of the remaining nuclear power plants was defined.
- Ambitious renewable targets were defined, too: The share of renewables in electricity generation is to increase to at least 35% (2020), 50% (2030), 65% (2040), and 80% (2050); the share of renewables in gross final energy consumption is set to be at least 18% (2020), 30% (2030), 45% (2040), and 60% (2050).
- Last but not least, ambitious targets for energy efficiency have also been defined.

Thus, the specifics of the energiewende in Germany, and a major disruptive force for conventional-based utilities, are the radical change of the electricity mix, and the incompatibility with the previous, fossil and nuclear-based one.

2.2.2 The Three Ds: Decarbonization, Decentralization, Digitalization

A closer look at the energiewende reveals that it contains the three disruptive elements that also shape restructuring processes in other jurisdictions:

Table 17.1 Main objectives of the energiewende

	Reduction of nuclear energy	Share of renewable energy		Reduction GHG emissions	Reduction of energy demand			
		Gross final energy	Electricity production		Primary energy	Domestic heat	Final energy transport	Electricity demand
2015	−47%							
2017	−56%							
2019	−60%							
2020		18%	35%	−40%	−20%	−20%	−10%	−10%
2021	−80%		40−45%					
2022	−100%							
2025								
2030		30%	50%	−55%				
2035			55−60%					
2040		45%	65%	−70%				
2050		60%	80%	−80% to 95%	−50%	−80%	−40%	−25%
Base	2010	−	−	1990	2008	2008	2005	2008

Source: Energy Concept 2050 (BReg, 2010), 13th Amendment of the Law on Nuclear Energy (*Atomgesetz, AtG*).

aIn fact, in addition to the disruption of the political framework for energy and climate framework, there is a set of exogenous, technology-driven disruptions, summarized as the 3D: decarbonization, decentralization, and digitalization.

Decarbonization of the energy system at the horizon 2050 is a global trend. Some European countries, such as the UK, France, Denmark, and the Netherlands are currently taking the lead, the U.S. is on its way, too, and even some emerging countries, such as India, are starting to look for a lower-carbon future energy system. According to the Paris Agreement on Climate Change, Europe has to achieve a 40% reduction in carbon dioxide emissions (compared to 1990 levels) by 2030, with ultimate levels being potentially higher. In this context, Germany has committed, in the framework of European pledges, to achieve a 40% and 55% reduction of GHG emissions, respectively, by 2020 and 2030, and to 80–95% by 2050 (basis: 1990). Broken down to the electricity sector, this implies almost 100% renewable energy. Fig. 17.1 shows that the percentage of lignite, in particular, of gross power generation in Germany has not really decreased, whereas the share of hard coal has dropped from about 25% to about 14%.

For the fossil-based Big 4 OldCos, the strict climate policy objectives represented a drastic loss of revenue. When excluding the (unrealistic) option of carbon capture, transport, and storage (CCTS) technologies, achieving ambitious climate objectives in Germany implies phasing out both hard coal and lignite.

Decentralization refers to technical progress that has made prosumage competitive and will further weaken the integrated utility world. This is where the idea of the smart grid comes in again and where new room for innovations arises. Even in a fully decentralized system, a central supplier or a group of central suppliers needs to ensure a very basic supply. Another task to be solved is the one of the central grid and load management, which

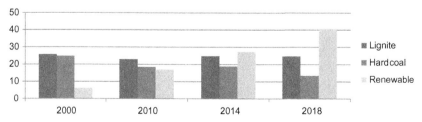

FIGURE 17.1 Share of coal power in German energy system. *(Source: Based on Arbeitsgruppe Energiebilanzen. 2018. Gross Electricity Generation in Germany from 1990 by Energy.)*

could operate in the format of a platform. As one can see, there is much room for creative thinking and different approaches that need to be evaluated. Variable prices are one of the very few elements being very likely to appear. A decentralized system could not only contribute to a reduction of costs and emissions, but also requires further investments in the grid the distribution management – keywords are grid flexibility, data security, and platform potential, as highlighted in other chapters in this book.

Last but not least, digitalization of the energy sector is both a disruptive factor for conventional utilities, but also an opportunity for new business development, e.g., innovative customer solutions. In particular, digitization offers new business models for prosumage, both at the central but also at the decentral level. Other applications are smart energy efficiency applications, and demand-side management. As also concluded by Chapter 1, digitalization leads to more flexible structure, both on the demand and on the supply side of electricity.

Smart meters are also part of the digital revolution, i.e., digital electricity meters that can collect information concerning the consumption and transmit it to the producer in real time. This data collection and connectivity, in conjunction with other technologies, such as the networking of one's home to a "smart home," forms the basis of the network conversion and expansion. The aim is to build an intelligent power grid, or "smart grid," which allows a group of (small-scale) producers, power plant-like wind and solar farms, and consumers to connect beyond the mere supply of electricity. This type of networking can be realized by the rapid development of the Internet, and the telecommunication and information industry (Eissler and Zorn, 2018). Such an intelligent distribution system could manage, which kinds of loads can extract energy to what time off the system. Blackouts through overuse can be avoided through this technology. The problem of the "duck curve"[3] can at least partly be controlled, e.g., through variable prices. The term "Industry 4.0" refers to a far-reaching networking of industrial systems using state-of-the-art technology. However, the digitalization of the electricity market only is not enough to meet the demands of the energy market of tomorrow. The path to an intelligent network requires not only the integration of new, digitally controlled technologies, but also

---

[3]The "duck curve" describes the low energy consumption over the day, when, for example, the energy generation peak of solar-PV is reached, and the peak of consumption when the energy generation of the same technology is low. In the case of California over the last years, for example, this ramp of the "over the day"-low to the "from six to nine pm"-high, in terms of consumption, has increased. See also Chapter 12.

comprehensive network expansion measures and further flanking technologies – the keywords are: energy efficiency and storage.

3. THE STRATEGY SPACE FOR DISRUPTIVE CHANGE OF THE INCUMBENT ENERGY SUPPLIERS

Given the strength of the disruptive forces, both politically (endogenously) and technologically (exogenously) driven, it is no surprise to see the German utilities fully "creatively disrupted," between 2011 and approx. 2016. This section provides an in-depth look at the changing energy market environment of the past decade and how the disruptive change has influenced its structure as well as the deployed strategies of the incumbent ESCs. These changes, in combination with the already discussed internal and external forces on the market, forced the Big 4 to adjust, rethink, and change fundamentally. Chapter 15 by Bauknecht et al., discusses different concepts of decentralization in the German context in detail.

3.1 Strategies in the Previous Energy Market

Following up on the timeline for the analysis of an ever-changing energy market, this section characterizes the market environment up until 2010 in a Porters five-force format. In this bygone environment, the four incumbents have had the chance to develop and grow somehow independently without having to endure a lot of substantial change. All of them developed a highly vertical integrated portfolio reaching from the generation of energy, in their own thermal and nuclear power plants, upstream over through transmission to the b2b and b2c sale of energy downstream. During the early 2000s, they used their market power and their high revenue streams, originating from very generous profit margins, to grow to their highest market value at around 2008.

Continuing with Fig. 17.2, the best way to draw a thorough picture of the energy market in 2010 is to identify one main trend for each of the five forces that shape the markets. As described earlier, the *rivalry among existing competitors wa*s mainly shaped by an oligopolistic structure of large and established corporations that don't seek to differentiate in their activities or offered products but split almost the entire market among them. This makes the *threat of entry* of new competitors relatively small, as there are very high entry barriers. These barriers include high capex for generation capacity that can compete in its margin with the one already existing and capex for scaled operations and economies that are requirements to be profitable in

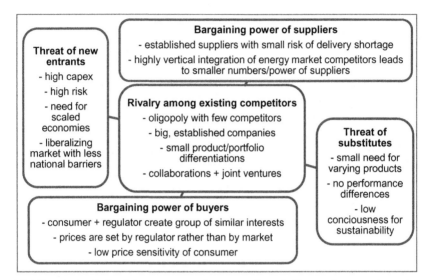

FIGURE 17.2 Analysis of the energy market up until 2010. *(Source: Company interviews and background research, using Michael Porter's (1985) 5-force approach.)*

a market with highly regulated margins. The *threat of substitutes* connects seamlessly to the previous trend, as there are no dramatic performance differences between the technologies. Together with a low consumer and regulator consciousness for especially environmental and efficiency aspects, this results in a very small need for varying products or substitutes.

Looking at the *bargaining power of suppliers and buyers,* it is easy to find that suppliers play a very small role compared to the buyers. Due to the high vertical integration of the incumbents, the number and power of suppliers is limited and the ones that are existing can fully deliver on the demand without any risks for shortages. Buyers have a low price sensitivity, which creates a very powerful buyer that acts as a counterweight to the rest of the market structure that is in favor of the existing incumbents. As laid out in the introduction to this book, and several companion chapters, bargaining power from incumbents to consumers is a key driver of the restructuring process, and particularly so in the case of the Big 4.

Table 17.2 presets some key financial indicators of the Big 4 (and their successor companies); return on capital (ROCE) and capital expenditures (CAPEX) are of particular interest. RWE and E.ON can maintain a relatively high level, whereas EnBW has slumped significantly since 2014. This suggests an inefficient handling of the capital employed. Vattenfall has consistently been at a lower value since 2014 than the other companies, although the strategic goal of exceeding the 9% threshold has been

Table 17.2 Overview of German electricity utilities

Category	Business unit and other	RWE AG	Vattenfall AB[a]	E.ON SE	Uniper SE	ENBW AG	Innogy SE
Absolute share of adjusted EBITDA (in Mio. €)	Sales	—	285 (8.4%)	847 (17%)	—	330 (15.6%)	592 (20%)
	Grid	—	906.7 (26.8%)	2,927 (59%)	—	1,045.9 (49.5%)	1,844 (62.3%)
	RG	4,331 (75.3%)	629.2 (18%)	785 (15.8%)	1,480.7 (85%)	331.7 (15.7%)	671 (22.7%)
	KG	1,134 (19.7%)	909.2 (26.8%)	654 (13.2%)	261.3 (15%)	377.1 (17.8%)	
	Other[b]	291 (5%)	655.5 (19.4%)	−258 (5.2%)		28.3 (1.4%)	−147 (−5%)
Total (sum)		5,756	3,385.6	4,955	1,742	2,113	2,960
Electricity sales (in Mrd. kWh)		261.1	157.3	141.8	725.9	122	262.4
Gas sales (in Mrd. kWh)		254.1	56.4	141.8	1,944	—	227.5
Costumers power/gas (in Mio.)		15.9/6.6	6.3/2.2	6.1	—	5.5	8.1
Investments in segments (in Mio. €)	Sales	—	—	595 (18%)	—	110.6 (6.2%)	51 (2.6%)
	Grid	—	520.3 (25%)	1,418 (42.9%)	—	787.5 (44.5%)	968 (68%)
	RG[c]	2,166[d] (82.4%)	537.1 (25.9%)	1,225 (37%)	—	706.4 (39.9%)	404 (28.4%)
	FG[e]	455 (17.3%)	352.8 (17%)	14 (0.4%)	740 (87.8%)	140.2 (7.9%)	—
	Other	8 (0.3%)	366.1 (17.6%)	56 (1.7%)	103 (12.2%)	—	—
Total (sum)		2,629	2,076.3	3,308	843	1,744.7	1,423
Employees		59,547	20,041	42,699	12,180	20,000	20,553

(Continued)

Table 17.2 Overview of German electricity utilities—cont'd

Business unit and other		RWE AG	Vattenfall AB[a]	E.ON SE	Uniper SE	ENBW AG	Innogy SE
Total power generation in segments 2017 in TWh	Nuclear	30.3	51.9				
	Hard coal	29.4	15.6				
	Lignite	74.2	0.3				
	Natural gas	53.9	15.6				
	Renewable	11.3	43.2				
	Other	3.1	0.7				
	Sum	202.2	127.3				
ROCE	2017	10.6%	7.7%	10.6%	n. a.	7.3%	n. a.
	2016	10.4%	8.7%	10.4%	n. a.	7.8%	n. a.
	2015	8.0%	7.3%	10.9%	–	9.5%	–
	2014	8.4%	8.2%	8.5%	–	10.0%	–
CAPEX in Mio €	2017	2,629	4,472	3,308	843	1,770	2,166
	2016	2,382	2,129	3,169	781	2,585	2,123
	2015	3,303	2,508	4,174	–	1,416	2,188
	2014	3,440	2,819	4,637	–	1,704	–
CO$_2$ intensity (in t/MWh)		0.676	0.520	0.281	0.547	0.556	0.495

[a]Exchange rate at that time: 1 SEK = 0.098 EUR.
[b]Heat, consolidation, other.
[c]RG means generation through renewables.
[d]RG accounted by Innogy.
[e]FG means generation through fossils.
Source: Annual reports from companies mentioned.

announced several times. For the Big 4, it is clear that RWE in particular has been able to significantly increase its ROCE since 2014 up to more than 10%. Vattenfall has a slightly lower ROCE, which always oscillates between 7% and 8%. By contrast, E.ON's ROCE is relatively constant at over 10%. The CAPEX is another economic key figure that needs to be compared in the context of the respective investment focus.[4] As we see in this table, RWE's CAPEX has fallen significantly since 2014, while Vattenfall's CAPEX, on the other hand, made a very significant jump after three equally declining years in 2017. The young companies Uniper and Innogy remain at a constant level, whereby Innogy has a volume almost three times as high in CAPEX as Uniper. At E.ON, similar to RWE, there is also a very strong drop in CAPEX before a light growth in 2017.

The interplay between the development of ROCE and CAPEX over the past business years is particularly interesting with respect to the future investment potential. Investments described with the CAPEX are not costs for the company, but conversion of assets that remain as fixed assets in the company. The high CAPEX thus suggests that companies have high confidence in the profitability of their investments. Therefore, the decreasing CAPEX of RWE and E.ON leads to a less risky but potentially less growing business. In contrast, Vattenfall experienced a big raise in 2017. EnBW, Innogy, and Uniper are showing stagnating investment levels.

3.2 Overview of "Creative Disruption" and Preliminary Results

This section contains the essence of the effects of the disruptive change on German corporate structures that were blown apart, to find themselves either

- converted to renewables-oriented companies as in the case of RWE-NewCo and E.ON-NewCo, and, perhaps in the near future, also EnBW-NewCo;
- reconverted (restored, counter-revolution) to fossil fuel activities as in the case of Uniper (now Fortum) and LEAG (Local Lignite-focused company in east Germany);
- to be nationalized as in the case of RWE-NukeCo and E.ON-NukeCo (called PreussenElektra), with more or less liabilities and waste left behind for the public sector to clean up (lignite and coal pits, nuclear waste, water pumping obligations, etc.); or
- or – very simply – disappearing as in the case of Vattenfall-OldCo.

[4]Capital expenditure describes the investments made by the company, which are not traditional costs. A high CAPEX indicates that a company is investing heavily in its future or even old business areas.

The phase of "creative disruption" is kickstarted with a spread of divestments and disintegrations taking place in almost all of the Big 4's portfolios. In a time, where decreasing gross margins for conventional energy generation are seen, the influx of regulatory measures ("energiewende") put additional financial pressure on the management of every ESC. It is now time to come up with ideas of how to contain the destruction of shareholder value.

In the following the elements of disruptive change, one by one, with a focus on the transformation of the previous Big 4 OldCos, are analyzed. Table 17.3 presents the structural changes that have taken place and the divestment and disintegration efforts for the respective portfolios of each ESC. Reviewing the first wave of structural changes, two main trends can be identified:

- First, there seems to be a strong drive for agility, both financially as well as in operational aspects, in order to keep up with a fast-paced regulatory and compatible market environment; and

- second, it seems like not one of the ESCs has yet been able to find a "master plan" for dealing with this disruptive change that transforms the industry. All of the four ESCs are struggling with decarbonization, decentralization, and digitization, with innovation demand as well as the cultural challenges that come with competing in newly formed growth markets, e.g., the customer solution business. The players are still struggling to redefine their role, their future prospects, & how they should reconfigure. This is not the end of the story, which is still unfolding with many uncertainties to follow.

Following section examines the energy strategies of the four major energy players in detail.

3.2.1 E.ON-OldCo

The structural disruption starts in 2016, when E.ON decided to disintegrate its conventional generation business together with its trading business into a newly formed and self-operational spin-off company called Uniper, of which it held a minority stake of 45.45%,[5] and has sold off that rest since. This decision marks the end of the past standard of highly vertical integrated ESCs. A move to give both companies more agility, while also providing a clearer reputational picture for the stakeholders. On one hand, there is a new green E.ON that combines the renewables and customer solutions business with the stable but stagnating revenue of the grids business, and on

---

[5] E.ON SE. 2016. "E.ON Press Release: Separation from the Uniper Group."

Table 17.3 Structural changes in the German energy sector

	Structural changes	Lignite	Hard Coal	Nuclear	Gas	Solar: PV	Wind (On/Offshore)	Grid	Customer-Solutions	Trading
EnBW AG	No restructuring as of now	X	X	X	X	X	X	X	X	X
E.ON SE	Disintegration of business with a minority stake (01.01.2016)	$ —→	$ —→	X	$ —→	X	X	X	X	$ —→
	Scission of Innogy's business through an asset swap (13.03.2018)					X •----$	X •----$	X •----$	X •----$	X •----$
Uniper SE	Formation as fully self operational company (01.01.2016)	X	X	–	X	–	–	–	–	X
RWE AG	Disintegration of business with a majority stake (01.04.2016)	X	X	X	X	$ —→ X	$ —→ X	$ —→ X	$ —→ X	X
	Scission of Innogy's business through an asset swap (13.03.2018)					X •----$	X •----$	X •----$	X •----$	$
Innogy SE	Formation as semi self operational company (01.04.2016)	–	–	–	–	–	–	X	X	–
Vattenfall AG	Divestment of Business to EPH-Group (18.04.2016)	$ —→	X	X	X	X	X	X	X	X
LEAG	Founded as a subsidiary to EPH-Group (18.04.2016)	•→ X	–	–	–	–	–	–	–	–

Legend

- renewable focus: ✳ - mixed/diversified: ✳   - owned: X

- fossil focus: ★ - divested/disintegrated: $ - not owned: –

- finished restructuring: —→   - planned restructuring: ----→

Source: Based on interviews with companies mentioned & background research.

the other hand Uniper, seeming to miss a strategic story, being left alone with the conventional generation and trading business, in hope for rising wholesale energy prices.

3.2.2 RWE-OldCo

Taking a look at the second big ESC RWE-OldCo, it is easy to recognize a similar story with appropriate focuses taking place. Beginning in the second quarter of 2016, Innogy was formed as green spin-off combining the renewables and customer solutions business with the grid operations.[6] Contrary to E.On, RWE held a majority stake of 76.8% of Innogy, ensuring for operational control and profiting from the hoped-for growth of its business.[7] This left RWE with all its conventional generation efforts and the trading business, while also keeping Innogy underneath the same roof as a semi-self-operational company. A decision that could be seen purely as an attempt to increase capital, accounting for the financial pressure mentioned here.

3.2.3 EnBW-OldCo

EnBW OldCo was a fully integrated, largely coal- and nuclear-based public company, owned by the federal state of Baden-Wuerttemberg, and some smaller communities. After a failed flirt with the French nuclear giant Electricité de France (EdF), EnBW had lobbied, like the other OldCos, for lifetime extensions for the nuclear power plants, and had invested heavily into coal-based plants, in the 2000s. The energiewende and the creative disruption imply the separation of its nuclear plants, ideally spun off to a state-owned (perhaps German-wide) nuclear company ("NukeCo"). There are also rumors that EnBW is seeking buyers for its coal plants, e.g., Uniper/Fortum. The future of EnBW-NewCo, then, is grids, renewables, and customer services, but the company is not there yet.

3.2.4 Vattenfall-OldCo

The creative disruption of Vattenfall OldCo is quickly told: From one of the Big 4 OldCo, the company vanished from the federal scene, by a decision of the Swedish government (as owner) to get rid of the carbon-intensive lignite business, which was sold to a Czech investment company (EPH). The nuclear part of the business, now Vattenfall NukeCo, was split off. After this disruption, the only parts of the old Vattenfall OldCo to stay around are

[6]RWE AG. 2016. "RWE Press Release: Future business with new subsidiary Innogy."
[7]RWE AG. 2017. "RWE Press Release: future perspectives for Innogy."

a trading company, two distribution companies (Berlin and Hamburg), as well as some thermal power plants for district heating (mainly in Berlin and Hamburg, too).

3.3 Moving Forward?

Fig. 17.3 provides a strategy analysis of the companies moving forward, still based on Porters five forces. As explained in detail, the market environment has changed fundamentally since 2010 leading to some sort of restructuring of almost every ESC's portfolio to a more focused and less vertical integrated portfolio. The regulatory environment has also hardened its grip. The closure of nuclear power plants is planned for 2022, renewable generation capacity is still being pushed, and an explicit coal phase out is omnipresent in the light of stricter climate goals. Interesting to note in Fig. 17.3 is the change of the threat of being substituted.

After completing the visualization of the market development by creating the second and more recent five-force analysis, the core trends and central changes can be identified. If one compares the *rivalry among existing competitors* from previous Fig. 17.2 and the one of today's Fig. 17.3, it can be found that the market environment has changed quite a bit with a more diverse competition structure due to the spin-off strategies and continuing market liberalization. Today, strategies need to be more focused, and the portfolios adapted accordingly. This is also due to the higher *threat of new entrants*

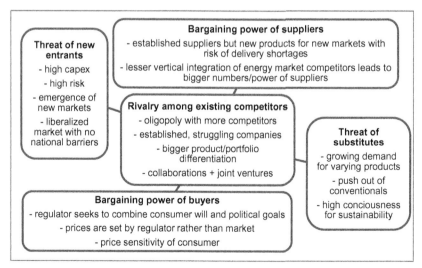

FIGURE 17.3 Analysis of the energy market from 2018 going forward. *(Source: Company interviews and background research, using Michael Porter's (1985) 5-force approach.)*

into the market that has still high capex and entry barriers but has opened up to international energy-supplying companies and consumer-focused companies such as consumer electronics and automotive in a race to leverage the emerging consumer solutions business and to develop a profitable strategy. Connected to this trend, the *threat of substitutes* is higher as well. The growing consciousness of consumers and regulators to green energy supply and the slow phase out of conventional energy generation, has seen the demand for substitutes, both in house and big project generation, rise.

Turning to the *bargaining power of suppliers,* a shift from a point of small power in the traditional picture to a bigger stand in the market has happened. This is due to the emergence of new markets and technologies that rely on new product and manufacturing lines that struggle to meet the demand. Therefore, the risk of shortages in the supply chain makes this environment more volatile and strengthens the power of the suppliers. The *bargaining power of buyers* is still as high as it has been in the traditional energy market with the regulator and the consumers of energy forming a group of shared interests.

4. CASE STUDY I: DISRUPTED UTILITY BUSINESS MODELS FOR RWE AND E.ON

Two case studies can highlight the key topic of this book, i.e., how the new technological, policy, and innovation environment (can) disrupt previous business models. The first case study focuses on shifting strategies by incumbent utilities, the second one on market entry of a new service company at the nexus of energy and transportation.

4.1 Unbundling the Unbundling: The 2018 RWE-E.on Deal

Zooming in on the strategies of the two biggest "OldCos," E.ON-OldCo and RWE-OldCo, provides insights not only into the way disruption has altered the course of the utilities, but also the specifics of the German low-carbon transformation. This section therefore focuses on the deal between the two, of spring 2018, to unbundle the unbundling of 2016, and to seek a way to leave the decade like "phoenix from the ashes." In fact, in 2018, the two largest restructured utilities, let's call them RWE-2018 and E.ON-2018 (to designate the status of the companies in 2018), announced a strategic move whereby one of them, RWE-2018, would focus on renewables, taking over E.ON-2018's renewable business developed thus far, whereas the other, E.ON-2018, would focus on distribution grids, a well-remunerated, regulated business, and some customer solutions.

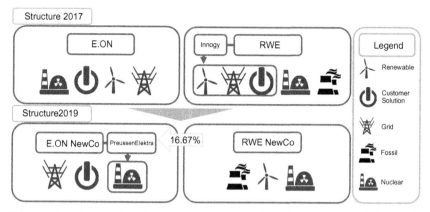

FIGURE 17.4 Creating two focused energy companies. *(Source: Own depiction on the basis of E.ON SE. 2018. "Creating the Future of Energy".)*

The 2018 deal consists of an extensive asset swap, valued at around 22 bn Euro, paired with the division of the merely 2-year-old Innogy spin-off.[8] As seen in Fig. 17.4, the details of the agreement include that E.ON-NewCo acquires RWE-2018's 76.8% stake in Innogy, while also making an offer of 40 Euro per share to all minority stakeholders. In return, RWE-NewCo obtains a 16.67% minority stake of E.ON-NewCo, its minority shares in RWE's nuclear power plants plus all of Innogy's gas storage efforts. On top of that, RWE-NewCo receives Innogy's due dividends for 2017 and 2018, while making a compensation cash payment of 1.5 bn Euro to E.ON.

4.2 Driving Considerations

To summarize the new outcome for both incumbents, there are two different strategies taking shape. RWE will change its reputation of the German "Bad Bank" to a diversified energy generation giant that will receive 60% of its EBITDA from the newly acquired growth business: E.ON's and Innogy's renewables. It seems like there is a clear story for RWE with the newly identified upstream focus and the disintegration of noncore businesses like the customer solution and grid operations. This gives RWE a better position for regulatory changes such as a capacity market. At the same time, E.ON will become a customer-solution-focused company with the fusion of its own and Innogy's customer solutions and Europe's first exclusive downstream energy player. E.ON is scaling up its total customer base from 31 m

---

[8]E.ON SE, and RWE AG. 2018. "Combined Press Release: Two European Energy Companies focus their Activities."

to approximately 50 m. Its regulatory grid asset base will grow from 23 bn to 37 bn Euro annually and its overall EBITDA is supposed to increase from 6 bn to 8 bn Euro.[9]

Comparing the two, E.ON is comfortably built around a highly regulated and lucrative (though nongrowth) grid business with decent cash flow. These fixed rates of return can secure its much-needed engagement in the customer solutions business that is not known for a high rate of return. It needs to develop a masterplan how to increase these and transform it to a market of growth.[10]

5. CASE STUDY II: DISRUPTION AT THE ELECTRICITY – TRANSPORT NEXUS DECENTRAL INNOVATION IN ELECTRIC MOBILITY

5.1 Energiewende and Electrification of Transport

This companion case study highlights another process of creative destruction, but – contrary to the electric utilities described – one with an open outcome. By ignoring the low-carbon transformation, or even openly working against it, the Big 4 German car manufacturers (VW, Daimler-Mercedes, BWM, and Ford) have for a long time underestimated the importance of low-carbon electric mobility. Among other opportunities, they ignored a very lucrative business, i.e., the development of an electric delivery vehicle that had been proposed to them by the German postal services. The Postal Services then decided to "make" instead to "buy," and are putting the Big 4 under pressure to follow suit, with a yet open outcome.

This case study illustrates that the energiewende affects a wave of changes among all sectors and consists mostly of both new arising technologies and new business models. The transportation sector is affected by these fundamental changes, too, and in order to fulfill the climate goals, the transportation sector of tomorrow will have to change fundamentally. Although there are different estimates out, there is a consensus that the energiewende will include a large-scale electrification of the transportation sector, not only in private transport, but also in goods transportation. Signs of this are appearing on the horizon, such as in California and in Norway.

---

[9]E.ON SE. 2018. "Creating the Future of Energy."

[10]One major challenge of both NewCos is how to deal with the nuclear liabilities. In fact, both have some nuclear power plants remaining, bundled in Preussen-Elektra (for E.on), and in the portfolio of RWE; this, however, is not part of this chapter.

5.2 German Postal Services Occupy a Strategic Niche: Electricity-Based Distribution Services

Amid polluted cities and rising public calls for decarbonized transportation, particularly in cities, the German Postal Services, by far the largest distributor of parcels, put out a tender for electric delivery vehicles. In fact, many German cities and communes are working on concepts on how to reduce the amount of fossil-fuel-powered vehicles – the idea of banning diesel engines is one discussed regulatory approach. Under these circumstances, in 2014, the Postal Services reached out to experienced automotive companies for a design and, subsequently, large-scale production of an electric delivery vehicle. However, none of the Big 4 reacted positively. They may have been reluctant because most of their income is still based on fossil-fuel-based products, and they do not seem to be eager to shift this focus toward sustainable, nonfossil transportation, contrary to other manufacturers like Tesla (100% electric) or Volvo, that has pledged to end the production of internal combustion engines from 2019 onwards. Furthermore, electric vehicles differ fundamentally in the way they are constructed and seemed to be (at this point of time) not as lucrative in terms of size of target groups as well as the way or intensity of usage (Lienkamp, 2012).

Ironically, and against all odds, the German Postal Services then created its own startup company, called streetscooter, based on an initial research project developed at Aachen University of Technology (RWTH). Streetscooter designs, manufactures, and sells a series of electric delivery vehicles (as well as electric motorcycles). From an initial experimental factor design for a few hundred vehicles per year, capacity rapidly increased to the 5-digit numbers. In May 2018, streetscooter even opened up a second factory, raising the production capacity to 20,000 vehicles annually.[11] As of late 2018, street scooter has become a unique commercial success story, with ever-increasing demand, and a high public profile. It is likely that all delivery postal vehicles will move to electric mobility. It will be interesting to see what other distributors will do, such as DHL, FedEx, Amazon®, & others.

5.3 What Future for Big-4 Vehicle Manufacturers?

The story of streetscooter is but one element of the German energiewende, but it follows a similar pattern as electricity generation itself: In the context of the three Ds, the very business model of the fossil-fuel-based car

---

[11]Compare: https://de.reuters.com/article/deutschland-deutsche-post-idDEKCN1IV1BA, visited on June 6th 2018.

manufacturers (the Big 4) is under threat. Decentral innovation is facilitated by digitization and decentralization of innovative capacities; on top of this, decarbonization of the transportation sector is gaining ground.

Will disruptive change for the Big 4 German vehicle manufacturers be as drastic as for the Big 4 electric utilities in the previous case study? Contrary to the utilities, where disruption has swept the entire sector, it is too early to draw conclusions on the electricity-transportation nexus:

- On the one hand, the speed of technical change, and the public and private pressure to develop nonfossil–fuel-based modes of transportation, are strong drivers of disruptive strategies;
- on the other hand, the capacity of the old, fossil-based system to resist and combat change is stronger than in the utility sector, based on notions of (national) incumbent industrial and innovative strength, and – last but not least – current employment.

In that respect, electric mobility is likely to become another battlefield in the new energy world, not only for the energiewende, but also for business models internationally. Decentral innovation is likely to be a driver of change. As one element of proof: after resisting collaborating, BMW and Ford have in the meantime changed their minds and agreed to cooperation with streetscooter.[12]

6. CONCLUSIONS

In this chapter, the strategies of the German utilities undergoing fundamental change have been analyzed. Disruption is omnipresent and the external forces of decarbonization, decentralization, and digitization spare nobody. Add to this the specifics of an ambitious energy and climate policy, called "energiewende," and you get the German case of creative disruption, a particularly drastic one. Over the last decade, not a single one of the Big 4 OldCos has survived. Combined, these disruptive forces have shaken up the market; washed away the old, 20th century Big 4; and created a new playing field for electricity companies going forward. After a decade of disruptive change, the OldCos have opted for one of three different strategies, respectively:

- To convert to renewable producers, sustainable customer solutions, and power grids (RWE-NewCo, E.o-NewCo, eventually also EnBW-NewCo);

[12]Compare: https://www.handelsblatt.com/unternehmen/dienstleister/streetscooter-post-und-ford-wollen-kooperation-vertiefen/20194552.html, visited on August 27th 2018.

- to opt for the "dark side" and continue to make money with fossil fuels and/or nuclear (Uniper/Fortum, LEAG); or
- to simply disappear (Vatenfall-OldCo).[13]

The case study of the utilities has shown how far creative disruption has gone: One of the two former fossil fuel-nuclear giants (RWE-NewCo) is focusing on renewables, the other (E.ON-NewCo) on the (boring but lucrative) grid business, with the hope of generating enough revenue to cross-subsidize a risky customer solution business. The second case study showed the vulnerability of the incumbents' positions and emphasized the importance of progress not only in the previous daily business, but also concerning the business of the day after tomorrow, if necessary from outside the sector (case of German Postal Services). If it comes to the question of shaping the way of generating the income for the time after creative disruption, not only the present incumbents are the big players, but also the start-ups and innovative spirit of those that are not handicapped with old structures.

REFERENCES

BMWi and BMU, 2010. Energy concept – for an environmentally sound, reliable and affordable energy supply. Berlin, Germany http://www.bmwi.de/English/Redaktion/Pdf/energy-concept,property=pdf,bereich=bmwi,sprache=en,rwb=true.pdf.

Eissler, M., Zorn, P., 2018. The economics of prosumage business opportunities in Germany, California, India, South Africa and Australia. Berlin.

Krause, F., Bossel, H., Müller-Reissmann, K.-F., 1980. In: Öko-Institut Freiburg (Ed.), Energie-Wende: Wachstum und Wohlstand ohne Erdöl und Uran. S. Fischer, Frankfurt am Main, Germany.

Lienkamp, M., 2012. Elektromobilität: Hype Oder Revolution? VDI. Springer Vieweg, Berlin.

Matthes, F.C., 2017. Energy transition in Germany: a case study on a policy-driven structural change of the energy system. Evol. Inst. Econ. Rev. 14 (1), 141–169. https://doi.org/10.1007/s40844-016-0066-x.

Porter, M.E., 1985. Competitive Advantage: Creating and Sustaining Superior Performance. Free Press/Collier Macmillan, New York/London.

von Hirschhausen, C., Gerbaulet, C., Kemfert, C., Lorenz, C., Oei, P.-Y., 2018. Energiewende 'Made in Germany' Electricity Sector Reform in the European Context. Springer, Berlin/Heidelberg/New York.

---

[13]A fourth option is not discussed here, i.e., to try to reach the safe haven of nationalization, for the high-risk-no-perspective nuclear plants to be decommissioned (RWE-NewCo (to be defined) and E.ON-NukeCo (PreussenElektra)).

CHAPTER 18

Who Will Fuel Your Electric Vehicle in the Future? You or Your Utility?

Jeremy Webb*, Jake Whitehead†, Clevo Wilson*
*Queensland University of Technology, Brisbane, QLD, Australia
†The University of Queensland, St Lucia, QLD, Australia

1. INTRODUCTION

A fundamental change to grid supply and demand will be generated by the progressive electrification of the world's automotive vehicle fleet. Of critical importance will, therefore, be the way in which electric vehicles (EVs) are charged: either directly from the grid or via distributed energy resources (DERs), and in particular through the use of residential rooftop solar (RRS). Equally, the way in which domestic standalone batteries will promote integration of the means of powering households and EVs, and change their relationship with the grid, are further key issues explored. The cases of Australia, the state of Queensland – both of which have one of the highest rates of RRS in the world – and California, which has a similar climate to much of Australia's major population centers, are examined. To provide insights into these issues, a detailed individual case study is used. It gives an indication of the extent to which ownership of an EV, rooftop solar and a standalone battery offers an integrated solution to domestic power needs. Additionally, a survey of Australian EV owners is used to collect observational data on these issues. These studies therefore give insights into how the uptake of EVs may change the way and the time frame under which households move from being power consumers to prosumers, prosumagers and acquire the possibility of becoming nonsumers.

This chapter is organized as follows:
- Section 2 discusses the transformation of the global automotive fleet to EVs and the likely effect on power grids.
- Section 3 outlines Australia's energy profile.
- Section 4 describes the way in which EVs, batteries, and RRS are being integrated into interconnected power systems.
- Section 5 outlines future projections of EV market growth.

Consumer, Prosumer, Prosumager
https://doi.org/10.1016/B978-0-12-816835-6.00018-8

- Section 6 adds to Section 5, with a specific focus on EV market projections for Australia.
- Section 7 examines a household case study of EV charging integrated with RRS and a standalone battery.
- Section 8 includes the results of a survey of Australian EV owners.
- Section 9 provides the chapter's conclusions and policy prescriptions.

2. THE EV TRANSITION AND ITS EFFECT ON POWER GRIDS

The impending rapid transition to EVs over the coming decades is occurring precisely at a time of three important trends in electricity supply and storage. Firstly, most national electricity grids are experiencing an increase in the proportion of commercial-scale renewable energy in their electricity mixes. This is being driven in part by government policies flowing from the Paris COP21 agreement on the reduction of greenhouse gases (GHG) (Pachauri et al., 2014). Road transport presents itself as an increasingly important mechanism for delivering the required GHG emission reductions, given that the sector accounts for approximately 20% of the global total (International Energy Agency, 2016). Moreover, the transport sector's GHG emissions have been increasing at a higher rate than other economic sectors. Between 1990 and 2012, total GHG emissions decreased by almost 18% but those from transport increased by 14% (Santos, 2017).

Secondly, while until recently a number of studies showed that costs were a major barrier to reducing transport GHG emissions (see Liu and Santos, 2015 and the US National Research Council, 2013), it is now widely accepted that cost parity between conventional vehicles and EVs will be achieved by the mid-2020s. The rapid fall in EV costs is based on both the falling price and the rising power/weight ratio of batteries (both automotive and standalone). Such has been the extent of this fall, it is being claimed that if volume production of EVs was currently comparable to that of conventional cars, cost parity would already have been achieved for some models.

Thirdly, the sharp fall in photovoltaic (PV) solar panel costs – now equal to or below that of wind power (Australian Renewable Energy Agency, 2017) – is leading to a rapid increase in RRS, and is beginning to spread to commercial buildings (Webb et al., 2017). This is opening the opportunity for its use as a means of powering EVs, and thus the opportunity for distributed and largely renewable power sources to be a significant means in supporting the transition to EVs, and vice versa.

To what extent distributed solar, battery storage and a combination of the two will be used to power EVs, and in what ways EVs will utilize public charging networks is, therefore, a key issue examined in this chapter. It is argued that, based on Australian EV users, home and/or workplace charging will continue to be the most prevalent means of charging EVs in the absence of a readily available network of workplace charging facilities, at least in the short run. The direct and indirect sources of this charging will be a mix of distributed energy resources and grid electricity, given the energy demands of a single EV can represent over 25% of a household's overall electricity consumption.

To examine this further, this chapter explores a range of literature and data sources. The US Department of Energy's Pacific Northwest National Laboratory (Kintner-Meyer et al., 2007) calculated that the US power grid could support 150 million EVs or 75% of light vehicles currently on US roads. That, however, would depend on managed demand and smart charging regimes to reduce pressure on peak load periods and an ability to overcome the issue of charging stress on electricity grids (Habib et al., 2015; Richardson, 2013; Mwasilu et al., 2014). A Californian study by Coignard et al. (2018) provides projections of the effect of unmanaged and managed EV charging on the electricity grid in term of its effect on the daily cycle of electricity consumption (graphically represented by the "duck curve" see Fig. 18.1) and ramp mitigation. At the outset, they find that the progressive transformation of the state's automotive fleet to EVs would not substantially harm the system-wide net load, even if all EVs are subject to uncontrolled charging; although they note some negative effects would nevertheless occur. Such a finding is largely replicated in other projections for European countries (McKinsey and Company, 2018) and Australia[1] (Kolokathis and Hogan, 2018; Australian Energy Market Operator, 2016) given the need for substantial generation capacity to meet early morning and evening usage but which is otherwise in excess. That is illustrated in the projected effect on California's duck curve (Fig. 18.1). It should be noted here that the revolution that has taken place in solar technology, and the subsequent impact on price, is also most likely to take place with battery technology development and its impact on price. Prices of both technologies are likely to continue to fall as will

---

[1]According to AEMO (2016) estimates, the 20-year impact of electric vehicles on energy consumption in Australia is projected to be small adding only around 4% to 2035–36 projections of electricity use.

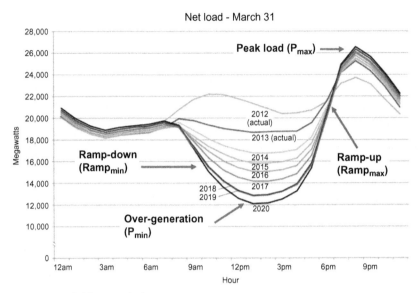

FIGURE 18.1 Californian duck curve.

the cost of installation and use of such technologies. Innovative ways of installing both solar and batteries in commercial and residential properties will also take place.

Coignard et al.'s (2018) calculations further show that a large fraction of the new 1.3 GW storage mandated by the Californian State Government could be obviated by smart EV charging from the grid (V1G) at a cost of $US150 million for installation of V1G-enabling equipment. This compares to an estimated outlay of $US1.45–$1.75 billion for additional new stationary storage. With a mix of V1G and two-way vehicle to grid and grid to vehicle charging (V2G) capable vehicles,[2] EVs could provide the equivalent of 5 GW of stationary storage (valued at between $12.8–$15.4 billion if provided through the construction of new stationary storage). Further savings are identified given the Californian system embodies 13–15 GW of non-dispatchable generating resources (largely combined cycle gas generators), which are difficult or highly undesirable to ramp down. While this is not seen as an urgent issue at present – in 2014, the net load on the Californian grid fell below the critical 15 GW level for only 0.03% of the year – by 2025 with the rise of renewables in the grid's power mix, the net load is forecast to fall below 15 GW for 14.2% of the year.

---

[2]Vehicle-to-grid (V2G) describes a system in which EVs can either send power to the grid or draw from it. That is it is a smart demand response system where EVs either return electricity to the grid or throttle back their charging rate.

3. ELECTRIC VEHICLES AND AUSTRALIA'S ENERGY PROFILE

The issues faced by California are no less significant in most other OECD countries, including Australia, which are simultaneously increasing the proportion of renewable energy in their power mixes and witnessing a transition to EVs, albeit at different rates. By using Australia as a case study, this chapter explores how EV-charging habits are evolving, and how this is likely to shape the role of EVs in power distribution and storage. In this context, the effect of Australia's globally high level of RRS is examined as a potential future trend in other countries with increasingly high levels of EV ownership, and how these two trends can be mutually supportive.

The extent to which a country may benefit from V1G and/or V2G will depend, in part, on the level of variability that can be expected as the proportion of renewable energy increases. For example, the state of Queensland in Australia has an identical renewable energy target to that of California – 50% by 2030 – although for Australia as a whole, this target is more modest at 20% by 2025. However, the Australian electricity grid remains heavily dominated by fossil fuels, which currently account for approximately 85% of energy generation – Table 18.1.[3]

Given coal-fired plants are more costly than combined cycle gas turbines (CCGT) to ramp up or down, for coal-dependent countries such as Australia, there are substantial potential financial gains to be made from using V1G and V2G to flatten the duck curve.

The extensive use of RRS in Australia, and regions such as California, has become an important part of residential energy generation and use. With the introduction of EVs – which, if used regularly for commuting, can add a further 25% to household energy use – RRS provides an added means for

Table 18.1 Renewable energy mix in Australia's national energy market

| Energy TWh | Wind & PV share of demand | | | | |
	NSW	QLD	Vic	SA	Total
Rooftop PV (cap factor 14%)	1.8	2.4	1.5	1.1	6.8
Utility PV (cap factor 28%)	0.9	1.7	1.0	0.5	4.1
Wind (cap factor 35%)	5.3	0.7	5.2	6.7	17.9
Total wind + PV supply	**8.0**	**4.8**	**7.7**	**8.2**	**28.8**
Electricity demand	**72.5**	**58.6**	**46.2**	**12.9**	**190.2**
Wind + PV share of total	11%	8%	17%	64%	15%

[3]The jurisdictions of Queensland, NSW, ACT, Victoria, Tasmania, and South Australia are all linked into a single grid – the National Energy Market (NEM) – the longest in the world.

increasing the cost effectiveness of a household's electricity consumption. This is particularly so in Australia, which has one of the highest penetration rates of RRS in the world (around 25% of all residences and close to one-third in Queensland). Consequently, RRS now represents over 14% of the national energy market's capacity (Australian Energy Regulator, 2017) (Table 18.1).

Globally, RRS is set to increase its penetration as the price of PV solar continues its sharp decline. In countries such as Australia, current assessments project that, in light of exceptionally high retail power prices[4] and the falling cost of PV, the high rate of RRS adoption will continue, but at a faster pace. For Queensland, projections (Jacobs Group, 2016) put the installed capacity of RRS rising from around 5000 MW in 2018 to between 5 and 6000 MW by 2030, with some building firms now integrating solar rooftop systems into their design (Burtt and Dargusch, 2015).

However, the direct use of RRS for EV charging currently faces a number of constraints, particularly given the uneven 24-hour duck curve consumption cycle. Fig. 18.2 shows the high level of daily variability of wind and solar power available to supply Queensland householders, which has some similarity to Californian households. Clearly, if EVs are used for commuting to and from work, then daytime charging using RRS – when residential demand is low and RRS power generation is at its peak – is not an option for a one-car family. However, as Coignard et al. (2018) note,

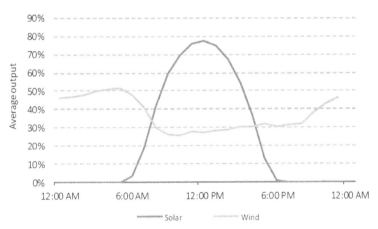

FIGURE 18.2 Daily variation in PV solar and wind power supply: Queensland.

[4]While Australia is one of the world's largest gas producers, almost all supply is locked into long-term export contracts.

flattening the duck curve then needs to rely on workplace charging. This is becoming an attractive economic proposition now that the cost of PV solar has fallen to a point which is beginning to make distributed commercial enterprise installations profitable without subsidies (Webb et al., 2017). A study by Neumann et al. (2012) estimated that if RRS were installed in parking lots of a medium-sized Swiss city, 14–50% of the passenger transport energy demand could be economically supplied depending on seasonal irradiation factors.

The issue for Australian EV owners is that they face some the highest grid supplied residential electricity prices in the world.[5] That has provided a major incentive to find ways of using RRS as an EV power source. Another key mechanism now emerging as an economic proposition is the use of residential standalone batteries. The Australian Climate Council (2017) points to a recent survey indicating that some 70% of households expected standalone batteries to be commonplace over the next decade. Not surprisingly, given the high penetration of RRS in Australia, the chief reason for this uptake was reported to be its role in linking up to RRS to reduce household power bills. The same report also notes that the uptake of standalone batteries has risen to over 20,000 in 2017, from a low base of around 7,000 in 2014. In light of these trends, a number of home builders are offering solar and battery packages built into the design and cost of new homes.

In the state of South Australia, the government has announced plans to provide a subsidy of around $2,500 for purchase of standalone home batteries and to eventually create connected micro-grids of residential standalone batteries for storage and feed-in to the grid when required. In Queensland, a support scheme was recently announced, which includes a $3,000 grant and $6,000 interest-free loan to encourage the uptake of home batteries.[6]

For Australia as a whole modeling has indicated that, by 2050, customer-owned generators (i.e., RRS) and storage could be supplying 30–45% of Australia's electricity consumption (Department of Environment and Energy, 2017a,b) involving a cumulative investment of around $200 billion.

---

[5]It should be noted that even with such high electricity prices, there is still >60% saving by switching from petrol to electricity for Australian residents, due to the energy efficiency of electric vehicles.

[6]For more details see: https://www.qld.gov.au/community/cost-of-living-support/loans-grants-battery-storage.

The use of standalone batteries also has potential in assisting cost-effective fast charging of EVs. While overnight home charging is the least expensive in terms of the cost of both electricity and charging hardware, for some – especially for those living in apartments, using on-street parking and long-distance travelers – it may not be viable or convenient. Fast charging points are, however, currently far more expensive to install – up to $150,000 in the US – reflected in the fact that they account for only 2,000 of the 16,000 charging stations currently deployed (McKinsey and Company, 2017). The rest are level two chargers which are capable of charging a 60-kWh battery (300–350 km of driving range) in 3–8 hours.[7] Level one chargers using a 120-VAC plug in the US (240-V plug in Australia) make up the majority of household EV chargers. A further issue attached to fast chargers is the demand charge that utilities typically apply to the rapid drawdown of power. However, McKinsey and Company (2017) points out that the use of standalone batteries at fast-charging stations could be used to help overcome the imposition of a rapid charge levy by being charged slowly during periods of low demand, and therefore at a lower cost. In this way, peak demand charges could be reduced by as much as 70%, thereby lowering the operating costs of charging stations.

Currently, in Australian states, there are varying restrictions on the extent to which power from rooftop solar can be fed into electricity grids, along with varying levels of remuneration. In Queensland, for instance, single-phase households are limited to 5 kW of grid feed-in (RRS and battery storage combined). Moreover, the future shape of the relationship between residential and grid power generation is yet to be clarified in Queensland where power generation and wholesale distribution is highly profitable and wholly state owned. Overall then, Australia faces a lack of a coherent and comprehensive policy driving the parallel demands of reducing GHG emissions, facilitating the increase in grid renewable energy and commercial accommodation of RRS and residential/EV battery storage. However, this can be expected to change due to increasing demands placed by the rapidly increasing number of consumers using solar/battery technology and EVs.

4. EV BATTERIES, STANDALONE BATTERIES, AND RRS

The integration of RRS, standalone batteries, and EVs into household energy usage regimes clearly presents greater flexibility and scope for householders

---

[7]Based on a 7–22 kWAC charging infrastructure.

to cost effectively manage their electricity consumption. This potential is described by one Brisbane Tesla owner who invested $AU18,000 in a 6.5-kW rooftop solar system and a standalone battery. The combination was sufficient, he reported, to meet most of the household's daily electricity usage (40 kWh) and charge the 7-kWh Tesla Powerwall battery. Savings were estimated at around $2500 a year on power bills and a payback period of 7 years was projected.

A more detailed analysis of an EV owner's domestic consumption patterns is provided in Section 6. This analysis more clearly demonstrates that access to both an EV and a standalone battery (especially if both are programmed for charging from and discharging to the grid) provides greater flexibility in terms of lowering power bills in the face of additional power consumption created by EVs. In particular, such a combination reduces dependence on workplace charging, can contribute to flattening the duck curve, as well as lowering ramping up and down costs as the proportion of grid renewables increases.

A study by Black and Veatch (2017) calculated that if the 251 million cars Americans driven in 2014 were electrified, the storage provided by the EVs' batteries could not only obviate future needed storage investment but also be profitable for EV owners. A review of the relevant literature by Richardson (2018) indicates that V2G systems could provide owners with a profit of between $100–300 annually.

5. EVS: ADOPTION FUTURE TRENDS

As of January 2018, there were over 3.3 million EVs globally with over 150 different electric models available (EV-Volumes, 2018). The majority of the EV fleet is concentrated in OECD nations and in particular in China, where national and regional governments have actively supported improvements in vehicle fuel efficiency and emissions standards. Globally, 39% of all EVs sold occurred in 2017 (1.3M), indicating that sales are tracking up on an exponential curve.

Bullish studies have predicted that the global share of EV sales will rise to as high as 56% of all new cars by 2040 (Bloomberg New Energy Finance, 2018) (Fig. 18.3). This projection is based on estimates that EVs will be cheaper to purchase than internal combustion engine (ICE) vehicles in most countries by 2025–2029 (Bloomberg New Energy Finance, 2017), and given the substantially lower cost of electricity compared to gasoline.

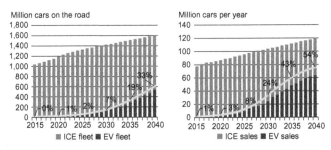

FIGURE 18.3 Projection of global light-duty EV vehicles sales and fleet penetration: 2015–2040.

6. CASE STUDY: AUSTRALIA'S EV MARKET

EVs are not currently a major component of vehicles sales in Australia. As of early 2018, there were approximately 8,500 EVs (EV-Volumes, 2018), out of a total fleet of 14 million passenger vehicles (Australian Bureau of Statistics, 2017). While EVs represented only 0.2% of new vehicle sales in 2017, sales are increasing rapidly, with early 2018 figures suggesting a 60% increase compared to 2017 (Fig. 18.4).

Australia's sluggish track record in EV uptake is in large part due to the almost complete lack of government incentives for EVs, the absence of supportive policies for increasing fuel efficiency and limited government support for reducing vehicle emissions.

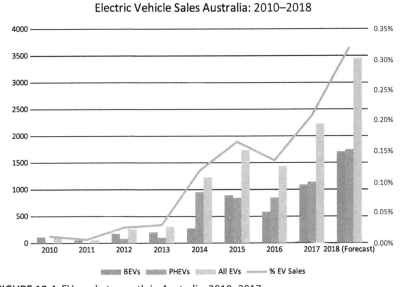

FIGURE 18.4 EV market growth in Australia: 2010–2017.

Predictions of future EV sales in Australia vary significantly across different studies. Energeia (2016) estimates there will be 2.2 million EVs on Australian roads by 2030. Moreover, even with only moderate policy intervention, Energeia projects that 49% of all new vehicles sales will be EVs by 2030, rising to 100% by 2040 (Energeia, 2018).

In line with gradually increasing EV sales, the provision of public charging infrastructure has also increased in Australia over recent years. As shown in Fig. 18.5, as of April 2018, over 700 standard charging stations were available nationally, in addition to 92 fast chargers and 22 Tesla superchargers.

At a national level, there are effectively no major incentives for EVs or other low emissions vehicles. In fact, unlike many other countries, Australia does not even have mandatory fuel efficiency standards. The Australian Government released a Vehicle Emissions Discussion Paper in 2016; however, no actions or policy measures have yet been generated through this process.

Moving forward, a key issue is the absence of a national policy which seeks to use an increasing EV population as a means of reducing GHG emissions. This is despite Australia's current vehicle fleet being a major contributor to CO_2 emissions. Another issue is a lack of policies which seek to increase the uptake of EVs and thereby provide the storage needed as the proportion of grid renewables rises. That stands in contrast to California which has a more holistic policy toward reducing CO_2 emissions through both legislating an increase in electric vehicles and driving toward zero emissions housing. This is further explored by Sioshansi, in Chapter 14.

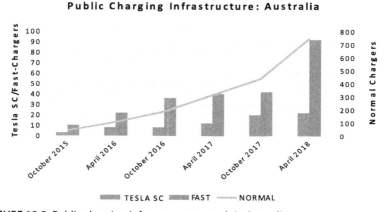

FIGURE 18.5 Public charging infrastructure growth In Australia.

7. EV HOUSEHOLD/GRID CHARGING REGIME CASE STUDY

In order to provide an example of residential EV charging using distributed energy resources, the following case study of a Brisbane house has been included in this chapter. This Brisbane house has a 6-kW solar system (6-kW REA Solar microinverter system[8]/12 degree tilt/30 degree azimuth), a Tesla Powerwall 2 battery (13 kWh), a Mitsubishi Outlander PHEV (50 km driving range/10 kWh battery), heated swimming pool, air-conditioning, electric hot water, and electric kitchen appliances. Table 18.2 provides an overview of the electrical generation and load figures for the case study house.

Examples of the house's electricity generation and consumption during a summer and winter day are also shown in Figs. 18.6 and 18.7. On a clear summer day, the house's rooftop solar system produces a maximum of 40 kWh. This is more than sufficient to power the house's electricity loads, including charging the EV. As such, the excess electricity generated by the solar system is exported to the grid after the battery is charged (as denoted by "grid export (solar)" in Fig. 18.6). While there is little to no pool heating load during the summer, this is partly offset by increased air-conditioning use, particularly during the evenings.

In contrast to summer, on a clear winter day, the house's rooftop solar system will produce a maximum of 26 kWh. While this is generally sufficient to power the house's average daily electricity loads, it depends on the prior day's weather. As shown in Fig. 18.7, while this winter day had near

Table 18.2 Household energy consumption and generation

Household energy consumption:	25 kWh per day (9,125 kWh p.a.)
- Pool (averaged over year)	- 5 kWh per day (20%)
- Pool heating (averaged over year)	- 4 kWh per day (16%)
- Hot water (averaged over year)	- 4 kWh per day (16%)
- Electric vehicle (35 km per day)	- 6 kWh per day (24%)
- Other loads	- 6 kWh per day (24%)
Day/night consumption split:	70% day/30% night
- Per day	17.5 kWh (day)/7.5 kWh (night)
- Per annum	6,389 kWh (day)/2,737 kWh (night)
Tesla Powerwall 2 capacity:	13.4 kWh (90% roundtrip efficiency)
- Night energy requirement	8.3 kWh per day (3,042 kWh p.a.)
Total solar energy required:	6,389 kWh + 3,042 kWh = 9,429 kWh p.a.
6-kW solar PV system energy generation	26 kWh per day (9,490 kWh p.a.)

[8] 6 kW of LG Neon R Panels connected to 5 kW of Enphase Microinverters.

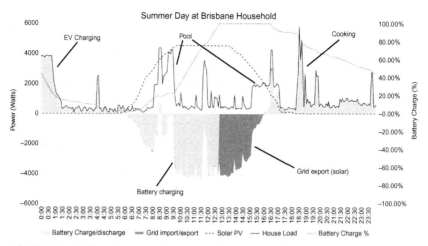

FIGURE 18.6 Brisbane household consumption and generation – summer.

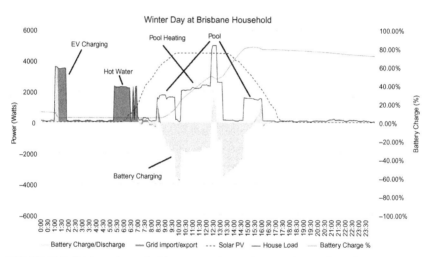

FIGURE 18.7 Brisbane household consumption and generation – winter (as mentioned, the illustration of a winter day's energy generation and consumption for this household shows an ideal, clear sunny day's RRS generation, which leads to provision of enough energy to meet the household's daily requirements, including EV charging. This compares to the previous cloudy day, which did not generate significant solar energy, and led to grid reliance during the early morning for hot water heating and EV charging).

ideal solar generation, the prior day was cloudy. As a result, the battery did not store sufficient electricity to charge the EV and power the hot water system overnight, and therefore, grid electricity had to be relied upon for these electrical loads during the early morning. Even after accounting for the higher pool heating loads during a winter's day, the system still charged the battery close to full, providing enough electricity to charge the EV for the next day's travel.

On the basis of green electricity[9] consumption rates averaging $AUD 0.35 per kWh over the next 5 years, the household's annual electricity cost would normally be $AUD 3,194 ($AUD 798 per quarter) – excluding connection fees.

The combined cost of the solar PV system and battery, including installation and off-grid capabilities, was approximately $AUD 21,000. Ignoring the minor amount of surplus solar energy generated (after accounting for the 90% roundtrip efficiency of the battery, and the low solar feed-in tariff rate of 0.14 per kWh), this system results in a payback period of approximately 6.6 years. While this system already makes economic sense based on current battery/solar pricing, on the basis of continuing reductions in prices, the payback period for new systems will continue to fall further, increasing the attractiveness of installing distributed energy resources at residential premises.

The house's battery is warranted for 10 years and the solar PV system for 25 years. Even after assuming the battery will need to be replaced/supplemented after 15 years (at an additional cost of $AUD 5,000), and accounting for degradation of the solar system's performance, this house's solar and battery system still equates to locking in electricity rates at approximately $AUD 0.12 per kWh for 25 years – a 65% saving over estimated grid electricity costs.

Focusing on the cost of charging the house's EV, on the basis of electricity costing $AUD 0.12 per kWh, this equates to a transport energy cost of $AUD 2.06 per 100 km. The equivalent gasoline Mitsubishi Outlander uses approximately 7 liters per 100 km. Given the volatility of oil prices, it is difficult to forecast future pricing, but even based on current Australian gasoline pricing of $AUD 1.50 per liter, this equates to $AUD 10.50 per 100 km. In other words, the switch to an EV will result in an 80% saving in transport energy costs.

It's important to note, however, with a price premium of approximately $AUD 15,000 for the Outlander PHEV over the equivalent gasoline model, even with the lower operating costs, the payback period is approximately 13 years. However, as this price premium continues to fall over the coming 5–10 years, EVs will become increasingly cost competitive from a total cost of ownership perspective.

---

[9] 100% renewable energy credits or offsets.

While this house's distributed energy resources come close to eliminating the need for grid electricity, this is dependent on reliably clear weather, which is not guaranteed, despite Brisbane's relatively sunny climate. As such, while the house's grid dependency has been significantly reduced, at the current level of electricity consumption, the grid connection is still required to provide additional energy security.

It could be argued that if the house installed additional battery capacity, it may be able to disconnect from the grid. However, the constraining factor in the achievement of nonsumer status is roof space and panel efficiency. Given most suburban homes in both Australia and California have gabled roofs, only 25–50% of this roof space is facing in the correct direction for solar. Thus, for the average 3–4 bedroom Australian house, the utilizable space available is in the region of 30–40 m^2, which would at most accommodate a 6–8 kW system RRS. Accepting that solar panels have only around 20% efficiency,[10] such a system would generate around 40–50 kWh in summer – more than sufficient to power the average suburban home including 150–200 km worth of electric driving per week. However, in winter on a clear day, power output is likely to fall to around 20–25 kWh; roughly equal to daily consumption. Thus, even with a standalone battery, grid backup will likely be required in order to maintain an adequate level of household energy security.[11]

Furthermore, in Queensland, solar PV systems cannot export more than 5 kW per day to the grid (at single-phase households), meaning that any electricity generated in addition to this which is not consumed by the house or stored in the battery, is lost. This can have significant cost implications for solar PV systems with inverters greater than 5 kW.

The assessment of this case study highlights the fact that while single-vehicle households may be able to significantly reduce their grid dependency, the addition of even one more vehicle – assuming a similar utilization rate of 35 km per day on average (Australian average distance; requiring approximately 6 kWh per day) – would increase the total house's energy consumption by almost 25%, with two EVs accounting for almost 40% of the house's daily electricity consumption. As such, despite RRS and batteries leading to decreased dependency on the grid, on average, EVs are likely

[10]The case study RRS is one of the most efficient and high wattage panels available on the market at 350W per panel (LG Neon R). The panel is 1700×1016 mm taking up approximately 1.7 m^2 per panel.
[11]However, as outlined by Sioshansi in Chapter 14 in regard to new Californian residences, such interdependence does not mean they cannot be classified as carbon neutral.

to necessitate some level of grid dependency. Moreover, grid utilization provides support not only for the uptake of EVs but also facilitates (through V1G and V2G bidirectional charging technologies) the possibility of greater battery storage as the uptake of grid renewables rises. These trends should be viewed as a positive – given the significant investment of governments in grid distribution assets (poles and wires).

8. RESULTS OF SURVEY ON CHARGING HABITS OF EV OWNERS

A survey of members from EV owners' associations from across Australia was carried out during April and May 2018, producing 153 responses – after filtering out electric bicycle owners, after-market electric vehicle conversions and incomplete responses. A comparison of the distribution of EV survey respondents with EV owners across Australia is shown in Table 18.3.

85% of respondents were battery-electric vehicle (BEV) owners and 15% plug-in hybrid electric vehicle (PHEV) owners. In terms of vehicle models, 43% were Tesla, 18% Nissan, and 25% Mitsubishi. Reflecting the high proportion of BEVs, vehicles had an average battery driving range of 242 km and an average battery capacity of 48 kWh.

The average daily distance traveled was 46 km per day (320 km per week), considerably higher than the all vehicle average of around 20–25 km indicated in surveys of Australian cities. The greater usage level clearly relates to the high proportion of surveyed EVs used for commuting. On the issue of cost, it is notable that most owners (over 70%) indicated that the overall lifetime costs of an EV would be less than that of a comparable internal combustion engine vehicle (ICV). Moreover, given that a majority of respondents also owned an ICV in addition to an EV, the choice of the latter for daily commuting also suggests they are taking advantage of the considerably lower fuel costs of EVs.

Nevertheless, in terms of the ranking of reasons for buying EVs, power and performance were top of the list, with "innovative technology" ranking similar to "lower running costs" in third place. It is therefore clear that the surveyed early adopters of EVs are paying the not-so-insignificant premium for an EV (over a comparable ICV) not primarily for cost-based or environmental reasons, but in order to acquire a new experience in automotive performance.

The charging profile of respondents clearly reflects a lack of workplace and public charging facilities in Australian cities. In terms of charging duration, on average, Australian EV owners sampled charged 93% of the time at

Table 18.3 Distribution of survey respondents across Australian States

	Queensland	New South Wales/ACT	Victoria	Tasmania	South Australia	Western Australia	Northern Territory
Proportion of respondents	15.6%	27.9%	14.3%	10.4%	7.1%	23.4%	1.3%
Proportion of EV fleet	14.7%	28.4%	26.5%	2.0%	19.6%	7.8%	1.0%

home (based on number of times charged multiplied by the average duration of charging), 3% at their workplace, and an identically small percentage at public AC chargers. The remaining 1% of time charging was carried out at public DC chargers. In terms of distinct charging events, 80% of charging occurred at home, 7% at work, 8% at public AC chargers, and 5% at public DC chargers.

While roughly one quarter of Australian residences have rooftop solar, that proportion was far higher for EV owners included in the survey sample at 73%, with an average install cost of $AUD 13,708 and an average capacity of 5.7 kW. The main reason indicated for installing RRS was to reduce electricity bills, although charging EVs comes in as equal second most important reason together with taking advantage of high feed-in tariffs. The proportion of those who placed importance on EV charging was higher among later installers (that is, the 30% who installed on or after 2014 when EV sales first became significant).

EV owners also proved to be leaders among Australian households in the use of standalone battery storage. 22% already own standalone batteries. Moreover, a further 53% said they would purchase a battery sometime in the future. This is despite the not-so-insignificant cost of a typical battery (an installed Tesla Powerwall costs around $AUD 11,000). The Boston Consulting Group (BCG) (2017) estimated that for Australia, residential and small-commercial battery storage would become cost effective in 2018. It is pointed out that the early break-even achievement is in large part due to Australia's wholesale electricity prices, which, as noted at around $AUD 130/MWh, are some of the highest in the world. By 2020, BCG projects that 30–40% of new RRS installations in Australia will be accompanied by battery storage (BCG, 2017). Other estimates put the number of households acquiring battery storage at between 500,000 to 1 million by 2020 (Reneweconomy, 2018) – an exponential increase from the 30,000 owners in 2017. Thus, with 2 million Australian households already having invested in PV rooftop solar, standalone batteries are presenting a cost-effective means to further reduce power bills, the more so for those intending to purchase an EV.

Another interesting finding was that survey respondents who had an EV, rooftop solar, and a home battery used an average of 23% of their annual solar generation to charge their primary EV. Most of this charging was carried out overnight (77% of all respondents). This closely aligns with the Brisbane household case-study where, on average, charging of the primary EV represented 24% of the home's daily electricity consumption, and 23% of the average daily solar generation (over the course of a year). It should also be noted that the case study household's solar system was closely aligned with the average solar system size of surveyed respondents (5.7 kW).

Both the case study and survey provide a profile of a typical suburban household in Australia with characteristics that are generally similar to households in other high RRS penetration regions such as California which has similar size of residence, climate, and energy use, along with relatively high levels of commuting by automobiles. Moreover, the overall energy use of the household in the case study and those surveyed is roughly the same once EV usage is taken into account. That usage is shown to account for around 23% of a household's power consumption. The survey further confirms the case study results, which indicate EVs in Australia are overwhelmingly charged overnight (the period averaging 5 hours over a 24 hour period) either from the standalone battery or off-peak grid.

The case study indicates that, even with the added power usage of EVs, the average 6-kW RRS system generates sufficient energy in total to meet a typical EV owning household's energy needs of around 25 kWh per day. However, it is equally clear that seasonal and daily variability – e.g., an intervention of successive cloudy days – will continue to make reliance on the grid (that is, overnight charging off-peak) an essential option for almost all households – even if a standalone battery is installed.

The exception may be where grid connection fees are particularly high – for example for those in remote areas – and where a fossil fuel generator may become an economic option as a means of complete separation from the grid. Utilities therefore need to accept that uptake of such a carbon-intensive alternative is likely to be encouraged by high grid connection fees. A literature search reveals an absence of studies of the economics of ancillary generators, which takes into account the fact that complete separation from the grid would remove the capacity to not only draw from, but also to be paid for, feeding into the grid.

Continued dependence on grids in the future when they are largely powered by renewables in Queensland and Californian, poses the question of how adequate storage is to be effected. That need is well indicated by climatic variability common to both California and Queensland. The prospect that standalone and automotive batteries – via V1G and V2G systems – could become a cost-effective and substantial part of either a grid's, micro grid's, or household's storage systems is, therefore, an enticing one and one which the EV owners' survey indicates could well be a cost effective reality.

There are, however, a number of impediments. It is noted that when EV batteries draw from the grid simultaneously in substantial numbers without smart charging systems and micro-grid storage arrangements, grids can be severely stressed. Such integration can also create other commercial issues where, as in the state of Queensland, the power utility is a state monopoly. In this situation, integration is likely to bring with it a progressively shrinking market for commercial-scale grid generation. This may call for a completely new business model, which embraces residential and EV-based DERs. Such a model could position power utilities to create and manage appropriately sized micro-grids by tying together the output of RRS and the storage provided by residential standalone and EV batteries.

A further advantage of bringing standalone and EV batteries into the storage system is that given the gold-plating of Australia's electricity grid, they could provide a cost-effective means of paying off this investment and drawing customers into a continuing partnership with the commercial grid. That is, by making EVs and standalone batteries interactive commercial partners in power supply and storage, a pathway is created for electricity utilities to ensure that grid dependency is maintained. More generally, such a development would allow the costs of electricity infrastructure to be spread across a wider range of consumers, resulting in greater price equity so that the benefits are not solely derived by those who own property and can afford to install solar and battery storage systems.

9. CONCLUSIONS

The survey and case study indicate that a rising number of Australian EV owners are also investing heavily in RRS (70%) and standalone batteries. By integrating their power generation and storage capabilities, EV owners are demonstrating they are able to cost effectively reduce their overall household power and transport energy bills. Batteries offer the opportunity to reduce residential grid dependence, and where permitted, feed excess solar power to the grid at times of peak tariffs. The high uptake of standalone batteries by early EV adopters is set to continue, being driven in part (as demonstrated by the case study) by its role in helping to greatly reduce transport energy costs. Equally, the case study indicates that, in summer months at least, standalone batteries can have a dual role of both charging EVs overnight and flattening the evening residential duck curve peak.

These developments are therefore moving households further away from prosumer status to prosumagers and considerably closer to being – but not wholly – self-sufficient (which, for most households at the moment, is not an option without a further major improvement in PV efficiency). But it is equally evident that once households acquire more than one EV (in Queensland the average is 1.8 vehicles per household) and the lower power-generating capacity of RRS in winter months are factored in, a more complex system of residential power generation and storage will be called for in an era of increasing use of renewable energy.

Utilities will consequently need to develop new business models that accommodate rapid technological advances, market forces, and consumer willingness to switch and take advantage of these emerging benefits. In doing so, utilities need to also carefully factor in the near-term EV cost parity with ICVs. As our survey shows, even with substantial current cost differentials between EVs and ICVs, most EV owners feel their investment is cost effective, particularly when they are also owners of RRS and standalone batteries. Consequently, this study indicates a cost-effective component of a new business model which takes advantage of the impending EV era, can be the utilization of the growth of both standalone and EV batteries as a means to expand the grid's storage system whose power sources are becoming progressively more based on renewables. Such an integration of EV and standalone batteries within power grids will require embracing a combination of V1G, V2G, higher RRS grid feed-in limits, as well as facilitation of PV-linked workplace charging.

REFERENCES

Australian Bureau of Statistics, 2017. Motor vehicle census, Australia, 31 Jan 2017. http://www.abs.gov.au/ausstats/abs@.nsf/mf/9309.0.

Australian Climate Council, 2017. Fully charged: renewables and storage powering in Australia. https://www.climatecouncil.org.au/battery-storage-2018.

Australian Energy Market Operator, 2016. AEMO insights: electric vehicles. August 2016 https://www.aemo.com.au/Media-Centre/~/-/media/5A0AB3A41BC8468BB-B97A1C79E8AD1BA.ashx.

Australian Energy Regulator, 2017. https://www.aer.gov.au/system/files/AER%20State%20of%20the%20energy%20market%202017%20-%20A4.pdf.

Australian Renewable Energy Agency, 2017. Large Scale Solar Projects, 2017. ARENA, Australian Government. https://arena.gov.au/assets/2017/06/AU21509_ARENA_Large_Scale_Solar_Brochure_v6-1.pdf.

Black and Veatch, 2017. Whose driving electric vehicle charging? https://www.bv.com/sites/default/files/17%20BV%20Electric%20Vehicle%20Report.pdf.

Bloomberg New Energy Finance, 2017. Electric vehicle outlook: 2017. https://data.bloomberglp.com/bnef/sites/14/2017/07/BNEF_EVO_2017_ExecutiveSummary.pdf.

Bloomberg New Energy Finance, 2018. Electric vehicle outlook: 2018. https://about.bnef.com/electric-vehicle-outlook.

Boston Consulting Group, 2017. How batteries are disrupting electricity markets. http://img-stg.bcg.com/BCG-How-Batteries-and-Solar-Power-Are-Disrupting-Electricity-Markets-Jan-2017_tcm30-152400.pdf.

Burtt, D., Dargusch, P., 2015. The cost-effectiveness of household photovoltaic systems in reducing greenhouse gas emissions in Australia: linking subsidies with emission reductions. Appl. Energy 148, 439–448.

Coignard, J., Saxena, S., Greenblatt, J., Wang, D., 2018. Clean vehicles as an enabler for a clean electricity grid. Environ. Res. Lett. 13 (5), 054031.

Department of Environment and Energy, 2017a. Australia's emissions projections 2017. December 2017 http://www.environment.gov.au/climate-change/climate-science-data/emissions-projections.

Department of Environment and Energy, 2017b. Australian energy update 2017 August 2017. https://www.energy.gov.au/sites/g/files/net3411/f/energy-update-report-2017.pdf.

Energeia, 2016. Shifting gears: the Australian electric vehicle market to 2030. http://energeia.com.au/wp-content/uploads/2014/02/Shifting-Gears-The-Australian-Electric-Vehicle-Market-to-2030.pdf.

Energeia, 2018. Australian electric vehicle market study. https://arena.gov.au/assets/2018/06/australian-ev-market-study-report.pdf.

EV-Volumes, 2018. Electric vehicles sales and infrastructure database. Supplied, 14 May 2018 http://www.ev-volumes.com/.

Habib, S., Kamran, M., Rashid, U., 2015. Impact analysis of vehicle-to-grid technology and charging strategies of electric vehicles on distribution networks—a review. J. Power Sources 277, 205–214.

International Energy Agency, 2016. C02 emissions from fuel combustion by sector in 2014. In: CO2 Emissions From Fuel Combustion. IEA. in CO2 Highlights 2016 -Excel tables http://www.iea.org/publications/freepublications/publication/co2-emissions-from-fuel-combustion-highlights-2016.html.

Jacobs Group (2016). Projections of uptake of small scale systems: Final report. Australian Energy Market Operator. https://www.aemo.com.au/-/media/Files/Electricity/NEM/Planning_and_Forecasting/NEFR/2016/Projections-of-uptake-of-smallscale-systems.pdf.

Kintner-Meyer, M., Schneider, K., Pratt, R., 2007. Impacts assessment on plug-in hybrid vehicles on electric utilities and regional U.S. power grids part 1: technological analysis. Pacific Northwest National Lab., U.S. Dept. of Energy, Richland, WA.

Kolokathis, C., Hogan, M., 2018. Keys to integrating electric vehicles already in hand. In: Regulatory Assistance Project. https://www.raponline.org/blog/keys-to-integrating-electric-vehicles-already-in-hand/.

Liu, J., Santos, G., 2015. Decarbonising the road transport sector: breakeven point and consequent potential consumers' behaviour for the US case. Int. J. Sustain. Transp. 9 (3), 159–175.

McKinsey and Company, 2017. Electrifying insights: how automakers can drive electrified vehicle sales and profitability. https://www.mckinsey.com/~/media/McKinsey/Industries/Automotive%20and%20Assembly/Our%20Insights/Electrifying%20insights%20How%20automakers%20can%20drive%20electrified%20vehicle%20sales%20and%20profitability/Electrifying%20insights%20-%20How%20automakers%20can%20drive%20electrified%20vehicle%20sales%20and%20profitability_vF.ashx.

McKinsey and Company, 2018. Charging Ahead: Understanding the Electric-Vehicle Infrastructure Challenge. McKinsey and Co. August, 2018 https://www.mckinsey.com/industries/automotive-and-assembly/our-insights/charging-ahead-understanding-the-electric-vehicle-infrastructure-challenge.

Mwasilu, F., Justo, J.J., Kim, E.K., Do, T.D., Jung, J.W., 2014. Electric vehicles and smart grid interaction: a review on vehicle to grid and renewable energy sources integration. Renew. Sust. Energ. Rev. 34, 501–516.

National Research Council, 2013. Transition to Alternative Vehicles and Fuels. http://www8.nationalacademies.org/onpinews/newsitem.aspx?RecordID=18264.

Neumann, H.-M., Daniel, S., Franz, B., 2012. The potential of photovoltaic carports to cover the energy demand of road passenger transport. Prog. Photovolt. Res. Appl. 20 (6), 639–649.

Pachauri, R.K., Allen, M.R., Barros, V.R., Broome, J., Cramer, W., Christ, R., Church, J.A., Clarke, L., Dahe, Q., Dasgupta, P., Dubash, N.K., 2014. Climate Change 2014: Synthesis report. Contribution of Working Groups I, II and III to the fifth assessment report of the Intergovernmental Panel on Climate Change. IPCC151.

Reneweconomy, 2018. Electric vehicles to reach cost parity with petrol cars by 2018. https://reneweconomy.com.au/ubs-electric-vehicles-to-reach-cost-parity-with-petrol-cars-by-2018-2018/.

Richardson, D.B., 2013. Electric vehicles and the electric grid: a review of modeling approaches, impacts, and renewable energy integration. Renew. Sust. Energ. Rev. 19, 247–254.

Richardson, P., 2018. The Economics of Renewable Energy. Lecture QUT, March, 2018 Department of Natural Resources, Mines and Energy.

Santos, G., 2017. Road transport and CO2 emissions: what are the challenges? Transp. Policy 59, 71–74.

Webb, J., Steinberg, W., Stein, W., Wilson, C., 2017. Solar grid parity and its impact on the grid. In: Sioshansi, F. (Ed.), Innovation and Disruption at the Grid's Edge: How Distributed Energy Resources Are Disrupting the Utility Business Model. Elsevier.

CHAPTER 19

Distributed Energy Resources in the US Wholesale Markets: Recent Trends, New Models, and Forecasts

Udi Helman
Helman Analytics, San Francisco, CA, United States

1. INTRODUCTION

The preceding chapters in this book are primarily focused on the new service options available to consumers, prosumers, and prosumagers, based in large part on the rapid expansion of cost-effective behind-the-meter assets, and their impact on industry business models. This chapter addresses how distributed energy resources (DERs), which are defined to include both behind-the-meter assets and small in-front-of-the-meter resources, and alternative service options, participate in the wholesale electric power markets and affect power system operations and reliability. While the chapter is focused on the United States, similar regulatory developments and market issues are relevant to other countries with expanding retail customer choices and high and rising penetration of DER.

The US wholesale power markets (Fig. 19.1), operated by independent system operators (ISOs),[1] are expected to be a large source of economic value for the existing and new types of DER – which, depending on the region, may consist of small-scale generation, energy storage, types of demand response, and energy efficiency. These wholesale markets include energy, ancillary services, and capacity. ISOs also administer procurement of some ancillary services using various payment formulas, such as voltage control/reactive power and blackstart. In addition to the wholesale value, DERs obtain economic value from a range of other services, which are not considered

---

[1] The term ISO is used generically to describe all regional market operators, including those which are formally designated in the United States as Independent System Operators (ISOs) and Regional Transmission Operators (RTOs).

Consumer, Prosumer, Prosumager
https://doi.org/10.1016/B978-0-12-816835-6.00019-X
431

FIGURE 19.1 US and Canadian ISOs, 2018. *(Source: ISO-RTO Council, September 2018.)*

in this chapter, including transmission and distribution deferral, distribution operations, and retail customer bill reductions and backup power.

When eligible to provide the different types of wholesale services, entities with DERs can participate directly in the markets, or they may affect the markets indirectly. In turn, direct participation can be "active" through submission of bids and offers, which if they clear the markets, are financially settled at market-clearing prices, or "passive" in providing self-scheduled or as-available energy or preshaped profiles, which are also settled financially through the markets. When DER do not participate at all in the wholesale markets, they may still affect the requirements and costs in those markets of the load-serving entity. For example, rooftop PV installed in response to retail customer incentives may change customer load shapes during peak hours and reduce load-serving entity capacity obligations. DER of different types may also cause costs, which can be incurred directly by the DER operator or may be shifted to other wholesale or retail customers. For example, the large capacity of PV installed in California has increased power system ramps and thereby caused additional operational costs to other wholesale buyers. In some regions, which are implementing "value of DER" retail tariffs, wholesale market prices will affect the rates offered to customers with behind-the-meter DERs (e.g., in New York).

This chapter focuses on how these resources will participate in the US ISO wholesale markets, alongside the large-scale (or bulk) generation and storage resources, which will continue to comprise the majority of electric power resources for several decades. Several examples are shown in which types of DER have already substantially entered particular wholesale markets, notably demand response and energy efficiency in the capacity markets, demand response in the contingency reserve markets, distributed storage in some of the frequency regulation markets, and different types of DER in the energy markets. Although DER definitions vary, by some measures, DER already constitute about 20% of the capacity (MW) in California and 16% of the capacity in the ISO-New England markets (ISO-New England, 2018c), and have provided as much as 25% of system energy in some hours in the California ISO.

Although most of the chapters in this book address new models for responsive retail load, this chapter uses the broadest definition of DER as small-scale ($\leq 20\,\text{MW}$) installations connected to the transmission and distribution network and customer-sited resources (including load management) of all sizes. This definition helps to capture the trends toward smaller resources generally being led by photovoltaics, which can be installed at different scales all over the grid, as well as at the customer site. In addition, all the wholesale markets and some state regulators are moving toward greater flexibility in accommodating aggregations of different types of distributed resources.

The chapter is organized as follows:

- Section 2 is a brief overview and description of the US wholesale markets;
- Section 3 provides a survey of how what are now called DER first participated in these markets and the transition to the most recent models;
- Section 4 is an inventory of existing and forecast DER, showing that by some measures, some ISOs are already close to 20% DER by capacity;
- Section 5 describes how DER participate in the wholesale markets;
- Section 6 examines some key further issues in DER participation followed by the chapter's conclusions.

The chapter, however, does not consider other technical aspects of the DER participation in the ISO markets, such as interconnection standards and procedures, metering, communications, telemetry requirements, and forecasting of DER production or net load reductions.

2. OVERVIEW OF THE US WHOLESALE MARKETS

In the United States, the organized wholesale markets operated by ISOs were introduced beginning in the late 1990s on a single-state or multi-state basis, subject to regulation by the Federal Energy Regulatory Commission (FERC), with the exception of most of the Texas market, which is regulated by the Public Utilities Commission of Texas (PUCT). As shown in Fig. 19.1, there are now seven such markets, which cover more than 75% of the nation's electric power systems measured by demand.[2] The details of ISO tariffs and market rules are found on the ISO websites, and market performance can be tracked in the state of the market reports put out by the ISO market monitors. While FERC regulates the rules of the ISO wholesale markets outside Texas, entry of DER is largely driven by state policies, which themselves may reflect policy preferences for the structure and resource mix of the electric power industry within the state.[3]

The four primary types of wholesale products are energy, ancillary services, capacity, and financial transmission rights. This chapter focuses on the first three of these.[4] Each of the ISOs runs wholesale markets in a sequence. The capacity markets are implemented months or years ahead of actual operations. The day-ahead energy and ancillary service markets clear on an hourly basis simultaneously over the 24 hours of the next operating day. The day-ahead markets establish schedules for each selected resource

---

[2]These are, in alphabetical order, California ISO (CAISO), Electric Reliability Council of Texas (ERCOT), ISO-New England, New York ISO (NYISO), Midcontinent ISO (MISO), PJM, and Southwest Power Pool (SPP). In addition, the CAISO operates the Energy Imbalance Market (EIM) in several other western states.

[3]In some states, the investor-owned utilities comprising the electric power industry were largely "restructured" in the late 1990s requiring a separation between ownership of generation (through divestiture), transmission and in some states implementing competitive retail choice. In California, and some other states, there is currently further restructuring underway, which is allowing community choice aggregators to become load-serving entities and third-party installers to profit from installation of photovoltaics, which reduce load and potentially shift costs to other retail customers. In other states, the utilities largely remain vertically integrated, but nonutility entities are allowed to invest in generation, storage, and demand response.

[4]Financial transmission rights (FTRs) are awarded to load-serving entities to allow them to hedge marginal congestion charges, or to other parties through auction markets and secondary sales. Location of DER can affect the value of FTRs indirectly by affecting power flows on the grid and possibly relieving congestion. These DER impacts are taken into account by FTR market participants during the monthly and annual allocations and auctions. Some research papers have evaluated the impact of distributed storage, which could be used to affect congestion on FTR allocations and valuation.

for the next day, as well as the financial settlement of those schedules at market-clearing prices. The real-time markets begin at midnight of the prior day and run within each operating hour on 5-minute intervals, with CAISO also having a 15-minute market. In these markets, 5-minute prices are calculated for energy along with hourly prices for ancillary services (and also 15-minute prices in CAISO). The remainder of this section examines basic design characteristics and offers some comments on trends in market prices. Section 4 focuses in more detail on the rules for DER, some market experiences, and ongoing reforms.

2.1 Energy Market Designs

Energy is defined in the wholesale markets as the injection or withdrawal of real power. The energy markets are the primary source of wholesale market value, typically accounting for over 80% of the cost of wholesale power procurement to buyers. Energy market prices are discussed further in Section 2.4. Under locational marginal pricing (LMP) of energy now utilized in each US ISO, each pricing location shows the cost of three components in each market interval: marginal energy (i.e., the marginal bid cost of the resource supplying the marginal MWh), marginal congestion, and marginal losses (as discussed next, there is also some degree of locational pricing by zone in ancillary services and capacity). LMP provides the most accurate price signal for where energy is most valuable on the transmission grid, which can encourage both short-term and long-term economic efficiency. For utility-scale renewable resources, locational energy pricing has been less important to date, as most such resources are sited based on forecast production (i.e., high wind or solar irradiation locations); however, for DER of different types, which can be located at, or closer to load, LMP is more important to signal the highest value locations. In some regions, locational pricing on the distribution network is also being examined, which would reflect the LMP plus the impact of distribution-level constraints.

Table 19.1 shows some of characteristics of the ISO energy markets. Two ISOs (CAISO and MISO) have recently implemented a ramping reserve in the energy markets. These reserves are intended to ensure that there is sufficient ramping range to address uncertainty about ramping requirements during real-time operations. Although not shown in the table, historically the minimum size for generation to participate in the energy markets has been 1 MW, but with small sizes allowed for demand response (of as little as 100 kW). Under new requirements from FERC, the minimum size of energy storage will also be reduced to 100 kW (FERC, 2018a).

Table 19.1 ISO energy market pricing characteristics

	PJM	ISO-NE	NYISO	MISO	SPP	ERCOT	CAISO
Name of energy pricing method	Locational marginal price (LMP)	LMP	Location-based marginal price (LBMP)	LMP	LMP	LMP	LMP
Name of ramping reserve, if implemented				Ramp capability product			Flexible ramping product
Number of supply nodes	1,950	900	500	2,380	750	750	3,000+
Number of load zones	20	8	11	6	17	4	3
Energy offer caps[a] ($/MWh)	$1,000	$1,000	$1,000	$1,000	$1,000	$9,000	$1,000
Energy price cap ($/MWh)	No	No	No	$3,500	No	No	No
Energy offer floor ($/MWh)	−$1,000	−$150, DR: −$75	−$1,000	−$500	−$500	−$250	−$150

[a]Each FERC jurisdictional market also allows offers greater than $1,000/MWh and up to a $2,000/MWh bid cap for resources which obtain approval based on cost justifications.

Source: Based on tables in EPRI (2016).

Aggregated DER will eventually be allowed to meet a minimum size in the 100–500 kW size. In the day-ahead markets, the time interval for transactions is 1 hour.

2.2 Ancillary Services

There are two types of ancillary services procured by ISOs: market-based ancillary services and tariff-based ancillary services. The market-based ancillary services include frequency regulation (usually called just regulation), contingency reserves (which include spinning reserves and nonspinning reserves), and in the future may include frequency responsive reserves if needed to meet NERC's Frequency Response Obligation (e.g., NERC, 2017). The tariff-based ancillary services include voltage control/reactive power and blackstart. If they meet eligibility requirements, DER can provide any of these market and nonmarket ancillary services.

Tables 19.2 and 19.3 show current minimum sizes to participate in these markets. As with energy, FERC (2018a) requires that energy storage be allowed to participate with a minimum size of 100 kW; we anticipate that subsequent requirements will be established for aggregated DER. The remainder of this chapter will focus on the market-based ancillary services.

Ancillary services generally account for under 5% and as little as 0.5% of wholesale market costs, but have high potential benefit for some DER resources, notably demand response and storage, and may account for more market value as conventional generation retires and production shifts to variable energy resources.

2.2.1 Frequency Regulation

Frequency regulation is energy injected or withdrawn, typically on time frames of 2–6 seconds, for purposes of maintaining system frequency in between the 5-minute dispatch. The quantity of this service needed in each ISO is a function of the system size, whether it is a part of a larger regional interconnection, and the impact of production deviations by variable energy resources. Table 19.2 provides details on the key characteristics of the regulation markets in each ISO. As is shown, they all procure a range for providing regulation from eligible resources, which is called regulation capacity (MW), and all except for ERCOT pay for performance on the basis of actual movement (also called mileage) by the selected resources. However, differences in the procurement methods and the pricing rules can lead to significant differences in the value of the product.

Table 19.2 Key characteristics of the ISO regulation markets

	ISO-NE	NYISO	PJM	MISO	SPP	ERCOT	CAISO
Product name	Regulation	Regulation	Regulation	Regulation	Regulation up, regulation down	Regulation service	Regulation up, regulation down
Regulation capacity name	Regulation capacity	Regulation capacity	Regulation capability	Regulating capacity	Regulation-up service, regulation-down service	Regulation service, fast responding regulation service	Regulation capacity
Performance component name	Regulation service	Regulation movement	Regulation performance	Regulating mileage	Regulation-up mileage, regulation-down mileage	N/A	Regulation mileage up regulation mileage down
Pricing locations	3 zones	3 zones	System	7 zones	4 zones	1 zone	2 fixed zones; up to 8 add'l subzones
Day-ahead procurement		✓		✓	✓	✓	✓
Real-time procurement	✓	✓	✓	✓	✓		✓

Minimum eligible resource size (MW)	5 MW (gen.); 1 MW (ATRR, which can be aggreg.)	1 MW (can be aggreg.)	0.1 MW	Varies by resource type, 1–5 MW	1 MW	0.1 MW	0.5 MW
Minimum offer size (MW)	0.1 MW	0.1 MW	0.1 MW	0.1 MW	0.1 MW	0.1 MW	0.01 MW
Offer cap ($/MW)	$100 for reg. capacity; $10 for Reg. Service	$1,000	$100	$500	$500	$7,000	$250
Offer floor ($/MW)	$0	$0	Not specified	−$500	−$500	$0	$0

Source: Based on tables in EPRI (2016).

Of relevance to DER, the table shows minimum sizes for market participation and the number of pricing zones, which can indicate where the higher value locations are. In addition to the details in the table, there are differences in the operating rules for regulation in the different ISO markets. For example, both PJM and CAISO have offered 15-minute energy neutral control signals to facilitate participation by energy limited storage; further discussion of these rules is in Section 4. Otherwise, generation resources have historically been expected to have a minimum continuous capability to follow the control signal for 30–60 minutes.

Market prices for Regulation are often closely correlated to the energy price, as marginal regulating resources are typically also available for energy and are paid an opportunity cost payment for providing regulating reserve capacity. A case study on the entry of distributed storage into the PJM Regulation market is provided below.

2.2.2 Contingency Reserves

The other major category of ISO ancillary service markets is contingency reserves, which are reserves held to recover from major contingencies such as unplanned outages of the largest generation or transmission elements. Spinning reserves are online resources, including demand response with economic bids, which can offer the range of output (or load drop), which they can achieve in 10 minutes and sustain from 30 minutes to 1 hour (see Table 19.3); nonspinning reserves are from offline generation and both economic and reliability demand response, which can respond within the time requirements (typically either 10 minutes or 30 minutes) and sustain for similar periods. Table 19.3 shows some of the relevant characteristics of the contingency reserve markets; some acronyms in the table are explained below the table. As discussed here, FERC (2018a) requires the minimum sizes for energy storage to be 100 kW. In all ISOs, excess faster responding online reserves can substitute for slower responding reserves if this lowers total procurement cost.

2.3 Resource Adequacy Requirements and Capacity Markets

Each of the U.S. ISOs, with the exception of ERCOT, has a resource adequacy requirement, which establishes the peak demand and reserves (denominated in MW) for each capacity zone, which load-serving entities must meet collectively through forward-capacity contracts or self-owned resources. The quantity of resource adequacy capacity needed to meet this requirement is established by the ISOs or state regulators, and load-serving

Table 19.3 Key characteristics of the ISO contingency reserve markets

	ISO-NE	NYISO	PJM	MISO	SPP	ERCOT	CAISO
Product name—spinning reserve	Ten-minute spinning reserve	Spinning reserve	Synchronized reserve	Spinning reserve	Spinning reserve	Responsive reserve	Spinning reserve
Product name—nonspinning reserve and supplemental reserve	Ten-minute nonspinning reserve; 30-minute operating reserve	Nonspinning reserve	Nonsynchronized reserve	Supplemental reserve	Supplemental reserve	Nonspinning reserve	Nonspinning reserve
Forward procurement	✓						
Day-ahead procurement		✓	[a]	✓	✓	✓	✓
Real-time procurement	✓	✓	✓	✓	✓	✓	✓
Minimum eligible size (MW)	Gen.≥1 MW; DR ≥0.1 MW	1 MW (can be aggregated)	0.1 MW	1 MW	1 MW	0.1 MW	0.5 MW
Minimum offer size (MW)	Not specified	0.1 MW	0.1 MW	0.1 MW	0.1 MW	0.1 MW	0.01 MW

Continued

Table 19.3 Key characteristics of the ISO contingency reserve markets—cont'd

	ISO-NE	NYISO	PJM	MISO	SPP	ERCOT	CAISO
Offer cap ($/MW)	FRM: $14/ kW-month	$1,000	SR–Tier 2: resource's O&M cost + $7.50/ MWh margin	$100	$100	$7,000	$250
Offer floor ($/MW)	FRM: not specified	Not specified	Not specified	−$100	−$100	$0	$0
Pricing locations	3 zones	3 zones	System; subzones may be defined	7 zones	4 zones	System	2 fixed zones; up to 8 add'l subzones
Minimum continuous energy when dispatched	30 min	30 min	30 min	30 min	1 hour	30 min	30 min

FRM, forward reserve market (ISO–New England); *SR*, synchronized reserve (PJM).
[a]PJM uses a day-ahead scheduling reserve in the day-ahead market.
Source: Based on tables in EPRI (2016).

entities are allocated a load-ratio share. Demand response is the primary type of DER currently participating in these markets, but other types of DER resources are now entering, as described in detail in Section 4. For DER, the higher capacity value in certain transmission-constrained zones, particularly around larger cities, is proving to be a growing market driver in regions such as California and New York.

Table 19.4 shows that three ISOs have fully centralized capacity markets, in which all such capacity procurement is transacted or self-provided at transparent market-clearing prices. Supply offers clear against a demand curve. MISO has a residual capacity auction, while load-serving entities in CAISO and SPP meet state resource adequacy requirements through self-owned or bilaterally contracted resources (CAISO conducts some very limited residual capacity procurement through its backstop mechanisms). In these bilateral markets, there is not a transparent market price for capacity. In California, state regulators and the CAISO have also added a "flexible capacity" requirement, which establishes that some of the procured capacity must be capable of supporting the evolving system ramps being created largely by solar energy production (CAISO, 2018). As noted, ERCOT does not have a resource adequacy requirement (and is called an "energy-only" market), but conducts periodic assessments of supply adequacy, which are used to set energy market bid caps, which are higher than in other markets (see Table 19.1).

In the ISOs where there are full-capacity markets with transparent prices, procurement of capacity by load-serving entities can range from 10–20% of total market costs. Capacity prices are highest when new capacity resources need to clear the auctions, and are lowest when prices are set by existing resources (i.e., during periods of low load growth). When energy market revenues decline, capacity market prices in principle act to support the "going forward" costs of existing capacity resources, to avoid mothballing and retirement, and to support new investment. A complicating factor in some regions is that much of new capacity is being introduced through state policies, such as renewable portfolio standards (RPS) and more recently, storage policies. Further details relevant to DER are examined in Section 4.

2.4 Considerations for DER Wholesale Market Participation

Because the ISO markets do not discriminate against new entrants, the wholesale markets are an important source of potential value for the new DER, and as installed costs of DER come down, many states are seeking to reduce subsidies to these resources and increase reliance on wholesale

Table 19.4 ISO centralized capacity market designs

	PJM	ISO-NE	NYISO	MISO
Name	Reliability Pricing Model (RPM)	Forward Capacity Market (FCM)	Installed Capacity Market (ICAP)	Planning Resource Auction (PRA)
Sloped demand curve	Yes	Yes (only for system-wide)	yes	no
Max. price	Net CONE	Net CONE	Net CONE	Net CONE
Minimum offer price rule	Yes	yes	yes	no
Number of locations	9 zones	3 zones	4 zones	10 zones
Must–offer requirement	DAM energy	DAM energy and RTM energy	DAM energy	DAM energy
Forward period	3 years ahead	3 years ahead	1 month prior	2 months prior
Commitment period	1 year	1 year	6 months	1 year
Product definition	Generic MW	Generic MW	Unforced capacity	Unforced capacity

Source: Based on tables in EPRI (2016).

market revenues or DER tariffs pegged to wholesale market value.[5] Some key features of the wholesale markets are that all resources scheduled or with bids accepted through the auction markets are paid the market clearing price, these prices are public, and barriers to further entry for DER are being reduced. Under most conditions, energy and ancillary service market clearing prices in energy are set by the bids of resources which have marginal fuel costs, and hence in most regions energy market prices will remain positive as long as those resources remain in operations. However, as discussed later, a number of further factors must be considered when considering DER business plans based on wholesale market participation or indirect valuation.

2.4.1 Administrative Costs

There is a financial cost to different types of market participation (e.g., active participation which requires metering and telemetry), which can be prohibitive to residential or commercial & industrial (C&I) customers with small DER installations. These costs can inhibit certain types of DERs from "active" participation, limiting them to either passive energy generation or demand response, which does not necessarily incur such costs.

2.4.2 Market Design Risk

ISO market rules are complicated, can vary in important details between ISOs, and at times rules can change dramatically in general or specific details, which can create both opportunities and risk for new technologies, including those which are DER. A recent example of this type of risk due to market rule changes is examined later in the case study of distributed battery storage in the PJM regulation market.

2.4.3 Market Price Risk

In the author's experience, new DER entrants often do not have a sophisticated understanding of how wholesale market prices are formed and their sensitivity to external factors. Market prices can change dramatically over time, even from year to year, creating uncertainty for different types of DER, particularly storage but also distributed PV. The trend in recent years has been toward lower energy value due primarily to low natural gas prices and in some regions, the increased penetration of variable energy resources. For example, FERC has calculated that from 2014 (the highest energy price

---

[5]To date, there are such tariffs in New York and Minnesota.

year over the past 5 years) to 2017, the average on-peak day-ahead energy market prices in the United States dropped from an average of $52/MWh to $33/MWh (prices are higher than this average in the coastal regions, and lower in the Midwest). These types of market price declines have negatively affected conventional generation, but DER continues to enter in many regions due to declining costs and policy support.

In regions with higher renewables, such as California and Texas, the impact on prices in certain high renewable production hours is already significant. For example, in 2017, the author calculates that the day-ahead CAISO energy market value of a solar profile in Southern California was about $25/MWh, which is around $10/MWh lower than the average annual energy price of $35/MWh, due to the impact of solar generation on market prices in those hours. Simulation studies suggest that with more solar coming online in California, the prices in most solar production hours will collapse to zero or negative within a few years (e.g., Eichman et al., 2015). As most new DER generation in California is forecast to be distributed PV, this trend suggests that the wholesale energy value will be minimal or may require new DER, which are intending to supply energy to the grid to have active controls to curtail during surplus hours. However, in other parts of the United States, this impact will take many more years to evolve.

2.4.4 Impacts of State Policies on the Wholesale Markets
In the United States, state governments (rather than the federal government) have established the primary policies, which provide incentives for DERs of different types (including through financial incentives, variants on net energy metering and value of DER tariffs, renewable portfolio standards, and utility DER procurement requirements), some of which are now entering the wholesale markets. The states also have the jurisdiction to determine rate recovery for utility-owned or contracted DER deployed for distribution deferral as well as how benefits from wholesale market participation are allocated between the utilities and nonutility entities. In addition, several states (in particular New York and California) are requiring refinements to distribution resource planning and operations, which will be the location of many if not eventually most DER, which will be seeking wholesale market participation. Hence, the way in which different types of DER are eligible for wholesale market participation has varied across the United States, creating both opportunities and sometimes barriers to entry. ISOs are having to adapt their systems and markets to accommodate these developments.

Finally, not all U.S. states have opted to join or create ISOs. The utilities in these regions remain vertically integrated, but nonutility resources can in principle locate on the transmission system and offer services to utility buyers (some services under tariff rates, and others under bilaterally contracted rates), or sell into neighboring ISO wholesale markets.[6] Second, some states in these regions have robust policies to support DERs, notably net energy metering policies (which offset retail rates), while the utilities may be themselves be required to meet state policies, which encourage development of distributed renewable resources. The primary difference with the regions with wholesale markets is that there isn't a transparent market for valuation of system energy and the other services.

3. THE HISTORICAL PHASES OF WHOLESALE MARKET PARTICIPATION BY DISTRIBUTED RESOURCES

Over the past few decades, there have been several waves of expansion in distributed resources, some in response to reliability needs, such as the large expansion in emergency and stand-by generation provided by reciprocating engines, and some due to other federal and state regulations which facilitated entry by small resources (EPRI, 2004). In recent years, some state policies, which earlier had been aimed at improving reliability and addressing peak demand through on-site generation were reoriented toward renewable energy and other new technologies such as fuel cells.[7]

With transmission open access and the start of the competitive US wholesale markets operated by ISOs in the late 1990s, there were new market participation opportunities for existing and new small generation[8] and end-use customer participation, facilitated by many other federal rules, which supported demand response and subsequently newer technologies such as distributed energy storage. These phases are examined briefly next.

---

[6]With respect to how DER resources sited in the nonmarket regions can interact with ISOs, at least in some locations, they can in principle be dynamically scheduled (which requires them to follow ISO dispatch) or otherwise schedule energy into a neighboring ISO market. Some of the Western utilities outside the CAISO have joined the Energy Imbalance Market operated by the CAISO, and other parts of the Western region are also examining creating organized wholesale markets.

[7]Such as the California Self-Generation Incentive Program (SGIP).

[8]The policy determination to allow competition in wholesale electricity generation was motivated in part by declining economics of scale in electricity production, notably smaller-scale natural gas-fired plants, which could enter the markets more rapidly than very large-scale fossil or nuclear plants.

3.1 The Demand Response Model

The emergence of demand response (DR) in wholesale markets has in many respects been the connective thread between small on-site generation, responsive load, and the newer attempts at an expanded DER aggregation model. DR is a method for compensating retail customers to participate in the wholesale markets, primarily by curtailing load but later extended in some markets also to cover provision of frequency regulation. There are generally two types of DR – load, which participates directly in the markets through economic bids; and load, which is only available for reliability-based curtailment instructions. The expansion of DR was supported by FERC over a series of orders, including Order 890 (2007), Order 1000 (FERC, 2011a), and Order 745 (FERC, 2011b), on demand response compensation, which will not be reviewed in detail here.

While DR has limitations on its capacity contribution to wholesale services, a next phase of DR may be the integration of such demand response capability into the more generalized aggregated DER model, allowing for more flexible aggregations, which can supply multiple market services utilizing different resource types at different times.

3.2 The New DER Technologies and Resources

The new types of DER, which are participating in the wholesale markets, include notably variable energy resources, such as photovoltaics (PV), other small renewable resources, and energy storage. Some states have also provided support for energy efficiency (which is categorized as DER in some regions but not others) and fuel cells. These resources have in some cases required new market participation models, and some modifications of the existing DR models. Four categories of DERs are outlined:

3.2.1 Variable Energy Resources

Integration of variable energy resources of various sizes and locations on the distribution and transmission networks or at the end-use customer site has required some modifications of conventional generator participation models. These include improved forecasting of variable energy production and requirements to submit bids into the markets for purposes of curtailment. The primary driver of the new DER participation is rooftop solar photovoltaics (PV) as well as different configurations of small in-front-of-the-meter PV systems. Beginning in the western states with high solar irradiation, but now penetrating rapidly in many other parts of the country, distributed PV is both reshaping load profiles and, as penetration of behind-the-meter installation increases, providing energy backflow to the distribution and transmission networks.

3.2.2 Limited Energy Storage

With the declining costs of lithium-ion batteries, and some increased installations of other types of small energy storage such as flywheels, there has been growth in distributed storage. Such devices located on the transmission and distribution networks and at the customer site are already eligible to provide wholesale markets services in some markets, and design initiatives are underway to facilitate further penetration. Most notably, FERC Order 841 (2018a) has required that all jurisdictional ISOs establish an Energy Storage Resource (ESR) market participation model, which establishes a minimum size for market participation of 100 kW, and provides rules for each market product as well as nonmarket ancillary services. However, as discussed further, there remain barriers to types of multiple-use application projects in some states.

3.2.3 Aggregated DER

The aggregated DER model is an extension of the prior distributed market participation models to incorporate newer small distributed technologies, which can be aggregated into a larger resource with potentially complicated operating and market characteristics. In particular, the addition of distributed storage to PV provides an opportunity for greater controllability of these resources, which can be paired also with controllable loads. Most ISOs are in the process of defining requirements for aggregated DER, including locational requirements for individual aggregations and metering and telemetry needed for them to actively participate in the markets (e.g., NYISO, 2017).

3.2.4 Potential Prosumer Models Which Incorporate DER

For the types of prosumers discussed in this book, who are interested in participating in the wholesale markets directly or via different intermediaries – e.g., a third-party aggregator, or a distribution system operator, which facilitates transactions with the ISO – there are several possible configurations. In a recent roadmap on DER participation in the wholesale markets, New York ISO (2017) has provided a useful typology of how these prosumers may participate under eight "use-cases," summarized in Table 19.5, which is modified somewhat from the original to remove acronyms and make the descriptions more generic.

Table 19.5 NYISO DER prosumer types and use cases

#	Type	Description	Wholesale services
1	Dispatchable load	Small-to-large size aggregated residential customers, dispatchable to partial load	Energy and possibly capacity
2	Dispatchable load	Medium-to-large size C&I customers dispatchable to partial load; not aggregated	Energy
3	Dispatchable load and generation	Small-to-large size residential customers with dispatchable load and generation with electronic communications to the ISO going through an aggregator	Energy, capacity, and reserves
4	Dispatchable load and generation	Similar to #3 but the electronic communications are direct to the distribution system operator (which interfaces with the ISO)	Energy, capacity, and reserves
5	Dispatchable load and storage	Similar to #3 except generation is replaced with storage	Energy, capacity, reserves, regulation
6	Dispatchable load and storage	Similar to #4 except generation is replaced with storage	Energy, capacity, reserves, regulation
7	Dispatchable load, storage, and generation	Similar to #3 except it includes storage	Energy, capacity, reserves, regulation
8	Dispatchable load, storage, and generation	Similar to #4 except it includes storage	Energy, capacity, reserves, regulation

Source: Based on the tables in NYISO (2017).

4. CURRENT STATUS AND REGIONAL FORECASTS OF DISTRIBUTED ENERGY RESOURCES IN THE UNITED STATES

Given the rapid current expansion in DER (using the broad definition), analysis of existing resources and future expansion has become a critical element in resource and transmission planning, as well as in understanding the evolving effects on system operations and wholesale markets. For certain distributed resource types, notably solar PV and more recently battery storage, there are periodic estimates of resource penetration in the trade press; for other types of resources, such analysis requires more data collection. In addition, forecasting of DER expansion for planning and reliability purposes has become a necessary function in the ISOs as well as many state regulators.

4.1 Existing DER Capacity

While different types of flexible consumers are the focus of this book, the largest component to date of DER participating (or potentially participating) in the wholesale markets are the small generators and storage, which can be located in front or behind the retail meter. To provide perspective on these resources, there are a few national inventories. Table 19.6 shows that in mid-2017, using data on in front of the meter generation resources from the U.S. Energy Information Agency (EIA) Form 860, there

Table 19.6 EIA inventory of small generation listed as electric power resources, 20 MW and under, in the United States, August 2017

	Aggregate MW	Number of installations	Number of installations ≤ 1 MW
Renewable and hydrogeneration			
Conventional hydroelectric	9,713	3,031	1,027
Solar photovoltaic	9,188	2,205	573
Onshore wind turbine	2,399	473	75
Geothermal	1,051	146	11
Biomass – total	2,512	403	109
Landfill gas	2,091	1,656	981
Municipal solid waste	522	42	0
Fossil fuel and other generation			
Natural gas and other gases	13,652	2,125	241
Petroleum products	8,660	3,139	802
Conventional steam coal	1,110	129	1
Other energy sources	424	54	3

Source: Compiled by author from EIA (2017).

are around 50 GW of small generation, defined here as between 1 MW and 20 MW, connected to the transmission and distribution systems in the United States, of which about half are hydroelectric and renewable, with the remainder using fossil fuels, including coal, oil, and natural gas. Small hydro had the largest installed capacity of nonfossil fuel DER until recently, when solar PV capacity exceeded it. Behind-the-meter PV accounts for another approximately 20 GW of generation. Further, demand response contributed about 28.7 GW in wholesale programs in 2016, and also 33 GW in retail programs (FERC, 2017). There are also a few GW of energy efficiency programs sometimes classified as DER (e.g., in PJM and ISO-NE) and counted toward wholesale market obligations. More details on these contributions are provided later. In some regions, combined heat and power (CHP) is also counted as DER, which adds another approximately 83 GW of distributed resources nationally, but which is not considered further here.

4.2 DER Capacity by ISO

As of December 2018, the state of California has by far the greatest capacity (MW) of distributed generation resources within its boundaries, over 12 GW of distributed renewable generation (by the CEC definition of resources at any location of 20 MW or less), of which 10 GW are solar PV, with expectations of continued expansion (CEC, 2018b). About half of these resources are behind-the-meter, with the remainder being small generators connected to the transmission and distribution networks. For the behind-the-meter generation and storage (CEC, 2018a), in 2017 the CEC counted about 5.4 GW toward peak reductions. Despite the policy drivers, non-PV distributed renewable generation in California has remained fairly stable in recent years, with small hydro at about 1 GW, biomass fluctuating around 0.5 GW, small wind around 350–400 MW, and geothermal around 130 MW (CEC, 2018b). In addition, California has 200–300 MW of fossil-fueled distributed generation, which can participate in the markets. There is also about 1.7 GW of wholesale economic and reliability demand response, but only 170 MW is counted by the CEC against peak demand. Collectively, with a state noncoincident, net peak load in 2017 of around 60.7 GW (Kavalec et al., 2018), there is a contribution of around 12 GW of supply-side and demand-modifying distributed resources measured against peak demand, or around 20% of the total (there is no exact estimate in the reported data), or possibly higher if all demand response is counted.

Other ISOs have lower DER penetration levels on the supply-side than California, but in some cases higher penetration of certain distributed resources, such as demand response, and much higher levels of active participation in the ancillary service and capacity markets.

ISO-New England has estimated recently that DER, defined as resources connected to the distribution network but providing wholesale services, comprise about 16% of total capacity (ISO-New England, 2018c), as further described in Section 5.

PJM has a high penetration of demand response in the capacity market, but as of yet less distributed renewable generation. However, in particular PJM submarkets, there has arguably been greater penetration than elsewhere; for example, as also shown in Section 5, in just 3 years, small battery systems (up to 30 MW, but most smaller and many in the 1–2 MW range) have at times comprised almost 50% of the PJM Regulation market. PJM and NYISO also have significant participation by demand response in the spinning reserves market.

Of note, the NYISO markets currently have low penetration by supply DER (other than CHP), but are being prepared for a significant expansion due to New York state's policy initiatives on distributed resources (NYISO, 2017).

While due to policy and market interest there is progressively more specific data being provided on DERs, ISOs do not necessarily provide consistent information on what wholesale services different DER are providing. Hence, this chapter uses the data from different ISOs to illustrate how different types of DER participate in the markets.

4.3 ISO DER Forecasting for Planning Functions

As DERs, including renewable generation and new types of storage, rapidly penetrate in some regions, ISOs have mostly deferred to state regulators and other external parties to provide DER growth forecasts. This approach is now changing as operational and planning impacts of DER become more significant, and several ISOs have been developing new methods for DER capacity and operational forecasting to assist in planning for system operations and transmission upgrades, and to anticipate resource adequacy capacity requirements. For example, ISO-New England develops annual 10 year-ahead planning forecasts of distributed PV and energy efficiency capacity in its region (ISO-NE, 2018a,b). The 2018 edition of this forecast anticipates an expansion in distributed PV from about 2.4 GW in 2017 to about 6 GW in 2027 (ISO-NE, 2018a).

In one ISO, DER forecasting is already being used for operational forecasting: The CAISO now includes the impact of distributed PV on its annual next-year system ramp forecasts used to establish flexible capacity requirements (CAISO, 2018).

Finally, although not necessarily integrated into ISO planning, utilities in states with high DER policy objectives are conducting more sophisticated DER capacity forecasting for purposes of distribution resource planning. In California utilities distributed resource plans, high forecasts of DER penetration over the next 10 years reach 30% of total supply.

5. DER IN WHOLESALE MARKETS AND OTHER ISO FUNCTIONS

This section examines how DERs are currently participating in the wholesale markets, and what avenues are being developed for expanded participation. The section first describes the market participation models being used for DER, and then turns to each product market, including energy, ancillary service, and capacity. The details of participation in these markets can be found in the technical manuals available for each ISO market, and will not be heavily referenced in this chapter. In addition, there are two case-studies in the section illustrating the state of DER participation.

5.1 Wholesale Market Participation Models

"Market participation models" are the set of rules, which govern the requirements and parameters for different classes of resources to participate in the wholesale markets. In each of the ISO markets, DER can utilize several different market participation models, some still to be implemented under FERC orders.[9] Table 19.7 shows that there are a range of such models, including the models, which govern conventional small generator and loads, those which are intended for limited energy resources, including storage, and the different demand response and emerging aggregated DER models.

5.2 Participation in Energy Markets

Wholesale energy markets allow for generators and storage resources to obtain payments ($/MWh) for all their energy (real power) production delivered to the bulk power system, whether these resources are utility

---

[9]Notably, the Electric Storage Resource (ESR) model, which is required under FERC Order 841 (FERC, 2018a).

Table 19.7 Current DER market participation models

ISO	Generator and load models	DER market participation models	
		Demand response and DER models	Limited energy and storage models
ISO-NE	Generator Asset (dispatchable, nondispatchable), Settlement Only Resource (<5MW)	Dispatchable Asset-Related Demand (DARD), Real-Time Demand Response	Alternative Technology Regulation Resource (ATRR), Electric Storage Resource (ESR)
NYISO	Special Case Resources (SCRs)	Day-Ahead Demand Response Program (DADRP), Demand Side Ancillary Services Program Resources (DSASP), Emergency Demand Response Program (EDRP), Behind-the-Meter Net Generation (BTM: NG)	Energy Limited Resources, (ELR), Limited Energy Storage Resources (LESR), Special Case Resources (SCRs), Electric Storage Resource (ESR)
PJM	Generation Resources (includes Capacity Storage Resource, Energy Storage Resource)	Demand-Side Resources (Emergency Load Response, Economic Load Response)	Regulation market – RegD resource, Electric Storage Resource (ESR)
SPP	Dispatchable Resource, External Resource, External Dynamic Resource, Quick-Start Resource	Demand Response Resource	Electric Storage Resource (ESR)
MISO	Generation Resource	Demand Response Resource (DRR) – Type I, Demand Response Resource (DRR) – Type II, Load Modifying Resource (LMR), Demand Resource, Behind the Meter Generation, Emergency Demand Response Resource	Stored Energy Resources (SER), Use-Limited Resources, Electric Storage Resource (ESR)
ERCOT	Distributed Generation (under 10MW)	Load Resources	
CAISO	Participating Generators, Participating Load	Proxy Demand Resources (PDR), Reliability Demand Response Resources (RDRR), Distributed Energy Resource Aggregation (DERA)	Nongenerator Resources (NGR), NGR–Regulation Energy Management (REM), Electric Storage Resource (ESR)

self-owned or merchant resources. As noted earlier, locational pricing of energy can help with siting DER in the highest value locations for energy, which is one of the primary advantages of these resources.

There are two methods for resources to participate in the energy markets: self-schedules and bid-based. A "self-schedule" requires submitting a production quantity, fixed or forecast, for each interval of the market, and to be a "price-taker" of the market's resulting locational marginal price for that interval. This mode of participation is also sometimes called "passive." However, even passive participants face financial exposure in the event of production deviations following the submission of the schedule. The second participation method is to submit a bid ($/MWh) and let the energy auction market optimization determine in which intervals to produce energy at a particular quantity, and in which intervals not to produce energy. This mode of participation is also called "active."

Whether self-scheduled or bid, the ISO markets are designed such that positive deviations from day-ahead schedules are financially settled at real-time prices, while negative deviations require the entity to "buy-back" its day-ahead position at real-time prices. For variable energy resources (primarily wind and solar), their short-term forecasts become their real-time schedules heading into the operating hour, with different rules in the different ISO markets for settling deviations from those forecasts during actual operations.

For distributed energy storage, there are additional characteristics, which complicate energy market operations. Most notably, the energy storage device has to be operated to reflect state-of-charge management and roundtrip efficiency (FERC, 2018a). This requires the storage operator to determine when to charge the device and when to discharge to ensure that energy (and ancillary service) market revenues are maximized, as further described in Chapter 3 by Baak and Sioshansi.

The integration of DER into wholesale energy markets as "price-takers" is fairly straightforward, as the ISOs have accommodated large numbers of self-scheduled small generation since the start of these markets. However, historically most of these resources, as shown in Table 19.6, were small fossil and hydro whose generation was predictable and steady. The emergence and rapid expansion of large and small variable energy resources is now sufficient to require modifications to ISO forecasting of DER output and, in some cases, revisions to the financial settlement rules. In addition, there are other reasons why DER are likely to largely remain as price-takers. First, to become dispatchable resources will require investments in telemetry. Most supply DER in the future will be variable energy resources, which do not have a fuel cost, and hence for that reason generally do not submit positive price offers. For distributed storage, FERC (2018a) has required that they are able to set market prices, but it is equally likely that these resources will prefer to be optimized directly by the ISOs as price-takers.

There is another development in the US energy markets, which will affect all resources including DER. If energy market prices continue to be low due to low natural gas prices and become negative more often during periods of surplus generation (a condition, which over the next few years will affect the CAISO energy markets much more than the other ISO markets due to the large solar penetration in California), "passive" DER will face the challenge that energy production has a cost, and this may encourage precurtailment or submission of bids to manage market price exposure. This may happen through direct participation, or via the use of "value of DER" retail rates, which are linked to wholesale market values.

5.3 Participation in Ancillary Services Markets

To participate in the ancillary service markets, all resources have to demonstrate that they can meet all control and telemetry requirements required for their particular resource. Resources can typically either submit offers into the auction for each product, but some ISOs also allow "self-scheduling" meaning that the resource is a price-taker. All self-scheduled resources providing ancillary services must follow ISO dispatch, whether the automatic control signals for frequency regulation, or economic dispatch instructions for contingency reserves in the event of contingencies. Unlike the energy markets, the sale of ancillary services in the day-ahead market cannot be "sold back" in the event that the resource cannot perform or has other uses in real-time operations; rather, there can be penalties for nonperformance, as well as possibly reductions in payments for poor performance.

DER participation in the ancillary service markets is fairly advanced in certain ways. Demand response has well-established qualification rules for contingency reserves, and in some markets, also for frequency regulation. For other resource types, there is, with a few exceptions (as discussed later), less history of participation, but under the evolving rules in the US wholesale markets, DER will be eligible for all of these ancillary services in the future, particularly those with energy storage and/or smart inverters (NYISO, 2017; FERC, 2018a).

As noted, most ISOs are currently accommodating demand response in the contingency reserve markets and PJM and NYISO also allow participation in frequency regulation. For example, demand response resources provided 8.8% of PJM's Tier 2 synchronized reserves in 2016, and 24.3% in 2017 (Monitoring Analytics, 2018). In NYISO, demand response resources provided 16% of spinning reserves in 2016 (NYISO, 2017).

Most ISOs have created market participation models and rules for small, limited energy storage resources to provide frequency regulation, with the example of PJM examined next. In addition, one of the advantages of lithium-ion batteries and smart inverters recently observed is the high performance in providing frequency regulation (Monitoring Analytics, 2018). These factors further allow for displacement of conventional generation and may result in reduced emissions from power system operations as a further benefit.

5.4 Case Study: Distributed Storage Resource Participation in the PJM Regulation Market

To date, one of the most interesting examples of large-scale penetration of an ISO market in the United States by actively participating distributed resources is the rapid expansion of small battery and flywheel storage resources, and to a lesser extent demand response, in the PJM Regulation market. Beginning in 2012, PJM introduced a new, "faster" automatic generation control (AGC) signal called RegD in addition to the RegA control signal, which conventional resources were following. PJM designed the market rules to allow RegD and RegA to be substitutable in meeting the system's regulation requirement. In addition, PJM initially offered the RegD resources a 15-minute energy neutral AGC signal, which was essentially designed to facilitate entry by very limited duration (15–20 minute) lithium-ion batteries (but was applied to all RegD resources).

This new market design was extremely successful in encouraging entry of new distributed storage projects, which could provide RegD – a few as large as 30 MW, but mostly 20 MW and under in size and located on both the transmission and distribution systems, as well as behind-the-meter supporting demand response.[10] As shown in Table 19.8, over just 4 years, 2013–2017, these new distributed resources expanded from essentially providing none of the Regulation requirement to almost 50% of the requirement, while coal generation was largely displaced from this service (Monitoring Analytics, 2017).

---

[10]The Demand Response qualified to provide regulation in PJM includes storage, electric water heaters, and generation.

Table 19.8 Market shares and average revenue to batteries in the PJM Regulation market, 2014–2018 Q1

Year	Battery share of market (%)	Battery revenue, average $/MW of Regulation provided
2014	16	36.78
2015	27.6	27.07
2016	41	15.39
2017	46.5	13.70
2018 Q1	34.1	28.32

Source: Monitoring Analytics, annual and quarterly PJM State of the Market reports.

Over this period, PJM changed the design in several ways due to operational constraints being experienced because of the increasing number of resources following the RegD signal. These changes included suspending new entry of RegD resources, and modifying the RegD 15-minute signal to a 30-minute energy neutral signal conditioned on system reliability. This resulted in greater costs of operation to the short-duration batteries, while market revenues declined, eventually leading to some exit of battery units by 2018 (as shown in Table 19.8).

However, this market development clearly demonstrates that new distributed resources can take on the most complex functions in system operations on a large scale. Within 5–10 years, it seems likely that due to state policies promoting storage and renewables, declining PV and lithium-ion battery costs, and if market prices remain reasonably stable, most frequency regulation will be supplied from batteries and smart inverters from both large and small installations. How this market entry unfolds in the different ISO markets, and the degree to which it is focused on distributed resources of various types, will depend on market prices, market rules, ISO software capabilities, and policy drivers. For example, in California, most new storage contracts are at fixed prices over 20 years, leaving either the utility or the storage developer (depending on the contract terms) to recover any available market revenues from energy and ancillary services regardless of what those prices are. This will likely cause Regulation market prices in California to decline rapidly as these projects come online (e.g., see analysis in Eichman et al., 2015).

5.5 Participation in Resource Adequacy Requirements and Capacity Markets

Capacity markets could be a major source of future revenues for DER, but significant barriers have to be overcome to the participation by variable energy resources and limited-energy storage. As noted earlier, demand response resources have been the primary type of distributed resource participating to date in the capacity markets (see each ISO's state of the market reports). There are large number of demand response types with different requirements as capacity resources; key requirements include the number of allowed load interruptions (which can range from a small number to unlimited) and the minimum duration of the interruption, which can range from 1 hour to 10 hours or more, depending on the resource type and ISO. Fig. 19.2 shows the potential contribution to peak reduction as a percentage of peak load of demand response resources from 2011–2016 in each market (FERC, 2012–2017). These consist primarily of reliability DR, with lesser participation by economic DR.

ISOs still differ in the types of other distributed resources, which can qualify as capacity resources. For example, in several markets (PJM and ISO-New England), energy efficiency projects have been incorporated in recent years.

As an example, Fig. 19.3 shows the quantities (MW) of both demand response and energy efficiency which cleared the PJM capacity market in recent years (the market clears 3-years ahead, so the quantities are shown

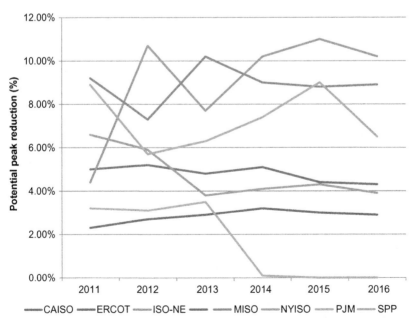

FIGURE 19.2 Demand response capacity (MW) as percentage (%) of potential peak reduction, 2011–2016. *(Sources: FERC Assessments of Demand Response and Advanced Metering, 2012–2017.)*

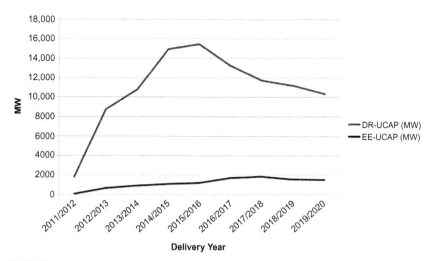

FIGURE 19.3 Demand response (DR) and energy efficiency (EE) cleared in PJM RPM capacity auctions, 2011/12–2019/20. *(Source: Monitoring Analytics, 2017 PJM State of the Market report.)*

for the delivery year). In PJM, between 15–23% of demand response in the capacity market is from small on-site fossil generation (PJM, 2018).

More recently, rules are being developed for participation by smaller distributed storage devices, with most ISOs to date rating these resources by their output (MW) which can be sustained over 4 hours. California will be the first region to have a large number of small energy storage resources with full capacity ratings. In addition, many behind-the-meter storage installations in California and elsewhere are being valued in part by their impact on the capacity obligations of load-serving entities (and also reductions in retail demand charges).

For aggregated DER, participation rules are still in development, but given that aggregations can consist of multiple types of resources, there is the opportunity to combine resources, which on their own would not achieve the minimum requirements to qualify as capacity resources.

Among the most complicated issues in measuring capacity ratings of DER resources will be the ratings on distributed solar plants, expected to be the dominant distributed energy resource in the future. Whether in-front-of-the-meter or behind-the-meter, solar resources have the characteristic that they typically experience declines in their contribution to meeting utility or regional peak demand in the range of 5–10% penetration by annual energy. This is because the "net load" peak demand shifts to the early

Table 19.9 Solar marginal ELCCs required for 2018 Integrated Resource Plans by CPUC-jurisdictional load-serving entities

ELCC values	2018	2022	2026	2030
Marginal solar ELCC (including BTM PV)	13%	2%	2%	2%

evening. The California Public Utilities Commission (CPUC) is the first state regulator to develop a probabilistic model to estimate the annual effective load-carrying capability (ELCC) of additional solar. When new solar generation was first entering the California market, it was generally credited with a capacity rating in the range of 65–75% of nameplate capacity (MW), due to the coincidence of production with annual peak demand. As shown in Table 19.9, the CPUC (2018a) has estimated that in 2018, with solar already providing over 11% of annual energy, additional solar PV located in any domain had reached a marginal ELCC rating of 13% of nameplate capacity, and for planning purposes this rating was assumed to decline to only 2% by 2022 and beyond, unless augmented by integrated storage. Hence, distributed solar has very little capacity value as a stand-alone resource in California from 2018 onwards.

5.6 Case Study: Categorizing DER Participation in the ISO-New England Wholesale Markets

Most ISOs disseminate data on which types of resources are using particular participation models on an ad hoc basis, although market monitoring reports are increasingly explaining more about the evolving resource mix.[11] As an example, ISO-New England has recently inventoried that in 2018, about 16% of its wholesale markets, measured by capacity (MW), comprises different types of DER (defined as resources located on the distribution network), operating under two different participation models: the settlement only resource (SOR), which allows resources of under 5 MW to schedule on an as-available basis, and as different types of Demand Resources. This is shown in Table 19.10, excerpted directly from ISO-New England (2018c). The table shows that of the 5.6 GW of DER catalogued, about 73% participate in the wholesale markets, 26% as energy resources and 47% primarily

---

[11]To date, the PJM state of the market reports along with other PJM technical reports provide the most data on which resources, including DER, are providing market services or supporting demand response. In addition, FERC provides a useful survey in its annual assessments of demand response and advanced metering. See the chapter references.

Table 19.10 ISO-New England Distributed Energy Resources, 2018

Distributed energy resource (DER) category	Settlement only resource (SOR) Nameplate capacity (MW)	Demand resource (DR) maximum capacity (MW)	Total DER capacity (MW)
Energy efficiency	–	1,765	1,765
Demand response (excluding behind-the-meter DG capacity)[a]	–	99	99
Natural gas generation	26	331	357
Generation using other fossil fuels	75	268	344
Generation using purchased steam	–	19	19
Nonsolar renewable generation (e.g., hydro, biomass, wind)	523	126	649
Solar PV generation participating in the wholesale market	810	48	858
Electricity storage	1	–	1
Solar PV generation *not* participating in the wholesale market	–	–	1,532
Total DER capacity	1,436	2,656	5,625
Total DER capacity/total wholesale system capability[b]	4.1%	7.5%	15.9%

[a]To avoid double-counting, demand response capacity reported here excludes any behind-the-meter DG capacity located at facilities providing demand response. Registered demand response capacity as of 01/2018 (MW): 684.
[b]System Operable Capacity (Seasonal Claimed Capability) plus SOR and DR Capacity as of 01/2018 (MW): 35,406.
Source: ISO-New England (2018c).

as demand resources; in addition, there are additional demand response resources not tabulated as DER. For a less complete inventory of how DER participate in the NYISO markets, see NYISO (2017).

6. KEY DESIGN ISSUES FOR EXPANSION OF DER PARTICIPATION

This section reviews several key design issues for the further expansion of DER participation. These include the further development of market participation models to support diverse mixes of distributed resources, a more structured interface between the wholesale market and resources located on the distribution network or at the customer site, how ISOs will assess the costs of any DER impact on ISO system operations and reliability, and the rules for multiple-use applications as well as removal of other regulatory barriers to market participation by DERs providing such applications.

6.1 Further Development of Market Participation Models and Market Rules Relevant to DER

As noted in Section 5, DER currently participate in the ISO wholesale markets via a range of different participation models, which establish the requirements for different technology configurations. As noted earlier, FERC Order 841 (2018a) has established common requirements for energy storage resources, including distributed storage eligible to participate in the wholesale markets, and FERC has indicated that further reforms will forthcoming for market participation by aggregated DER models. In the order, FERC also offered ISOs some discretion in how rapidly they allowed small storage resources to enter the auction markets, given the potential impact on market solution times. For certain market products, most notably the capacity product, there is also likely to be further evolution in market rules. For example, there is no consensus method yet for determining how much energy duration is needed for energy storage to qualify as capacity resources, and changes in these requirements will affect aggregated DER. Also, as noted, the experience with solar capacity ratings in California has indicated the importance of considering the effect of aggregate solar penetration on the capacity rating of additional (or marginal) solar at any location or scale, a complicated calculation, which has not yet been incorporated effectively into resource adequacy requirements.

6.2 The Interface of the Wholesale Market With the Distribution System and the Role of the Distribution System Operator

The current wholesale markets were designed to calculate spot energy pricing on the high-voltage transmission network operated by ISOs, although ISOs have differed in the voltages, which they initially utilized for market and system operations. With the expansion of DER, various options are being evaluated for improved market integration of DER connected to the distribution network into the wholesale markets, including having ISOs extend wholesale market pricing to the distribution system or the creation of a separate distribution system operator (currently the distribution utility), which operates a separate market transaction system for distribution-connected resources coordinated with the ISO markets (see also Chapter 6 by Stanley et al.).

The state of New York has undertaken the most detailed examination to date of how an independent distribution system operator or platform (DSP) would be implemented. Such an organization would potentially be solving a much larger optimization problem than the ISOs, potentially modeling up to millions of individual small resources. Several New York utilities are now conducting demonstration projects on DSP operations (NYDSP, 2018).

6.3 DER Impact on ISO System Operations and Reliability

While this chapter is focused on wholesale markets, most ISOs and some regulatory entities have also been examining the potential impacts of types of new DER on system operations and reliability, which in turn will affect how those resources participate in the wholesale markets. These assessments and operating experiences may result in new operational requirements, which in turn can deter or facilitate DER market entry. ISOs and both federal and state regulators have begun to examine these issues in more detail.

In a recent survey, FERC (2018b) identified several improvements in planning and operations to ensure reliable integration of DERs, and has also been reflected in a number of ISO reports and technical comments. These include "The lack of DER data and the resulting implications for the operation, planning, and design of the bulk power system; the need for coordination between the settings and capabilities of resources connected to the bulk power system and DERs; the need for improved modeling practices and capabilities for DERs; the effect of DER daily generation profiles on system unit commitment and ramping needs; and the effect of distribution connected variable PV and wind output on day-ahead load forecasts." Mechanisms for correcting for these impacts could include new technical requirements for DER, assigning costs of DER integration, and provision of some integration services by the DER installations.

6.4 Multiple-Use Applications and Regulatory Barriers

Many DER installations, which are intended to provide wholesale services but are located on the distribution network or behind-the-meter at a customer location, will have other uses, potentially including retail customer services, transmission and distribution upgrade deferral (also known as "non-wire alternatives"), and contribution to distribution system operations. The distribution utility and state regulators will have jurisdiction over these latter applications. In California, these are being called "multiple-use applications" (CPUC, 2018b). While such installations are still a very small portion of the wholesale markets (in part due to regulatory barriers), they present coordination issues, which will require new market rules, which can be enforced by each off-taker of the project's services. The most obvious requirement is a set of enforceable rules, which establish the constraints on DER operations. For example, just like all resources interconnected to the bulk power system, if DERs offer wholesale reliability services (such as ancillary services and operating as a capacity resource), they must perform according to the market rules or face penalties (CPUC, 2018b).

Whether particular types and configurations of DER providing multiple-use applications can participate in the wholesale markets is in part a function of the regulatory rules, which are evolving at both the federal level and in each state as they examine the implications for industry structure and investment incentives.

There are several types of these barriers. In some states, distribution utilities cannot seek rate recovery for distribution system assets which provide both distribution deferral while earning additional revenues through wholesale market services, such as could be offered by distributed storage. Historically, this has been to preserve the distinction in the competitive markets between infrastructure seeking rate recovery and resources able to enter through market-based investment. Recently, a number of alternative contractual structures have been proposed to allow for such multiple-use DER investments, including having the distribution utility auction the rights to the eligible storage ranges for wholesale services or having regulators retract some or all of the wholesale revenues from the utility's allowed rate of return.

Moreover, aggregations of DER developed as nonwires alternatives to ISO transmission upgrades are not eligible as ISO transmission assets with rate recovery through transmission access charges. Hence, they may be approved by the ISOs within the transmission planning process as a least cost solution to a transmission need, but will need to obtain state regulatory approval for cost recovery or obtain sufficient revenues otherwise through bilateral contracts and wholesale market value.

7. CONCLUSIONS

The US wholesale markets are anticipating a large expansion in participation by DER over the coming decades. There are historical precedents for such expansion, and new types of distributed resources are often building on or extending existing market participation models. Demand response pioneered participation by large numbers of small, aggregated responsive load resources in the capacity markets, and to a lesser degree in the operating reserves markets. Some ISOs already have a much larger number of small generation, storage and demand response resources than others, and hence integration of DER into the markets will likely proceed at different paces in different regions for some time. In some regions, the types of consumers, prosumers, and prosumagers reviewed in this book will comprise a growing share of the DERs actively participating. By some measures, certain ISO markets already have penetration of close to 20% in terms of DER capacity, and forecasts of over 30% of the wholesale market in California and New England comprising DER within the next 5–10 years are plausible. Other markets, such as NYISO, may not be far behind given the acceleration of policy support. And although its states are not as focused on policies to promote DERs, PJM provides examples of distributed resources, primarily demand response and small batteries, already supplying 10% of capacity, 16% of spinning reserves, and at times almost 50% of frequency regulation.

The evolution to wholesale markets with increasing participation by DERs, seems fairly straightforward given these existing examples of high penetration by these resources. Of interest to market operators is the problem of optimizing auction markets with very large numbers of small resources, but this does not seem to be a significant long-term barrier. More likely is the prospect that for many years most of the new DER providing energy will be largely "passive" participants. However, as the penetration of such resources continues to increase, there will be an increasing value for active power controls, reflecting in system ramp periods and in ancillary services. A significant challenge facing both large and small resources in the wholesale energy markets is the declining value of energy given low natural gas prices and increasing penetration by low or no marginal cost renewable resources. If this trend continues, it seems inevitable that a growing percentage of market value will flow through the ancillary service and capacity markets.

REFERENCES

California Energy Commission (CEC), 2018a. California Energy Commission—tracking progress: energy storage. August. [Online] Available: http://www.energy.ca.gov/renewables/tracking_progress/documents/energy_storage.pdf.
California Energy Commission (CEC), 2018b. California Energy Commission—tracking progress: renewable energy. July. [Online] Available: http://www.energy.ca.gov/renewables/tracking_progress/documents/renewable.pdf.

California Independent System Operator (CAISO), 2018. Flexible capacity needs assessment. various years. [Online] Available: http://www.caiso.com/planning/Pages/ReliabilityRequirements/Default.aspx. (Accessed 2018).

California Public Utilities Commission (CPUC), 2018a. Decision setting requirements for load serving entities filing integrated resource plans. February 8. [Online]. Available: http://docs.cpuc.ca.gov/PublishedDocs/Published/G000/M209/K709/209709519.PDF.

California Public Utilities Commission (CPUC), 2018b. Decision on multiple-use application issues. Rulemaking 15 03 011, Decision 18-01-003, Issued January 17, 2018. [Online] Available: http://docs.cpuc.ca.gov/PublishedDocs/Published/G000/M206/K462/206462341.pdf.

Eichman, J., Denholm, P., Jorgenson, J., Helman, U., 2015. Operational Benefits of Meeting California's Energy Storage Targets. National Renewable Energy Laboratory (NREL). December. Technical Report NREL/TP-5400-65061, [Online]. Available: http://www.nrel.gov/docs/fy16osti/65061.pdf.

Electric Power Research Institute (EPRI), 2004. Distributed Energy Resources: Current Landscape and a Roadmap for the Future. EPRI, Palo Alto, CA. 1008415.

Electric Power Research Institute (EPRI), 2016. Wholesale Electricity Market Design Initiatives in the United States: Survey and Research Needs. EPRI, Palo Alto, CA. 3002009273.

Energy Information Agency (EIA), Department of Energy (DOE), 2017. Form EIA-860, annual and monthly. [Online] Available: https://www.eia.gov/electricity/data/eia860/. (Accessed November 2017).

Federal Energy Regulatory Commission (FERC), 2011a. Order No. 1000, 136 FERC ¶ 61,051.

Federal Energy Regulatory Commission (FERC), 2011b. Order No. 745, FERC Stats. & Regs. ¶ 31,322.

Federal Energy Regulatory Commission (FERC), 2012–2017. Assessments of Demand Response and Advanced Metering. [Online] Available: https://www.ferc.gov/industries/electric/indus-act/demand-response/dem-res-adv-metering.asp.

Federal Energy Regulatory Commission (FERC), 2018a. Order 841, electric storage participation in markets operated by regional transmission organizations and independent system operators. 162 FERC ¶61,127, 18 CFR Part 35 [Docket Nos. RM16-23-000; AD16-20-000], Issued February 15, 2018a.

Federal Energy Regulatory Commission (FERC), 2018b. Staff paper, distributed energy resources: technical considerations for the bulk power system. February. [Online] Available: https://www.ferc.gov/EventCalendar/EventDetails.aspx?ID=10920&CalType=%20&CalendarID=116&Date=4/1/2018&View=Listview.

ISO-New England, 2018a. Distributed generation forecast. [Online] Available: https://www.iso-ne.com/system-planning/system-forecasting/distributed-generation-forecast/. (Accessed 2018).

ISO-New England, 2018b. Energy Efficiency Forecast. [Online] Available: https://www.iso-ne.com/system-planning/system-forecasting/energy-efficiency-forecast. (Accessed 2018).

ISO-New England, 2018c. Statement of Henry Yoshimura. ISO New England Inc. Panel 1 - Economic Dispatch, Pricing, and Settlement of DER Aggregations. April 10. [Online] Available: https://www.ferc.gov/CalendarFiles/20180410100927-Yoshimura,%20ISO%20New%20England.pdf.

Kavalec, C., Gautam, A., Jaske, M., Marshall, L., Movassagh, N., Vaid, R., 2018. California Energy Demand 2018-2030 Revised Forecast. California Energy Commission, Electricity Assessments Division. Publication Number: CEC-200-2018-002-SD. [Online] Available: http://www.energy.ca.gov/publications/displayOneReport.php?pubNum=CEC-200-2018-002-SD.

Monitoring Analytics, LLC, Independent Market Monitor for PJM, State of the Market Report for PJM, 2017, [Online]. Available: http://monitoringanalytics.com/reports/ PJM_State_of_the_Market/2017.shtml.

Monitoring Analytics, LLC, 2018. State of the market report for PJM, 2017. March 8. [Online] Available: http://www.monitoringanalytics.com/reports/PJM_State_of_the_ Market/2018.shtml.

New York Department of Public Service (DSP), 2018. Webpage on "REV— Demonstration Projects". [Online] Available: http://www3.dps.ny.gov/W/PSCWeb. nsf/All/B2D9D834B0D307C685257F3F006FF1D9?OpenDocument. (Accessed July 2018).

New York Independent System Operator (NYISO), January 2017. Distributed energy resources roadmap for New York's wholesale electricity markets. [Online] Available: https://www.nyiso.com/public/webdocs/media_room/press_releases/2017/Child_ DER_Roadmap/Distributed_Energy_Resources_Roadmap.pdf.

North American Electric Reliability Corporation (NERC), 2017. BAL-003-1 Frequency Response Obligation Allocation for Operation Year 2017. North American Electric Reliability Corporation (NERC).

PJM, January 2018. 2017 distributed energy resources (DER) that participate in PJM markets as demand response, PJM demand side response operations. [Online] Available: https://www.pjm.com/-/media/committees-groups/subcommittees/ders/post-ings/2017-ders-annual-report.ashx?la=en.

EPILOGUE

In the good old times, life was simple. Energy consumers were generally passive, with little choice other than turning on the light and paying the bill. In developed countries, the quality of service was generally good and the end user price was regulated, more or less expensive depending on the energy mix. The electrification of our countries was made possible by the genius and enthusiasm of thousands of talented engineers and technical workers. It was a galvanizing period in the history of energy.

We are now on the threshold of a new Era.

The energy transition and the digital revolution are transforming the energy market, and especially the electricity market. Renewable energies (RE) and battery storage are more and more competitive, grid parity for photovoltaic electricity is being achieved in many places, and as a result energy systems are becoming more and more decentralized.

For the energy consumers, this is a new world of opportunities, which are explored in the first part of the book:

- In competitive retail markets, consumers can freely choose among a large number of suppliers and offers: for instance 100% renewable, or fixed price for several years, or simply the best financial deal;
- Thanks to smart meters, they can get precise information on their consumption. If they accept to give access to these data to a third party, they will receive specific offers to reduce their bill, as well as demand response opportunities to help the system during peak periods;
- They can produce renewable electricity, and choose to become self-consumers, possibly with some batteries to help match their consumption and their production. They can also be part of a collective self-consumption project;
- They can have an electric vehicle, with simple apps and incentives helping them to optimize the charge/discharge of the EV;
- They can finance a local renewable energy project via a crowdfunding platform; or
- They can participate in a peer-to-peer platform, to sell their production in excess to, or buy from a local energy producer.

Large commercial and industrial (C&I) customers are generally more advanced than residential customers depending on their size, energy consumption, and willingness to engage in the energy transition. Large multinational companies are more and more engaged in power purchase agreements with RE producers and in 100% renewable contracts.

There is, however, no guarantee that consumers, especially the residential consumers, will effectively take advantage of these opportunities – as noted by Ron Ben-David in the book's Preface and explored in other chapters in the book. The new world offers new opportunities but also adds new complexities. Those who can navigate the complexities welcome the opportunities – especially when the value of the new options is apparent to the public. Opportunities in energy that were unreachable are now affordable.

It is somewhat puzzling to clinch to the certainty that consumers are willing (at best) to be active in their choice of supplier; that they are willing to allocate some of their time to something as mundane as their energy bill. One may think that the real emancipation toward energy is precisely in not having to deal with it.

Moreover, the energy sector has to cope with the growing suspicion regarding any risk of intrusion or invasion of privacy that comes with smart meters and the digitalization, topics extensively covered in this volume. The main forces hindering consumers' commitment in the energy transition are, beyond inertia, the fear of change and anxiety due to complexity and digital intrusion.

The result is a growing trend of segmentation of customers, which leads to real differences of how they use the distribution network, how much value they gain from it, and how much cost they impose on it. Whereas in the old world, all energy consumers were more or less equal and treated in the same way, this may no longer be the case. The passive consumers – the "good" ones from the point of view of the incumbents – unable or unwilling to seize the opportunities, will be billed more and more, while others will enjoy the benefits of innovation while bargaining for new service offers.

This is a matter for regulators. The second part of the book shows that their role is becoming much more important than in the past, with an impact on the speed and spread of the disruption.

The case of self-consumption is especially illustrative. In many countries, self-consumption is encouraged or subsidized by public authorities. It turns out that most self-consumers are owners of large houses or companies like supermarkets in sunny places – South of France for instance. They may end up receiving subsidies, paying less taxes on energy, and paying less in network tariff. As the whole energy + tax system is, at a given time, a zero sum game, other less privileged customers will have to pay more to compensate as a number of chapters in this book explain. This cannot be a good outcome for two basic reasons:

- Efficiency: in the long run, it is inefficient to distort economic signals. For instance, net metering may help encourage self-consumption, but it is very costly for the electric system if the renewable energy is produced when the value of power is low, or potentially negative; and
- Equity: a public policy ending up in poor or middle-class people potentially subsidizing the wealthiest doesn't make much sense.

In France, the regulator CRE has made public this kind of analysis, recommending to limit tax exemptions to self-consumers <9 kVA. CRE has also set a network tariff option for self-consumers reflecting only the network costs savings that occurs if production and consumption are well matched.

CRE has been criticized for this, has been called pronuclear, anti-innovation, anti-renewables, and so on. However, good economic signals must prevail and it is not the regulator's remit to decide which users of the network have to be subsidized. This, CRE believes, is a sentiment broadly accepted by regulators around the world.

Beyond self-consumption, one of the main tasks of energy regulators is to set network tariffs. They must take into account the increased diversity and complexity of network users: distributed generation, self-consumers, storage, demand response operators, electric vehicles, and other behind-the-meter assets. As shown in several chapters of the book, innovative ideas are required to convey the right economic signals and to allocate network costs and/or benefits to those who generate them.

In this context, distribution system operators must be innovative too, which may not be their most obvious characteristic, since they are regulated entities. Once again, the regulators must find new mechanisms to ensure distribution operators have the right incentives to innovate to the benefits of energy consumers. In this case, incentive regulation plays the role of competitive market pressure.

Another fundamental task for the regulators is to allow optimal network access to all users, and especially the new kind of users. The aggregation of large numbers of small sources of flexibility shall be made possible, and such aggregated bodies must be able to participate in all the elements of the electricity value chain. These lines of thinking are broadly accepted among regulators in the US, Europe, Australia, and elsewhere, which is encouraging.

The "Clean energy package," the new European legislation, which was passed at the end of 2018, seeks to adapt the internal market to this new world.

A fully competitive retail market, with distribution system operators as neutral market facilitators, is an essential part of the market design and shall help energy consumers to reap the benefits of innovation.

However, any innovation must, in due time, find a viable business model and this question of business model is the central matter of the third part of the book.

First, the rollout of smart meters and the development of distributed flexibility resources will change the way distribution networks are managed. Self-consumption, local energy communities, positive energy areas, and micro-grids will challenge traditional business models of distribution operators, who will see less energy withdrawn from the grid. The ultimate disruption is the development of independent, nonconnected micro-grids. It appears that such standalone micro-grids will be rare in developed countries with good existing networks, but they will play a major role to electrify the last billion of people in the world still without access to electricity, with innovative business models such as pay-as-you-go systems described in the book.

Incumbents, in particular former monopolies, will be especially challenged, as more and more options will be available to more end users. They may have to make bold strategic decisions, as it has been the case recently in Germany, further explored in this volume.

And, of course, there are all the newcomers, from the simplest business model of low-cost energy supplier to the most sophisticated ones like blockchain peer-to-peer platforms, VPPs, demand response operators, and others. At the moment, we see a large number of companies entering the market in many countries, with very different business models and innovations. This initial phase will most probably be followed by subsequent consolidation, when the winning business models will emerge – perhaps the topic of a sequel volume?

One very strong newcomer is the transport sector, which may be able by itself to disrupt the energy sector, if bullish forecasts of electric vehicles penetration turn out to be true. The vehicle to grid business model has the potential to fundamentally change the way flexibility is procured and managed on electricity networks, and to allow for very large proportions of renewable intermittent electricity sources to be stored during sunny daylight hours when energy is plentiful and cheap.

Energy is a fascinating sector, both the source of our prosperity and the main cause of climate change, which may doom our civilization. And this is a fascinating period to work in the energy sector, given the scale of change we are witnessing. As regulators, this is not the right time to repeat the old recipes, we have to welcome and anticipate change, to create an open system able to take the most of new opportunities and engage consumers in the energy transition. This book helps grasp the spirit of the times, the importance of the stakes as well as the uncertainty of the outcomes.

Jean–Laurent Lastelle and Dominique Jamme
Commission de régulation de l'énergie (CRE),
Paris, France

INDEX

Note: Page numbers followed by *f* indicate figures, *t* indicate tables, *b* indicate boxes, and *np* indicate footnotes.

Printed in the United States
By Bookmasters